CW00435653

1985

Roger Stonebridge Martin Moran
J.M. Gear Jane O'Donovan May Grant
Brenda D. Griffin Mervyn Griffin
Jennifer M. Irving Joe Stewart Ron Payne
Alan Douglas Isobel M. Hughes
Ian S. Hughes Ian T. Stalker
Roger Chapman John Limbach
Allan MacLeod Sandra Gordon
Douglas Gordon Donald D. MacAusland
Peter R. Mills David S. Simpson
Ken Falconer J. Brewster Alan MacIntyre
William S. Lockyer Len Cerajowski
Lorna Liddell Brenda Jones Ray Peel
David MacFadzean Paul Morgan
Barbara Morgan Gareth Morgan
Caroline Morgan Alex G. Cousins
George Wostenholme Catherine McVean
Kenneth McVean Eleanor Christie
James MacKay James Macrae
Graham R. Wyllie Brian D. Souness
Ian R.F. Ross Mark McCann
Arthur C. Dickie Brian Shackleton
David Matthews Margaret K. Foster
James D. Foster Bill Barlow
Dorothy Batchelor Leslie A. Knight
Peter Keillar Alan Wilson
Beryl Leatherland Tom Leatherland
Sheila Murray David Smith Jim Chalmers
John Hetherington Paul K. Williamson

1986

Dan Doherty Alan Ingram
Gordon M. McAndrew Ann Bowker
Walter M. Stephen John G. Crummett
A. Laurence Rudkin Dave Atkins
James A. Bloomer Fiona Cameron
Alan J. Henderson C.W. Pringle
Ian V. Douglas Roger Booth
William R. Morrison J.G. Cooney
Jim Barton James Byers Ronald E. Dow
Trixie Robertson Nick Kempe
Graeme Cornwallis Francis H. Scott
Stephen E. Powell Kathleen Slocum
Stephen Scobie Ronald Torano
Margaret MacLennan Mark Kirby
Jack R.F. Burt James S. Bell
Andrew Finnimore Stephen Poulton
Shirley Poulton Peter Ilieve Jeremy Wray
Graeme Morrison David Alexander
Timothy C. Outten David H. Purser
W.A.B. Kerr Ashley Cooper
Jacqueline Brodie Nigel F. Toothill
John B. McKay J.A. Scott
Margaret Cadenhead Charles Cadenhead
Malcolm Lamont James V. Mathieson
Thomas H. MacEwan Ian M. Williams
John Harrison Brian McKay
Hugh Ormiston G.A.C. Binnie Dave Myles
Stan Stewart Cyril Henderson Colin Scales

1987

Peter Bellarby Robert Ward Mike West
Neville Kale Jane Kale Andrew Kale
David Kale Terry Butterworth
David S. Adam Edna Stewart
J. Stanley Stewart Douglas Wylie
Vaughan Hammond Graham S. Wilson
Iain Crosbie Ian R. Young
Alex M. Drummond D.H.W. Taylor
Raymond G. Porter Dawn Strickland
M.R. Lees Chris W. Lilley
Robert T. Waalker R.J. Buchan
Ian C. McCallum William Harrower
J.A. Baird Julian Lines Coll Findlay
Sandy Donald Leon D. Firth
Peter Warburton John Town John Crombie
William Harkins Diana J. Harkins
Janet Sutcliffe Geoff Eccles
George R. Craig Andrew Mackin
Kenneth Layhe Elizabeth Layhe
Jim Montgomery Keith Relzin

John Cameron Uinseann M.
Edward A. Dick Georgie M
James Tarvet Michael A. Taylor
Brian Covell Fiona Torbet Ian
Charles L. Scott H. Gordon /
Hugh R. Shercliff George I
Jadwiga Kowalska Anne M
Bill Miller Maggie Mill
Harold R.E. Clarke W. Shaw
Peter A. Dawes Fergus Ma
Pamela Harper J. Mitche.

1988

William S. Gray Alexander Baxter
G. Collinson Jack Veitch Douglas Rennie
Douglas M. Fraser Tommy Hepburn
F.G. North John Blair-Fish Donald Shiach
James R. Brocklehurst G.D. Moylan
Cyril M. Smith John Green Keith Skeens
Dave Cording Alec M. Synge
David R. Bird Helen Steven
Marcus H. Ward Harry Robinson
David W. Eadington T.E. Edwards
Fraser Hamilton David F Geddes
W. Brian Carlyle Andrew C.B. Dempster
Stewart Lang Brian R. Johnson
Andrew Kerr John Gibson James Taylor
Christopher Allan Irvin John Cushnie
Kay Turner Nev Wiseman Mal Newlyn
Ian Holland Mark Elsegood
Alasdair MacLennan Seonaid Wood
Dairena Gaffney Roger D. Everett
Andrew Tibbs Roger Owen
Hamish H. Johnston A. Kinghorn
Norrie Muir Alistair Milner Robert Wilson
Maurice Watson John C.S. Vaughan
Katherine Jamieson Peter H. Nall
Neil D. Robertson John M. Burley
Kay Simpson C. Clinch W.A. Simpson
John Adams John Allen Robert Dale
C. Andrew Scott Geoff Skeaping
James G. Bell Charles R. Haigh
J. Stanley Roberts W.G.C. Lamb
Tommy Kilpatrick Fraser Brown
Arthur C. Custance H.G. Sillitoe
John Inglis W.A. Simpson
Graham H. Howie Robert B. Robertson

1989

Roger D.L. Guthrie Frank W. Garforth
Ann Wakeling Matthew Bramley
William A. Nimmo Smith Allan R. Neil
David E. Purchase Jack Ashcroft
Darrell Pickles Iain H. Ogilvie
William R. Mowbray James Binnie
James Brown Paul Riley Innes Mitchell
Leslie B. Aird Irene D. Aird
W. Douglas Allan David McGill
N. Keith Rutter Kenneth Brown
Douglas A. Anderson David A. Smith
Paul Gillies Matthew G.D. Shaw
John Barker Ruth Barker Elsie Middlemiss
John Coop Jim F. Stuart Ian Henderson
Anne M. Marker Willis B. Marker
Mike Paterson Anne Bennet Stuart Benn
Peter Williams Garth Broomfield
George Graham Iain M. Brown
S.J. Henderson Nigel K. Saxton
Derek G. Sime David McAvoy
Graham Tutton Anne H. Lindsay
Ian A. Jones David J. Broadhead
Roderick L.G. Brodie Chris R. Peart
Arnold T. Morrison Donald F. Maclean
John C.M. Blair J. Michael Barron
Michael Thomson John M. Uytman
Cherie Chapman Terry McDonagh
Archie Given Ellen Sanderson
J. Kenneth Oakley Peter Lomax Yates
John S. Alexander Michael W. Kelly
Robert F. Gibson Michael Milmoe
James W. Stewart Robert L. Cameron
Alex A. Hanton Richard G. Ross

... ... R. Sharren J. Smith

1990

Jack Greenway Dave Duff V.R. Davey
John R. Davis Eric Campbell Knox
Robert MacCallum Kenneth Critchley
Bill Lackenby Peter Ellis Paul Russell
B.E.H. Maden Duncal L. Murray
Bertha Rostron James W. Rostron
Neil Clough Graham North
William Paterson Ian J.B. Murray
Dan A. Carmichael Andrew R. Kilbride
Kenneth Pierce Ian Turner W. John Webb
John Barrett James C. Waterton
Leonard J. Thomson Raymond Horner
Marion Faulds David A. Henderson
Gerry Bowes Philip Massey
Andrew Brown J.W. Quine John Norrie
Alistair M. Beeley David M. Clark
Chris B. Cormack Brian D. Curle
Andrew S. Templeton Andrew Grundy
John Leftly Dee Lacy Tony Rogers
Tony Taylor Alexander Laing John Russell
Robert D. Worth George G. Sim
Andrew Murdoch Peter Malone
D. Nairne Gray Hugh Symonds
J.E.R. Ullock James Haddow
Eddie Sutherland Norma Sutherland
Guy Semple Frances A. Wilson
Peter Wilson John W. Richardson
Jonathan de Ferranti Neil Williams
Klaus Schwartz Malcolm J.J. Arney
James D. Gentles Bethan Steele
David Steele Andrew M. McCosh
Iain A.J. Coker Dennis Alexander
David Stallard Alexander H. MacCalman
Margaret Graham Bertram W. Logie
Neil G. Spalding Andrew J. Matheson
D.C. Hunter Scott John Barnard
David Jones Martin Wilson
Stuart Clements Katharine Weyman
Dennis J.W. Usher Andrew R. Beckett
Rob H. Woodall John Patrick
Molly Johnstone Alasdair M. Dutton
Rory N. Dutton Jack Sugden
Harry E.M. Dott Bernard Smith Ian Young
Pete Craven Gordon Colthart
Connie McCreath J. Peter S. Gray
Les Rothnie Jonathan D. Groves
Margaret Guy Allan Boath
Bruce G. Lindsay Gordon F. Lindsay
Ian S. Robertson Allan Downie
Michael A. Underwood Marjorie Powrie
Hew B. Fraser John M. Knight
A.J. Muston Nick Picozzi
Douglas McHardy Alan W. Patrick
Peter Norman Hughill Lynn M. Youngs
Gerald Orchard Alan J.L. Rodger
Dave Crawford Wal Clark Jennie Boulter
Peter Boulter Andrew McD. Craig
Elizabeth S. Heath Teresa Lingard
John Barrowman Paul Howard
Harry Hartley Malcolm Gray

1991

Angela Soper Robert F. McKay
Iain M. Gilbert Ivan McA.G. Smith
Peter Sellers Sylvia Sellers Tom Anderson
Iain D. Shepherd David A. Kydd
Alastair Grant Stephen J. Hagan
John Wainwright Robert Gordon Buchan
William Knowles Wolf Gruellich

THE
MUNROIST'S
COMPANION

Compiled and Edited by
Robin N. Campbell

This book is compiled from information and experience provided by members of the Scottish Mountaineering Club and other contributors. The book is published by the Scottish Mountaineering Trust, which is a charitable trust.

Revenue from the sale of books published by the Trust is used for the continuation of its publishing programme and for charitable purposes associated with Scottish mountains and mountaineering.

Published by
The Scottish Mountaineering Trust

PUBLISHED BY THE SCOTTISH MOUNTAINEERING TRUST: 1999
© THE SCOTTISH MOUNTAINEERING CLUB

First Published 1999

British Library Cataloguing in Publication Data
ISBN 0 907521-50-9

A catalogue record of this book is available from
the British Library

Cover Illustrations.
      Front: *Ben Lomond from the north* (detail), watercolour on paper
      Back: *Stob Binnein and Ben More from Glen Dochart,* watercolour on paper
These illustrations are reproduced from original works by George Fennel Robson, O.W.S.
(1788 - 1833) by kind permission of the Heather Newman Gallery, Cranham, Nr. Painswick,
Gloucestershire GL6 6TX

Production by Scottish Mountaineering Trust (Publications) Limited
Graphics & typesetting by Just, Kirkintilloch, Glasgow
Printed and bound by The Bath Press Limited

Distributed by Cordee, 3a DeMontfort Street, Leicester, LE1 7HD

THE
MUNROIST'S
COMPANION

An Anthology
Compiled and Edited by
Robin N. Campbell

The Scottish Mountaineering Club

Contents

Editor's Preface   1

Chapter 1   The Pioneers – Munro

1.1	Hugh Thomas Munro, 1856 – 1919		4
1.2	Munro and his Mountains	T. Weir	9
1.3	Reminiscences of a Solitary Walk in Early Club Days	H.T. Munro	17
1.4	Winter Ascents in the Cairngorms	H.T. Munro	20
1.5	Hot Nights and Days on the Mountains in June	H.T. Munro	25
1.6	Three Nights on the Cairngorms	H.T. Munro	29
1.7	Munro and the Salvationist Tendency	R.N. Campbell	32
1.8	Obituary of Munro	W. Douglas	41

Chapter 2   The Pioneers – Robertson

2.1	Archibald Eneas Robertson, 1870 – 1958		46
2.2	Robertson's Round of the Munros	A.E. Robertson	49
2.3	The 'Munros' of Scotland	A.E. Robertson	67
2.4	Robertson Observed	J.L. Aikman	71
2.5	Obituary of A.E. Robertson	J.H.B. Bell	76

Chapter 3   The Pioneers – Four Early Completers

3.1	Burn, Parker, Corbett and Dow		79
3.2	Finishing the Three-thousanders in the Cairngorms	R.G. Burn	81
3.3	The Scottish 'Threes'	J.A. Parker	87
3.4	Munros, Beards and Weather	J. Dow	90

Chapter 4   Defining and Classifying

4.1	On Defining Munros: Introduction		94
4.2	Munro on Definition	H.T. Munro	95
4.3	Preface to the 1921 Tables	W.N. Ling	100
4.4	Notes on Munro's Tables	R.G. Burn	101
4.5	Munro's Tables – Two Contrasting Views	J. Dow & E.C. Thomson	104
4.6	Some Observations on Munro's Tables	R.M. Gall Inglis	107
4.7	The Separation of Mountains and . . .	F.F. Bonsall	111
	. . . the Separation of Munros		114
4.8	Munro's Tables, 1891 – 1991	R.N. Campbell	117
4.9	On the Classification of Mountains	D. Purchase	123
4.10	Some Unsolved Problems in Munroology	G. Cohen	156
4.11	For the Next Revision of the Tables	J. Gall Inglis	158
4.12	Tables of Scottish Mountains before Munro	C. Huntley	162

Chapter 5   The History of Munro's Tables

5.1	The Published Tables		165
5.2	A Variorum Table of the Munros and Tops	R.N. Campbell	167

Chapter 6   Technical Advice to Munroists

6.1	Introduction		204
6.2	Joseph Stott's 'Practical Hints for Pedestrians'	R.N. Campbell	205
6.3	Naismith's Rule . . . and Naismith Reviewed	T.J. Ransley	211
6.4	How to Stop a Fall on Hard Snow or Ice	W.W. Naismith	214
6.5	On Route Finding in Mist	W. Douglas	215
6.6	On the Height of Some of the Black Cuchullins in Skye	J.N. Collie	218
6.7	Aneroid Barometers	J. Gall Inglis	225
6.8	The Height of Slioch	J.A. Parker	228
6.9	Aneroid and Munros	J. Rooke Corbett	231
6.10	Orientation	H. Raeburn	238
6.11	Steering in Mist by Dead-Reckoning	J.A. Parker	243
6.12	Drug Addiction in Scottish Mountaineering	G.J.F. Dutton	246

Chapter 7   Predicaments

7.1	Introduction		249
7.2	Benighted on Ben More Assynt	W.W. Naismith	249
7.3	Beinn Dearg and the Fannichs	H.G.S. Lawson	253
7.4	Stuchd an Lochain and the Upper Part of Glen Lyon	F.S. Goggs	259
7.5	An Experience of the Hills of Ey	E.M. Corner	265
7.6	A Fifteen-Hour Walk in Benderloch	F.S. Goggs	271
7.7	Midnight Wanderings in the Lairig	E. Backhouse	276
7.8	A Far Cry to Lochow	J.F.A. Burt	279
7.9	The Breath of the Gods	*Various authors*	282

Chapter 8   The Modern Munroist

8.1	Introduction		288
8.2	Hillwalking from Cape Wrath to Glasgow	A.G. Cousins	289
8.3	Ben Feskineth – A Lost Munro?	J.C. Donaldson	299
8.4	From Sea to Shining Sea!	I.A. Robertson	301
8.5	That Elusive Final Munro	I. Waller	307
8.6	Rampant Munrosis: The Scottish Disease	W.D. Brooker	309
8.7	A Posthumous Completion	R.N. Campbell	314

Index of Mountains and Tops	318
General Index	325

Illustrations and Poems

List of Munroists by Year of Completion — *Endpapers*

Highland Landscape (poem)   *Douglas J. Fraser* — 3

Portrait of Sir Hugh T. Munro (chalk on paper)   *National Galleries of Scotland* — 5

Application Form of Hugh T. Munro   *SMC Archives* — 7

Tom Weir — 9

The Ruins of Lindertis House   *R.N. Campbell* — 15

An Tudair and Sgurr na Lapaich from Pollan Buidhe   *A.E. Robertson* — 19

Braeriach and Sgoran Dubh from Carn Eilrig   *J.R. Young* — 22-3

Sgurr Dubh an Da Bheinn, Gars-Bheinn and Sgurr nan Eag   *D.J. Bennet* — 27

Hygienic Hymn (poem)   *Alexander Nicolson* — 31

Hely H. Almond in 1895   *Elliot & Fry, photographers* — 32

The Inaccessible Pinnacle of Sgurr Dearg   *A.E. Robertson* — 37

The Grave of Sir Hugh T. Munro   *R.N. Campbell* — 40

William Douglas (See Note 1)   *SMC Archives* — 41

Sir Hugh T. Munro at the Dower House of Drumleys   *SMC Archives* — 43

Portrait of the Rev. A.E. Robertson (Oil on canvas)   *Keith Henderson, R.S.W.* — 47

Rev. A.E. Robertson on Salisbury Crags   *SMC Archives* — 51

Application Form of Archibald E. Robertson   *SMC Archives* — 54

Buachaille Etive Mor   *A.E. Robertson* — 65

Rev. A.E. Robertson   *SMC Archives* — 67

Sgurr a' Mhadaidh from Sgurr Thuilm   *A.E. Robertson* — 68

J. Logan Aikman (see Note 2)   *SMC Archives* — 71

SMC Annual Dinner Menu – Drawing of the CIC Hut, Ben Nevis   *W.R. Lester* — 74

James H.B. Bell   *SMC Archives* — 76

Rev. A. Ronald G. Burn, at 80 years of age   *P. Duffy* — 82

Cairn Toul and Sgor an Lochain Uaine from Ben Macdui   *D.J. Bennet* — 85

James A. Parker (See Note 1)   *SMC Archives* — 87

Beinn Sgritheall   *D.J. Bennet* — 88

Map of Eididh na Clach Geala to Beinn Dearg   *One-Inch O.S. Map, 1881* — 96

Map of Eididh na Clach Geala to Beinn Dearg   *Six-Inch O.S. Map, 1881* — 97

The Bidean nam Bian Range from the north-east   *D.J. Bennet* — 106

Robin M. Gall Inglis   *SMC Archives* — 107

Frank F. Bonsall — 111

The Liathach Range from the south-east   *D.J. Bennet* — 115

Robin N. Campbell — 117

David Purchase — 123

SMC Annual Dinner Menu – Drawing of Abseiler   *A.H.H. Ross* — 154

Kedgeree (poem)   *James Smith* — 155

Ben Vane (poem)   *W.P. Ker*   157

James Gall Inglis   *SMC Archives*   159

Chris Huntley   162

Expostulation with Cruachan (poem)   *W.P. Ker*   164

Joseph G. Stott on Cruach Ardrain summit   *SMC Archives*   205

The Song of the Scottish Mountaineering Club   *J.G. Stott and J. Bland*   209-10

Trevor J. Ransley   211

William W. Naismith   *SMC Archives*   214

Bidein a' Ghlas Thuill (sketch)   *Robert Dawson Scott*   217

J. Norman Collie   *SMC Archives*   218

Map of 'The Cuchullin Hills' (The Cuillin of Skye)   *C. Pilkington*   219

The Pinnacle Ridge of Sgurr nan Gillean from the west   *D.J. Bennet*   222

'Doing the Dubhs' (poem)   *Traditional*   224

Sir Hugh T. Munro's Pocket Thermometer and Barometer   *R.N. Campbell*   225

Slioch from the south side of Loch Maree   *R.N. Campbell*   229

J. Rooke Corbett   *Rucksack Club Archives*   232

Harold Raeburn   *SMC Archives*   238

The Magnapole – an early marching compass   *H. Raeburn*   242

The Northern Corrie of Lochnagar (sketch)   *Robert Dawson Scott*   245

Geoffrey J.H. Dutton   246

Map of Conival and Ben More Assynt   *A. Kassyk*   250

Frank S. Goggs (See Note 1)   *SMC Archives*   259

Map of Upper Glen Lyon   *A. Kassyk*   261

Map of Glen Ey to Glen Thaitneach   *A. Kassyk*   267

Beinn Laoigh from the north   *D.J. Bennet*   280

Theme and Variations (poem)   *W.P. Ker*   287

Alexander ('Sandy') G. Cousins on the summit of Mullach Fraoch-choire   289

Alexander ('Sandy') G. Cousins in the West Perthshire Hills   *D.J. Bennet*   297

Iain A. Robertson   301

William ('Bill') D. Brooker   309

'Munro' before his first posthumous outing   *R.N. Campbell*   315

'Munro' completes the Munros   *R.N. Campbell*   316

'Munro' prepares to complete the Tops   *D.G. Pyper*   317

1. This picture is a detail from A.E. Robertson's group photograph of the 1906 SMC Meet at Clachaig Inn, Glencoe. The photograph, together with a key identifying all those who appear in it, was reproduced in *SMCJ* 1910, XI, 9.

2. This group photograph is from a handprinted menu of a Dinner at the CIC Hut convened by Aikman. Others present, and presumably shown in the photograph, were G.G. Jackson, J.G. MacLean, J.G. Robinson, G.F. Todd, W. Waddell and G.C. Williams.

Acknowledgements

I WOULD like to record a debt of gratitude to the following people and institutions.

To Heather and Derek Newman for Fennel Robson's gorgeous watercolours. To the Keeper of the List, Chris Huntley, for supplying up-to-date Munroist data. To Heather Moncur for her father Douglas Fraser's poem *Highland Landscape*. To Susanna Kerr, Deborah Hunter and the National Galleries of Scotland for the chalk drawing of Sir Hugh Munro. To Olive Geddes and the National Library of Scotland for archival assistance. To Graeme Hunter, Custodian of the SMC Slide Collection, for archival photographs. To Maude Tiso, Keeper of the A.E. Robertson Collection, for photographs and for the Henderson portrait of Robertson. To Patrick Duffy for the photograph of Ronald Burn. To Gordon Adshead, Secretary of the Rucksack Club, for the photograph of Rooke Corbett. To Adam Kassyk for the watercolour map drawings used in Section 7. To Donald Bennet for cracking the whip, for assistance with illustrations and for contributing his own excellent photographs. To Dave Hewitt of The Angry Corrie for advice and encouragement. To Derek Bearhop, the Master of the Tables, for contributing the 1997 edition to the Variorum Table. To Bob Richardson for assisting with entering other components of the Variorum Table. To Gordon Adshead and David Purchase, fellow Munroologists, for their valuable advice about the Variorum Table. To Douglas Anderson, Convenor of the SMC Publications Sub-Committee for support and encouragement. To Lynden Astill of Just for his patient attention to detail and sensitivity in setting the book. To the various Editors of the SMC and Cairngorm Club Journals down the years whose work I have plundered.

Finally, I offer thanks to all those authors or relatives of authors who freely contributed their work and supplied portrait photographs.

Robin N. Campbell

Preface

THERE have been many books about the Munros and about the pastime of collecting them.[1] So it is necessary to offer some justification for providing yet another. My excuse is that the existing books are either manuals describing the Munros and how best to climb them or personal accounts of a traverse of them (quickly, many times, without a car, in winter, carrying a bicycle, etc.). There is then a danger that the mountaineer beginning a traverse of the Munros may be misled into thinking that this is a pastime with only a technical aspect, and, moreover, a pastime in which a spirit of competitive achievement runs strongly – a sport, in a word. Not so. Munro-bagging has a rich and colourful history stretching right back through the hundred or so years of Scottish mountaineering. So in this Companion I have included without alteration or abbreviation selected writings from the pioneers Hugh Munro, Archie Robertson,[2] Ronald Burn, James Parker, John Dow, Rooke Corbett and James Gall Inglis with the object of providing the contemporary bagger with a sense of this history and the opportunity to share in the experience of the pioneers. And, although there is a section containing accounts written by modern Munroists, I have excluded the writings of the swift, the multiply-completing, the 277-in-one-gulpers, etc. – for these are not typical Munroists. With almost 2,000 now having completed the Munros and reported their completions,[3] it is clear that the typical Munroist takes several years to make the traverse, does it (or reports it) only once, climbs in all seasons and in all weathers and, if they have a competitive spirit running through them, they leave it behind when they go on the hill. Indeed, there are a number of well-known figures in Scottish mountaineering who have stopped at the brink of completing the traverse, leaving a handful of Munros unclimbed, perhaps because of a fear that they may turn a satisfying pastime into a treadmill ruled by the setting of goals and achieving of targets. These, then, are the readers for whom this book is intended to be a Companion.

If history is one aspect of Munroing which is neglected, then philosophy is another! From the very earliest days, there have been animated debates about the status of hills. Even if a top is 3,000 feet high it does not follow that it should be included in the Tables, for there are many pimples, warts, pinnacles and shoulders that have no individuality in the context of the mountain that supports them. And ever since Munro conceived the brilliant idea of distinguishing some Table-worthy tops as a special class more 'distinct and separate' than the others, Masters of the Tables – and ordinary baggers – have worried about the physical or metaphysical basis of this distinction. I have responded to this thirst for philosophy by including a lengthy section on defining and classifying Munros and Tops. This section begins with the tight-lipped thoughts of Munro himself and passes

---

[1] It may seem odd to describe Munro-bagging as collecting. But experiences may be collected as well as objects, witness the efforts of Don Juan. And the obsessive zeal which animates the collector of experiences may be just as strong.

[2] Robertson's diary of his traverse – a substantial work – is selectively abbreviated.

[3] Some of these reports are now in the public domain. The SMC have now deposited in the National Library of Scotland an extensive collection of papers, accessible in the Manuscript Collection, catalogued as Accession 11538. Items 47 through 58 are reports to the then Keeper of the List, Bill Brooker, of all completions between 1971 and 1993. A catalogue of these deposits is available in the Library's Manuscript Reading Room.

through the ideas of other early Munroists to modern discussions, which begin with Frank Bonsall in the 1970s and end with David Purchase's searching analyses.

In addition, I have been very much aware that the typical Munroist feels somewhat irritated by the seemingly never-ending changes in the published Tables, and perhaps suspects that this is all a stratagem of the SMC, pursued in order to sell more books![4] The situation is really much more complex. Munro himself struggled to make these distinctions in a manner that satisfied him, and the changes that occurred between the original Tables of 1891 and the first revision of them in 1921 (Munro's responsibility until his death in 1919) were far greater and more radical than any we have seen since. Moreover, the data provided by the Ordnance Survey were originally grossly defective and errors in the height and position of tops have persisted to the present day. For example, it is only in the most recent maps that Spidean Coire nan Clach of Beinn Eighe is given the marked height that it was long known to deserve. A third factor has been the fallibility of Masters of the Tables. It is hard to keep track of 540-something tops, even if you have climbed them all once or twice. Mistakes have been made, subsequent editors have corrected them, and gone on to make new mistakes of their own! In order to make the point absolutely clear that the Munros and Tops are a very movable feast, and to guide future revisions, I have included a Variorum Table of the Munros, which keeps track of the astonishing changes which have occurred between 1891 and 1997 for all of the 591 tops appearing in the Tables through these years.

Two sections of the Companion remain to be introduced. Although I wanted to include a section on Techniques, it was clearly absurd to attempt to duplicate the kind of advice obtainable in books dedicated to ensuring fitness, good equipment and safe movement and navigation. So, although I have included a few wise words about movement and navigation from master mountaineers such as Willie Naismith and Harold Raeburn, the core of the section is about the determination of height. It is a mistake to imagine that this is entirely the province of the professional surveyor. Certainly, we are not as useful to the Ordnance Survey as amateur astronomers are to astronomy, but the mountaineer has always had a role to play in map-making on the mountains, and I am sure that there are still questions about height and even location that will not be settled without the assistance and guidance of mountaineers. Indeed I hope very much that reading this section of the Companion will encourage Munroists (or Corbettists) to carry poles, aneroids and levels with them once again, just as the pioneers did. After all, an organization which used to publish spot mountain heights to the first decimal place of one foot and now offers up heights to the nearest metre deserves what it gets!

Lastly, every Munroist comes to grief on some occasions. And these are events which seem to me to be part of the pastime: if not a cause for celebration they are certainly badges of experience that may be worn with a certain kind of grim but dignified pride. So I have

---

[4] Profits from the sale of all books by the Scottish Mountaineering Trust, which is a registered charity, are used for the general benefit of Scottish mountaineering – for the repair of footpaths, the refurbishment of Club Huts (provided these are accessible to the mountaineering public) and to assist the purchase of mountain land by appropriate bodies.

included a section entitled *Predicaments* in which mountaineers, sometimes quite celebrated ones, become shamelessly and hopelessly lost, or suffer other ignominious reversals. These stories provide amusement, *via* Schadenfreude, and also useful warnings of the dangers that lurk on high. Mountaineering is not golf – which produces the grossest sorts of humiliation for its participants on a regular basis – but there are plenty of banana-skins up there, waiting for the technically-perfect and super-fit to step on them.

A final word about some matters of spelling and usage. (1) The use of Compleation strikes me as twee, or should it be twea, and I have studiously avoided and expunged it in favour of completion. (2) I have also stuck to 'Munros'. This is surely better than the grammatically-awful 'Munro's' used by Robertson, but I am almost persuaded that the 'Irish spelling' of 'Munroes' is better (see Ivan Waller in Chapter 8.5). After all, it is not unusual for a Munro to resemble a potato in other respects, so why not in this? However, the -es plural ending is usually reserved for words of recent foreign origin, which counts against it, as does the worry that were they to be spelled 'Munroes' it would not be long before someone began to write of 'climbing a Munroe', following the shining example of U.S. Vice-President Dan Quayle's correction of a child's 'potato' to 'potatoe'. (3) So far as the naming of hills and the spelling of hill-names is concerned, I have not attempted to 'correct' the names or spellings of the original authors, since such a process would be unending and, in any case, unpleasantly presumptuous. Hills which have changed their names or spellings may be securely identified by use of the Index and the Variorum Table. (4) Since the Tables have avoided Gaelic accents for some time now, so have I. (5) I have added footnotes freely where I felt that the reader deserved some extra clarification. In chapters where there are author's footnotes as well as mine, I have distinguished them, otherwise it may be assumed that any footnote is mine. (6) Frequent reference is made to the *Scottish Mountaineering Club Journal*, usually abbreviated to *SMCJ*, to the *Cairngorm Club Journal*, abbreviated to *CCJ*, and to the SMC's Deposits in the National Library (see footnote 2) as *NLS Acc. 11538*.

Highland Landscape

Here, there is beauty every sense can share
Against the moving back-cloth of the sky;
The murmur of the stream, the scented air,
The various enchantments for the eye.
About my feet the moor is yellow-starred
With tormentil, the friendliest of flowers;
Above, the mighty peak that stands on guard
Forms and dissolves between the passing showers.
Wherever near or far the eye may dwell,
All things contribute to a sense of fitness
So integral, it would be hard to tell
Which of them bears the more impressive witness –
The splendid sweep of the enclosing hill,
The neat perfection of the tormentil.

Douglas J. Fraser

CHAPTER 1

The Pioneers - Munro

1.1 Hugh Thomas Munro 1856 – 1919

WE begin, as we should, with Munro himself. For although he didn't complete the round of either the Munros or the Tops, Munro was undoubtedly a collector, or 'bagger' of tops and possibly the first to conceive of the idea of a complete round. The first edition of his Tables contained many tops whose height, configuration and even location was uncertain, since it was at that time not of any particular importance that our mountains should be accurately mapped. So it is hardly surprising that Munro should want to visit as many of his tops as possible, in order to produce a better second edition. But he went far beyond what was required by these editorial duties, visiting 535 of his 538 tops and, of course, many other tops, shoulders, cairns, etc. as well. When did it occur to Munro that he might climb them all? And when did his collection reach the point where completion became a definite possibility? These are interesting questions, not so far answered.

The selection of writings that follows attempts to give the reader a well-rounded picture of Munro. Tom Weir's piece concentrates on Munro's activities in the years 1889-91, the period during which he was compiling his Tables and helping to shape the character of the newly-formed Scottish Mountaineering Club, and it ends with a fascinating account of Weir's visit to Munro's home in Angus. Four pieces by Munro follow, describing visits to different kinds of mountain country and spanning 25 years or so. My own article about Munro tries to add to what we know about him in a general way, but particularly focuses on the question of what Munro's own climbing goals were and what were the tops that he didn't climb. The section ends with Willie Douglas's obituary – a characteristically painstaking, thorough and sympathetic piece.

For those wishing to read more of Munro's writings, and for later reference, there follows a list of his mountaineering notes and articles. Those articles marked with an asterisk were published as contributions to the SMC's Guide Book project. Later references to Munro's writings will be as 'Munro 1' through 'Munro 88'.

1. Winter Ascents. *SMCJ* 1890, I, 20-24
2. Suggestions as to Maps. *SMCJ* 1890, I, 43-44.
3. Winter Ascents No. 2 – The Braes of Angus. *SMCJ* 1890, I, 98-105.
4. Notes on Mam Sodhail, Sgurr Fhuaran and Beinn Fhada. *SMCJ* 1890, I, 129-130.
5. The Drumochter Hills. *SMCJ* 1891, I, 176-177.
6. Ascent of Ben More, Mull. *SMCJ* 1891, I, 177.
7. Club Expeditions. *SMCJ* 1891, I, 178.
8. Review of J. Bartholomew, 'New Series of Reduced O.S. Maps Nos. 11, 12, 13, 15, 16, 21'. *SMCJ* 1891, I, 180-183.
9. Club Meet at Dalmally, Easter 1891, *SMCJ* 1891, I, 239.

Chalk drawing of Sir Hugh T. Munro by an unknown hand
SCOTTISH NATIONAL PORTRAIT GALLERY

10. Notes on Carn Liath and Beinn Vuroch. *SMCJ* 1891, I, 243.

11. Notes on Glenfinnan and Lochaber Hills. *SMCJ* 1891, I, 243-245.

12. Dalwhinnie to Tyndrum. *SMCJ* 1891, I, 245-246.

13. Review of J. Bartholomew, 'New Series of Reduced O.S. Maps Nos. 17, 20'. *SMCJ* 1891, I, 248-249.

14. Winter Ascents No. 3 – The Rum Mountains. *SMCJ* 1891, I, 259-264.

15. Tables giving all the Scottish Mountains exceeding 3,000 feet in height. *SMCJ* 1891, I, 276-314.

16. Club Meet at Dalwhinnie, Easter 1891, *SMCJ* 1891, I, 321.

17. Ben Lomond, etc. , *SMCJ* 1892, II, 31-32.

18. Craigowe (Sidlaw Hills), *SMCJ* 1892, II, 33-35.

19. Cairns on Mountain Tops. *SMCJ* 1892, II, 38.

20. Winter Ascents No. 4 – The Cairngorms. *SMCJ* 1892, II, 45-50. See Chapter 1.4

21. The Lochnagar Range. *SMCJ* 1892, II, 133-134.

22. Review of J. Bartholomew's 'Geological Map of Scotland'. *SMCJ* 1892, II, 154-155.

23. Dark Lochnagar. *SMCJ* 1893, II, 190-200.

24. Review of J. Bartholomew, 'New Series of Reduced O.S. Maps Nos. 19, 25'. *SMCJ* 1893, II, 210-211.

25. Supplementary Note on Ben-y-Gloe. *SMCJ* 1893, II, 239-245.

26. Sgoran Dubh and the Western Cairngorms. *CCJ* 1893, I, 26-28.

27. Loch Eunach, Sgoran Dubh and the Western Cairngorms. *SMCJ* 1893, II, 296-300.

28. Review of J. Geikie, 'Fragments of Earth Lore'. *SMCJ* 1893, II, 326-327.

29. Review of W. Martin & Co., 'Solid Alto-Relievo Model of Scotland'. *SMCJ* 1893, II, 327-328.

30. Additions, Corrections and Remarks. *SMCJ* 1893, II, 330-336.

31. An Teallach, Ross-shire. *SMCJ* 1894, III, 10-18.

32. Review of J. Bartholomew, 'New Series of Reduced O.S. Maps No. 24'. *SMCJ* 1894, III, 49-50.

33. Boot Trees. *SMCJ* 1894, III, 169-170.

34. Review of W.M. Conway, 'Climbing and Exploration in the Karakorams-Himalayas'. *SMCJ* 1894, III, 172-173.

35. Beinn a' Chroin and Ben Vorlich. *SMCJ* 1895, III, 235.

36. Beinn a' Chaoruinn, Creag Meaghaidh and the Monadh Liaths. *SMCJ* 1895, III, 235-237.

37. The West Highland Railway. *SMCJ* 1895, III, 238-239.

38. Review of J. Murray, 'Handbook for Travellers in Scotland'. *SMCJ* 1895, III, 240-242.

39. Review of E. Whymper, 'On the Top of Ben Nevis'. *SMCJ* 1895, III, 245.

40. Review of J. Bartholomew, 'New Series of Reduced O.S. Maps Nos. 12, 16, 26'. *SMCJ* 1895, III, 246.

41. Cruach Ardran by the North-West Face. *SMCJ* 1895, III, 306-307.

42. The Buchaille Etives. *SMCJ* 1895, III, 348-350.

43. Note on A.E. Robertson, 'Two Days in Lochaber'. *SMCJ* 1895, III, 354.

44. Suggestions as to Raising of Subscription, etc., *SMCJ* 1896, IV, 68-69.

45. West Monar. *SMCJ* 1896, IV, 175-177.

46. Snow Cornices and Crevasses. *SMCJ* 1897, IV, 253.

47. Club Meet at Loch Awe, New Year 1897, *SMCJ* 1897, IV, 284-287.

48. Club Meet at Fort William, New Year 1898, *SMCJ* 1898, V, 77-79.

Munro's application to join the Scottish Mountaineering Club (Scottish climbs only)

49. Club Meet at Ballachulish, Easter 1898, *SMCJ* 1898, V, 80-81.
50. Note to Prof. Heddle's 'South West Ross'. *SMCJ* 1898, V, 114-115.
51. A Summer Night on the Glenshee Hills. *SMCJ* 1898, V, 116-120.
52. Bens Laoghal, Hope and Clibrig. *SMCJ* 1899, V, 182-187.
53. Creag Meaghaidh Range, East of the 'Window'. *SMCJ* 1900, VI, 37.
54. Geal Charn (3,036 ft.), Monadhliaths. *SMCJ* 1900, VI, 37.
55. The Freevater and Glen Strathfarrar Mountains. *SMCJ* 1900, VI, 46-48.
56. The Corrour Hills. *SMCJ* 1900, VI, 65.
57. A' Mhaighdean. *SMCJ* 1900, VI, 99-101.
58. Meall na Cuaich. *SMCJ* 1901, VI, 130-131.
59. Beinn Chonzie*. *SMCJ* 1901, VI, 244-245.
60. Beinn Chaluim, Beinn Dheiceach, Meall Chuirn*. *SMCJ* 1902, VII, 28-29.
61. The Drumochter Hills*. *SMCJ* 1903, VII, 234-235.
62. Caiplich and Cairngorm. *SMCJ* 1903, VII, 238-239.
63. The Drochaid Glas. *SMCJ* 1903, VII, 298.
64. The Braes of Angus*. *SMCJ* 1904, VIII, 125-132.
65. Mount Blair*. *SMCJ* 1904, VIII, 166.
66. The Cairnwell and Glas Thulachan Groups*. *SMCJ* 1904, VIII, 167-171.
67. Ben Vrackie*. *SMCJ* 1904, VIII, 173.
68. Beinn Dearg and Carn a' Chlamain*. *SMCJ* 1904, VIII, 174-176.
69. An Sgarsoch and Carn an Fhidleir*. *SMCJ* 1904, VIII, 176-177.
70. Clunie Forest*. *SMCJ* 1905, VIII, 262 266.
71. Beinn Fhada*. *SMCJ* 1905, VIII, 275.
72. Note to Mam Sodhail*. *SMCJ* 1905, VIII, 279.
73. Slioch and Beinn Lair*. *SMCJ* 1906, IX, 88-89.
74. A' Mhaighdean and Beinn Dearg Mhor*. *SMCJ* 1906, IX, 89-90.
75. The Fannichs*. *SMCJ* 1906, IX, 95-98.
76. Hot Days and Nights on the Mountains in June. *SMCJ* 1906, IX, 126-131. See Chapter 1.5.
77. Beinn Laoghal*. *SMCJ* 1907, IX, 204.
78. Beinn Cleith Bric*. *SMCJ* 1907, IX, 205-206.
79. An Teallach, Ross-shire. *SMCJ* 1907, IX, 289-290.
80. Ben More, Assynt. *SMCJ* 1907, IX, 290.
81. Letter to the Editor. *SMCJ* 1909, X, 231-232.
82. Tomdoun. *SMCJ* 1912, XII, 177-181.
83. Letter about Munro's Tables. *SMCJ* 1913, XII, 221-224.
84. North Africa, 1913, *SMCJ* 1914, XIII, 51.
85. Letter about Lindertis Meet, May 1915, *SMCJ* 1915, XIII, 216.
86. Note about Mr. Reid, 'The SMC in Clover Again'. *SMCJ* 1916, XIV, 55.
87. Three Nights in the Cairngorms. *CCJ* 1918, IX, 59-63. See Chapter 1.6
88. Reminiscences of a Solitary Walk in Early Club Days. *SMCJ* 1918, XV, 67-71. See Chapter 1.3.

1.2 Munro and his Mountains

Tom Weir[1]

I HAVE just been into Angus, stravaiging round Kirriemuir, enjoying two worlds, up in the shining snows above Clova and Isla, and down among the green haughs of the South Esk. On the low ground it was spring, with skylarks pouring out torrents of song and peewits tumbling in the fields. But on Mount Keen it was still bitter winter, as I knew, for I had just been up there, bagging my first new 'Munro' for a very long time.

It was a dose of tonsilitis and 'flu which sent me up there. While I was swallowing and sneezing, I had opened Volume I of the Scottish Mountaineering Club *Journal* to take my mind off the confines of bed. Soon I was forgetting gargling and pills as a remarkable man stood out from the pages – Sir Hugh Munro, of Lindertis.[2]

I saw him as a lone figure in an Inverness cape with a Balmoral on his head, the snow crunching under his boots in that rolling world of mountains which stretches from Angus to Braemar. I see him stopping on top after top, to get out his aneroid and make an entry in a notebook, or sit on some commanding height to work out the exact details of the topography around him, for he was a great cataloguer of mountain views.

Then, as the pink of sunset gilds the summits, I can see him hitch his pack and set off at some speed for the Milton of Clova or the Spittal of Glen Shee, for Munro was a great cross-country traveller, preferring to traverse his mountains than to retrace his steps to the point of departure.

I like to think how he arrived in Glasgow for the SMC dinner of 1890, held in December. He would be thirty-three years of age then, bearded and wearing the kilt, for he had changed out of his knickerbockers after a morning in the thick mist and deep powder snow of Carn na Caim. Upon this 3,000 ft. summit he had stood at 10 a.m., the early hour of the climb allowing him to catch the 1.15 p.m. train from Dalwhinnie to Glasgow.

---

[1] This appreciation by TomWeir is taken from his book *Scotland*, pp. 61-68 (Gordon Wright Publishing, 1980).

[2] At the time of publication of Volume I of the *SMC Journal*, Munro was plain Mr Munro. He did not acquire the title until the death of his father in 1913.

He had been climbing at Dalwhinnie for three days before the dinner. This was about the time he wrote in the *Journal*.[3]

> 'I should be glad at almost any time during January, February, and March to join small parties of members of the club on expeditions of one or several days' duration. I am willing to go anywhere, but the districts I am most anxious to explore are – the Sutherland Hills, the Ullapool and Loch Maree country, the Cuchullins, Western Inverness-shire, the Blackmount, Glencoe, Glen Nevis, and Glen Lyon Hills. During the months mentioned I can almost always find time for a trip, but later I am much engaged. I am sometimes free, however, for a few days, and if it fitted my movements I would be glad to join any climbing party on learning of it.
>
> H.T. Munro, Lindertis.'

Well, he did explore all these districts, some in company, but mostly alone for he was never put off for lack of a companion. See him on Beinn a' Ghlo on the 22nd January, a day of wind with snow blowing,[4] '...in spiral columns several hundred feet high, penetrating everything, filling pockets and drifting between my waistcoat and shirt, where it melted and then froze into a solid wedge of ice. In all my winter experience in hills I have never suffered so severely from cold.'

Yet the cold did not prevent him from recording the details of the views, though the description is mercifully short compared with a tendency towards topographical excess in other accounts. That day he merely says – 'View good – Cairngorms and Ben Alder groups, the Glencoe Hills; Schiehallion (which does not show to advantage from here); Ben Lawers looking well, with Stobinian over his left shoulder, Ben Chonzie; the Fifeshire Lomonds and Sidlaws showing well, with the smoke of Dundee behind. The special feature, however, is the fine view of the higher peaks of Beinn a' Ghlo.'

He had started his walk from Blair Atholl, but finished that night two miles above Kirkmichael. 'Heavy walking all day in soft snow. At Diranean they had to scrape me down with a knife to get the frozen snow off me before I could enter the house.'

The date then was 1891, and just a month later he achieved one of his great desires, a landing in Rhum, where the landowner put the lodges at his disposal.[5] He writes – 'In the grey dawn of a drizzling morning – the 4th of February last – I landed in Rum. The day was not tempting for climbing so I went out to try for woodcock, accompanied by a keeper whose broad Lancashire accent seemed out of place in the Highlands.'

Rhum was unknown to mountaineers when Munro got permission to land. The weather was unsettled. Consider his resource therefore, when he climbed into the mist two

---

[3] See Munro 7.

[4] See Munro 10.

[5] See Munro 14. The proprietor of Rum, John Bullough, died about the time of Munro's visit. It was, of course, his son Sir George Bullough, who later transformed Kinloch House – using stone from Arran and soil from Ayrshire – into an extraordinary chateau furnished with Japanese gardens and alligator ponds, and who changed the spelling of Rum to Rhum. After a decent interval, the O.S. have now changed it back to Rum.

days later to see what he could achieve on the rocky ridges. He got to the top of Allival at midday, seeing in front of him Askival, clear of cloud and looking impressively difficult with a rock pinnacle blocking the way. He describes himself as being 'out for a stroll,' but continues – 'After casting about a little, I struck an easy way to the col, and a few minutes' ascent by the very narrow ridge brought me face to face with the *Gendarme*, which, as anticipated was quite perpendicular and probably one hundred feet high. The east face, however though steep – real climbing – presented no particular difficulty. Several attempts to regain the ridge proving abortive, I therefore kept to the face, reaching the summit almost without knowing it at 1.5 p.m.

So far so good. His Munro blood was really up; the day was still young, so now he dropped to the Ashval col for 'a nice bit of real rock climbing with some rather awkward smooth slabs of rock.' This was done in mist, as was the continuation onwards to Sgurr nan Gillean, 2,503 ft. The only unpleasant problem of the day occurred on the way down when he got into a constricted gully of steep grass and broken rock, 'as steep and disagreeable a piece of climbing as I wish to experience alone.' But he was back to his usual high spirits in Glendibidil which he thought 'vied with Glencoe in rugged grandeur, while its contrasts of glorious views far surpasses it.'

I like to think of him leaving Rhum by open boat for Arisaig, its prow pointed towards more snowy mountains in Glen Finnan and Lochaber where his axe was in constant play as he explored Streaps and its neighbours[6] before walking to Corpach 'in wild wind and sheets of rain.' He makes the observation – 'Members will be taken at this homely and comfortable inn at 8s 6d per day.'

From Corpach he climbed to the Carn Mor Dearg arête, enjoying some airy step-cutting and the proximity of the Nevis cliffs. He headed into Glen Nevis next day for a traverse of the An Gearanach ridge which demanded much care on its very narrow crest. The following morning saw him aboard the *Fusilier* heading home, another mountain journey successfully accomplished. Indeed, he never had an accident.

Nor did he go looking for difficulty. If there was an easy way, then Munro would take it. If not, then as on Rhum, he would not shirk the problem, nor did he refuse invitations from more technically-minded mountaineers. I like his description of climbing a gully on Ben Eunaich in March,[7] when he was 'much hampered too, by having an Inverness cape on', a remarkable garment for a place so constricted that he could not wield his axe properly. And the day was so wild that descent from the summit was 'as if wrestling with a man. There were some moments when I could not make a foot of ground.'

It must have been a very bad day indeed to tax a man of Munro's fitness. No journey was too long. To get to Dalmally from Dalwhinnie he walked over the Ben Alder peaks (spending a day climbing) to Loch Rannoch, thence to Glen Lyon and over the hill to the railway at Bridge of Orchy.[8]

---

[6] See Munro 11.

[7] See Munro 9.

[8] See Munro 12.

Munro[9] loved change, and was, in fact, a world traveller, though the only reference I can find to a foreign ascent is of the extinct volcano Irazu, in Costa Rica, made with his wife. Maybe he was too busy on his travels, for he was a King's Messenger, a professional courier who carried foreign despatches for diplomats, though many of his later journeys were done mainly for pleasure.

The climb in Costa Rica was made on Easter Sunday, 1894, just a year after he had unravelled the topography of An Teallach which was very much a mystery mountain at this time. Pennant and McCulloch had described it as 'awful' and 'terrific'.

But the SMC party which included Munro, were stirred in a different way when they saw 'the glorious hills themselves, suddenly bursting through the storm clouds, black, snow-slashed, and jagged against the setting sun,' a sight encouraging enough for them to hope 'that a vague tradition of an unclimbed peak might prove a reality.' Certainly they were the first to traverse An Teallach completely, fix the heights of the peaks, and determine its structure by photography.

The information was published in Volume III of the Journal in meticulous detail, with sketches and photographs showing the disposition of the peaks and corries. Munro had a 'guidebook' mind but was a dispenser of titbits as well as important information. In Sutherland, for example, he observes – 'The charges for forwarding luggage by the Sutherland mails are somewhat high, so pedestrians and cyclists would do well to make up brown paper parcels not exceeding eleven pounds each, and forward them by parcel post.'

He explored Sutherland by bicycle, but was a keen user of the West Highland Railway from the time of its opening, pointing out that 'by taking the early train, 7.35 a.m. from Glasgow, it is quite possible, without unduly hurrying, to cross Carn Dearg, 3,084 ft; Sgor Gaibhre, 3,128 ft; and Sgor Choinnich, 3,040 ft; and descending to the foot of Loch Ossian, return over Beinn na Lap, 3,066 ft; in time to continue your journey to Fort William by the evening train.'[10]

While on the Inverness line he notes that it is possible to dovetail Meall Cuaich, east-north-east of Dalwhinnie, 3,120 ft., into a break in the journey from Glasgow or Edinburgh. Of the railway north of Dingwall he had no good word to say.[11]

The motor car in Munro's life does not occur until Volume XII, when he writes, 'Without doubt, the motor car offers possibilities, and brings within the scope of a day or two's expedition, regions which formerly, even with the help of a bicycle, would have taken thrice as long.' The theme of the article is 'Tomdoun,' and since he drove the 130 miles between Glen Garry and Lindertis in five hours forty minutes the surface must have been reasonable, even if the Loch Laggan stretch was 'scandalously bad'.

He gives a summary of the road. 'Between Spean Bridge and Invergarry (sixteen miles) the road is moderate, except at two places with notice boards 'three water-courses across

---

[9] Three paragraphs have been omitted from Tom Weir's piece: they describe Munro's experiences in the Cairngorms given in full below as Chapter 1.4.

[10] See Munro 56.

[11] See Munro 58.

roadway' and 'seven ditto ditto'. These places cannot be taken too slowly. Above Invergarry the road is stony, narrow, and twisty, and requires careful driving.'[12]

The date was 1912 and Munro was fifty-six. Only seven years of his life were left. He was with his friend Rennie, a companion of An Teallach, whose photography and knowledge of botany delighted him. Together they explored the high peaks of Knoydart, from the top of Sgor na Ciche above Loch Nevis to the peaks of Loch Hourn. As always Munro notes the wild life in some detail, but reflects 'on the whole, I have never seen less animal life on the mountains.'

No doubt he would be thinking back to Easter, 1897, when he was glad of the shelter of these lochs after being driven out of Skye by atrocious weather. The occasion was a famous yachting meet. The boat was to be used as a base for climbing on the Cuillin, but foul weather and seasickness drove the twenty members and nine guests eastward to Knoydart. Munro was president of the Club then, and the decision to lift anchor and get out was his.

Walter Barrow gives a good account of the cheerful end to the meet, when sailing back to Oban. 'The black peaks of Rum stood out against the rich golden light reflected in the glassy surface of a rolling swell. And on the deck of the yacht, members of the Club, headed by the President in Highland kilt and sporran, danced a reel and Strathspey to the drone of the Scottish pipes.'[13]

I have given you, I hope, something of the spirit and character of the man, as I got to know him from his writings. The time had now come to visit his home, talk with his son, and meet anyone I could find who remembered him. I found the house of 'Drumleys' just three miles south of Kirriemuir, and when I rang the bell and the door was opened by a man in a red kilt and tweed jacket I knew I was looking at Sir Torquil Munro, 5th Baronet of Lindertis. "Come in," he said when I told him I wanted to talk to him about his father, to complete a picture I had of him in my mind's eye.

"I don't know that I can tell you very much," he said, "I never really knew him, you know. He was a great traveller, away a lot. He wasn't a very tall man, always wore a beard and dressed in the kilt."

He would not be so unlike his son, I imagined, who is compact, square-shouldered, with a wiry frame, a neatly-built man. Nor do I imagine the Scots voice would be so different, for Sir Torquil was educated at Crieff, Winchester, and Magdalene College, Cambridge, while his father was born in London, studied German at Stuttgart at the age of seventeen, taking a business training at nineteen, and going in 1880 to be Private Secretary to Sir George Colley, Governor of Natal. Out there he had fought in the Basuto War as a cavalryman, returning home with a black boy, a monkey, and a host of curios.

---

[12] See Munro 82.

[13] Barrow's reminiscence of the Meet appeared in *SMCJ* 1939, XXII, 29-31. The original account, by Professor R. Lodge, (in *SMCJ* 1897, IV, 288-293) notes that these deck celebrations marked the first appearance of decent weather of the Meet and without a trace of shame confesses that 'a piper was discovered among the crew'!

"My father was a widower," Sir Torquil continued. "I was two when my mother died. Although I never really knew him he was very kind. He often came to see me at school in Crieff, and would take me runs in the car. I remember Harold Raeburn staying here, and we went bird nesting. He showed me a long eared owl's nest in a tree out there.

"I was eighteen when my father died in 1919. He died of Spanish 'flu in France. He ran a canteen for French troops in Tarascon during the war, but he is buried between here and the old family home of Lindertis. He was very fond of the music of Wagner, and he played the flute. He was a great dancer. He had very small feet and neat ankles – I know that because although I have a small foot I couldn't wear his shoes. He never drank tea, just milk, or water, wine at dinner time. He was a water diviner, you know. He had the gift, although he didn't practice it, and I inherited that from him. It's my hobby, and most valuable it has proved to me as a farmer.

"He believed in ghosts. Once when he was staying at an old castle, coming down a narrow stairway for dinner, he met a little old woman coming up, and as it was a narrow stair he stood aside for her to pass. He noticed she was dressed in curious clothes, with an old-fashioned cap and long skirts. He happened to remark at dinner that a servant he had met on the stair wore decidedly odd clothes, when there was a silence from his host who then told him seriously it was the castle ghost he had seen. He also believed in heavenly music. He had heard it several times in the mountains.

"He loved children. This house was always full of them. He loved to give them treats. He was a great story teller, and could always make people laugh. One story that always left him in chuckles was of the man who wrote his will leaving £500 to a nephew and £500 to each of his nieces, but nothing to his wife because she wasn't a relative."

Lindertis is a 3,000 acre estate and 260 acre farm, famous today for its pedigree bulls. One was sold for the world-record price of £60,000 in 1963. Seed potatoes are also exported from its fields of light soil. I asked Sir Torquil if his father had been interested in farming. "He was really a forester," he replied "He did become interested in farming, and grew a lot of food when the war crisis demanded it. He went heart and soul into farming then, but he was really an estate manager. He managed Lindertis for his uncle, then for his father, before he fell heir to it in 1913."

From where I sat in Sir Hugh's favourite room I looked across a park of green sward to the swell of low hills. Behind me, out of sight, was the old mansion house of Lindertis, where two notable SMC meets had been held in 1915. Sir Torquil invited me to go up there. The mansion, alas, is no more. The house where so many of Munro's mountain journeys started is a ruin, all but the wings, which are inhabited by a farm worker, a retired forester, and the county rabbit trapper. The main building, Sir Torquil told me, was unroofed because of the expense of its upkeep.

Round the farm steadings where the Aberdeen-Angus bulls are housed, I spoke to Mr Nicol, who remembered Sir Hugh, but could not think of him as a mountaineer because he "didna look very strong." But he could tell me: "A' the high hills o' Scotland are ca'd efter him. They ca' them Munros," he said.

The Ruins of the Munro seat, Lindertis

And that itself is an irony, because Munro had no use for personal names in mountaineering. He was such a traditionalist that he wrote a criticism of the use of 'Angel's peak,' for a summit in the Cairngorms because it had been bestowed by a well-known climber.[14] Only two 3,000-footers did not fall below Munro's feet, Carn Cloich-Mhuilinn in the Cairngorms, which he was keeping for 'the last one,' and the Inaccessible Pinnacle in the Cuillin which he had tried just four years before he died.[15]

The cemetery where he lies buried with his wife is not easy to find, sandwiched as it is by a farm hedge on one side and a high garden wall on the other. In that sunny corner I found a small marble cross. Munro's wife was a general's daughter, and she died ten years after their marriage. That decade was Munro's richest as a climber.

The canvas of his life was very much in my mind as I left the grave and took the road which winds from Kirriemuir into Glen Clova. And appropriately it was a day when you could feel the sting of the wind from the gleaming snow wreaths – a day for the hill, and I could almost hear the clip-clop of the horse pulling Sir Hugh's dog-cart as it passed through

---

[14] Munro's rebuke appeared in *SMCJ* 1909, X, 232, "This mountain is often, though most incorrectly, called 'the Angel's Peak'. It is generally understood that this name was given to it by a prominent member of the Cairngorm Club. The contrast between it and the severe appearance of the (lower) Devil's Point . . . may well have suggested the name of Angel's Peak . . . I hold that there can be no justification for altering existing names, especially such as are given on the O.S. maps . . . even [in the Cuillins] the practice of calling what are merely minor tops of well-known mountains after climbers, however distinguished, must be deprecated".

Henry Alexander, in the SMC Guidebook to The Cairngorms (Edinburgh, 1928) notes on p. 146 that 'the name Angel's Peak . . has no historical warrant, having been invented by a well-known Cairngorm enthusiast, the late Alexander Copland, as a counter-balance to the Devil's Point.' On p. 144 Alexander explains that the name Devil's Point is a 'euphemistic rendering' in English of the Gaelic name Bod an Diabhail. Adam Watson's SMC Guide (SMT, Edinburgh, 1975, p. 145) gives this name as Bod an Deamhainn and offers an accurate English rendering 'the penis of the Devil'. One can only speculate about what part of the Angel Mr Copland had in mind.

[15] In fact, three Tops eluded Munro. See Chapter 1.7 below. Munro's grave and headstone are described there also.

the little farms, the passenger in the Inverness cape and Balmoral, about to leave one world for another, on another resourceful mountain journey.

Nor could I leave it here. Not until I had been to the head of Glen Isla could I feel my pilgrimage complete, where the Caenlochan glen swings between escarpments and a variety of steep gullies offer challenge, couloirs which were climbed on the January meet at Lindertis so many years ago when Munro kept his guests so busy that none of them saw his house in daylight. They left in the dark and came back in the dark.[16]

Following their route I climbed into the snowy corrie by the stumps of a vanished wood, reaching the summit by a gully fringed by a miniature glacier.

It led into the mist, over a cornice of hard snow to the summit plateau where I was able to discard the compass as the sun broke the mist, a fine moment made charming by a flock of snow-buntings rising from my feet, while on another snow patch some thirty ptarmigan waddled about like domestic hens. Dazzling snow patches among black menacing clouds gave a feeling of immensity to these great hill shapes which stretch without break to Lochnagar.

The hills were, I felt, very much as Munro had described them in one of his earliest articles. Listen to this:

'The enhanced beauty of the mountains in their winter clothing when the corries are filled with snow, the freedom to roam over the country unchecked by landlords or shooting tenants, the glorious views enjoyed, and, above all, the increased interest of the climb when the rocks are coated with ice, when slopes of hard frozen snow often compel the use of the axe, when every *arête* has an overhanging cornice of snow, then in short, our Scottish hills present most of the characteristics and many of the difficulties of mountains in the Alps, three or four times their height.'[17]

Turning away from the Braes of Angus that night into a blaze of sunset tingeing the snows with fire I felt grateful to that bout of 'flu which sent me north to lay the ghost of an exceptional Scot, whose spirit will be somewhere around each time I tick off another of the few Munros which are outstanding from his list.

And as a postscript to this, I would like to acknowledge my thanks to the wife of the late George Tertius Glover, who presented me with her husband's set of the *SMC Journal* from which I obtained the information for this article.

Glover wrote to me long before I met him. A constant attender of SMC meets from 1899 Glover got to know Munro as a friend. So George Glover, who was my friend, has been a stepping stone to a great figure of the past.

I am glad that I met some of the grand old men before they died, though Munro was not one of them. I was four years old when he passed on.

---

[16] Tom Weir has mixed two Meets at Lindertis together. The first, in January 1915, is described by W. Inglis Clark in *SMCJ* 1915, XIII, 268-272. Then indeed, according to Clark, they arrived in darkness and left in darkness, but climbed only in Glen Clova. It was the second Meet, in May 1915, and described by Walter Reid in *SMCJ* 1915, XIII, 337-340, which explored the Glen Isla side of Glas Maol.

[17] See Munro 3.

1.3 Reminiscences of a Solitary Walk in Early Club Days

Sir Hugh T. Munro[1]

LANDING at Corpach about 5 on a glorious May evening in 1889, I walked out to Inverailort. At the head of Upper Lochiel two seals were basking on the still surface of the loch, close to the shore, their bodies rigid, and half out of the water. They allowed me to approach comparatively near to them before lazily submerging.

In those days this part of the West Highland Railway was not even commenced, and the beauty of the scenery, now so familiar to many, was a revelation to me. I remember being particularly struck with the little pine-covered island on Loch Eilt, where the Loch narrows to only the width of a few yards on each side of the island. Also with the situation of Inverailort, and with the shores of Loch nan Uamh (the Lake of the Cave).

The hour of the *Clansman's* departure from Arisaig was uncertain. Arriving at the Arisaig Hotel about 2.30 p.m. the next day, I was told that she was just coming in, but that her point of call was in the next bay to the south, a walk of some four miles. However, I got a sailing boat to put me across the loch, a seal following only a few feet behind the boat for several hundred yards. A few minutes' walk across a narrow neck of land, and I just caught the ship without five minutes to spare.

At Inverie the laird, who turned out to be the late Mr Baird of Knoydart, not only kindly put me ashore in his boat, but would not hear of my going to the inn, and took me up to the lodge for the night. I had intended going on to Skiary, but a heavy thunderstorm, following an intensely hot morning, had left the mists hanging low, and I was anxious for a clear day for the lovely walk over the pass.

Next morning the laird insisted on showing me his farm buildings and his gardens, where he prided himself on being able to grow plants which were not hardy enough for Kew. He had come from London to fetch some keys which he had forgotten. It was not till after luncheon that I set out for Skiary, and the mists had completely cleared off, leaving the air intensely still and clear. Shall I ever forget the descent on to Loch Hourn, that most beautiful of all Highland lochs? Later, as I fished from a boat till near eleven at night for codlings, it was difficult to tell where the reality of the rocks and promontories ended and the reflection in the glassy surface of the water began. Skiary must certainly be one of the most primitive inns (!) in Europe. A beehive crofter's cottage on the shores of the loch, with just a 'but and a ben,' and, but for the codlings, I should have been dependent on oatmeal and very bad whisky, which probably had contributed nothing to the revenue of the United Kingdom.

A mile or two on my journey the next morning, I was met by my boatman of the night before, who insisted on my going to his cottage and drinking milk, introducing me with: "This is my wife. Isn't she fat?" She·was! He was full of stories and traditions of 'the Prince,' told with a veneration that would have suggested that the '45 had been in the

---

[1] See Munro 88. This piece by Munro was his last contribution to the *SMCJ*, and was published just 6 months before his death. However, it describes a very early excursion through territory that was not only unknown to most Scots, but most rigorously preserved by its American proprietor.

nineteenth and not the eighteenth century. He accompanied me as far as Glenquoich Lodge, where Mr Malcolm, the factor for the property, most hospitably gave me an excellent luncheon, and, moreover, drove me down the Glen to Invergarry. I had still eight miles to tramp, and it was late before I reached Fort Augustus.

The Loch Ness steamer deposited me at Drumnadrochit at an early hour the next day, and in due course I made my way through Glen Urquhart, and over to Invercannich. This road gives no indication of the superlative beauty of the scenery immediately to the west, but the descent into Strath Glas through the sweet smelling birk woods was very fascinating. After an early luncheon I made my way to Fasnakyle, for at that time the whole of the country to the west, as far as Shiel Inn, was under the sway of Mr Winans,[2] and arrangements had to be made for next day. Now it happened that my uncle had been one of the principal witnesses for Lord Tweedmouth in the cross actions for interdict between him and Mr Winans. The latter, while endeavouring to exclude the public from the whole of the vast tract of country which he rented, tried at the same time to establish a right of way across a part of his neighbour, Lord Tweedmouth's property. Lord Tweedmouth, then Mr Marjoribanks, had first seen Guisachan[3] as the guest of my uncle, who had a lease of the lodge and shootings, and my uncle was able to prove that one of the paths over which Mr Winans claimed a right of way had been made by his – my uncle's – orders, and at his expense, and had not existed previously. I frankly told the head stalker at Fasnakyle who I was, and after a palaver, it ended in his giving me a passport, merely saying: "You must not talk about it when you go south." Moreover, on my saying I was going on to Guisachan, he guided me by a short cut over a bridge, which I afterwards heard was a very high mark of favour.

At Guisachan nothing was good enough for me. I had to be shown all the sights, and especially a certain waterfall some three or four miles beyond the lodge. In consequence it was late before I got back to the hotel, and I had put in a good many miles since leaving Drumnadrochit. This was the first of many visits to the Glenaffric Hotel, and though I do not think the Falkeners were there at the time I should like to pay a tribute to the care and attention I have ever received from Mrs Falkener. I have been there at all seasons of the year. I have stalked from there in Glen Cannich in December, when there was not a shovelful of coal in the house; I have walked, I have driven, I have bicycled, and I have motored there, and always with the same kindly welcome.

An early start was made next morning, for the day was to be a long one. Turning up to the right out of Strath Glas, Glen Affric, the most beautiful of the larger glens of Britain, came as a revelation. Nowhere else are rock and heather, lochs and islands, natural forests of Scots firs and birks, river and falls blended in such beauty. Every few miles would one of Mr Winans' sentries step up and, quite civilly, ask whence I was from and where I was

---

[2] William Louis Winans, who owned more than 200,000 acres in Affric and Kintail. Winans' zealous approach to access is described by J. Parker Smith, M.P. in *Blackwood's Magazine* 1891 , No. 169, 259-262 – "his stopping roads and breaking down bridges, his deer fences, his watchers doubled and posted in bothies at short intervals along his march like sentinels around a Soudan zareba". Parker Smith also describes a celebrated case (Court of Session, 4th series, vol. xii – June 3, 1885) in which Winans fails in an action of interdict against a crofter's trespassing pet lamb!

[3] Guisachan House, 2 miles south-west of Tomich (south of Glen Affric).

Sgurr na Lapaich, Glen Affric - a Munro spurned?

going. Of course I was on a public right of way, and need not have answered, but had I not a passport? One of these sentries, according to the instructions, accompanied me over Sgurr na Lapaich – the lower Sgurr na Lapaich, above Loch Affric, not the higher hill of the same name to the north of Glen Cannich. From it an easy ascent leads to Mam Sodhail, from which we had a gorgeous view. Hence south-west to the col, where we struck a rough track, which my companion was careful to tell me was an undoubted right of way leading from Glen Cannich to Glen Affric.[4] On reaching the Glen we parted, he for the east, I for the west. The day was getting on, but the weather was glorious, and I determined to diverge at the eastern base of Beinn Fhada and visit the Falls of Glomach. Although the weather was so dry, and the water so low, that I crossed the stream just above the falls dry shod, and although it was only a few months since I had seen Niagara, I was still impressed with the magnificence of the surroundings, and the sheer plunge of the waters for a height of 370 feet. Dorus-duain (the crooked door) was reached in the dusk, and I had to wake up the hotel on reaching Shiel Inn (alas, now closed). When I found they were out of beer, I sat down and cried – or nearly so.

My principal recollection of the following day is the interminable grind of a thirty-five hundred feet ascent up the north-west ridge of Sgurr Fhuaran (Scour Ouran) of uniform and monotonous steepness. The name, 'the mountain of the springs', was certainly here inappropriate, for never a sign of water was encountered from base to summit. At the col I had an hour's sleep, choosing the windy and shady side of a big boulder. Then an easy ascent to the summit of Sgurr na Carnach – 3,270 feet (name and height from the 6 in. O.S. map) – and a quick run down to the hotel.

---

[4] See Munro 4, in which he identifies the various rights-of-way by means of which one might cross this country, and indicates what mountains might be attempted 'without much risk of unpleasantness or interference'.

Next morning up the steep road to the top of Mam Ratagan, and then over the moor to Ben Sgriol, visiting both summits. Comparisons are odious, but the view remains in my mind as perhaps the most beautiful I have seen in Scotland. The atmosphere was so clear that the Minch seemed like a lake, and the whole chain of the Outer Hebrides appeared only a few miles off. And so still was the air that every stroke of the oars of a boat on Loch Hourn could be plainly heard, and the note of a dozen cuckoos shouting in all directions. An hour and a half was spent at the cairn, again choosing the shady and windy side. Then a descent was made to the south, to the shores of the loch. For many hundred feet the cool sound of an underground runnel could be heard before its beautifully clear and cold granite waters appeared at the surface. I am one of those who hold that all things should be reserved for their proper use. Water is intended for ablutionary purposes. But there are occasions when exceptions are excusable. A hot day on the mountains is one of these.

A walk along the north shore of the loch, and then a short (?) cut across the moor to Glenelg. Next morning I joined the *Clansman*, and twenty-four hours later landed in Glasgow, and dined in London that night.

Will these random recollections of twenty-nine years ago be of interest to any members of the Club? I scarcely dare to hope so, but to one who can never again undertake anything so strenuous their memory is still sweet.

1.4 Winter Ascents in the Cairngorms

Hugh T. Munro[1]

ALREADY more than one interesting article on the Cairngorms has appeared in the pages of the Journal, and I should hesitate to trespass on grounds so well described by Mr McConnochie, had I not been reminded by the Editor of a promise made in a previous paper (Vol. I, p. 105) that I would, at some future date, give my first experience of this district. The perusal, moreover, of the following account may serve as yet another warning that an ample margin of time should invariably be allowed, especially in solitary winter climbing, and that the half-hour lost in the morning will most infallibly be regretted before the day is over.

As recorded in the paper referred to above, I had, on the 6th February [1890], crossed the Braes of Angus to Braemar. The weather had been glorious, so on the morning of the 7th I was rather disappointed to find the clouds hanging low on the hills. Having abandoned all idea of the mountains, I dawdled away some time in a cottage by the Linn of Dee, and some more at Derry Lodge. In Glen Luibeg the mist was reached, but as the low beallach between it and Glen Dee was topped, suddenly, floating apparently in mid air, and

---

[1] See Munro 20. This is the last of a series of four pieces written by Munro for the early *Journals* and describing solitary winter ascents. Although nowadays solo climbing is sometimes thought to be foolhardy, there is no doubt that it was a common occurrence amongst the pioneers. Despite being in other respects notably gregarious, Munro plainly enjoyed climbing alone, and the three pieces I have selected from his voluminous writings all describe solo traverses.

seemingly 10,000 feet high, the grand crag of the Devil's Point stood out, framed in cloud, with its snows dazzlingly white in the mid-day sun, and then the mist rolled down from the hills, shrinking back into the valley to the south, and all in a few moments – disappeared. The temptation to ascend Cairntoul or Braeriach was great, but it was too late in the day, and prudence, combined with a wish to see the Learg Ghrumach, prevailed. This celebrated pass, the meaning of which is 'the gruesome' or 'mis-shapen pass', is a narrow cleft, which, for upwards of seven miles, divides Cairntoul and Braeriach on the west from Carn a' Mhaim, Ben Macdhui, and Creag na Leacainn on the east. Frowning cliffs tower sometimes as much as 2,400 feet above the pass, and although in most places they are not so steep as to be inaccessible, the two sides approach so closely to one another that the track in the upper portions of the pass is lost among a chaos of huge granite boulders, which winter frosts have disintegrated from the crags above. A little south of the summit the 'Wells of Dee' – tiny tarns of crystal-clear water – have been formed by these fallen granite blocks. They have no visible outlet, but the water percolates through the rocks and forms one of the principal sources of the Dee. The walking on this occasion was much facilitated, as the glen in its upper and rougher parts was full of hard frozen snow, as smooth and as good to walk on as a turnpike road. At 2.30 a halt of half an hour for luncheon at the Wells. The sun almost too hot, though all around was snow and ice; the stillness only broken by the incessant calling of the ptarmigan, already pairing, very tame, and every few minutes by the sound of falling rocks – some of them of considerable size – from the slopes of Ben Macdhui; indeed, a lookout had to be kept to avoid them. None fell from the western side, as it was not exposed to the sun.

The Beallach, only a little way beyond the Wells, is some 2,700 feet above the sea, and consists of a chaotic heap of boulders. The northern side of the pass is even wilder than the southern, and the view from it, in the sensuous evening light, surpassingly lovely. The sun set in a soft pink haze, graduating through many tints of yellow to an ethereal blue, – a sunset of that peculiar type, rare in Scotland, rarer still in England, which always recalls to my memory Egypt and the desert. It was already nearly five when the first trees of Rothiemurchus Forest were reached, and one by one the stars were peeping out; then, when darkness had closed in, one, bigger and ruddier than the rest, blazed from the brow of Craigellachie, above Aviemore. It is to this rock, and not to the village near Dufftown, that the slogan of the Grants', 'Stand fast, Craigellachie!' refers. Immediately it was answered from a neighbouring cairn, and in a few minutes beacon fires from a score of heights were celebrating the election of Grant of Rothiemurchus to the first Inverness-shire County Council.

Finding on reaching Aviemore station at 6.30 that a train was leaving in a few minutes, I decided to go to Kingussie.

8th February

The following morning I returned to Kincraig station, which I reached at 8.30. A hard white frost and an intensely cold morning made a quick walk of three or four miles up Glen Feshie agreeable. The glen in its lower parts is flat and uninteresting. A good bridle path strikes off up the Allt Ruadh (Red Burn), through a wood, on to the moor, where it ceases. By this time it was 10.15, and the sun very hot, though still a hard frost. An easy

Braeriach and Sgoran Dubh from Carn Eilrig

ascent of another hour and three-quarters over heather, grass, and club moss, and the top of Sgoran Dubh (3,658 feet) is reached at twelve. Some way below the summit two eagles were seen, one of which had just killed a grouse. Here one is surprised to find oneself at the edge of a precipice of 2,000 feet, descending to Loch Eunach, grandly situated in an amphitheatre of cliffs. The north summit, some three-quarters of a mile to the north, although locally called Sgoran Dubh Mhor, is in reality twenty-three feet lower than the south top. From almost every other point of view, however, it looks the higher. On the edge of the cliffs between the two summits is a semaphore, doubtless to signal to the bothy at the foot of the loch the position of the deer. To the south and west stretches away a vast and comparatively level tableland, with the deep clefts of different glens – Feshie, Dee, Geldie, etc. – opening from it. Here I suddenly changed my plans, and instead of ascending Braeriach first and descending to Braemar, I reversed the direction, so as to return to Speyside. Striking south-east, to round the cliffs at the head of Loch Eunach, a descent to about 2,800 feet has to be made, and after half an hour for luncheon, another hour and a half placed me at the top of Cairn Toul (4,241 feet) at 2.45. A quarter of an hour here for the view, and another twenty minutes more to the top of Sgor an Lochan Uaine ('The mountain of the little green loch'). This, although only named on the 6-inch O.S. map, is a fine peak.[2] No height is given, but a considerable 4,000 feet contour on the 1-inch map, and, according to Mr Hinxman's aneroid, its approximate height is 4,095 feet. Hence along the tops of the great flat tableland, on which cricket, football, or even polo might almost be played, to Braeriach (the 'greyish' or 'speckled brae'), 4,284 feet, the third highest summit in Britain, at 4.20.

---

[2] Munro's attitude to O.S. naming is discussed below in Chapters 4.8 and 4.9. He seemed to attach undue importance to whether or not the O.S. or Bartholomew's editors had seen fit to name a peak on popular maps.

The views from Cairntoul and Braeriach are very similar. From the former the view down Glen Geusachan and Glen Dee, with the Devil's Point looking quite small below, is rather finer; while from the latter the foreground to the north, over Rothiemurchus Forest, is better, as is also the view of Ben Macdhui and Cairngorm over the narrow chasm of the Learg Ghruamach. The evening was absolutely perfect, and the view most extensive. South-east, Lochnagar shows its graceful north-west outline; then turning to the right the Braes of Angus, Glas Maol, etc.; Beinn Iutharn (B. Uarn) and Glas Thulachan, with the black cone of Mount Blair, between them and Glas Maol. Due south, and very prominent, the several peaks of Beinn a' Ghlo. Next, Ben Chonzie, then Ben Lawers, looking very massive. Schiehallion from Cairntoul shows no sky line, being entirely backed by Ben Lawers; from Braeriach, however, a small piece of him shows against the sky. The twin peaks of Am Binnein and Ben More. Beinn Laoigh next, and in shape very like the last two. Ben Cruachan south-west and 70 miles away; and over his right shoulder, and much further away, a hill which, if not Ben More, is some other of the Mull hills. The Blackmount and Glencoe hills, the mountains of Rum nearly due west, Ben Nevis, etc., and range upon range of Inverness and Ross-shire hills, Mam Sodhail (Mamsoul); the hills round Loch Maree, Scour Vuillin; and the big bulky mass of Ben Wyvis to the north-west, very unmistakable; the valley of the Spey in front, and Ben Rinnes away to the north-east.

It was 4.30 before the summit of Braeriach was left. A north-west course was shaped, and a descent made by an easy *arête*, with cliffs on each side, which at first required a little care owing to the ice on the rocks. Leaving Loch Coire an Lochan on the left, and keeping to the hard frozen snow in the bed of the Allt na Beinne Bige, the road in Glen Eunach was reached at six and Lynwilg Inn at nine.

9th *February*

The following day Lynwilg was not left till 8.45, and bitterly the lost hour was regretted before the day was over. I failed to find the bridge over the Morlich, and stripped to ford it, having to break the ice at the edges.

There are few more beautiful places than Rothiemurchus Forest, with its fine old Scotch firs and luxuriant heather, its herds of red deer – at this season of the year very tame – its open glades and glistening tarns, its views across Loch Morlich and Glen More to the Cromdale hills, and over Strath Spey to the Monadhliaths; but that same luxuriant heather is uncommonly troublesome walking, every rise seems to have a corresponding dip on the other side, the distances in the clear air are most deceptive, and the numerous tracks are all shaped like corkscrews, and all of them lead to nowhere. Added to this a blazing hot sun without a breath of wind, although the frost was keen, and it was 2.40 before Cairn Gorm (4,084 feet) was reached, the ascent being made by the shoulder, which terminates to the north in An t-Aonach. The day hitherto had been lovely, but by this time the mist was rolling over the top of Braeriach, and creeping up the valleys to the south-west. Prudence certainly dictated a return to Speyside, but I was well accustomed to finding my way among the mountains alone, in winter and in all weathers, and I started for Ben Macdhui without misgivings. I hurried down the three or four hundred feet to the foot of the peak, and then over the extensive snow and ice fields round the crescent-shaped ridge. I was soon in dense mist, which froze to one's hair, clothes, and beard. I had no difficulty in reaching the summit of Ben Macdhui (4,296 feet), but the necessity of continually consulting the map, compass, and aneroid, had wasted time, and it was already 4.30. I dashed off down the snow, in what I believed to be the direction of Loch Etchachan, but whether I had omitted to reckon the deviation, or whether a slight change of wind, which I afterwards found had taken place, had put me wrong, I found myself at five p.m. having descended about one thousand feet, just at the bottom margin of the mist on the top of the precipices overhanging Loch Avon. Here was a balmy place to be in! – dangerous cliffs all round, the cold so intense that one could scarcely have lived an hour without moving. It was long after sunset, and the chances of getting out of difficulties before it became quite dark seemed slight. I had no flask, little food, and there was not enough safe ground to make it possible to walk up and down through the long night. Dashed up a steep hard snow slope – no time to cut steps, but hauling myself up by the point of my axe, crossed an intervening ridge, and again descended, only to find myself among even worse cliffs still above Loch Avon. For a moment I hesitated whether to attempt to cut down a dangerously steep *couloir* of hard snow, which seemed to descend to the loch but even if practicable at all for one man without rope, which is very doubtful, it would certainly have taken far too long. One last look at the map and compass in the dim light, and then another race up a long steep slope with the help of the axe. I thought I should have burst, but time was too precious to stop to take breath even for a minute. A wide sweep round, and then, bearing left, an easy descent over snow that evidently filled the bed of a burn, and I was deeply thankful to find myself at 5.45, on a dark night early in February, 3,100 feet above the sea, on the shores of the frozen Loch Etchachan. A tedious walk in the dark brought me at 8.30 to Derry Lodge, where I was hospitably entertained by Fraser, the head stalker, and his wife.

In spite of the undoubted danger I ran on this occasion, I still hold that solitary winter climbing, with proper precautions, is perfectly safe. This is the only time I have run any serious risk, although I have been on the mountains alone in winter many scores of times. The one inexcusable fault is to allow oneself to get benighted. With an hour more daylight – and I might easily have started two hours earlier – the mistake in the mist, even if it had been made at all, would have been easily retrieved.

1.5 Hot Nights and Days on the Mountains in June

Hugh T. Munro[1]

Bidein a' Choire Sheasgaich and Lurg Mhor

BY the kind invitation of Mr and Mrs Colin Phillip, who are spending the summer at Glen Brittle, I was enabled to pay a visit to that most inaccessible region the Southern Cuillins under exceptionally favourable conditions. To catch the mail for Skye it is necessary for me to go as far as Perth or Blair Athole overnight. Instead of so doing I left home on the morning of 4th June, and reached Strathcarron Station at 6 p.m. After a light meal I started out at seven for Lurg Mhor and his neighbours. Lurg Mhor, lying above the west end of Loch Monar, is undoubtedly somewhat un-get-at-able.   From Strathcarron it can be approached either by a rough driving road to Loch Calavie, or more directly by a bridle path over the moor to the head of Loch an Laoigh. I chose the latter route. About a mile from the station the track branches, and the left branch should be followed. Having misunderstood the directions given me I took the right, which terminates at the little Loch nan Graobh, and had in consequence a rough walk across the moor till the correct path was again struck. This path rises to a height of some 1,500 feet, and then drops to about 800 feet at the loch. In the twilight the west face of Bidein a' Choire Sheasgaich looked craggy, and I accordingly bore away to the left for the north ridge. It afterwards appeared that this west face was anywhere easily climbable. The summit, which has no cairn, is according to the six-inch O.S. map 3,107 feet – the one-inch map only gives a 3,000 feet contour. It had taken four and a half hours to reach this, but the night was very hot, and at least an hour might have been saved. The big north-east corrie between this hill and Lurg Mhor was still very full of snow. Between the two hills there is a considerable dip, but the ground is very easy. Lurg Mhor (3,234 feet) has a large cairn. Beyond this the ridge narrows, and is in places slabby with an abrupt drop to the north, and requires some dodging, but even at the darkest hour of the twenty-four there was no difficulty in finding an easy way. Meall Mor rises to a pretty and very distinct little top with a small cairn (3,190 feet from the six-inch O.S.). In returning I kept over the southern shoulder of Bidein a' Choire Sheasgaich, but otherwise followed the same route, and reached the hotel at 6 a.m. in time for a good rest before the mail left for Skye.

It was after 9 p.m. before Glen Brittle Lodge was reached.

---

[1] See Munro 76.

Sgurr Sguman and the Dubhs

Though I had written some days before, I was unable to secure John McKenzie, as he was permanently engaged to Mr A.E. Robertson, who was staying at Sligachan. Accordingly, on 6th June I started out alone and ascended Sgurr Sguman by his easy western shoulder. The day was again very fine and hot, and the views beautiful. An easy descent was made into Coir a' Ghrunnda and a line struck for Sgurr Dubh na Dabheinn on good snow patches below the cliffs of Sgurr Alasdair. Mr Phillip tells me that in company with Mrs Phillip and Dr Collie he had once descended these cliffs from Alasdair by a narrow but perfectly easy scree-filled chimney which they had accidentally struck. It is so hidden that it can neither be seen from above nor below unless one is close to the very base of the cliffs. John McKenzie told me that he knows this chimney, and that it is as easy as the Stone Shoot from Coire Labain.[2] Many newly fallen stones on the snow induced me to avoid keeping too close to the cliffs, and consequently I entirely failed to see any sign of it.

By the time I reached Dubh na Dabheinn the mist had come down thick, and it was not easy to choose the best route. However, no difficulty was experienced in reaching Dubh Mhor. Hence I returned again over Dubh na Dabheinn, and down Coir a' Ghrunnda home. The descent of Dubh na Dabheinn is tedious and irksome, as it consists entirely of big blocks of very rough gabbro. The mist only extended to just below the loch.

Sgurr Alasdair and Sgurr Tearlach.

Next morning, 7th June, was again intensely hot, the air perfectly still, and all the tops clear. In company with the two Miss Protheros, nieces of Mr Phillip, I climbed Alasdair by the Stone Shoot. From Alasdair we went on to Tearlach. I suppose this mountain is almost always climbed by those who have either just come from Mhic Coinnich or crossed the Alasdair-Dubh gap, and by comparison it seems easy. I admit, though, that with two young ladies under my care I regretted that we had not brought the rope. They, however, climbed with ease and confidence, notwithstanding that Ben Vorlich was their only previous ascent of a 3,000-foot mountain. The height of Sgurr Alasdair has now been fixed trigonometrically at 3,309 feet. At the most I do not think that Tearlach can be 50 feet lower, and it may very possibly prove to be the second highest peak of the Cuillins.[3] The day was absolutely perfect, and only the necessity of returning home for dinner induced us to leave the summit. On the Alasdair side of the Stone Shoot there was still a considerable depth of snow, on which we got several short standing glissades. About two-thirds of the way down is a spring of the coldest and most delicious water, which, however, *might* run dry late in the summer.

---

[2] Presumably the chimney taken to avoid the appalling 'Bad Step' on the Alasdair-Sgumain ridge is what Phillip intended.

[3] In fact the heights of Cuillin Peaks remained mysterious for some time, certainly until the interesting article by Guy Barlow, 'The Relative Heights of the Cuillin Peaks', *SMCJ* 1923, XVI, 244-249. Barlow surveyed the Tearlach-Alasdair difference as 50 feet, agreeing with Munro. However, he also found that the O.S. had over-estimated the height of Sgurr Dearg by nearly 30 feet, and Sgurr Alasdair by nearly 60 feet!

Sgurr Dubh an Da Bheinn, Gars-bheinn and Sgurr nan Eag

Sgurr nan Eag and Garsbheinn

If possible 8th June was even hotter and more beautiful than the previous day. We had decided, however, to climb at night, and accordingly at 11 p.m. started for Coir a' Ghrunnda. Just as we left the Lodge the mist came down thick, and of course many were the lamentations that we had wasted so beautiful a day. Spite of the mist it was intensely hot. In June there is no night, and the way into Coir a' Ghrunnda is easy enough to find once you know that you must avoid the burn and bear well away to the left close to the cliffs of Sgurr Sguman. Still it is wonderful how time is lost in thick fog, especially fog at midnight, and already the evening twilight, which lingers through the night, was giving place to the dawn, when some 300 or 400 feet below the loch (*i.e.* 1,800 feet above the sea) we rose above the mist, the full moon shone out, and the rocky cirque of summits appeared clearly silhouetted against a cloudless sky. A short halt for a light breakfast at the base of Sgurr nan Eag by a spring which rivalled that in the Alasdair Stone Shoot, and then we hurried on over unpleasant stony ground until the ridge was struck.

The view from here onwards was one we shall never forget. I have often, of course, had the experience of being in sunshine with the mist below, but except once – from the summit of Monte Rosa, in 1875 – I have never before seen the effect so continuous and lasting; usually the sun dissipates the mists, or they rise and envelop the mountaintops. Today we remained on the summits for several hours basking in the hot sun, revelling in the gorgeous views, and photographing, and during the whole time a white sea of cloud lay 1,000 to 1,500 feet below us, perfectly still, looking like a padding of cotton-wool, and appearing so solid as to give the impression that a stone, if rolled down on to it, would rest on the top and not penetrate it. We got also some beautiful and varied fog bow effects. Once a perfect bow appeared high *above* the sun, although there did not seem to be any vapour in the upper air. Now and then a tongue of mist would creep up until it filled the hollow in which lay Loch Coir a' Ghrunnda, which for a few moments it would obscure, and then again slowly recede to its original position a few hundred feet lower. Except this loch no water could be seen, all was covered and hidden by this white quilt of mist, but above it every mountain which it can ever be possible to see, stood out intensely clear and black and close-looking. The Long Island from Barra to Harris, Rum, Mull, and the mainland from Ben Nevis and the Glencoe hills to the Sutherlandshire mountains, Blathbheinn and Clach Glas looking like islands, and the whole range of the Cuillins from Sgurr nan Gillean to Garsbheinn. By the way, I must entirely dissent from the statement in Mr Douglas's list of the Cuillins[4] that the main ridge ends in Sgurr Dubh Bheag, or indeed that either Dubh Bheag or Dubh Mhor are on the main ridge at all. They form a branch ridge just as much as do Sgurr a' Coir an Lochan or Druim nan Ramh, and the main ridge from Sgurr Tearlach passes through Sgurr Dubh na Dabheinn, Caisteal a' Gharbh Choire, Sgurr nan Eag, and Sgurr a' Choire Bheag, and terminates in Garsbheinn. I had often been puzzled to reconcile Mr Douglas's dictum with the map, and these clear days on the spot have confirmed my view, with which Mr Alfred Harker agrees.[5]

From Eag our original idea had been to go to the Dubhs, but the young ladies seemed to fancy Garsbheinn, which fitted in well with my views as it enabled me to round off this end of the range. It was only the possible anxiety of our friends if we stayed away too long which finally compelled us to descend from the last-named summit, and about the time that they were breakfasting at Sligachan and Glen Brittle we plunged down into the mist which, opaque as it had seemed from above, proved to be very thin and dry when we got into it; but neither at Sligachan or Glen Brittle did they see the tops of the mountains or blue sky all that day. We reached home having been out just twelve hours – surely record time, but photography and the magnificent views, the delight of drinking in the pure crisp air, and basking in the sun on the ridges, possibly also *anni domini* on the side of the writer, must be held answerable, and by no means any want of energy on the part of the young ladies.

That afternoon I drove up to Sligachan intending to go on on Sunday evening to Portree, but the offer from Mr Robertson of John McKenzie's services on the Monday was too good to be refused, the only condition being that we should remain on the top of the third pinnacle until he had photographed us from the fourth.

Sunday was another lovely and very hot day.

Pinnacles and Western Ridge of Sgurr nan Gillean

When we started at 8.30 on Monday, 11th, the mist again lay low but thin, and by the time we reached the base of the first pinnacle two hours later it had broken up and disappeared, but the rocks were already quite warm, showing that from here upward the sun had shone

---

[4] *SMCJ* 1897, IV, 212-213. This is the first version of the list of peaks and passes of the Cuillins which has persisted through many revisions into current guidebooks. The Munro/Harker view prevailed and Douglas modified the list accordingly in the first Guidebook to Skye, which appeared as *SMCJ* 1907, IX, 293-367.

[5] Harker's version is in 'Notes, Geographical and Topographical, on the Cuillin Hills, Skye', *SMCJ* 1900, VI, 1-13.

all the morning. The day was intensely hot, but the distance not as clear as on the previous days. The party consisted of A.E. Robertson, Mrs Urquhart, John McKenzie and his nephew Archie (who promises to be a good climber), and the writer. The rope was put on at the base of the third pinnacle. The pinnacles took four hours, but upwards of one hour of this was occupied with photography and luncheon; one and a half hours to the base of the first pinnacle and two hours thence to the summit should be sufficient in these splendid conditions. We descended by the western ridge, the rope being only required to cross the 'policeman' and the few steps immediately above it.

After dinner I drove up to Portree, and next morning returned home.

I could not help contrasting this scorching week with my last icy experience of the Cuillins at the Easter Meet, 1905. It may be worth recording that John McKenzie tells me that in company with Mr Wickham King and another member he once climbed the gully leading up to the Bealach Coire na Banachdich, which, led by Raeburn, we had attempted at the above Meet.[6] Had we known it had already been climbed we might possibly not have spent so much time over it. I do not, however, regret it, for it gave us a most interesting and enjoyable climb.

---

[6] Harold Raeburn describes this adventure with Munro, and others, in 'Ridge-Walking on the Coolins at Easter, 1905', *SMCJ* 1906, IX, 67.

1.6 Three Nights on the Cairngorms

Sir Hugh T. Munro[1]

AS I was a contributor to the first number of the *Cairngorm Club Journal,* the Editor has asked me to write something for the fiftieth number. I respond readily; but as my climbing days began upwards of forty-three years ago in the Alps, it is inevitable that anything I now write must be rather the reminiscences of a dotard than the experiences of an active climber. Nevertheless, I still aspire to stand on the summit of the only three 'tops' in Scotland exceeding 3,000 feet in height which I have not yet climbed. Raeburn, Collie, Garden, and others, however, must combine to haul me up on a rope; otherwise the ascents will not be made!

I am minded to tell briefly of three night adventures on the Cairngorms.

[The first of these is an account of his day crossing the central Cairngorms from Lynwilg in 1890, which is reproduced above as part of *Winter Ascents in the Cairngorms*. It concludes with his arrival in the late evening at Derry.]

This was the first of many visits paid to Derry Lodge; and I should like here to pay a tribute to the kindness, hospitality, and courtesy of Donald Fraser, the late stalker. His daughter, too, was most assiduous in her attentions. She collected post-cards, and I have had the pleasure of sending her some from many, outlandish parts of the world.

---

[1] See Munro 87. These are the last words from the pen of Munro.

Fraser had, of course, as most of the Cairngorm Club know, many reminiscences of the Royal Family and of foreign princes, including the Kaiser, who had stalked in Mar Forest. He told me that the finest rifle shot he had ever known was Prince Henry of Battenberg. On one occasion he was stalking with the Prince and had brought him in sight of the deer, but said – "We can't get within shooting distance." The Prince replied, – "Surely you can take me to those peat hags." "Yes," Fraser responded, "but they are more than 400 yards away from the stag." "Take me there, and I will shoot it through the heart." He did so. Years after, in 1914, I had the honour of sitting next to Princess Henry at luncheon. As it happened, she had on a coat the buttons of which were made of deer's teeth taken from deer which Prince Henry had killed. I told her Fraser's verdict on her husband's shooting and I think she was pleased.

Fraser spent the long months of winter in mounting deer's heads. He had the opportunity of getting any number of the cast horns of stags, and, as he himself told me, he could usually make a much better and more symmetrical head than nature could produce, for as a rule the two sides of a stag's head differ very considerably.

Mrs. Fraser, when a child of twelve, accompanied by a girl two years older, walked from Braemar to some place in the Carse of Gowrie. Her parents had arranged that the two girls should spend two nights on the way. The first night was to be spent at the Kirkton of Glenisla but as their route lay down Glenshee, this would have taken them out of their way, so they decided to go on to the next sleeping-place. When they reached it, however, they became ambitious of doing the whole journey in one walk, so they continued on, and did the whole fifty miles without a rest. I doubt if there are many, members of the Cairngorm Club, or of the Scottish Mountaineering Club, who could do as much.

But this has very little to do with the Cairngorms or with mountaineering,

I will now tell of two other nights, this time voluntarily spent on the Central and Eastern Cairngorms.

Once, a dozen or more years ago, I and a friend left Aviemore in the late afternoon of the 18th of June – Waterloo Day. We made our way through the Rothiemurchus and Glenmore Forests until, at about 10.30 at night, we found ourselves at the foot of what on the Ordnance map is called Fiacaill Coire an t-Sneachda. It is a narrow and steep ridge running up to the summit plateau, which, in spite of some snow lying about, was quite easy, and did not even suggest the rope. Here we got into a thin mist. As most members of the Cairngorm Club will know, the big pasture-like land extending from Cairngorm by Coire an t-Sneachda to Ben Muich Dhui is an undulating moorland, across which it would be possible to canter a pony. The Cairngorms are, in fact, not true mountains, but rather a tableland which denudation has raised to the rank of mountains. And while no one would venture to compare them with the wild boldness of the Western hills, such as the Cuillins – *facile princeps*, the first among Scottish mountains – the Glencoe or the Dundonald mountains, for instance, not to mention many another range, the Cairngorms – the central range of the Grampians – have a certain reposeful grandeur, an indication of *strength*, which is unique in Scotland.

The original programme had been ambitious. I don't quite remember what we had meant to do, but I know our plan had included Beinn Mheadhoin and half the Eastern Cairngorms. We did not accomplish it. My friend did not like the very thin mist on the hills, and, although it had not been thick enough to make the use of the compass necessary between Fiacaill Coire an t-Sneachda and Ben Muich Dhui, my friend contended that it was not weather for a night on the hills, and that we had better seek a lower elevation as soon as possible. I gave in to him, but insisted on crossing the top above Coire an Sput Dheirg (4,095 ft.) and Sron Riach (3,534 ft.). The names and heights of these two subsidiary summits of Ben Muich Dhui are found only on the 6-inch map. The walk down the glen to Braemar will ever linger in my memory. The short summer night – it was within three days of the longest day – was already past before we reached the glen. The unnatural midnight twilight had already given place to daylight. Suddenly a bird – a thrush, I think – began to sing, and in a few moments the whole countryside seemed to be alive with the songs of the birds. Great stags were all over the place, peacefully grazing by the roadside. I had a rather long walking-stick, and on one occasion I lunged out, saying "Here! You get out of that!" and hit a big stag – a Royal – on the haunch. We reached Braemar about 4.30 on a glorious summer morning, and actually disturbed a dozen big stags feeding in the flower gardens in the centre of the village. With some trouble we woke up the people at the Fife Arms, and were royally entertained.

One more Cairngorm excursion I may perhaps be permitted to describe. One hot afternoon in July, Garden, Duncan, and I left Aberdeen by train. We dined at Ballater, and, later, drove up Glen Gairn to a point which I am now unable to indicate, but it was somewhere very near Loch Builg. Our first point was the big brae of Ben Avon. In turn, we topped all the summits of Ben Avon as well as of Beinn a' Bhuird. For an hour we lay down and dozed near the summit of Ben Avon, but, though the days were intensely hot, the proximity of a big patch of snow chilled the air, and we did not care to rest for very long. It was 5.30 the following evening before we reached Braemar, and I have still a vivid recollection of the rankness of the heather and the 'glegs' in Glen Quoich ; also of the luxury of a tepid bath, a plate of clear turtle, and a bottle of champagne at the Fife Arms that Sunday night.

Hygienic Hymn'

A happy man was I
On that Sabbath day alone,
Worshipping there, in the silent air,
Steeped in the pure Ozone.

I breathed the blest Ozone,
On the crown of Sgurr nan Gillean,
With gladsome mind, of mountain wind
I drank a plenteous fill in.

Drinking the blest Ozone,
On the crest of that awful hill,
I thanked the Lord, who the world had stored
With the life that the air did fill.

Great is the dome of St Paul's
Arching o'er altar and throne;
Greater still is that silent hill
Bathed in the pure Ozone!

Alexander Nicolson

1.7 Munro and the Salvationist Tendency

Robin N. Campbell[1]

IN Volume II of the Club Journal, Hely Almond[2] drew a distinction between two tendencies within the new Club. It is a false distinction, since many early members – notably Naismith – cut right across it. However, the labels stuck and they serve as a handy basis for grouping some at least of the prominent figures in the Club's early history. He wrote: –

Hely Almond

'Members of the Mountaineering Club may be divided into 2 classes. There are those [the Ultramontane] whose ambition is to scale the in-accessible side of peaks with un-pronounceable names, who look upon a quarry face with fond enthusiasm, as affording chances quite as great, and nearly as glorious, of getting badly hurt, as a genuine mountain does . . But let me confess, with all due humility and shame, that I have permanently enlisted in the Salvation Army, which is the name I give to the second class of mountaineers. As our name implies, we like to know that we are safe – absolutely safe. We don't like contusions; we would rather go home to dinner than lie on the ground till people came to set our bones, or carry us off on a stretcher; we have no desire to be the conscious element of an avalanche or land-slip. And yet, like Mark Twain on his celebrated ascent of the Riffelberg, we like something of the pomp and circumstance of glorious war – an alpenstock, a bit of rope, blue spectacles – a good deal of noise and fuss about it when we come home again.'

Among the prominent Salvationists of the early Club, Joseph Stott, Colin Phillip, Hugh Munro, Archibald Robertson, and Ronald Burn deserve special mention. Stott had already been active with the Edinburgh Tramps for many years before 1889[3]. His only recorded expedition of note after 1889 is a trip with Munro on December 21, the shortest day of 1891,

---

[1] *SMCJ* 1989, XXXIV, 219-227. I am indebted to several people for help in compiling this piece: Tom Weir and James C. Donaldson supplied wise guidance, John M. Ross unearthed the Kirriemuir Observer from its unlikely resting-place, Robert Aitken lent a willing, if sceptical ear to my theories about Munro, and, along with Geoffrey J.F. Dutton, made bitter complaint about the dullness of the writing!

[2] See 'Ben-y-Gloe on Christmas Day', *SMCJ* 1892, II, 235-239. The portrait is taken from R. J. Mackenzie's biography *Almond of Loretto*, Constable & Co., 1905.

[3] Stott's wanderings with the Tramps are described in my article, 'Stott's Mountaineering Club', *SMCJ* 1974, XXX, 257-263, part of which appears later in this volume as Chapter 6.2. Of course, Stott left Scotland for New Zealand in 1892, and remained there in miserable exile.

in which they climbed all the tops of the Tarmachans and Meall Ghaordie for good measure, in vile conditions. This gives an idea of the prodigious feats of walking achieved by the pioneers: this was in no way considered an exceptional expedition.

Colin Phillip was an artist in watercolour, the son of John Phillip of Aberdeen whose paintings of quotidien Scottish and Spanish life hang in many Scottish galleries. He evidently knew the mountains extremely well: Munro and other walkers were often at pains to acknowledge Phillip's superior knowledge and to defer to him in matters of mapping or nomenclature. His doings are unfortunately rather spottily recorded and we are left with a very inadequate picture of him.

Among the members of the Tendency, however, none is better known than Munro. His likeness appears in numerous books, sporting Balmoral bonnet, full Highland fig and – often – a large and mysterious bag of dark cloth; he and his deeds are described here and there, most notably in a typically effective piece by Tom Weir.[4] Of course, we need not seek far to discover the reason for Munro's fame. He volunteered for the task set by the early Club of compiling a list of all the Scottish mountains, and, completing it, began a hill-walking game that continues to fascinate the climber of today.

Munros and Tops

Munro's compilation rests upon three foundations: the criterion of 3,000 feet for mountainhood, a distinction between Tops and mere wrinkles, shoulders or undulations, and a distinction between ordinary Tops and an officer class of Separate Mountains, or 'Munros' as they have been called since shortly after publication of the original list, which enumerated 538 Tops and 283 Munros. It is noteworthy that even today no satisfactory account of the physical or metaphysical basis of these foundations has been offered. Robin Gall Inglis[5] argued that whereas 'maximum amount of dip encountered *en route* to the nearest (higher) summit' served as a workable basis to explain Munro's first distinction, this criterion fared very badly in accounting for the second. Then F.F. Bonsall offered a formula[6] to deal with both distinctions, namely 'the Naismith-Rule time to reach the peak from the nearest higher ground'. However, Bonsall's criterion leaves several major anomalies unexplained. The matter is complex and I will not explore it further here, save to remark that it may be necessary to cast the net well beyond the purely topographic criteria so far considered if Munro's own criteria are to be captured. Criteria such as possession of a name, or a decent cairn, seem to have mattered to Munro. He also seemed reluctant to grant more than one Munro to ranges bearing a singular name distinct from that of any constituent peak, such as Buachaille Etive Mor, Liathach, An Teallach, etc. Although we learn from William Douglas[7] of 'a great visit paid (by Munro) to Sir Colin Phillip's in Arran, where 'hills and tops' were discussed for three days and three nights with but little intermission', we can only lament the fact that none of the contemporary discussion of these issues has survived.[8]

---

[4] See Chapter 1.2

[5] See Chapter 4.6

[6] See Chapter 4.7

[7] See Chapter 1.8

[8] I may have exaggerated the deficiency. See Chapter 4.2

Munro, Robertson and Burn: What did they climb?

History teaches us that the first Munroist was the Reverend Archibald Eneas Robertson, who completed the Munros on Meall Dearg, Aonach Eagach in 1901,[9] and that the first man round the Tops was the Reverend Ronald Burn who completed the Munros and Tops on Beinn a' Chroin in 1923.[10] However, what of Munro himself? Munro suffered from rheumatism[11] and his climbing seems to cease in 1915, although he continued to attend Meets until 1918. He died without completing either the Munros or Tops. The official wisdom about what he climbed is given by James Donaldson,[12] 'When Sir Hugh died of pneumonia in 1919 he had climbed all the Tops except the Inaccessible Pinnacle and Carn Cloich-mhuilinn'. This is very close to Ling's account,[13]'He had . . visited all the 3000-foot tops in Scotland except one or two'. It is also very close to the truth, so far as one can uncover that commodity amongst the leavings of the long-dead.

However, some unofficial histories tell a different story. It would be invidious to identify those responsible, but we read in various quarters stories that imply (a) that Munro was trying to complete the Munros, and (b) that he was thwarted in this attempt by the Inaccessible Pinnacle. For example, (passing over blatantly erroneous stories to one that is more subtly wrong) I have read that Munro would have been mortified by the demotion of Carn Cloich-mhuilinn to ordinary Top, since he had left it specially for his last ascent. Sir Hugh might well have been mortified by the demotion, since there is no indication that he wished it to be demoted. However, it would only have affected these supposedly-intended celebrations if his object had been to complete the Munros. Since his object was not the Munros but the Tops, the demotion of Carn Cloich-mhuilinn would not have mattered a jot: it would still have been his last Top.

How do we know that his object was to complete the Tops? Well, he climbed all but a few of them, which is a fair indication. Besides, accounts of his early doings are plentiful in the Journal and these make it plain that he never lost an opportunity to visit a Top, however humble or downright dubious it might be.

So, Munro's object was to complete the Tops. If, however, it had been to complete the Munros, the Inaccessible Pinnacle would have constituted no obstruction, since the Pinnacle is listed as an ordinary Top in the original Tables,[14] and Sgurr Dearg is the Munro. In Section 17 of the Tables the two peaks are listed as follows:-

---

[9] See Chapter 2.3

[10] Burn's achievement is recorded in *SMCJ* 1923, XVI, 329 – a brief, triumphant Note. "I believe I am the first and only one to have done everything."

[11] In 'Lochnagar Corrie', *SMCJ* 1893, II, 246, Douglas wrote – 'On the afternoon of the 10th of March, J.H. Gibson and I took train to Kirriemuir, where we were met by Munro who drove us up the same evening to the charming little inn of Clova. Next day, in a blowy but fine morning, we shouldered our rucksacks and started to cross the Capel Mount to Glen Muick. We had barely reached the top of the pass when, alas! poor Munro received such a stern reminder of the near presence of his old enemy, rheumatism, that he had to turn back.' A lucky escape, perhaps, in view what transpired later that day! It is interesting that this affliction struck Munro so early: in 1893 he was only 37.

[12] Foreword to *Munro's Tables*, *e.g.* 1974 edition.

[13] See Chapter 4.3

[14] See Munro 15.

Mtn	Top	Height	Name
157	279	3234	Sgurr Dearg (Ordnance Point)
-	256	3250 ap.	Do ('Inaccessible Peak')

Exactly the same numberings and heights appear in the Altitude Tables.

This state of affairs may strike us as curious, but there is no help for it. The heights are given correctly, or at any rate the Pinnacle is correctly listed as higher than Sgurr Dearg. There cannot be any clerical error, since the order of the heights is confirmed by the order of the Top-numberings, and the Mountain-numbering for Sgurr Dearg (157) is as it should be, given the stated height. Besides, if there had been any clerical error, it is remarkable that Munro never saw fit to correct it – he was quick enough to correct other errors in the Tables, and elsewhere.[15] Indeed, so far as I can see the question of the bizarre status of these two peaks is discussed nowhere in the Journal and simply 'corrected' without comment in the 1921 revision of the Tables. So, Munro could have completed the Munros, and possibly before Robertson, had he chosen to ignore the Pinnacle.

Robertson's case is further confirmation of the perverse status of the Pinnacle. It is not at all likely that Robertson had climbed the Pinnacle when he claimed completion. In his notebooks[16] there is mention of climbing Sgurr Dearg, but no mention of the Pinnacle: on the other hand, his other roped ascents in the Cuillin and elsewhere are described in minute detail.[17]

Robertson claimed completion on 28th September 1901, and wrote about his feat as follows:-

> 'The first thought that strikes one in looking back over the hills of Scotland as a whole, is that there are almost none that have not some fairly easy route to the top – and I regret to say it. For although the most incorrigible of peak-baggers, I love a climb as well. Like the keeper I once asked if he would have a dram or a pint of beer, I most emphatically reply 'Both is best!'. I only wish I could tell the Club of some faraway unknown peak bristling with difficulties on all sides, but in fact there are none. The only hills where there are no easy ways to the top are certain of the Coolins in Skye, Sgurr Dubh for example or Mhadaidh or perhaps Sgurr Alasdair, although on Alasdair you have got the Stone Shoot which leads to within 125 feet of the top.'

No mention of the Pinnacle, which surely 'bristles with difficulties on every side' if any peak does! So, for those who insist that Munro was thwarted, it seems that poor Robertson must be

---

[15] See Munro 30.

[16] These notebooks are described in Chapter 2.2. The references to his visit to Skye occur on pp. 64-70 of Volume I. According to Robertson, his account of the trip is based on a letter 'written by me at the time to my cousin Miss K.C. McFarlan'. However, he adds the words 'no details recorded' to the brief description of his day round Coire Lagan, and to two other excursions on Skye. It is difficult to know what to make of these notes. Why would he need recorded details of an expedition undertaken less than a year before the date of the notebook? Perhaps he meant no details of views, since it was his frequent – and irritating – practice to record verbal panoramas throughout the notebooks. Perhaps not. In an effort to clear this matter up, I searched the Sligachan Hotel Visitors' and Climbers' Books (*NLS Acc. 11538* items 15 & 16) but without result. A version of Robertson's Mountaineering Notebooks appears below as Chapter 2.2

[17] *e.g.* Pinnacle Ridge, Sgurr nan Gillean, *Notebook I*, pp. 64-67, Bhasteir Tooth, *Notebook I*, p. 68 and Tower Ridge, *Notebook II*, pp. 22-23.

considered thwarted as well! Robertson returned to the Cuillin in 1906: although it is not made absolutely clear that he climbed the Pinnacle then, it is likely that he did.[18] He was there on a fine day with MacRobert and other able climbers and took a photograph of the Pinnacle.[19] He was certainly capable of climbing it: his boast that 'Both is best!' is amply substantiated by other routes climbed. In passing, it is perhaps worth mentioning that scrutiny of Robertson's notebooks results in a tick placed by every one of the 283 Munros of the original list, except for Ben Wyvis. He made an early visit there alone[20] – ,'I followed the usual way up, but near the top it came on heavy rain and as I did not want to get soaked, I turned.' Although Robertson makes various returns towards the end of his notebooks to correct other half-finished peaks, there is no later mention of Ben Wyvis. So perhaps Robertson was thwarted in more ways than one!

Whatever doubts there may be concerning Robertson, there are none at all regarding the next claimant, Burn. Burn completed the Tops, and so certainly climbed the Pinnacle. Indeed his ascent is recorded in the Journal.[21] In Burn's obituary E.C. Thomson recalls Burn's visit to Skye, and the heartless leg-pulling which he endured there at the hands of the young members who dragged him up![22] Burn was obsessively meticulous and I have no doubt at all that his completion would withstand the most sceptical scrutiny. It is likely – given the foregoing discussion of Robertson – that he was the first Munroist as well as the first over the Tops.

To return to Munro, after this lengthy traverse, it is clear that his object was to complete the Tops, but which tops did he fail to ascend? Tradition, codified by James Donaldson, specifies the Inaccessible Pinnacle and Carn Cloich-mhuilinn. However, that is not quite correct.

In 1917 Munro wrote a short piece for the Cairngorm Club Journal.[23] He remarked there,

'I still aspire to stand on the summit of the only three 'tops' in Scotland exceeding 3,000 feet in height which I have not yet climbed. Raeburn, Collie, Garden, and others, however, must combine to haul me up on a rope; otherwise the ascents will not be made!'

My own guess is that he was alluding here to his rheumatism rather than to any Salvationist weaknesses. So in 1917 (possibly slightly earlier) there were three outstanding tops, and probably these remained so, given his condition. But what were they?

An obvious step was to check through Munro's Card Index of Tops and personal copy of the Tables.[24] Only three tops were not crossed off. The Inaccessible Pinnacle, Carn Fhidleir (that featureless lump above the Tilt, Feshie and Geldie), and Carn Cloich-mhuilinn.

---

[18] This question can now be settled. In Robertson's papers there is a 'Brief Record of all my mountaineering ascents from 1882-1904' [*NLS Acc. 11538* item192]. There is a record of the Inaccessible, climbed with John Mackenzie and Meares on June 13, 1905. Moreover, it is the only record of the Inaccessible in the whole list.

[19] *SMCJ* 1907, IX, opposite p.153 and pp.162-165.

[20] *Notebook I*, p. 6.

[21] *SMCJ* 1923, XVI, 300.

[22] *SMCJ* 1973, XXX, 200. An additional account of Burn's ascent of the Pinnacle is given in J.H.B. Bell's *A Progress in Mountaineering*, pp. 175-176, Oliver & Boyd, 1950, or more accessibly in *Bell's Scottish Climbs*, pp. 118-119, Gollancz, 1988 – now with Magna Books, 1995. Apparently Burn was helped up by Bell, if not pulled up by the leg, and was made 'to stand upright on the small summit block' to make doubly sure of the conquest.

[23] See Munro 87 and Chapter 1.6

[24] *NLS Acc. 11538* items 116 (Tables) and 117 (Card Index).

The Inaccessible Pinnacle – temporary summit of Sgurr Dearg

He had failed on Carn Fhidleir in extraordinary circumstances on July 11th, 1908. The account is given by William Garden[25] and is worth reproducing in full. Although Garden does not say so, it is likely that it was because of Munro's 'fanatical belief in the exclusive rights of proprietors in land' that they made their attempt in darkness.[26] Certainly Munro made many other ascents in summer under cover of darkness.

> 'I accompanied Munro through Glen Tilt. Dining early at Blair Atholl, we drove to Forest Lodge, arriving there at 7.40 p.m. The threatening afternoon had settled down to a night of persistently heavy rain. By the time we reached the Belford Memorial Bridge (9.40) we were thoroughly well soaked, and the Tarf and Tilt were already in high flood. From the bridge we followed the left side of the Tarf, but kept well on the high ground, about a quarter of a mile from the stream, and took advantage of innumerable sheep tracks when we could strike them in the rapidly increasing darkness. At 11 p.m. we reached the remains of an old shepherd's bothy, where we rigged up a tent with a mackintosh, under which we took our bearings by aid of compass, map, and matches. From the bothy we bore away in a north-west direction over gently rising moorland. The rain poured harder than ever, and we heard the low growl of the angry Tarf dying away as we left it. As we ascended we got into dense fog, and at 1.05 a.m. we reached the large cairn on the summit of An Sgarsoch with some difficulty, as the summit is very flat and extensive. It was now quite chilly, very dark, and, what was worse, we had been unable to keep our powder dry, and so could neither read our compasses nor see our maps. We knew the wind was north, so going into its biting teeth, we dropped down by the side of the Allt a' Chaoruinn and struck the Geldie. Carn an Fhidleir, originally included in the programme, had to be abandoned, which was more regretted by Munro than I, because in consequence it still remains one of the few three-thousanders undone by him.'

I might have saved myself the trouble of rooting through Munro's copy of the Tables. Some months ago I discovered an article by Ronald Burn[27] describing his final Tops. Burn reports a visit to Munro at Lindertis in January 1919, just two months before Munro's death and notes that that at that time Munro had still to climb three tops – 'Carn an Fhidleir Feisidh, Carn Cloich-mhuilinn and the Inaccessible of Skye'.

Munro the Man

About Munro the man I have little to add to the accounts given elsewhere. There is ample evidence of his clubbable nature: his many years of service on Committee; his devotion to Dinners and Meets, attended at great expense and personal inconvenience, and latterly with little prospect of a hill; his 85 contributions to the Journal; the two Meets convened at Lindertis at his own expense, etc., etc. However, there are hints that he was by no means universally amiable. Douglas describes him as a curious mixture of courtesy and

---

[25] *SMCJ* 1909, X, 230.

[26] *SMCJ* 1903, VII, 282. Reporting the Sligachan Meet, Douglas wrote- 'We had an eloquent re-statement of what may be called the Munro Doctrine, *viz.*, the strict, almost fanatical recognition of the exclusive rights of private property in land'.

[27] See Chapter 3.2

pugnacity.[28]   The Club Minute-Books[29] record disagreements between Naismith and Munro over finance, with Naismith always on the side of parsimony.

Munro could be obdurate, too, when the Members' and his own interests failed to coincide. Many of us nowadays have Journal sets which lack the first or second volume, which were produced in rather careful quantities. This shortage was apparent as early as 1903 when a motion was put to the AGM by Mr Alex Fraser to reprint these volumes.[30] This motion was vetoed by Munro on the grounds that it violated his copyright in the Tables, thus striking a valuable blow on behalf of authors! As noted above, a landowner himself, and a politically active Tory to boot, Munro took a very uncompromising position in relation to rights of exclusion and it may be suspected that he played a large part in shaping the docile policies of the Club in respect of access. However, none of this amounts to any more than the observation that he was a man of his times, no worse and probably better than many of his peers. Further, although it might be supposed that a landowning hereditary baronet who was a member of the Royal Household would be some sort of a snob, this seems unlikely. His first act on acceding to the Presidency on the death of Veitch was to propose a motion that the Committee, qua scrutineers of aspirant members, 'should adjudicate solely upon a candidate's qualifications and not upon his social status', leaving such dubious judgments to the ballot of members (a motion regrettably defeated). A survey of his companions on the hill certainly shows no sign that he preferred the company of any particular class of men. On the contrary, he was ready to go on the hill with any member that came to hand.

The Death of Munro

One final point may be settled here. Where does Munro lie? The Journal tells us only that he died on 19th March 1919 in Tarascon, near Avignon in Provence, where he was running a canteen for troops after the War. Douglas' obituary suggests that he may have been buried there, quoting a report from the local paper, as follows (my translation):-

> 'The funeral service (*les funerailles*) of Sir Hugh Munro, founder of the canteen at the station in our town, took place on Saturday 22nd March at 1.30 p.m. This foreign gentlemen, rich and elderly, who died in a small hotel room, had, with his sister and his two daughters, left Scotland, his country house and his estates and comfortable rural life, to come to our small town and do good amongst us, to establish a charity and devote to it his time, nights as well as days, his wealth, his health and finally his life.'

However, Sir Torquil – Munro's son – showed Munro's grave to Tom Weir some years ago. The graveyard is private, created by Munro after a falling-out with the local kirk at Airlie (Munro's wife Selina was Roman Catholic): it is located in a small patch of waste ground between a farmhouse and a walled garden about 200 yards west of Drumleys, just north of the main road.[31] There are three graves, one of which is very recent. Of the two old graves

---

[28] See Chapter 1.8

[29] *e.g.* Minutes of 13th Committee Meeting in *NLS Acc.11538* item 1.

[30] *SMCJ* 1904, VIII, 74.

[31] Grid Reference NO 339 508.

The Grave of Sir Hugh T. Munro

one was for Munro's mother and the other for his wife, both of whom predeceased him. The latter grave has a headstone, bearing details of both Munro and his wife. Although it seemed possible that Munro might only have been commemorated here, rather than buried, there is no doubt that his remains were brought home and buried here.

The local paper[32] reports the funeral, on 2nd April 1919, 'when his remains were laid to rest in the family burial ground, in the near vicinity of the mansion of Lindertis . . The body was brought to this country and reached Lindertis on Monday (31st March). The coffin, wrapped in the Union Jack, reposed in the stately hall of the mansion . . . The first portion of the funereal service was conducted there by the Bishop of St Andrews, assisted by the Reverend J.A. Philip, Kirriemuir. An imposing cortège, including many school children, wound its way through the umbrageous branches of the evergreens to the graveside, where the final rites were performed by the Bishop of St Andrews and Mr Philip.'

---

[32] *Kirriemuir Observer*, 4th April, 1919. This valuable Scottish historical record may be consulted at the British Newspaper Library, Colingdale, London – after a visit to view the Elgin Marbles, perhaps.

1.8 Obituary of Munro

William Douglas[1]

SIR HUGH MUNRO has gone. He died while running a canteen for French soldiers. The Club and Munro have been inseparably linked from its inception to the date of his death. When it was possible for him to attend, at no meet, dinner, general or committee meeting did he fail to be present, and on the few occasions when he was absent the blank was at once marked and felt. He took the liveliest interest in every phase of the Club's welfare, and his racy comments on all that passed were one of the striking features of our gatherings. His joy at being elected President was intense. He even, in the exuberance of his delight, went the length of saying that he held the honour in higher esteem than he would have done had he been made Prime Minister of Great Britain.

I think it will be found that his attendances at our various gatherings were more numerous, whether on the hills or at the dining table, than those of any other member of the Club, and few amongst us knew the Highland hills so well as he did. With the exception of some half a dozen or so, he had reached the summit of all the 538 'tops' named in his 'Tables.' He was a most delightful companion, and to have him in a climbing party ensured a happy day for all present. His flow of capital talk and story was endless, and it cheered many a weary mile at the end of the day. A tale went the rounds some time ago that he and a great talker had a day on the hills together, and when they returned both complained they had been silent all day as neither could get a word in edgeways. Munro's talk was always good, and his stories excellent and well told.

Munro was unique – a laird, a politician, with a strange mixture of courtesy and pugnacity. His hostile comments in general meetings were always vigorous, but he never failed to give opposite views fair consideration. His hospitality to the Club and Club members was great, and those who were able to take advantage of it will hold the occasions in loving memory. One has only to look over the pages of the Journal to see what an indelible impression he has made on the life of the Club during his nearly thirty years of membership; but no doubt his most important contribution was his 'Tables giving all the Scottish Mountains exceeding 3,000 feet in height,' which appeared in the first volume of the Journal. These Tables involved an immense amount of research, of much poring over 6-inch maps, and of special visits to certain tops to decide doubtful points. I remember

---

[1] *SMCJ* 1919, XV, 214-219.

meeting him one evening at Joe Stott's[2] when the list was in preparation, and I have a vivid recollection of his enthusiasm as we discussed what was a mountain and what was a top till the small hours of the morning. I afterwards heard of a great visit paid to Sir Colin Phillip's in Arran, where 'hills and tops' were discussed for three days and three nights with but little intermission. This list of 'Munros' – as a 3,000-foot hill is now called – will be a lasting monument to his memory.

Professor Ramsay, his old friend and neighbour,[3] sends a few words of appreciation which we are glad to possess. He says: "Munro was keen at everything he undertook, a keen sportsman, a keen politician, devoted to music; as keen a dancer as a climber, a warm-hearted host, and a promoter of good fellowship in every form, he combined all the qualities of a clubable man, and nothing could exceed the whole-heartedness with which he devoted those qualities to the interests of the S.M.C."

Miss A.K. Munro, his sister, in response to a request for a few biographical details, has sent me the following to use in this notice. I am sure we would all wish to have the words as they were written, so I give them as they stand:-

"Hugh Thomas Munro was born in London, 27 Eaton Place, in 1856 – the eldest of a large family of nine. As a boy he was a great collector, and started collections of butterflies, birds' eggs, shells, fossils, &c. He had even then a great love of children, and used to save up all his pocket money to give the school children at Lindertis treats, and organised sports followed by tea, and always ending up with a great display of fireworks.

"When he was seventeen he went to Stuttgart to learn German, and while there developed his intense love of the mountains, spending some of his holidays in the Alps, and began climbing.

"He also then began to love travelling, and when, two years later, he came home, and went into Messrs Rathbones' house in the city to get a business training – which it was thought would be useful to him in later life – used to save up his money and take first one sister and then another for little trips abroad.

"He lived in London in his parents' house in Eaton Place, and enjoyed to the full the London seasons. He was a magnificent dancer, and had a wonderful ear and memory for music. About this time General the Honourable W. Fielding, who was sent to attend the Italian manoeuvres, knowing his love of travel, took him as A.D.C., and thus he saw Rome under most favourable circumstances.

"After some years of this life he had a bad attack of pleurisy, and the climate of the Cape was recommended. He went in 1880 as Private Secretary to Sir George Colley, Governor of Natal, and much enjoyed the social life and the interest of the flora and magnificent scenery of the Cape. On the outbreak of the Basuto War he volunteered for active service, and

---

[2] Joseph Stott, the first editor of the *SMC Journal*, who commisioned Munro to produce the Tables. Stott emigrated to New Zealand after Volume I and was replaced as Editor by Willie Douglas.

[3] George G. Ramsay, first President of the SMC, was a neighbour in the country landowning sense: he lived in Glen Isla.

Sir Hugh T. Munro at the Dower House of Drumleys

joined an irregular corps of cavalry, Landrey's Horse. He was all through that campaign, and had a most perilous experience carrying dispatches through the heart of the enemy's country. At the end of the war, and after Sir George Colley's death, he returned, bringing a fine collection of Basuto and Zulu curios, antelope heads, a black boy, and a monkey, home to Eaton Place.

"After this he lived principally in Forfarshire at Lindertis, managing the property, first for his uncle, Sir Thomas Munro, and then for his father, Sir Campbell Munro, and no year passed without his spending many days on the mountains he loved so well.

"From this time forward he took a deep and most active interest in politics. In 1885 he stood for Kirkcaldy Burghs, a forlorn hope; but it was thought well to contest that seat in the Conservative interest, and no one else was willing to come forward. He made a splendid fight, but at that time Scotland was entirely Radical, and no Conservative had a chance of success. It was the only time he ever stood for Parliament, though frequently asked to do so for his own county – Forfarshire; for though he loved the contest, he would have hated the life in London of an M.P. He preferred pulling the strings and working for others, and no election took place without his working most strenuously for the Unionist candidates, speaking several times a day at contested elections not only in Forfarshire, but also in Perthshire, Fife, and Kincardine – organising the various meetings, putting up speakers at his home, Drumleys, and, on the day of the election, driving the electors from early morning till the close of the poll in the evening.

"He organised the political life of Forfarshire on the Unionist side; was long on Central Council of Conservative party in Scotland; Chairman of Tay Divisional Committee of National Union of Conservative Associations for Scotland; and Chairman of Forfarshire Unionist Association; member of County Council for Forfarshire since its formation; member of School Board; Secretary of the Primrose League; and later on, Chairman of the Unionist Associatiom He was also a most active member of the County Council and of the Airlie Parish Council. He married, in 1892, the daughter of General Byrne, and taught her to love travelling as much as he did himself. They went together to the West Indies and the Spanish Main, as well as many trips nearer home – Switzerland, Holland, Germany, Spain, Tangier, Morocco, &c. She died in 1902, and when his children grew old enough he took his daughters for many delightful tours. His eldest daughter went to Albania, Greece, Italy on one tour. Another time he took both his daughters to Algiers, Biskra, the Riviera, &c., and in December 1913 he started with his eldest girl round the world, going by America, visiting Niagara, the Grand Cañon, Yosemite Valley, &c., thence to Honolulu, Japan, China, Singapore, Ceylon, and so home. They were away five months. He also acted several times as an extra King's Messenger through the kindness of a friend at the Foreign Office, who, knowing his love of travel, procured this pleasant way of seeing Berlin, and Petrograd, and Vienna, and Constantinople, to all of which he carried the Foreign Office dispatches. He was a wonderful courier, and his varied interests and knowledge of many subjects, architecture, art, nature, geology, &c., made him a most interesting and efficient guide.

"I say nothing about the mountaineering; you know that better than I do; and for many years he spent some time climbing amongst either the Alps or the Scotch mountains. I think this was the paramount interest of his life.

"When the war broke out, as he was past military age, he put his services at the disposal of the Red Cross, and went during the winter of 1915-16 to Malta to trace the missing. He returned in June very unwell, and suffering from some sort of malarial fever, which he never threw off completely. He devoted himself heart and soul to farming, raising stock, bringing land under cultivation, increasing the food supply in every way. In the spring of 1918 he went to Tarascon, in the south of France, with his two daughters, and under the auspices of the French Croix Rouge started his own canteen for the French troops, which has remained open ever since. When it was in complete working order he returned home to look after things at Lindertis. In the spring of the year he returned to Tarascon, and after a month's work at his canteen got a chill which developed into pneumonia, and the end came after a week's illness."

The following is an extract from a French local paper: –

"TARASCON. – OBSEQUES. – Samedi 22 mars, à 13 h.30, ont eu lieu les funérailles de Sir Hugh Munro, fondateur de la cantine de gare de notre ville.

"Ce gentilhomme étranger, riche, âgé, qui vient de mourir dans une petite chambre d'hotel, avait, avec sa soeur et ses deux filles, quitté l'Ecosse, son chateau, ses propriétés, une vie paisible et confortable, pour venir dans une petite ville faire le bien parmi nous, fonder une belle oeuvre et lui consacrer son temps, ses nuits comme ses jours, son argent, sa santé et enfin sa vie.

"A l'issue de la cérémonie, Monsieur le Président de la Société de Secours aux blessés méleurs a retracé en termes éloquents et émus l'oeuvre généreuse du défunt, qui, ne pouvant s'engager comme combattant, avait demandé a faire son devoir sur ce champ d'honneur le seul qui fut permis, où il a trouvé une mort glorieuse. Désolé de ne pouvoir relater en entier ce beau discours, je ne puis m'empecher d'en citer les derniers mots: "et Mesdemoiselles, nous garderons pieusement le souvenir de votre pere, de votre frère. Permettez dans votre lointain pays la reconnaissance de vos amis de France."

CHAPTER 2

The Pioneers - Robertson

2.1 Archibald Eneas Robertson 1870 – 1958

WHILE Hugh Munro may have been the first 'bagger', he was a bagger of Tops rather than Munros, and of course he did not complete his bag. Archie Robertson was the first to complete the round of the Munros. Once he conceived the notion, he went at it hammer and tongs, accounting for 70-odd in each of 1898 and 1899, and 20-odd in 1901. The rapidity of his round, particularly in its latter stages, is a reminder that the Munro-gobbling practices of more recent times – sometimes criticized by those who see Munro-bagging as an acceptable form of mountaineering only if it is practised slowly – were endorsed by the Original Munroist.

Robertson is the subject of a book – *The First Munroist* by Peter Drummond & Ian Mitchell (Ernest Press, 1993) – and in Chapter 7, 'Transports of Delight', Mitchell makes it clear that Robertson enjoyed facilities of access (using traps, trains and his bicycle) and of accommodation (living with keepers and others inhabiting remote houses deep in the glens) which were in fact superior to what is available to the present-day Munroist. Moreover, the absence of hydro-electric damming of the glens and the ready availability of boats and boatmen when lochs or rivers must be crossed meant that pedestrian movement within the Highlands was in many places freer then, land-owners permitting!

Robertson recorded his mountaineering days in minute detail in notebooks and diaries, which have all been preserved. Some of these are identified in the next chapter, which describes Robertson's Round. They are all deposited in the Manuscript collection of the National Library of Scotland and accessible to the public in their Reading Rooms, for anyone who might be interested in getting more detail than I have been able to provide here. A typical notebook entry will give timings throughout Robertson's day and ample detail of the route that he followed, as well as weather, views, etc. He also took up photography in a serious way after completing, and his photographs have been a mainstay of the *SMC Journal* and of the Club's many publications ever since. Some 95 of these photographs were reproduced in *The First Munroist* and so I have included only a few in the present book. Limited access to the Robertson collection of photographs may be made available through application to the SMC Secretary.

As well as the account of Robertson's round, I have included three other pieces. The first is Robertson's own reflections on completing the Munros, which he published in 1902. This is written in typical racy style, peppered with jokes and anecdotes. As the second piece – Logan Aikman's diary record of a chance meeting with the 59-year-old Robertson at the CIC Hut – makes clear, this raciness can wear a little thin! The third item included is Jim Bell's obituary, which contains some interesting details of Robertson's later life.

In pieces of my own which appear in this book (Chapters 1.7 and 4.8) I draw attention to some apparent defects in Robertson's round: he may not have climbed Ben Wyvis and he certainly didn't climb the Ridge South of Creag a' Choire Aird. In the latter case, the omission

Portrait of the Rev. A. E. Robertson by Keith Henderson, R.S.W.

arose because of a mistake in the printing of the Tables, and in the former we cannot be sure that he didn't remedy the deficiency. It is interesting that his *Brief Record* (see notes to next chapter) records an ascent of Creag a' Choire Aird in June 1902 and that his Notebook ends a day or so before this ascent! So it may be that diligent study of Robertson's papers may turn up a *mea culpa* somewhere. It may be, too, that scrutiny of the account of his round that follows may uncover further omissions – I haven't had the heart to make this search! However, I do not believe that any of this matters greatly. There is no reason to doubt that when Robertson claimed completion, he honestly believed he had done them all, and who is there amongst the 2000 or so completers who can put hand on heart and say that it is absolutely definitely the case that I have stood on the precise summit of all of the Munros!?

Although it is not an incident that had anything to do with Munro-bagging, readers may be interested in another unique property of Robertson. He may have been the first mountaineer to have been struck by lightning in the Highlands. He recorded the incident in his Brief Record as follows:–

'April 5th 1905. Left Imperial Hotel Fort William at 9.05 for Ben Nevis *via* path. Struck by lightning about 1 on ridge of corrie overlooking Glen Nevis. Got home at 4.15. Dr MacArthur dressed my head for 2 hours. 20 stitches! Temperature about 1° above normal at 10 p.m.'

Robertson did not write a report of this accident for the *SMC Journal*, but the following note appeared in the *Cairngorm Club Journal* for 1905 (Volume 5, p. 59). From the exaggerated style of the report, it may have first appeared in a newspaper.

'A distressing and somewhat peculiar accident occurred on Ben Nevis on 6th April last, by which Rev. A.E. Robertson, Edinburgh, the well-known mountaineer, was severely injured. Notwithstanding that the day was a most unsuitable one for climbing, there being an almost continuous fall of snow, accompanied by thunder and lightning, Mr Robertson set out alone to make the ascent of Ben Nevis. He succeeded in reaching the summit, and on his downward journey the severity of the blizzard which prevailed made him rather keep further to the south than the line of the bridle path in order to avoid the cliffs, but owing to the mist and driving snow he had unconsciously deviated further than had been his intention. He distinctly recollects that the thunder and lightning seemed very near, and that the steel of his ice-axe hissed with electric sparks, doubtless St Elmo's fire. It is Mr Robertson's belief that a flash of lightning struck either his ice-axe or the ground near where he was, thus rendering him unconscious. On falling he must have been hurled with terrific force down a thousand feet over the frozen boulders strewn upon the hillside, but of what actually took place he has not the faintest recollection. He can recall nothing until he found himself making for the path from the direction of Glen Nevis, and at an altitude considerably over a thousand feet lower than the point where he calculates he was rendered unconscious. He had lost his cap and ice-axe, his clothes were torn, and blood was oozing freely from his wounds, but, as already stated, he managed by a supreme effort of will to walk unaided to Fort William, which was distant three miles. Mr Robertson has, we are glad to say, now quite recovered, but bears more than one mark of his terrible accident'.

Clearly, this story opens up an opportunity for some archaeological research in Five Finger Gully, with the First Munroist's cap and ice-axe as a possible prize!

2.2 Robertson's Round of the Munros

A.E. Robertson

[THIS account of Robertson's traverse is based on his two-volume *Mountaineering Notebook* and his *Brief Record of all my Mountaineering Ascents from 1882-1904*, – manuscripts which are now in the National Library of Scotland.[1] Volume I of the Notebook is 72 pages, dated March 1st 1899, and Volume II is 31 pages, dated February 1936. In fact, the hand in which the volumes are written changes at the entry for 20th June 1898, which is on page 64 of Volume I, so it seems that Robertson may have completed Volume I only as far as page 64 in 1899, adding the concluding pages in 1936. I have also made some use of an earlier editing of these notebooks by J.H.B. Bell and J.D.B. Wilson which appeared as *SMCJ* 1948, XXIV, 25-31 and *SMCJ* 1949, XXIV, 81-86

The expeditions of the early years of his round are recorded in fair detail, with commentary which is often interesting. However, later expeditions are recorded in a more perfunctory style. Accordingly, I have adopted different strategies in presenting this material. Until the end of 1898, the round is described in the first person and I have altered Robertson's words as little as possible, except for frequent omission of matter with no bearing on his progress around the Munros and of descriptions of summit views. From 1899 onwards I have freely paraphrased the Notebook, again omitting irrelevant matter, and presenting, of course, a third-person account.]

In August 1889 Aunt Lizzie and mother had a house jointly at Loch Awe near the station. From there I with some other lads climbed Cruachan. We rowed down to the Cruachan burn. Just as we were starting at the falls, a stranger came up and asked if he might accompany us as he had the same object in view and was alone. Rose had just been murdered by Laurie on Goatfell, the murderer was still at large, and we boys were much suspicious that the stranger was he![2] However, after much whispering together and scanning him well, up and down, we allowed him to join us! He turned out to be some Inspector of Schools in Edinburgh.

In the summer of 1890 we were at Onich, and there, in this year, my love for the hills was generated. On 25th August I climbed Ben Nevis alone. I took $2\,^{1}/_{4}$ hours to go up and it was very misty on top. I had tea in the Hotel at the top. On 29th August Dr Whyte took me with him to Bidean nam Bian – a red-letter day for me. The party was – Dr Whyte, Mr Peyton of Broughty Ferry, Dr John Sutherland Black, Mr Cassie of Hopeman, and myself. This day first shewed me the delights of scientific mountaineering – the use of maps, aneroid, compass, etc. – and ever since that day I have steadily pursued the Quest. I well remember how struck I was with Dr Black's aneroid and map, and with Mr Peyton's knowledge of geology and his general skill in directing and guiding the whole party. How he skipped about with his hammer, peering here, peering there, whacking at this, tearing at that – he was never still!

---

[1] *NLS Acc.11538* items193-4 and 192, respectively.

[2] This is a reference to the famous Arran Murder case (see William Roughead's *John Watson Laurie* in the Famous British Trials series), in which John Laurie was apprehended after much public excitement and convicted of murdering Edwin Rose in the course of a climb on Arran.

We drove to Clachaig Inn and ascended by the burn into the great north corrie. Mr Cassie had to get sips of grog on the way up, and Mr Peyton was much scandalized at him, when he found halfway up that he had no nails in his boots. "It adds 1000 feet to a hill," he said – something which I have never forgotten.

In the spring of 1892 Mr Alex Somerville invited me up to stay with him at Aviemore in June for a week. On 24th June we climbed Braeriach – one of the most lovely days for climbing and clear views I have ever had. We drove to the first bothy in Glen Einich and ascended by the zigzag path. On this day I had my taste for scientific mountaineering deepened and confirmed. Mr Somerville had an aneroid, compass and maps, and the use of them greatly charmed me. In his house at Aviemore (Lower Tullochgrue) he had with him a number or two of the SMC Journal, and these I read with the greatest interest. We reached the cairn in brilliantly clear weather, with all that was possible to be seen, visible; and he and I picked out all the better-known hills. When thus engaged, two other climbers joined us, and helped us greatly in identifying the view. By their talk, gait and equipment we could see they were no mere 'tourist' walkers, and they turned out to be Mr W. Douglas, Editor of the SMC Journal, and a friend. From Mr Douglas I learned a great deal more anent the SMC and mountaineering generally, which whetted my appetite keener than ever. We exchanged cards and I promised to look him up in Edinburgh – which I did at the first opportunity. This was indeed a notable day for me.

Next day with Mr Shepherd of Cambuslang I climbed Cairngorm. This day was as bad as the last had been good – thick mist, rain and hail and a fearful wind which burst on us from the south-east. I was steering by compass, not allowing for magnetic variation[3] and so we never reached the cairn. We were very high up nearly 4,000 feet before we turned.

From Aviemore I went north for two months to Ewan Grant at Nigg. From here in August I did Ben Wyvis, taking train to Auchterneed from Tain. I followed the usual way up, but near the top it came on heavy rain and as I did not want to get soaked I turned.

In September I paid a visit to the Whytes at Bonskeid. On 17th September Dr Whyte, Jack Geddes and I climbed Schiehallion.

A day or so after Christmas I went alone to Kenmore and thence to Fearnan Temperance Hotel. I walked well upon to Meall Gruaidh (3280 ft.) amusing myself by glissading on strips of snow. This was the first time I had ever been on snow. I had no Alpine stock or axe yet.

In the spring of 1893 I began to lay in a proper mountaineering outfit. I bought an ice-axe through Douglas from Chamonix. It cost me almost 21 shillings all told, 20 francs + postage from A. Simond. I also bought an aneroid through Lord Kelvin from his instrument-maker, James Pitkin, 56 Red Lion St. Clerkenwell, E.C. It cost me £3 and it has been ever a most reliable instrument to me. Every hill I have gone to ever since, I have had it with me. I bought a compass (9 shillings) from White, Glasgow. Last, but by no means least, James Wright, Edinburgh, made for me a pair of boots – 'my old hobnailers'. I will never get a better pair, never. They carried me always from this date in every mountain expedition I had until 1896, then very frequently till the summer of 1898. I suppose they

---

[3] About 18 degrees West!

must have taken me over about 100 hills over 3000 feet, a thing unique in boots! They are now among my treasures.

In April I went with some New College friends to Loch Awe (G.R.S. Reid, J.B. Smith, Wilson and Magee). We climbed a snow gully on Stob Garbh of Cruachan and then glissaded some slopes between Stob Garbh and Stob Diamh. We all slid away with howls of delight, nearly killing ourselves. Another day we climbed Cruachan over Meall Cuanail. Reid and I then traversed the ridge to the horseshoe and so home, glissading down much the same place as before. After another day off Wilson and I started for Ben Lui by train to Dalmally then trap to Socach Farm. We went over Beinn a' Cleibh and so to the top. After another off day Reid and I went to Crianlarich and climbed Stobinian and Ben More.

Robertson modelling his newly purchased Wettermantel

On Saturday 22nd April I climbed Ben Vorlich and Stuc a' Chroin from Lochearn-head, then down by Gleann an Dubh Choirean to Callander.[4]

In May I bought my rucksack from Silver, London (21s.) and ordered through Douglas a wettermantel[5] from Frey, Munich, which reached me early in June at Aviemore. I spent the month of June at Aviemore, with rooms at Charlie McDonald's, Coylum Bridge. I did a great deal of climbing this month in the Cairngorms and got into a 'condition' that has served me well ever since. I climbed Creag na Leacainn (1st June), Braeriach (5th), Cairngorm (10th), Sgoran Dubh (12th), Ben Macdui (17th) – Mr Fraser of Walker, Fraser & Steele with me, Sgor an Lochan Uaine and Cairn Toul (20th), and The Devil's Point (26th).

During the beginning of July 1893 I started on my first walking tour, rucksack on back, Alpine Stock in hand. I took in my rucksack in that tour a flannel shirt and drawers, slippers, U-Sohn's binocular, wettermantel, raisins, figs, chocolate. Nor have I changed my list of articles very much since. I would not take my wettermantel now, in summer, and I always now carry a sweater.

---

[4] This outing is out of sequence in the *Notebook*, placed amongst 1894 climbs.

[5] According to Harold Raeburn, writing in *Section A of the SMC Guide*, in 1921, 'For an outside or overall garment in bad weather, there is nothing to equal the Tyrolese wettermantel of loden cloth. It is merely two sheets of natural wool cloth, like a herald's tabard. These button up the sides when on. The yoke is a double layer of cloth, one lying loose on the other. It has loose wide sleeves, which can button close around the wrist. It is very light, and the skirts, which ought not to come much below the knee, can be stowed away through the rope when climbing is to be done.'

Taking the early train from Aviemore on Tuesday 4th July, I got out at Dalwhinnie and hired a trap which took me down to Loch Ericht Lodge. Passing the lodge and the gardener with some trepidation, I struck up the shooting-path which comes down here from Loch Pattack, and in about another 2 miles I got another which took me up by the side of the Culrea burn. After walking up this for a good bit, enjoying the loneliness and beauty of the scene, suddenly I came upon a party of men supposed to be mending the path, but all sound asleep. I gave a shout, and how they jumped! – it afterwards transpired that Sir John Ramsden (the proprietor) was half-expected up that day. One of the men turned out to be the keeper, John Clark, and he was very friendly. He walked with me for a long way, giving me advice as to how I should go. He asked me for my card, "in case Sir John might want to know", which of course I readily did.

This was my first real experience of unknown deer forest land. I had set my heart on exploring this region: Mr Stott's and Prof. Ramsay's articles in the *SMCJ* having fired my ambition.[6] I heard from McCallum, a keeper at Aviemore, of possible night quarters at Ben Alder Lodge (McCook's), so I just planned it out and went, and my boldness was in no way regrettable. McCook's has been quite a favourite haunt for me ever since and I have received nothing but the greatest kindness and hospitality from them always.

I left the path at a height of 2,100 feet, crossed the burn and made straight up the steep north face of Ben Alder. It was very steep, but quite easy, and I got into a kind of gully which took me out on the great, high plateau. The mist, which had been threatening all day, now came down on me, but with compass and map I made the cairn at 3 p.m. I descended by the south-east shoulder and reached McCook's at 5.35. With some trepidation I knocked at the door. Out comes Mrs McCook, smiling and neat and clean as she always is "Can you put me up for the night?" "Yes, sir, we shall be delighted." Thus was I admitted to McCook's, and in the many times I have revisited I have always gone with the greatest pleasure and been received with the greatest courtesy.

[Next day Geal Charn was climbed]

As there appeared to be no cairn, I promptly made one. I then made for Aonach Beag. I was half an hour on top, and then packed my traps and made off for Beinn Eibhinn. Going down the ridge I started an old raven with her young. At the bealach I dipped down the south slope for about 100 feet to an inviting spring and had my lunch, and at 2.05 was on the top of Beinn Eibhinn. After picking my way down the north ridge and going down the Allt Cam, a long, hot and toilsome walk (oh, those flies !) brought me to Lublea, where the keeper (McIntosh – an old Ben Alder ghillie and friend of McCook's) gave me a good welcome and refreshment. He put me across the River Spean in a crazy boat which nearly sank with the two of us in midstream. I reached Moy Inn at 6 p.m. There I stayed several days and did a lot of walking. My expeditions were a) Beinn a' Chlachair and Mullach Coire an Iubhair, b) the Creag Meaghaidh range[7] and c) the twin tops of Beinn a' Chaoruinn. I had a fearful thunderstorm on the hill, the air being so charged with electricity that the point of my stock fizzled when held up.

---

[6] Stott's article 'Ben Aulder' appeared in *SMCJ* 1890, I, 70-75; Ramsay's 'Ascent of Ben Alder' in *SMCJ* 1891, I, 135-138.

[7] This expedition is described in full detail in *SMCJ* 1894, III, 23-27.

Leaving Moy I walked up the east side of Loch Treig to Creaguaineach Lodge (Archie Cameron's). Next day I walked up the Amhainn Reidh and so to the top of Binnein Mor.[8] Next day from Steall I climbed Aonach Beag, Carn Mor Dearg and Ben Nevis. From Fort William I walked on to Onich where I stayed some 7 or 8 days. During my stay I climbed Sgorr Dhonuill and Sgorr Dhearg of Beinn a' Bheithir. From Onich I walked up Glencoe to Altnafeadh. I had hoped to climb Buchaille Etive Mor, but it came on to rain, so I stopped the night with the keeper (Dan McKay). The other keeper Cameron of Laggangarbh was over and we spent a pleasant evening. Next morning the weather was still unpropitious and I did not start for the Buchaille, preferring the Capuan luxuries of McKay's kitchen and my pipe to the buffetings of wind and rain. I went on to Inveroran and stayed with John McGregor, who was gardener at Forest Lodge. Next day was Sunday. Next day McGregor put me across Loch Tulla and I made for the bealach between Ben Dothaidh and Ben Doran, then down to Loch Lyon and down Glen Lyon to Bridge of Balgie. Here I found mother and Kate.[9] We spent a month in Oakwood Cottage (Mrs MacNaughton's) and I did a lot of climbing. My 'days' were The Tarmachans; Meall Corronaich and Meall a' Choire Leith; Meall Ghaordie; Stuchd an Lochain; Carn Gorm and Meall Garbh; Creag Mhor and Carn Mairg with Mr Somerville; Meall Garbh, An Stuc, Ben Lawers and Beinn Ghlas.

I returned home in September, and in this month applied for admission to the SMC, my application form, with statement of hills climbed, being signed by W. Douglas and Professor Ramsay respectively.[10] At the Fifth Annual General Meeting, held on 15th December, I was admitted a member, and at the end of the month attended my first Club Meet at Dalmally – every hour of which I enjoyed. On the first day Tough, Burnett and I ascended Beinn a' Bhuiridh by a gully on the north-east face. On 1st January 1894 a party of us climbed Ben Lui by the north-east face, led by Tough. This was my first experience of real hard snow and rope work, and I learned much from Tough's excellent skill and guiding.

On April 13th I went to Inveroran with Harry Tod, W.S. We walked from Tyndrum, taking Ben Doran en route. Next day we did Stob Ghabhar by the south-east ridge returning by Corrie Ba. On the 16th we were put over in a boat to the east side of Loch Tulla and climbed up the steep north ridge of Beinn Dothaidh, then down to Bridge of Orchy and home.

On Monday, 23rd April, I was joined at Blair Athol by W.P. Fell, and we walked up Glen Tilt to Falar Lodge (Donald Lamond), where we spent the night. I think this may be almost the highest house in Scotland: it is 1760 feet. It was very cold in the lodge and there was a great bank of snow right up the walls of the house. Next morning was very wet and stormy, and the mist was down thick to the very doors. However, we started, mist or no mist, on our walk to the Braemar side. It was about the longest and most intricate piece of steering I have ever done. We emerged out of the mist at the Baddoch burn just where we expected, although the ground was all perfectly new to me – this shows what may be done by an intelligent use of map, compass and aneroid. From Falar we followed the road for $1\frac{1}{2}$ miles

---

[8] See 'Two Days in Lochaber', *SMCJ* 1895, III, 267-271.

[9] Kate was Robertson's cousin, Kate McFarlan, who appears frequently in the *Notebook*, and eventually becomes his wife.

[10] Robertson's Application Form is reproduced on page 54.

Scottish Mountaineering Club.

STATEMENT OF THE QUALIFICATIONS FOR MEMBERSHIP OF

(Candidate's Full Name), Archibald Æneas Robertson

(Designation), M.A. (Glasgow)

(Address), 17 Hartington Place. Edinburgh.

Extract from Rule XIV.:—
"Every Candidate for admission to the Club must forward to the Secretary (on a special Form to be obtained from him) at least one month before the Annual General Meeting in December (or any other General Meeting), a list of his Scottish ascents, stating the month and year in which each ascent was made. The list must be signed by the candidate and by two members of the Club acting as proposer and seconder."

Note.—Ascents elsewhere than in Scotland should also be given.

DATE OF ASCENT (ONLY THE YEAR AND MONTH NEED BE STATED).	ASCENT.	REMARKS (if any).
August 1889.	Ben Cruachan.	
July 1890	Bidean nam Bian	
August "	Ben Nevis.	
June 1892	Braeriach	
" "	Cairn Gorm	
August "	Ben Wyvis	
Sept "	Schiehallion	
Dec. "	Meall Gruaidh	
March 1893	Stob Garbh and Beinn a Bhuiridh (Cruachan)	ascent via Coire Creachainn step cutting
April 1893	Ben Cruachan, Drochaid Glas, Stob Dearg.	
" "	Ben a Chleibh, Ben Laoigh (Lui)	
" "	Ben More, Am Binnein	
" "	Ben Vorlich, Stuc a Chroin	
June "	Creag na Leacainn (Cairngorms)	
" "	Braeriach	
" "	Cairn Toul, Sgor an Lochain Uaine	
" "	Ben Mac Dhui	
" "	Cairngorm	
" "	Sgoran Dubh	
July "	Ben Alder	
" "	Beal Charn: Aonach Beag; Ben Eibhinn.	
" "	Ben a Chuoruinn (Loch Pattack)	
" "	Creag Meagaidh range.	
" "	Mullach Coire an Iubhair, Ben a Clachair.	
" "	Binnein Mòr (Ben Nevis)	
" "	Aonach Beag, Carn Mòr Dearg, Ben Nevis.	from Aonach Beag along ridge to Carn Mòr Dearg, thence along the arête to B. Nevis.
" "	Ben a Bheithir (Sgor Dhonuill & Sgor Dearg)	
August "	Meall Connaraich, Meall a Choire Leith (Lawers)	
" "	Meall Garbh, An Stuc, Ben Lawers, Beinn Ghlas.	
" "	Meall nan Tarmachan.	
" "	Meall Ghaordie.	
" "	Carn Gorm, Meall Garbh (C. Mairg range)	
" "	Stuchd an Lochain (Rannoch)	
" "	Creag Mhòr (C. Mairg range)	
" "	Cairn Mairg.	

Candidate's Signature, Archd. Robertson.

Proposer's Signature, William Douglas.

Seconder's Signature, G. G. Ramsay.

Date, Sep 1st 1893.

Archie Robertson's SMC Application Form

till it crosses the Allt a' Ghlinne Bhig and then followed up this stream. Near the top of Beinn Iutharn Mhor the wind and the drift were very bad, and at the cairn we were only too glad to shelter from the icy blast. We soon left for Beinn Iutharn Beag, which we duly reached by dint of careful steering. We now made for the Baddoch, great care being needed not to get into Glen Ey in the thick mist. A weary walk down the Baddoch brought us to the road in Glen Cluny, and we reached our destination (Mrs Downie's at Newbigging) at 6 – soaked to the very skin. On Friday 27th we walked to Lochnagar over Cairn Taggart and the Cairn of Corbreach. Next day we walked to the Shanspittal and up to Carn an Tuirc, Cairn na Glasha, Tolmount, Cairn Bannoch and Fafernie. On Monday 30th we left Mrs Downie and traversed to Glen Shee by way of the Glas Maol and Creag Leacach. We stayed with a Mrs Patton, Lealach, Spittal and were very comfortably put up. Next day we climbed Glas Thalachan and along to Carn an Righ, then home via Lochan Eun. We returned by mail cart to Blairgowrie next day, and so to Edinburgh.

On Saturday May 19th I climbed Ben Lomond with a party of Crichtons, Browns, etc.

On Friday June 1st I went to Loch Ericht Lodge at Dalwhinnie (Jemima and John Clark, very kind). Next day I climbed Carn Dearg from the Culrea Burn, descending by Lochan Sgor and over the Bealach Dubh and round to McCook's. On the Monday I returned by Sron an Iolaire and Beinn Bheoil to Dalwhinnie where I caught the train to Aviemore and that evening found myself in my old quarters at McDonald's, Coylum Bridge, and was there for three months, during which time I had the following walks, in chronological order: Braeriach; Cairngorm with the Dalys; Cairn Toul; Braeriach; Stac Meall na Cuaich, Glen Tromie; Braeriach with Dr Whyte and a large party; Cairngorm, thence to Ben Macdui and home by the Larig with the Crichtons, Dalys and Iverachs; Braeriach with the Whytes, Mr and Mrs S.R. Crockett, Dr Sutherland Black and Charles Douglas; Cairngorm and down to see Loch A'an with the Whytes, Crocketts, etc.; Bynac, A' Choinneach, right along Loch A'an to the Shelter Stone, up Coire Raibert to Cairngorm and home – Mrs Crichton, Miss C., Mr Daly and self; Braeriach with Hugh Black.

In September we were in Glen Lyon at Mrs MacNaughton's, but I was very busy studying and only got a few climbs done. These were Garbh Meall above Lochs; Beinn Heasgarnich and Creag Mhor from Sheanvore (Mrs Monro), which I reached by bicycle; Ben Creachan with Kate in a trap to Invermeran, then up easily and rapidly from Glen Meran.

In the afternoon of Saturday 29th December Sandy Taylor, J. Parker and I climbed Ben Narnain in a fearful wind and then joined the SMC Meet at Tarbet Hotel. On Monday 31st Parker, Rennie, Taylor and I did Ben Vorlich by the north-east corry, and on 1st January 1895 we had a grand climb traversing the Cobbler from end to end. Our party was Maylard, Naismith, Rose, Thomson, J. Drummond and myself. It was the best as well as the most difficult day I had done from a climbing point of view . On 2nd January Parker, Thomson, Drummond and I did Beinn Chabhair.

On Thursday 11th April I took train to Fort William for the Easter SMC Meet at the Alexandra Hotel. On Friday a large party of us drove up Glen Nevis. Munro, Parker, Howie, Gunn and myself walked up to Sgor a' Mhaim. Munro, Parker and I continued the circuit of Coire a' Mhail. We traversed successively Sgurr an Iubhair, Am Bodach, Stob

Choire a' Chairn, An Garbhanach and An Gearanach. On Monday Parker and I had a splendid day peak-bagging among the Easains. From Roy Bridge we struck up the moor to Stob Coire nan Ceann. We then traversed the ridge in brilliant sunshine and deep snow, bagging Stob Coire Claurigh, Stob Coire an Laoigh and Sgor a' Choinnich Mor. On Wednesday Myres and myself climbed Stob Bhan and Mullach nan Coirean. On Thursday I was joined by Sandy Moncrieff and Mirylees, who arrived with 60 yards of rope instead of 60 feet as I had told him. On Friday we took the stage coach to the head of Glen Shiel to begin a ten-days walking tour. We tramped up Glen Finnan, pretty heavily laden, to Corryhully, then went up to Sgor Choileam and glissaded down the other side and on to Glen Dessary farm house, where we were received by a bevy of about 30 dogs. Next day in perfect sunshine we started off up Glen Dessary for Sgor na Ciche.

[After climbing Sgor na h-Aide in mistake for Sgor na Ciche, the party descended to the head of Loch Nevis in search of lodgings.]

The near view of the cottages did not greatly please us: they were dirty, damp and badly thatched. "I'm not going to sleep there," said Mirylees emphatically. However, 'any port in a storm', so I knocked at the door of one. Imagine our surprise when out stepped a Highlander in full costume. Kilts, cap, shoes and even a dirk. We told him our tale. One or two other men emerged from sundry peat-smoked dwellings and a prolonged dispute arose among them in Gaelic. At last one – the keeper at Carnoch – came forward and bid us welcome. "I have only one bed and there are 3 of you, but you will have to make the best of it!". This we did. Mirylees, who had just returned from roughing it in South Africa and was up to the thing, pulled a long 'kist' alongside the bed, re-made the bed across it, and we three slept transversely, and very comfortably too!

Next day we scaled Sgor na Ciche, using the rope for the last 200 feet, then descended by the N.E. spur and Coire nan Gall to Kinlochquoich (tea, scones and treacle) and so to Quoich Bridge (James Henderson).[11]   Next day we we went up to Alltbeath and over the Bealach Dubh-leac to Shiel Inn. Tuesday 23rd was a rest day and Mirylees had unfortunately to leave us. On Wednesday Sandy and I did Scour Ouran, then along the ridge over Sgurr na Carnach and Sgurr na Ciste Duibhe, descending into Glen Shiel. On Thursday I did the Saddle myself in mist. On Friday we walked up to Cluny Inn and on Saturday I did Crawlich [A' Chralaig] and Sgurr nan Ceathramhan [Mullach Fraoch-choire]. On Sunday we walked back to Shiel Inn. On Monday we climbed Ben Attow: fording the River Croe gave us grand sport and the wee lochan – a dew drop – that we suddenly came on as we toiled up the steep slope, will always remain in my mind as one of my most beautiful pictures. Here, too, we were the fortunate spectators of a fight between two ravens and an eagle, which the former won easily, driving the royal bird right off the ground. On Tuesday we shifted our quarters to Glen Elg, intending to climb Ben Screel, but alas bad weather and laziness prevailed and after waiting two days we took the Clansman to Oban. From Oban I went north to Barriemore where I joined Kate. On Monday 6th May we climbed Ben Sguliaird, driving to the head of Loch Creran.

---

[11] These establishments were both submerged when Loch Quoich was dammed.

On Wednesday 22nd May my friend the Rev. James Harvey of Free Lady Glenorchy's, Edinburgh, and I took the early mail train to Beauly. We left Beauly about 1 p.m. and coached to Struy Bridge, arriving there about 3 p.m. Thence we walked up Glen Strathfarrar to Deannie Lodge (Campbell, Keeper). Next morning, heavily laden, we struck up the path N. to the ridge, then W. to Sgurr Ruadh, Carn nan Gobhar and Sgurr a' Choire Ghlais. Heavy rain came on at the cairn and as we had now had about enough of it we gave up Sgurr Fhuar Thuill and took the shortest road S. to the main road, which we followed along to Monar Lodge (McLennan) in the evening.

Next day we walked along the loch side to Strathmore Lodge (McPhail). On Saturday we climbed Maoile Lunndaich from Loch Mhuilich, then over Carn nam Fiaclan to the bealach. Here McPhail and Mr Harvey went round to the right (N.). I went straight up the fine steep rugged ridge to the top of the Spidean (Bidein an Eoin Deirg). Distinct traces of lightning were seen, the ground being all torn up. McPhail and Mr Harvey struck down for home here, while I ran along the ridge to Sgurr a' Chaoruinn and Sgurr Choinnich, returning by the Allt Bealach Crodhain and the Amhainn Strath Mhoir.[12] On Sunday we rested, Harvey giving them a sermon. Then on Monday we three of us walked up to the Bealach an Sgoltaidh and then S. to Bidein a' Choire Sheasgaich – no cairn, pronounced "Spidean an Heasgich". We then went on to Lurg Mhor – fine steep cliffs on the N. side, then along to Meall Mor and down past an old whisky still which McPhail showed us. The next day we were put over in a boat to the S. side of the loch. McPhail came with us and his son carried our rucksacks to the bealach between Sgurr na Lapaich and Riabhachan. From there they went slowly up to Lapaich, while I went W. to Riabhachan – cairn and stick, then 300 yards to the E. another cairn – same height. I soon ran back to the bealach and joined the others on Sgurr na Lapaich. We said goodbye at the top and made our way down to Ben Ula Lodge. Roderick McLean the Keeper put us up in the Lodge: with baths and easy chairs we were very comfortable. Next day Harvey had to leave, but I stayed on and had a magnificent day, going up by the path easily to Tom a' Choinnich, then along the fine ridge to Carn Eige and on to reach Mam Soul at 3 p.m.[13] The cairn is a regular tower. On the east side, out of wind and weather, is a shelter used by Winans' keepers.[14] Next morning I walked down to Cannich from Ben Ula and went home.

On 23rd July I went to Miss Seton's at Blair Athole and was there joined by Reid. On the 24th we climbed the three peaks of Beinn a' Ghlo: Carn Liath, the "Turkey Peak"[15] and Carn nan Gabhar. On the 26th we climbed Beinn Dearg – a wet stormy day with thick mist. Then on the 29th we did Carn Chlamhain. On the 30th we left Blair by goods train to Dalnaspidal and walked by Loch Garry and Loch Rannoch to Mrs Ross's at Cul a' Mhuilinn (3/6 per night). In the morning we were driven to Rannoch Station and went by train to Bridge of Orchy. From there we climbed Beinn Achallader and got down by Glen Cailliche to Sheanvore in Glen Lyon. I stayed at Oakbank Cottage in Glen Lyon through August and September, working hard for my B.D., and did no climbing.

---

[12] The Amhainn Strath Mhoir and Strathmore Lodge were both submerged by the damming of Loch Monar.

[13] The present Loch Mullardoch was at that time two lochs, with Ben Ula Lodge at the road end, between them.

[14] See Hugh Munro's 'Solitary Walk ..' above, Chapter 1.3, for the story of the awkward Mr Winans.

[15] A disused name for Braigh Coire Chruinn Bhalgain.

At the SMC New Year Meet 1896, conditions were very bad, but Beinn Chaluim was climbed. At the end of March I went off with Reid. On 1st April we crossed over the two sisters – Stob Choire an Easain Mhor, Stob a' Choir Mheadhoinache – from Creaguainsach Lodge to Tulloch then caught the train to Fort William for the SMC Meet at the Alexandra. On the 3rd we climbed Ben Nevis with Lamond Howie – a misty day. We had coffee in the Observatory, then stood at the edge of Tower Ridge, shouting at a party stuck on the Tower – very grisly looking in the mist and twilight. I went back to Edinburgh the next day.

On February 9th 1897 Sandy Moncrieff, Reid and I took the early train to Crianlarich and climbed Cruach Ardran by the north face – stepcutting and the rope and a fearful wind on top.

On July 14th Mr Urquhart, Miss Nerta [?], Maud MacLaren and I drove from Dalwhinnie to Drumochter Lodge, thence up the ridge to the Athole Sow [given as 3175 feet, so Robertson means A'Mharconaich]. Mr Urquhart lay on the top reading Shairp's Poems and I then walked on to Beinn Udlamain and returned the same way.

On May 2nd 1898 I left for a three month climbing tour with my bicycle. From Spean Bridge I bicycled to Lianachan and climbed Aonach Mor, returning to the Spean Hotel. Next day I rode to Tomdoun Inn. Then on the 4th I climbed Spidean Mialach and Gleourach. On the 5th I rode on towards Cluny Bridge Inn and left my bike and rucksack at the top of the hill – not happy about doing so by reason of a party of tinkers which I saw approaching. I went up a good shooting path to Creag a' Mhaim. Back at the road I went down at a furious pace with both brakes on to the Inn. On the 6th I left my bike under a bridge and climbed Carn Ghluasaid and on from there to Sgurr nan Conbhairean – large sappers' cairn on top – and Tigh Mor 3,222 ft. I then retraced my steps skirting around the W. side of Sgurr nan Conbhairean. On the 7th I left Cluny at 9.55 and crossed to Alltbeath via the Allt a' Chaoruinn Mhoir. I crossed the river, then up the steep slopes by the Allt Reithe Garbh. Turning west I scrambled up the steep cone to the top of Sgurr nan Ceathramhnan at 3.05 – a large sapper-built cairn with a stick – a magnificent hill and a magnificent day. I descended to Altbeath (Scott's) at 4.35, where I got a good tea. Mrs Scott was a fine young Shetland woman and was busy sorting and carding wool. I was back at Cluny by 8.40. That evening my friend Jack Methuen arrived very late and shared my bedroom. On May 9th at 9.35 I rode west for 4 $^1/_2$ miles and left my bike at a shepherd's barn, then struck north to Saileag and east along the ridge to Sgurr a' Bhealaich Dearg, Aonach Meadhoin, Carn Fuarlach and Sgurr na Ciste Dubh [Robertson means Ciste Dhubh], which I reached at 4.45. I got back to Cluny at 6.30. May 10th was very wet and thick mist the whole time. I left Cluny at 9.45 and went up to Drum Sionnaich then west along the ridge to Aonach air Chrith, Maol Cheann Dearg, Sgurr a' Doire Leathain, Sgurr an Lochan and Creag nan Damh, getting there at 4. From here I struck down the N.E. ridge, picked up my bike where I had left it the day before and so home to Cluny Inn.

[On May 16th Robertson made his way from Methuen's farm at Balmacara by Kyle of Lochalsh and *The Claymore* to Glenelg which he reached at 4 a.m. on the 17th. He went on to Ellanreoch Farm where he had breakfast at 9.]

The rain was coming down in torrents, so things did not look promising for Ben Screel. The memory of several days' delay with Sandy Moncrieff in 1895 came up before me –

a fate seemed to hang over my climbing Screel. It began to clear up at 11.30, and I made a desperate effort. Tearing myself out of my very comfortable chair, I sallied forth. A long tramp up the east side of Meall Buidhe then up the west slope of Ben Screel brought me to the cairn at 3. There was a great deal of fresh snow for the last 1,000 feet. I descended in a south-easterly direction to Arnisdale. Mr and Mrs Macmorran put me up for the night and did their utmost for me. Macmorran had engaged an old crofter to take me across Loch Hourn in his boat. The crofter had been at sea a lot in his early days and had seen many foreign parts. He was much impressed with my ice-axe. "Ah, that's a grand tomahawk that you've got!" was his remark, which amused me greatly. We reached the other side just to the west of Eilean a' Mhuineil, and I struck up the ridge of Stob a' Choire Odhair, then to the top of Ladhar Bheinn by the fine ridge to the left of the rocks in the Coire Dhorrcail. I left the top at 4 and retraced my steps, later walking along the rough hill and shore side to Barrisdale where I stayed with the keeper McMaster. He has some friends staying on holiday who were shooting rats and playing the bagpipes when I arrived.

On the 19th I went south up the excellent Inverie path to the bealach then sharp left up the ridge to Luinne Bheinn and on to Meall Buidhe. On 20th May – a lovely day – I walked along Loch Hourn side by a very up-and-down path past Skiary to Kinlochourn. I had intended to leave my rucksack at Skiary and stay there for the night, but things did not look at all likely – there was neither beer nor whisky in the place and the rooms were dark, damp and dirty – so I walked on to Kinlochhourn and arranged to stay at Captain Campbell's house (he was Captain of Lord Burton's yacht). I left my rucksack and climbed Sgurr a' Mhoraire getting back to Kinlochhourn at 6.40. From there, on 21st May, I proceeded northwest by shooting-path for Sgurr na Sgine and reached the top at 1.35, descending by the Bealach Choire Mhalagain to Shiel Inn. When I got there I proceeded to gobble up a cold roast of beef and a dish of potatoes, much to the astonishment of the girl who served me. I had not tasted anything meaty since I had left Balmacara six days before, and I was dying for meat! Some men gave me a lift to Totaig and then after some fun in hooting with an old tin horn for the ferry we got over to Ardelve. Here I found my bicycle which Methuen had conveyed thither for me some days before. I was soon back at Coillemore (Methuen's) enjoying all the comforts of the saltmarket at his most hospitable board.

[On Thursday May 26th Robertson and 'a young fellow McLean' climbed Sgorr Ruadh and Beinn Liath Mor. Sgorr Ruadh was climbed by a steep gully on its north-east face – the first recorded route on the mountain. He then caught the train to Achnasheen, ascended Fionn Bheinn the following morning and cycled over to Kinlochewe in the afternoon. On Saturday 28th, he cycled to Heights of Kinlochewe and climbed Mullach Coire Mhic Fhearchair and Sgurr Ban. On the 29th, he climbed A' Mhaighdean by the same method, spending the entire day in heavy rain and seeing nothing.[16] On the following day Slioch was done in company with the keeper at Smiorasair on the north side of Loch Maree, an unusual route. In the afternoon Robertson's friend George Reid arrived. On the 31st the pair set out for Beinn Eighe, proceeding over the 'Black Men' to Sgurr Ban.]

Here George, who had been going very poorly up to this, thought it best not to go further. I went on alone. The day was wet and misty and I saw nothing. I was soon on

---

[16] I think this may be the only occasion in the *Notebook* where Robertson climbs on a Sunday.

Spidean Coire an Leachan and then Coinneach Mor – about here I lost a stocking (Harris) which I was using for a comforter around my neck! From Coinneach Mor I struck north to Ruadh Stac Mor, and then took north-east down a snow slope. This soon stopped and I found myself upon the edge of very steep rocks indeed. I was loath to return so I just climbed down very carefully, but found some places pretty stiff. When I got down to the foot of the glen and looked up where I had come from, it looked mighty bad. In fact, had I known what it looked like, I should never have tried it. It was not a place for a man alive.[17] With a thankful heart I rounded into the Allt Toll a' Ghiubhais, over the bealach and so back to the Hotel – a long day. That evening I got a wire from Kate letting me know how ill dear mother was and next morning about 9 I got another telling me she was gone. I instantly and hastily packed up, jumped on my bike, rode off to Achnasheen, caught the mid-day train and was in 3 Whitehouse Loan that night – a sad journey for me.

On Tuesday 7th June I returned by the early mail to Achnasheen, retrieved my bike and rode down to Fannich Lodge.

[On the 8th, accompanied by a keeper, Fraser, Robertson climbed An Coileachan, Meallan Rairigidh, Sgurr Mor and Beinn Liath Mhor Fannaich. On the 9th they went over Sgurr nan Each to Sgurr nan Clach Geala and Meall a' Chrasgaidh. On the 10th they rowed to Cabuie at the west end of the loch. "The keeper had had enough of climbing the last two days, being fat and lazy," so Robertson went on alone to Sgurr Breac, which he measured at 3251 feet.]

I then turned west along the ridge to A' Chailleach. On this ridge, before you come to A' Chailleach, there is a well-defined top not marked at all in the O.S. and therefore not noticed by Munro in his Tables. I made it out to be at least 3100 feet, the bealach between it and Sgurr Breac being 2875 feet, and the other bealach being 2710 feet.[18]

[Robertson then proceeded by bike and train to Coulags in Strathcarron, where he climbed Maol Chean-dearg, continuing to his friend Methuen's at Balmacara the same day. From there he climbed A' Ghlas-bheinn (Glen Elchaig) on the 16th before cycling on to Skye on the 20th where he met up with J.A. Parker and Dr and Mrs Inglis Clark at Sligachan Hotel. On Tuesday 21st June they climbed Sgurr nan Gillean by the Pinnacle Ridge, descending by the Tourist Route. On 22nd June Parker and Robertson traversed Clach Glas and Blaven.]

On the following day we all did Bruach na Frithe. Clark and I went east along the ridge to the Bhasteir Tooth. We got up this to within 10 feet of the top when a fearful storm of wind, hail and cold rain burst in full fury upon us. The wind was roaring. I was first and lying out spread-eagled on a steepish face of rock. The last 10 feet rose right up from this point, but, in the conditions it would not have been safe to try it, so we beat a retreat as

---

[17] The Torridonian mountains of course abound with such places: it is unwise to descend any convex slope not known from below.

[18] This provides a perfect example of a) the need to revise the Tables, and b) the extreme reluctance of Masters of the Tables to act ahead of the O.S. This top, now known as Toman Coinich (935m.), was certainly notified to Munro by Robertson, but not included in the 1921 Tables. Again, its claims were firmly endorsed in Burn's 1923 *Notes* (see Chapter 4.4) and by Corbett in 1932 (see Chapter 6.9). Yet, because the maps showed only a 2750 foot contour, nothing was done until 1981 – 83 years later! – when it was eventually included, no doubt to the accompaniment of a deal of grumbling.

hastily as we could. We got off the rocks in due time, but oh, how cold I was! – I don't think I ever was so cold in my life. Part of the way down was a gully, which by this time was a torrent. I had to lie with the water pouring over me while I paid out the rope to Clark. When clear of the rocks we took to our heels and ran. Ran. Gracious, we ran for miles, ending by coming up to the Inn at the double. I think the people thought we were mad. Clark had a bottle of whisky in his room and he gave me half a tumbler of it – neat. I never drank so much whisky in my life. He took the same, and I hurried off to my room and dried myself. The next hour was rather an oblivion to me. I know I got into bed and fell fast asleep, being wakened by the dinner bell. I ate a dinner worthy of the occasion, simply clearing off everything, and felt as fit as a fiddle: the next day I would never have known I had been out. Clark did not fare so well. He was violently sick and had to lie in bed all evening. Parker and I came up to see him after dinner, and I remember standing at the foot of his bed and reproaching him for his excesses![19]

On the 25th Parker, Clark and myself traversed the 4 tops of Sgurr a' Mhadaidh and Sgurr a' Ghreadaidh. On the 27th we went to Glen Brittle House, and on the 28th we climbed Sgumain, Alasdair and Sgurr Dearg – no details recorded.[20] On the 30th we had a very long day. We climbed Sgurr nan Eag and Sgurr Dubh an Da Bheinn then Sgurr Dubh and down to Loch Coruisk, and so back to Sligachan by Druim Hain and the glen. On 2nd July I climbed Sgurr na Banachdich from Sligachan with Dr Alfred Harker, the famous geologist who was surveying the Coolin on behalf of H.M. Geological Survey, and I well remember the rapidity with which he traversed the ground, and how well he knew the easy and quick routes to go by.[21]

On July 3rd I left Sligachan on my bike for Kyleakin where I spent the night with a friend of Methuen's at the mansion house there. I arrived soaked with rain and was taken in hand by an Indian servant, and bathed and dressed like a baby in luxurious comfort.

[Robertson enjoyed another break at Balmacara before taking the train across to Grantown-on-Spey, stopping on the way to bag Moruisg between trains. From there he cycled on to Tomintoul and Inchrory Lodge where he was put up for 3 nights by the keeper, MacLean, and remembered 'waking up one night to find a swarm of rats gnawing at some remains of sandwiches I had left on the table. I flung my stockings at them and went back to sleep.' From Inchrory he made a strange traverse of the Eastern Cairngorms on the 9th July, first crossing Beinn a' Bhuird to drop down into the upper Quoich, then climbing to Ben Avon over Carn Eas and Creag an Dail Mhor, and following the ridges north-east over Big Brae, etc. to Inchrory. On the 11th he cycled over to Braemar by Loch Builg, 'one of the highest driving roads I know in Scotland', and on to Miss Gruer's at Inverey for a long stay. Making profitable use of his bicycle, he bagged Carn Cloich-mhuilinn, Beinn Bhrotain and

[19] This episode looks very like a classic case of hypothermia exacerbated by whisky!

[20] Clark provided more details in his interesting account of this visit to Skye, given in *SMCJ* 1898, V, 144-145. Perhaps understandably, he makes no mention of the whisky episode, but he notes that the party approached Sgurr a' Mhadaidh by the exciting ridge from the Thuilm-Mhadaidh bealach, and that the round of Coire Lagain included Sgurr Tearlach but avoided Mhic Coinnich (at that time not recognized as a Munro) by descending the stone shoot and reascending to the ridge. The Inaccessible 'was reached at too late an hour to permit of its ascent.'

[21] These 'easy and quick routes' were all marked by Harker on the wonderful Cuillin Map included in the Club's Guide to Skye (*SMCJ*, IX, 293-367).

Monadh Mor on the 12th; Beinn Mheadhoin, Beinn a' Chaoruinn and Beinn Bhreac on the 13th; An Sgarsoch and Carn an Fhidhleir on the 14th; Derry Cairngorm and Ben Macdui on the 15th; An Socach and Carn Bhac on the 16th; and Devil's Point and Carn a' Mhaim on the 18th.]

[Aside from a second ascent of Lochnagar, Robertson did not climb again in 1898 and it was not until late in April 1899 that he once again sallied forth].

On April 27th 1899 I left Edinburgh by mail train at 4 a.m. with a heavily-laden bicycle (Beeston Humber), bag in carrier at the back, diamond-shaped bag within the main frame, bag on front carrier, U. Sohn's binocular in a wire (sponge) basket hanging from the front forks, ice-axe strapped along the top tube. I arrived in Lairg at 1 and then rode N. to Altnaharra. There was no wind and the gradient was easy so I managed to ride a good deal more of the hill than I had expected. The run down was fine and the two brakes acted well. I was well received at Altnaharra, no guests but myself, when I arrived at 4 o'clock, after 22 miles. Dinner was soup, a delicious salmon cutlet, fresh out of the loch, meat, pudding, cheese, a bottle of beer – everything grand.

Next day breakfast was home-cured bacon and eggs and more salmon.. I got off at 9 and had another long pull up over a wild wild moor and then down Strath More to Muiseal at 10.40, 13 miles. I stabled my bike in an old outhouse and started up the hill for Ben Hope. The rain was now on and the mist pretty well down, so map and compass were in constant requisition. I reached the cairn at 12.45 – not a thing to be seen – and got back down to Muiseal at 1.45 and Altnaharra at 4. Next day there was fresh snow well down. I started for Ben Clibreck at 10.10 and reached the cairn at 12.30. There was a terrible gale on the top, with drift, very cold hard frost and deep snow. My beard was frozen stiff, but being well 'battened down' I did not feel it. Clibreck is a beautiful graceful cone of a hill, quite easy. I got back to the hotel at 2.20, being joyfully received by the landlady, who was much alarmed at my venturing out on "such an awful day". It seems a shepherd was lost on just such a day, on the very place I was, only a month previously and she was afraid of another catastrophe – she did not know me!! I had a good dinner at 3 and started off at 4, being fairly blown up the hill by the gale on my back. It was a lovely afternoon, the hills all white, Clibreck on my left a perfect sugar cone. I got to Dalchork (Mundell's – relatives of of Rev. Archie Gossip's who had given me an introduction) at 6, bike and bags all 'doing fine'. On May 1st I left Dalchork and cycled across to Inchnadamph, helped by an east wind. Next day I left the hotel at 9.10 and got to the top of Connival at 11.40, then on to the top of Ben More Assynt at 12.30, returning to the Hotel by the same route. May 3rd was another beautiful day. I cycled to Ullapool. The weather looked so settled I thought it better to make for the Teallachs at once, as I wanted fine weather on them very much. I crossed the ferry and up a fearful steep hill. A man who came over with me in the ferry gave me a hand to push my loaded cycle up the brae, otherwise I would hardly have managed it.[22] I reached Dundonell in the evening – a lovely spot with a nice wee inn. May 4th was a splendid clear day. I left Dundonnell at 8.55

---

[22] According to the bicyclist's *vade mecum*, Harry Inglis' *Contour Road Book of Scotland*, 1899, this road from Altnaharrie to Dundonell is 'abominable, with a precipitous descent to Loch Broom – certainly vying with the Foyers road as being the worst road in Scotland.' Gradients for this descent are given as '1 in 16-6-9-5, this last being at the foot.'

up by the path at the back of the steading, and then by easy slopes to Bidean a' Ghlas Thuill at 11.30, and Sgurr Fiona at 12.20. Left cairn at 12.50 – Corrag Bhuidhe buttress at 1.45. Glissaded down 1,000 feet from the Cadha Gobhlach and reached Loch Toll an Lochain at 2.35. Left the loch at 3.30 and was back at Dundonnell at 5.15.

[On May 5th Robertson cycled to Inverlael Farm on Loch Broom, where he stayed for two days and climbed Beinn Dearg, Meall nan Ceapraichean, Cona' Mheall and Am Faochagach on the first and Eididh nan Clach Geala and Seana Bhraigh on the second, after which he moved on to Torridon. "I cycled from Inverlael to Torridon House (Duncan Darroch). I left at 7.30 and arrived at 3.30 – 52 miles." With the head keeper Willie Macdonald he climbed Liathach on 12th May and Alligin the day after.

The second half of May was spent in the Glen Strath Farrar and Glen Cannich areas. In Strathfarrar he stayed with the keeper Euan Macdonnell at Ardchuilk. He climbed Sgurr Fhuar-Thuill with Macdonnell on the 19th and Creag Dhubh and Carn nan Gobhar on the 20th. On the 22nd he cycled round to Loch Mullardoch and found accommodation at the west end of the loch with Donald Finlayson, keeper at Coire na Cuilean.]

"He is quite a young fellow – say 24 – but one of the best of his kind I have ever met. So intelligent, so eager for knowledge. He is not married but he has a fine old housekeeper who does things very well. She has not 'the English' or at least very little of it and you would laugh to hear her and me at it. He has got a fine wee house, all beautifully lined with wood inside and 'as dry as a cork' to use his own expression. Finlayson came here from Camban. He is a great reader and the books he has astonish me. Travels of all sorts. I'm sure there are 50 of them."

[Robertson climbed An Socach (west of An Riabhachan) on the 23rd. On the 24th Finlayson went with him to Beinn Fhionnlaidh and, skirting Carn Eige, to Mam Soul, then along the ridge to Creag a' Chaoruinn and west by Bealach Coire Ghaidheil to An Socach, returning by Gleann a' Choilich. On the 25th he climbed Tuill Creagach and on the following day cycled round to Affric Lodge, where "the Maclarens put me up – not too willingly!" From there he climbed Sgurr na Lapaich, Mam Soul (again!) and Saoiter Mor (An Tudair) on the 27th. He then cycled in stages to Spean Bridge, stopping off at Kilfinan to bag Sron a' Choire Gairbh on the way. Leaving his bicycle, he went on foot to Stob Ban (Grey Corries) on the 30th, and round to the head of Loch Treig where he stayed for two nights with the keeper George Ross. On the 31st he climbed Binnein Beag and Sgurr Eilde Mor and on the Ist June he returned to Spean Bridge via Beinn na Lap, Cnoc Dearg and Stob Coire Sgriodain. He next cycled to the Stage House Inn at Glenfinnan and went over to Glen Dessary via Sgor nan Coireachan. On Sunday June 4th he "took the service in the school for the missionary – Hebrews 13-8." On the 5th he climbed Sgor nan Coireachan (of Sgor na Ciche) and Sgurr Mor, on the 6th Scour Gairoch (Gairich)[23] and on the 7th he made a long return to Glenfinnan taking in Gulvain on the way.

After a break of 5 days with Kate at Barriemore in Appin (Mrs Campbell), Robertson climbed Beinn Fhionnlaidh and Sgor na h-Ulaidh on the 13th. On the 15th he took the steamer to Salen and bicycled across Mull to climb Ben More, enjoying a view which moved him to the following effusion:]

---

[23] There is no entry in the *Notebook* for June 6th, but Gairich is reorded in the *Brief Record* for that day.

"The evening view from the summit of Ben More was an unforgettable one. I have never had quite the like of it either before or since – the sun setting into the Atlantic is making for itself, on the mist below, a shining path of light. As I sit watching and waiting and looking the wisps of mist are gathering together forming a thick ribbed cloud below me which is slowly creeping up the valley and rolling over the bealachs, leaving the tops bright and clear in the evening sun. Looking westward, the cloud has wholly covered Loch na Keal, leaving only the peak of Gometra rising, Proteus-like, out of the cloud sea. The shoulder of the hill below me is now shrouded, mantled in the wrinkled folds of white, and then, in the twinkling of an eye, the mantle is lifted off and it is all clear again. One could hardly tell where the mist ended and where the sea began. Along the line of the setting sun the rays have made a way for themselves and have pierced through the cloud mist, and you can see the sea along the path of light. Iona and the Sound of Iona was specially noticeable, Staffa also and the Treshnish Islands, Ardnamurchan Point, Rum, Ladhar Bheinn – a wondrous sight."

[After another short break at Barriemore, Robertson moved to Clachaig Inn on the 21st, from which he climbed Sgorr nam Fiannaidh, Buachaille Etive Beag, and "to near the crest of the north ridge of Glencoe by 'the Black Tongue', to the west of the Study."[24] Moving on to Kingshouse, he climbed Buachaille Etive Mor en route and Meall a' Bhuiridh and Clach Leathad on the following day, the 25th. He then cycled down to stay with the schoolteacher at Loch Etive head for two nights, climbing Stob Coir' an Albannaich and Meall nan Eun on one day and Ben Starav, Beinn nan Aighenan and Glas Bheinn Mhor on the other. On the 28th he cycled to Inveroran and from there accounted for Beinn Toaig (Stob a' Choire Odhair) and on the 30th Beinn a' Chuirn and Beinn Mhanach.

On July 1st Robertson joined Kate at Bridge of Orchy station and they went to McCook's at Ben Alder where they stayed for two weeks, during which he collected the southern group of Carn Dearg, Sgor Gaibhre and Sgor Choinnich. He then went on the 17th by train and bicycle via Tulloch to Lublea where he stayed with Mackintosh, the keeper at Moy, and climbed Creag Peathraich [Pitridh], then on to the Laggan Free Church Manse for Geal Charn (Monadh Liath) and to Newtonmore, for Carn Dearg, Carn Mairg [Carn Ban] and Carn Ballach on the 20th and Carn Sgulain and A' Chailleach on the 21st. From a base at Insh Inn he then accounted for Geal Charn (Sgoran Dubh), Carn Ban, Meall Dubh-achadh and Meall Tionail [Mullach Clach a' Bhlair] before cycling down to Dalwhinnie where he stayed for three nights with the station master and climbed his outstanding Drumochter Munros: Carn na Caim, Meall a' Chaoruinn and Glas Meall Mor to the east and Geal Charn and Sgairneach Mhor to the west. He concluded his long tour in fine style on the 28th by climbing Sgairneach Mhor on the same day as he bicycled to Perth.

In 1900 Robertson took part in a number of climbs with SMC members, but did not add to his tally of Munros. However in April 1901 he began to round up the stragglers.

On the 4th and 5th he climbed Beinn a' Chroin and Cruach Ardrain with Kate and George Hall, going on himself to bag Beinn Tulaichean. On the 15th with George Hall he climbed Ben Oss and Beinn Dubhchraig from Tyndrum and stayed on alone to collect An Caisteal. In June

---

[24] This entry, repeated in his *Brief Record*, is interesting in two respects: the abstention from Meall Dearg, which suggests that he had already elected it as his final Munro; and the reference to this aspect of Am Bodach as 'the Black Tongue' – a name I have not been able to confirm elsewhere.

Buachaille Etive Mor – a Munro forever

he set off on a bicycle trip to the Grampians with Kate. On the 3rd they climbed Carn Geoidh and Carn Bhinnein from Glenshee and, having got their bikes up the Devil's Elbow, he climbed Cairnwell and Carn Aosda before they rode down to Ballater. From there he climbed Mount Keen, then the pair took their bikes over the Capel Mounth to Clova Inn on the 6th. From there he bagged Tom Buidhe, Tolmount, Cairn Bannoch and Broad Cairn on the 7th and Mayar and Driesh on on the 8th.

On 23rd July he climbed Beinn Eunaich and Beinn a' Chochuill and on the following day he went round Meall a' Churain and Beinn Dheiceach [Cheathaich] between trains from Luib.

Robertson's final flurry of Munros began on September 16th[25] when a bicycle ascent of Rest and Be Thankful was followed by a round of Beinn Ime and Ben Vane, proceeding to catch up with Kate at Cairndow. On the 17th he climbed Beinn Bhuidhe and on the 18th the couple cycled across to Lawers Hotel, Robertson stopping to bag Beinn an Lochain then tearing along to catch up. From Lawers Inn he climbed Meall Gruaidh on the 19th and then on the 20th he found a very complicated method for Ben Chonzie, crossing Loch Tay to Ardtalnaig and then enduring the 14-mile round trip to the hill by Gleann a' Chilleine, returning by the steamer, on which he enjoyed "a very welcome and unexpected bottle of beer". On the 21st they cycled to Crianlarich where they left their machines and made a brief return to Edinburgh before resuming on bicycle to Clachaig on the 23rd. The bag was now complete apart from Meall Dearg, and after spending the week taking Kate up other Glencoe hills, on the 28th the concluding ascent was made with Sandy Moncrieff, who had come up from Edinburgh for the occasion.]

Climbed Meall Dearg, 3,118 feet, Aonach Eagach ridge, east end. This was a great day for me! The last of my 283 separate mountains over 3,000 feet in Scotland according to Munro's Tables *SMCJ* Volume I.

From Clachaig Inn, with Kate and Sandy Moncrieff, we took the main road east up Glencoe for 2 1/2 miles and then north up a horrible loose scree gully (with the Black Tongue on our left) to the ridge. A short scramble westwards took us to the cairn. On the cairn we broached the champagne which Sandy had provided and I had carried up (a quart of Ayala), and we toasted ourselves and the day and the event! Sandy made me first kiss the cairn and then my wife! We inserted a card with our names and the special event into the now empty bottle, which we carefully packed away among the stones of the cairn. This bottle, intact, was still there in 1930. Cameron, Allt an Righ, the keeper, was on the top with Lord Strathcona and they handled it with interest and replaced it. We descended the steep scree gully with ease!! I, at any rate, never descended a scree slope with less trouble! The screes melted away under my feet and were not: such is the effect of much champagne!!

---

[25] It is interesting that these last bagging expeditions were conducted at the height of the stalking season!

2.3 The 'Munros' of Scotland

A.E. Robertson[1]

PEAK-BAGGING and record-breaking are somewhat, I fear, looked down upon by the members of the SMC. And outside of the Club they are as a rule regarded in the same unfavourable light. The other day, when telling a friend some of my experiences in endeavouring to climb every hill over 3,000 feet in Scotland, he could not see the point of it at all. "Why should you want to climb every hill?" he queried, and then irreverently added, "no one has ever kissed every lamp-post in Princes Street, and why should any one want to?" Yet it must be confessed that the writer has never looked at it in this profane light, and that for many years past he has very much wanted to kiss every summit that finds a place in the historic 'Tables'. And in a word be it said, after many vicissitudes and exertions, he at length, last September, in Glencoe, wiped out the last of the 3,000 footers, some 283 separate mountains in all, according to Munro's list.

The Editor has asked me in view of this to give some of my impressions of the hills of Scotland as a whole, and I gladly respond, though I must say his request has been found far from easy to fulfil.

The campaign has been a desultory one, and has occupied about ten years. It was begun with no thought of ever climbing them all, but simply from a desire to obtain a general knowledge of the Highland hills. In this way about a hundred, scattered up and down through the country, were climbed. In 1898 a three months' holiday added some seventy-five to the list. The thought then occurred to me that the thing might be completed, and another three months' holiday in 1899, in which some seventy-two new hills were 'bagged', brought the goal in sight, which was at length attained this autumn.

The first thought that strikes one in looking back over the hills of Scotland as a whole, is that there are almost none that have not some fairly easy route to the top – and I regret to say it. For although the most incorrigible of peak-baggers, I love a climb as well. Like the keeper I once asked if he would have a dram or a pint of beer, I most emphatically reply, "Both is best!" I only wish I could tell the Club of some faraway unknown peak bristling with difficulties on all sides, but the fact is there are none. The only hills where there are no easy ways to the top are certain of the Coolins in Skye, Sgurr Dubh for example or Mhadaidh and perhaps Sgurr Alasdair, though on Alasdair you have got the Stone Shoot which leads to within 125 feet of the top.

[1] *SMCJ* 1902, VII, 10-14.

The West-north-west Ridge of Sgurr a' Mhadaidh from Sgurr Thuilm

When one asks what are the best climbing hills, provided you are willing to seek out difficulties, the list widens at once. First and foremost I would place the Coolins, then the north face of Ben Nevis, Glencoe, the Torridon Hills, the Teallachs, for rock work; while as regards snow craft, on almost every one of the 3,000 feet hills one can get excellent climbs provided the north or north-east face be taken and there be frost to put the snow into proper order. The inland mountains carry the most snow, for example Mam Soul, Sgurr nan Conbhairean, the Cairngorms, Ben Alder, Beinn Heasgarnich.

The difficulty of getting at the remoter hills and securing a suitable base of operations, was often a very serious one. In this connection I found my bicycle simply invaluable, and many of the more distant expeditions which would have involved a night out, or a long tedious and expensive hire,[2] were brought by the aid of the wheel within the compass of a long day from some fixed point. Take for example the districts of central Ross-shire and

---

[2] Of a gig, etc., or even a pony. Horse-powered transport was available in almost every Highland glen in the 1890s.

north-west Inverness-shire. One can cycle up Glen Strathfarrar as far as Monar Lodge, up Glen Cannich as far as the west end of Loch Mullardoch, and up Glen Affric as far as Affric Lodge; in this way all the remote summits at the head of these glens can be reached in the course of a long day from Affric Hotel or Struy Bridge Inn. Likewise Glen Quoich can be got at from Tomdoun, and the head of Glen Lyon from Bridge of Balgie. Don't be afraid your bike will run away, or be stolen in your absence! Turn him loose to browse in the heather, and he will be waiting for you when you return. For the few up there who could ride away with him, would not, and those who would ride away with him, could not!

But there are regions where neither trap nor bicycle are of the least avail, and where hotels are gloriously conspicuous by their absence – and long may such regions exist. When you go to Glen Dessary, to Loch Hourn, and to the more distant parts of Kintail, you have to renounce all ideas of cycling or driving, not to speak of the Capuan luxuries of a roadside inn. There is nothing for it but to tramp it, carrying your all in your own rucksack, taking your chance for quarters at the shepherds' shielings, or keepers' houses passed on the way

What delightful weeks I have spent in this manner. The long fine spring and early summer days, the loneliness and the wonder of the wild and unknown country; no trains, no coaches, no villas, far out of the track of that baneful and vulgar modern product, the guidebook tourist.[3] You set forth to traverse your peak, and the only house within fifteen miles is that keeper's there, where you must be put up for the night. You sight it with your glass as you lie away up among the tops far down in the glen below. Towards evening you approach the house not without apprehension, the dogs rush out barking vociferously, half in welcome, half in anger. You knock at the door, there is a parley. You are admitted, and once admitted, treated with all the courtesy, dignity, and hospitality that are the prime characteristics of the Celtic nature. In all my wanderings I have never been refused a night's shelter. The Highlander is nothing if he is not hospitable. Of course this has to be gone about in the right way. If a man comes up to a keeper's house and demands a bed in the same tone of voice as he would engage a room at the Metropole he will be refused – and quite right too – for even a Highland keeper's house is his castle. But if he approaches his would-be host and hostess with fitting politeness, with a certain sense of obligation in his voice and bearing, he will certainly be received and welcomed and given the run of whatever is in the house.

What fine characters these shepherds and keepers are – well read, well informed, interested, capable, God-fearing.

> *"There dwelt a shepherd, Michael was his name,*
> *An old man, stout of heart and strong of limb,*
> *His bodily frame had been from youth to age*
> *Of an unusual strength: his mind was keen,*
> *Intense, and frugal, apt for all affairs."*[4]

---

[3] Prejudice against the tourist (presumed to be English) was rife amongst the natives in the late 19th century. For some especially gross examples of such prejudice, see 'Practical Advice to Pedestrians', by Joseph Stott, Chapter 6.2 below. The 'guidebook' deprecated is probably Murray's (1894) – an excellent book still available in a modern reprint today.

[4] From William Wordsworth's poem *Michael*.

And what lonely lives they lead, an isolation scarcely credible in these railway days. In one family that I know well, the eldest girl though fourteen years of age, had never seen a church or a school in her life, yet for all that, quick witted, intelligent, far more truly *educated* by nature and the occasional visit of a peripatetic teacher, than the many town sparrows, crammed with superficial smatterings in our city Board Schools. And what *naive* ideas many of them have! I well remember the air with which one good woman opened the door of a tiny room in which was a sitz-bath standing up on end, and the pride with which she exclaimed, "This is the bathroom, if such a thing should ever be required."

And what pawky humour too. There is more sly fun in the Celt than he gets credit for. I could fill pages with their stories, but let one reminiscence suffice. "Well, Donald," I remarked one evening as we sat with our pipes over the peat fire, "this must be a wild place in winter." "Oh, yes, sir, a wild place in the winter time." "Big storms, I daresay." "Hoo, yes, storms." "And wrecks?" "Ach, aye, wrecks, the weemans will be taalking about them whiles; but it will be years since she didn't see any." "And strange animals, perhaps?" "Heuch, aye, strange beasts and wild beasts." "Serpents?" "Yes, serpents, aye and sea serpents, great sea serpents. There was waane, it wass two years ago, her heid cam thro' the Kyle on the 7th of June, and it wass the 12th of August before her tail passed oot. I wass tired waatching her."

In the interest of sporting rights, most, if not all the hills under deer were climbed either in spring or early summer. This time of the year has many advantages. The days are long, the high ground is all under snow, the weather is generally settled, for May and June are undoubtedly the driest months in the Highlands, and last but not least, one is free to move where'er he please without let or hindrance.

In conclusion, let me say that I look back upon the days I have spent in pursuing this quest as among the best spent days of my life. Amid the strange beauty and wild grandeur of rock face and snow slope, scaling tops where literally almost foot hath never aforetime trod, I have indeed come face to face with the sacred sanctities of Nature, and he would be indeed dull of heart who could see her beauties thus unfolded, feel her hand on his brow, her breath on his cheek, who could see and feel that unmoved. When I call to mind the cast-iron peaks of the Black Coolins, the ridges on Ben Nevis, the gullies on the Buchaille, the rich and varied hues of the Lochinver and Assynt hills, the seascapes from the Torridons, the wild, lonely, rolling uplands of the Mam Soul range, or the region in and around Ben Alder – the memory of these things is a priceless possession.

> "... these beauteous forms
> Through a long absence, have not been to me
> As is a landscape to a blind man's eye,
> But oft in lonely rooms, and 'mid the din
> Of towns and cities, I have owed to them,
> In hours of weariness, sensations sweet
> Felt in the blood and felt along the heart."

Nor is it altogether mere retrospect, Othello's occupation is not gone! And to the silly people who ask me, "What will you do now since you have no more worlds to conquer?" I can only say, "I am going to climb them over again."

2.4 Robertson Observed

From the diaries of J. Logan Aikman[1]

IT was with joy that at last we observed the squat shape of the Hut looming up in the midst of its stony surroundings. The Coire na Ciste burn was in spate, but we splashed through without being badly soaked and while plodding up up the brae towards the door we espied a white face peering out of the window and a little whiff of smoke from the chimney telling of a warm welcome from within. Our fear had been that a mob would be in residence – I had heard that there would likely be five there – but to our surprise but one figure met us as we entered the rather gloomy interior.

Logan Aikman (arrowed) and friends on their way to the CIC Hut, 1930

---

[1] Logan Aikman was an original JMCS member and became SMC Secretary eventually. His extensive diaries cover the period from April 1924 until September 1930. They have been deposited in the National Library (NLS Acc.11538 items 63-73). The present excerpt deals with a visit to the newly-opened Charles Inglis Clark Hut on Ben Nevis, where Aikman and his friend Tom Grieve enjoy an unexpected encounter with the redoubtable Robertson. The story begins with the pair approaching the Hut on Sunday 22nd September 1929.

The figure turned out to be the Rev. A.E. Robertson, who talked cheerily to us, bade us remove our wet clothes, explained that he had been two nights there alone, that he was glad to see us, that the stove was going well, and boiling water for tea would be forthcoming as soon as we liked. He got our names by a direct interrogation, was suitably surprised to feel the weight of my old rucksack and to see the jam pots, tins of this and that, loaves of bread, clothes, etc., that I had produced from it like rabbits from a hat. In fact, Tom and I had the utmost difficulty in getting a word in edgeways, and were ordered about to 'go here' and 'do this' in a way that might have been highly objectionable, but in this instance was not.

AER must light the lamp himself – he knew how – and was helped on to a stool with planks across while he fiddled with it. AER must attend to the stove himself – we weren't competent – he knew exactly the way to poke the glowing anthracite and diddle the handle up and down. We must get changed – Had we been at the Hut before? – Ah! it was good to hear of you, Aikman, being so assiduous and keen in visiting it – (I felt quite bucked at this, and felt I might be trusted on my own here) – Come, come, what about a meal? – Ah, yes Aikman, give us white pudding! – Beans? No, I never take baked beans, but you boys have them – Soup? Excellent! – I haven't had soup the last two nights – A pan, yes – Don't disturb that kettle! – Must keep plenty water for washing up – Tomato soup, good – Yes it will be a good idea to boil the pudding in it – No, a bigger pan – Grieve, get a bigger pot out of the locker there – Put butter in the soup – Add water – No, not too much! – Now put it on the fire – Yes, shorts are an excellent thing to wear up here in the evenings, but not for an old fellow like me – You young fellows don't realise the easiness of climbing nowadays – When I and other pioneers were doing the big things we had a hard time of it – No, Grieve, don't disturb that pot – Plates for the oven, come on – in that cupboard – Aikman knows where they are – I must say I am glad to see you boys – Even an old buffer like me enjoys company – Ah! this is going to be a grand dinner!

No, Aikman, whitewash on the ceiling wouldn't do at all. This is specially treated wood – Look at my handiwork – These shelves all put up – Yes, I made the table and presented it – also the bookcase – I told the Ladies' Club what would be acceptable – No, MacRobert hadn't very much to do with the furnishing. The others and myself put our heads together and made all these wooden things. Ha! Ha! Not a bad joke for an old boy! – These plates will be hot enough – soup spoons forward – Bread, I have some loaves there, use them up first – Some men have been leaving all sorts of scraps – That won't do at all – Look at that great meat bone – I brought up a roast – My friends didn't like the weather and wouldn't stay – Ha! Ha! – Oh! the white pudding's burst – Still, it will taste as good – Put it on that plate and in the oven to steam – That soup smells good . . and tastes delightful – You boys are great cooks, best soup that ever was – This is a great meal.

When did you boys start climbing? – Yes, I spent ten years before I had done all the Munroes – No, never was a great rock climber, no routes called after me,[2] but I was in several very good expeditions, and with famous climbers – Raeburn was a wonderful man, very sad his end. Bell, too, and Naismith – Yes, Graham Napier, the Napier brothers,

---

[2] In view of Robertson's good opinion of himself, it is perhaps a surprise that this statement is untrue! Robertson's Gully on Sgorr Ruadh is his and was described by him in Chapter 2.2.

splendid climbers – long reach – Are you his partner? Indeed? – White pudding – now – full of vitamins – A big oilskin and gum boots would be a great asset – See my old cloak – I have been more or less storm-stayed except for a few necessary excursions. Ha! Ha! Never could take baked beans – Grieve, you know about sardine tins – Open that one – I'll leave you two sardines – Don't you like sardines, Aikman – Well! – I managed to find a young lad in Fort William and gave him 7/6 to carry up my stuff, shelves and things. An old boy like me can't carry those colossal loads like you boys.

Come and see the snow guard on the outer door – Oh! it's stuck – Aikman, you're the smallest – Get through the window there – Yes, it falls down if the door is slammed – That's fixed it now! – The architect let his fancy go on that door, strong as the gate of a fortress – No, the stone walls are only a protection. The whole thing is a timber structure, though it looks as if it were really stone-built – Four feet thick? No, no, only 2 feet 6 inches – And an air space under the flooring – It was a great job building it – Young fellow Gibson stuck to it and encouraged the men – Fearful storms up here. Why, the teak lintel was found one morning tossed away quarter of a mile by the wind and half-buried in the bog – That was a good idea that water trough affair, well made by young Spiers and Mowbray – Yes, the way down to the river is very awkward.

Now, let's wash up – much easier with really hot water. I'll do the washing, you boys dry – Put each thing away at once, much the best plan, saves time – No, no, I'll put the coal on – Don't tickle it up that way – Care and knowledge required for the stove – Open the other window there – Cold, are you? Grieve, you look very funny huddled up in that chair in a blanket before the fire, the convalescent invalid – Ha! Ha! I should have got you lads in a photo like that – Took two interiors today, an hour's exposure – Had this camera for donkey's years, some wonderful photos with it, too. I show them as slides at my various lectures.

Now for a smoke – It's nice to see you lads so keen – You sweep up the floor there – Oh! this is fine – I have to go away tomorrow – Where shall I stay tomorrow night? Connel, good – I have my car down at the distillery – Shall I be able to change my clothes there? – Staying with shepherds? Oh yes, I always make myself very pleasant to them, not patronising, you know – Tell them all about myself – Find their relatives have other houses in other parts – very useful to get so far ben with these people, and they say when I've gone, 'What a nice man!'

Accidents? Slingsby's Chimney – You did it? – A terrible winter night, man slipped at pitch at top, companion staggers into Fort William. Police don't know Slingsby's Chimney. Someone says, 'Old parson Robertson at Rannoch, he'll know' – telegraph – I come up, go direct to place, find body in horrid mess, tell the ghillies to pull themselves together, rope him up and drag him down – The Club has never had a fatal accident – great record – may go some day – Always climb within your powers.

That boy Dinsmore and friend Forsyth, is it? – Must explain that first night – Big party of us – ex-Presidents – Inglis Clark, his wife – all sitting at that table in the corner there – Elton attending to the stove – Suggestion that I give a blessing – Said something like this to finish – 'May this house be a shelter from the storm and a refuge for the distressed' –

Carn Dearg of Ben Nevis and the CIC Hut

Scarcely finished – banging at door – bursts open – Man reels in, staggering and talking gibberish. Dinsmore follows, not so bad – explain plight – crash in Gardyloo – Calm them down – hot tea – Inglis Clark whispers to me, 'Your prayer has been answered rather sooner than expected' – Having patted them and soothed them into sense, sent them back down to Fort William – Dinsmore a strong fellow who could have won through – Saw him next day at the Opening Ceremony, told him straight who was he to think of leading another up a climb as difficult and tricky as could be found? – Might have had Forsyth's blood on his hands, poor fellow wrecked with nervous fatigue, would probably have collapsed completely had the Hut not been there – Spoke kindly to him all the same – You lads must learn to creep before you can walk.

This sort of thing went on for many hours. It was most enjoyable, but it could probably pall before long. However, we sat rather stunned before it all and, as the reader can see, it was difficult to make remarks oneself, for AER rippled on in his racy fashion. He reminded us strongly of K.P. in the way he pulled at his moustache and smoothed his bald pate with his hand. The time passed delightfully slowly too and at 10 or so we got the water boiling again and had coffee, which AER would however not touch. So Grieve got into his pyjamas, collected an immense heap of blankets, and retired to his bunk, AER to his, and myself after the labours of blowing out the lamp to mine. We talked a bit in the dark while the stove looked on with one red eye. The wind blew and the rain splashed in the pitch dark night outside, and altogether it was very jolly to be simply indoors.

Unfortunately, I couldn't get off to sleep. I grew hotter and hotter till I was bathed in perspiration. This I attempted to stem by removing sweaters and blankets, with only partial success, and I continued to creak uneasily from position to position till very late – about 3 a.m. it must have been – I slipped off to a sound if belated slumber.

Monday 23rd September 1929. Once I did get to sleep, I slept well, and the first consciousness of the young day was my hearing AER padding around tinkering with the stove. So I got up too, it wasn't too early. Tom Grieve lay beneath his mountain of blankets, occasionally blinked a sleepy eye at us and then pretended to be asleep when we suggested that another pair of hands would be useful.

The fire soon brisked up a bit and we put on kettles. Robertson was great for letting the stove take its own time and was horrified at suggestions to throw in old bread or pour paraffin to brighten things up. What should we have for breakfast? AER said he had heaps of eggs, so eggs it should be. I suggested an omelette, which was agreed to, though in a dubious sort of way, the other two making no bones about whether I was competent to produce an edible one. They magnanimously allowed me to proceed, however. So I got six eggs, mixed them up, added butter and poured the resulting mess on to a frying pan. I also cut up bacon and made it an ingredient, for it was to be a savoury omelette. There was no parsley, however. AER wondered whether the parsley fern to be found on the Nevis rocks wouldn't do, but he didn't offer to out and get it. The fire was found to be so slow that we roped in a Primus for the purposes of the omelette, which needs a hot fire. We got it started without any trouble. Thanks perhaps to Robertson's advice? He certainly gave plenty. Tom Grieve had meanwhile been improving the shining hour by a wash and by setting the table and infusing the tea, so we sat down to breakfast with the sense of labour rewarded.

The omelette was certainly very good, though it had got a bit broken due to the regrettable omission of a fish slice from the Hut cutlery, but AER sang its praises along with his own. He was most racy on the subject of a new chaplancy job he had just got in Edinburgh. 'So much a year, you know and scarcely any work to do for it – Preach occasionally and talk to the inmates once a week – Tell them about myself and the hills and this sort of breakfast.' I mentioned that I had once heard him preach and he bowed his head in his hands and groaned – so unlike a clerk in Holy Orders and more like a schoolboy on some tragic occasion being recalled when he gave a Greek recitation or something at a school show.

Robertson got his gear packed up eventually and with many protestations of his joy in having our company set off for civilisation about 9.30.

2.5 Obituary of A.E. Robertson

James H.B. Bell[1]

WITH the passing of the Rev. A.E. Robertson, a great Scottish mountaineer and an honorary member of our Club, we may note the end of the epoch of topographical exploration of the Bens and Glens of the Scottish Highlands – if indeed that phase of the history of our Club and of Scottish mountaineering has not already given place to the newer epoch of more specialised rock and ice climbing some years ago.

In order to understand and appreciate the achievements of the early pioneers we must bear in mind that modern roads, easy transport, light equipment and miniature precision cameras did not exist during the active climbing years of A.E.R.[2] He took little over 10 years to climb the 283 Munros in the original list, his explorations covering the years 1889 to 1901. Nowadays this is by no means regarded as an unusual achievement, but A.E.R. was the first to complete it. For transport over very bad roads to his base he used a bicycle. The base itself may not have been very near the hills, and he accepted the true wanderer's risk for

---

[1] *SMCJ* 1959, XXVI, 362-366.

[2] As I have indicated in Chapter 2.1, it may be that Bell exaggerates these disadvantages. So far as cameras are concerned, work of exceptional quality and durability was achieved with the cumbersome plate cameras of Robertson's time, as Bell later concedes.

securing accommodation, which he nearly always obtained in the cottages of keepers or shepherds, a welcome visitor as he talked their own language and shared their own interests.[3] He was a magnificent photographer and, like Dr Inglis Clark and a few others, thought nothing of carrying a whole-plate camera up the slopes of Carn Mor Dearg, to Coire Mhic Fhearchair or other remote corries. Of course he had an advantage over many of us moderns. It was a more leisured age, and his diaries record that in two of these years (1898 and 1899) his circumstances allowed him long holidays. In 1898 he added 75 Munros to his list within 3 months. On many of such expeditions he was alone, so he became a self-reliant path-finder. On quite a number he was accompanied by his close friend Alexander (later Lord) Moncrieff, and it was with him that he completed his Munros in September 1901, with a traverse of the Aonach Eagach ridge in Glencoe.

Needless to say, he made many contributions to the SMC Journal, perhaps not so many full-length articles, but numerous topographical notes on the more remote mountains, and he wrote quite a number of these for the first SMC Guide Book which appeared serially in the Journal. He was an eager and careful student of the history of the Highlands and the old passes and routes. In *Old Tracks and Coffin Roads and Cross-country Routes in the North-West Highlands*[4] he gave a comprehensive yet concise account of his researches, which was afterwards re-issued in pamphlet form with a wide circulation.

It was natural that, with these interests, he was for many years associated with the Royal Scottish Geographical Society and the Scottish Rights of Way Society. He became a member of Council of the 'Geographic' in 1941, was elected Vice-President in 1945 and was awarded the Honorary Fellowship in 1956, the presentation of the scroll (for services to the society and to Scottish topography) taking place in his own home, as by then he was unable to receive the honour in public. He became a Director of the Rights of Way Society in 1923, Chairman in 1931, and after the reorganisation of the society he became its first President in 1946. In this year also he was elected a Fellow of the Royal Society of Edinburgh. It may be noted that the Scottish Rights of Way Society is now raising funds for a memorial to him, which, it is intended, will take the form of a bridge over the River Elchaig in Wester Ross, to facilitate access to the Falls of Glomach.

A.E.R. was born at Helensburgh in 1870. He was educated at Glasgow Academy and the University of Glasgow. There he attended Lord Kelvin's class in Natural Philosophy and, later on, he obtained with Lord Kelvin's help an aneroid barometer especially suited for checking the heights of the Scottish Bens. This aneroid accompanied him thereafter on every hill and proved perfectly reliable. Mrs Robertson has now presented it to the SMC for the personal use of the President during his term of office.

Later, after completing his B.D. course at Edinburgh University, he entered the ministry of the Church of Scotland and was assistant at North Esk (Musselburgh) and St Matthew's (Edinburgh) before being ordained to Rannoch in 1907, where he maintained that his congregation had a greater proportion of men in it than any other in Scotland. He retired

---

[3] Although Robertson eventually learned Gaelic, this was some years after he completed his round. There is no indication in his *Notebook* that he knew anything of the language.

[4] *SMCJ* 1941, XXII, 327-352. This article is reproduced in *The First Munroist* – see Chapter 2.1.

and went to live in Edinburgh in 1920, but continued to serve as Chaplain to the Astley-Ainslie Institution until 1939, and then until the end of the war as Chaplain to the Forces when the institution became a military hospital.

He was twice happily married, climbing numerous hills with his first wife before her death in the middle 1930s, and once again finding happy companionship on the hills with the second Mrs Robertson, their last Munro together being the Clachlet in 1940. After the war he attended several Meets, but mainly for shorter walks and photography. A.E.R., in his spare time, was an accomplished craftsman and cabinet maker, doing beautiful work in his own home, and also making a table for the C.I.C. Hut. He was one of the small party who occupied the Hut before its official opening at Easter 1929.

He joined the SMC at its fourth AGM. in 1893, along with J.A. Parker. He served as Slide Custodian, 1903-6, and many of his own slides enriched the collection, besides illustrating the Journal and Guide Books. He was Vice-President, 1927-29, and President, 1930-32. This did not end his activities, however, for he acted as General Editor for the Guide Books from 1931 to 1945. Later he was made an Honorary Member, a fitting recognition of his prolonged service.

It would be wrong to consider that his climbing was restricted to expeditions devoid of technical difficulty. There was much less rock climbing done in his active years and it was more difficult to find skilled partners. Yet A.E.R. did some good rock climbs in his day – on the Cobbler and the Buachaille, with Inglis Clark on the ridges of Ben Nevis, in the first attack on the Rose Ridge of Sgoran Dubh (rather more snow than rock at Easter time) and all over the Cuillin (some of this, too, at Easter 1893). He climbed only once in the Alps, in the poor summer of 1908, when he ascended the Matterhorn and the Rimpfischhorn, but made the comment that he preferred his 'good, sound Scottish snow' – on which, indeed, he was an excellent and reliable performer.

I first met him at the Easter 1925 Meet at Fort William in his bearded days. I had Frank Smythe with me as a guest, and he impressed us both with his terse greeting, "I'm Robertson, who are you?" Since then I have been ever happy to count him as a good friend and an encouraging helper after I took over the Editorship of the Journal. Robertson was an excellent after-dinner speaker, and no one present at the jubilee Dinner of the Club in 1938 will forget the vivid brilliance and feeling with which he proposed the 'Bens and the Glens' – all within a speech (or was it an incantation) of 3 minutes' duration. He was a good story-teller at meets, an interesting conversationalist and lecturer with a broad fund of humour, often very short and to the point. In his fullness of years he ever remembered his days on the Scottish mountains and his old climbing friends, and the Club has assuredly lost one of its most colourful personalities.

CHAPTER 3

The Pioneers - Four Early Completers

3.1 Burn, Parker, Corbett & Dow

IN THE FOOTSTEPS of Robertson came the Rev. A. Ronald G. Burn, who completed 'everything' in 1923; James A. Parker, who completed the Munros in 1927 and established the extension to the 'Furths' in 1929; J. Rooke Corbett, who completed Munros and Tops in 1930 and John Dow, who completed the Munros in 1933.

Burn is the subject of a recent book,[1] which presents edited excerpts from his surviving diaries. He made his traverse largely alone and indeed seems by all accounts to have been a solitary individual throughout his life and work. He was a classical scholar and applied great rigour and energy to the task of ensuring that Gaelic place-names were spelled and explained correctly, advice that often fell on deaf ears, I fear. I have appended a list of his mountaineering writings for those who would like to know more about him. His last job was as a reader for Oxford University Press, and the excellent photograph kindly supplied by Pat Duffy (a colleague at the Press) dates from this last post. According to Mr Duffy, Burn "was a shy person of eccentric dress, but . . highly regarded by management for his knowledge of the Classics. Most readers occupied very small cubicles of barely 8ft. by 6ft., but Burn had one of only three of around 20ft. by 8ft. in order to accommodate his books. He was fortunate to have the other large rooms occupied by kindred spirits, a mathematician P. Barrett and a linguist Dr P. Naish, who took it upon themselves to look after him by bringing hot soup, etc. into him each day . . His [climbing] feats were all the more remarkable considering how poorly equipped he was at all times. Sadly we lost touch with him when he retired as he never came to the annual reunions, and I was very surprised that he never went back to his beloved hills, where he could have lived much more cheaply than in Oxford's always expensive bedsitters . . Most of the baggers seem to be of a class that dislike publicity and are basically loners, but I always felt that there was an especial loneliness about RB, of the type summed up by the Welsh expression *hiraeth*.".

Although Burn became a member of the SMC and clearly valued his membership, he was naturally not at all 'clubbable' and his involvement with other members was slight, and sometimes not particularly encouraging to him. For example, although his attendance at the Club Meet in Skye in May 1923 resulted in a number of ascents useful to his goal of completion, the account of the Meet given by J.H.B. Bell[2] suggests that a certain amount of fun was had at Burn's expense, such as forcing him to stand upright on the perilous summit

---

[1] *Burn on the Hill*. By Elizabeth Allan. Bidean Books. 1995.

[2] See *A Progress in Mountaineering*, 175-6. Oliver & Boyd. 1950. Also as *Bell's Scottish Climbs*, 118-9. Magna Books. 1995.

block of the Inaccessible Pinnacle on the grounds that it was the true summit. Indeed it may be, but who else has felt obliged to stand upright on it!?

Burn is represented in this volume by the account of the last tops of his traverse, which follows, and by his fascinating notes about the Munros and Tops in Chapter 4.4. An obituary – disappointingly brief – appeared in *SMCJ* 1973, XXX, 200.

James Parker was an engineer who joined the SMC in 1893 and went on to become President in 1925-6. He was an active rock-climber and all-round mountaineer, thus one of those many climbers who do not fit the Hely Almond moulds of Salvationist and Ultramontane. He moved to a post with the Great North of Scotland Railway Company in Aberdeen in 1906 and became a prominent member, and eventual President in 1928-30, of the Cairngorm Club. His enthusiasm for engineering led him into campaigns for new roads, bridges and mountain indicators which nowadays would be regarded as excessive. He contributed many interesting topographical articles to both *SMCJ* and *CCJ* and also edited the SMC's *Western Highlands* guidebook. His close friend William Garden provided an interesting obituary following his death in 1946[3]. He is represented here by the account of his traverse which follows, and by his careful analysis of the height of Slioch (Chapter 6.8).

Rooke Corbett is of course best known for his definition and compilation of 2,500ft. summits.[4] He was a Cambridge mathematician who became a District Valuer based in Bristol and an enthusiastic original member of the Rucksack Club. He joined the SMC in 1923 and was a joint Editor of the Club's *Northern Highlands* guidebook. His obituary[5] notes that shortly before his severe heart attack in 1943 'he accomplished a long-cherished ambition of completing the ascent of every 2,000ft. eminence in Scotland'. A slightly longer obituary appeared in the Journal of the Rucksack Club.[6] He is represented here by 'Aneroids and Munros' (Chapter 6.9).

John Dow was an Inland Revenue officer based in Dumfries and an enthusiastic member of the SMC. Like Parker and Corbett, he was involved in the Club's guidebook program and produced a Galloway section for a planned *Southern Uplands* guidebook. Unfortunately this project lapsed due to lack of interest. As his contributions to the present volume show, he was a man of some considerable wit and also not slow to speak his mind. In 'Munros, Beards, and Weather' (below) the august beard of A.E. Robertson is given a jovial tug, and in a later section he cheerily offers radical opinions about the Munros to that grey and somewhat grim conservative, E.C. Thomson (Chapter 4.5). The same Thomson provided a short obituary following Dow's death (in his 90s) in 1972.[7]

Some writings by or about Ronald Burn

1.   Out of the Golden Remote Wild West. *SMCJ* 1917, XIV, 155-169 & 207-223.
2.   Notes on Munro's Tables – see Chapter 4.4 below.
3.   Note recording his completion. *SMCJ* 1923, XVI, 329.

---

[3] *SMCJ* 1947, XXIII, 432-434.

[4] References to Corbett's writings may be found in David Purchase's Chapter 4.9 below.

[5] *SMCJ* 1950, XXIV, 244.

[6] *RCJ* 1950, XI, 249-251.

[7] *SMCJ* 1973, XXX, 200-201.

4.   Account of Sligachan Meet, May 1923. *SMCJ* 1923, XVI, 310-317.
5.   A climb on Blaven with George Sang. *SMCJ* 1923, XVI, 326-329.
6.   Note concerning Sgurr Dhomhnuill. *SMCJ* 1925, XVII, 221-223.
7.   Note about the meaning of Bhasteir. *SMCJ* 1925, XVII, 223-224.
8.   Finishing the Tops .. – see Chapter 3.2
9.   Note about the Invergarry & Kinlochquoich Mail Car. *SMCJ* 1926, XVII, 300.
10.   Note about Sgurr a' Mhuilinn. *SMCJ 1926*, XVII, 300-302
11.   Edited extract from Burn's diary (ascent with Harold Raeburn). *SMCJ* 1990, XXXIV, 400-402.

3.2 Finishing the Three-thousanders in the Cairngorms

Ronald Burn[1]

YOU WILL REMEMBER, gentle reader, the excellent Jubilee Number of this Journal, and the all too short article by the late Sir Hugh Munro,[2] in which he states that he had only three more 'tops' in Scotland over 3000 ft. to climb in order to have ascended all the 538 points in his classic Tables. These three were Carn an Fhidhleir Feisidh (3276), Carn Cloich Mhuilinn and the Inaccessible of Skye. His ambition was also mine, and to my great satisfaction I have achieved it and a little more.[3] I think that I am the first and only one to have completed all the 3000 ft. points – 558 in all.

Alas! Yes deliberately I write alas. For glad though I was to have accomplished a long dreamed-over project, I would far sooner dear old Munro had not died with three undone so that he might have been the first to do all in his own Tables and also to revise his Tables and then do all the peaks he had added. He was revising (fitfully) his Tables a little before his death, and in January 1919, three months before he passed away, I had the great privilege of spending two nights at Lindertis and of copying into my maps all the notes in his.

But this would give me no right to trespass on another club's Journal (of which I have a complete set, by rare luck). So perforce I shelter myself behind the Editor, who himself asked me for an article on my experiences in doing the tops "with more especial reference to the Cairngorms". Well, I have few experiences except kindness and hospitality unbounded from very many keeper friends, in most parts of Gaidhealtachd, and no startling adventures that I remember of during June and July 1923. So, being given a large tract of country to write about, I will try to pick out expeditions that included some of the out-of-the-way and little-climbed tops that within this range I had yet to do that summer, just in case by any chance there may be one single Cairngormer who has not been there. My narrative must be confined to those done in 1923, for memory soon fades.

---

[1] *CCJ* 1923, XI, 147-153. —RNC

[2] Munro 87. See Chapter 1.6 —RNC

[3] See *SMCJ* 1923, XVI, 329, where it is stated that I have done every point tabled over 3000 ft., *i.e.* not only every point in Munro's original Tables, which was Munro's ambition, but also all those added (20) to the revised Tables lately published by the SMC (543 in all) – as well, of course, as those excluded (15) from the revised Tables but given in Munro's original edition. —RB

Ronald Burn at 80

First, then on Wednesday, June 27th, I did that little group above and east of the railway at Dalnaspidal, seldom climbed and yet very accessible, and comprising Glas Meall Mor (3037), Meall a' Chaorruinn (3004), A' Bhuidheannaich Mhor (3046) and Carn na Caim (3087).

Could the Railway Company not work up Dalnaspidal into a mountaineering Strathpeffer for Easter and Christmas meets, providing a runabout car for the Ben Alder range? This would open up a country at present almost unexplored. Or are winter sportsmen forever to go to Switzerland, and interesting hills to be made inaccessible to those who love them most?[4]

Next day I did Meall na Cuaich, (leaving Truimbank Hotel at 10.55 and reaching the summit, 3120, at 12.10, and descended to Bhran Cottage in Glen Tromie, whence I tramped by Ruthven and Kingussie to Insh (I thought it was never going to come into view) where Mrs. Cameron of Rose Cottage (once the inn) made me exceedingly comfortable. Her husband was most interesting and gave me several words and meanings not in the Gaelic dictionaries for my collection, which at the time of writing has reached its 2100th. It is a great pity that Insh is not nearer the hills (or that the Camerons have not bought Derry Lodge!)

Next day I went to Kincraig for letters and then back along the Feshie to climb on the Monadh Ruadh and ended it by finishing all the points on the Braeriach massif that I had not done, by visiting every top from the 4149 cairn to Sron-na-Lairig and back over several. But this day includes only well-known peaks and will not be detailed.

Next day I started at about 9.30 from Tolvah in Glen Feshie where I had slept, and once more took the Allt Fhearnachan path. There are two tracks after one gets well beyond the bridge and wood.[5] The map marks a cart road going north and then ceasing. Actually it turns east uphill till past Glaic na Meirlich (on the ridge ending at Carn Ban Beag). This is not to be used. It looks the better and quicker way as reaching high ground sooner but its conspicuousness is due to streams having used it and made it their bed. This track avoids (by keeping higher up) the bridge over the Allt Fhearnachan, whereas to get the good footpath marked on the map one goes to the bridge (not of course crossing it) crosses the wee burn from Coir' Arcain and then up and close to its left bank as in map. The old track does not cross this little stream till east of where the map makes it end. By gentle uniform slopes this gravelly footpath lands one on the 3000 contour (or even 3250?) opposite the big snow patch called Ciste Marad (not Mairearaid). Further on is a broken pony shelter where lies a sheet of corrugated iron. It would now have been no exertion to bag Carn Ban Mor 3443. But I had done it some years ago and had to get as far as Cairntoul and the Devil's Point[6] that day.

On the previous day, in order to avoid the awful ground drained by the head streams of the Eideart, knolls and dips and knolls again (also water), I had headed well towards

---

[4] An interesting suggestion (though many would find it deplorable), eventually fulfilled by the Highlands & Islands Development Board in the 1960s – of course, at Aviemore rather than Dalnaspidal. - RNC

[5] The name of the wood is Barlan Mosach. —RB

[6] The Gaelic name is Bodan Deamhain. Other names are Bod an Diabhoil, Pioc (peak) an Donais, Creag Bhiorach (sharp) Gleann Giuthsachain. —RB

Loch Einich. But all in vain: if I missed haggs I gained upsy downy knowes and stones. This bad bit cannot be avoided and there is no comfortable route. Today I kept the continuation of Ross's path on the right bank of the Allt na Sgornaich (gullet) and so amid moraine heaps (best tackled by circumvention) with several pools and snow patches at their foot I toiled on past the south end of Loch nan Cnapan, crossed the Glais Fheith (bog-stream) Inbhir Fheisidh (Feshie) or Fhaisidh, the left head stream of the Allt Luinneag (little purler – a beautiful and very true name for this lilting burn). I now kept up the corrie of the other stream (Glais Theith Luinneag) till near its top when I crossed it and mounted a snow patch and then stones and so gained the smallish cairn of Sgor an Lochain Uaine[7] (1.49). It is a great pity that the contours of 'Parker's new map' seem here ambiguous, as one would like to know within 50 feet the height of a peak made 4095 ap. by Hinxman's aneroid (given with no ap. caution in Bartholomew). Corner made it less high than Cairngorm, someone else 4205 approximate.

Having previously done Cairntoul I did not ascend it, leaving it for the return journey if time should allow. I almost missed the Coir' an t-Saighdeir (soldier) top 3989 and its rudimentary cairn (or are the stones there natural?) The way down to the wettish sandy col (An Diollaid, the saddle) between Cairntoul and the Devil's Point was very stony. I reached the cairn of Bod an Deamhain (3303) at 3.16. Looking down the cliffs on the east side I felt sure (as I had long before on looking up at them from below) that their reputation for unclimbableness starting direct from the Dee is exaggerated. Those down to the Giuthsachan side seem also feasible. Opposite loomed the huge and impossible boiler-plates of Beinn Bhrodain shining with water. The day had been misty with sharp showers soaking me from knees downward. On my way back I skirted lower down on Cairntoul to just under the 3975 ap. col to Sgor an Lochain Uaine in order to cut across to (cairned) 3705 top on the march over a mile north-by-east of Lochan na Stuirteig (black-headed gull).

On Monday the whole Beinn Bhrodain massif was completed and more besides.

Having crammed two days' work into one I had only Druim nam Bo to do on my way to Inverey, and to finish all that I had not done of the Cairngorms which were baggable from Glen Feshie side. There is nothing to say about this seldom-ascended mere shoulder[8] except that having started at 11.01 I reached the top 3005 about 1.30. This consists of stones leant one overlapping the other somewhat like what would be the result if an earthquake tipped up at a gentle angle the floor as panto chorus girls were dancing by holding each others' shoulders in Indian file.[9] The granite was red and flat as though schistose.

The rest of Monday was spent in getting to Inverey and Tuesday to Spital of Glen Shee, for I had missed in the Monadh Minigeig range Meall Odhar Mor feeling sure it could not be on the Tables, and Glas Meall Beag because I simply didn't see it and had forgotten its

---

[7] Called Pioc an Donais by one informant, but he belongs to the younger generation who are less reliable. My two old authorities assure me that this name belongs to the Devil's Point alone. —RB

[8] Druim nam Bo is as Burn says 'a mere shoulder' and disappeared never to return in 1921. Munro gives its location as half a mile south-west of Meall Tionail, now known as Mullach Clach a' Bhlair. —RNC

[9] A highly unusual sermon in stones! —RNC

Cairn Toul and Sgor an Lochain Uaine from Ben Macdui

existence.[10] Having accomplished these I returned to Miss Gruer's at Inverey. Friday July 6th was spent in doing 11 tops on Beinn a' Bhuird and Beinn Athfhinn ('Avon') that I had not done (including one or two duplicates). But as this ground is quite familiar I need detail nothing. I would however suggest to anyone who contemplates climbing Beinn a' Bhuird from Glen Quoich, that after crossing the Dubh Gleann burn (there is a wooden bridge – none across Clais na Fearna burn), one should keep well up above the wood and not attempt the purgatorial task of following the Quoich. I have read somewhere that there was once a path along it right up to that from Slugan Lodge, but there is no trace of it and the fallen trees and brushwood and long heather are beyond the limit. (There is a curious figure cut on the grass of the lower slopes of Carn 'Elrig' Mor depicting a Highlander playing the pipes, visible from the road).

Next day though heavier was pleasanter and is worth detailing if my space will allow. I had 14 tops, all new, to polish off, starting from the right bank of the Derry and so round to the right bank of the 'Luibeg'.

I started from Inverey at 10.20. Once in Glen Derry with the bridge in sight I headed to the left and began to climb just before the river's slow big elbow and thence into a corrie that led me to near the top of Carn Gorm Beag na Doire (now called Little Cairn Gorm of Derry) (3375 ap.) cairnless (2.00). The dip to the north-north-west is short but well stoned (3325 ap.) as is also the slope up to the main peak (3788) whose name must surely refer to its blue loom when seen from a distance. It is not a particularly green hill except for a little

---

[10] Burn is obviously talking about what are usually called Meall Odhar and Little Glas Maol. The range to which these hills belong is sometimes called the Monega. Evidently Burn thought that this name Monega was a version of the name Monadh Minigeig, which is applied to the East Drumochter group. This is a typical example of Burn's committed approach to place names. Holding Ordnance Survey Gaelic in justified contempt, he went his own way, although in many cases - as here - it is difficult to follow him! —NC

on the glen side, but it is a handsome cone and has a bonny conical cairn to deck it (2.19). The dip to the north-east was long and made deeper by my not following the col ridge further to the left. More stones and then Sgor an Lochain Uaine (3175 ap.) This is a good top. The col from Derry Cairngorm is 3325 ap. but I went directly west by north to Creagan a' Choir' Aiteachain[11] and the dip is 3125 ap. The hill 3529 is cairnless (3.15). I now headed for Beinn Mheadhoin, and, using the path for as long as I could, descended to Loch 'Etchachan' and crossed it at its east end.

My next move was, I think, a mistake. I ought to have taken the 3750 top to the north-east second or third in order, but on descent to the Loch I had thought it more direct to climb it at once. The ascent was over boulders and steepish, and it was not conquered till 3.50 (no cairn) – hardly I think worth including in the Tables as a top, and it was queried by Munro in his annotated copy. There followed a longish descent (3525 ap.) over stones to the handsome 3551 cone which is much more of a real mountain – cairn, 4.07. Then over grass and a burn missing the 3725 ap. col between the south-west 3750 top and the main peak, and so I gained the massive Beinn Mheadhoin (3883).

I had time to scramble up only the barn that supports the cairn, 4.20. The usual stones lay on the way down to (cairnless) Stacan Dubha (3330 ap., 5.00) from which there was a good view over lonely Loch Avon. I had little time to absorb it, but picked out the Shelter Stone. Bumpy ground followed a short descent and then I was under the slabby cliffs of Carn Aiteachain (3673). I got a fairly easy way up its steep side and reached the cairn at 5.44. Then came a long ridge of stones (col 3625 ap.) on which I cut out the 3926 point as being unimportant. At length I reached the top over Coir' Sputan Dearg, 4095 (no cairn – 6.44). It had been conspicious most of the day, which though sunny was close. It is a handsome peak. A shelter nestles on the top. The 3811 point above Lochan Uaine had not to be done and I cut it to go lower and escape the stones and so reached Sron Riabhach (3534) cairned (7.04). It looks more conspicuous from 4095, but on Carn a' Mhaim it shows itself no top and the dip from 3811 to it is almost invisible, whereas between 4095 and 3811 there is a fairish drop, (comparatively) but 3811 to 3534 is really only a gently falling ridge: see 'Parker.' I now had but one more hill to crown my day and descended sidelong among those eternal stones to reach the grassy col of Carn a' Mhaim (2625 ap.) The ridge was bumpy and long but at last I gained the top (3375 ap.) no cairn(8.03). This is the real summit, but the Sappers' one has a cairn, 3329 (col 3310 ap.) (8.15). Then once past a stone-belt I hurried down on goodish going, moss with stones far enough apart to let one step out quickly. At about the 2750 contour stands a (guide?) cairn. I reached Luibeg at 9.05 and Linn of Dee at 10.30.

Next day I did 10 tops between Sron Riabhach of Ben Macdhui and Cairngorm in the thunderstorm of July that carried away the four bridges on the railway near Carr Bridge. There is a crowd of useless cairns on Ben Macdhui round the main one and the Club would do a useful deed in demolishing all but those pointing north-east, south and west. Such are a few days of a wonderful holiday.

---

[11] The true spelling of the name and Loch 'Etchachan' (3075 ap.) has the same name. It means juniper place. So Ruigh-Aiteachan in Glen Feshie. — RB

3.3 The Scottish 'Threes'

James A. Parker[1]

ACCORDING to the SMC's official list there are 276 mountains in Scotland which are 3,000 feet or over in height.[2] In the late spring of 1926 I found myself in the enviable position of having ample leisure, a recently acquired motorcar and the ability (?) to drive it, and thanks to a very successful fortnight at the SMC's Easter Meet at Tomdoun and Cluanie, a total of no less than 187 of the three thousand feet mountains already to my credit. It was therefore perfectly obvious that the correct thing to do was to set about the climbing of the remaining eighty-nine peaks as early as possible.

A list of the wanted hills was therefore prepared towards the end of May and it showed that the majority of them were fairly conveniently placed in the vicinity of Killin, Tyndrum, Ballachulish, and Spean Bridge; but that there was a very formidable minority of scattered peaks to the west of the Great Glen ranging from Ben More in Mull to Ben Hope in Sutherland and that many of them, such as A' Mhaighdean, Seana Bhraigh, and Meall Buidhe (Loch Nevis) were extremely awkwardly placed even for a man with a motorcar. A careful examination of the list showed, however, that with methodical grouping and a good bit of luck the whole of the eighty-nine might be climbed in fifty-one working (*i.e.* climbing) days. This being, of course, quite a different thing from consecutive days.

As the result proved, the operations extended from the 4th June 1926, Ben Chonzie, to the 19th July 1927, Ben Hope, and occupied fifty-six working days. Bad luck was experienced with some of the more optimistic groups on account of bad weather and, of course, climbing was not practicable in many of the districts during the deer stalking and winter seasons.

Now that the work has been accomplished it is interesting to look back on the whole undertaking and recall one's impressions. The first thing that struck me was the tremendous monotony of some of the more uninteresting hills and the second was the great beauty of many of the regions into which the quest led me, districts which are seldom visited other than by sportsmen in search of game if even by them. Fortunately the uninteresting hills were in a very small minority and there were few days if any that could

---

[1] *CCJ* XI, 290-294.

[2] Parker is referring to the 1921 Tables.

compare as regards sheer unrelieved monotony with the circuit of the five Monadh Liaths from Newtonmore on a dull day with a bitterly cold east wind and no view. But it is more pleasant to think of the good hills, of which there were many.

One of the finest of these was undoubtedly Ben More in Mull which was climbed from Salen on the 15th June, 1926. It is a beautiful hill of volcanic origin similar to the Cuillin and has a bold precipitous north face with a rugged *arête*, which called for careful handling by the solitary climber, running down eastwards to its graceful outlier A' Chioch. The view from the summit must be superb on a clear day; but unfortunately the ascent was made on a hazy day and distant view there was none.

Ben Sgriol, which was climbed from Glenelg on the 21st July, is another fine hill and was interesting on account of its narrow and steep western summit ridge and for the magnificent views that it commanded on account of its isolated position between Skye and the mountains of Loch Hourn and Loch Duich. Its 3,196 feet drop southwards to the shores of Loch Hourn in rather less than one mile is magnificent and is comparable to – but not so impressive as – the 1,972 feet drop from the summit of Slieve League in Co. Donegal in less than half a mile to the shores of the Atlantic.

Beinn Sgritheall

Kinloch Rannoch as a climbing centre, with a car, was a great discovery and the summit views from the hills on the confines of 'mountain girdled' Rannoch Moor on peerless days in early spring a revelation. The Ballachulish Hills were done during the Easter Meet of the SMC and their memory is mostly one of arduous days in the worst of weather, with the glorious exception of Ben Starav at the head of Loch Etive. But two of the best of the Ballachulish Hills, Sgor na h-Ulaidh and Beinn Fhionnlaidh, climbed from Glen Coe in the thickest of mists, afforded a most delightful problem in route finding, the tricky descent from the latter mountain under such conditions into the rain drenched upper recesses of Glen Creran being wonderfully impressive.

The Beinn Dearg Group in Ross-shire gave three most interesting days in perfect weather; but with Ladhar Bheinn on the south shore of Loch Hourn I was just a wee bit disappointed, probably because it was climbed by its uninteresting southern slope and perhaps because I was just getting a bit *blasé* – it was the eighty-seventh.

A good hill, Ben Hope, was reserved for the last and it was climbed with R.T. Sellar on the 19th July, 1927. Most unfortunately the weather was very bad, it was the beginning of the summer weather of that year; but the ascent along its narrow north ridge was extremely interesting. View there was none and with just a kind word of congratulation from Sellar and a hasty handshake we ran down the easy south and south-west slopes to the car that was waiting on the roadside.

Most of the ascents had unfortunately to be made alone but out of the fifty-six climbing days the weather on no fewer than forty-seven was excellent and in many cases simply superb. The bulk of the work was done in the months of March, April, May and June, the record month being May 1927, during which twenty-nine of the hills were climbed and of these thirteen were climbed in seven consecutive days. A result of careful grouping, good staff work, and perfect weather!

Many of the hills were difficult to get at and involved long and laborious days; but on the other hand some of the hills that gave the greatest cause for anxiety in this respect fell with unexpected ease. Of these latter Ladhar Bheinn was a conspicuous example. I went to Mallaig prepared if necessary to charter a special motorboat or even to sleep out on the mountain as the Hotel (*sic*) at Inverie was impossible, when to my surprise the peak was done most comfortably between the morning and afternoon runs of the ordinary boat from Mallaig to Inverie for a four shilling return fare and with afternoon tea served up by the crew of the boat on the homeward journey.

The longest day was undoubtedly the one devoted to that most un-get-at-able of all hills, A' Mhaighdean, which was done with Gordon Wilson from Kinlochewe by way of Glen Bianasdail and the east end of Lochan Fada. Being grouped with Sgurr Ban and Mullach Coire Mhic Fhearchair, its ascent took twelve hours almost continuous going. But it is a fine hill and has a grand western precipice. Another long day was that devoted to Meall Buidhe, Loch Nevis, from Tomdoun via Kinlochquoich through the very wonderful pass of Lochan nam Breac.

Another long day must be mentioned although it was done in April 1926, *viz.*, Sgurr nan Ceathreamhnan (3,771 feet) which stands on the north side of Glen Affaric fully four miles west of Mam Soul. It is the fourth highest peak west of the Caledonian Canal and is undoubtedly one of the finest mountains in Scotland. Its ascent along with that of its northern outlier Creag a' Choir' Aird from Cluanie took eleven hours steady going; but it was worth it.

Some one asks, "Now that you have climbed all the 3,000 feet mountains in Scotland, which, in your opinion, are the finest?" It is a difficult question to reply to, and I do so with much hesitation because there are many fine peaks and many opinions. East of the Caledonian Canal I would say, not in order of merit, Ben Cruachan, Bidean nam Bian, Ben Lui, Ben Lawers, Ben Nevis, Lochnagar, Cairn Toul, Braeriach, and Ben Macdhui. And west of the canal, Ben More in Mull, The Saddle (Loch Duich), Ben Attow, Sgurr nan Ceathreamhnan, Sgurr Ruadh (Achnashellach), Sgurr na Lapaich in Strathfarrar, Liathach, Beinn Eighe, Slioch, An Teallach, Beinn Dearg (Ross), Ben More Assynt, and all the Black Cuillins, especially Sgurr Alasdair.

And now that the quest is finished I am harassed with the awful thought that for the ascent of perhaps seventy-five per cent of the hills I had no witness with me and that it is open to any one to challenge the statement, which is hereby confirmed, that I have climbed all the three thousanders. All that I have to show in proof is a carefully compiled list dating from the 19th July 1883, with the ascent of Ben Lomond, the most southerly 3,000 feet hill in Scotland, and ending curiously enough with Ben Hope in Sutherland, the most northerly, forty-four years later. In view of the recent English Channel swimming dispute, the correct thing is apparently now to go and climb them all over again with press representatives and other responsible witnesses, but this I absolutely refuse to do. I would rather tackle the 'Twenty Fives'; but that is another story. Fortunately they have not yet been listed, and probably never will.[3]

3.4 Munros, Beards and Weather

J. Dow[1]

THE EDITOR has suggested to me that following precedent I should let him have some notes on the 'Munros'. I am not sure that I have much to report which is in the least degree new, but I shall try to avoid repetition.

Subject to my remarks below, Robertson's pioneer work in ascending for the first time all the 3,000-foot mountains of Scotland was certainly a feat. Again, subject to my later remarks, to cover all the subsidiary tops as well as the main mountains, as Burn and Corbett did, was also somewhat of a feat, and similarly to ascend all the 3,000-foot mountains in Great Britain and Ireland as Parker has done was a very meritorious performance; but when I have said this I would like to make it quite definite that to complete the ascent of the 277 Scottish Munros under modern road and transport conditions is very far from being in the slightest degree a feat. This will be very clearly seen when I have to admit that never once had I to spend a night out, never once did I fail to return to a hot bath and a comfortable bed, and very rarely did I even miss dinner, so that in actual fact the whole affair was in my case pretty much of a luxury progress. Fifty-five of the hills were climbed on day excursions from my former home in Edinburgh, and in every other case the return was to a fully equipped and licensed hotel (the latter adjective is inserted, I should explain, for the benefit of *other* Club members). If nowadays any kudos is to be obtained by ascending all the hills on the Munro list it

---

[3] No marks for prophecy!

[1] *SMCJ* 1933, XX, 113-118.

will, I fear, have to be earned by climbing them all on dates between, say, 1st December and 31st March, or in some such fashion.[2]

I am not prepared, however, to be too modest about the matter, and I would therefore quote two points in my favour. The first is that the hills were all ascended by me after the age of forty-five, though this is a very trifling thing in these days of longevity; when someone does the lot after he reaches sixty I shall be willing to take off my hat to him.[3] The other point is, however, much more important – that no one before me has climbed the 277 mountains without the assistance of a beard. I do think that this is a really vital consideration; and indeed one might argue with considerable force that bearded men cannot, in a civilised society, be reckoned, and that therefore to me belongs the glory and honour of being the first to count as a conqueror of the Munros.

While I would not be prepared to press this contention to the bitter end, or even to go to the length of arguing that to call in the extraneous assistance of a beard is as illegitimate from the mountaineering point of view as would be, for example, the making of all the ascents seated in a caterpillar tractor, I am still strongly of opinion, however, that it is not quite playing the game; and when one contemplates in particular Robertson's conduct in this connection, it is difficult to find suitable language in which adequately to describe it. Burn, Parker and Corbett, while they certainly completed the list in each case with the aid of a beard, have had the grace not to play the hypocrite in the matter; but Robertson, after making no doubt full use of this artificial and (I repeat) semi-illegitimate aid, most basely and callously after his performance sacrificed that which I have no doubt really made the performance possible. I am content to draw attention to this, and to leave judgment to others, but a more lamentable example of sheer ingratitude I should have difficulty in conceiving.

One more word before leaving this subject of beards. Those who have had may I say the pleasure and privilege (please do not insert a query, Mr Editor) of ascending Munros with me may, on occasion, have marvelled somewhat at my solemn and respectful demeanour and behaviour when at the summit cairns. I should therefore explain that at these supreme moments there was always in my mind the thought that on this peak four grave and reverend men have at one time stood, and that over this cairn, on four great days of the past, four dignified and (more or less) flowing beards have wagged. Such thoughts, it will be admitted, would induce awe and reverence even in the most frivolous, and I hope that I am not of the most frivolous.

On the question of transport one point might be mentioned. I find that 214 out of the 277 hills were ascended with the help of a motor car – somebody else's when available, or my own in the last resort. These cars were left lying, generally for many hours at a time, here and there all over the Highlands without the slightest precaution ever being taken, and not only was there never any theft, but never once was anything even disturbed unless on one single occasion in Glencoe when the road reconstruction work was in full swing there. I do not think that a higher compliment could be paid to the people of the Highlands of

---

[2] Cleverly anticipating Martin Moran's traverse – see *The Munros in Winter*. David & Charles. 1986.

[3] Ivan Waller's traverse (see Chapter 8.5) does not quite qualify, but Dow might have given his hat a firm touch.

Scotland than merely to state this fact; and I do not believe that in any other country in the world could such a record have been possible.

Coming to statistics, I find that the ascent of the 277 Munros and of 153 of the subsidiary tops in the Tables, most of which tops were taken as being either on the route or reasonably near, required a total of 150 days out, spread over 6 years. I have sometimes been asked as to weather experiences, and I am giving a short analysis which may be of some slight interest in this connection. To the 150 days noted other 8 days have been added which were occupied by repeat ascents, and it must further be explained that owing to the necessity in my case invariably of making arrangements in advance, none of the days was picked for weather reasons but all had to be taken just as they happened to come. I have assumed the three main enemies to be wind, mist and rain in the order stated, Class 3 comprising days when none of these was troublesome and Class 0 days in which they were all troublesome more or less. The result is as under:–

	Class 3	Class 2	Class 1	Class 0	Total
January	2	2	1	1	6
February	2	2	1	0	5
March	2	1	1	2	6
April	7	6	5	5	23
May	13	15	2	3	33
June	9	7	3	2	21
July	4	2	1	0	7
August	3	4	7	2	16
September	1	0	0	1	2
October	5	8	8	3	24
November	1	1	1	0	3
December	3	7	1	1	12
					158

On classifying, roughly, days in Classes 3 and 2 as good and in Classes 1 and 0 as bad, the following percentage results are obtained:–

	Good	Bad		Good	Bad
January	67	33	July	86	14
February	80	20	August	44	56
March	50	50	September	50	50
April	57	43	October	54	46
May	85	15	November	67	33
June	76	24	December	83	17

In fully half of the months the totals are, of course, too small for the results to be of any value, but the preponderance of good weather in May and June and of bad weather in August is certainly striking, and the figures for the winter months are also interesting although as noted of little real value.

As an interference with enjoyment mist is the greatest nuisance, and out of the 277 Munros 114 were mist-capped when ascended. For a variation of the proverbial pastime of hunting in a pitch-dark room for a black hat worn by a bare-headed nigger[4] who isn't there, I can confidently recommend searching the summit plateau of a flat-topped Munro in thick cloud for a cairn which may not exist! – though in actual fact it almost always does. Only 20 Munros have summits without marking of any kind, and 10 of these are reasonably sharp-topped; but in a fair number of cases the cairn is not on the actual highest point of the hill.

With regard to relative difficulty from the point of view of the hill walker, to which class will normally belong the type of man who will desire to complete all the Munros, it can quite definitely be repeated that there is nothing whatever out of Skye which cannot be ascended under normal conditions without the compulsory use of the hands. In Skye the Inaccessible Pinnacle is the only summit for the ascent of which a rope might be desirable, and even here if the hill walker finds, as he probably will, that the ascent of the shorter side is beyond his powers, and has to go up the eastern arête, he may feel that any help he can get from the rope is more moral than physical. None of the other Skye Munros need trouble the hill walker at all provided he goes to them in good weather.

And now, finally, a few remarks with regard to the Tables themselves. I understand that the new edition of the General Guide is to be issued with the Tables unaltered, but as the Club by including them in the Guide is to some extent accepting responsibility for them, more or less, I think that sooner or later their revision will have to be tackled, and possibly in the near or distant future the Club will appoint a Sub-Committee to take the job in hand. I am not personally aware of the rules which Sir Hugh Munro applied in deciding which were separate mountains and which were tops – if indeed he did apply any rigid rules at all – but my own idea is that a businesslike classification would have to take into account the following factors, of importance in the order named, (1) dip, (2) distance and (3) difficulty. A formula could no doubt be evolved for dealing with the first two factors automatically, and, while the third might to some extent be a matter of opinion, general agreement as to the facts in each individual case would probably be found to exist.

As an example of the changes which might be found necessary, were the list to be reconsidered on these or similar lines, I might mention the following – as examples merely, not as an exhaustive list by any means: An Teallach and Beinn Eighe might each rank as three Munros; the two Buachailles of Etive, Bidean nam Bian and Liathach might in each case rank as two Munros; Am Bathaich of Sgurr a' Mhaoraich might be a separate Munro: while on the other hand the number of Munros in the Cluny Ridge might be reduced from seven to five; Mam Sodhail might be a top of Carn Eige; in the Ardverikie Forest, Aonach Beag might be a top of Geal-Charn and Creag Pitridh a top of Mullach Coire an Iubhair; Carn Ban in the Monadhliaths might be a top of Carn Dearg; and An Garbhanach and Stob Coire a' Chairn in the Mamores might perhaps hardly be considered as separate Munros. There would also be many possible adjustments in the list of tops, but my notes are lengthy enough already.

---

[4] For those who take an interest in these matters, the Editor responsible for publishing this dastardly word was Charles W. Parry. He was succeeded by James H.B. Bell in 1936.

CHAPTER 4

Defining and Classifying

4.1 On Defining Munros: Introduction

HUGH MUNRO'S original task was to enumerate the Scottish mountains over 3,000 feet in height. Whether independently or on Committee or other advice is not known, but he took on the additional task of picking out those mountains that were 'distinct and separate'. It is worth considering the nature of his task briefly. Available to him, besides a range of small scale popular maps, were the Ordnance Survey One-Inch and Six-Inch survey sheets. Nowadays we would regard the map corresponding to the Six-Inch map – the 1:10,000 sheet – as a base map from which other smaller-scale maps are derived. However, the map sheets of the 1870s available to Munro contained quite different and independent information: the Six-Inch contained numerous spot heights and names, etc., but no contours; the One-Inch had 250-foot contours, but few spot heights or names.[1] So to arrive at his enumeration of mountains, Munro had to shuffle back and forth between these two map series, and, in the worst case where a mountain lacked a spot height, he had only the very inaccurate contour height to go by. Although his personal knowledge of the mountains was growing apace, his SMC Application Form shows that in 1890 it was still quite limited.[2]

In view of these mapping difficulties, the fierce deadline to which Munro worked, and the shocking state of the contemporary maps in areas such as Skye, it was inevitable that his Tables would contain errors. It is therefore quite wrong to regard the original Tables of 1891 as the Holy Writ of Munro: rather, they were a series of hurried stabs in the dark. If Munro had lived long enough to produce a second edition of the Tables, that edition would have been based on much more accurate maps and on close personal knowledge, supplemented by the experience of his fellow-mountaineers over some 30 years of careful exploration and observation. It might indeed have been the Holy Writ of Munro. But the circumstances of his death in 1919 and the ambiguities surrounding the authorship of the second edition of 1921, leave it to some degree open to question what was Munro's idea of a 'distinct and separate mountain'.

Present-day Masters of the Tables have to strike a balance of faith. They must keep faith with the terrain, of course, and they must also keep faith with Munro. And this same ambivalence defines two strands of work on the problems of definition and classification. Some mountaineers have been primarily interested in the orographic question – What combinations of height and conformation define mountains? Others have pursued the historical question – what can we conclude about Munro's definition of mountain from study of his Tables and his writings. And there are others who oscillate uneasily between these distinct goals. Amongst the various chapters that compose this section, these various tendencies are all represented. For example, my own chapter is aimed at the historical

---

[1] See illustrative maps on pages 96 and 97.

[2] See Scottish part of Munro's Application Form on page 7.

question, David Purchase's chapter tackles the orographical question, whereas Frank Bonsall looks for an orographic principle that will coincide with Munro's principle of classification.

In addition to these rather academic efforts, I have included what I consider to be basic reading (apart from the Tables themselves) for anyone interested in joining in these endlessly fascinating quests, namely a compendium of Munro's own wise words, Robin Gall Inglis' analysis of Munro's Card Index and personal copy of the Tables, President Ling's description of the nature of the 1921 Tables, and the thoughts of Ronald Burn and John Dow about the Tables. Papers by the other early completers – Parker, Corbett and James Gall Inglis – appear elsewhere in the book. Finally, Geoff Cohen's agenda for 'theoretical Munroology' seems like light relief now, but it shows that for the academically-minded bagger, completion is a distant mirage!

4.2 Munro on Definition

Hugh T. Munro

[IT IS convenient to begin this section with a collection of Munro's own views on the question of how a mountain should be defined. While I have done my best to make this comprehensive, I am sure there will be comments which I have overlooked. Munro's observations are presented in chronological order. When he comments on a particular top I have indicated its status in the 1891 Tables by a following 'M' or 'T'.]

1. 'In the Preface to the first number of the *Journal* it was correctly stated that there are more than three hundred mountains in Scotland whose height exceeds 3,000 feet. The exact number cannot be determined, owing to the impossibility of deciding what should be considered distinct mountains. For instance, Braeriach[M] and Cairn Toul[M] are always counted as separate mountains, and so are the various peaks of the Cuillins, in Skye; and yet these are no more distinct than are Sron Isean[T] or Stob Diamh[M] from the two main peaks of Ben Cruachan, one and a half miles to the west. The names of these peaks, though, are not even given on the Ordnance sheet, but are generally included under the name Ben Cruachan.

In the following tables, therefore, it has been thought best to include every 'top' which attains an elevation of 3,000 feet; while in the first column only such as may be fairly reckoned distinct mountains are numbered.'[1]

2. 'The decision as to what are to be considered distinct and separate mountains, and what may be counted as 'tops', although arrived at after careful consideration, cannot be finally insisted on.'[2]

3. 'It will be seen that although on the 1-inch [map] unnamed and only a 3750 contour given, Stob Coire Claurigh[M] is the culminating point of the large portion of the Lochaber Hills, of which Stob Coire Easain[M] appears on most maps as the most prominent.'[3]

---

[1] See Munro 15, p. 276. Munro's writings are listed in Chapter 1.1

[2] *ibid.*, p. 281.

[3] *ibid.*, p. 289.

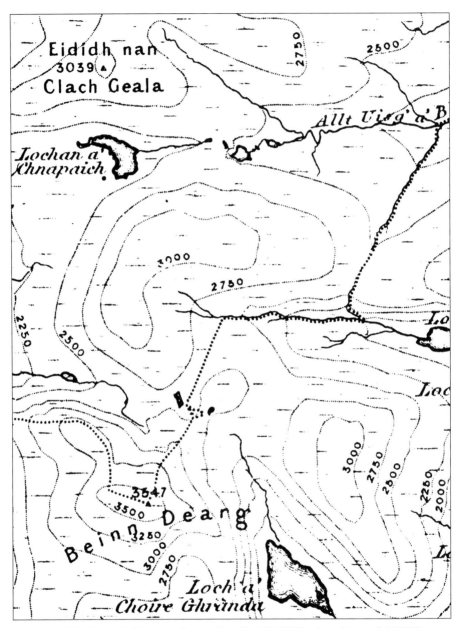

*An extract of the **One-Inch Ordnance Survey Map** Sheet 92 (1881) enlarged to a scale 1:25000 showing the Beinn Dearg to Eididh nan Clach Geala group of mountains*

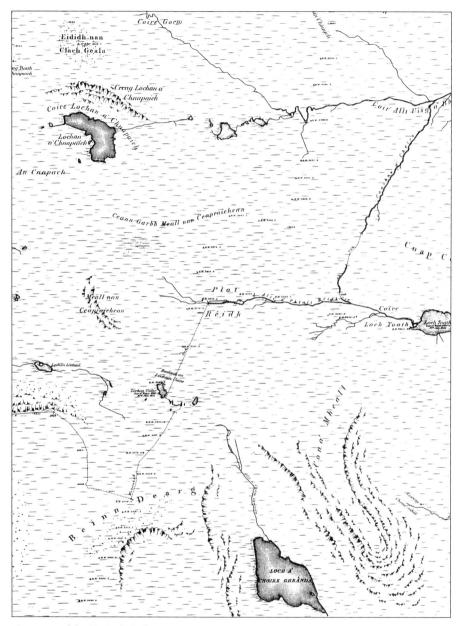

*An extract of the **Six-Inch Ordnance Survey Map** Sheet xxxvi (1881) reduced to a scale 1:25000 showing the Beinn Dearg to Eididh nan Clach Geala group of mountains*

4. 'It will be seen that although unnamed and only a 3500 contour given on the 1-inch map, Geal Charn[M] is the culminating point of the large range immediately to the N. of Ben Alder.'[4]

5. 'Sgor Iutharna[T] is the 'lancet edge' mentioned on pages 73, 138, and 245 [of *SMCJ* Volume I]. Having stood on the top of it, and of every top in the district, I fancy it must be fully 3400 feet, and standing well out is almost worthy to be considered a separate mountain.'[5]

6. 'It is difficult to decide what should be considered "tops" in the big plateau between Braeriach and Cairntoul.'[6]

7. 'In the Eastern Grampians it is especially difficult to decide what are to be considered separate mountains, tops, or merely shoulders. Little Glas Maol[T], Druim Mor[T], Creag Leachdach[T] and Cairn of Gowal[T] are all very doubtful tops.'[7]

8. 'From Creag a' Ghlas-uilt (Lochnagar, T), the south-west shoulder, ten minutes' walk off, appeared a very distinct top, I therefore went off and measured it, making its approximate height 3,470 feet. It is certainly a good top . .'[8]

9. 'A third of a mile to the S.E. [of Geal Charn[M], Glenfeshie], a very small 3,000 feet contour on the 1-inch map indicates a pretty little stony top; the slight depressions on each side do not, however, justify its being counted. Meall Buidhe[T] is the local name for the N.W. end of the next 3,000 feet contour; it is a good top, unmarked by any cairn – height, from the 6-inch map, 3,185 feet. Between it and the north top of Sgoran Dubh[T] – called locally Sgoran Dubh Mor – is another doubtful top. Sgoran Dubh Mor has a large cairn. The southern and highest summit, locally known as Sgoran Dubh Bheag[M], has only a natural cairn. Between the two, at the edge of the cliffs, is a semaphore for signalling to the bothy at the foot of Loch Eunach. A third of a mile S.S.W. from Sgoran Dubh, in the direction of Carn Ban[M], some rocky ground on the moor is dignified on the 6-inch map with the name of Sgor Gaoithe.

Carn Ban[M], which has a cairn with a stick on it, is a mere swelling on the moor, – a good 'top', but it should not in [the 1891 Tables] have been reckoned a separate mountain. Meall Dubh-achaidh[M] . . is very similar, and is also a doubtful 'mountain'. Meall Tionail[M], separated from it by the fine corrie of the Garbhlach, may more properly be considered a mountain, both on account of its distance from Sgoran Dubh and of the corries which partially isolate it. . . Druim nam Bo[T] is a mere shoulder – not even a top. Diollaid Coire Eindart[T] . . is the point marked 3,184 feet on the 1-inch map. Although undignified by any cairn, its distance from Meall Tionail – one and a quarter miles east, as well as its nearly equal height, entitles it to be considered a 'top'.

---

[4] *ibid.*, p. 289.

[5] *ibid.*, p. 289.

[6] *ibid.*, p. 301.

[7] *ibid.*, p. 303, repeated on p. 305.

[8] See Munro 21. This top, not in the 1891 Tables, was included in 1921 as Stob an Dubh Loch, although the location given for it is wrong.

From here it is an hour's walk to the mossy excrescence which constitutes the top above Lochan nan Cnapan[T] . . without a cairn, it is difficult to say where the highest point is, so broad and flat is the moor. Still it falls away decidedly all round, and is an undoubted 'top'.

The 4,149 feet[T] and 4,061 feet points [of the Braeriach plateau] have well-built cairns, though the latter should scarcely be considered a top, and has not been counted in the tables – the 4,036 feet top above Loch Coire an Lochan has no cairn.'[9]

10. 'Keeping west . . over boggy moorland . . I reached Snechdach Slinnean[T], 'the snowy shoulder' (3,011 feet), merely a slight rise in the wet and peaty moor, without a cairn. Returning over Carn Mairg[M], I followed round the angle of the fence north, and afterwards north-east over the same kind of ground to Carn Ballach, the two summits of which [M,T] . . are a little difficult to identify in mist, so level is the moor.'[10]

11. 'I ascended both of the Buchailles. . .[On Buchaille Mor] there is little dip between [Stob na Broige][T] and Stob Coire Altruim[T]. . The next summit, Stob na Doire[T] . . is a fine isolated top. . . [On Buchaille Bheag] Stob Coire Raineach[T] comes next. There is a considerable dip between this and Stob Dubh, the southern and highest summit. I visited in turn all the tops of both.'[11]

12. 'Bidein an Eoin Deirg[M] . . is a mere subsidiary top, and notwithstanding its distance from Sgurr a' Chaoruinn[M], its nearly equal height of 3,430 feet, and big cairn, ought not to be considered a separate mountain.'[12]

13. '[Carn Bhinnein][M], though a good 'top', is a very doubtful mountain, the depression between it and . . Carn Geoidh [M], not being great.'[13]

14. 'Mam nan Carn[T] is unnamed, except on the 6-inch map, but is marked on the 1-inch map by a height of 3,217 feet. A hundred and fifty yards to the S.S.W. of this point, however, the 6-inch map gives a height of 3,224 feet. It is a long, almost level ridge, extending east and west, and although the depression between it and Beinn Iutharn Mor[M], which lies to the north of it, is not great – only some 300 feet – its nearly equal height and its bulk almost entitle it to the rank of separate mountain. So flat is it, though, that without its very small cairn it would be difficult to 'locate' its summit. . . The dip between Mam nan Carn and Beinn Iutharn Beag[M] though marked is not very great. The latter, which has a small cairn, is 3,011 feet, and should really be considered a subsidiary peak of the former, although it is named on all the maps, which the former is not.'[14]

---

[9] See Munro 27. Druim nam Bo was deleted in the 1921 Tables, but Carn Ban Mor and Meall Dubh-achaidh retained their status as separate mountains.

[10] See Munro 36, p. 236. Despite these negative comments, the Monadh Liath hills retained their status in the 1921 Tables, except for the lower top of Carn Ballach, which was eliminated by James Gall Inglis.

[11] See Munro 42. Plainly Munro was not sufficiently moved by Stob na Doire's 'fine isolation', nor by Stob Coire Raineach's 'considerable dip' to worry about their status in his Tables.

[12] See Munro 45. Bidein an Eoin Deirg was demoted to Top in the 1921 Tables.

[13] See Munro 51, p.117. Carn Bhinnein was demoted to Top in the 1921 Tables.

[14] *ibid.*, p. 118. In 1921, Mam nan Carn remained a Top and Beinn Iutharn Beag was demoted to Top.

15. 'To the north-north-east[15] of [Bynack More] is a shapely little top of some 3,400 feet, with however only a slight depression between it and Caiplich[M], as the highest summit (3,574 feet) of Ben Bynac is called. . . A' Choinneach[M] is a long flat-toppoed shoulder with sufficient dip between it and Bynac to constitute it a top, but with certainly none of the characteristics of a distinct mountain.'[16]

16. 'Although the dip between the Drochaid Glas[T] and Stob Diamh[M] is not very great, I am still of the opinion that the latter summit is worthy to be reckoned a separate mountain, not only on account of its distance from the main peak of Cruachan, but because it forms a distinct centre from which three ridges radiate, two of which constitute the well-known Dalmally Horse-shoe.'[17]

[Finally, amongst the various notes to the 1921 Tables which are attributed to Munro, only one – apart from those which are repetitions of notes to the 1891 Tables – is relevant. The note applies to Glas Leathad Beag, Centre Top[T] (Ben Wyvis) and consists simply of a height, 3030 feet, and the remark 'almost a separate mountain'.]

---

[15] I presume that this is a typo for 'north-north-west'. At any rate Bynack Beag is plainly intended. Bynack Beag had no status until 1981, when it became a Top.

[16] See Munro 62. Despite Munro's disparagement of A' Choinneach, it remained a Munro in the 1921 Tables and lingered until 1981.

[17] See Munro 63.

4.3 Preface to the 1921 Tables

William N. Ling[1]

IT is much to be regretted that Sir Hugh Munro did not live to carry through the press this revised edition of his Tables, for which he had been collecting material for many years. As he always welcomed information on the subject, and had himself visited all the 3000-feet tops in Scotland except one or two, his knowledge of them was probably second to none.

Unfortunately, his revision was only partially completed at the time of his death, and no definite information has been found as to his views on many facts that had been brought to his notice. In these circumstances, it has been thought desirable simply to reissue the Tables substantially as he left them, leaving the debatable questions of inserting additional tops, or of deleting old ones, to be settled when more complete information is available.

The main revision of the Tables was carried out by the late Mr J.R. Young, in consultation with various members of the SMC, from –

(a) A card index[2] left by Sir Hugh Munro, on which he had recorded changes in classification, new tops, cancelled tops, and other notes.

---

[1] This note from President Ling introduces the first revision of Munro's Tables, published as part of the *SMC Guide, Volume I, Section A* in October 1921 – later editions of this clumsily-named book were given the title *General Guide*. The note is important because of its authoritative assessment of Sir Hugh's contribution to this revision – see my discussion of this question in Chapter 4.8

[2] The Card Index is in the National Library: *NLS Acc. 11538* item 117.

(b) A list – prepared for Sir Hugh by Mr A.W. Peacock – of the many alterations made in the O.S. maps subsequently to the first publication of the Tables. The latest available maps were the Revised six-inch Survey of about 1897 onwards, and the Second Revision of the one-inch Survey, of about 1904-1907. The nature of these changes will be found on page 115.[3]

The re-classifications of the new tops, cancelled tops, and separate mountains are all from Sir Hugh's card index, with only a few exceptions; but the sequence of the individual tops has been considerably modified by the replacement of many 'contour' heights by 'approx.' heights, gleaned from the *SMC Journal*, the hill-shaded 1-inch O.S. maps, and other sources mentioned in the footnotes, by Mr J.G. Inglis. He has also rearranged the individual tops under their respective 'separate mountains', has prepared an alphabetical index, and has revised the 'Position' and 'Best Ascended From' columns.

The Scottish Mountaineering Club takes this opportunity of thanking Sir Hugh Munro's executors for handing over to the Club for publication his card index, and other papers relating to the Tables. The many gentlemen who gave assistance in the revision of the Tables are also thanked for their help.

W.N. LING, President, Scottish Mountaineering Club, September 1921.

---

[3] These revised Tables were produced by James Gall Inglis, whose thrilling account of the misbehaviour of 'Aneroid Barometers' may be enjoyed below. His meticulous approach made him an ideal Master of the Tables, which role he filled until his death in 1939, and was also a hallmark of his family business, Gall & Inglis of Newington, which produced 'Contour Road Books' and 'Ready Reckoners'. His name does not figure in the published list of Munroists, but this is an inexcusable oversight: his obituary notice (by F.S. Goggs; *SMCJ* 1939, XXII, 140-141) reports that he climbed his last Munro, Meall a' Chrasgaidh, in 1938. This ascent is in the report of the Easter Meet on 15th April, so he is Munroist No. 6.

4.4 Notes on Munro's Tables

Ronald G. Burn[1]

HAVING climbed a number of out-of-the-way hills in Ross and Inverness, etc., and made systematic use of an aneroid, I enclose a few notes, which I trust, Mr Editor, you will think of sufficient interest to publish.

FANNICHS – The 2,750 contour between A' Chailleach and Sgurr Breac (3,286 by my aneroid) has long been more than suspected of possessing standard height. Its name is Tom Choinnich (round hill of the moss), and height, 3,131. Beinn Liath Mhor Fainich I made 3,137.

BEINN DEARG – Ceann Garbh of Meall nan Ceapraichean is the lowest of three summits, though its height alone seems to have been ascertained. The south top is highest

---

[1] *SMCJ* 1920, XV , 339-341. These notes may not have been in time for consideration by J. Gall Inglis, Master of the 1921 Tables. However, it is remarkable how little notice was taken of them in successive revisions. Since 1981, however, some of Burn's suggestions have been taken up, though it may be doubted whether these changes owe much to Burn's advice!

(3,192), and there is 80 feet dip to the mid top (3,177), so that Ceann Garbh (3,063) is actually the lowest top. But the mid top seems the least important.

Visiting Munro, two or three months before his death, I went right through his own copy of the Tables; and one remark, pencilled against hill 116, struck me. It was that Douglas had discovered a peak on Mullach Coire Mhic Fhearchair, but no height was given. The name of the peak I have found to be Tom Choinnich, and height 3,229. This peak shows best from Sgurr Ban, and it lies east by south of the Mullach. It should certainly be included. A' Mhaighdean I make 3,140.

Talking about Munro's own copy, I might here insert that he had been told that Foinaven (Eriboll district) was over 3,000 feet. I have been lucky enough to secure Heddle's *Geological Map of Sutherland* (1881), and there, sure enough, the hill is marked 3,013, the top lying east by north of 2,980 (trig. pt.) of the new 1-inch O.S. and named Ganu Mor on both maps. Presumably this is an aneroid height, though not so marked.

Carn Gorm Loch of Stravaich was also pencil-noted as over 3,000 – I make it 3,010. Its south-west neighbour Faochag (misnamed Am Fraochagach in the Tables, following O.S.) has a south top 3,010, perhaps worth inclusion. I suspect that Meall Gorm near by to south-east is also of standard height, but lacked time to investigate.

BEINN EIGHE – Spidean Coire nan Clach, the finest peak on the ridge and the hinge on which all the rest turn, is certainly a separate mountain. It is the second highest of the range (3,275) and I suggest that Ruadh Stac Mor (and possibly Sail Mor) be reckoned as the Munros of this range. The next 3,000 top to Spidean is Mullach a' Choinnich Mhoir (top of the big moss, 3,030 in the Tables), and its west summit is perhaps 3,185.

LIATHGHAICH – The most easterly peak is called Stuc a' Choire Dhuibh, without the addition of Bhig. It is 3,001. Next is Bidein Toll a' Bheathaich (peak of the hole of the [herd or flock] beast), not a' Mhuic (3,136). If Creag Dhubh a' Choire Leith must be included, it is 3,191. Perhaps Spideanan nam Fasairinen (3,060) should be a separate hill, as the ridge to Mullach na Rathain is long and contains a shoulder of some small importance – Coinneach an Tuill Bhain (moss of the white hollow, 3,200).

The top between Beinn Fhionnlaidh and Carn Eite (not Eige – see W.J Watson's *Place-Names of Ross*), at the head of Glen Cannich, called in the Tables Coire Lochain Top, is named Friamhnach (the rooty hill ?), but it does not deserve to be in the Tables at all.

AFFRIC – The small top between Sgurr na Lapaich of Glen Affric and Mam Sabhal (not Sodhail) is called Mullach Cadha Rainich. The ridge running parallel from Ciste Dubh (nearly) contains an equally dubious mid top (nameless), 3,482. It ends in a 3,500 contour, requiring insertion, whose name is Sugh Doire Mor, not An Tudair, ?arising from An t-Sugh Doire misheard. I make the height 3,497 or even less, and this after doubly-checked reading. Coire Coulavie (*i.e.*, cul na fiadh=deer's food) Top should be deleted. The new map quite rightly gives no name to the 3,462 top, as the name Creag a' Chaorruinn applies to its south-east heel.

Only one peak of the Taigh Mor massif needs inclusion – the 3,285 one, plus the 3,045 top named Tom a' Choinnich and Sail Chaorruinn (3,040).

Aonach Mheadhoin of Sgurr a' Bhealaich Dheirg should be omitted. It is almost invisible.

The name Ceum na h-Aon Choise (on Beinn Fhada) does not belong to any top, nor is it anywhere near even a 2,000 contour. The place is a low gully of Coire Garbh at about 1,000 contour west of Sgurr a' Choire Ghairbh. If it is to have a name, it can only be Plaide Mhor top (3,140). But more prominent than this round end of the beautiful grass blanket that stretches west from the summit of Beinn Fhada, is the top above Bealach an t-Sealgaire and to east of it (3,020). It is worth inclusion and so, too, is the top south by east of the 3,383 summit (nameless, and not easy to find a name – ?West Top of Sugh Doire).

No amount of trying to 'cook' my aneroid results would allow more than 2,973 to Faochag=the whelk (not Fraochag) of Sgurr na Sgine (Glen Sheil), despite the map's 3,000 contour. But I fear the contour will secure this peak's place in the Tables.

Gurr Thionail of Sgurr a' Mhoraire (not Mhaoraiche), Glen Quoich, 3,065 by aneroid (2,750 contour), is offered as a prospective candidate. It looks higher than Am Bathaiche (3,045) both from that peak and from the main hill. (Query:– may not Sgurr a' Chlaidheimh be over 3,000 feet?

On the other hand, Meall an Teanga of Loch Lochy should be deleted: I make it 2,991.

LOCH LAGGAN – Beinn a' Chlachair has an important north-east top which ought to be included (3,138).[2]

Between Creag Mhoir and the head of Coir' Arder are some bumps divided between 1 and 6 inch maps. None need inclusion. Uinneag Coire a' Chaorruinn (3,180) should go, and perhaps Meall a' Ghoire (peak 345).

Geal Charn Mor (255) is the true name of the south-west outlier of the Monadhliaths.

CAIRNGORMS – The Loch (not Lochan) nan Cnapan top of the Tables is named Cnapan Alasdair Mhoir – Ian Alasdair Mor having been the grandfather of Finlay Macintosh, who has just removed to Loch Ericht, after spending twenty years in Glen Feshie.

On Sgarsaich Mhor (not An Sgarsoch), famed for its still visible market-stance, are two tops to the east and south. The east one is in Tables, the south is 3,178. Either both should be deleted or both shoulders retained.

Càrn Bhac of Fealar should be Carn a' Bhathaiche (byre-like stony hill).

Meall Gorm of Glas Maol is not worth its place in the Tables, and still less is Druim Mor, a mere fence turn on a uniformly rising ridge. Not so Creag Leachdach of Fafernie (3,150).

Sron a' Chadha No (3,338) of Cairngorm is no top, for the col is very small.

---

[2] This is a very justifiable observation which has unaccountably been ignored by recent editors of Munro's Tables.

LOCHNAGAR – Perhaps the south-west top of Creag a' Ghlais Uillt (3,476) is worth insertion and Stuc Eoin (3,571).

Beinn a' Chaorruinn Bheag (Glen Derry) seems, perhaps, a dubious top, and Bynac Beag to north-west of Caplaich is, though a poor thing, a genuine top – not so the 3,400 point, north by east. Bynac Beag is 3,191.

4.5 Munro's Tables - Two Contrasting Views

1. John Dow[1]

AT THE GENERAL MEETING there was some criticism of the proposal to reprint unaltered in the new edition of the General Guide Book the Munro List of Mountains and Tops, one member alleging inconsistency in the combination of a revised Guide Book with unrevised Munro's Tables. As noted on p. iii of Section II of the 1933 edition, Sir Hugh's untimely death did not permit him to complete his task, and it is not unreasonable to assume that, had he lived, he would himself have removed a number of the anomalies which are obvious to anyone who has visited all the listed heights, including the 'Tops'. It is of course true, as the Guide Book Editor remarked, that general agreement as to what constitutes a 'Munro' and what a 'Top', apart from the 3,000 feet requirement, could not be obtained. Sir Hugh himself attempted no exact definition, and my own view, for what it is worth, is that each doubtful case would have to be decided on its merits after careful examination of the ground; the contour lines shown on the Ordnance Survey Map are not always infallible!

In a previous article[2] I suggested that the important factors to consider are distance, dip and difficulty, which can be roughly judged by time taken from point to point. On my journeys I always kept a record of times, and after giving due weight to all these points I submit a list of summits which, in my opinion, might fairly be added to the roll of separate mountains as being at least as well defined as many of the heights already included in the total of 276. All of these were entered in the Tables as Tops, with the exception of Beinn Tarsuinn in Section 11.

I might add that most people who have completed the traverses would probably agree that Buachaille Etive Mor, Bidean nam Bian, Liathach, Beinn Eighe and An Teallach could fairly be described as mountain ranges rather than as single peaks with outliers.[3]

Effectively to revise the list of 267 Tops would be a much more difficult proposition, as deletions as well as additions would be involved. In any case the necessary space is not available in this issue of the Journal.

---

[1] *SMCJ* 1949, XXIV, 118-122.

[2] 'Munros, Beards and Weather', Chapter 3.4 above.

[3] Dow's suggestions for promotion have a familiar ring to us today, apart from the very last one! Since his criteria of *dip* and *distance* (to Am Basteir) are absolutely trivial, Dow must have had *difficulty* in mind in designating Bhasteir Tooth as a Munro. It is an interesting historical question whether it was the difficulty of reaching Cuillin tops that persuaded Munro to designate 9 of them as mountains in 1891 and to add Am Basteir, Sgurr a' Mhadaidh and Sgurr Mhic Choinnich in 1921. It may be that it was simply distinctness of mountain form (of which difficulty is occasionally a consequence) that moved him. Certainly, if Dow's suggestion had been adopted, then it would have been soon followed by claims for Crowberry Tower (Buachaille), the Great Tower (Ben Nevis), etc.

Dow's suggestions for promotion to Munro status

Section 3.	Feet
An Stuc (Ben Lawers group)	3,643
Beinn nan Eachan, W. Top (Tarmachan group)	3,265

Section 4.	
Stob na Doire (Buachaille Etive Mor)	3,250
Stob na Broige (Buachaille Etive Mor)	3,120
Stob Coire Raineach (Buachaille Etive Bheag)	3,029
Stob Coire nan Lochan (Bidean nam Bian)	3,657
Beinn Fhada, Stob Coire Sgreamhach (Bidean nam Bian)	3,497

Section 7.	
Garbh Cioch Mor (Sgurr na Ciche, Knoydart)	3,365
Am Bathaich (Sgurr a' Mhaoraich)	3,055

Section 8.	
Sgurr nan Carnach (Sgurr Fhuaran)	3,270
Stuc Mor (Sgurr nan Ceathreamhnan)	3,496
Sgurr na Lapaich (Mam Soul)	3,401

Section 9.	
Creag Dubh (Carn nan Gobhar)	3,102
Bidean an Eoin Deirg	3,430

Section 10.	
Tom na Gruagaich (Alligin)	3,021
Mullach an Rathain (Liathach)	3,358
Meall Dearg (Liathach)	3,150
Sail Mhor (Beinn Eighe)	3,217
Spidean Coire nan Clach (Beinn Eighe)	3,220
Creag Dubh (Beinn Eighe)	3,050

Section 11 .	
Beinn Tarsuinn	3,080
Glas Meall Mhor (An Teallach)	3,176
Sgurr Fiona (An Teallach)	3,474
Sail Liath (An Teallach)	3,100

Section 12.	
Glas Leathad Beag (Centre Top)	3,007

Section 14.	
Carn Eas	3,556
Creag an Leth Choin, S. Top	3,448
Sgor an Lochan Uaine	4,095

Section 15.	
Beinn Iutharn Beag	3,121
Carn Bhinnein	3,006

Section 17.	
Bhasteir Tooth	3,000

Bidean nan Bian, one of three Glen Coe mountains to achieve double-Munro status in the 1997 revision of the Tables

2. E.C. Thomson

A General Guide Book Sub-Committee has recommended that Munro's Tables be republished without alteration, and the Club has endorsed this recommendation. In my view the decision is a wise one. It has been argued against it that Munro was not infallible. We revise 'Goudie' on the Law of Bankruptcy or Grove's Dictionary of Music, why not Munro's Tables? They would still be Munro's Tables. And certainly, if the whole country were thoroughly re-surveyed and substantial differences in heights discovered, something would have to be done about it. Or if a sound scientific principle were laid down which truly reflected the complexities of mountain structure and stood up to the criticisms of geographers and statisticians, as well as the mere mountaineer, some valuable progress might be made. But such a task would be very difficult and, so far as I know, has never been seriously attempted.

Munro simply attempted to enumerate the 'separate mountains' and 'tops' over 3,000 feet in height, viewing the matter very objectively and recognising that a 'separate mountain' might be a simple, single formation like Schiehallion or a complex structure with twin peaks and a lot of subsidiary tops like Bidean nam Bian. When we consider that ranges, peaks of ranges, separate mountains, peaks of separate mountains, subsidiary tops on ranges, subsidiary tops of mountains, plateaus, ridges, shoulders and what you will are all reduced to the common denominators of 'separate mountains' and 'tops', we must realise that there are bound to be anomalies, and the less we worry about them the better. In my view Sir Hugh only went seriously astray when he allowed his common sense to be overruled by the fear that an anomaly would arise if he counted Braeriach and Cairn Toul as two mountains and Ben Cruachan as only one. He, therefore, split Ben Cruachan into a western and an eastern mountain because the dips and distances were rather similar to an example in the Cairngorms.[4] To my mind there is no comparison between the well-defined, compact mass of Ben Cruachan, falling, on all sides, apart from a narrow neck, for practically 100 per cent. of its total elevation, and the wide plateau above the Garbh-Choire, losing only one-third of its elevation to the Lairig Ghru.

But let that be. Until we can agree on an accurate scientific principle, let us stick to Sir Hugh as the commonly accepted yardstick.

---

[4] See 'Munro on Definition', Chapter 4.2 above.

4.6 Some Observations on 'Munro's Tables'

Robert M. Gall Inglis[1]

THE EDITOR of the 1933 edition of 'Munro's Tables', in his suggestions for a subsequent revision, proposed that a beginning might be made by casting out unworthy 'tops'. The present Guide Books General Editor, who is responsible for the new edition shortly to be published, ventures, by tabulating and applying data on Sir Hugh Munro's Card Index relative to the Appendix of Reductions and Deletions which follows the Tables (which changes were in the main Sir Hugh's own recommendations), to suggest, first of all, a basis on which unworthy 'tops' might be judged; and at the same time, by comparing this data with other hitherto unpublished notes on the original Card Index, to see if an indication may be obtained as to what may have been in Sir Hugh's mind when he made these notes toward what, as is stated in the Preface to the 1921 edition (quoted in subsequent editions), was 'his revision, for which he had been collecting material for many years'.

That there are seeming anomalies in 'Munro's Tables' cannot be doubted, for example:–

(a) The inclusion of Carn Ban, Monadhliaths, as a 'separate mountain',between which and its *higher* neighbour, Carn Dearg, only 5/8 mile distant, there is a maximum possible drop of only 150 feet.

(b) The classification as 'tops' of Stob Coire Raineach of Buachaille Etive Beag, Am Bathaich of Sgurr a' Mhaoraich, Mullach an Rathain of Liathach, each with a drop of between 450 and 500 feet from their immediate neighbouring 'top'. Compare these 'tops', and Stob

---

[1] *SMCJ* 1953, XXV, 132-136.

na Broige of Buachaille Etive Mor, with Stob Diamh of Ben Cruachan (drop 475 feet), Beinn Ghlas of Lawers (drop 400 feet), and Geal Charn of Sgoran Dubh (drop 170 feet), which, although also 'ridge tops', with similar or much less dip, are counted as 'separate mountains' in the Tables.

(c) The inclusion of many 'tops' which are but rising eminences in a ridge, or flat outlying shoulders, having less than 50 feet of dip between them and their neighbouring higher top or summit. Such are: Mam Coire Easain and Stob a' Choire Ghlais of Clachlet, Sron a' Cha No on Cairngorm, and many others.

That 'dip 'was a relevant factor in the 1921 revision of the Tables is indicated by notes on 'dips' on the cards of the following 'tops' deleted from the original Tables. The first three are Sir Hugh's own notes; the fourth, that of Mr J.R. Young, editor of the 1921 edition:–

	Dip per Map	Card Index Note
Beinn a' Chuirn	270 feet	'Rise 242 feet. Delete.'
Beinn a' Chaoruinn, Middle Top	94 feet	'Rise on either side 27 feet and 84 feet.'
Leachd Riach	99 feet	'Drop only 26 feet.'
Beinn Creachan, Top of Coire Dubh	95 feet	'Rise only 43 feet.'

A distance factor was also suggested by the editor of the 1933 edition, but it seems doubtful if Sir Hugh intended this to be taken into consideration, since Sgurr na Lapaich of Mam Soul, two and a half miles along a ridge, was relegated from an original 'separate mountain' to a 'top'.

TOPS PROMOTED TO BE SEPARATE MOUNTAINS

	Section.	Dip per map.
Na Gruagaichean	5	342 feet
Meall na Teanga	7	1000+ feet

SEPARATE MOUNTAINS REDUCED TO TOPS.

	Section.	Dip per map. (feet)
Beinn a' Chuirn	3	270
Beinn Iutharn Bheag	15	371
Bidean an Eoin Deirg	9	280
Carn Bhinnein	15	206
Carn Eas	14	106
Creag Dubh	9	352
Creag na Dala Moire	14	239
Creag na Leth Choin	14	198
Glas Mheall Mor	15	287
Meall a' Chaoruinn	15	104
Sgor Choinnich	5	290
Sgor an Lochan Uaine, Cairntoul	14	300
Sgurr na Lapaich, Mam Soul	8	401

TOPS DELETED FROM THE TABLES

	Section.	Dip per map. (feet)
An Socach, Ben Wyvis	12	50
Beinn a' Chaoruinn, Middle Top	6	94
Beinn na Socaich, Stob Coire Easain	5	99
Big Brae, Ben Avon	14	125
Blaven, S. top	17	81
Carn Ballach, S.W. Top	6	59
Creag a' Bhraghit	1	75
Creag Meaghaidh, East Top	6	50
Cruach Ardrain, N.E Top	1	50
Druim na Bo	14	55
Leachd Riach	14	99
Sron dha Murchdi	3	50
Sron a' Ghaothair	6	50
Top between Cruach Ardrain and Stob Garbh	1	84
Top of Coire Dubh, Beinn Creachan	3	95

FURTHER NOTES FROM SIR HUGH MUNRO'S CARD INDEX

	Section.	Dip per map.	Sir Hugh Munro's Comments on Relative Card.
Stob Diamh, Cruachan	4	472 ft.	It is a question if Cruachan should be reckoned as two separate mountains.
Stob an Cul Coire, Aonach Mor	5	250 ft.	Should this not be a separate mountain? (Dip 180 feet. J. R. Corbett.)
Carn Sgulain, Monadhliaths	6	115 ft.	Very doubtful separate mountain.
Beinn Fhionnlaidh, Carn Eige	8	594 ft.	Doubtful separate mountain.
An Coileachan, Fannaichs	11	515 ft.	Is this a separate mountain?
Meall Gorm, N.W. summit	11	359 ft.	Is this a separate mountain?
Creag Leacach	16	238 ft.	Should this be a separate mountain?
Carn Dearg Mheadhonach	5	73 ft.	Doubtful top. (Dip 73 feet: 6-inch O.S. Map; 75 to 85 feet on several occasions. R.G.I.)
Carn Beag Dearg	5	50 ft.	Doubtful top. (Dip 15 to 25 feet on several occasions. R.G.I.)
Creag Mhor, Creag Meaghaidh	6	50 ft.	Doubtful top. (Dip 16 feet: 6-inch O.S. Map.)
Creag a' Coir' Aird, East Top	8	50 ft.	Is this a top? (Dip 15 to 20 feet. J. Dow.)
Bhraigh a' Choire Bhig, Sgurr na Lapaich	9	50? ft.	Not a very good top. (O.S. contours doubtful. R.G.I.)
Ruadh na Spreidhe, Sgurr na Lapaich	9	50 ft.	Not a very good top.
Creag a' Chaoruinn, Sgurr na Lapaich	9	295 ft.	Not a very good top, but to be counted.
Fiacaill Coire Cas, Cairngorm	14	50 ft.	This is a doubtful top.
Beinn Mheadhoin, S.W. Top	14	150 ft.	A very doubtful top.
Beinn Bhreac, West Top	14	95 ft.	Doubtful top. (Dip 50 feet. J.R. Corbett.)
Stob Bac an Fhurain, Ben Avon	14	133 ft.	Consider if this new top should be counted.

NOTE.-'Dip', as quoted, is the maximum approximate drop between the eminence named and its immediately neighbouring summit or top), as indicated by the 1-inch O.S. Map (Popular Edition) contours. These contours, although admitted to be only approximate, prove, by observations, both visual and by aneroid, to be reasonably accurate in the great majority of cases, and for the purposes of this article, the figures quoted may be so considered. Notes in brackets are later observations, not on cards.

A study of the foregoing tables indicates the virtual impossibility of inferring what was in Sir Hugh's mind as to the qualification of a 'Separate Mountain' as distinct from a 'Top' in his intended revision, for why has he promoted Na Gruagaichean, which has an indicated dip of 350 feet between it and Binnein Mor, and yet degraded Beinn Iutharn Beag and Sgurr na Lapaich of Mam Soul, with dips of 370 feet and 400 feet respectively? His notes on the cards of Beinn Fhionnlaidh (Carn Eige), and An Coileachan, Fannaichs, make the issue even more confused.

In view of this, and the statement in the Preface to the 1921 Tables regarding the impossibility of deciding what should be 'separate mountains,'the writer suggests that, despite seeming anomalies, such as those quoted earlier in this article, their claims to higher status be passed over, and that in any future revision of the Tables, the 'Separate Mountains' of the 1933 and 1953 editions be left unchanged.

But when the list of approximate dips of the deleted 'tops' in the Appendix is similarly considered, we are on surer ground. Every one, with the exception of Big Brae, whose card bears no note in Sir Hugh's hand, has a maximum probable dip of less than 100 feet. The table, giving approximate dip according to the 1-inch O.S. Map (Popular Edition), and also hitherto unpublished comments by Sir Hugh Munro on the relative cards in his Index, seems to confirm this figure of 100 feet of dip as a probable basis of minimum qualification for a 'top' to be in Sir Hugh's mind.

On this basis, therefore, all 'tops' whose summit is enclosed by no, or only one, contour ring (indicating a maximum probable dip of 100 feet) *should* be considered unworthy of status. The writer estimates that some eighty tops in the Tables would be thus affected. However, in order not to be too drastic, he suggests that in any future official revision of the Tables that only 'tops' without any contour ring, which observation on the ground proves to have dip of 50 feet or less, and one-ring contour tops, which by observation are proved to have a dip of less than 50 to 75 feet, be *noted* as unworthy of inclusion as such, excepting 'tops' on ridges that involve good climbing or scrambling, such as the Coolin, and possibly Liathach, Teallach and Aonach Eagach.

The writer suggests, too, as stated in the Preface to the 1953 edition of 'Munro's Tables', that they, as an historic document, should be left as they are at present, and that any subsequent approved list of unworthy 'tops' be added under a separate heading to the existing Appendix.

It is hoped that this article may stimulate renewed interest in what is an intriguing problem, and that continued observations of the dips of the no, and one-ring, contour tops, as well as the heights of the numerous 'approximates', may be sent in to the writer, with a view to collecting evidence for consideration in subsequent editions of 'Munro's Tables'.

4.7 The Separation of Mountains . .

Frank F. Bonsall[1]

THERE is ample evidence that H.T. Munro thought deeply about the problem of selecting the separate mountains from his list of tops, but he has left us very little guidance on the principles underlying his solution. Perhaps his most explicit statement is in a note[2] where he justifies counting Stob Diamh in the Cruachan group as a separate mountain on grounds which include distance from the main peak, the intervening dip, and the structure of the group. By contrast, P. Donald, in the Introduction to his list of Hills in the Scottish Lowlands, gives an explicit rule for determining the tops that are not to be counted as separate hills: 'Tops are not more than 17 units from the main top of the hill to which they belong, where a unit is either $^1/_{12}$ mile measured along the connecting ridge or one 50-feet contour between the lower top and its connecting col.' But he qualifies the rule with 'except where inapplicable on topographical grounds.'

It seems to be generally agreed that it is not possible to give a satisfactory rule for determining the separate mountains among a list of tops. As in the somewhat analogous problem of determining the distinct species of living organisms, it is agreed that the only valid solution is a list acceptable to experts in the field. However, to abandon the problem in this way does not commend itself to a mathematician, and my purpose in this note is to suggest a simple explicit solution. I should say at once that the solution involves no mathematics.

It is clear that for our purpose the appropriate measure of separation of a point B from a point A is the time taken to walk from A to B; and we cannot do better than accept the Naismith rule to determine this time: 20 minutes for every mile of horizontal distance and 3 minutes for every 100 feet of ascent. I denote this Naismith time by $t(A => B)$ minutes, so that $t(A => B)=20d+3a$, where d is the horizontal distance in miles and a is the ascent in 100 feet units.

Our next step is to fix some arbitrary interval of time, say 30 minutes, that will be regarded as sufficient separation. Donald's rule then takes the following form. List the highest top as a separate mountain and call it A. Then regard all tops P with $t(A => P)$ less than 30 as subsidiary tops of A, which are not to be listed as separate mountains. Next, let B be the

---

[1] *SMCJ* 1973, XXX, 153-156.

[2] *SMCJ* 1903, VII, 298.

highest remaining top, list *B* as a separate mountain, find *B*'s subsidiary tops, and so on. This certainly is an effective rule, but it leads to some most unsatisfactory results. Walking along a ridge away from *A*, we pass over *P* which is a subsidiary top of *A*, and arrive at *Q* which is a separate mountain. But *Q* may be close to *P* and inferior to it (see Figure 1).

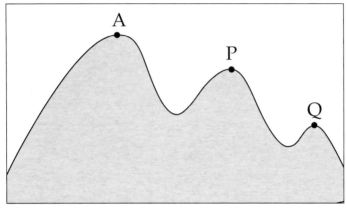

Figure 1

Again, if *A* has a massive top, an insignificant pimple *Q* on the flank of *A* may qualify as a separate mountain (see Figure 2).

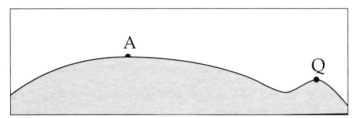

Figure 2

Common sense leads us to reject *Q* In both cases. No doubt it was the recognition of results like these that caused Donald to qualify his rule and persuaded others to abandon hope of a satisfactory rule.

The key to my proposed solution is to consider the separation of a top from *all higher ground* rather than from higher tops. Thus if we still regard 30 minutes as the appropriate separation, I propose to list a top *P* as a separate mountain if it is not possible to walk to *P* from any higher ground in less than 30 minutes. The number 30 here has been chosen arbitrarily, and I shall indicate how an appropriate number can be chosen.

The proposed rule does not suffer from the defects that we have noted in Donald's rule. It also has the merit that the listing of a top as a separate mountain does not depend on decisions made about other tops.

In detail the procedure is as follows. We take a list of tops, for example Munro's list of 545 tops (including Beinn Tarsuinn). For each top *P*, other than the highest, we determine a number which I call the *separation* of P and denote by s(P). We find s(P) by finding the minimum of t(X => P) for all points X that are higher than P. In other words s(P) is the least number of minutes in which we can walk to P from higher ground. We now arrange the list of tops in order according to their separations. We put the highest top at the head of the list, then the top with the greatest separation, then the top with the second greatest separation, and so on. Finally we decide how many separate mountains we wish to have, and take that number from the beginning of our list. For example, if we decide that 277 is an excellent number of separate mountains, we take the first 277 from our ordered list.

The calculation of s(P) sounds formidable, but in reality there is little difficulty. Firstly, we need only consider those points X that lie on the boundary of the ground higher than P, because to walk to P from any higher ground we must pass through such a point X. Secondly, there will usually be at most three significant ridges running from P, and so we shall need to measure t(X => P) for at most three points X, and very often for only one. Moreover it would suffice to do a very rough preliminary measurement of s(P) for all tops P and reserve careful measurement for the borderline cases. The last few difficult cases could well be settled by practical experiment with stopwatch and aneroid.

I have not carried out even a rough determination of the separations of Munro's tops. However, I suspect that if we selected a list of 277 mountains by this rule, most of Munro's list of separate mountains would remain unchanged, but a few familiar injustices would be put right. For example, Liathach might become two mountains, Beinn Eighe three, while Carn Ghluasaid (Cluanie), Meall Dubhag (Cairngorms), and Carn Ban (Monadh Liath) might be deleted.

Very rough measurements for Section 1 of Munro's Tables[3] carried out on a well worn one-inch map give complete agreement in the sense that the 18 Munros are also the 18 tops with the greatest separations. Most of the Munros have very large separations, only Beinn a' Chleibh (s(P)=27) and Beinn Tulaichean (s(P)=29) having separations less than 45. Among the remaining tops the greatest separation is for Meall na Dige (s(P)=24). Section 1 may be exceptional in that most of the mountains have very simple structures.

For comparison, I have carried out similar rough measurements for Section 10[4], where the mountains have much more complicated structures. Here again the 6 Munros are also the 6 tops with the greatest separations, the least separation being s(P)=52 for Beinn Liath Mhor. However in this section there are 4 other tops with quite high separations:—Spidean Coire nan Clach (s(P)=49) and Sail Mhor (s(P)=45) on Beinn Eighe, Mullach an Rathain (s(P)=38) on Liathach, and Tom na Gruagaich (s(P)=30) on Beinn Alligin.

When more accurately surveyed maps of the Scottish Highlands become available, presumably with the heights given in metres, it will become appropriate to construct new tables of tops and separate mountains. I would suggest that these tables should list

---

[3] Old Section 1.

[4] Old Section 10 (now 13).

mountains over 900 metres in height. To choose 1000 metres would throw away too many good mountains; 900 metres, being a little less than 3000 feet, would bring in some fine new ones.[5]

It is my hope that this note will provoke discussion of the principles on which these new tables should be constructed.

. . and the Separation of Munros

Frank F. Bonsall[6]

MY purpose is to report the results of a rough measurement of the separations of the tops in Munro's Tables, carried out on the one-inch O.S. maps. It may be recalled[7] that the separation $s(P)$ of a top P is defined to be the least number of minutes taken to walk to P from higher ground, and that it is crucial that we determine $s(P)$ with reference to all other higher ground and not merely other tops. The best way to measure $s(P)$ would be to record the walking times of a large number of walkers of varying weights and ages. Lacking such records, we must use maps, and, at least for the mountains on the Scottish mainland, we are not likely to do serious injustice by using the familiar Naismith rule to estimate walking time. For a large part of the Highlands it would now be possible to measure the separations accurately on the revised six-inch and 1:10,000 maps. However, the present report is based on measurements on the one-inch maps, occasionally supplemented by larger scale maps when the one-inch map is excessively obscure or plainly erroneous, as for example with Buachaille Etive Beag. Since the measurement of the separation of the Cuillin tops involves special problems, the following remarks apply only to sections 1 to 16 of Munro's tables.

My main finding is a remarkable agreement between theory and practice, as represented by measured separation and Munro's selection of his separate mountains. In each of the eight sections 1, 2, 3, 5, 10, 13, 15, 16, each Munro has a greater separation than each non-Munro.[8] In nine sections, all Munros have separations of at least 26, and in eight sections all non-Munros have separations less than 26. Altogether, I find only seven Munros with separations less than 23, and only twelve non-Munros with separations greater than 30. These nineteen exceptional tops are listed in Tables 1 and 2 below.

The seven rather miserable Munros in Table 1 all occur as minor protuberances on bulky mountains or plateaus. The wooden spoon is won by Carn Ban in the Monadh Liath with a separation of 14 measured on the one-inch map. This was confirmed on the ground last summer with a walking time of 16 minutes.

---

[5] This suggestion of Professor Bonsall's was first made by Robin Gall Inglis in *SMCJ*, 1969, XXIX, 169. In the present volume it is also advocated by David Purchase. In my view it would be dangerous folly to break faith with Munro in such a radical fashion.

[6] *SMCJ* 1974, XXX, 254-256.

[7] See above.

[8] Bonsall is referring to Old Section numbers here.

The gold medal for the most separated non-Munro is won by Sgurr na Lapaich in Glen Affric. The omission of this fine mountain which dominates so much of Glen Affric, from the list of Munros is doubly strange, in that it was listed as a separate mountain in the 1891 edition of the tables.[9] Munro's intuition seems to have been least reliable in the roughest mountain regions. The main concentrations of well separated non-Munros occur in Glencoe and Torridon. On the present measurements, Buachaille Etive Mor and Beinn Eighe become mountain ranges, each with three well separated peaks. Buachaille Etive Beag and Liathach each have two well separated peaks.

Liathach, the great Torridonian mountain that gained a second Munro in the 1981 revision of the Tables

The Cairngorms include four Munros with very small separations and one non-Munro, Cairn Lochan, with a very large separation. One other non-Munro in the Cairngorms deserves special mention, namely Braeriach South Plateau. If this were accepted as a separate mountain it would become the fifth highest mountain in Scotland, and as such would surely deserve a better name. It would be very bold of me to propose a name, but the Wells of Dee lie close to its summit, and I am indebted to Mr W. Matheson[10] for the suggestion that, accordingly, an appropriate name would be Beinn an Fhuarain.

A brief inspection of a few of the new large scale maps has convinced me that the changes in the heights of mountains given by the new survey make a revised set of Tables necessary. For example, in that splendid tract of country between Loch Maree and

---

[9] Sgurr na Lapaich is a real Munro mystery. As Bonsall says, it has a large separation and it was included in the 1891 Tables. Munro had climbed it (see Chapter 1.3), so his decision to count it as separate was fully informed. And yet it was demoted to Top, presumably on Munro's recommendation, in the 1921 Tables!

[10] Reader in Celtic in the University of Edinburgh —FFB.

An Teallach there are two new 3000 ft. mountains, both of them well separated. These are Beinn a' Chlaidheimh (3000 ft.) and Ruadh Stac Mor (3013 ft.). The latter is the shapely peak nearly a mile northeast of A' Mhaighdean, and is therefore even more remote than that remote mountain. Many of us have admired Ruadh Stac Mor from a distance; the new survey shows that it is essential to stand on its summit.

Table 1: Munros with Separation less than 23

Section	Sep. Mt.	Top	Name	Separation
6	224	425	Carn Ban	14
8	126	234	Tigh Mor na Seilge (S.S.W. top)	21
8	194	366	Carn Ghluasaid	21
14	222	423	Carn Cloich-mhuillin	19
14	140	253	Meall Dubhag	20
14	75	145	Carn Ban Mor	18
14	265	511	Geal Charn	18

Table 2: Non-Munros with Separation more than 30

Section	Top	Name	Separation
4	269	Stob na Doire	40
4	389	Stob na Broige	37
4	499	Stob Coire Raineach	39
7	459	Am Bathaich	32
7	170	Sgurr na Lapaich	53
10	193	Mullach an Rathain	38
10	296	Sail Mhor	43
10	290	Spidean Coire nan Clach	48
12	437	Glas Leathad Beag (Centre top)	45
14	16	Cairn Lochan	44
14	6	Braeriach South Plateau	32
15	488	Glas Mheall Mor	31

4.8 Munro's Tables, 1891–1991

Robin N. Campbell[1]

IN THE YEAR of the centenary of publication of these Tables it is worth pausing to look back at the original list. In the eight editions that have appeared since 1891, much has been changed. However, there have only been two major revisions. The first of these was Munro's own revision, which appeared in 1921 when the Tables were published in Section A of the Club's Guide (known in later editions as the 'General Guide'). The second major revision occurred in 1981 when Jim Donaldson and Hamish Brown corrected several anomalies, possibly following the prescriptions of Frank Bonsall.[2] In the intervening period of 60 years the only changes made were consequent on changes in mapped heights and hill names. It is generally recognised that the 1981 revision was a substantive one: indeed Donaldson and

Brown have been castigated by many commentators for daring to tamper with the Holy Writ of Munro! However, it is not widely recognised that Munro's own revision was also substantive, involving an altered view of the significance of height in deciding what constituted a separate mountain. So my purpose in the present article is to establish the nature of the changes between 1891 and 1921 and to offer an account of the criteria operated by Munro.

Since Munro died in 1919, the 1921 Tables are posthumous. President Ling made the following observations in his Prefatory Note:-

'Unfortunately, [Munro's] revision was only partially completed at the time of his death, and no definite information has been found as to his views on many facts that had been brought to his notice. In these circumstances, it has been thought desirable simply to reissue the Tables substantially as he left them, leaving the debatable questions of inserting additional tops, or of deleting old ones, to be settled when more complete information is available.'

Before 1969, editions of the Tables were supplemented by clarifying Notes. While most of those in the 1921 edition were supplied by Munro, there are various other notes added. Fortunately these are clearly marked as 'foreign' additions and so it is reasonably easy to distinguish in this edition what is attributable to Munro and what is not. In the quotation from Ling the weasel word 'substantially' implies that there may have been some tampering after

---

[1] *SMCJ* 1991, XXXV, 21-27.

[2] See Chapter 4.7 above.

all, and this possibility is kept open later in Ling's Note, when he observes that 'the re-classifications of the new tops, cancelled tops, and separate mountains are all from Sir Hugh's card index, *with only a few exceptions.*' So it may be that the 1921 Tables are not quite the Holy Writ (Revised) of Munro. My own guess is that there was very little tampering, and that little rather unimportant. At any rate, subject to this small doubt, it is clear that the 1921 Tables represented Munro's view of what constituted a 3,000ft. mountain, just as did the 1891 Tables.

The 1891 Tables

Munro drew up these Tables at the Club's request between December 1889 and the summer of 1891. He was 33 years old: no doubt the vigour of youth was an essential tool for the job! His other tools were the O.S. One-Inch and Six-Inch sheets,[3] supplemented by advice from other climbers – notably Norman Collie and Colin Phillip – whose knowledge greatly exceeded his own. When he began to compile the Tables he had visited only 42 tops (counted from his Application Form and early articles in Volume I). The 3,000ft. tops are spread over thirty One-Inch sheets. The number of Six-Inch sheets to be consulted would obviously vary considerably, with a maximum of thirty-six per One-Inch sheet. An estimate of 600 maps in total would not be far off the mark. The two sheets provided quite different information: there were no contours on the Six-Inch; on the other hand, there were very few names and spot heights on the One-Inch. So Munro's effort was indeed heroic. That there were a number of anomalies and even a mistake or two in his Tables is hardly surprising. The surprising thing is that there were so few.

Three years ago I published a piece about Munro in the Journal in which I drew attention to the anomalous listing of the Inaccessible Pinnacle in the 1891 Tables. Although listed as higher than Sgurr Dearg and clearly marked as belonging to Sgurr Dearg, Sgurr Dearg summit is counted as the Munro, and the Pinnacle as a mere Top (I use Top with capital T to mean top that is not a Munro). What I did not realise at the time was that this type of anomaly was to be found elsewhere in the Tables. The anomaly may be defined as follows:–

1) Two tops are such that each is the nearest top to the other and one must be counted a Munro.

2) The lower top is designated as a Munro and the higher only as a Top.

In fact, as Table 1 shows, there are 8 such anomalies in the 1891 Tables. In the Table I have indicated the current name for each top where it is substantially different. The names of some tops are marked with an asterisk. This signifies that the top is named only on the Six-Inch sheet available in 1891. Absence of an asterisk means that the top is named on both One-Inch and Six-Inch sheets. Hereafter I shall use 'unnamed' and 'named' with these meanings. The heights given are those of the 1891 Tables and follow the conventions described on p. 278: that is, a plain height signifies that a height is given on both One-Inch and Six-Inch sheet and that these heights agree. If they disagree, or no spot height is given on the One-Inch, then the Six-Inch height is given first and the One-Inch height or contour is given in brackets. When no Six-Inch height is available, the One-Inch contour height is given, or an approximate height from members' own surveys.

---

[3] Examples of these sheets are shown on pages 96 and 97.

Table 1: 'Inaccessible Pinnacle' anomalies in the 1891 Tables

Case	Name	Height	Munro No.	Top No.	Section
1a.	Beinn Dheiceach (Beinn Cheataich)	3074	231	423	3
1b.	Meall Glas*	3139(3000)	-	363	
2a.	Meall Chuirn (Meall a' Churain)	3007	274	499	3
2b.	Sgiath Chuil*	3050ap	-	445	
3a.	Crom Leathad* (Stob Poite Coire Ardair, East Top)	3441	80	140	6
3b.	Creag an Lochan* (Stob Poite Coire Ardair, West Top)	3460(3250)	-	128	
4a.	Maoile Lunndaidh	3294	126	214	9
4b.	Creag Toll a' Choin* (deleted 1981)	3295(3250)	-	213	
5a.	Meall nan Ceapraichean*	3000c	282	529	12
5b.	Ceann Garbh*	3063(3000)	-	430	
6a.	Meall a' Chaoruinn (deleted 1981)	3004	279	509	15
6b.	Fuar Bheinn (A' Bhuidheanach Bheag)	3064(3054)	-	428	
7a.	Carn Bhac (Carn Bhac, S.W. Top)	3014	269	491	15
7b.	Top of Coire Bhousneag* (Carn Bhac, N.E. Top)	3098	-	402	
8a.	Sgurr Dearg (Ordnance Point)	3234	157	279	17
8b.	Sgurr Dearg (Inaccessible Peak)*	3250ap	-	256	

In Case 5 there is a qualified height for Meall nan Ceapraichean, namely 3000c. This means that neither map offered an exact height; the top is above the 3000ft. contour but below the 3250 contour. Obviously this presented Munro with a difficulty! Whether it is rightly regarded as an anomaly is debatable.

What common factors can be discovered in the 7 remaining anomalies? Cases 1, 2, 4, 7 and 8 share the feature that the Munro is named on both sheets while the Top is named only on the Six-Inch. In case 6, while the name Fuar Bheinn appears on both sheets Munro notes that 'The point of which the height is given is $1^{1}/_{4}$ mile N. by E. of the *name* Fuar Bheinn on the maps', so in fact the Top is not named on either sheet, strictly speaking. Case 8 is a special case, since Munro states in the Table introduction that he took Cuillin names from Pilkington's Map and approximate heights from Collie's aneroid measurements. In fact it is clear from examining the entries that he did this only when O.S. heights and names were unavailable. Reference to Pilkington's Map[4] shows a name for Sgurr Dearg Summit, but – despite being clearly indicated as a peak – the Inaccessible Pinnacle is *not* named, a surprising piece of modesty by its conqueror! So, strange as it might seem, it looks very much as if Munro took the presence of a name on the popular sheet as an important condition for a top to be considered a distinct and separate mountain, so much so that the presence of a neighbouring unnamed top – known to be higher – was disregarded. Case 3 remains unexplained.

This proposal is fairly extraordinary, since (I presume) whether or not a base map name was transferred to the One-Inch map rested entirely on the whim of the Ordnance Survey. It seems very odd that Munro should have taken the Survey's preferences into account, unless he was so pressed for time that he felt that, having to start somewhere, he might as well start there.

An obvious first question to ask about these anomalies is whether Munro applied this curious rule in every case where he might have done so. What must be examined are cases where we have two tops in proximity, the lower named and the higher unnamed, one of which must be deemed a Munro. Apart from the 8 anomalous cases, there are 3 which are not anomalous, shown in Table 2.

Table 2: Pairs of tops where an unnamed higher top is a Munro.

Name	Height	Munro No.	Top No.	Section
Geal-Charn*	3688(3500)	31	51	5
Aonach Beag	3646	41	64	5
Stob Coire an Laoigh*	3659(3500)	35	57	5
Stob Coire an Easain	3545	-	100	5
Aonach Meadhoin*	3284(3250)	131	221	8
Carn Fuaralach	3241	-	274	8

Munro had visited the first two of these cases and gives interesting explanations (where none are required) in the accompanying Notes, as follows. 'It will be seen that although unnamed and only a 3500 contour given on the One-Inch map, Geal Charn is the culminating point of the large range immediately to the N. of Ben Alder.' Although Stob Coire an Laoigh is not mentioned, 'It will be seen that although unnamed on the 1-inch map and only a 3750 contour given, Stob Coire Claurigh is the culminating point of the large portion of the Lochaber hills, of which Stob Coire an Easain appears on most maps as the most prominent.' Similar comments are offered about the unnamed Munros west of Lochnagar in Section 16. It is plain from these Notes that Munro was tempted to treat these cases anomalously. Only his personal acquaintance with the topography stayed his hand! There is no evidence that Munro had climbed Aonach Meadhoin, but he did visit Glen Affric, traversing to Glen Shiel, in 1889[5] and may well have examined the group from a

---

[4] This map is reproduced on page 219.

[5] See Chapter 1.2 above.

distance, since he enjoyed fine weather. These cases then, with the possible exception of Aonach Meadhoin, tend rather to support the view that Munro strongly favoured – even to the point of height anomaly – tops marked prominently on popular maps.

Although the 8 anomalous cases are evidence enough for my claim – since they are otherwise quite inexplicable – it is interesting to examine other aspects of the Table for supporting evidence. For example, we might expect Munro to apply a rather high criterion of *separation* when considering the 'promotion' of an unnamed top to Munro but a low criterion of separation when contemplating the 'demotion' of a named top to Top – a kind of banker's spread! Various measures of separation were discussed by Bonsall in the articles referred to: I have used his own measure – the Naismith time to walk to any higher ground.

Considering the named tops first, there are 306 of these in the Table and 59 of these are 'demoted' to Top. All but a handful have separations of 22 minutes or less. There is an obvious factor common to the remainder, which is that they are tops in mountain groups with distinct *range* names – Liathach, Beinn Eighe, An Teallach and Ben Wyvis. In each of these ranges there is no top with the same name as the range, and in none of them did Munro designate more than one Munro. Yet Mullach an Rathain of Liathach has a separation of 42, Sail Mhor of Beinn Eighe 52, Glas Mheall Mor of An Teallach 30 and Feachdach of Ben Wyvis 52. So Munro plainly considered that such ranges should have only one Munro, regardless of separation, and so the criterion applied has to be modified as follows: named Tops must have low separations unless they are tops of distinctly-named ranges. I am left with one exception, which is Braeriach South Plateau. This named Top has a very large separation of 44 or so, as noted by Bonsall, and does not belong to any distinctly-named range.

There are 232 unnamed tops in the Table and 36 of these were 'promoted' to Munro. Thirty of these have separations of 32 minutes or more. Of the remaining 6, one is the inexplicable case of Crom Leathad already mentioned and another is An Gearanach (Mamores). This latter top was visited by Munro in 1891 and reckoned to be at least 3250 ft., thus higher than neighbouring Stob Coire a' Chairn (3219). However, he was plainly unsure of himself and entered it in the Table as 3200ap. It may be that he made both tops Munros because of these uncertainties. However, the remaining four unnamed Munros seem to have rather low separations and for some reason the presumed 'banker's spread' has not been applied to them. These are Stob a Choire Mheadhonache, Sgor Choinnich (Corrour), Creag na Dala Moire (Ben Avon) and Sgor an Lochain Uaine (Cairn Toul). The last three were demoted to Top in the 1921 revision.

A final fascinating product of my scrutiny of these Tables is the discovery of a serious clerical or typographical error. In Section 8 An Socach is listed as Munro 283 and the following top, Creag a' Chaoruinn, is listed as Munro 265. Creag a' Chaoruinn has a separation so low that it is barely measurable, easily the worst Munro in the Table. However, the top-number for An Socach is 486 and for Creag a' Chaoruinn it is 127. Evidently the Munro-numbers are far too high. What happened was that the Munro-number of 283 belonged to the preceding top – the Ridge South of Creag a' Choire Aird, and the Munro-number of 265 belonged to An Socach. Most unfortunately, these two numbers had slipped down the page a notch somewhere in the process! So Creag a' Chaoruinn was a mere Top and the Ridge South of Creag a' Choire Aird was a Munro. These designations and numberings are listed correctly in Table II of the 1891 Tables, which of course nobody reads. So here is a further flaw in Robertson's traverse of the Munros. His notebooks show that he took the trouble to climb Creag a' Chaoruinn but neglected the worthy Ridge South of Creag a' Choire Aird! Robertson must have remedied this deficiency later, since he is credited with supplying an aneroid height for this top in the Notes to the 1921 Tables.

The 1921 Tables

The 7 certain anomalies in Table 1 were all set to rights in these Tables, showing that Munro had come to the view we share today, that where relative height and other criteria are in conflict, height wins! Several named Tops were added, resulting from the demotion of unworthy Munros, showing that he had narrowed the previous 'banker's spread' of 10 minutes or so. This narrowing of the spread was applied only to the lower end, since the only genuine promotion of a previously unnamed Top was Na Gruagaichean. The application of the distinctly-named range principle remained in place, unchallenged until the Donaldson and Brown reforms. Of course, it would have been impossible for Munro to persist with his enthusiasm for named tops, since – as a result of his own efforts – the Ordnance Survey had now added 76 named tops to their One-Inch maps, bringing the total of named tops to 382.

A Moral for Baggers

Given the considerable differences between Munro's and the present Tables, a question which often presents itself is what the intending bagger should climb. Some advocate completing the original Tables, on the grounds that only these hills carry the *imprimatur* of Munro. But against this we can be perfectly sure that Munro would have included the Fisherfield tops had he known that they were of adequate height, etc. Moreover, as I have shown, the 1921 Tables are very largely Munro's own revision. Only very minor changes were applied in the revisions of 1933, 1953, 1969 and 1974: so all of these lists carry the stamp of Munro too. Most baggers adopt the strategy of completing the Tables current at the time of their own round. This occasionally presents difficulties when a new edition of the Tables appears *en route*! This strategy, though very satisfactory from the commercial point of view of the Scottish Mountaineering Trust, suffers from the drawback that, to the bagger, the arbitrariness of his quarry is very evident, particularly in the case of the pursuit of Munros, rather than Tops. In truth, this arbitrariness is inevitable. I have demonstrated, I hope, that Munro himself changed his mind about what were Munros between 1891 and his death, and in quite a fundamental way. As he wrote in 1891 (p. 281), 'The decision as to what are to be considered distinct and separate mountains, and what may be counted as 'tops', although arrived at after careful consideration, cannot be finally insisted on.' So no bagger should submit to bureaucratic constraints imposed by Masters of the Tables or Clerks of the List. The individual bagger should choose whichever one of the published lists suits best, or better still, make up his own Table. After careful consideration, of course, and bearing in mind the recommendations of Mr Bearhop, or whoever! Finally, these ruminations suggest an alternative for the bagger too weary or aged to contemplate moving on from the Munros to the Tops. Climb all the demoted Munros!

4.9 On the Classification of Mountains: a graphical approach

David Purchase

1. Introduction

*"Of making many lists there is no end, and the climbing of all
the hills therein is a weariness of the flesh."*

Many have been the comments that the number of Munroists grows at an ever-increasing rate. What was once a trickle is now a flood. I note, for example, that a completion year as recent as 1989 puts me firmly in the first half of the list. Less frequently noted is that the publication of lists of mountains appears to be following the same pattern. What used to occur about once a decade now seems to happen at least once each year, with no sign of abating. The frustration is that each author devises his or her own criteria for entry, in order that the resulting list may differ from all others. And then, when the list is published, there is often no information which would enable the user to check the validity of the entries or test for omissions.

There are three objectives for the current work. The first is to summarise the approaches that have been used to draw up lists of hills. The second is to propose a set of criteria which could be used throughout the British Isles for the listing and classification of hills; and the last is to suggest what should, and should not, be changed in currently published lists. In doing this I would emphasise that I think historical precedent is just as important as the use of criteria based on topographical data. Also, it is highly desirable that a basis is adopted which can be consistently applied not only in the Highlands but also in the Scottish Lowlands and the rest of the British Isles. In order to address these objectives the article will start, after a few points of definition, with a description of published lists.

This article was first prepared and submitted for publication before the announcement of the 1997 revisions to *Munro's Tables* [1] and in ignorance of them. However for the current volume the editor suggested that comments on those changes should be incorporated. This I have done, though as will be seen it is sometimes necessary to refer also to earlier editions of the *Tables*. It is natural that an exercise of this type should concentrate on the

---

[1] *Munro's Tables and Other Tables of Lower Hills.* Revised by Derek A. Bearhop. 1997. SMT.

Munros themselves. The basis to be proposed divides those current Tops which might be worthy of promotion into two quite distinct groups – one group of four hills which qualify very marginally, and another of five hills which are far more clear-cut cases. (These numbers were eight and nine prior to the 1997 changes.) The former group are almost balanced by twelve Munros which just fail to qualify, and I shall propose that all these marginal examples are left unchanged, with just the Group of Five becoming eligible for full Munro status.

2. A few definitions

It is hardly surprising that different writers have used different terminology in their tables and lists. However the current discussion will be helped by a consistent usage throughout, and so I adopt the following definitions. (When describing a previous approach, the author's usage will be stated; but my own definitions will otherwise be used except in direct quotations.)

mountain	Any point which is regarded, on the criteria being considered, as a 'separate mountain' (e.g. a Munro). For emphasis 'separate mountain' is sometimes used but the meaning is unchanged.
top	Any point which does not qualify as a mountain but which is regarded, on the criteria being considered, as a 'subsidiary top'.
minor top	Any local high point which does not qualify as a mountain or top.
hill	Any local high point; that is, mountains, tops and minor tops are all hills.
summit	When it is necessary to refer explicitly to the location of the highest point of a hill, the word 'summit' is used. Summit can apply whatever the status of the hill in question. But in context the words 'mountain', 'top' and 'hill' will often be used to describe the highest point.
separation	the separation between two points is defined in distance and height, with a time derived from them. As this concept is used throughout the article, it is described more fully in the next section.
the Tables	Unless otherwise stated, 'the *Tables*' refers to *Munro's Tables*, but excludes the *Other Tables of Lower Hills*.

For consistency with modern Ordnance Survey (OS) mapping, when describing the proposed system all distances and heights are given in metric units. When referring to earlier works, the units used are as in the original, with converted values where needed. These conversions are accurate when this is critical to the discussion (for example, the minimum altitude for a Munro is 914.4m) and are then shown in square brackets [ ]. Frequently precision is not of the essence; for example, 500ft and 150m will often be regarded as equivalent (and then the converted value will be in normal parentheses).

Throughout the article the heights of Munros and Tops, and the separations derived from them, are taken from the 1997 edition of the *Tables*. If changes from the previously accepted heights are material then an appropriate comment is made.

3. A note on separation

The concept of the 'separation' between two points is used throughout the article, and so a short description follows. Some more detailed matters are deferred until a later section. Note that horizontal (map) distances are always given in miles or kilometres ('km') to one decimal place, whereas heights are in feet or metres ('m').

In considering the separation of a hill from its neighbour, it is convenient to start from the *lower* summit. The distance to any other (higher) point is measured *along the connecting ridge* even if a shorter route is available which involves little extra loss of height. The 'reascent' or the 'drop' (the terms are used interchangeably) is defined as the altitude of the hill, *minus* the altitude of the lowest bealach traversed along that connecting ridge.

Determining a required distance from the OS map to 0.1 km (the normal accuracy of a grid reference) is difficult in only a few cases. However the drop is less easy, as although there is often a height given for the summit of even minor hills it is much less common to have a value at the bealach. But in practice I have found that a careful inspection of the contour lines near the bealach enables a value for the drop to be derived which is usually accurate to 5m or so. For the purposes of classification this is quite adequate, especially if (as in the case of the system to be proposed) small errors cannot lead to the exclusion of the summit under consideration.

Historically, separations were measured from one summit to another. In his important contribution to the subject, Bonsall[2] introduced in 1973 the concept of measurement to the 'nearest higher ground'; that is, in practice, to the first point reached along a connecting ridge that has the same altitude as the summit in question. Using nearest higher ground has, of course, no effect on the drop but will always reduce the distance – sometimes trivially, but often by a substantial amount. An example is shown in Figure 1. So far as I can tell, Bonsall's concept has not been used in any published lists, even recent ones, but I shall use it in my own proposals.

It is sometimes useful to express a separation in *time*. This is calculated from the distance and drop using a walking speed of 4 km per hour, plus 1 minute for each 10m of ascent; no account is taken of terrain. The result is taken to the nearer minute. This formula is somewhat less onerous than Naismith's Rule, and has been chosen for its practical convenience (and, for many, its greater realism); however the separation in time is not essential in what follows, and Naismith's Rule or other formulae could be used without altering any conclusions.

---

[2] See Chapter 4.7, Part 1.

4. A survey of mountain lists in the British Isles

Munro's Tables

Any discussion of mountain classification must start with *Munro's Tables*. However my reference to these can be brief, as much fuller descriptions appear elsewhere in this volume.

Munro himself gave no definitions of separate mountains or subsidiary tops, stating only that each decision, *"although arrived at after careful consideration, cannot be finally insisted on"*. However, there is strong evidence (see, for example, Campbell[3]) that an important influence was whether the hill was separately named on the 1-inch OS maps published in the late nineteenth century. Indeed in eight cases this was taken, in the first publication in 1891, to the extreme of identifying a named point as the Munro and a nearby, *higher* but unnamed point as a top; removal of these anomalies was among a number of corrections planned by Munro and implemented posthumously in the first revision in 1921.

Interestingly, the editor of the 1933 edition, James Gall Inglis, though making only one change (other than to names) to the 1921 *Tables*, included a note *'for the next revision'* with a description of the conditions that he deemed appropriate for deciding whether a point is a 'top'. He proposed a drop of 75-100ft (say 25m) *'of decided gradient'* and with *'some kind of individuality'*. He added that three classes required special consideration even if not quite meeting these conditions; these were:

- The rising end of a long, fairly level ridge, from which the hillside falls steeply for a long distance;
- Spur tops, branching off main ridges and much lower than the other tops; and
- Plateau tops, great distances apart.

All of these are adequately catered for by the proposals to be put forward later.

Twenty years later his son Robert M Gall Inglis discussed the matter further.[4] He concluded (wrongly in my view) that when considering the retention or deletion of tops, Munro had regard only to drop and not to distance, and that in his later work Munro thought that a top needed a minimum drop of 100ft (30m). However Inglis suggested that existing tops with drops over 75ft should be retained.

In his second article,[5] Bonsall demonstrated that the limit for a Munro was *in practice* equivalent to a separation in time to the nearest higher ground of 30 minutes or more. (He used Naismith's Rule; at the pace used herein that time is about 35 minutes.) However there were, and are, plenty of anomalies in both directions.

It should be noted that, though the words 'mountain' and 'top' are often used in the *Tables* in the same sense as in this article, sometimes 'top' is used for 'hill', that is, for any listed point *including* separate mountains. In current usage, Top is capitalised when referring to a point listed in the *Tables*, though originally it was printed as "top".

---

[3] See Chapter 4.8

[4] See Chapter 4.6

[5] See Chapter 4.7, Part 2.

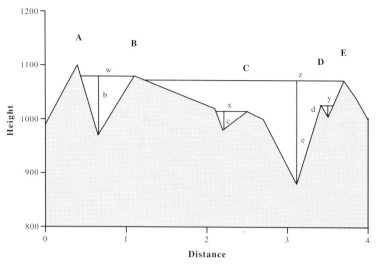

Figure 1 – Mountains, Tops and minor tops

The figure shows an outline of the elevation of a ridge comprising five hills, A to E, with A being assumed to be the highest in the neighbourhood. The 'reascent' components of the separations for B to E are indicated by b, c, d and e. The separations in distance to the nearest higher ground are shown as w, x, y and z. It can be seen that, while the separation of B is almost unaffected by using 'nearest higher ground' rather than measuring to a summit, that of E is significantly reduced and that of C is very greatly reduced.

Using 'nearest higher ground' A and E would be mountains, B and C tops and D a minor top. But if distances were measured to summits of adjacent mountains then C might qualify as a third mountain, since its separation from A would be large in distance, and from E large in drop.

Corbett's Tables

Although Corbett's list[6] of Scottish hills over 2500ft in height, published posthumously in 1952, appeared after that by Donald it is more logical to consider it first. In listing all hills between 2500 and 3000ft in height Corbett adopted a very simple criterion; there must be a reascent of 500ft [152.4m]. This is, by most standards, a severe test and no Corbett has any reason to fear for its status as a separate mountain. An equivalent metric rule would be a reascent of 150m with no regard to distance; this reascent would take 15 minutes at the standard pace.

However I have found only one Corbett summit less than 1 km from higher ground - Beinn na h-Eaglaise, which is 0.8 km away from Beinn Sgritheall and has a drop of 210m. Thus in practice they all have a separation of at least 30 minutes (that is, at least 15 minutes for distance plus at least 15 minutes for reascent, except Beinn na h-Eaglaise which is 12 plus 21 minutes). It would be a bold author who proposed a radically different classification for Corbetts. The list has great charm, and until recently was unique in having an upper as well as a lower height limit.

---

[6] Corbett, J. Rooke. List of Scottish Mountains 2500ft and under 3000ft in height. *SMCJ* 1952, XXV, 45-52 (Included in *Munro's Tables* from 1953).

Donald's Tables

Donald's Tables[7] of hills in the Scottish Lowlands were published in 1935. These showed all hills in Scotland south of the Highland Line and over 2000ft [609.6m] high. Like *Munro's Tables*, this list was divided into mountains and tops, though Donald used the word 'hill' to mean a separate mountain, and the word 'top' to include all listed hills including mountains. He also listed 15 'minor tops' which he defined as 2000ft contour rings which did not qualify even as tops. In the 1980 edition of the *Tables* a further 13 minor tops were listed, actually all well over 2000ft though the wording of the definition was not changed; but in 1997 Notman Law was transferred to the main list and all the rest of these minor tops were dropped.

Donald's is the first list we consider with a 2000ft limit. Figure 2 shows the dividing lines between mountains and tops, and if appropriate between tops and minor tops, for his and several other such lists. The dividing lines to be proposed later for these lists are also marked.

Donald's classification rules, which have never been altered, are as follows. He defines a 'unit' as one-twelfth of a mile or one 50ft contour of ascent. He then states that a mountain must be at least 17 units from other mountains, and that any hill with a reascent of more than 100ft that is not a mountain is a top, adding that a hill may be a top with a reascent as little as 50ft if it is of 'sufficient topographical merit'. He states that, in general, *"While the rules ... rather lack mathematical precision* [sic; a remarkable statement], *the actual result of their application is that ... an 80-feet drop determines a 'top' and the 17-unit rule a 'hill'."* For comparison with the proposed criteria, these rules must be metricated. A 'unit' is $15^{1}/_{4}$ m of height or 134 metres of distance; hence 17 units (260m or $2^{1}/_{4}$ km or some combination) correspond to a time between 26 and 34 minutes. It is not unreasonable to say that, as an equivalent rule, a mountain requires a separation of 30 minutes. So far as tops are concerned, Donald implies that any hill with a 25m drop qualifies and that some with lesser drops are included so long as this is 15m or more.

However, Donald measured separation, as already indicated, from the summit of one hill to the summit of a nearby mountain. This has produced anomalies of such degree that it is surprising that no editor has emended his classification. I take just one example – the ridge of the Ettrick Hills (Section 7) running north-east from Andrewhinney Hill. Trowgrain Middle is near enough to Andrewhinney Hill to be classified as a top. But Herman Law, which is lower than Trowgrain Middle and only a kilometre from it, is classified as a separate mountain – presumably because it is $1^{1}/_{2}$ miles (18 units) from Andrewhinney Hill. Measured from the nearest higher ground, Herman Law has barely enough separation to qualify as a top!

---

[7] Donald, Percy. Tables giving all hills in the Scottish Lowlands 2000ft in height and above. *SMCJ* 1935, XX, 415-438 (Included in *Munro's Tables* from 1953).

Early English, Welsh and Irish lists

During the period that ended with the publication of Corbett's Tables, a number of lists of hills in England, Wales or Ireland were prepared, though not usually with any great sophistication nor including any distinction between mountains and tops. Indeed Corbett himself was responsible for the first of these, showing hills in England and Wales above 2500ft and published in 1911[8] – over 40 years before his better-known table of Scottish hills! He revised and updated this list in 1929[9].

Several subsequent lists were issued, mostly with a 2000ft limit: by Carr & Lister[10] in 1925, Elmslie[11] in 1933, Simpson[12] in 1937, and Moss[13] in 1939 and 1940. The first lists of Irish hills were prepared by Hodge[14] and Wall,[15] both in 1939 though presumably independently. For reasons of space these lists will not be discussed here, but they are shown in Table 1 (described at the end of this section), and included in the references, to assist the interested reader. None had criteria for inclusion other than drop; most required merely a 50ft drop though 100ft and (once) 250ft were also used. Discussion was almost entirely on the difficulty of establishing a genuine 50ft drop, a problem which was normally overcome in practice by the use of a 50-foot contour ring, though the approximations thereby introduced were well understood. Indeed Moss in his two lists identified, for the first time outwith Scotland, some points as 'minor tops', though to achieve this 'anti-status' a hill had to have a single contour ring, no summit height *and* no name on the 1-inch OS map!

While all this was going on, and indeed subsequently, some authors in Scotland merely extended the *Tables* to include the 3000ft hills 'Furth of Scotland'; and, as the number of such hills was quite small, added a comment to the effect that "we do not know how to distinguish between mountains and tops consistently with *Munro's Tables*, so if you want to claim the Furths you had better climb them all" – though much more elegantly expressed, of course. Maxwell[16] in 1959, however, demanded a 500ft drop for a mountain and one of 150ft for a top. These values were however relaxed at greater distances; for example, though the 500ft drop for a mountain was required at distances up to a mile, a drop of only 50ft sufficed if the distance was two miles or more. Indeed his formulae are the closest

---

[8] Corbett, J. Rooke. Twenty-fives. *Journal of the Rucksack Club (JRC)* 1911, II, 61-65.

[9] Corbett, J. Rooke. Twenty-fives. *JRC* 1929, VI, 337-344.

[10] Carr, Herbert R.C. & Lister, George A. (eds). *The Mountains of Snowdonia in History, the Sciences, Literature and Sport.* 1925. Bodley Head.

[11] Elmslie, W.T. The Two Thousand Footers of England. *Journal of the Fell and Rock Climbing Club* 1933, IX, 344-351.

[12] Simpson, F.H.F. Concerning Contours. *Wayfarers' Journal* 1937, 18-24.

[13] Moss, E. Some New Twenty-fives. *JRC* 1933, VII, 273-4; *and* The Two-thousands of England. *JRC* 1939, IX, 184-189; *and* The Two-thousands of Wales. *JRC* 1940, IX, 239-243; *and* All Those Two-thousands. *JRC* 1952, XII, 67-70; *and* More Welsh Two-thousands. *JRC* 1954, XII, 276.

[14] Hodge, E.W. The Mountains of Eire. *Wayfarers' Journal* 1939, 67-73.

[15] Wall, Claude W. *Mountaineering in Ireland.* 1939. Federation of Mountaineering Clubs of Ireland (Second edition, 1976).

[16] Maxwell, D.C. *Tables giving all the 3000ft Mountains of England, Wales and Ireland.* 1959 [privately printed].

I have seen to those to be proposed later, though they are more stringent so far as mountains are concerned.

It will be seen from the above that there was much listing activity taking place outwith Scotland during the first half of the century. However there are no eponymous sets of hills corresponding to Munros, Corbetts and Donalds. That is fair enough; but it would, I feel, be inappropriate if the names of more recent compilers became attached to hills first gathered together so long ago.

Docharty's Lists

In 1954 Docharty published his *Selection of some 900 British and Irish Mountain Tops*,[17] which included most hills above 2500ft (except those in *Munro's Tables*) and many 'of interest' below that height. He followed this eight years later with a *Supplement* (in two Volumes) to the *Selection* which included 1,022 more hills under 2500ft. It seems unfortunate that, as all these volumes were privately printed and not widely available, Docharty's extensive lists did not have the influence that they might otherwise have done. However, it must also be added that the presentation of the actual lists, though elaborate and attractive, is not of the easiest for practical use. There is a significant amount of duplication and cross-referencing, and to find a top of a particular height you need to know the height band in which its parent mountain falls. But the essays in these three volumes are fascinating, and the panoramic photographs superb.

So far as classification is concerned (and the lists are elaborately classified), Docharty normally used a drop of 500ft to determine a mountain *('but with discretion')*, but in England (only) he found that 250ft was a more practical limit. If there is a criticism of the underlying concept of the lists, it is that Docharty did not include tops below 3000ft if they were part of a range whose highest point was over 3000ft. That is, a Corbett could have subsidiary tops in his list, but a Munro did not gain any additional tops below 3000ft. While the reasons, in terms of containing the length of the published lists, are entirely understandable, the result seems to me to be incomplete in a rather arbitrary manner. (It should be added that this restriction was not applied outwith Scotland, and even in the Highlands there were some 30 exceptions, hills which Docharty regarded as of particular interest often on account of distance from the relevant Munro.)

Bridge's Tables

Returning to England and Wales, the next set of tables to be published were those by George Bridge.[18] Like Donald, he used 2000ft as the height criterion, and evolved a system of classification into mountains and tops which depended on both the distance and the drop in height. (In fact, Bridge used both 'mountain' *and* 'top' in the sense of 'hill'; the distinction was conveyed by the phrases 'separate mountain' and 'subsidiary mountain'.)

---

[17] Docharty, W. McK. *A Selection of some 900 British and Irish Mountain Tops.* 1954 and *The Supplement to A Selection of some 900 British and Irish Mountain Tops, and a Selection of 1,000 Tops under 2500ft (in two volumes).* 1962 [all privately printed].

[18] Bridge, George. *The Mountains of England and Wales – Tables of Mountains of Two Thousand Feet and more in Altitude.* 1973. Gaston's / West Col Productions.

Bridge has a graphical approach to classification. Hills must have a drop of at least 50ft, and *any* separation between summits of more than 500ft, or more than 4 miles, will qualify a hill as a separate mountain. Intermediate points lie on a curve which includes a drop of 250ft at 1 mile, and 100ft at 2 miles. Arithmetically the rule is almost, though not quite, *'distance* x *drop = constant'* (200 to 250 in Imperial units). In metric units the equivalent product of kilometres of distance and metres of drop is, in the important region of the graph, about 100. The derived separation in time has a minimum of just below 27 minutes; it is exactly 27 minutes at 150m of drop and also at 1 km of distance, and is about 35 minutes at 2 km. Thus a separation of 30 minutes defines a mountain consistently with Bridge as well as Donald. (Bridge's rule produces greater times for more distant hills with smaller drops, but then the refinement of measuring to the nearest higher ground becomes even more necessary.)

More recent lists

There are many other, more recent lists of hills, of greater or lesser interest in the present context. It is outside the scope of this article to describe them all, but information about their criteria for classification is shown in Table 1 on p133. The following paragraphs are by way of amplification of the details in that table.

Among the most useful, if only because they come down to 600m [1968ft], are the lists of (nearly) all the hills in England and Wales contained in the four books by Terry Marsh.[19] I say 'nearly' because the few hills on Dartmoor (which Bridge includes) that qualify are not listed; nor is Snaefell on the Isle of Man, also included by Bridge, though that is a more reasonable omission! Marsh makes no attempt to distinguish between mountains and tops, listing all hills with a reascent of at least 30m (100ft); but he does also list 'minor tops' which he defines as having a reascent of between 15m and 30m.

In 1989 Dr E J Yeaman published his *Handbook*[20] which, despite the impression given by its title, is primarily an extensive list. It includes all hills in Scotland, regardless of altitude, with a drop of at least 100m or a separation in distance of at least 5 km – 2,435 hills in all. The presentation, however, is complex and to add to the confusion hills can appear in two or more regions. The information shown includes an indication of the 'energy' required to reach each hill (in arbitrary units which have been described as 'Mars Bar units'); in concept this could be similar to a classification by separation in time, though Yeaman measures every hill from the nearest road, not from any nearby higher ground or summit. Much interesting material about hill names, features and weather is also included.

The Grahams[21] were a list which, when first published late in 1992, contained hills in the Highlands that are between 2000 and 2500ft high, and *"having a descent all round of about 150m, or being the highest point all round for about 2 miles"*. This strange mixture of metric and

[19] Marsh, Terry. *The Mountains of Wales.* 1985. and *The Lake Mountains, Volumes One & Two.* 1987. and *The Pennine Mountains.* 1989 (all Hodder & Stoughton).

[20] Yeaman, Dr E.J. *Handbook of the Scottish Hills.* 1989. Wafaida.

[21] Graham, Fiona. *The Grahams.* (*The Great Outdoors*, Nov. 1992), XV, 10-13 (Included in *Munro's Tables* in 1997).

Imperial, with its double vagueness, was subsequently refined in cooperation with Dawson (see below), some errors corrected, and the concept extended to the whole of Scotland; so the Grahams are now Scottish hills within those height limits and with a reascent of 150m. This is almost identical to the Corbett rule and thus the list can be regarded as an extension of Corbett's Tables downwards to 2000ft. In 1997 the Grahams achieved the ultimate accolade of inclusion in *Munro's Tables*.

Earlier in 1992 Alan Dawson had published *The Relative Hills of Britain*.[22] This covered the whole of England, Wales and Scotland and their islands (but not Ireland) and listed all hills with a reascent of 150m *regardless of the height of the summit* (the lowest is Muldoanich, 153m, an island off the coast of Barra). He has called these hills 'Marilyns'. Originally there were 1,542 hills listed (now revised to 1,551); they include 205 of the 284 Munros, and, of course, all the Corbetts (if 'twin peaks' such as Buidhe Bheinn or, formerly, Corrieyairack Hill be excluded) and Grahams (as now defined). The concept does not assist in the classification of hills into mountains and tops, but it tends to confirm that no modern compiler requires a drop of more than 150m (500ft) to define a separate mountain in the British Isles.

The most extensive work for England and Wales is the recent *Mountain Tables*[23] by Michael Dewey. He lists all 2000ft (610m) hills, using a graphical approach rather similar to Bridge's to distinguish mountains and tops (in particular, a mountain requires a separation of at least 4 km or at least 120m, and between these limits *'distance* x *drop'* must exceed 60). On this basis there are 258 mountains and 175 tops. In addition all hills between 500m [1640ft] and 2000ft (373 in total) with a drop of 30m or more are given, and 332 'Notable Tops' below 500m are added for the benefit of readers living in less hilly regions! But the separation in the primary list is still between summits rather than to the nearest higher ground.

More recent still are the series of tables in booklet form published by TACit Press,[24] which normally use a drop of 150m to define a mountain and 30m for a top. These tables have the merit of giving notes on any doubtful values, and ample data to enable the user to check the entries or compile lists on different criteria. In passing, though the reasons are understandable, I wonder whether I am alone in finding it odd that current compilers seem content to use metric measures for the drop, yet persist in using 2000ft as the standard minimum height when 600m would seem to be just as reasonable a level? In this context TACit at least make the gesture of including lists of 'SubHills' which *inter alia* show all hills between 600m and 609m inclusive.

The standard list for Ireland was prepared by Vandeleur and Lynam in 1952, and published in 1976 in the second edition of the book by Wall,[25] though this is now difficult to find. In addition to the list in the 1992 book *The Mountains of Ireland* by Paddy Dillon,

---

[22] Dawson, Alan. *The Relative Hills of Britain*. 1992. Cicerone Press.

[23] Dewey, Michael. *Mountain Tables*. 1995. Constable.

[24] Dawson, Alan. *The Murdos*. 1995. and *The Grahams and the New Donalds*. 1995 and *The Hewitts and Marilyns of Wales*. 1997 and *The Hewitts and Marilyns of England*. 1997 (all TACit Press).

[25] See fn. 15.

TABLE 1 – PUBLISHED LISTS OF HILLS IN THE BRITISH ISLES

Compiler	Footnote Ref.	Date	Region	Lower limits for		
				Entry in List	Mountains	Tops
Munro	1	1891	S	3000ft	–	–
Corbett	8	1911	E, W	2500ft	–	–
Carr & Lister	10	1925	W	2000ft	–	100ft
Corbett	9	1929	E, W	2500ft	–	50ft
Parker	-	1929	F	3000ft	–	–
Elmslie	11	1933	E	2000ft	250ft	–
Donald	7	1935	S	2000ft	250ft*	50ft
Simpson	12	1937	E	2000ft	–	50ft
Hodge	14	1939	I	2500ft	–	–
Wall	15	1939	I	2500ft	–	–
Moss	13	1939–40	E, W	2000ft	–	50ft
Walsh	-	1950	E, W	2000ft	–	50ft
Corbett	6	1952	S	2500ft	500ft	–
Docharty	17	1954 &	S, W, I	2500ft	500ft	50ft
		1962	E	2500ft	250ft	50ft
Wainwright	-	1955–66	E	1000ft	–	–
Maxwell	16	1959	F	3000ft	500ft*	50ft
Bridge	18	1973	E, W	2000ft	500ft*	50ft
Wall	15	1976	I	2000ft	–	50ft
Brown	27	1977	F	3000ft	–	–
Mulholland	-	1980–83	F	3000ft	300ft	50ft
Marsh	19	1985–89	E, W	600m	–	30m
Buxton & Lewis	-	1986	E, W	2000ft	–	20m
Yeaman	20	1989	S	100m	100m	–
Nuttall, J & A	-	1989–90	E, W	2000ft	–	15m
Butterfield & Baines	-	1992	S	3000ft	250ft	–
Dawson	22	1992	S, E, W	150m	150m	–
Graham	21	1992	S	2000ft	150m	–
Dillon	-	1992	I	2000ft	–	–
Dewey	23	1995	E, W	2000ft	120m*	15m
Dawson	24	1995–97	S, E, W	2000ft	150m	30m
Clements	26	1997	I	2000ft	150m	30m
				& 150m	150m	–

In the column headed 'Region' S, E, W and I refer to Scotland, England, Wales and Ireland, and F to the Furth of Scotland at the 3000ft level. Lists usually cover the whole of their region, but in a few cases cover only a major part (such as the Highlands, the Lake District or Snowdonia). Values are quoted in the units used by the compiler.

The final columns show the minimum drops for qualification as a mountain and as a top. If a compiler shows only one drop limit this is shown in whichever column seems more appropriate. (If the entry is under 'Tops', the list is of hills and is not subdivided.) If the drop limit for mountains varies with the separation in distance then the figure shown, marked *, is that which applies if the distance is small; the mountain drop at large distances is then the same as that shown for tops. (The Donald 'Mountain' limit is inferred; the largest drop for a Donald Top is 220ft.)

there is *Irish Peaks* edited by Joss Lynam (Constable, 1982), which describes many hills down to 500m or so; but it does not claim to be complete and there is no accompanying list. The latest of the TACit booklets[26] just mentioned lists all hills in Ireland over 2000ft high with a drop of at least 30m (as well as the 453 hills with a reascent of 150m regardless of height, thus extending the list in Dawson's book to give 'Marilyns' throughout the British Isles).

Table 1 and Figure 2 have already been mentioned. The first shows all the mountain lists described in this section of the article, and some others too. Whenever possible it indicates the reascent criterion used by the compiler for mountains, tops or hills. The table is intended to be complete up to about 1970, but some more recent lists are not included if they neither record a significantly different set of hills from earlier ones, nor add to the development of classification methods. Figure 2 shows the dividing lines between mountains and tops (and if appropriate between tops and minor tops) for those lists using a 2000ft lower limit and where the criterion is not merely the drop. There is, of course, inadequate information to enable an equivalent diagram to be prepared for lists with a 3000ft limit.

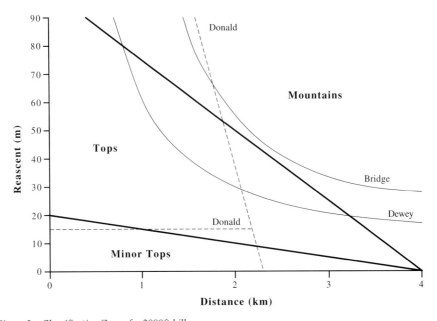

Figure 2 – Classification Zones for 2000ft hills

The figure shows the dividing lines between mountains and tops, and (Donalds only) between tops and the former minor tops, for the lists compiled by Donald, Bridge and Dewey. Also shown are the two dividing lines to be proposed later. However, unlike the three named lists, I shall be using the more severe criterion of 'distance to nearest higher ground'.

[26] Clements, E.D. *The Hewitts and Marilyns of Ireland.* 1997. TACit Press.

5. What are we seeking in a classification system?

Consideration of the historical precedents, experience of the hills throughout the British Isles, and a mathematical background lead me to suggest that a good classification system should meet the following criteria. I regard them all as important, and they are not listed in any particular order. They are hereafter referred to as C1 to C6.

C1   The system should be simple to apply. It should not require data that is not readily available, and it should be as insensitive as possible to any lack of precision (e.g. on OS maps) in that data.

C2   The system should achieve consistency throughout the British Isles.

C3   The results should match currently accepted lists as closely as possible.

C4   The system should classify hills as 'mountains', 'tops' and 'minor tops'.

C5   The system should produce a clear and unambiguous result for every hill, which should not depend on the result for any other hill. But …

C6   Editorial discretion must be preserved.

Some of these criteria (but not, I hope, C1 or C2) may require elaboration or explanation. For example, it seems to me important (C5) that the classification of any particular 'local high point' should not depend upon whether its neighbouring higher hill is a mountain, top or minor top. Donald, as we have seen, based his classification on separation from the nearest *mountain*, not even the nearest higher hill, and this is one reason for the anomalies already described. But it does not seem logical to suggest that, on a long, gently sloping but undulating ridge such as the Ettrick ridge already mentioned, or the northern Aran ridge in Wales, a *lower* point should achieve a *higher* status purely on account of distance from the main summit.

There are several reasons why it is essential that some discretion remains with the compiler of the list (C6). Firstly, the terrain can justify a higher ranking than the raw data suggest (though in practice this may apply only in the Cuillin of Skye). Next there may be local features which affect the classification. For example, in the south-east Grampians (Section 7 of the *Tables*) there are eight hills with separations all quite close to 2 km and 75m. A strict application of the basis to be proposed would split these into four Munros (Tom Buidhe, Cairn Bannoch, Carn a' Choire Bhoidheach and Cairn an t-Sagairt Mor) and four tops (Creag Leacach, Carn an Tuirc, Tolmount and Broad Cairn); but this would be a quite unjustifiable differentiation between very similar hills and the compiler of the *Tables* would rightly retain them all as Munros. Then there is the matter of historical precedent. This may not be significant for lists other than the Munros and Corbetts, but for them it is of great importance. Overall, a system based on physical parameters should not be regarded as definitive, but as a guide to the compiler. Decisions to override the system's results can then be taken for good reasons rather than by accident or oversight. (My own view is that discretion should be used more readily to promote than to demote a hill – but others may well disagree!)

More surprising may be C4, the suggestion that the classification should allow for minor tops as well as mountains and tops. This calls for some justification.

- The division into mountains and tops, however it may be achieved, reflects a natural and well-accepted concept. Lists which have only one grade of hill invariably have merely a minimum drop for inclusion: this is either large (as with the Corbetts) excluding many fine hills, or small (15m or 30m is often used) which leaves the feeling of many unworthy points being classed as mountains.

- If there is no *minimum* criterion for a top, then it is impossible both in theory and practice to produce a complete list. Even a list including every point defined by a separate contour ring will not do; for a map with a smaller contour interval would produce more points to record. In the extreme the compiler would need to include every trivial undulation, even every rock, if it is above the minimum altitude. (In general I do not favour the 'contour ring' approach though if compilers wish to include all separate contours of exactly the minimum height, e.g. 2000ft, then this is fairly harmless.)

- Thus it is useful to allow the classification of 'minor top'. This can include all those points which seem important to the compiler, for example because they are conspicuous on the ground or close to qualifying, even though they do not meet the criteria for a 'top'. The class will also include all points which are 'tops' in existing lists such as the *Tables*, even if they do not qualify as such. (In my view it should also extend to points which have ever been tops, now removed, though I admit that there are difficulties in the case of those former tops which have been found not even to be 'local high points'!) The list of minor tops is, of course, always subjective and can never be complete; but because it enables us to have a minimum criterion for tops it ensures that it is possible to include all *true* tops in any list.

Criterion C3, to match current lists, is important for the acceptability of any new approach. A geographer might propose a system in which each separate mountain had to be surrounded by large drops on all sides (e.g. Ben Lawers might be the only 'mountain' in the range north of Loch Tay), but such an approach, however scientific, would be of little value for walkers. This criterion leads us, I suggest, to conclude that classification purely by distance apart, or purely by drop, is inadequate to reflect the almost instinctive belief that the closer two hills are, the deeper the intervening drop needs to be to justify both as mountains. This is an explicit feature of the Donald and Bridge lists and was in my view clearly implied by Munro too. Of course, with a large drop requirement such as 150m a very satisfactory list of mountains *only* (such as the Corbetts and Grahams) can be compiled, but this is not suitable as a dividing line between mountains and tops.

Lastly I suggest that any list should include the data that justify the classification; in practice this will be the separation from the nearest higher ground in kilometres of distance and metres of reascent. This has a number of advantages. It will enable others to check the classifications if desired, highlight cases where editorial discretion has been exercised, and allow swift correction of errors. It will render it easy to give effect to any changes when new information is made available by the Ordnance Survey. And it also allows users to draw up their own lists on other criteria should they so wish.

6. A proposed system of classification

The system of classification to be put forward here has evolved over the best part of a decade of consideration of the principles and details. Approaches for the Highlands (with a 3000ft or 900m lower height limit) and the rest of the British Isles (with a 2000ft or 600m limit) were for a long time independent but it was heartening to find, towards the end of the work, that they could be combined.

An initial approach was based directly on Bonsall, ranking hills purely in order of their separation in *time*, but this soon proved unsatisfactory. The reason is that this method gives too much weight to distance and not enough to drop; for example a drop of 150m is equivalent to a distance of a kilometre, whereas in classification terms the former is a good deal more significant than the latter. (In Figure 2, a dividing line based on time would be close to, and even nearer the vertical than that for the Donalds, which already suffer from inadequate emphasis on the drop, especially having regard to the Lowland terrain.)

For a long time, influenced by this start, I classified hills by their separation in reascent and time, not reascent and distance. This was conceptually unsatisfactory, as time is in part a function of the reascent, and it led to the oddity of using impossible points (such as a drop of 80m with a separation time of zero) to define the boundary between mountains and tops. Nevertheless the use of this basis, through a large number of alternative parameters, led successfully to the final system based on distance and reascent as now described.

One early move was to plot the separations (to the nearest higher ground) of all the hills in each region. The results for the Munros are in Figure 3 on p139, for the Donalds in Figure 4 on p140 and for England and Wales in Figures 5 to 7 on p146-7. These diagrams led quickly to the realisation that, as might be expected on physical grounds, the reascent is correlated with the distance apart, and hills are clustered around an imaginary line (call it the 'centre line') rising 'NE from the origin' of the graph. For example, looking at the Munros and Tops, the centre line is approximately *'reascent in metres = 60 x distance in kilometres'* – and no hill has a reascent significantly less than 20 times the distance. (I am here referring only to smaller reascents, say up to 100m. For much larger reascents the separation in distance can be as great as you wish.)

It follows that the critical decision is the point on this 'centre line' at which a hill might qualify as a mountain. The way in which outlying points are dealt with is then less important, as relatively few classifications will depend on this. In particular it was realised that, however intellectually appealing was a curved dividing line using a formula similar to Bridge's, to adopt this would be complex and unsatisfactory. A study of Figures 4 to 7 in conjunction with Figure 2 led me to conclude that such a formula was either too generous near the centre line (as is Dewey), or too severe for close hills with larger drops (as is Bridge). In accordance with C1, the simplicity of dividing lines which are straight was to be preferred. Indeed these diagrams led me to wonder whether previous compilers had studied the actual distribution of drops and distances at all!

The two bases of classification, one for the Highlands and the other for use elsewhere in the British Isles, are now defined. In doing this a graphical approach is used (but for those interested, formulae are given in the Appendix). I emphasise that all separations in distance are to the nearest higher ground.

The Highlands

- Draw a line connecting the two points *"zero distance, 150m drop"* and *"4 km distance, zero drop"*. Then any hill on or above this line is a mountain (a Munro).

- Draw a further line connecting *"zero distance, 30m drop"* and *"4 km distance, zero drop"*. (The second point is the same as before.) Any hill below this second line is a minor top, while hills between the two lines, or on the lower line, are tops.

The end points defining these lines are selected both to match the current *Tables* as closely as possible (C3), and to use values which have gained widespread acceptability. 150m (500ft) and 30m (100ft) seem far and away the best values for height. There is no similarly obvious value to use for distance, so I have chosen the convenient one of 4 km (equivalent to 1 hour). Distance is the less critical parameter anyway.

The upper line goes through points such as "2 km, 75m drop" and "1 km, $112^1/_2$ m drop". A 'typical' hill (i.e. one on the 'centre line' described above) that qualifies as a Munro by a small margin would have a separation of $1^1/_2$ km in distance and 100m of reascent (about 1 mile and 350ft). Beinn Liath Mhor Fannaich and Conival are examples. A typical hill that just qualifies as a true top will have a reascent of 30m (100ft), or 25m with at least $^3/_4$ km of distance (80ft at half a mile or more).

To clarify the proposed dividing line between Munros and tops, I am suggesting that *any* hill with a reascent of 150m or more, or at a distance of 4 km or more, *must* qualify as a Munro. It could be argued that two very close hills should need a higher reascent, or that even 4 km of distance is not enough if the drop is small. But in real life there are no such hills! There is only one hill (Garbh Chioch Mhor, promoted in 1981) with a distance below 1 km and a reascent over 150m. There are six hills with distances between 1 and $1^1/_4$ km (up to $^3/_4$ mile) and reascents over 150m, all of which apart from Ruadh Stac Mor have always been Munros. At the other extreme, there is also only one hill with a distance separation of 4km or more and a drop of less than 100m. That hill is Beinn Bhreac; its separation is $4^1/_2$ km and 80m, and I would doubt that it has ever been suggested for demotion from Munro status. The most extreme outlier that I have found is Geal Charn in the Monadh Liath, with a drop of only 100m even though it is 10 km (6 miles) from higher ground! So far as tops are concerned, at 2 km a drop of 'only' 15m (50ft) is required; but there is *no* 3000ft hill in the Highlands 2 km or more from higher ground with a drop less than 40m. (The rather unusual hill with exactly these values is the East Top of An Socach in Section 6.)

The true test of the proposals is their effectiveness in the region of the graph where there *are* plenty of hills. Here Figure 3 shows that the proposed line is fairly close to the boundary between Munros and tops, with 12 current Munros falling just below the line and only one so far below as to be embarrassing. (Sgor an Iubhair was a second before the 1997 revision. For obvious reasons the Skye Munros are excluded from this analysis.) There are a similar number of tops above the line – a total of 9, of which 4 are very close to it and should not be promoted. This leaves 5 tops that, even after the 1997 revision, clearly justify promotion to Munro status.

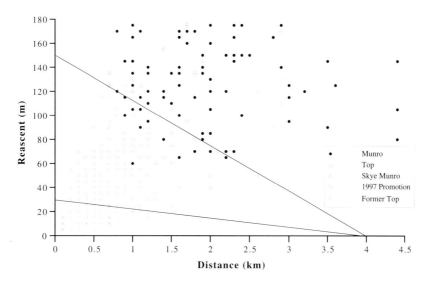

Figure 3 – Munros and Tops

The figure shows all Munros and Tops with a reascent of 180m (600ft) or less and a separation in distance to the nearest higher ground of less than 4¹/₂km (nearly 3 miles), plotted by their separation in distance and drop. The symbol indicates whether the hill is listed in the current Tables as a mountain or a top, or is a former top. Skye Munros and the 1997 promotions are distinguished. The proposed dividing lines are also shown.

Note that the separations are taken to the nearer 0.1 km in distance and the nearer 5m of drop. There is thus no physical significance, here or in subsequent figures, in the apparent horizontal and vertical alignments. However, it is clear that in only a handful of cases could more accurate measures affect the resulting classification.

South of the Highland Line

In the Highlands a minimum height of 3000ft (just over 900m) is used, but for the Donalds, England, Wales and Ireland the equivalent appropriate limit is 2000ft (just over 600m). A natural adjustment to the above rules is to reduce all the parameters relating to height to two-thirds of their 'Highland' values; it was pleasing to find that this matched almost exactly the system already derived independently for these hills. Thus the rule now becomes:

- Draw a line connecting *"zero distance, 100m drop"* to *"4 km, zero drop"*, and a further line connecting *"zero distance, 20m drop"* to *"4 km, zero drop"*. Then, as before, the lines divide the graph into three regions, of mountains, tops and minor tops.

There are two observations to make. Firstly, it might appear that the distance parameters should also be two-thirds of those in the Highlands, leading to either (say) 2¹/₂ km in this rule, or 6 km for the Highlands. The former would allow a few more current Donalds to remain as mountains, but seems far too lenient – at 2 km it would demand a reascent of only 20m. After all, the '50m at 2 km' of the proposed rule is hardly severe. The latter would significantly worsen the match to Munros with the *Tables*, and cannot be seriously considered. Hence it was felt better and simpler to use 4 km (1 hour) of separation throughout.

Secondly, it may be thought that the lower limit for tops, which allows all hills with a drop of 20m to qualify, is rather generous. However the rule as proposed is a better match for the Donalds than 30m would be, and Bridge has many tops which do not qualify even using a 20m drop. Hence I concluded that it was better, on a matter in itself of little importance, to maintain the 'two-thirds' relationship with the Highland rules.

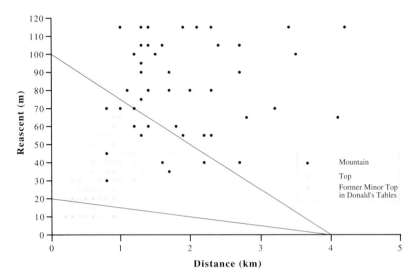

Figure 4 – The Donalds
The figure shows all Donalds with a reascent of 120m (400ft) or less, and at a distance of less than 4½ km, plotted by their separation in distance and drop. The symbols indicate whether they are listed in Donald's Tables as mountains, tops or the former 'minor tops'. The proposed dividing lines are also shown.

7. Some consequences . . .

It may be of interest to summarise the changes to the lists in Parts 1 – 3 of *Munro's Tables* that could follow from the adoption of the proposed classification rules. It is useful to have a simple 'measure' of the amount by which a hill meets, or fails to meet, the minimum requirement, and for this purpose I use a value in metres (and call it the 'excess' or 'shortfall', as appropriate). This is the difference between the *actual* reascent, and the minimum reascent needed for a hill *at the same distance from nearest higher ground* to qualify. Graphically, it is the length of the *vertical* line between the hill's plotted position and the dividing line; physically the 'excess' is the amount by which the height of the lowest intervening bealach could be raised without jeopardising the status as a mountain. Conversely a 'shortfall' implies that excavation of the bealach to that extra depth is needed!

It is worth noting that the likely error in estimating the drop, and hence the excess or shortfall, is typically 5m or less (rarely up to 10m). Similarly, an error of 0.1 km in the distance estimate would alter the excess or shortfall by less than 4m. In all cases where a change of status is proposed the relevant value is much greater than this.

As already stated, most significant would be the promotion of five tops to Munros. These are listed in Table 2 in descending order of 'merit' for promotion. The table also shows the tops which marginally qualify, but which I do not recommend for promotion. It is interesting (and convenient!) that there is such a large gap between the two groups of hills. (As explained in the caption to the table the tops which were promoted in the 1997 revision are also shown. All those promotions 'qualified' on my basis, but some were very marginal. By way of comparison, the three tops closest to promotion but which *fail* to qualify are Carn na Criche, Carn na Con Dhu and Sgurr nan Saighead.)

TABLE 2 – TOPS THAT QUALIFY AS MUNROS

| Top | Munro | Sect. | Separation | | | Excess |
			km	m	min	m
Spidean Coire nan Clach	Beinn Eighe	13	2.9	172	61	131
Stob Coire Raineach	Buachaille Etive Beag	3	1.7	177	43	91
Glas Leathad Beag	Ben Wyvis	15	2.9	132	57	91
Sgurr na Lapaich	Mam Sodhail	11	2.9	109	54	68
Sail Mhor	Beinn Eighe	13	2.6	120	51	67
Stob na Doire	Buachaille Etive Mor	3	1.9	145	43	66
Tom na Gruagaich	Beinn Alligin	13	1.4	155	37	58
Stob na Broige	Buachaille Etive Mor	3	1.8	135	41	53
Cairn Lochan	Ben Macdui (see text)	8	2.8	90	51	45
Stob Coire Sgreamhach	Bidean nam Bian	3	1.0	128	28	16
Beinn Iutharn Bheag	Beinn Iutharn Mhor	6	1.5	105	33	11
Sgurr na Carnach	Sgurr Fhuaran	11	0.7	135	24	11
Sgor Choinnich	Sgor Gaibhre	4	0.9	125	26	9
Creag Dubh	Carn nan Gobhar	12	1.7	94	35	8
Sgor an Lochain Uaine	Cairn Toul	8	1.0	118	27	5
An Stuc	Meall Garbh (Lawers)	2	0.7	127	23	3
Coinneach Mhor	Beinn Eighe	13	1.0	115	27	2

The 'excess' in the right hand column is described at the start of section 7. It is the difference in metres between the actual reascent, and the reascent at the point on the proposed dividing line between Munros and tops for a hill at the same distance from nearest higher ground. The nine tops in the upper half of the table were recommended for promotion in the original version of this article, but not the eight tops in the lower half.

The eight hills shown in italics were promoted to Munros in 1997. The values shown are derived from the altitudes in the 1997 Tables.

Comment could be made about each hill, but I will confine myself to a mention of three. Firstly, the Affric Sgurr na Lapaich was sometimes said to be the most worthy of Munro status, yet it ranked only fourth in the (pre-1997) list. Secondly, the separation quoted in Table 2 for Cairn Lochan is measured from Ben Macdui. The separation from Cairn Gorm is 2.8 km and 116m, and the corresponding excess is 71m; Cairn Lochan is even more worthy of promotion when compared with the Munro of which it is currently deemed to be a top. And lastly, as mentioned at the end of section 2, all values are based on heights in the 1997 *Tables*. The separation shown for Spidean Coire na Clach (Beinn Eighe) is therefore now measured from nearest higher ground on Ruadh-stac Mor. But even using 1990 data which gave a height of 972m (and hence implied that the nearest higher ground was on Coinneach Mhor) the separation was 2.2 km and 151m with a corresponding excess of 84m; Spidean Coire na Clach did not depend on the good offices of the Ordnance Survey to justify its promotion.

TABLE 3 – MUNROS THAT DO NOT QUALIFY AS SUCH

		Separation			Shortfall
Munro	*Sect.*	*km*	*m*	*min*	*m*
Carn Ghluasaid	11	1.0	60	21	52
Sgor an Iubhair	4	1.1	77	24	32
Carn an Tuirc	7	1.6	65	31	25
The Devil's Point	8	1.1	90	26	19
Sail Chaorainn	11	1.1	90	26	19
Creag a'Mhaim	10	1.4	80	29	17
Na Gruagaichean	4	0.9	100	24	16
Tolmount	7	1.8	70	34	12
Saileag	11	1.2	95	28	10
Creag Pitridh	4	1.0	105	26	7
Creag Leacach	7	2.0	70	37	5
Aonach Beag (Alder)	4	1.1	105	27	4
Broad Cairn	7	2.2	65	40	2
Sgurr an Lochain	10	0.9	115	25	1

The thirteen Munros shown do not qualify as such under the proposals herein. However for the reasons given in the text, only Carn Ghluasaid is suggested for demotion to top. (Skye Munros are excluded from this table. Sgor an Iubhair, demoted in 1997, is shown in italics.)

The 'shortfall' in the right hand column is described at the start of section 7. It is the difference in metres between the actual reascent, and the reascent at the point on the proposed dividing line between Munros and tops for a hill at the same distance from nearest higher ground. It can be seen that half of these Munros are very close indeed to the dividing line.

Next would be the thirteen Munros listed in Table 3 that could be demoted to tops. There is one clear candidate: Carn Ghluasaid, which falls short by over 50m. To put it another way, its drop is about half what it needs to be. Of the other Munros which fall below the dividing line, four are part of a compact group of eight hills in Section 7 of the *Tables*, all of which (as already discussed in section 5) should retain the same status. Nearly all the rest have reascents of 90m or more, are close to the line and should not, I feel, be demoted. It is interesting that although the South Glen Shiel Ridge is often regarded as having far more Munros than can be justified, only two of its seven mountains fail to qualify and one of those (Sgurr an Lochain) is extremely marginal. (Although Skye Munros cannot be assessed by the standard rules, I should mention Am Basteir and Sgurr Mhic Choinnich. Both have a reascent of under 60m, less than that of any other Munro, even Carn Ghluasaid; however in each case the separation by the 'easy' route is much greater.)

Sgor an Iubhair, which was promoted in 1981 and demoted in 1997, is also shown in Table 3. It is interesting because there are *two* drops, one of 77m and one of about 70m, between it and Sgurr a'Mhaim. In my view, as will emerge in a later section, I do not regard this feature as justifying special treatment; however its location where an important spur meets the main ridge could well have justified its retention as a Munro. I agree with the decision of the 1997 editor, who allowed it to subside gracefully to Top status, but (in the original version of this article) I refrained from recommending this. (All the other 1981 changes are quite clear-cut and their current statuses are consistent with my proposed rules.)

As I have said, there are now 4 (formerly 8) tops that 'just' qualify as Munros, and 12 Munros that could 'just' be demoted. The smallness of these two numbers is an indication that the dividing line is in the right place. It would be possible to move it slightly to reduce one of the numbers, or to ensure that all hills in the cluster in Section 7 of the *Tables* fall in the same region of the graph; but if this were done then the corollary is that the other number become larger. Such a change would also result in less memorable end points for the dividing line, and inconsistencies with the basis outwith the Highlands, and so I would prefer to let the inevitable blurring at the boundary fall exactly as shown in Figure 3. (When dealing with an *existing* list it seems sensible not to change the status of hills that fall very close to a boundary line, in what I regard as the 'zone of fuzziness'. When compiling a new list, of course, I would follow the rules precisely unless there were good grounds for discretion.)

Lastly affecting the *Tables* are hills that justify inclusion as tops. Here the additions in 1997 include all hills with a drop known to exceed 30m, and it is unnecessary to go into detail. It should be clear that my proposals would not require the removal of *any* current tops, as they will all qualify for retention in the 'minor top' category, however small the reascent.

All Corbetts have a drop of over 150m [actually 152.4m], and so they will clearly all continue to rank as mountains whatever the precise criteria adopted. I can therefore now consider the Donalds. There would be no promotions, and Table 4 shows the ten mountains which would become tops under the proposed rules. At least half of these are demoted because the use of nearest higher ground gives separations significantly less than those measured to a mountain summit. Only the last four in the table, with shortfalls of less than 10m, could perhaps be retained at their current status on grounds of historical precedent. (I think it is unfortunate that the 1997 revision did not at least tidy up the worst of these anomalies.) I have also identified six points not in the Donald list which justify the status of top – Shiel Dod (1.0 km, 27m) in the Lowther Hills is the most deserving example – but further work is needed to ensure that this list is complete.

TABLE 4 – DONALD MOUNTAINS THAT SHOULD BE DEMOTED TO TOPS

		Separation		Shortfall
Donald Mountain	*Section*	*km*	*m*	*m*
Herman Law	7	0.8	31	49
Bell Craig	7	0.8	47	33
Swatte Fell	6	1.7	35	23
Lowther Hill	8	1.6	40	20
Hillshaw Head	4	1.3	55	13
Stob Law	5	0.8	70	10
Talla Cleuch Head	5	1.2	62	8
Tarfessock	10	1.0	69	6
Middle Hill	5	2.2	41	4
Birkscairn Hill	5	1.4	62	3

The ten hills shown would be demoted to tops under the proposals herein. The 'shortfall' in the right hand column is described at the start of section 7. It is the difference in metres between the actual reascent, and the reascent at the point on the proposed dividing line between mountains and tops for a hill at the same distance from nearest higher ground.

So far as Bridge's Tables in England and Wales are concerned, the proposed rules are rather more generous than those he used, especially for hills close together but with a large drop. Thus it is hardly surprising that two Lake District hills (Starling Dodd and Harrison Stickle) and three Welsh ones (Moel yr Ogof, Pen y Brynfforchog, and Y Garn near Plynlimon), but none in the more gently sloping Pennines, justify promotion to mountain status. In contrast the use of nearest higher ground results in far more mountains being demoted to tops, the numbers being 15 in the Lake District, 10 in the Pennines and 21 in Wales. It is interesting to note how clearly Figures 4 to 7 demonstrate the differences in the underlying orography between the regions, with the Lake District hills generally being close together with deep drops, and the Pennine hills much further apart and with lesser drops. The Donalds and the Welsh hills are between these extremes, though more like the Lakes than the Pennines.

Finally, Table 5 gives information for the 3000ft hills 'Furth of Scotland', which are now shown in the *Tables* though not classified. (The 11 clear 'mountains' with very large separations are omitted.) A precise application of the classification system put forward here would give mountain status to Elidir Fawr, Y Garn, Tryfan, Carnedd Dafydd and Sca Fell, but not to others such as Foel-fras, Glyder Fach and Caher; the result would be 16 mountains and 18 tops. However several of the 'near misses' have been proposed for mountain status by previous writers (Maxwell has a total of 17 mountains and Brown[27] 20). My suggestion is, therefore, that the first four hills with 'shortfalls' in Table 5 (Foel-fras, Glyder Fach, Caher and Beenkeragh) should also be classified as mountains. This application of criterion C6 has an ulterior motive; the convenient result is that all Furth hills have the *same* classification as they do in their own regional lists using the rule 'south of the Highland Line'.

Also listed in Table 5 are the only three hills which are minor tops on the Highland rule, but tops in their own region. Though it is hardly critical, my preference would be to include these as Furths. The final list would then contain 20 mountains and 17 tops.

TABLE 5 – 'FURTH OF SCOTLAND'

| Hill | Status | Separation | | Excess |
		km	m	m
Elidir Fawr	M	3.5	213	194
Y Garn	M	1.8	236	153
Tryfan	M	1.0	190	77
Carnedd Dafydd	M	2.8	111	66
Sca Fell	M	1.1	133	24
Foel-fras	T	2.4	59	-1
Caher	T	1.2	100	-5
Glyder Fach	T	1.5	75	-19
Beenkeragh	T	1.0	92	-20
Crib-y-ddysgl	T	1.0	72	-40
The Big Gun	T	0.5	70	44
Crib Goch	T	0.6	65	39
Ill Crag	T	0.9	57	34
Cnoc an Chuilinn	T	1.0	55	32
Yr Elen	T	0.7	55	30
Broad Crag	T	0.5	52	26
Pen yr Ole Wen	T	1.0	45	22
Foel Grach	T	1.1	40	18
Maolan Bui	T	0.4	40	13
Garnedd Uchaf	T	1.2	32	11
Knockoughter	T	0.3	35	7
Cruach Mhor	T	0.3	32	4
Caher W top	T	0.2	30	2
Symonds Knott	N	0.3	21	-7
Helvellyn Lower Man	N	0.4	18	-9
Maolan Bui SW top	N	0.4	18	-9

This table shows all Furth hills less than 4 km from higher ground (which includes all with a drop less than 250m) listed in descending order of the excess. Negative values are shortfalls. Note that in the upper part of the table the excesses and shortfalls relate to the dividing line between mountains and tops, whereas in the lower part they relate to the line between tops and minor tops. The 'Status' column shows that which applies using the 'Highland' rules; this is discussed at the end of section 7. The last three hills are not included in Munro's Tables, but are the only ones which might be considered for listing as further tops.

---

[27] Brown, H.M. Furth of Scotland. *SMCJ* 1977, XXXI, 189-191.

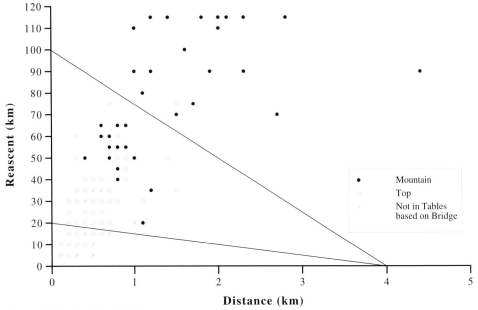

Figure 5 – The Lake District Hills

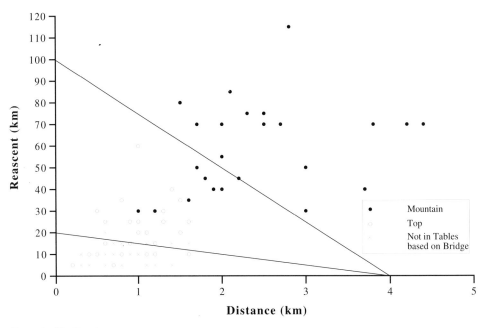

Figure 6 – The Pennines

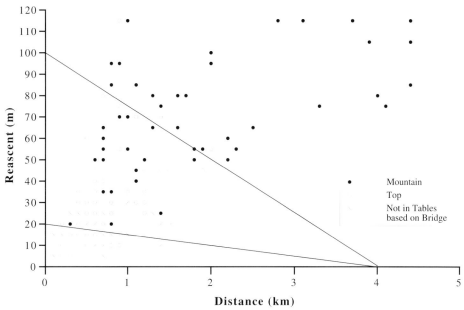

Figure 7 – The Welsh Hills

These figures show all the hills over 2000ft high with a reascent of 120m (400ft) or less, and at a distance of less than 4½ km, in their respective regions. The presentation is similar to Figure 4 and the symbols indicate whether the hills are listed in Bridge's Tables as mountains or tops, or are unlisted.

8. . . . and some comparisons

There have, of course, been several previous proposals for a reclassification of the hills in the *Tables* (quite apart from the changes made by successive editors), and it may be interesting to note how the current suggestions compare with some of these. In the early days most articles concentrated on establishing the actual heights of hills and bealachs in the less well-mapped regions; but once the information of this sort was more reliable (though changes are, as we have seen, still not unknown!) some contributors to *SMCJ* proposed significant changes.

The most important of these proposals are by Dow and Bonsall. In his 1933 article *Munros, Beards and Weather*,[28] Dow concluded with some brief thoughts on classification, suggesting that dip [drop], distance and difficulty, in that order, were the factors to be taken into account. He gave examples of tops which should be promoted and Munros which should be demoted. So far as potential promotions were concerned, a complete list was given in his later article, considered below. He suggested eight demotions. Two (An

---

[28] See Chapter 3.4

Garbhanach and Carn Ban) have indeed subsequently been demoted. The South Glen Shiel Ridge was to be reduced to five Munros (which is what my basis would achieve, though I do not propose that this should be done). Of the remaining four, Aonach Beag (Alder) and Creag Pitridh are noted in Table 3 as below the dividing line though not here recommended for demotion; only Stob Coire a'Chairn and Mam Sodhail, each with a drop of 125m, continue to qualify in their own right as Munros, though by margins of 20m or less.

In his second relevant article some 16 years later, forming the first half of *Munro's Tables – Two Contrasting Views*,[29] Dow listed no fewer than 31 hills which he suggested should be added to the list of Munros. (This time he did not consider demotions.) Six of these are quickly dealt with; Beinn Tarsuinn was added in 1953, and three more were promoted in the 1981 revision (in fact, all the promotions then made except Sgor an Iubhair which has already been discussed), whereas two (Am Bathaich [Sgurr a'Mhaoraich] and Creag Dhubh [Beinn Eighe]) have been found to be below 3000ft. Of the remaining 25, Dow included 8 of the 9 originally recommended here for promotion (all except Cairn Lochan) and 6 of the 8 which marginally qualify but were not recommended (all except Sgor Choinnich and Coinneach Mhor). Thus only 11 of Dow's 31 would, on my basis, deservedly remain tops. They include 3 quite close to the dividing line (Stob Coire nan Lochan, Glas Mheall Mor on An Teallach, and Bidean an Eoin Deirg), but others are, in terms of separation, quite modest tops. These include Carn Eas (Ben Avon), Stuc Mor (Ceathreamhnan), Meall Dearg (the Northern Pinnacles, Liathach), and the Bhasteir Tooth. Presumably some of these were recommended on grounds of difficulty (the third of Dow's criteria), though I suspect that others may have gained entry to his list only because of the inadequacies of the maps in some regions at that time.

Bearing in mind that Dow did not state any specific drop or distance criteria for qualification as a Munro, I conclude that overall my proposals are consistent with his ideas.

It is rather easier to compare the effect of my proposals with those in Bonsall's second article, already mentioned. He allows for discretion at the margin (my 'zone of fuzziness') by suggesting that Munros are demoted if their separation is less than 23 minutes, but that tops are promoted only if their separation is more than 30 minutes. (These times use Naismith's Rule; my equivalents are about 28 and 35 minutes.) He proposed the demotion of seven Munros, five of which (four in Section 8 and Carn Ban in the Monadh Liath) were indeed demoted in 1981. Of the other two, Carn Ghluasaid and Sail Chaorainn, one is here recommended for demotion and the other, being marginal, is not.

Bonsall suggested that 12 tops should be promoted. One was Am Bathaich (below 3000ft) and another Mullach an Rathain (promoted in 1981). Eight of the others are in my original list of nine proposed promotions (all except Tom na Gruagaich, the one with the smallest separation in distance), leaving just two which I feel should be left as tops: Glas Mheall Mor (Drumochter) and Carn na Criche ('Braeriach South Plateau'). The first has a separation of 2.1 km and 68m and the second 2.6 km and 50m; they are comparable with Broad Cairn (see Table 3). Both are, on my basis, *just* below the dividing line. Glas Mheall Mor presents no special features but Carn na Criche is more interesting. Of all the tops in

---

[29] See Chapter 4.5, Part 1.

the *Tables* not shown in Table 2 it has the largest separation in distance, and its altitude makes it the highest top of all now that the N Top of Ben Macdui has been deleted. Partly, I suspect, for this latter reason Bonsall wished to see Carn na Criche promoted. I do not agree. Even were its separation slightly greater, say 2.8 km, so that it just qualified I would recommend that it remained as a top. Editorial discretion is a wonderful thing; but if justification be required it is that a 'short cut' (initially going just east of north) to the nearest higher ground reduces the distance to 1.8 km and increases the drop by only 15m. The topography would override the arithmetic. If the promotion of Cairn Lochan, a conspicuous summit from many directions, seems controversial how much more so would be that of Carn na Criche with less than half the drop at a similar distance.

Close inspection of Bonsall's suggestions shows that *in practice* they are equivalent to allowing *any* separation of a mile (1.6 km) or more to justify Munro status, and demanding that *any* separation of under ³⁄₄ mile (1.2 km) leads to a demotion (distances between these limits representing the zone of fuzziness where no change was suggested). As I have already said, this places too much weight on distance apart and not enough on drop.

Finally it should be mentioned that some previous proposals have included suggestions for tops that should be added or deleted. There does not, however, seem to be any benefit to be gained from analysing these, as the process would be little more than a repetition of previous lists.

9. Some points of detail

It may be as well to cover a few less important matters, mostly of definition, relating to the proposed classification system.

When measuring the separation of a hill from the nearest higher ground, the distance should be measured along the connecting ridge. But in some terrain (Section 7 of the *Tables*, the south-east Grampians, provides excellent examples) 'the connecting ridge' is not clearly defined. In this case, and subject to the requirement that the route passes through the bealach (i.e. has minimum reascent) any natural route may be chosen. Indeed, as we have just seen in the case of Carn na Criche, it is occasionally appropriate to have regard also to a route that does not pass through the bealach, though this is quite rare. It is unusual for the choice of route to affect the emerging classification, but when it does the lesser status should be selected.

The reascent or drop is simply the hill's height minus the height of the lowest bealach traversed. This definition stands even if there are intervening undulations (e.g. as in going from E to B in Figure 1, or as in the case of Sgor an Iubhair already discussed); the extra height gain thereby incurred 'on the ground' is ignored. This is necessary as otherwise the accumulation of that extra height could lead to a top being quite unjustly promoted. (In theory, if not always in practice, the extra height can be avoided by contouring round the intervening bumps.)

There is a potential problem if a hill is connected to higher ground along two high ridges. (I have not found any instance where it is necessary to consider seriously three or more ridges.) In determining the hill's status, clearly the lower must be chosen if they are different. If both separations lead to the same status, then the separation to be recorded is that nearer to the dividing line, i.e. that with the smaller 'excess' (as described at the start of section 7; for an example, imagine the two separations given earlier for Cairn Lochan, plotted on Figure 3). This will usually result in the separation with the smaller reascent being chosen, but there are a few exceptions. Even in these cases a study of the actual topography confirms that the mountain to which the top 'belongs' should be determined by the 'nearer' separation.

This is a convenient place to mention one type of anomaly in recent editions of the *Tables*. Several tops are listed under the 'wrong' Munro and in some cases the separations are so different that it is difficult to see how this occurred. These are (with the 'correct' Munro in parentheses) Diollaid a'Chairn (Geal Charn), Creagan a'Choire Etchachan (Ben Macdui), Stob Coire na Cralaig (Mullach Fraoch-choire), and Toman Coinich (Sgurr Breac). There are others where the decision is marginal, such as Crow Craigies and Creag an Dubh-loch (both 'nearer' to Cairn Bannoch), and here I would not make any change. The position of Cairn Lochan has already been mentioned: if it is not promoted as proposed then it and other nearby tops should really be listed under Ben Macdui rather than Cairn Gorm, though I can see that this might be considered too radical a break with tradition!

One factor that does not enter into the proposed classification process is the difference in altitude of the two summits being considered. To do so would infringe C1, and perhaps C5 as well. However in marginal cases I can imagine that editorial discretion might keep the lower hill as a top. Consider as an example the range comprising Beinn Eibhinn, Aonach Beag and Geal Charn in the Alder region. The centre hill, in fact, has a separation of 1.1 km and 105m and just fails to meet the criteria for Munro status, but should certainly be retained as such on historical and other grounds. However if it were only 950m high instead of 1116m, even with the same separation (i.e. the same drop), there is no doubt that 'top' would be the right status. This instance is purely imaginary. In fact there are so few cases where a large difference between the heights of the hills might influence the allotted status that a formal rule would be overkill; the matter should be left for editorial judgement.

My final comment relates to the view that *"we should not promote Glas Leathad Beag* [or Tom na Gruagaich, etc. – the equivalent point arose with the 1981 promotion of Mullach an Rathain] *because Sir Hugh allowed only one mountain in cases like this"*. If this could be applied consistently, in a topographical sense, I would have no quarrel with it. But in fact, as Campbell has pointed out, it seems that Sir Hugh had regard to whether or not a mountain group had a *range* name distinct from the name of any summit in the group. This is just one example of the influence on the original *Tables* of the naming practice of the Ordnance Survey on their 1-inch maps in the late nineteenth century. Since they still, a hundred years later, seem reluctant to accept that walkers and climbers are among the major users and determiners of hill names, I refuse to concede that names shown on current maps, let alone early ones, should dictate the content of mountain lists.

A possible orographical interpretation of this view is that its advocates require a large drop between Munros. This would imply that many small groups or ranges of hills would have only one Munro; examples include Ben Cruachan, the two pairs adjacent to Loch

Treig, Carn Aosda and The Cairnwell, Ruadh Stac Mor and A'Mhaighdean, and Conival and Ben More Assynt. If you insist rigorously on a large drop between mountains a coherent list can be derived; but it is not the Munros. Perhaps such hills would be the Greater Corbetts. For example, a minimum drop of 150m would leave Lochnagar, Glas Maol and Mount Keen as the *only* Munros in Section 7. If the intervening bealach had to be below 600m in height Glas Maol and Mount Keen would disappear as well.

TABLE 6 – SUMMARY OF THE EFFECTS OF THE PROPOSALS

Hills	Current (1997)			Proposed				Proposed with lower limit			
	M	T	Total	M	T	N	Total	M	T	N	Total
Munros	284	227	511	288	172	122	582	314	201	142	657
Furths	20	14	34	20	17	5	42	22	18	5	45
Corbetts	220	–	220	219	–	–	219	209	–	–	209
Grahams	224	–	224	224	–	–	224	224	–	–	224
Donalds	89	51	140	79	67	27	173	88	82	40	210
Sub-totals *	807	292	1099	800	256	154	1210	826	301	187	1314
Lake District	74	76	150	61	61	31	153	64	61	39	164
Pennines	62	28	90	52	22	18	92	64	26	33	123
Wales	112	56	168	94	60	21	175	102	70	32	204
Ireland	156	101	257	175	58	24	257	185	63	30	278
Sub-totals	404	261	665	382	201	94	677	415	220	134	769
Totals *	**1191**	**539**	**1730**	**1162**	**440**	**243**	**1845**	**1219**	**503**	**316**	**2038**

The Table shows the numbers of Mountains (M), Tops (T) and Minor tops (N) in each of the regions under consideration on three bases. First, the current version of the published tables (using Hamish Brown's classification of the Furths, Bridge's Tables for England and Wales, and Wall's Irish list). Secondly, using the classification basis proposed herein (with discretion used as suggested in the text). And lastly, using that basis and also lower height limits of 900m, 750m or 600m as appropriate (and 150m as the Corbett reascent qualification).

The middle set of figures shows an increase of 4 in the number of Munros (i.e. 5, less 1 for Carn Ghluasaid). The final (right hand) set includes a further 21 mountains of 900m or more which are currently Corbetts, and five hills which would qualify as mountains despite not meeting the Corbett criterion. It is notable that the Corbetts would gain only 11 hills in the 750m–761m range from the Grahams, which is fewer than they would lose to the Munros; I have found no potential Corbetts with reascents of 150m but not 152m. The Grahams lose and gain equally at each end of the range.

In order to produce a fair comparison, minor tops are included above only if they are, or have ever been Tops in a published list or are very close to qualifying as tops. (The 'Pennines' row includes Dartmoor and the Isle of Man. Some of the Irish figures are estimates only.)

* Some totals in the first 'sub-total' row of the table are less than the sum of the preceding rows, as an adjustment has been made for the Corbetts and Grahams which are also Donalds. Similarly the final totals are adjusted to avoid double-counting the Furths. These sub-totals and overall totals are shown purely for interest, as it is not suggested that all the lists are comparable (even without the Furths, the total of all 600m hills in Scotland would be much larger).

10. Conclusion

Many readers, if they are still with me, will be saying *"What is all this about? Why should we not retain Munro's Tables, and the Corbett and Donald lists, as an historical record, rather than try to evolve any sort of formal classification rules? Let others, if they wish, produce tables of hills on whatever basis they choose."*

This is a perfectly valid approach, and one with which I have some lingering sympathy. However there are two reasons why I suggest that it is not the right one. Firstly, the pass has already been sold; many changes have been made to the *Tables* that have not resulted purely from resurveys. The tension between modernisers and traditionalists has meant that those changes have often been an unsatisfactory compromise. Secondly, there is clearly now a demand for hill lists covering all of the British Isles to a limit of 600m if not lower. To this sympathetic observer, it would be unfortunate if the SMC, by maintaining the 'historical' attitude, allowed its rôle to be taken over by others. One consequence is bound to be a plethora of systems; whereas if the Club took the lead I believe that its views would command respect.

Accordingly I conclude with a set of recommendations for the Club to consider. After the first, they are in what I expect to be the order of increasing sensitivity. It will be interesting to look back in a few years to see just how far down this list we have proceeded!

1. The SMC should endorse a system of classification. Of course I should like it to be the one put forward here; but the detail is less important than the endorsement.

   It would also be useful if a standard usage of 'mountain' and 'top' could be adopted and given effect to consistently throughout the introductions to Munro's and Donald's Tables.

2. The classification of the Donalds should be changed as described.

3. The five further tops recommended in Table 2 should be promoted to Munro, and Carn Ghluasaid should be demoted.

4. The minimum altitude for a Donald should be taken as 600m and that for a Munro should be 900m. For Corbetts the minimum altitude should be reduced to 750m, the maximum to 900m and the minimum reascent taken as 150m.

By way of a summary, Table 6 shows the number of mountains and tops (and my own count of minor tops) on three bases: the current published *Tables*; the *Tables* as modified by the rules proposed herein (with discretion exercised as suggested earlier); and finally with the addition of hills down to 900m or 600m as appropriate. (Interestingly, this last change would allow the inclusion of every hill that has *ever* been listed in the *Tables* – bar two; Am Bathaich north of Sgurr a' Mhaoraich, and Sgurr na Creige north of The Saddle. And the number of Corbetts would actually be reduced, to the benefit of the Munros.) I suggest that the numbers on the third basis support my view that all the above changes could be made without in any way detracting from the quality and authenticity of *Munro's Tables* and the other *Tables of Lower Hills*.

Finally, I should like to acknowledge the help given by the librarians of the SMC and the Alpine Club, without whose willing grant of access to their collections this article could hardly have been written, and also the constructive comments by the editor of this volume which have much improved the current version.

Additional References

The following are the references to the published lists in Table 1 that have not already been given above in footnotes.

Butterfield, Irving & Baines, Jack. 1992. *A Munroist's Log.* Ernest Press.

Buxton, Chris & Lewis, Gwyn. 1986. *The Mountain Summits of England and Wales.* Red Dial Publications.

Dillon, Paddy. 1992. *The Mountains of Ireland.* Cicerone Press.

Mulholland, H. 1980. *Guide to Eire's 3000ft Mountains,* and 1982. *Guide to Wales' 3000ft Mountains,* and 1983. *Guide to Lakeland's 3000ft Mountains.* (all Mulholland-Wirral).

Nuttall, John & Anne. 1989-90. *The Mountains of England and Wales: Vol. 1 – Wales and Vol. 2 – England.* Cicerone Press.

Parker, James A. Beinn Tarsuinn and the British 'Threes'. *SMCJ* 1929, XVIII, 336-343.

Wainwright, A. 1955-66. *A Pictorial Guide to the Lakeland Fells.* (In 7 volumes). Westmorland Gazette.

Walsh, A. St. G. The 2000-footers of England (and Wales). *Wayfarers' Journal* 1950, 31-37.

The following works contain useful discussions on classification criteria, or have otherwise contributed to the development of this article, but are not specifically referred to in the text.

Butterfield, Irvine. 1986. *The High Mountains.* Diadem Books

Campbell, Robin N. 1989. 'Munro and the Salvationist Tendency'. Chapter 1.7 above.

Dempster, Andrew. 1995. *The Munro Phenomenon.* Mainstream Publishing

Griffin, A. H. 1974. *Long Days in the Hills.* Robert Hale

Hodge, E. W. 1950. 'An Ancient Rage'. *Journal of the Fell and Rock Climbing Club.* pp. 298-302

Pyatt, E. C. & Clark, R. W. 1957. *Mountaineering in Britain.* Phoenix House

Smith, W. P. Haskett. 1894-5. *Climbing in the British Isles.* In two volumes (of the intended three)

The Irish section, by H C Hart, was reprinted as *Climbing in Ireland* in 1974, and the whole work was reprinted in one volume in 1986 by the Ernest Press

Wright, Nick. 1974. *English Mountain Summits.* Robert Hale

Appendix

The Classification Equations

When classifying a set of hills using the system put forward in section 6 above, it is of course necessary to determine for each hill its separation in distance and drop. However it is not essential to plot the results in graphical form to determine the hill's status, and it may in practice be more convenient to use the following equations (which can readily be used also to determine the excess or shortfall). In these, *km* is the separation in distance and *m* the separation in drop.

The Highlands

        If   *37.5 x km + m = 150 or more*,   the hill is a mountain.

        Otherwise, if   *7.5 x km + m = 30 or more*, it is a top.

South of the Highland Line

        If   *25 x km + m = 100 or more*,   the hill is a mountain.

        Otherwise, if   *5 x km + m = 20 or more*, it is a top.

THE ABSEIL

KEDGEREE

or A Windy Day in the Cairngorms[1]

The brindled limbs of Cairngorm
Cowered before the spiteful storm
Of rain-clouds hurling endless ranks
Against the mountain's sodden flanks.

So much for Art, you get the gist,
All wet and 'orrible and mist,
Which, far from promising dispersal,
Looked 'singularly universal'.

Beneath the showers' savage flurry
A tent, still redolent of curry,
Spewed forth two grubby mountain chaps,
Who, full of hope though short of maps,
Decided that the flood looked thinner;
"Cairngorm shall fall—but after dinner!"

Then, fortified by pints of tea
And quantities of kedgeree,
A certain SMITH emerged, and with
Him tagged along a second smith
(A smaller model, free of fame;
He almost blushed to bear the name).

The slope grew steep, the cairns flew past,
And still they galloped through the blast
Undaunted, till at ten to three,
The vanguard of the kedgeree
Sunk like a depth charge to the pit
Of smith's insides—a direct hit.
He crumpled up, deprived of breath
And gasped, his thoughts on choking death,
"Honour is all, press on, my friend"
—As all the best books recommend.

The SMITH, it seems, possessed a more a-
-thletic intestinal flora
And wheeched on up without a stop
To belch in freedom at the top;
While smith lay helpless, a balloon
Stretched taut between the fierce monsoon
That raged inside him, and the storm
Shrieking around his turgid form.

Before, I'd always thought it queer
That Indians seldom mountaineer.
The Himalaya's savage mould
Though on their doorstep, leaves them cold;
They are a most unclimbing nation,
Preferring shiftless contemplation.

The reason's clear. They live, you see,
On curried meat and kedgeree.

Jimmy Smith

---

[1] *Edinburgh University Mountaineering Club Journal, 1960-61. The hero of Jimmy Smith's witty and well-crafted poem is of course Robin Smith, who blew away the cobwebs from Scottish mountaineering from 1957 to 1962, when he died in an accident in the Pamirs.*

4.10 Some Unsolved Problems in Munroology

Geoff Cohen[1]

AS a rather intermittent practitioner and amateur student of Munroology, may I pose some questions that could be of interest to the more fastidious pedants of the subject?

1. I wonder whether there are any Munroists who can claim to have: (a) climbed all the Munros in true winter conditions, or (b) seen a clear view from the summit of each Munro, or (c) ascended each Munro separately (*i.e.* not as part of an interconnected ridge walk involving only a relatively short ascent from a high col).

These achievements are presented in ascending order of difficulty and I should be surprised if there were anyone who could claim the full absurdity of the last record. As an ultramontane with a tendency to pick up Munros in the back end of the year, I find that of a total of 125, some 60 per cent have been done in true winter conditions and, surprisingly, 65 per cent have yielded a view from the summit on at least one occasion.

2. It is generally recognised that as a science develops, its concepts pass from being purely classificatory to being capable of increasingly precise measurement. Concurrently more refined and mathematical models are proposed for the processes concerned. Perhaps the science of Munroology has reached sufficient maturity for such a quantitative approach to develop. In this spirit is a problem which has intrigued me since well before *Hamish's Mountain Walk*: the question of a minimum time path through all the Munros. The problem may be posed mathematically as follows: ignoring all logistical constraints, and defining the time between any pair of summits by a suitable version of Naismith's rule, what particular path from a given starting point would traverse all the Munros in the shortest possible time? Readers familiar with the nodes and links of graph theory may perhaps be able to offer an approximate solution to this computationally formidable problem.

3. A casual enquiry by a visitor front the south as to which area of Scotland contains the most Munros prompts the question of how best to define the (areal) density of Munros. This is related to problems like the isolation of Munros: which mountain or group of mountains is most isolated from peaks of similar height? It also has a connection with the '24 hour problem' of Blyth Wright: where should one try for the greatest number of Munros within the space of 24 hours? (An intriguing suggestion is the Cuillin Ridge followed by the North and South sides of Glen Shiel: but mechanical transport is surely unethical).

4. Ever more obscure problems abound for the ardent Munroological theoretician. Where, for instance, is the centre of gravity of the Munros – taking 'weight' as proportional to height above 3,000 feet? What, if anything, characterises the height distribution of Munros? (Unfortunately they do not follow Zipf's Law as might have been expected). All such problems can of course be extended to Munro tops, Corbetts or even Donalds and the 'furth of Scotland.'

Despite metrication, the subject of Munroology has apparently boundless horizons.

---

[1] *SMCJ* 1979, XXXI, 423-424.

Ben Vane[1]

Of mica schist, in many a twist
The goodly frame began
By Lomond shore, some time before
The Leven water ran.

First there was heat; to find a seat
Was inconvenient here,
And grievous then, in every glen,
Was many an atmosphere.

But, ages long, the fabric strong
Had time enough to cool,
When ice and snow their virtue show,
In every furrow full.

At last yielding, one lucky spring,
The winter shrank, and there
Beneath the face a resting place
Was offered to the bear.

And woolly elephants, they tell,
In Coiregrogan roamed;
Still on the bank you find the fank
Where they were clipped and combed.

Then, withering fast, the glaciers passed,
And there at length arrayed
With waters sheen and mosses green
The mountain was displayed.

The Bard would fain return, Ben Vane,
The strength of thee to scan,
But then, you see, his destiny
Has formed another plan.

W.P. Ker

---

[1]*SMCJ* (1912), Volume XII, No. 67, p. 46. The poem was written in atonement for failing to attend the 1912 New Year Meet of the SMC at Tarbet!

4.11 For the Next Revision of the Tables

James Gall Inglis[1]

THERE has been a gratifying revival of interest in mountain cartography of late, and the time seems to have arrived for beginning a systematic revision of Munro's Tables. Little can be done with the names and heights until the 6-inch map is revised, but a beginning could be made by casting out unworthy tops, and examining the claims of others to be promoted, the 'separate mountains' of the present Tables perhaps being allowed to remain unaltered.

Steps should also be taken to examine the 2750 contours of the O.S. maps in case some of them should actually be of 'Munro' height – at least one has been found since the Revised Tables were published. A few candidates evidently very near the 'Munro' line, but regarding which the evidence is conflicting at present, are given below.

In the Original Tables, the mountains being very little known, a large number of tops were included simply because the O.S. gave a contour, or the name or height of a point prominent from below. Many of these were found to be mere shoulders, and were therefore deleted in the Revision of the Tables; but others of the same type have been noted since, and from perusal of the 50-foot contours for this issue, others still will probably be hard put to it to preserve their status. On the other hand, from time to time many new tops have been proposed in the *SMC Journal* and obviously some kind of standard will have to be fixed.

What constitutes a 'Top'? While it is impossible to draw a hard-and-fast line, review of the doubtful 'tops' he has visited has led the writer to the conclusion that the definition depends a good deal on height and distance relative to the rest of the hill, and to individuality and geographical significance. What is fairly a 'top' on one hill may be obviously only a shoulder on another. The following are suggested as general conditions for deciding whether a point is a 'top' or merely a shoulder or spur:–

1. There should be a dip of some 75-100 feet, of decided gradient, to the col separating it from another top – though pinnacles and precipitous drops might perhaps be treated more leniently.

2. It should also have some kind of individuality. For instance, there should be something in the nature of a 'waist' in the contours below the col, or a branching from the main ridge, or peculiarity of formation, marking it off as a distinct portion of the ridge, not a mere undulation; or a sudden change in the character of the ridge from grass to rock, or from broad to very narrow.

3. Three classes of tops require special consideration, although not altogether up to the standard of the first two conditions: (a) The rising end of a long, fairly level ridge, from which the hillside falls steeply for a long distance. Where it is much lower than the rest of the ridge, it should in general be counted a shoulder, (b) Spur tops, branching off main ridges and much lower than the other tops, but with the 'waist,' or formation, or individuality feature prominent. Those with no particular individuality and with cols of easy gradient should not be accorded the higher status, (c) Plateau tops, great distances apart, as in the E. Grampians.

---

[1] From *Munro's Tables, etc.* SMC *General Guide-Book*. 1933. Pp. iv-v.

James Gall Inglis, second Master of the Tables and sixth Munroist

ADDITIONAL NOTES, TABLE I (1933)[2]

STOB AN FHIR-BHOGHA (B. Heasgarnich): evidently only a hummock; no 'top' found, but possible top N. of cairn, JRC.[3]

CARN DEARG N.W. (Ben Nevis) : 4020-4080 ft. approx., by aneroid. Actual top is on the edge of cliff, some 300 yards S. of the O.S. cairn shoulder, above which Mheall Bhanabhie (1071 ft.) showed prominently, JGI.

STOB COIRE AN FHIR DHUIBH (Aonach Mor) : 3325 ft. approx., JD

SGAIRNEACH MHOR : actual top is at the edge of the cliffs, as indicated by the hill-shading. The 3053 point to the W. is entitled to consideration as a top on account of its formation; the col, however, seems less than 53 ft., JGI.

A' BHUIDHEANACH (of Carn Liath): 3177 ft.; should be Centre Top, as name applies to the whole ridge.

MAOL CHINN-DEARG (South Cluanie): 3214 ft. ; should be W. Top, as name applies to the whole ridge.

CREAG A' CHOIR' AIRD (Sg. nan Ceathramhnan): S. Top (last edn., 'Southern ridge') ; the adverse comment on the inference drawn from the hill-shading should be deleted from the Note, as it does riot apply to the new position '1/2 m. S.' of the 3188-foot top. The '1 1/2 m. south' of the last edition seems to have been a clerical error, as HTM's card index has '1/2 m. S.', agreeing with JD.'s position, and height of 3215 ft.

TOM A' CHOINICH BEAG (Affric): 3450 ft. approx.; JD says 'certainly 50 ft. lower than An Leth-Chreag'; in view of several readings about 3450 ft., it seems possible that the O.S. height of An Leth-Chreag may not be that of the actual top.

AN RIABHACHAN: 3696 ft.; this is the correct height, the hill-shading, on which the 3730 estimate of the last edition was based, having been found to be erroneous, and the 3700 confirming contour now stated to be only approximate. The county boundary top is not more than 10 ft. lower, there being a point 3686 close to the boundary.

BEN WYVIS: 'Glas Leathad Mor', in the new 1-in. map, apparently refers to the lower slopes of the whole ridge, not the top.

CONA' MHEALL (Inverlael): 3225 ft. ap.; a S. Top, 3050 ft. ap., should be added, the summit of a fine narrow precipitous ridge: sharply-defined narrow col, dip about 75 ft., JGI.

MEALL NAN CEAPRAICHEAN: 3192 ft. approx., RB; 3175 and 3220, JGI; the top is at the south end of the ridge, where the O.S. has only a 3100 contour. The 3150 contour to the north is only an undulation in a rising ridge, some 25 ft. lower than the actual top, without individuality, and not a 'top';   Ceann Garbh is also a very doubtful top, without individuality, col some 50 ft. only, of slight gradient, JGI.

New 'Munro' : (on the other hand, RB and JRC make M. na Teanga only 2991 ft. ap.).

BEINN TARSUINN: 2850 contour, 6 3/4 m. N. of Kinlochewe ; 2980 ft., CP; 3080 ft., JRC, JGI,

---

[2] I have edited out references by JGI to Table pages and to SMCJ articles reproduced in the present volume.

[3] Initials refer as follows: RB – Ronald Burn; JRC – J. Rooke Corbett; EMC – Edred M. Corner; JD – John Dow; JGI – J. Gall Inglis; HTM – Hugh T. Munro; JAP – James A. Parker; ECT – Edward C. Thomson.

JAP; 3075 ft., and photo of B. Eighe shows it is not lower than Sg. an Tuill Bhain, Mr J. Hirst. The status of this hill seems well established. Note by Mr Colin Phillip: 'The map of this part was very casual: I think the O.S. had bad weather, and were hurried in order to meet the views of the then laird.'

Possible 'Munros': and Suggested Tops. Space and time limit this list to the less debatable items.

BEINN A' CHLAIDHEIMH, 2800 contour, 10 m. N.by E. of Kinlochewe : 3120 ft., at S. end, ECT; 2997, estimate by B. Dearg Mhor, 2976 by aneroid, new 1-in. map contours unsatisfactory, JRC. No near high-up setting available.

RUADH STAC MOR, 2850 cont.; 2940 ft., after making B. Tarsuinn 2970, A' Maighdean 3120, CP.

CARN GORM LOCH, 2950 cont., $1^{1}/_{4}$ m. E. of Am Faochagach; over 3000, note HTM; 3010 ft., RB; 3020, est. from Am Faochagach, JG1; 2910 (too low), JRC.

FOINAVEN, 2980 ft.; perhaps 3013 ft., RB.

CREAG MHOR (Glen Lyon); well-marked W. Top, JGI.

MEALL GARBH (Carn Mairg); E. Top, fairly well marked. The actual top is at the W. end of the ridge; a third top, not so well marked, is $^{1}/_{2}$ m. S.E., and 70 ft. lower; Meall Luaidhe, not a top, having only a 50 ft. col of small gradent, JGI.

B. A' CHLACHAIR : important N.E. Top, 3138 ft. approx., RB.

GURR THIONAIL (Sgurr a' Mhaoraich), 2965 feet : 3065 ft. approx., RB, JRC; looks higher than Am Bathaich

SGURR A' CHLAIDHEIMH ; ? over 3000 ft., RB.

BEINN FHADA (Kintail): two tops suggested, RB.

TOM COINNICH (Fannichs), top of Druim Reidh ridge, 1 m. E. of A' Chailleach, 2750 contour; 3131 ft. ap., RB: 'certainly over 3000, but not so high as RB's figures,' JRC.

MULLACH COIRE. MHIC FHEARCHAIR : a well-marked S.E. Top, Tom Choinnich, should be added, RB, JGI; 3229 ft. ap., RB; 3166, JRC; 3150, estimate, JGI.

CREAG AN DUINE (E. end Seana Braigh ridge, 2900 cont.); the ends appeared absolutely same height from 3000 ft. on Meall nan Ceapraichean, though the 3041 ft. point was nearer, but Mr J.A. Parker made C. an Duine only 2980 ft., JGI.

MEALL GORM (Am Faochagach): 2900 contour; worth examining, suggested as 3000 by RB, and as possibly, but probably under, 3000, by JGI. The S. top of Am Faochagach, doubtfully suggested by RB, is not worthy of the name, JGI.

BYNAC BHEAG should be added to the Tables, RB, JRC; 3194 ft., RB.

B. BHROTAIN; ? an E. Top, 3550 ft. ap., EMC; well-marked in hill-shading.

MONADH MOR; ? a S. Top, 3575 ft. ap., dip about 150 ft., EMC; other proposals dubious.

CARN BHAC: S.W. Top, 3014 ft. ; should be Centre Top ; the real S.W. Top of the ridge is CARN A' BHUTHA.

AN SGARSOCH ; ? a S. TOP, 3178 ft. ap., RB.

4.12 Tables of Scottish Mountains before Munro

Chris Huntley[1]

READERS of the 1997 edition of Munro's Tables will have been interested in the comment on pp.1-2 of the Introduction, that the SMC was aware of a publication predating the Tables in which, county by county, hills are listed in descending order. The initial correspondence which brought this to our attention is given below, followed by our reply.

Peter Warburton wrote to inform us that: "Before Sir Hugh Munro brought out his Tables of Heights over 3000 feet, in the first (1891) volume of the Scottish Mountaineering Club Journal, it was generally believed that only some 30 hills were of that altitude; the authoritative Baddeley's Guide, for instance, listed 31.

"A similar statement, rather more cautiously worded, appeared in the foreword to the 1974 edition of the Tables. It is surprising that such an unlikely assertion seems to have gone unchallenged, except for the qualification in the following sentence that perhaps a few early Club members thought they knew rather better. In the way of these things, the qualification has gone largely unnoticed and the 30/31 figure has been so widely quoted that the myth has come to be regarded as a fact, backed by the authority of the Tables.

"Baddeley's 31 did not claim to be a complete listing and any reader glancing casually at the many ½ inch to the mile maps included in the guides would have noticed dozens more mountains with spot heights above 3000 ft. The rival firm of Black were more prudent; their list of twenty-three 3000 footers was headed 'Some of the Principal Mountains in Scotland according to the Ordnance Survey'. It is a pity that, in trumping Black's 23, Baddeley chose the single line title 'Heights of Scotch Mountains'.

"The source for all serious guide book writers was the OS who had completed their large scale (6" to the mile) field survey of Scotland by 1877. This survey, with some later revision, became the basis for the 1-inch series, publication of which Baddeley noted, in June 1883, was 'all but complete' for the Highlands. Those who found that a smaller scale commercial map met their needs had a choice. One of the best was published by Johnson's of Edinburgh. Even at the scale of 10 miles to the inch their editions in the 1850s named and gave heights for 46 hills of over 3000ft. or 42 if hindsight is used to exclude 4 mistakes (Ben Ledi, Ben Vrackie, Foinaven and Beinn a' Bha'ach Ard).

---

[1] *SMCJ* 1998, XXXVI, 704-5. Chris Huntley, of course, is the present Keeper of the List.

"Before Sir Hugh's Tables appeared, the full listing of Scottish hills in order of height may well have been considered an eccentric and pointless pursuit, but it had been undertaken. Robert Hall's 'The Highland Sportsman and Tourist' (Third Edition, 1884) lists 236 heights of 3000ft. or more plus 1867 – yes, 1867 –lower hills, each with county and district. Mr. Hall was in business in London and Inverness as a shooting and estate agent and the 313 page 'Highland Sportsman', priced at 2/6d, was probably circulated *gratis* to clients. The extent to which he cast his bread upon the waters is indicated by the inclusion, among the end papers, of three pages of Press Opinions of an earlier edition - 40 quotations in all and all favourable. My copy is stamped 'With the Author's Compliments' and it is probable that many Highland proprietors received copies on that basis - perhaps one even reached the library at Lindertis?"

Peter Warburton's text arrived at what could be considered an inopportune time. The Scottish Mountaineering Trust and the Editor of Munro's Tables were putting together a new edition and the possibility that the Tables were pre-dated needed to be investigated.

My first attempts to acquire a copy of the book came to nothing, although most antiquarian booksellers I spoke to did seem to be familiar with this publication and others of a similar vogue by Mr. Hall. One bookseller told me he knew the book well, and had a copy which he would send. It duly arrived but was actually by a Herbert Hall, published in the 1850s, and was entitled 'The Highland Tourist'. This was also a tourist's compendium, very much aimed at the sporting Tourist. However, there were no lists of hills. Fortunately a call to the National Library of Scotland confirmed that they had a number of editions and so I finally managed to see a copy. Sure enough, there, chapter by chapter, were lists of hills although these were largely swamped by the salient information directed at the Victorian Tourist who was far more interested in the Shooting and Fishing opportunities than the Hills. I found that, in fact, the hills warranted almost no comment, and when I did come across a mention of Ben Lomond in the text I found that it wasn't on the list! The publication seems to have been annual from 1882-1885, and looking at each one I could not actually see any changes. Perhaps some of the detail on prices and estate owners necessitated new editions.

Having seen the Hall publication, I then went back to check the first publication of the Tables and found that the claim of there only being 31 summits exceeding 3000 feet did not originate from that time, and seems to have only appeared in the more recent editions. Therefore this observation did not come from Sir Hugh. Once this was clarified the element of doubt that Sir Hugh Munro had either not read up on the subject (i.e. searching out guides such as Hall's) or that he was not making good use of the existing maps, is removed. Instead what we have is Sir Hugh producing a publication which was using available information from the existing maps, enhancing it by setting a cut off point of 3000 feet, and then thoroughly exploring each area to search out the Mountains from the Tops.

In making a direct comparison of the lists there is much variation in the spelling of hills and even heights, making a straight copy very unlikely. In addition Sir Hugh created his own areas (The Sections) grouping together logical clusters of hills rather than using county boundaries. One issue that Hall had to resolve, and Sir Hugh avoided, was in which county should a top be listed when it falls on the county border (as many do)? For this reason we find Stob an t-Sluichd on Ben Avon being the only hill above 3000 feet listed in Banffshire, with all the other tops on Ben Avon found in the chapter for Aberdeenshire. Sir Hugh's reasons for selecting the 3000 feet limit is interesting, and never given as far as I know, although he was defining a sufficiently demanding, but feasible List to occupy a lifetime of hillwalking, given the conditions at that time.

In conclusion we have two very different publications, both of which have their origins in the maps of the 1880's. The first from Mr. Hall, a fascinating guide to the 'Sporting' opportunities of the Highlands, which, no doubt, was useful to the Tourists of its day but with little or no comment on the quality of routes on the Hills, and secondly Munro's Tables, which was directed to all those interested in the Hills and which is still generating much discussion and pleasure! And readers of the new Tables will find no mention of the '31 hills' in the Introduction.

Expostulation with Cruachan[1]

TUNE: Into thir dark and drublie dayis.

Of Crechanben the crewilté,
The driftis dreich, the hichtis hie,
It sair wald tene my tong to tell;
Quha suld reherss thy painis fell
Forgaitheris with the frenesie.

With fensom feiris thou art forfairn,
Ay yowland lyk ane busteous bairn;
With mauchie mistis thy mirth is marrit,
With skowland skyis the spreit is skarrit,
And seitis ar cauld upon thy cairn.

Quhair is thy lown illuminat air,
Thy fre fassoun, thy foirheid fair?
Quheir is thy peirles pulchritude?
Quhy stayis thou nocht as anis thou stude,
Quhy girnis and greitis thou evirmair?

Return agane fra drowpand dule!
Restoir thy pure wayfarand fule,
And lat him se thee quhair thou smylis,
With Mul, Arane, and the Owt-Ylis,
Into the lufsom licht of Yule.

Quod KER

---

[1]*SMCJ (1900), Volume VI, No. 32, p. 52. A poem by William.Paton Ker in the manner of William Dunbar. The 'tune' suggested by Ker is the first line of Dunbar's melancholic Meditatioun in Winter and could only be the dreariest sort of dirge! Ker was Professor of Poetry at All Souls, Oxford.*

CHAPTER 5

The History of Munro's Tables

5.1 The Published Tables

HUGH MUNRO'S original Tables appeared in September 1891 in the sixth and last number of Volume I of the *SMC Journal*. These Tables are now very inaccessible, since they have not been reprinted. They exhibit large differences of layout and nomenclature from later more accessible editions; they contain a number of anomalies and errors; the heights given are often very approximate, since in many cases only 250ft. contours or questionable aneroid readings were available; locations are given sometimes in the broadest terms – e.g. 'North of Loch Laggan' – but usually in terms of a rough distance and compass direction from other hills or from hotels, etc., and they are supplemented by sometimes lengthy and interesting notes. For all these reasons, I decided it was essential that this Companion should reproduce the original Table 1. At first I thought that a facsimile version would suit best. Certainly it would suit the reproduction of the thousands of 4-pt. fractions which the Table contains! But it would use 24 pages, include two columns of very little interest (the 'County' and 'Best ascended from' columns), and, besides, I would have to unstitch my priceless copy of Volume I to permit photography! In any event, consideration of the subsequent history of the Tables suggested a different plan.

The second edition of the Tables appeared in October 1921, two years after Munro's death, as the final chapter of *Section A of the SMC Guide*, a volume which was called the *General Guide* in later editions. Although based on Munro's Card Index and his annotated personal copy of the Tables, the new Master of the Tables, James Gall Inglis, used a different layout, in which Tops were indented under the Munro to which they were allocated. This necessitated a change in the order of tops, since Munro had followed a consistent directional principle when describing any group of tops (e.g. the Ben Lawers Range is described from south to north along the ridge). Inglis added to the notes left by Munro and distinguished his own notes from Munro's, but it is in general not obvious what in the new Tables is due to Inglis and what due to Munro. There were a great many changes: improvements in the spelling of hill names, refinements of height estimates, much more accurate locations using a resolution of about 100 yards and 32 compass directions. Moreover, forty-odd tops changed status, suffering promotion to Munro, demotion to Top or deletion and about twenty new tops were introduced, including some Munros such as Sgurr a' Mhadaidh and Sgurr Mhic Choinnich.

The 1921 Tables were published in almost exactly the same form in 1933 (as part of the *General Guide*, and in 1953 and 1969 as a single volume entitled *Munro's Tables and other Tables of Lesser Heights*. While Inglis and the succeeding editors James C. Donaldson and Wilfrid L. Coats flirted with the introduction of the Letterewe Munro Beinn Tarsuinn (known as an Ordnance Survey mistake for many years), it wasn't properly included. The only introduced top was Carn a' Bhutha, a satellite of Carn Bhac, which promptly disappeared. Other minor changes were the sharpening of contour heights to 50 ft., the correction of a mistake in the status of An Gearanach and An Garbhanach, and the addition of four-figure Grid References (the bottom left corner of the target square) as an aid to location.

So the first real revision after 1921 did not occur until 1974, when Donaldson edited the first metric version of the Tables. Although few metric heights were available, Donaldson pressed on zealously and converted the best Imperial height (often still only a contour height!) to metres for each top. Six-figure Grid References were provided for the first time. Donaldson also introduced Beinn Tarsuinn and two other Letterewe Munros (Ruadh Stac Mor and Beinn a' Chlaidheimh), juggled with the competing summit tops of some hills, and deleted Beinn an Lochain and other inadequate tops. But these changes of status occurred as a result of new Ordnance Survey heights, so although the 1974 Tables contained many changes and innovations, they did not break faith with the principles (whatever they are) governing the 1891 through 1969 versions of the Tables. Rather strangely, Donaldson did not specify his metric criterion for inclusion, nor the conversion factor used. In fact, his conversions to metric height were often erroneous or unexpected so that the top numbers did not reflect previous editions well. The new six-figure locations were also sometimes wayward.

In 1981 Donaldson and the heroic multi-completer Hamish M. Brown joined forces to produce a radical revision of the Tables. They set out to put right what they regarded as anomalies in the Tables, such as the miserly allocation of Munros to Liathach and An Teallach and the overgenerous provision of Munros and especially Tops in the Cairngorms and Grampians. The traditional Table Sections suffered only minor revisions but endured a major rearrangement, since the Cairngorm and Grampian sections were now described after the Lochaber-to-Drumochter section rather than as the last mainland area. In addition, most sections were now divided into named subsections. New metric map coverage was now almost complete, so that the heights and locations were much more accurate than in 1974. While Donaldson and Brown perhaps gained some favour by promoting Garbh Chioch Mhor, Mullach an Rathain and Sgurr Fiona, they also acquired a retinue of bitter detractors for demoting Carn Cloich-mhuilinn and six other eastern Munros!

The 1981 revision continued through new versions in 1984 and (under a new Editor, Derek A. Bearhop) in 1990, but without significant changes apart from the introduction of Beinn Teallach, which had been elevated by the Ordnance Survey. However, in 1997 Bearhop produced new Tables in which the reforms introduced by Donaldson and Brown were carried further. Eight Tops were promoted to Munro rank: for seven of them this was a new experience, but the eighth – Sgor an Lochain Uaine (formerly of Cairn Toul) – had been a separate mountain in the 1891 Tables! Bearhop continued the shake-out of inadequate Tops, being especially severe with those close to Munro tops, and also introduced nine Tops, including three Tops reinstated from older Tables!

Leaving minor revisions and reprintings aside, then, there have been five distinct versions of Munro's Tables – the 1891, 1921, 1974, 1981 and 1997 Tables. The hill-walker of today who consults the present Tables and compares these with the 1891 Tables will consequently encounter many difficulties due to changes in nomenclature, location, height and the scale used to measure it; the appearance, disappearance and re-appearance of tops; and, not least, the rearrangement and revision of Table sections. Accordingly, the next chapter presents a summary or variorum Table 1 which traces the movement of tops from 1891 to 1997 through these five major versions. Naturally, the Variorum Table contains every entry from the 1891 Table 1, and it is also constructed so as to preserve the order of the 1891 Table.

5.2 A Variorum Table of the Munros and Tops

THE FIRST REQUIREMENT for such a table is a method of referring to tops that is independent of name, height, location, etc., since all of these are liable to change. This was achieved by using a two-letter mnemonic derived from the existing subsection names, followed by a one or two-digit number corresponding to the order of appearance of the top in the Tables. The order in which tops are described in the 1891 Tables provided the original numbering and later-introduced tops are added in sequence of publication. Thus Blaven is SK01 and Knight's Peak is SK23, etc. The Subsection mnemonics together with Old and New Section numbers and 1997 Subsection names are shown below in Table 5.1.

1997 Subsection Name	Code	Old Section	New Section	1997 Subsection Name	Code	Old Section	New Section
Ben Lomond & the Arrochar Alps	AR	1	1	Eastern Cairngorms	EC	14	8
Ben Lui Group	LU	1	1	Loch Laggan Hills	LA	6	9
Balquhidder	BQ	1	1	Monadh Liath	ML	6	9
Crieff and Loch Earn	SE	2	1	Loch Lochy Hills	WL	7	10
Glen Lochay Hills	MF	3	2	Glenfinnan	FI	7	10
Bridge of Orchy Hills	OR	3	2	Glen Dessary-Kingie	DK	7	10
The Lawers Group	LT	3	2	Knoydart	KN	7	10
Glen Lyon	LY	3	2	Loch Quoich	QO	7	10
Cruachan Group	CR	4	3	Sgritheall	SG	7	10
Etive Hills	ET	4	3	South Glen Shiel (Saddle)	SA	7	10
Blackmount	BL	4	3	South Glen Shiel (S. Cluanie)	SS	7	10
Appin	AP	4	3	The Five Sisters-Ciste Dhubh	NS	8	11
Glencoe	CO	4	3	A' Chralaig-Conbhairean Gp	ES	8	11
Aonach Eagach	AE	5	3	Ben Attow	AT	8	11
The Mamores	MA	5	4	Glen Affric	AF	8	11
Ben Nevis and the Aonachs	NE	5	4	Sgurr na Lapaich Group	NM	9	12
Grey Corries	GC	5	4	East of Achnashellach	EA	9	12
Loch Treig and Loch Ossian	OT	5	4	Strathfarrar Hills	SF	9	12
Loch Ericht to Loch Laggan	EL	5	4	Coulin Forest	WA	10	13
The West Drumochter Hills	WD	5	5	Torridon	TO	10	13
The East Drumochter Hills	ED	15	5	Letterewe and Fisherfield	LF	11	14
Tarf and Tilt	TT	15	6	The Fannichs	FA	11	14
West of the Cairnwell Pass	WC	15	6	An Teallach	TE	11	14
Glas Maol Hills	GM	16	7	Ben Wyvis	WY	12	15
Glen Doll Hills	DO	16	7	Beinn Dearg Group	GU	12	15
Lochnagar	SD	16	7	Assynt	AS	13	16
Glen Feshie Hills	FE	14	8	Klibreck and Hope	KH	13	16
Western Cairngorms	BC	14	8	Mull	MU	17	17
Macdui-Cairngorm	MC	14	8	Skye	SK	17	17

Table 5.1 Unique Two-Letter Mnemonic Codes for Subsections of 1997 Table 1

Codes requiring additional explanation: SE–Strathearn; MF–Mamlorn Forest; LT–Lawers and Tarmachan; OT–Ossian-Treig; SD–South Deeside; BC–Braeriach-Cairn Toul; WL–West Lochy; NS–North Shiel; ES–East Shiel; NM–North Mullardoch; WA–West Achnashellach; GU–Garve-Ullapool.

Numbering the tops in this way and following the sequence of Old Sections thereby preserves the order of the 1891 Table, apart from two minor departures needed to keep Subsections intact: Stuchd an Lochain/Meall Buidhe are placed beside the other Glen Lyon Hills and Driesh/Mayar beside the other Glen Doll Hills. From each of the five Tables the following information was collected: Name; Height in feet; Height in metres (employing conversion at 1m=3.2808ft. where necessary); Location; (for Tops) which Munro they are considered to be a top *of*); (for Munros) Separate Mountain Number; Top number; Table Section Number and 1-inch or 2-cm. Map Number. New tops were allocated new identifiers in sequence of publication, as described above. The five Tables were then combined in a single Variorum Table, with five lines of information for each top.

Proceeding in this fashion through the five versions yielded 591 tops, of which only 413 have the same status in each version – 248 constant Munros and 165 constant Tops. Thus an astonishing 178 tops have been introduced, deleted, promoted or demoted since 1891! Amongst these are 146 straightforward cases in which a single change is involved: 10 introduced Munros, 27 introduced Tops, 26 Munros demoted to Top, 23 Tops promoted to Munro, 3 deleted Munros and 57 deleted Tops. So an additional 62 tops have become or ceased to be a Munro. The remaining 32 varying tops are the result of 'third or fourth thoughts' by successive Editors. For example, rival tops with very small mutual separations have jostled for the positions of summit of Ben Lui, Beinn a' Chaoruinn (Laggan), Carn Ballach, Creag a' Choire Aird, Maoile Lunndaidh, Slioch and Sgurr Dearg; Sgurr an Iubhair and Sgor an Lochain Uaine have enjoyed promotion and also suffered demotion; Sgurr Dearg (Cairn) has made the ignominious traverse from Munro to Top to deletion. But who knows?: it may come back! After all, Editors have reinstated 13 tops which their predecessors had seen fit to delete! Taking account also of these wavering tops, then, there is (I think!) a grand total of 324 tops which have enjoyed the status of Munro in one or other version of the Tables.

Notes on interpretation of the Table

The 5 versions of Table 1 are identified by: [91] – 1891; [21] – 1921; etc.

The first line of each entry contains a unique top Identifier (already described), a coded History, and Remarks about the top, either referred to a version, or general [G].

History: The first 5 letters give the status of the top in each of the 5 versions of Table 1: M – a Munro; T – a Top; x – absent. Following a semi-colon, up to three letters specify other aspects of the top's history: N – a change of name; H – a variation in spot height greater than 50ft. between Tables; L – a variation greater than 400 metres in location between Tables.

Remarks: These draw attention to changes or features that seem important and also describe typos, errors or other peculiarities in the 5 versions of the Tables. Where something is marked as a typo or error, the value has been corrected. So an entry such as '[74] typo: Northing 453 should be 253' means that the GR in the 1974 Table ended in 453, but this has been changed to 253 in the Variorum Table entry.

Up to 5 lines follow, each headed by a version identifier – [91], etc. and giving the top's Name, Height in feet, Height in metres, Location, 'Parent' Munro, Munro Number, Top Number, Section Number and Map Number.

Names: An asterisk indicates that the name appears only on the base map and not on the 1-inch/2-cm. map. A hash signifies that the name is a local name, not appearing on either map.

Heights: Square brackets indicates that the height is a conversion from the best available height in the other standard. Imperial heights follow these rules:-

1. If a single height is given, then either:-
   a. the 1-inch and 6-inch maps give the same spot height - no indication
   b. the 6-inch gives a spot height and no 1-inch height or contour is available - indicated by '*'
   c. the 1-inch gives a contour and no 6-inch height or contour is available - indicated by 'c'
2. If 2 heights or contours are given, the first is the 6-inch and the second, in brackets, is the 1-inch
3. Any height followed by an 'a' is an approximate height measured by climbers

Editors of metric Tables have published only a single height, so the entries are simpler. However, policies have differed: 1974 heights are 10-cm. map heights; 1981-to-1990 heights are 2-cm. map heights where these are available and from larger-scale maps – "or other sources" – when there is no 2-cm. height; 1997 heights are taken from the most recent larger scale map.

Map Numbers: No map numbers were supplied in 1891. In 1921, the numbers are those of the 2nd Revision of the 1-inch (1905-7). A hill-shaded version of this revision was produced around 1912, and this is sometimes referred to in notes. In 1974, the numbers are for the 7th Series 1-inch and in all later Tables for the 2 cm. Landranger Series.

Finally, there may be a line of Notes. These Notes reproduce those of the published Tables, perhaps with some extra abbreviation. Notes having to do with the location or condition of Hotels, etc., have not been included. Munro's 1891 Notes are included in full, except where these are repeated in Chapter 4.2. In the 1921 Tables Notes 'not passed by Munro' were printed in square brackets. This usage is repeated here.

General Principles: The policy followed in relation to Table errors has already been described, under *Remarks* above. Of course, not all such errors have been detected, and new errors will have been introduced. Please report any further errors found. Where the status, height and location of a top did not vary between versions it seemed pointless to include all 5 lines, so in such cases only the first and last/most recent appearance in that status is included. In very many cases the only difference between the entries for 1891 and 1921 was an improved location, so in such cases – provided the top did not subsequently change status in 1974 – the 1921 entry was not included, but the improved location was – as a Remark.

Abbreviations, etc. Any possible abbreviations (L. for Loch, etc.) have been applied where the meaning is sufficiently clear. 'Appended' is abbreviated to 'App.' Fractional distances have been replaced by decimal parts of a mile.

No. Yr.	Code Name	Status	Remarks Feet	Metres	Location	Of Mtn.	Top	Sect.	Map
AR01		MMMMM	[21] 2.75m NbyE of Rowardennan						
[91]	Ben Lomond		3192	[973]	3m NbyE of Rowardennan	179	315	1	
[97]	Ben Lomond		[3195]	974	NN 367 028	184	297	1	56
AR02		MMMMM	[21] 2.25m NW of Arrochar						
[91]	Beinn Narnain★		3036 (3000)	[925]	1.5m SE of AR03	254	462	1	
[97]	Beinn Narnain		[3038]	926	NN 271 066	259	454	1	56
AR03		MMMMM							
[91]	Beinn Ime		3318 (3250)	[1011]	3.75m NW of Arrochar	117	198	1	
[97]	Beinn Ime		[3317]	1011	NN 255 084	118	190	1	56
AR04		MMMMM							
[91]	Ben Vane		3004	[916]	3.75m NNW of Arrochar	278	506	1	
[97]	Ben Vane		[3002]	915	NN 277 098	283	507	1	56
AR05		MMMxx	[21] 3m SEbyE of Cairndow Inn [G] 3021 ht. confirmed by O.S. in 1933! Deleted 1981.						
[91]	Beinn an Lochain		3021	[921]	3m ESE of Cairndow Inn	262	480	1	
[74]	Beinn an Lochain		3021a (2992)	[921]	NN 217 079	265	511	1	53
Notes: [91] The 3021 top is 150 yards NE of 2955 pt. (1-in.)									
AR06		MMMMM							
[91]	Ben Vorlich, South Top		3092	[942]	2.5m SW of Ardlui	222	405	1	
[97]	Ben Vorlich		[3094]	943	NN 295 124	229	391	1	56/50
AR07		TTTTT							
[91]	Ben Vorlich, North Top		3055	[931]	2.25m SW of Ardlui		440	1	
[97]	Ben Vorlich, North Top		[3054]	931	NN 294 130	AR06	434	1	56/50
AR08		MMMMM							
[91]	Beinn Buidhe		3106	[947]	4m N of head L. Fyne	211	385	1	
[97]	Beinn Bhuidhe		[3110]	948	NN 203 187	216	371	1	56/50
LU01		MMMMM	[21] 1m SWbyW of LU02						
[91]	Beinn a' Chleibh		3008	[917]	1m SW of LU02	273	498	1	
[97]	Beinn a' Chleibh		[3005]	916	NN 250 256	281	502	1	50
LU02		MMxMM	[G] Deleted in favour of LU05 1974 (error?). Reinstated 1981.						
[91]	Beinn Laoigh (Ben Lui)		3708	[1130]	6m E of Dalmally	26	46	1	
[97]	Ben Lui		[3707]	1130	NN 266 263	28	42	1	50
Notes: [91] The actual top is in Perthshire									
LU03		MMMMM							
[91]	Beinn Oss		3374	[1028]	1.5m ESE of LU02	102	172	1	
[97]	Ben Oss		[3376]	1029	NN 287 253	101	161	1	50
LU04		MMMMM	[74] Typo: Height 3024 should be 3204.						
[91]	Beinn Dubh Chraige		3204	[977]	3.25m SSW of Tyndrum	170	300	1	
[97]	Beinn Dubhchraig		[3209]	978	NN 307 254	175	282	1	50
LU05		xxMTx	[74] GR is Ben Lui, NW Top; possibly an error. [G] Introduced 1974. Deleted 1997.						
[74]	Ben Lui		3708	[1130]	NN 265 264	27	50	1	53
[81]	Ben Lui, N.W Top		[3697]	1127	NN 265 264	LU02	48	1	50
BQ01		MMMMM							
[91]	Beinn Chabhair		3053	[931]	3.5m ENE of Ardlui	242	442	1	
[97]	Beinn Chabhair		[3061]	933	NN 367 179	244	426	1	50/56
BQ02		MMMMM	[21] 3.75m S of Crianlarich						
[91]	An Caisteal★		3265 (3250)	[995]	1m NE of BQ01	145	241	1	
[97]	An Caisteal		[3264]	995	NN 378 193	147	238	1	50/56
BQ03		TTTTT	[21] .63m WbyS of BQ04 [74] Height 929 in Table 2 is wrong, producing wrong Top No.						
[91]	Beinn a' Chroin, West Top		3078 (3000)	[938]	4.25m SbyE of Crianlarich		419	1	
[97]	Beinn a' Chroin, West Top		[3077]	938	NN 385 185	BQ04	410	1	50/56
BQ04		MMMMM							
[91]	Beinn a' Chroin, East Top		3101	[945]	4.25m SbyE of Crianlarich	216	394	1	
[97]	Beinn a' Chroin		[3084]	940	NN 394 186	233	403	1	50/56
BQ05		MMMMM	[21] 4m SEbyE of Crianlarich						
[91]	Beinn Tulachan		3099	[945]	4.25m SSE of Crianlarich	219	401	1	
[97]	Beinn Tulaichean		[3104]	946	NN 416 196	220	380	1	56
BQ06		Mxxxx	[G] Soon mapped lower than BQ07, so deleted 1921.						
[91]	Cruach Ardran, N.E. Top		3477 (3250)	[1060]	3m SSE of Crianlarich	72	124	1	
Notes: [91] The W top is given on the 6-in. as 3429; the E top —77, the first 2 digits obliterated. So the height is probably 3477, as it is only slightly higher than the W top									
BQ07		TMMMM	[74] Typo: Mtn. No. 86 should be 87. [G] Promoted 1921.						
[91]	Cruach Ardran, S.W. Top		3429 (3250)	[1045]	.25m of BQ06		148	1	
[21]	Cruach Ardrain		3428 (3250)	[1045]	3m SEbyE of Crianlarich	83	158	1	46
[97]	Cruach Ardrain		[3432]	1046	NN 409 212	87	138	1	51/56
Notes: [21] [The '—77' pt. (NE top, BQ06) is revised to 3377 in the 6-inch and so now deleted]									

No. Yr.	Code Name	Status	Remarks	Feet	Metres	Location	Of Mtn.	Top	Sect.	Map
BQ08		Txxxx	[G] Deleted 1921.							
[91]	Top btw. Cruach Ardran & Stob Garbh			3034 (3000)	[925]	Btw. BQ06 & BQ09		465	1	
BQ09		TTTTT								
[91]	Stob Garbh			3148	[960]	2.5m SE of Crianlarich		349	1	
[97]	Stob Garbh			[3146]	959	NN 411 221	BQ07	341	1	51/56
BQ10		MMMMM								
[91]	Ben More			3843	[1171]	3m EbyS of Crianlarich	17	28	1	
[97]	Ben More			[3852]	1174	NN 432 244	16	24	1	51
BQ11		MMMMM; N	[G] Renamed 1974.							
[91]	Am Binnein (Stobinain)			3827	[1166]	1m S of BQ10	18	29	1	
[97]	Stob Binnein			[3822]	1165	NN 434 227	18	27	1	51
BQ12		TTTTT	[21] .5m SEbyS of BQ11							
[91]	Stob Coire an Lochain			3497	[1066]	.5m SE of BQ11		120	1	
[97]	Stob Coire an Lochain			[3504]	1068	NN 438 220	BQ11	109	1	51
BQ13		Txxxx	[G] Deleted 1921.							
[91]	Creag a' Bhragit*			3000c	[914]	Btw. BQ12 & BQ14		538	1	
BQ14		TTTTT	[21] 1m E of BQ11							
[91]	Meall na Dige			3140 (3000)	[957]	.75m E of BQ12		362	1	
[97]	Meall na Dige			[3169]	966	NN 450 225	BQ11	317	1	51
SE01		MMMMM								
[91]	Ben Vorlich			3224	[983]	4m SE of Lochearnhead	162	284	2	
[97]	Ben Vorlich			[3232]	985	NN 629 189	165	264	1	57
SE02		MMMMM	[21] 1.25m SW of SE01							
[91]	Stuc a' Chroin			3189	[972]	1m SW of SE01	180	318	2	
[97]	Stuc a' Chroin			[3199]	975	NN 617 174	182	295	1	57
SE03		MMMMM								
[91]	Ben Chonzie			3048	[929]	Head of Gl. Turret	244	448	2	
[97]	Ben Chonzie			[3054]	931	NN 773 308	250	433	1	51/52
LY01		MMMMM	[21] 4m SEbyE of Kinloch Rannoch							
[91]	Schichallion			3547	[1081]	4m SE of Kinloch Rannoch	59	98	3	
[97]	Schiehallion			[3553]	1083	NN 713 547	59	90	2	51/52
LY02		MMMMM; N	[91] 'Carn Mairg Range' app. [21] 3.25m WNW of Fortingal [G] Renamed 1997.							
[91]	Creag Mhor			3200a (3000)	[975]	3m WSW of Fortingal	171	301	3	
[97]	Meall nan Aighean			[3218]	981	NN 694 496	169	271	2	51

Notes: [91] Mr Colin Phillip's aneroid measurement [21] The name on the 1-in. is .5m E. of the top. [Another well-marked top, .33m WSW, was made 10ft. lower]

LY03		TTTTT; H	[91] 'Carn Mairg Range' app.							
[91]	Meall Liath*			3261 (3250)	[994]	.5m EbyS of LY04		244	3	
[74]	Meall Liath			3261 (3250c)	[994]	NN 692 511	LY04	266	3	48
[97]	Meall Liath			[3320]	1012	NN 693 512	LY04	189	2	51
LY04		MMMMM	[91] 'Carn Mairg Range' app. [21] 4m NWbyW of Fortingal							
[91]	Carn Mairg			3419	[1042]	4m WNW of Fortingal	90	155	3	
[97]	Carn Mairg			[3415]	1041	NN 684 512	91	144	2	51
LY05		TTTTT	[91] 'Carn Mairg Range' app. [21] 1m WNW of LY04							
[91]	Meall a' Bharr*			3250c	[991]	1m WbyN of LY04		260	3	
[97]	Meall a' Bharr			[3294]	1004	NN 668 515	LY04	208	2	51

Notes: [21] The name on the 1-in. is .5m S. of the top

LY06		TTTxx	[91] 'Carn Mairg Range' app. [21] .75m SEbyE of LY07 [G] Deleted 1981.							
[91]	Meall Luaidhe*			3000c	[914]	.75m SE of LY07		515	3	
[74]	Meall Luaidhe			3035a (3000)	[925]	NN 656 510	LY07	484	3	48
LY07		MMMMM; L	[91] 'Carn Mairg Range' app. [21] 2.25m W of LY04 [81] Height & GR are for the 'top .33m E'! [G] See *SMCJ* 1922, XVI, 161-70							
[91]	Meall Garbh			3200a	[975]	2.5m W of LY04	173	303	3	
[74]	Meall Garbh			3200a (3150c)	[975]	NN 649 517	173	316	3	48
[81]	Meall Garbh			[3159]	963	NN 651 515	186	333	2	51
[97]	Meall Garbh			[3176]	968	NN 647 517	186	311	2	51

Notes: [91] Mr Colin Phillip's aneroid measurement [21] [Another well-marked top, .33m E., was made 10ft. lower]

LY08		TTTTT	[91] 'Carn Mairg Range' app. [21] .63m SW of LY07							
[91]	An Sgor*			3002 (3000c)	[915]	2.75 WbyS of LY04		512	3	
[97]	An Sgorr			[3031]	924	NN 640 509	LY09	461	2	51
LY09		MMMMM	[91] 'Carn Mairg Range' app. [21] 1.75m NEbyN of Free Church							
[91]	Carn Gorm			3370	[1027]	1.5m NNE of Free Church	103	174	3	
[97]	Carn Gorm			[3376]	1029	NN 635 500	103	163	2	51

No. Yr.	Code Name	Status	Remarks Feet	Metres	Location	Of Mtn.	Top	Sect.	Map
LY10		TTTTT					470	3	
[91]	Sron Chon a' Choirein★		3031 (3000)	[924]	.75m EbyS of LY11		470	3	
[97]	Sron Chona Choirein		[3041]	927	NN 493 445	LY11	452	2	51
LY11		MMMMM	[21] Btw. Gl. Lyon & L. Giorra						
[91]	Stuchd an Lochain		3144	[958]	Btw. Gl. Lyon & L. Girrie	191	353	3	
[97]	Stuchd an Lochain		[3150]	960	NN 483 448	197	338	2	51
LY12		MMMMM; N	[21] Btw. Ls. Giorra & Rannoch [G] Renamed 1921.						
[91]	Garbh Mheall		3054 (3000)	[931]	Btw. Ls. Girrie & Rannoch	241	441	3	
[97]	Meall Buidhe		[3058]	932	NN 498 499	248	430	2	51
Notes: [21] ['Garbh Mheall' on 1-inch map is .38m NNE of summit]									
LY13		TTTxx; N	[21] .75m SbyE of LY12 [G] Renamed 1921. Deleted 1981.						
[91]	Garbh Mheall, S.E. Top		3004 (3000)	[916]	.67m SbyE of LY12		505	3	
[74]	Meall Buidhe, S.E. Top		3004 (3000c)	[916]	NN 501 489	LY12	540	3	47
LT01		MMMMM; N	[91] 'Ben Lawers Range' app. [21] 2.75m NEbyE of LT05 [G] Renamed 1921.						
[91]	Meall Gruaidh		3280	[1000]	3m NE of LT05	134	225	3	
[97]	Meall Greigh		[3284]	1001	NN 674 438	136	217	2	51
LT02		MMMMM	[91] 'Ben Lawers Range' app. [74] Typo: Top No. 63 should be 62.						
[91]	Meall Garbh		3661	[1116]	1.5m NNE of LT05	34	56	3	
[97]	Meall Garbh		[3668]	1118	NN 644 436	35	51	2	51
LT03		TTTTM	[91] 'Ben Lawers Range' app.						
[91]	An Stuc★		3643 (3500)	[1110]	1m NbyE of LT05		66	3	
[81]	An Stuc		[3668]	1118	NN 639 430	LT05	56	2	51
[97]	An Stuc		[3668]	1118	NN 639 431	34	50	2	51
LT04		TTTTT	[91] 'Ben Lawers Range' app.						
[91]	Creag an Fhithich★		3430	[1045]	.5m N of LT05		147	3	
[97]	Creag an Fhithich		[3435]	1047	NN 635 422	LT05	133	2	51
Notes: [91] Local name Spicean nan Each									
LT05		MMMMM	[91] 'Ben Lawers Range' app. [21] L. Tay, North side						
[91]	Ben Lawers		3984	[1214]	N side of L. Tay	10	15	3	
[97]	Ben Lawers		[3983]	1214	NN 635 414	10	13	2	51
LT06		MMMMM	[91] 'Ben Lawers Range' app. [21] .88m SW of LT05						
[91]	Beinn Ghlas		3657a (3500)	[1115]	1m SW of LT05	38	60	3	
[97]	Beinn Ghlas		[3619]	1103	NN 625 404	47	72	2	51
Notes: [91] Dr Heddle's aneroid measurement									
LT07		Txxxx	[91] 'Ben Lawers Range' app.						
[91]	Sron dha-Murchdi★		3040a (3000)	[927]	.5m SSW of LT08		458	3	
Notes: [91] Mr Munro's aneroid measurement									
LT08		MMMMM	[91] 'Ben Lawers Range' app.						
[91]	Meall Corranaich		3530a (3250)	[1076]	1.25m W of LT05	63	105	3	
[97]	Meall Corranaich		[3507]	1069	NN 615 410	68	105	2	51
Notes: [91] Mr Munro's aneroid measurement									
LT09		MMMMM	[91] 'Ben Lawers Range' app.						
[91]	Meall a' Choire Leith		3033	[924]	2m NW of LT05	259	469	3	
[97]	Meall a' Choire Leith		[3038]	926	NN 612 439	261	457	2	51
LT10		MMMMM							
[91]	Meall nan Tarmachan		3421	[1043]	3.75m NbyE of Killin	89	154	3	
[97]	Meall nan Tarmachan		[3425]	1044	NN 585 390	89	141	2	51
LT11		TTTTT	[21] .5m SW of LT10						
[91]	Meall Garbh★		3369a (3250)	[1027]	.5m SSW of LT10		176	3	
[97]	Meall Garbh		[3366]	1026	NN 578 383	LT10	169	2	51
Notes: [91] Dr Heddle's aneroid measurement. Reckoned somewhat higher by Mr Munro									
LT12		TTTTT	[21] 1m WSW of LT10 [G] Called 'W. Top' 1921 & 1974.						
[91]	Beinn nan Eachan★		3265a (3250)	[995]	1m SW of LT10		240	3	
[97]	Beinn nan Eachan		[3281]	1000	NN 570 383	LT10	221	2	51
Notes: [91] Dr Heddle's aneroid measurement. Reckoned somewhat higher by Mr Munro									
LT13		xTTxx	[G] Introduced 1921; Deleted 1981.						
[21]	Beinn nan Eachan, East Top		3110a (3000)	[948]	.25m E of LT12	LT10	394	3	46
[74]	Beinn nan Eachan, E. Top		3110 (3000c)	[948]	NN 574 383	LT10	405	3	48
LT14		xxxTT	[G] Introduced 1981.						
[81]	Creag na Caillich		[3005]	916	NN 563 377	LT10	512	2	51
[97]	Creag na Caillich		[3005]	916	NN 562 377	LT10	504	2	51
LT15		xxxxT	[G] Introduced 1997.						
[97]	Meall nan Tarmachan, S.E. Top		[3028]	923	NN 589 385	LT10	468	2	51

No. Yr.	Code Name	Status	Remarks Feet	Metres	Location	Of Mtn.	Top	Sect.	Map
MF01		MMMMM	[21] Btw. Gl. Lochay & Gl. Lyon [74] Typo: Mtn. No. 90 should be 91.						
[91]	Meall Ghaordie		3407	[1038]	5.5m NW of Killin	92	157	3	
[97]	Meall Ghaordie		[3409]	1039	NN 514 397	93	149	2	51
MF02		TTTxx	[G] Deleted 1981.						
[91]	Stob an Fhir-Bhogha★, B. Heasgarnich		3381 (3250)	[1031]	.5m S of MF03		168	3	
[74]	Stob an Fhir-Bogha		3380 (3300c)	[1030]	NN 411 372	MF03	180	3	47
MF03		MMMMM	[21] 1.75m SE of L. Lyon						
[91]	Beinn Heasgarnich		3530	[1076]	1.5m SE of L. Lyon	64	106	3	
[97]	Beinn Heasgarnich		[3537]	1078	NN 413 383	62	96	2	51
MF04		MMMMM; H							
[91]	Creag Mhor		3387	[1032]	2.25m SW of MF03	97	165	3	
[74]	Creag Mhor		3437 (3387)	[1048]	NN 391 361	82	152	3	47
[81]	Creag Mhor		[3386]	1032	NN 391 361	96	162	2	51
[97]	Creag Mhor		[3435]	1047	NN 391 361	84	134	2	50
Notes: [91] 3305ft. on 1-inch O.S.									
MF05		TTTTT	[21] .67m SbyW of MF04						
[91]	Stob nan Clach★		3146 (3000)	[959]	.67m S of MF04		351	3	
[97]	Stob nan Clach		[3136]	956	NN 387 351	MF04	354	2	50
MF06		MMMMM	[21] 3.75m ENE of Tyndrum [G] Called 'N. Top' 1921 & 1974.						
[91]	Beinn Chaluim		3354	[1022]	3.5m ENE of Tyndrum	107	184	3	
[97]	Ben Challum		[3363]	1025	NN 386 322	106	170	2	50
MF07		TTTTT							
[91]	Beinn Chaluim, S. Top		3236	[986]	.5m S of MF06		278	3	
[97]	Ben Challum, South Top		[3274]	998	NN 386 315	MF06	226	2	50
MF08		TMMMM	[G] Promoted 1921, since higher than MF09.						
[91]	Meall Glas★		3139 (3000)	[957]	1m WbyS of MF09		363	3	
[21]	Meall Glas		3139 (3000)	[957]	Btw. Gls. Dochart & Lochay	196	370	3	46
[97]	Meall Glas		[3146]	959	NN 431 321	199	340	2	51
Notes: [91] Locally called Meall Glas Mhor									
MF09		MTTTT; N	[G] Renamed & Demoted 1921, since lower than MF08.						
[91]	Beinn Dheiceach		3074	[937]	Btw. Gls. Dochart & Lochay	231	423	3	
[21]	Beinn Cheathaich		3074	[937]	.88m ENE of MF08	MF08	439	3	46
[97]	Beinn Cheathaich		[3074]	937	NN 444 326	MF08	413	2	51
MF10		TMMMM; H	[G] Promoted 1921, since higher than MF11.						
[91]	Sgiath Chuil★		3050a (3000c)	[930]	.5m S of MF11		445	3	
[21]	Sgiath Chuil		3050a (3000)	[930]	2.5m NNW of Luib Station	244	464	3	46
[74]	Sgiath Chuil		3016 (3000c)	[919]	NN 464 318	267	513	3	47
[81]	Sgiath Chuil		[3068]	935	NN 463 318	237	433	2	51
[97]	Sgiath Chuil		[3022]	921	NN 462 317	270	476	2	51
Notes: [91] Measured by Dr Heddle & Mr Colin Phillip									
MF11		MTTTT	[G] Demoted 1921, since lower than MF10.						
[91]	Meall Chuirn		3007	[917]	Btw. Gls. Dochart & Lochay	274	499	3	
[21]	Meall a' Churain		3007	[917]	.5m N of MF10	MF10	528	3	46
[97]	Meall a' Churain		[3012]	918	NN 463 325	MF10	486	2	51
OR01		MMMMM	[21] 2m SbyE of Br. of Orchy						
[91]	Beinn Doireann		3523	[1074]	Head of Gl. Lyon Hills	65	108	3	
[97]	Beinn Dorain		[3530]	1076	NN 325 378	64	98	2	50
OR02		MMMMM	[21] 2.25m ENE of Br. of Orchy						
[91]	Beinn an Dothaidh		3283 (3250)	[1001]	Head of Gl. Lyon Hills	132	222	3	
[97]	Beinn an Dothaidh		[3294]	1004	NN 331 408	129	206	2	50
OR03		TTTTT	[21] .88m SSW of OR04						
[91]	Beinn Achallader, South Top		3288	[1002]	Head of Gl. Lyon Hills		218	3	
[97]	Beinn Achaladair, South Top		[3287]	1002	NN 342 420	OR04	211	2	50
OR04		MMMMM	[21] Head of Gl. Lyon						
[91]	Beinn Achallader, North Top		3404	[1038]	Head of Gl. Lyon Hills	93	159	3	
[97]	Beinn Achaladair		[3405]	1038	NN 344 432	94	150	2	50
Notes: [91] The point 3404ft. is a little to the S. of that marked 3399 on the 1-inch O.S. [21] 200 yds. SW of the pt. 3399 on the 1-in.									
OR05		TTTTT	[21] 1m WSW of OR06						
[91]	Meall Buidhe		3193 (3000)	[973]	Head of Gl. Lyon Hills		314	3	
[97]	Meall Buidhe		[3209]	978	NN 359 438	OR06	284	2	50
OR06		MMMMM							
[91]	Beinn Creachan		3540	[1079]	Head of Gl. Lyon Hills	62	102	3	
[97]	Beinn a' Chreachain		[3547]	1081	NN 373 440	61	93	2	50

No. Yr.	Code Name	Status	Remarks Feet	Metres	Location	Of Mtn.	Top	Sect.	Map
OR07		Txxxx	[G] Deleted 1921.						
[91]	Top of Coire Dubh		3145	[959]	7m Inveroran/2.5m Invermeran		352	3	
OR08		MTTTT	[G] Demoted 1921.						
[91]	Beinn a' Chuirn		3020 (3000)	[921]	Head of Gl. Lyon Hills	263	481	3	
[21]	Beinn a' Chuirn		3020 (3000)	[921]	.75m WbyS of OR09	OR09	509	3	46
[97]	Beinn a' Chuirn		[3028]	923	NN 360 409	OR09	466	2	50
OR09		MMMMM							
[91]	Ben Vannoch		3125	[953]	Head of Gl. Lyon Hills	202	374	3	
[97]	Beinn Mhanach		[3127]	953	NN 373 411	211	363	2	50
CR01		TTTTT	[91] 'Cruachan Range' app. [21] .5m WNW of CR02						
[91]	Stob Dearg#		3611	[1101]	Most W. peak of Ben Cruachan		77	4	
[97]	Stob Dearg (Taynuilt Peak)		[3622]	1104	NN 062 307	CR02	71	3	50
CR02		MMMMM	[91] 'Cruachan Range' app.						
[91]	Ben Cruachan		3689	[1124]	Btw. Ls. Awe & Etive	30	50	4	
[97]	Ben Cruachan		[3694]	1126	NN 069 304	31	45	3	50
CR03		TTTTT	[91] 'Cruachan Range' app.						
[91]	Meall Cuanail		3004	[916]	.5m S of CR02		508	4	
[97]	Meall Cuanail		[3012]	918	NN 069 295	CR02	487	3	50
CR04		TTTTT	[91] 'Cruachan Range' app.						
[91]	Drochaid Glas		3312	[1010]	1m E of CR02		201	4	
[97]	Drochaid Ghlas		[3310]	1009	NN 083 306	CR02	197	3	50
CR05		MMMMM	[91] 'Cruachan Range' app. [21] .75m EbyN of CR04						
[91]	Stob Diamh#		3272	[997]	.75m E of CR04	140	233	4	
[97]	Stob Diamh		[3274]	998	NN 094 308	143	231	3	50
CR06		TTTTT	[91] 'Cruachan Range' app. [21] .5m S of CR05						
[91]	Stob Garbh#		3215 (3000)	[980]	Halfway btw. CR05 & 3091 Top (1-in.)		292	4	
[97]	Stob Garbh		[3215]	980	NN 095 302	CR05	278	3	50
CR07		TTTTT	[91] 'Cruachan Range' app.						
[91]	Sron an Isean#		3163 (3000)	[964]	NE Spur of Cruachan		338	4	
[97]	Sron an Isean		[3169]	966	NN 099 311	CR05	318	3	50
CR08		MMMMM							
[91]	Beinn a' Chochuill		3215	[980]	3.5m NbyW of L. Awe Hotel	167	293	4	
[97]	Beinn a' Chochuill		[3215]	980	NN 109 328	172	275	3	50
CR09		MMMMM							
[91]	Beinn Eunaich		3242	[988]	3.5m NbyE of L. Awe Hotel	153	271	4	
[97]	Beinn Eunaich		[3245]	989	NN 135 328	156	253	3	50
Notes: [91] The S. top of Beinn Eunaich, 3174 feet, is really only a shoulder									
ET01		MMMMM							
[91]	Beinn nan Aighean		3141	[957]	2m SE of ET03	195	358	4	
[97]	Beinn nan Aighenan		[3150]	960	NN 148 405	196	333	3	50
ET02		TTTTT	[21] .67m SSE of ET03						
[91]	Meall Cruidh*, Ben Starav		3049 (2750)	[929]	.67m S of ET03		447	4	
[97]	Meall Cruidh		[3051]	930	NN 129 415	ET03	436	3	50
ET03		MMMMM	[21] East of Upper L. Etive						
[91]	Ben Starav		3541	[1079]	E end of L. Etive	61	101	4	
[97]	Ben Starav		[3537]	1078	NN 125 427	63	97	3	50
ET04		TTTTT; H	[81] Too high! Pt. 1068 is ET09; but GR is ET04.						
[91]	Stob Coire Dheirg, Ben Starav		3372	[1028]	.33m E of ET03		173	4	
[81]	Stob Coire Dheirg		[3504]	1068	NN 131 426	ET03	115	3	50
[97]	Stob Coire Dheirg		[3373]	1028	NN 131 426	ET03	166	3	50
ET05		MMMMM	[21] 1.75m E of ET03						
[91]	Glas Bheinn Mhor		3258	[993]	2m E of ET03	149	249	4	
[97]	Glas Bheinn Mhor		[3271]	997	NN 153 429	145	233	3	50
ET06		MMMMM	[21] 3.25m EbyS of Lochetivehead						
[91]	Stob Coir' an Albannaich		3425	[1044]	2.5m EbyS of Lochetivehead	87	150	4	
[97]	Stob Coir' an Albannaich		[3425]	1044	NN 169 443	90	142	3	50
ET07		MMMMM	[21] 5.75m WNW of Inveroran						
[91]	Meall nan Eun		3039	[926]	5.5m WNW of Inveroran	252	460	4	
[97]	Meall nan Eun		[3045]	928	NN 192 449	254	445	3	50
ET08		xxxxT	[G] Introduced 1997.						
[97]	Stob an Duine Ruaidh		[3012]	918	NN 124 410	ET03	492	3	50
ET09		xxxxx	[G] SE Top of ET03 at NN 128 425 and 1068m. Wrongly listed as 'Stob Coire Dheirg' in 1990. Corrected 1997.						

No. Yr.	Code Name	Status	Remarks / Feet	Metres	Location	Of Mtn.	Top	Sect.	Map
BL01		TTTTT	[91] 'Stob Ghabhar' app. [21] 1.5m WbyN of BL03						
[91]	Stob a' Bruaich Leith★		3083	[940]	1.5m W of BL03		413	4	
[97]	Stob a' Bhruaich Leith		[3087]	941	NN 208 459	BL03	401	3	50
BL02		TTTTT; L	[91] 'Stob Ghabhar' app. [21] .33m WbyN of BL03 [G] Since 1974 has moved West, but not very convincingly!						
[91]	Sron a' Ghearrain		3240	[988]	.33m W of BL03		275	4	
[74]	Sron a' Ghearrain		3202 (3200c)	[976]	NN 224 457	BL03	310	4	47
[81]	Sron a' Ghearrain		[3251]	991c	NN 221 457	BL03	253	3	50
[97]	Sron a' Ghearrain		[3248]	990	NN 220 457	BL03	251	3	50
Notes: [91] A point a little NW marked 3159 on the 1-in. map [21] [3159 pt. is .25m WNW of top]									
BL03		MMMMM							
[91]	Stob Ghabhar		3565	[1087]	3.75 NW of Inveroran	55	92	4	
[97]	Stob Ghabhar		[3576]	1090	NN 230 455	55	83	3	50
BL04		TTTTx	[91] 'Stob Ghabhar' app. [21] .5m NNE of BL03 [G] Deleted 1997.						
[91]	Sron nan Giubhas		3174 (3000)	[967]	.5m NE of BL03		330	4	
[81]	Sron nan Giubhas		[3195]	974	NN 231 462	BL03	307	3	50
BL05		TTTTx	[91] 'Stob Ghabhar' app. [21] .33m ESE of BL03 [G] Deleted 1997.						
[91]	Aonach Eagach★		3272 (3250)	[997]	SE Shoulder of BL03		234	4	
[81]	Aonach Eagach		[3251]	991c	NN 236 454	BL03	252	3	50
BL06		MMMMM	[21] 1.75m EbyN of BL03						
[91]	Stob a' Choire Odhair★		3058 (3000)	[932]	.25m NW of B.Toaig/1.75m EbyN of BL03	240	438	4	
[97]	Stob a' Choire Odhair		[3100]	945	NN 257 459	226	387	3	50
BL07		MMMTT	[G] Demoted 1981.						
[91]	Clach Leathad (Clachlet)		3602	[1098]	3.5m SSW of Kingshouse	50	83	4	
[74]	Clach Leathad		3601 (3602)	[1098]	NN 241 493	48	88	4	47
[81]	Clach Leathad		[3602]	1098	NN 240 493	BL10	81	3	41
[97]	Clach Leathad		[3606]	1099	NN 240 493	BL10	77	3	50
BL08		TTTxx	[G] Deleted 1981.						
[91]	Mam Coire Easain★		3506	[1069]	.5m N of BL07		110	4	
[74]	Mam Coire Easain		3508 (3506)	[1069]	NN 239 499	BL07	118	4	47
BL09		MMMMM	[21] 2.75m SbyW of Kingshouse						
[91]	Meall a' Bhuiridh★, Clach Leathad		3636 (3500)	[1108]	.67m EbyN of BL08	44	69	4	
[97]	Meall a' Bhuiridh		[3635]	1108	NN 250 503	45	65	3	41
BL10		TTTMM; N	[G] Renamed 1921. Promoted 1981.						
[91]	Top btw. Mam C. Easain & Stob Glas Ch.		3600 (3500)	[1097]	1m N of BL07		85	4	
[74]	Creise		3608 (3596)	[1100]	NN 238 507	BL07	87	4	47
[81]	Creise		[3609]	1100	NN 238 507	48	79	3	41
[97]	Creise		[3609]	1100	NN 238 506	50	75	3	41
Notes: [91] Locally known as Creise, although the point named Sron Creise on the 1-in. map is .75m to N & beyond Stob Glas Ch.									
BL11		TTTTT; H							
[91]	Stob Glas Choire★, Clach Leathad		3207 (3000)	[978]	.25m S of Sron Creise (2952,1-in.).		298	4	
[74]	Stob a' Ghlais Choire		3268 (3150c)	[996]	NN 240 517	BL07	260	4	47
[97]	Stob a' Ghlais Choire		[3268]	996	NN 240 516	BL10	237	3	41
CO01		MMMMM	[91] 'Buchaille Etive Mor' app. [74] Typo: Mtn. No. 196 should be 106!						
[91]	Stob Dearg		3345	[1020]	NE end of Buchaille Etive Mor	109	188	4	
[97]	Stob Dearg		[3350]	1021	NN 222 542	110	175	3	41
CO02		TTTTT; H	[91] 'Buchaille Etive Mor' app.						
[91]	Stob na Doire★		3250a (3000)	[991]	1.25 SW of CO01		255	4	
[74]	Stob na Doire		3316 (3200c)	[1011]	NN 207 533	CO01	216	4	47
[97]	Stob na Doire		[3317]	1011	NN 207 532	CO01	192	3	41
Notes: [91] Mr Colin Phillip's aneroid measurement									
CO03		TTTTT	[91] 'Buchaille Etive Mor' app. [21] .63m WSW of CO02						
[91]	Stob Coire Altruim#		3065 (3000)	[934]	.5m WSW of CO02		427	4	
[97]	Stob Coire Altruim		[3087]	941	NN 197 530	CO04	402	3	41
CO04		TTTTM	[91] 'Buchaille Etive Mor' app. [G] Promoted 1997.						
[91]	Stob na Broige★		3120	[951]	SW end of Buachaille Etive Mor		379	4	
[81]	Stob na Broige		[3133]	955	NN 191 526	CO01	366	3	41
[97]	Stob na Broige		[3136]	956	NN 190 525	207	353	3	41
CO05		MMMMM	[91] 'Buchaille Etive Bheag' app. [21] Btw. Glencoe & Glenetive						
[91]	Stob Dubh★		3129	[954]	Glencoe & Glenetive	200	371	4	
[97]	Stob Dubh		[3143]	958	NN 179 535	201	345	3	41
Notes: [21] [150yds. NNE of 3129 pt. on 1-inch map]									
CO06		TTTTM	[91] 'Buchaille Etive Bheag' app. [G] Promoted 1997.						
[91]	Stob Coire Raineach★		3029	[923]	NE end of Buchaille Etive Bheag		473	4	
[81]	Stob Coire Raineach		[3035]	925	NN 191 548	CO05	472	3	41
[97]	Stob Coire Raineach		[3035]	925	NN 191 548	263	460	3	41

No. Yr.	Code Name	Status	Remarks Feet	Metres	Location	Of Mtn.	Top	Sect.	Map
CO07		TTTTT	[91] 'Bidean nam Bian' app. [21] .75m NE of CO08						
[91]	Beinn Fhada		3064 (3000)	[934]	Glencoe		429	4	
[97]	Beinn Fhada, N.E. Top		[3054]	931	NN 164 543	CO08	432	3	41
CO08		TTTTM	[91] 'Bidean nam Bian' app. [21] .75m ESE of CO09 [74] Typo: Named 'Stob C. Sgriodain'! [G] Promoted 1997.						
[91]	Stob Coire Sgrenach#		3497 (3250)	[1066]	.75m SE of CO09		119	4	
[81]	Stob Coire Sgreamhach		[3517]	1072	NN 155 536	CO09	106	3	41
[97]	Stob Coire Sgreamhach		[3517]	1072	NN 154 536		65	3	41
CO09		MMMMM	[91] 'Bidean nam Bian' app. [21] 1.5m S of L. Achtriochtan						
[91]	Bidean nam Bian		3766	[1148]	Glencoe	24	38	4	
[97]	Bidean nam Bian		[3773]	1150	NN 143 542	23	32	3	41
CO10		TTTTT	[91] 'Bidean nam Bian' app.						
[91]	Stob Coire nam Beith#		3621 (3500)	[1104]	.33m NW of CO09		75	4	
[97]	Stob Coire nam Beith		[3632]	1107	NN 139 545	CO09	67	3	41
CO11		TTTTT	[91] 'Bidean nam Bian' app. [21] .5m NNE of CO09 [81] Typo: Northing 459 should be 549!						
[91]	Stob Coire nan Lochan		3657	[1115]	.5m NE of CO09		61	4	
[97]	Stob Coire nan Lochan		[3658]	1115	NN 148 548	CO09	56	3	41
CO12		xTTTT	[G] Introduced 1921.						
[21]	Beinn Fhada, Centre Top		3120a (3000)	[951]	.5m NE of CO08	CO09	392	4	53
[97]	Beinn Fhada		[3123]	952	NN 159 540	CO08	367	3	41
AP01		TTTTT							
[91]	Stob an Fhuarain★		3160a (3000)	[963]	.5m NE of AP02		340	4	
[97]	Stob an Fhuarain		[3176]	968	NN 118 523	AP02	312	3	41

Notes: [91] Dr Heddle's aneroid measurement. The summit of Aonach Dubh a' Ghlinne (on both 1 & 6-inch maps) is the name of the ridge of which Stob an Fhuarain is the summit

No. Yr.	Code Name	Status	Remarks Feet	Metres	Location	Of Mtn.	Top	Sect.	Map
AP02		MMMMM							
[91]	Sgor na h-Ulaidh		3258	[993]	Head of Gl. Creran	148	248	4	
[97]	Sgor na h-Ulaidh		[3261]	994	NN 111 518	149	240	3	41
AP03		MMMMM							
[91]	Beinn Fhionnlaidh		3139	[957]	Head of Gl. Creran	198	364	4	
[97]	Beinn Fhionnlaidh		[3146]	959	NN 095 497	198	339	3	50
AP04		MMMMM	[21] 2.75m E of Head of L. Creran						
[91]	Beinn Sguliaird		3058	[932]	3m NE of Head Gl. Creran	239	437	4	
[97]	Beinn Sgulaird		[3074]	937	NN 053 460	237	414	3	50
AP05		MMMMM	[91] 'Beinn a Bheithir' app. [21] 1m WbyS of AP06						
[91]	Sgorr Dhonuill		3284	[1001]	2.5m S of Ballachulish Hotel	130	220	4	
[97]	Sgorr Dhonuill		[3284]	1001	NN 040 555	137	219	3	41
AP06		MMMMM	[91] 'Beinn a Bheithir' app. [21] 2.75m SbyE of Ballachulish Hotel						
[91]	Sgorr Dhearg		3362	[1025]	2.5m S of Ballachulish Hotel	106	180	4	
[97]	Sgorr Dhearg		[3360]	1024	NN 056 558	107	171	3	41
AP07		TTTTT	[91] 'Beinn a Bheithir' app. [21] .33m ENE of AP06						
[91]	Sgorr Bhan#		3104 (3000)	[946]	2.5m S of Ballachulish Hotel		389	4	
[97]	Sgorr Bhan		[3107]	947	NN 062 560	AP06	377	3	41
AE01		MMMMM	[21] W end of Aonach Eagach Ridge						
[91]	Sgor nam Fiannaidh		3168	[966]	1.25m NNE of Clachaig Inn	184	332	5	
[97]	Sgorr nam Fiannaidh		[3173]	967	NN 140 583	188	315	3	41
AE02		TTTTT	[91] 'Aonach Eagach' app.						
[91]	Stob Coire Leith★		3080 (3000)	[939]	.5m EbyN of AE01		416	5	
[97]	Stob Coire Leith		[3084]	940	NN 149 584	AE01	404	3	41

Notes: [91] This mountain is named Meall Garbh on the 1-in. map, but Stob C. Leith on the 6-in.

No. Yr.	Code Name	Status	Remarks Feet	Metres	Location	Of Mtn.	Top	Sect.	Map
AE03		MMMMM	[91] 'Aonach Eagach' app. [21] 1.38m E of AE01						
[91]	Meall Dearg		3118	[950]	1.5m NE of Clachaig Inn	207	381	5	
[97]	Meall Dearg		[3127]	953	NN 161 583	212	364	3	41
AE04		TTTTT	[91] 'Aonach Eagach' app.						
[91]	Am Bodach		3085 (3000)	[940]	.5m ESE of AE03		410	5	
[97]	Am Bodach		[3094]	943	NN 168 580	AE03	390	3	41
MA01		MMMMM; N	[21] Above L. Eilde Mor [G] Renamed 1921.						
[91]	Sgor na h-Eilde		3279 (3250)	[999]	1.25m NW of Locheilt Lodge	135	226	5	
[97]	Sgurr Eilde Mor		[3314]	1010	NN 230 657	123	196	4	41
MA02		TTTTT; N	[21] Top of Ridge, .88m SEbyS from MA06 [G] Renamed 1921.						
[91]	Sgor na h-Eilde Beag★		3140 (3000)	[957]	Top of Ridge, 1m SE of MA06		361	5	
[97]	Sgor Eilde Beag		[3136]	956	NN 219 652	MA06	351	4	41
MA03		TTTTT; N	[G] Renamed 1921.						
[91]	Top of Coire nan Laogh★		3475 (3250)	[1059]	.5m S of MA06		125	5	
[97]	Binnein Mor, South Top		[3484]	1062	NN 211 656	MA06	113	4	41

No. Yr.	Code Name	Status	Remarks	Feet	Metres	Location	Of Mtn.	Top	Sect.	Map
MA04		TMMMM; N	[G] Promoted & Renamed 1921.							
[91]	A' Gruagach★			3442 (3250)	[1049]	1m SW of MA06		139	5	
[21]	Na Gruagaichean★			3442 (3250)	[1049]	1m SW of MA06	77	148	5	53
[97]	Na Gruagaichean			[3465]	1056	NN 203 652	74	116	4	41
MA05		TTTTT; N	[G] Renamed 1921.							
[91]	A' Gruagach, N.W. Top			3404 (3250)	[1038]	.25m NW of MA04		160	5	
[97]	Na Gruagaichean, N.W. Top			[3415]	1041	NN 201 654	MA04	145	4	41
MA06		MMMMM	[21] Btw. Gl. Nevis & L. Eilde Mor							
[91]	Binnein Mor			3700	[1128]	3m NE of Kinlochmore Lodge	28	48	5	
[97]	Binnein Mor			[3707]	1130	NN 212 663	27	41	4	41
MA07		MMMMM	[21] Head of Gl. Nevis, Mamore Forest							
[91]	Binnein Beag			3083	[940]	Head of Gl. Nevis	228	414	5	
[97]	Binnein Beag			[3094]	943	NN 221 677	230	392	4	41
MA08		MTMMM	[21] .5m N of MA09 . Demoted by mistake, corrected 1933.							
[91]	An Gearanach★			3200a (3000)	[975]	1.25m S of Steall, Gl. Nevis	174	305	5	
[21]	An Gearanach			3200a (3000)	[975]	1.25m S of Steall, Gl. Nevis	MA09	311	5	53
[74]	An Gearanach			3230 (3200c)	[984]	NN 186 670	160	3289	5	47
[97]	An Gearanach			[3222]	982	NN 187 669	166	268	4	41

Notes: [91] The N end is named An Gearanach, the S end – almost exactly the same height, & rather more than .25m S – An Garbhanach. The arete connecting them is extremely narrow, & the height of both must be very near, if not over, 3250 ft.

No. Yr.	Code Name	Status	Remarks	Feet	Metres	Location	Of Mtn.	Top	Sect.	Map
MA09		TMTTT	[21] 1.5m S of Steall, Gl. Nevis. Promoted by mistake, corrected 1933.							
[91]	An Garbhanach★			3200a (3000)	[975]	.33m S of MA08		306	5	
[21]	An Garbhanach			3200a (3000)	[975]	.33m S of MA08	172	310	5	53
[74]	An Garbhanach			3206 (3200c)	[977]	NN 187 665	MA08	309	5	47
[97]	An Garbhanach			[3199]	975	NN 188 665	MA08	292	4	41
MA10		MMMMM	[21] .88m NE of MA11							
[91]	Stob Coire a' Chairn★			3219 (3000)	[981]	.33m S of MA09	164	288	5	
[97]	Stob Coire a' Chairn			[3218]	981	NN 185 660	171	274	4	41
MA11		MMMMM	[21] Btw. Gl. Nevis & Head of L. Leven							
[91]	Am Bodach			3382	[1031]	Gl. Nevis, Mamore Forest	99	167	5	
[97]	Am Bodach			[3386]	1032	NN 176 650	99	156	4	41
MA12		TTTMT	[21] .75m S of MA13 [G] Promoted 1981; Demoted 1997!							
[91]	Sgor an Iubhair			3250c	[991]	About 1m S of MA13		266	5	
[74]	Sgor an Iubhair			3284 (3250c)	[1001]	NN 165 655	MA13	242	5	47
[81]	Sgor an Iubhair			[3284]	1001	NN 165 655	133	221	4	41
[97]	Sgor an Iubhair			[3284]	1001	NN 165 655	MA13	218	4	41

Notes: [91] The height marked 2424, & named Sgor an Iubhair on the 1-inch map, is merely a hump on the ridge. The top is a small 3250 cont., nearly 1m to the N & the same distance S of MA13

No. Yr.	Code Name	Status	Remarks	Feet	Metres	Location	Of Mtn.	Top	Sect.	Map
MA13		MMMMM								
[91]	Sgor a' Mhaim			3601	[1098]	Gl. Nevis, Mamore Forest	51	84	5	
[97]	Sgurr a' Mhaim			[3606]	1099	NN 164 667	51	78	4	41
MA14		MMMMM								
[91]	Stob Ban			3274	[998]	Gl. Nevis, Mamore Forest	138	230	5	
[97]	Stob Ban			[3278]	999	NN 147 654	140	225	4	41
MA15		TTTTT; N	[21] .75m SE of MA16 [G] Renamed 1921.							
[91]	Top of Coire Dearg★			3004 (3000)	[916]	1m W of MA14		507	5	
[97]	Mullach nan Coirean, S.E. Top			[3008]	917	NN 131 654	MA15	499	4	41
MA16		MMMMM	[G] Called 'N.W. Top' 1921/74.							
[91]	Mullach nan Coirean			3077	[938]	Gl. Nevis, Mamore Forest	229	420	5	
[97]	Mullach nan Coirean			[3081]	939	NN 122 662	236	407	4	41
MA17		xxxTT	[G] Introduced 1981. Recommended (and named) by Edred Corner in 1909 and by many others since!							
[81]	Stob a' Choire Mhail			[3182]	970c	NN 163 659	MA12	316	4	41
[97]	Stob Choire a' Mhail			[3248]	990	NN 163 659	MA13	252	4	41
NE01		MMMMM								
[91]	Ben Nevis			4406	[1343]	Lochaber	1	1	5	
[97]	Ben Nevis			[4409]	1344	NN 166 712	1	1	4	41
NE02		TTTTT	[74] Typo: Top No. 201 should be 200.							
[91]	Carn Dearg			3348	[1020]	Spur 1m SW of NE01		186	5	
[97]	Carn Dearg (South-west)			[3346]	1020	NN 155 701	NE01	176	4	41
NE03		TTTTT; HL	[97] Typo: Easting 559 should be 159! [G] Original O.S. cairn and height 300yds N of true top.							
[91]	Carn Dearg			3961	[1207]	Spur .75m NW of NE01		17	5	
[74]	Carn Dearg, N.W. Top			3975 (3961)	[1212]	NN 159 722	NE01	17	5	47
[97]	Carn Dearg (North-west)			[4006]	1221	NN 159 719	NE01	10	4	41

No. Yr.	Code Name	Status	Remarks	Feet	Metres	Location	Of Mtn.	Top	Sect.	Map
NE04		TTTxx	[21] 1m NNW of NE06 [G] Deleted 1981.							
[91]	Carn Beag Dearg			3264	[995]	Btw. NE01 & NE07, NE08		242	5	
[74]	Carn Beag Dearg			3300 (3265)	[1006]	NN 171 737	NE06	227	5	47
NE05		TTTTT; L	[74] GR is for small top .25m to North; probably an error							
[91]	Carn Dearg Meadhonach			3875	[1181]	Btw. NE01 & NE07, NE08		21	5	
[21]	Carn Dearg Meadhonach			3873 (3750)	[1181]	.5m NNW of NE06	NE06	22	5	53
[74]	Carn Dearg Meadhonach			3870 (3850c)	[1180]	NN 173 731	NE06	22	5	47
[97]	Carn Dearg Meadhonach			[3868]	1179	NN 176 726	NE06	21	4	41
NE06		MMMMM								
[91]	Carn Mor Dearg			4012	[1223]	Btw. NE01 & NE07, NE08	8	12	5	
[97]	Carn Mor Dearg			[4003]	1220	NN 177 721	9	11	4	41
NE07		MMMMM	[21] 2m NEbyE of NE01							
[91]	Aonach Mor			3999	[1219]	2m NE of NE01	9	13	5	
[97]	Aonach Mor			[4006]	1221	NN 192 729	8	9	4	41

Notes: [91] Aonach an Nid, 1m N of NE07 (3774 ft., 6-inch map)is really only a shoulder & not to be considered a top

No. Yr.	Code Name	Status	Remarks	Feet	Metres	Location	Of Mtn.	Top	Sect.	Map
NE08		MMMMM								
[91]	Aonach Beag			4060	[1238]	2m E of NE01	7	10	5	
[97]	Aonach Beag			[4049]	1234	NN 196 715	7	8	4	41
NE09		TTTTT; NH	[21] 67m EbyN of NE07 [G] Renamed 1921.							
[91]	Top of An Cul Choire★			3580a	[1091]	.75m E of NE07		89	5	
[74]	Stob an Cul Choire			3600c (3500c)	[1097]	NN 203 732	NE07	91	5	47
[81]	Stob an Cul Choire			[3599]	1097	NN 203 732	NE07	83	4	41
[97]	Stob an Cul Choire			[3504]	1068	NN 203 731	NE07	108	4	41

Notes: [91] Dr Heddle's aneroid measurement

No. Yr.	Code Name	Status	Remarks	Feet	Metres	Location	Of Mtn.	Top	Sect.	Map
NE10		TTTxx	[21] 1m NE of NE07 [G] Deleted 1981.							
[91]	Stob Coire an Fhir Dhuibh★			3250c	[991]	.33m NE of NE09		267	5	
[74]	Stob Coire an Fhir Duibh			3225c (3250c)	[983]	NN 208 735	NE07	292	5	47
NE11		TTTTT	[21] 1.5m NE of NE07							
[91]	Tom na Sroine★			3000c	[914]	1.5m NE of NE07		533	5	
[97]	Tom na Sroine			[3012]	918	NN 207 748	NE07	495	4	41

Notes: [91] The 3000 cont. – 1-in. map – is about .75m S of the name Tom na Sroine on the 6-in.

No. Yr.	Code Name	Status	Remarks	Feet	Metres	Location	Of Mtn.	Top	Sect.	Map
NE12		TTTTT; N	[21] .5m SE of NE08 [G] Renamed 1921.							
[91]	Top of Coire Bhealaich★			3644	[1111]	1.5m SE of NE08		65	5	
[97]	Stob Coire Bhealaich			[3609]	1100c	NN 202 709	NE08	76	4	41
NE13		TTTTT	[21] 1m SEbyS of NE08							
[91]	Sgor a' Bhuic★			3165	[965]	1m SE of NE08		335	5	
[97]	Sgurr a' Bhuic			[3159]	963	NN 204 701	NE08	322	4	41
GC01		TTTTT	[21] .63m WSW of GC02 [74] Typo: GR 228 715 should be 220 711.							
[91]	Sgor a' Choinnich Beag			3175	[968]	Gl. Nevis North Side		329	5	
[97]	Sgurr Choinnich Beag			[3159]	963	NN 220 710	GC02	323	4	41

Notes: [91] 3108 on 1-inch O.S. [21] [200yds. NE of the 3108 pt. on the 1-in.]

No. Yr.	Code Name	Status	Remarks	Feet	Metres	Location	Of Mtn.	Top	Sect.	Map
GC02		MMMMM	[21] 3.75m E of NE01							
[91]	Sgor a' Choinnich Mor			3603	[1098]	Gl. Nevis North Side	49	82	5	
[97]	Sgurr Choinnich Mor			[3589]	1094	NN 227 714	52	80	4	41
GC03		TTTTT	[21] 4.25m EbyN of NE01							
[91]	Stob Coire an Easain			3545	[1081]	Gl. Nevis North Side		100	5	
[97]	Stob Coire Easain			[3543]	1080	NN 234 727	GC05	94	4	41
GC04		TxxTT	[G] Deleted 1921. Restored 1981!							
[91]	Beinn na Socaich			3000c	[914]	.75m N of GC03		516	5	
[81]	Beinn na Socaich			[3304]	1007	NN 236 734	GC05	206	4	41
[97]	Beinn na Socaich			[3304]	1007	NN 236 734	GC05	200	4	41
GC05		MMMMM	[21] .33m EbyS of GC03							
[91]	Stob Coire an Laoigh★			3659	[1115]	.33m SbyE of GC03	35	57	5	
[97]	Stob Coire an Laoigh			[3661]	1116	NN 239 725	38	54	4	41
GC06		TTTTT	[21] .75m ENE of GC03							
[91]	Caisteal★			3609	[1100]	.75m EbyN of GC03		80	5	
[97]	Caisteil			[3629]	1106	NN 246 729	GC05	68	4	41

Notes: [21] W. end of the 3500 cont.

No. Yr.	Code Name	Status	Remarks	Feet	Metres	Location	Of Mtn.	Top	Sect.	Map
GC07		TTTTT	[21] .33m EbyN of GC06							
[91]	Stob Coire Cath na Sgine★			3529	[1076]	.33m EbyN of GC06		107	5	
[97]	Stob Coire Cath na Sine			[3540]	1079	NN 252 730	GC05	95	4	41

Notes: [21] E. end of the 3500 cont.

No. Yr.	Code Name	Status	Remarks	Feet	Metres	Location	Of Mtn.	Top	Sect.	Map
GC08		TTTTT	[21] .33m WbyS of GC09							
[91]	Stob a' Choire Leith★			3629	[1106]	1.5m ENE of GC03		72	5	
[97]	Stob a' Choire Leith			[3625]	1105	NN 256 736	GC09	69	4	41

No. Yr.	Code Name	Status	Remarks	Feet	Metres	Location	Of Mtn.	Top	Sect.	Map
GC09		MMMMM	[21] 4.5m S of Roy Bridge [G] Called 'S. Top' 1921/74.							
[91]	Stob Choire Claurigh★			3858	[1176]	1.75m ENE of GC03	15	25	5	
[97]	Stob Choire Claurigh			[3862]	1177	NN 262 738	15	22	4	41
Notes: [91] See Chapter 4.2										
GC10		TTTTT								
[91]	Stob Coire nan Ceann★		·	3720a	[1134]	.33m NNE from GC09		45	5	
[97]	Stob Coire na Ceannain			[3684]	1123	NN 267 745	GC09	46	4	41
Notes: [91] Dr Heddle's aneroid measurement										
GC11		TTTTT								
[91]	Stob Coire Gaibhre★			3150a (3000)	[960]	1.25m N of GC09		343	5	
[97]	Stob Coire na Gaibhre			[3143]	958	NN 261 757	GC09 ·	343	4	41
Notes: [91] Height estimated by Mr Colin Phillip										
GC12		MMMMM	[21] 4m NWbyN of Head of L. Treig							
[91]	Stob Ban			3217	[981]	3.25m NW of Head of L. Treig	166	290	5	
[97]	Stob Ban			[3205]	977	NN 266 723	178	287	4	41
GC13		xTTxx	[G] Introduced 1921. Deleted 1981.							
[21]	Stob Choire Claurigh, N. Top			3719a (3500)	[1134]	.33m N of GC09	GC09	48	5	54
[74]	Stob Choire Claurigh, North Top			3719a (3650c)	[1134]	NN 262 744	GC09	46	5	47
OT01		MMMMM; N	[G] Renamed 1921.							
[91]	Stob Choire an Easain Mhoir			3658	[1115]	1.5m W of L. Treig	36	58	5	
[97]	Stob Coire Easain			[3658]	1115	NN 308 730	39	55	4	41
OT02		MMMMM; N	[G] Renamed 1921.							
[91]	Stob a' Choire Mheadhonaiche★			3610	[1100]	.67m NE of OT01	48	79	5	
[97]	Stob a' Choire Mheadhoin			[3625]	1105	NN 316 736	46	70	4	41
OT03		MMMMM	[91] Located W. of L. Soir a' Ghiubhas [21] .75m E of L. Treig [G] Called 'N. Top' 1921/74.							
[91]	Stob Coire Sgriodain★			3210 (3000)	[978]	E of L. Treig	169	296	5	
[97]	Stob Coire Sgriodain			[3212]	979	NN 356 743	174	281	4	41
OT04		TTTTT; N	[21] .33m SSE of OT03 [G] Renamed 1921.							
[91]	Crags above Glac Bhan★			3132 (3000)	[955]	.25m SW of L. Soir a Ghiubhais		368	5	
[97]	Stob Coire Sgriodain, South Top			[3143]	958	NN 359 739	OT03	344	4	41
OT05		MMMMM; N	[G] Renamed 1921.							
[91]	Cnoc Dearg			3433	[1046]	2m E of L. Treig	83	144	5	
[97]	Chno Dearg			[3432]	1046	NN 377 741	86	137	4	41
OT06		TTTTT; L	[G] Location seems rather variable.							
[91]	Meall Garbh★			3197 (3000)	[974]	Shoulder .75m SW of OT05		308	5	
[74]	Meall Garbh			3206 (3150c)	[977]	NN 371 731	OT05	308	5	47
[81]	Meall Garbh			[3205]	977	NN 372 727	OT05	295	4	41
[97]	Meall Garbh			[3202]	976	NN 371 727	OT05	290	4	41
OT07		MMMMM								
[91]	Beinn na Lap			3066	[935]	1m NW of L. Ossian	233	425	5	
[97]	Beinn na Lap			[3068]	935	NN 376 695	241	419	4	41
OT08		MMMMM								
[91]	Carn Dearg			3084	[940]	1.5m SE of L. Ossian	226	411	5	
[97]	Carn Dearg			[3087]	941	NN 417 661	231	399	4	42
OT09		MMMMM	[21] Btw. L. Ossian & L. Ericht							
[91]	Sgor Gaibhre			3128	[953]	Btw. Ls. Ossian & Ericht	201	372	5	
[97]	Sgor Gaibhre			[3133]	955	NN 444 674	208	356	4	42
OT10		MTTTT								
[91]	Sgor Choinnich★			3040 (3000)	[927]	.5m N of OT09	249	455	5	
[21]	Sgor Choinnich			3040 (3000)	[927]	.63m N of OT09	OT09	482	5	54
[97]	Sgor Choinnich			[3048]	929	NN 443 683	OT09	437	4	42
EL01		TTTTT								
[91]	Mullach Coire nan Nead★			3025 ·	[922]	1m W of EL03		478	5	
[97]	Mullach Coire nan Nead			[3025]	922	NN 430 734	EL03	474	4	42
Notes: [91] 2965 on 1-inch O.S.										
EL02		TTTTT; N	[G] Renamed 1981.							
[91]	Uinneag a' Ghlas-Choire★			3041 (3000)	[927]	.67m WSW of EL03		453	5	
[97]	Meall Glas Choire			[3031]	924	NN 436 727	EL03	463	4	42
EL03		MMMMM	[21] 3m WbyN of EL13							
[91]	Beinn Eibhinn			3611	[1101]	3m WNW of EL13	47	78	5	
[97]	Beinn Eibhinn			[3615]	1102	NN 449 733	48	73	4	42
EL04		MMMMM	[21] 2.75m WNW of EL13							
[91]	Aonach Beag			3646	[1111]	2.75m NW of EL13	41	64	5	
[97]	Aonach Beag			[3661]	1116	NN 457 741	37	53	4	42

No. Yr.	Code Name	Status	Remarks	Feet	Metres	Location	Of Mtn.	Top	Sect.	Map
EL05		MMMMM								
[91]	Geal-Charn★			3688	[1124]	1m ENE of EL04	31	51	5	
[97]	Geal Charn			[3714]	1132	NN 469 746	26	39	4	42
Notes: [91] See Chapter 4.2										
EL06		TTTTT; H								
[91]	Sgor Iutharna★			3250c	[991]	2m E of EL04		263	5	
[21]	Sgor Iutharn			3300a (3250)	[1006]	2m E of EL04	EL05	222	5	63
[74]	Sgor Iutharn			3350 (3250c)	[1021]	NN 490 744	EL05	198	5	47
[81]	Sgor Iutharn			[3327]	1014c	NN 490 743	EL05	189	4	42
[97]	Sgor Iutharn			[3373]	1028	NN 489 743	EL05	165	4	42
Notes: [91] See Chapter 4.2										
EL07		TTTTT	[21] 1.25m WSW of EL08							
[91]	Diollaid a' Chairn★			3029 (3000)	[923]	1m WSW of EL08		474	5	
[97]	Diollaid a' Chairn			[3025]	922	NN 488 758	EL08	471	4	42
EL08		MMMMM								
[91]	Carn Dearg			3391	[1034]	3m N of EL13	96	164	5	
[97]	Carn Dearg			[3392]	1034	NN 504 764	98	155	4	42
EL09		MMMMM	[21] 4.25m NNW of EL13							
[91]	Beinn a' Clachair			3569	[1088]	4m NNW of EL13	54	91	5	
[97]	Beinn a' Chlachair			[3566]	1087	NN 471 781	56	85	4	42
EL10		MMMMM	[21] 6m N of EL13							
[91]	Creag Peathraich			3031	[924]	4.75m N of EL13	260	472	5	
[97]	Creag Pitridh			[3031]	924	NN 487 814	264	462	4	42
EL11		MMMMM; N	[21] 1m E of EL10 [G] Renamed 1981.							
[91]	Mullach Coire an Iubhair			3443	[1049]	4.5m N of EL13	79	138	5	
[81]	Geal Charn			[3442]	1049	NN 504 812	78	134	4	42
[97]	Geal Charn - Mullach Coire an Iubhair			[3442]	1049	NN 504 811	81	129	4	42
Notes: [21] [This name only on 6-in.; 1-in. has 'Geal Charn']										
EL12		TTTxx; H	[21] Surely direction is EbyS? [74] Typo: Northing 819 should be 809. [G] Deleted 1981.							
[91]	Sron Garbh★			3206 (3250)	[977]	Shoulder .5m E of EL11		299	5	
[21]	Sron Garbh			3320a (3250)	[1012]	Shoulder .5m SbyE of EL11	EL11	209	5	63
[74]	Sron Garbh			3357 (3350c)	[1023]	NN 508 809	EL11	192	5	36
EL13		MMMMM	[21] West side of L. Ericht							
[91]	Ben Alder			3757	[1145]	L. Ericht	25	39	5	
[97]	Ben Alder			[3766]	1148	NN 496 718	25	35	4	42
EL14		TTTTT	[21] .75m SSW of EL15							
[91]	Sron Coire na h-Iolaire★			3125 (3000)	[953]	1.25m SE of EL13		376	5	
[97]	Sron Coire na h-Iolaire			[3133]	955	NN 513 704	EL15	357	4	42
EL15		MMMMM								
[91]	Beinn Bheoil			3333	[1016]	1.25m E of EL13	114	193	5	
[97]	Beinn Bheoil			[3343]	1019	NN 516 717	112	178	4	42
WD01		MMMMM; HL	[74] GR and height are for 1891 spot height (not the top)!							
[91]	Sgairneach Mor			3160	[963]	3m W of Dalnaspidal Station	189	341	5	
[21]	Sgairneach Mhor			3210a (3160)	[978]	3m W of Dalnaspidal Station	166	302	5	54
[74]	Sgairneach Mhor			3160	[963]	NN 595 728	188	352	5	48
[81]	Sgairneach Mhor			[3251]	991	NN 599 731	151	254	4	42
[97]	Sgairneach Mhor			[3251]	991	NN 598 731	155	249	4	42
Notes: [21] [3160 pt. is on a rising ridge; actual top is .33m to NE]										
WD02		MMMMM								
[91]	Beinn Udlamain			3306	[1008]	4m W of Dalnaspidal Station	121	203	5	
[97]	Beinn Udlamain			[3317]	1011	NN 579 739	119	191	5	42
WD03		MMMMM; NL	[21] 3m NWbyW of Dalnaspidal Station [74] GR and height given are for Bruach nan Iomairean! [G] Renamed 1921.							
[91]	Marcaonach			3185 (3000)	[971]	1.75m W of County March	182	322	5	
[74]	A' Mharconaich			3174	[967]	NN 601 759	183	343	5	37
[97]	A' Mharconaich			[3199]	975	NN 604 762	179	291	5	42
Notes: [91] Bruach nan Iomairean (3175ft., .5m SbyW of Marcaonich) is merely a shoulder of Marcaonich										
WD04		MMMMM	[21] 4.5m SWbyW of Dalwhinnie							
[91]	Geal Charn			3005	[916]	4.5m SSW of Dalwhinnie	277	503	5	
[97]	Geal Charn			[3008]	917	NN 596 782	279	498	5	42
LA01		MMTTT	[G] Demoted 1974.							
[91]	Beinn a' Chaoruinn, S. Top			3437	[1048]	N side Gl. Spean	82	142	6	
[21]	Beinn a' Chaoruinn, S. Top			3437	[1048]	North Side Gl. Spean	79	151	6	63
[74]	Beinn a' Chaorainn, South Top			3445 (3437)	[1050]	NN 386 845	LA02	146	6	36
[97]	Beinn a' Chaorainn, South Top			[3442]	1049★	NN 386 845	LA02	128	9	34/41

No. Yr.	Code Name	Status	Remarks Feet	Metres	Location	Of Mtn.	Top	Sect.	Map
LA02		TxMMM; H	[74] Typo: Mtn. No. 75 should be 76. [G] Deleted 1921. Restored & Promoted 1974!						
[91]	Beinn a' Chaoruinn, Middle Top		3394 (3250)	[1035]	N side Gl. Spean		163	6	
[74]	Beinn a' Chaorainn, Centre Top		3453★	[1052]	NN 386 851	76	142	6	36
[81]	Beinn a' Chaorainn		[3451]	1052	NN 386 851	76	128	9	34
[97]	Beinn a' Chaorainn		[3442]	1049★	NN 386 851	80	127	9	34/41
Notes: [74] New 6-inch height.									
LA03		TTTTT	[21] .75m NbyW of LA01						
[91]	Beinn a' Chaoruinn, N. Top		3422	[1043]	N side Gl. Spean		153	6	
[97]	Beinn a' Chaorainn, North Top		[3422]	1043	NN 383 857	LA02	143	9	34/41
LA04		MMMMM	[91] ind. 'Creag Meaghaidh Range'						
[91]	Creag Meaghaidh		3700	[1128]	3m NNW of Foot of L. Laggan	27	47	6	
[97]	Creag Meagaidh		[3701]	1128	NN 418 875	30	44	9	34/42
LA05		Txxxx	[91] ind. 'Creag Meaghaidh Range' [G] Deleted 1921.						
[91]	Creag Meaghaidh, East Top		3594	[1095]	.67m EbyN of LA04		86	6	
LA06		TTTTT	[91] ind. 'Creag Meaghaidh Range' [21] 1.33m SbyE of LA04						
[91]	An Cearcallach		3250	[991]	1.25m S of LA04		254	6	
[97]	An Cearcallach		[3258]	993	NN 422 853	LA04	241	9	34/42
LA07		TTTTT; NH	[91] ind. 'Creag Meaghaidh Range' [21] 1m SE of LA04 [G] Renamed 1921.						
[91]	Meall Coire Coille na Froise		3299 (3250)	[1006]	1.25m SE of LA04		209	6	
[74]	Meall Coire Choille-rais		3370 (3299)	[1027]	NN 432 864	LA04	186	6	36
[81]	Meall Coire Choille-Rais		[3369]	1027	NN 433 862	LA04	171	9	34
[97]	Meall Coire Choille-rais		[3373]	1028	NN 432 862	LA04	164	9	34/42
LA08		TTTxx	[91] ind. 'Creag Meaghaidh Range' [G] Deleted 1981.						
[91]	Creag Mhor		3496 (3500c)	[1066]	1.5m E of LA04		121	6	
[74]	Creag Mhor		3507 (3496)	[1069]	NN 444 873	LA04	126	6	36
Notes: [91] The summit named Creag Mhor (3496 ft.) on the 6-in. is the very small 3500 cont., about .33m N of the name Creag Mhor on the 1-in.									
LA09		TTTTT; II	[91] ind. 'Creag Meaghaidh Range'						
[91]	Crags above Coire Ard Dhoire		3591	[1095]	1m E of LA04		87	6	
[74]	Puist Coire Ardair		3510 (3591)	[1070]	NN 436 873	LA04	111	6	36
[81]	Puist Coire Ardair		[3510]	1070	NN 436 873	LA04	108	9	34
[97]	Puist Coire Ardair		[3514]	1071	NN 437 872	LA04	102	9	34/42
Notes: [91] Mrs Grant in 'Letters from the Mountains', published1806, speaks of the whole range as 'the lofty Corryarder'									
LA10		TxxTT; NH	[91] ind. 'Creag Meaghaidh Range' [G] Deleted 1921. Restored & Renamed 1981.						
[91]	Sron a' Ghaothair★		3150a (3000)	[960]	.5m ENE of LA08		345	6	
[81]	Sron a' Choire★		[3284]	1001	NN 448 878	LA04	224	9	34
[97]	Sron a' Choire		[3284]	1001	NN 448 878	LA04	220	9	34/42
LA11		TMMMM; N	[91] ind. 'Creag Meaghaidh Range' [G] Promoted (higher than LA12) & Renamed 1921.						
[91]	Creag an Lochan★		3460 (3250)	[1055]	.75m SW of LA12		128	6	
[21]	Stob Poite Coire Ardair★, W. Top		3460 (3250)	[1055]	1m NE of LA04	70	137	6	63
[97]	Stob Poite Coire Ardair		[3458]	1054	NN 428 888	76	119	9	34/42
Notes: [91] Crom Leathad is the 3441 pt. at the NE end, & Creag an Lochan is the SW end of the large 3250 cont. on the 1-in., commencing .75m NE of Creag Meaghaidh [21] [The name 'Creag an Lochan' is .67m from the top and refers to another feature]									
LA12		MTTTx; N	[91] ind. 'Creag Meaghaidh Range' [74] Typo: Easting 734 should be 437. [G] Demoted (lower than LA11) & Renamed 1921. Deleted 1997.						
[91]	Crom Leathad★		3441	[1049]	1.5m NE of LA04	80	140	6	
[21]	Stob Poite Coire Ardair★, E. Top		3441	[1049]	.83m ENE of LA11	LA11	149	6	63
[81]	Stob Poite Coire Ardair, East Top		[3448]	1051	NN 437 892	LA11	131	9	34
Notes: [91] See notes for LA11 [21] [The name 'Crom Leathad' is .67m from the top and refers to another feature]									
LA13		TTTTT; N	[91] ind. 'Creag Meaghaidh Range' [21] 1.38m ENE of LA11 [G] Renamed 1981.						
[91]	Sron Garbh Choire		3248 (3250)	[990]	2.25m NE of LA04		270	6	
[97]	Sron Coire a' Chriochairein		[3258]	993	NN 447 899	LA11	244	9	34/42
Notes: [21] [91] The small 3250 contour .33m E of the name Sron Garbh Ch. on the 1-in.									
LA14		TTTTT; N	[91] ind. 'Creag Meaghaidh Range' [21] .88m WbyN of LA15 [G] Renamed 1921.						
[91]	Top of Coire a' Chaoruinn★		3180 (3000)	[969]	.75m WbyN of LA15		326	6	
[97]	Meall an t-Snaim		[3179]	969	NN 459 904	LA15	308	9	34
LA15		MMMMM	[91] ind. 'Creag Meaghaidh Range' [21] 3.5m W of L. Laggan Inn						
[91]	Carn Liath		3298	[1005]	3.5m WbyN of L. Laggan Inn	125	210	6	
[97]	Carn Liath		[3300]	1006	NN 472 903	127	203	9	34
LA16		TTTxx; N	[91] ind. 'Creag Meaghaidh Range' [21] .33m ENE of LA15 [G] Renamed 1921. Deleted 1981.						
[91]	Buidh' Aonach		3177 (3000)	[968]	3.25m WNW of L. Laggan Inn		327	6	
[74]	A' Bhuidheanach		3171 (3177)	[967]	NN 481 907	LA15	346	6	36
LA17		TTTTT; N	[91] ind. 'Creag Meaghaidh Range' [21] 1.75m NEbyN of LA15 [74] Typo: Easting 749 should be 497. [G] Renamed 1921.						
[91]	Top of Coire Dubh★		3002 (3000c)	[915]	1.5m ENE of LA15		511	6	
[97]	Stob Coire Dubh		[3005]	916	NN 496 916	LA15	505	9	34

No. Yr.	Code Name	Status	Remarks / Feet	Metres	Location	Of Mtn.	Top	Sect.	Map
LA18	xxxxM		[G] Introduced 1984.			282	506	9	34/41
[97]	Beinn Teallach		[3002]	915	NN 361 859				
ML01	MMMMM		[91] ind. 'Monadh Liath Mountains' [21] 9.75m W of Newtonmore						
[91]	Geal Charn		3036	[925]	10m W of Newtonmore Station	255	463	6	
[97]	Geal Charn		[3038]	926	NH 561 987	260	456	9	35
ML02	TTTxx		[91] ind. 'Monadh Liath Mountains' [G] Deleted 1981.						
[91]	Snechdach Slinnean		3011 (3000)	[918]	.67m WSW of ML03		494	6	
[74]	Snechdach Slinnean		3014 (3011)	[919]	NH 621 027	ML03	523	6	37
ML03	MMMTT; N		[91] ind. 'Monadh Liath Mountains' [21] 5.75m WNW of Newtonmore [G] Renamed 1921. Demoted 1981.						
[91]	Carn Mairg		3087	[941]	6m WNW of Newtonmore Station	225	409	6	
[74]	Carn Ban		3089 (3087)	[942]	NH 632 032	225	425	6	37
[81]	Carn Ban		[3091]	942	NH 632 031	ML04	407	9	35
[97]	Carn Ban		[3091]	942	NH 632 031	ML04	394	9	35
ML04	MMMMM		[91] ind. 'Monadh Liath Mountains' [21] 5.5m WNW of Newtonmore						
[91]	Carn Dearg, N.W. Top		3093 (3000)	[943]	.5m SE of ML03	221	404	6	
[97]	Carn Dearg		[3100]	945	NH 635 023	225	385	9	35
ML05	TTTTT		[91] ind. 'Monadh Liath Mountains' [21] .5m SE of ML04						
[91]	Carn Dearg, S.E. Top		3025 (3000)	[922]	1m SE of ML03		477	6	
[97]	Carn Dearg, S.E. Top		[3028]	923	NH 637 017	ML04	467	9	35
ML06	Mxxxx		[91] ind. 'Monadh Liath Mountains' [G] Demoted & Deleted 1921.						
[91]	Carn Ballach, S.W. Top		3009 (3000)	[917]	1m NE of ML03	272	496	6	
ML07	TMMTT		[91] ind. 'Monadh Liath Mountains' [G] Promoted 1921. Demoted 1981! Also see Endnotes.						
[91]	Carn Ballach, N.E. Top		3000c	[914]	1.25m NE of ML03		517	6	
[21]	Carn Ballach, N.E. Top		3020a (3000)	[921]	1.25m NE of ML03	264	510	6	73
[74]	Carn Ballach		3017 (3009)	[920]	NH 643 045	269	517	6	37
[81]	Carn Ballach		[3018]	920	NH 643 045	ML04	491	9	35
[97]	Carn Ballach		[3018]	920	NH 643 045	ML04	477	9	35

Notes: [21] [The SW Top is deleted, being practically indistinguishable]

No. Yr.	Code Name	Status	Remarks / Feet	Metres	Location	Of Mtn.	Top	Sect.	Map
ML08	MMMMM		[91] ind. 'Monadh Liath Mountains' [21] 3.75m NW of Newtonmore						
[91]	A' Chailleach		3045	[928]	4m NW of Newtonmore	245	450	6	
[97]	A' Chailleach		[3051]	930	NH 681 041	251	435	9	35
ML09	MMMMM		[91] ind. 'Monadh Liath Mountains'						
[91]	Carn Sgulain		3015	[919]	4.5m NNW of Newtonmore	267	488	6	
[97]	Carn Sgulain		[3018]	920	NH 683 058	271	479	9	35
WL01	MMMMM								
[91]	Sron a' Choire Ghairbh		3066	[935]	2m W of L. Lochy	234	426	7	
[97]	Sron a' Choire Ghairbh		[3074]	937	NN 222 945	239	417	10	34
WL02	TMMMM		[G] Promoted 1921.						
[91]	Meall an Teanga*		3050a	[930]	1.75m S of WL01		446	7	
[21]	Meall na Teanga		3050a (2750)	[930]	1.75m SbyW of WL01	245	467	7	62
[97]	Meall na Teanga		[3012]	918	NN 220 924	275	488	10	34

Notes: [91] Meall an Teanga only appears on the O.S. maps as a 2750 cont. Dr Heddle, with careful aneroid measurements, & levels from other hills, makes the height 3050ft.

No. Yr.	Code Name	Status	Remarks / Feet	Metres	Location	Of Mtn.	Top	Sect.	Map
FI01	MMMMM; N		[G] Renamed 'Gaor Bheinn' 1921. Old name restored 1997.						
[91]	Gulvain, N. Top		3224	[983]	Btw. L. Eil & L. Arkaig	161	283	7	
[97]	Gulvain		[3238]	987	NN 002 875	161	258	10	41

Notes: [91] The N top of Gulvain is locally called Gulvain Mor, the S top Gulvain Beag

No. Yr.	Code Name	Status	Remarks / Feet	Metres	Location	Of Mtn.	Top	Sect.	Map
FI02	TTTTT; N		[21] .75m SSW of FI01 [G] Renamed 'Gaor Bheinn' 1921. Old name restored 1997.						
[91]	Gulvain, S. Top		3148	[960]	Btw. Heads of L. Eil & L. Arkaig		348	7	
[97]	Gulvain, South Top		[3156]	962	NM 996 864	FI01	328	10	40
FI03	MMMMM; N		[G] Renamed 1921.						
[91]	Sgor Choileam		3164	[964]	Head of Glenfinnan	187	336	7	
[97]	Sgurr Thuilm		[3159]	963	NM 939 879	193	326	10	40
FI04	MMMMM								
[91]	Sgor nan Coireachan		3133	[955]	2.25m W of FI03	199	367	7	
[97]	Sgurr nan Coireachan		[3136]	956	NM 902 880	206	352	10	40
DK01	MMMMM		[21] 2.5m NEbyN of Head of L. Nevis						
[91]	Sgor na Ciche		3410	[1039]	Head of L. Nevis	91	156	7	
[97]	Sgurr na Ciche		[3412]	1040	NM 902 966	92	148	10	33/40
DK02	TTTMM		[G] Promoted 1981.						
[91]	Garbh Chioch Mor*		3365a (3250)	[1026]	.5m SE of DK01		179	7	
[74]	Garbh Chioch Mhor		3350c		NM 908 961	DK01	213	7	35
[81]	Garbh Chioch Mhor		[3323]	1013	NM 909 961	113	190	10	33/40
[97]	Garbh Chioch Mhor		[3323]	1013	NM 909 961	116	187	10	33/40

Notes: [91] Dr Heddle's measurements

No. Yr.	Code Name	Status	Remarks	Feet	Metres	Location	Of Mtn.	Top	Sect.	Map
DK03		TTTTT; H								
[91]	Garbh Chioch Bheag★			3100a (3000)	[945]	1m ESE of DK01		397	7	
[97]	Garbh Chioch Bheag			[3176]	968	NM 918 959	DK02	310	10	33/40
Notes: [91] Dr Heddle's measurements										
DK04		MMMMM	[21] North of Gl. Dessary							
[91]	Sgor nan Coireachan			3125	[953]	Gl. Dessary	203	375	7	
[97]	Sgurr nan Coireachan			[3127]	953	NM 933 958	213	365	10	33/40
DK05		MMMMM								
[91]	Sgurr Mor			3290	[1003]	1.5m S of Head of L. Quoich	128	217	7	
[97]	Sgurr Mor			[3291]	1003	NM 965 980	132	210	10	33/40
DK06		MMMMM; N	[21] 1.5m S of Middle of L. Quoich [G] Renamed 1921.							
[91]	Scour Gairoch			3015	[919]	1.5m S of L. Quoich	266	487	7	
[97]	Gairich			[3015]	919	NN 025 995	272	482	10	33
KN01		MMMMM								
[91]	Meall Buidhe			3107	[947]	2m NNW of Head of L. Nevis	210	384	7	
[97]	Meall Buidhe			[3104]	946	NM 849 989	222	382	10	33/40
KN02		MMMMM								
[91]	Luinne Bheinn			3083	[940]	3.5m N of Head of L. Nevis	227	412	7	
[97]	Luinne Bheinn			[3081]	939	NG 869 007	234	405	10	33
KN03		MMMMM	[21] Btw. L. Nevis & L. Hourn							
[91]	Ladhar Bheinn			3343	[1019]	4.5m NE of Inverie	110	189	7	
[97]	Ladhar Bheinn			[3346]	1020	NG 823 039	111	177	10	33
KN04		TTTTT	[74] Typo: Easting 820 should be 830 - or wrong top located?							
[91]	Stob a' Choire Odhair			3138	[956]	.33m ENE of KN03		365	7	
[97]	Stob a' Choire Odhair			[3150]	960c	NG 830 043	KN03	336	10	33
Notes: [91] This height is taken from the Admiralty chart, none is given on the O.S. maps										
KN05		xxxTT	[G] Introduced 1981.							
[81]	Meall Buidhe, S.E Top			[3051]	930	NM 853 987	KN01	451	10	33/40
[97]	Meall Buidhe, S.E. Top			[3091]	942	NM 852 987	KN01	396	10	33/40
KN06		xxxTT	[G] Introduced 1981.							
[81]	Luinne Bheinn, East Top			[3074]	937	NG 872 007	KN02	428	10	33/40
[97]	Luinne Bheinn, East Top			[3074]	937	NG 872 007	KN02	416	10	33
SG01		MMMMM								
[91]	Ben Sgriol			3196	[974]	North Side L. Hourn	175	309	7	
[97]	Beinn Sgritheall			[3195]	974	NG 835 126	183	296	10	33
SG02		TTTTT	[21] .25m NNW of SG01							
[91]	Ben Sgriol, N.W. Top			3034 (3000)	[925]	North Side L. Hourn		466	7	
[97]	Beinn Sgritheall, N.W. Top			[3045]	928	NG 834 131	SG01	440	10	33
SA01		TTTTT								
[91]	Sgurr Leac nan Each			3013	[918]	1.25m W of SA04		492	7	
[97]	Sgurr Leac nan Each			[3015]	919	NG 917 133	SA04	483	10	33
SA02		TTTTT; N	[G] Renamed 1921.							
[91]	Sgurr na Creige			3082	[939]	.75m WbyS of SA04		415	7	
[97]	Spidean Dhomhuill Bhric			[3081]	939	NG 922 129	SA04	408	10	33
Notes: [91] Locally the Sgurr na Creige of the O.S. is called Bidean an Dhonuill Breac, while the top, .5m N of The Saddle, is known as Sgurr na Creige										
SA03		TTTTx	[21] .5m WSW of SA04 [G] Deleted 1997.							
[91]	The Saddle, W. Top			3196 (3000)	[974]	.5m W of SA04		310	7	
[81]	The Saddle, West Top			[3176]	968c	NG 928 128	SA04	319	10	33
SA04		MMMMM								
[91]	The Saddle			3317	[1011]	Btw. Heads of L. Duich & L. Hourn	118	199	7	
[97]	The Saddle			[3314]	1010	NG 936 131	121	194	10	33
SA05		TTxTT; H	[G] Relocated in 1974. See note to SA09.							
[91]	Sgurr na Forcan#			3100a (3000)	[945]	.5m E of SA04		395	7	
[21]	Sgurr na Forcan#			3100a (3000)	[945]	.33m E of SA04	SA04	409	7	72
[81]	Sgurr na Forcan			[3150]	960c	NG 941 131	SA04	345	10	33
[97]	Sgurr na Forcan			[3159]	963	NG 940 130	SA04	324	10	33
Notes: [91] Mr Colin Phillip's measurement – levels from the Saddle										
SA06		TTxxx; N	[G] Renamed 1921. Deleted 1974.							
[91]	Top half mile N. of Saddle			3000c	[914]	.5m N of SA04		534	7	
[21]	Sgurr na Creige			3100a (3000)	[945]	.5m N of SA04	SA04	413	7	72
Notes: [91] Locally the Sgurr na Creige of the O.S. is called Bidean an Dhonuill Breac, while the top, .5m N of The Saddle, is known as Sgurr na Creige [21] [Name on 1-inch map is .5m N. of the top. Local name is Sgurr Nid na h-Iolaire]										

No. Yr.	Code Name	Status	Remarks / Feet	Metres	Location	Of Mtn.	Top	Sect.	Map
SA07		TTxxx	[G] Deleted 1974.						
[91]	Fraochag★		3000c	[914]	End of shoulder 1m NE of SA08		518	7	
[21]	Faochag		3010a (3000)	[917]	End of shoulder 1m NE of SA08	SA08	525	7	72
SA08		MMMMM	[21] 1.25m SEbyS of SA04						
[91]	Sgurr na Sgine		3098	[944]	1.25m SSE of SA04	220	403	7	
[97]	Sgurr na Sgine		[3104]	946	NG 946 113	223	383	10	33
SA09		xxTTx; N	[74] GR is Saddle, E. Top; possibly an error. [G] Introduced 1974. GR given is Saddle, E.Top; possibly an error.						
Renamed 1981.Deleted 1997.									
[74]	Sgurr nan Forcan		3050c	958	NG 938 131	SA04	374	7	35
[81]	The Saddle, East Top		[3143]	958	NG 938 130	SA04	357	10	33
SA10		xxxTx	[G] Introduced 1981. Deleted 1997!						
[81]	The Saddle, Trig Point		[3314]	1010	NG 934 131	SA04	200	10	33
SA11		xxxTT	[G] Introduced 1981.						
[81]	Sgurr na Sgine, N.W Top		[3097]	944	NG 944 115	SA08	402	10	33
[97]	Sgurr na Sgine, N.W. Top		[3091]	942	NG 943 115	SA08	398	10	33
QO01		TTxxx	[G] Deleted 1974.						
[91]	Am Bathaiche★		3000c	[914]	.67m NNE of QO02		519	7	
[21]	Am Bathaich		3055a (3000)	[931]	.75m NNE of QO02	QO02	459	7	72
QO02		MMMMM; N	[21] 2.25m E of Lochhournhead [G] Renamed 1921.						
[91]	Sgurr a' Mhoraire		3365	[1026]	2.5m E of Lochhournhead	105	178	7	
[97]	Sgurr a' Mhaoraich		[3369]	1027	NG 983 065	104	167	10	33
QO03		TTTTT; N	[G] Renamed 1921.						
[91]	Sgurr a' Mhoraire Beag★		3101 (3000)	[945]	.5m WbyN of QO02		393	7	
[97]	Sgurr a' Mhaoraich Beag		[3110]	948	NG 977 067	QO02	372	10	33
QO04		MMMMM							
[91]	Gleourach		3395	[1035]	1.75m N of L. Quoich	95	162	7	
[97]	Gleouraich		[3396]	1035	NH 039 053	97	154	10	33
QO05		TTTTT; N	[G] Renamed 1981.						
[91]	Gleourach, E. Top		3291 (3250)	[1003]	.67m EbyS of QO05		216	7	
[97]	Craig Coire na Fiar Bhealaich		[3300]	1006	NH 047 051	QO04	204	10	33
QO06		MMMMM	[21] 1.75m N of Foot of L. Quoich						
[91]	Spidean Mialach		3268	[996]	2m N of Foot of L. Quoich	142	237	7	
[97]	Spidean Mialach		[3268]	996	NH 066 043	146	236	10	33
SS01		MMMMM	[21] 2.63m SSE of Clunie Bridge Inn						
[91]	Creag a' Mhaim		3102	[946]	2.5m SSE of Clunie Bridge Inn	215	392	7	
[97]	Creag a' Mhaim		[3107]	947	NH 087 077	218	375	10	33
SS02		MMMMM							
[91]	Drum Sionnach★		3222 (3000)	[982]	1m NW of SS01	163	286	7	
[97]	Druim Shionnach		[3238]	987	NH 074 084	160	257	10	33
SS03		MMMMM							
[91]	Aonach air Chrith		3342	[1019]	2.5m WbyN of SS01	111	190	7	
[97]	Aonach air Chrith		[3350]	1021	NH 050 083	109	174	10	33
SS04		MMMMM							
[91]	Maol Cheann-dearg		3214	[980]	1.25m WbyN of SS03	168	294	7	
[97]	Maol Chinn-dearg		[3218]	981	NH 032 087	168	270	10	33
Notes: [91] The name Maol Cheann-dearg is applied to the whole ridge – both to this top & Aonach air Chrith									
SS05		MMMMM	[97] Typo: Northing 199 should be 099!						
[91]	Sgurr an Doire Leathain★		3272 (3250)	[997]	.67m SE of SS06	141	235	7	
[97]	Sgurr an Doire Leathain		[3314]	1010	NH 015 099	122	195	10	33
SS06		MMMMM	[21] South Side Gl. Shiel						
[91]	Sgurr an Lochain		3282	[1000]	4.5m WbyS of Clunie Inn	133	224	7	
[97]	Sgurr an Lochain		[3294]	1004	NH 005 104	131	209	10	33
SS07		MMMMM	[21] 1.5m WNW of SS06 [97] Typo: Easting 913 should be 983!						
[91]	Creag nan Damh		3012	[918]	South Side Gl. Sheil	270	493	7	
[97]	Creag nan Damh		[3012]	918	NG 983 111	274	485	10	33
SS08		xxxT	[G] Introduced 1997.						
[97]	Druim Shionnach, West Top		[3077]	938	NH 062 082	SS02	411	10	33
NS01		MMMMM	[91] ind.'Beinn Mhor Range' [21] 3m ESE of Shiel Bridge						
[91]	Sgurr Fhuaran (Scour Ouran)		3505	[1068]	North Side Gl. Sheil	67	112	8	
[97]	Sgurr Fhuaran		[3501]	1067	NG 978 166	70	110	11	33
NS02		TTTTM	[91] ind.'Beinn Mhor Range' [21] .63m S of NS01 [G] Promoted 1997.						
[91]	Sgurr na Carnach★		3270 (3250)	[997]	.5m S of NS01		236	8	
[81]	Sgurr na Carnach		[3287]	1002	NG 977 159	NS01	218	11	33
[97]	Sgurr na Carnach		[3287]	1002	NG 977 158	134	213	11	33

No. Yr.	Code Name	Status	Remarks	Feet	Metres	Location	Of Mtn.	Top	Sect.	Map
NS03		MMMMM	[91] ind. 'Beinn Mhor Range' [21] 1m ESE of NS01							
[91]	Sgurr na Ciste Duibhe			3370	[1027]	1m SbyE of NS01	104	175	8	
[97]	Sgurr na Ciste Duibhe			[3369]	1027	NG 984 149	105	168	11	33
NS04		TTTTT; H	[91] ind. 'Beinn Mhor Range' [21] .67m E of NS03							
[91]	Sgurr nan Spainteach#			3129 (3000)	[954]	.5m E of NS03		370	8	
[97]	Sgurr nan Spainteach			[3248]	990	NG 991 150	NS03	250	11	33
NS05		MMMMM	[21] 1m WbyN of NS06							
[91]	Saileag★			3124 (3000)	[952]	1m W of NS06	204	377	8	
[97]	Saileag			[3136]	956	NH 017 148	205	350	11	33
NS06		MMMMM	[21] N Side of Head of Gl. Shiel							
[91]	Sgurr a' Bhealaich Dheirg			3378	[1030]	N Side of Head of Gl. Sheil	100	169	8	
[97]	Sgurr a' Bhealaich Dheirg			[3399]	1036	NH 035 143	96	152	11	33
NS07		MMMMM	[21] 2.25m NWbyN of Cluanie Inn							
[91]	Aonach Meadhoin★			3284 (3250)	[1001]	.2m WbyS of NS08	131	221	8	
[97]	Aonach Meadhoin			[3284]	1001	NH 049 137	135	214	11	33
NS08		TTTTT; N	[21] .33m ENE of NS07 [G] Renamed 1921.							
[91]	Carn Fuaralach			3241	[988]	2m NW of Clunie Inn		274	8	
[97]	Sgurr an Fhuarail			[3238]	987	NH 054 139	NS07	259	11	33
NS09		MMMMM	[21] 3.25m NNW of Cluanie Inn							
[91]	Ciste Dhubh			3218	[981]	3.25m NbyW of Clunie Inn	165	289	8	
[97]	Ciste Dhubh			[3212]	979	NH 062 166	173	279	11	33
NS10		xxTTT	[G] Introduced 1974.							
[74]	Sgurr nan Saighead			3050 (3000c)	929	NG 975 178	NS01	470	8	35
[97]	Sgurr nan Saighead			[3048]	929	NG 974 177	NS01	438	11	33
ES01		MMMMM; N	[21] 3.5m NNE of Cluanie Inn [G] Renamed 1921. Called 'Centre Top' in 1921/74.							
[91]	Sgurr nan Ceathramhan			3614	[1102]	3.5m NbyE of Clunie Inn	46	76	8	
[97]	Mullach Fraoch-choire			[3615]	1102	NH 095 171	49	74	11	33
ES02		TTTxx; N	[21] .33m ENE of ES01 [G] Renamed 1921. Deleted 1981.							
[91]	Sgurr nan Ceathramhan, N.E. Top			3435	[1047]	.33m NE of ES01		143	8	
[74]	Mullach Fraoch-choire, N.E. Top			3435 (3400c)	[1047]	NH 100 175	ES01	150	8	35
ES03		TTTTT; N	[G] Renamed 1921. Renamed again 1981.							
[91]	Coire Odhar			3295 (3250)	[1004]	.5m SSW of ES01		211	8	
[21]	Mullach Fraoch-choire, S. Top			3295	[1004]	.67m SSW of ES01	ES01	227	8	72
[97]	Stob Coire na Cralaig			[3307]	1008	NH 091 163	ES04	199	11	33
ES04		MMMMM; N	[21] 2.25m NNE of Cluanie Inn [G] Renamed 1921.							
[91]	Garbh-leac			3676	[1120]	2.25m NNE of Clunie Inn	32	52	8	
[97]	A' Chralaig			[3674]	1120	NH 094 148	33	48	11	33
ES05		TTTTT; H								
[91]	A' Chioch★			3000c	[914]	1.5m NE of ES04		520	8	
[21]	A' Chioch			3050a (3000)	[930]	1.25m ENE of ES04	ES04	468	8	72
[74]	A' Chralaig, A'Chioch			3100c	948	NH 108 153	ES04	406	8	35
[81]	A' Chioch			[3110]	948	NH 108 153	ES04	387	11	34
[97]	A' Chioch			[3107]	947	NH 108 152	ES04	374	11	34
ES06		TTTTT; N	[74] MA12 & ES06 are both Top 242; ES06 is Top 250 in Table 2, but with wrong height 999. [G] Renamed 1921. Renamed again 1981.							
[91]	Tigh Mor, Centre Top			3276	[999]	Btw. L. Affric & L. Clunie		227	8	
[21]	Tigh Mor na Seilge, Centre Top			3276	[999]	.33m NNE of ES08	ES08	242	8	72
[97]	Carn na Coire Mheadhoin			[3284]	1001	NH 134 158	ES08	215	11	34
	Notes: [91] 3222 on the 1-in. The pt. marked 3276 on the 6-in. is about 200 yds SSW from the 3222 pt.									
ES07		TTTTT; N	[21] .75m NNE of ES08 [G] Renamed 1921.							
[91]	Tigh Mor, N.N.E. Top			3045 (3000)	[928]	.33m NNE of ES06		449	8	
[97]	Tigh Mor na Seilge			[3048]	929	NH 140 166	ES08	439	11	34
ES08		MMMMM; N	[G] Renamed 1921. Renamed again 1981.							
[91]	Tigh Mor, S.S.W. Top			3285 (3250)	[1001]	.33m S of ES06	129	219	8	
[21]	Tigh Mor na Seilge, S.S.W. Top			3285 (3250)	[1001]	Btw. L. Affric & L. Cluanie	126	234	8	72
[97]	Sail Chaorainn			[3287]	1002	NH 133 154	133	212	11	34
ES09		TTTxx	[21] 1m ESE of ES08 [G] Deleted 1981.							
[91]	Sail Chaoruinn★			3000c	[914]	1m SW of ES06		521	8	
[74]	Sail Chaoruinn			3025 (3000c)	[922]	NH 141 148	ES08	505	8	35
ES10		MMMMM	[21] 2.25m N of L. Cluanie							
[91]	Sgurr nan Conbhairean			3636	[1108]	N of L. Clunie	43	68	8	
[97]	Sgurr nan Conbhairean			[3638]	1109	NH 129 138	44	63	11	34
	Notes: [91] 3634 on 1-inch map									

No. Yr.	Code Name	Status	Remarks	Feet	Metres	Location	Of Mtn.	Top	Sect.	Map
ES11		TTTTT	[21] .5m WSW of ES10							
[91]	Drochaid an Tuill Easaich★			3250c	[991]	.5m SW of ES10		257	8	
[97]	Drochaid an Tuill Easaich			[3284]	1001	NH 120 134	ES10	216	11	34
ES12		TTTTT	[21] .63m SE of ES10							
[91]	Creag a' Chaoruinn★			3260 (3250)	[994]	.5m SE of ES10		246	8	
[97]	Creag a' Chaorainn			[3274]	998	NH 137 131	ES10	229	11	34

Notes: [21] [The eastmost of two small 3250 contours]

No. Yr.	Code Name	Status	Remarks	Feet	Metres	Location	Of Mtn.	Top	Sect.	Map
ES13		MMMMM	[21] 1.75m N of L. Cluanie							
[91]	Carn Ghluasaid			3140 (3000)	[96]	1.5m N of L. Clunie	196	359	8	
[97]	Carn Ghluasaid			[3140]	957	NH 145 125	203	347	11	34
AT01		MMMMM	[21] 3.25m ENE of Croe Bridge							
[91]	A' Ghlas-Bheinn			3006	[916]	3.5m ENE of Croe Bridge	275	501	8	
[97]	A' Ghlas-bheinn			[3012]	918	NH 008 230	273	484	11	25/33
AT02		TTTTT; N	[91] ind. 'Beinn Fhada' [G] Renamed 1974.							
[91]	Ceum na h-Aon Choise★			3150a (3000)	[960]	1m WbyN of AT03		346	8	
[97]	Meall an Fhuarain Mhoir			[3130]	954	NG 999 196	AT03	359	11	33

Notes: [91] Mr Colin Phillip's aneroid measurement in very uncertain weather

No. Yr.	Code Name	Status	Remarks	Feet	Metres	Location	Of Mtn.	Top	Sect.	Map
AT03		MMMMM	[91] ind. 'Beinn Fhada'							
[91]	Beinn Fhada (Ben Attow)			3383	[1031]	4m E of Head of L. Duich	98	166	8	
[97]	Beinn Fhada			[3386]	1032	NH 018 192	100	157	11	33
AT04		TTTTT; H	[91] ind. 'Beinn Fhada'							
[91]	Sgor a' Dubh Doire#			3000c	[914]	1m ESE of AT03		522	8	
[21]	Sgurr a' Dubh Doire#			3100a (3000)	[945]	1m ESE of AT03	AT03	411	8	72
[97]	Sgurr a' Dubh Doire			[3156]	962	NH 034 185	AT03	329	11	33

Notes: [91] The height of this top is probably nearly 3100. The only height on the 6-in. is 3014, a little to the S of the county march, apparently not on the top

No. Yr.	Code Name	Status	Remarks	Feet	Metres	Location	Of Mtn.	Top	Sect.	Map
AF01		TTTTT; N	[21] 1m NbyW of AF03 [81] Formerly named Stuc Bheag! [G] Renamed in 1981 - swap with AF02!							
[91]	Stuc Beag#			3250c	[991]	1m N of AF03		258	8	
[97]	Stuc Mor			[3415]	1041	NH 053 242	AF03	146	11	25/33

Notes: [91] The name Stuc Bheag on the 6-inch map is at least 1m NNE of the 3250 cont. locally known by that name

No. Yr.	Code Name	Status	Remarks	Feet	Metres	Location	Of Mtn.	Top	Sect.	Map
AF02		TTTTT; N	[21] .75m NNW of AF03 [81] Formerly named Stuc Mor! [G] Renamed in 1981 - swap with AF01!							
[91]	Stuc Mor#			3250c	[991]	.5m N of AF03		259	8	
[97]	Stuc Bheag			[3527]	1075	NH 053 237	AF03	99	11	25/33
AF03		MMMMM	[21] 6.5m EbyN of Head of L. Duich [G] Mis-spelled 1891. Called 'Centre Top' in 1921.							
[91]	Sgurr nan Caethreamhnan, E. Top			3771	[1149]	7m EbyN of Head of L. Duich	23	36	8	
[97]	Sgurr nan Ceathreamhnan			[3776]	1151	NH 057 228	22	31	11	25/33
AF04		TTTTT	[21] .25m W of AF03 [G] Mis-spelled 1891.							
[91]	Sgurr nan Ceathreamhnan, W. Top			3737	[1139]	.5m W of AF03		42	8	
[97]	Sgurr nan Ceathreamhnan, West Top			[3750]	1143	NH 053 228	AF03	37	11	25/33
AF05		TTTxx	[21] 1m WNW of AF03 [G] Deleted 1921.							
[91]	Creag nan Clachan Geala★			3282 (3000)	[1000]	1m WbyN of AF03		223	8	
[74]	Creag nan Clachan Geala			3282 (3250c)	998	NH 043 232	AF03	256	8	26
AF06		TTTTx; N	[21] 1m EbyS of AF03 [G] Renamed 1921. Deleted 1997.							
[91]	Top of Coire nan Dearcag★			3089 (3000)	[942]	1m E of AF03		406	8	
[81]	Stob Coire nan Dearcag★			[3084]	940	NH 071 225	AF03	413	11	25/33
AF07		TTTTT; N	[G] Renamed 1981.							
[91]	Creag a' Choir' Aird★			3188 (3000)	[972]	3m ENE of AF03		320	8	
[21]	Creag a' Choir' Aird★, N. Top			3188	[972]	2.75m NEbyN of AF03	AF09	328	8	72
[97]	Mullach Sithidh			[3195]	974	NH 082 264	AF30	301	11	25/33

Notes: [91] A 3000 cont. on the 1-inch map extends 2.25m nearly N & S, with an apparent width of under .25m. The NW end is Creag a' Choir Aird

No. Yr.	Code Name	Status	Remarks	Feet	Metres	Location	Of Mtn.	Top	Sect.	Map
AF08		TTTxx	[21] .5m ENE of AF07 [G] Deleted 1981.							
[91]	Creag a' Choir' Aird, E. Top			3058 (3000)	[932]	.5m E of AF07		439	8	
[74]	Creag a' Choire Aird, East Top			3058 (3050c)	[932]	NH 087 266	AF09	456	8	26
AF09		MMxTT; N	[91] Typo: Mtn. No. is missing but should be 283! [G] Demoted & Renamed 1981. See Endnotes							
[91]	Ridge S. of Creag a' Choir' Aird★			3000c	[914]	1.5m S of AF07	283	535	8	
[21]	Creag a' Choir' Aird★, Southern Ridge			3210a (3000)	[978]	1.5m S of AF07	167	303	8	72
[81]	Carn na Con Dhu★			[3176]	968	NH 073 242	AF30	321	11	25/33
[97]	Carn na Con Dhu			[3173]	967	NH 072 241	AF30	314	11	25/33

Notes: [91] No height or name is given to the southern portion of the ridge, but from the shaded 1-inch map it appears at least higher than Creag a' Choir Aird [21] [Inference in 1891 note doubtful. Dr Corner's measurements: Tops 1m, 1.33m & 1.83m from AF28; heights 3060, 3080 & 3075]

No. Yr.	Code Name	Status	Remarks	Feet	Metres	Location	Of Mtn.	Top	Sect.	Map
AF10		MMMMM	[91] Typo: Mtn. No. is 283 but should be 265. See Chapter 4.8							
[91]	An Socach★			3017 (3000)	[920]	2m E of AF03	265	486	8	
[97]	An Socach			[3022]	921	NH 088 230	264	475	11	25/33

No.	Code	Status	Remarks							
Yr.	Name			Feet	Metres	Location	Of Mtn.	Top	Sect.	Map
AF11		TTTTT; N	[91] Typo: Mtn. No. is 265, but this belongs to AF10! See Chapter 4.8 [G] Renamed 1981.							
[91]	Creag a' Chaoruinn★			3462 (3250)	[1055]	1.5m SbyW of AF15		127	8	
[97]	Creag Coire nan Each			[3461]	1055	NH 113 232	AF15	117	11	25
AF12		TTTxx; N	[G] Renamed 1921. Deleted 1981.							
[91]	Top of Coire Coulavie★			3508	[1069]	1m SW of AF15		109	8	
[74]	Stob Coire Coulavie			3508	1069	NH 111 240	AF15	121	8	26
AF13		TTTxx	[21] .5m SW of AF15 [G] Deleted 1981.							
[91]	Ciste Dhubh★			3606	[1099]	1.5m SW of AF15		81	8	
[74]	Ciste Dubh			3606 (3600c)	1109	NH 114 246	AF15	75	8	26
AF14		TTTTT; N	[21] 1m SEbyS of AF15 [G] Renamed 1921.							
[91]	Saoiter Mor★			3500c	[1067]	1m SE of AF15		117	8	
[97]	An Tudair			[3524]	1074	NH 127 239	AF15	100	11	25
AF15		MMMMM								
[91]	Mam Sodhail (Mam Soul)			3862	[1177]	2.5m NW of L. Affric	14	23	8	
[97]	Mam Sodhail			[3875]	1181	NH 120 253	14	19	11	25
AF16		MMMMM	[21] .5m NNE of AF15							
[91]	Carn Eige			3877	[1182]	.5m N of AF15	13	20	8	
[97]	Carn Eighe			[3881]	1183	NH 123 262	12	17	11	25
AF17		TTTTT; N	[21] 1.25m EbyS of AF15 [G] Renamed 1921.							
[91]	Top btw. Mam Sodhail & Sg. na Lapaich			3262 (3250)	[994]	Btw. AF15 & AF18		243	8	
[97]	Mullach Cadha Rainich			[3268]	996	NH 139 246	AF15	235	11	25
AF18		MTTTT	[G] Demoted 1921. Claims remain strong!							
[91]	Sgurr na Lapaich			3401	[1037]	2.25m ESE of AF15	94	161	8	
[21]	Sgurr na Lapaich			3401	[1037]	2.25m ESE of AF15	AF15	170	8	72
[97]	Sgurr na Lapaich			[3399]	1036	NH 154 243	AF15	153	11	25
AF19		TTTTT; N	[21] .67m NNW of AF16 [G] Renamed 1921.							
[91]	Top of Coire Lochain			3006 (3000)	[916]	.67m NbyW of AF16		500	8	
[97]	Stob Coire Lochan			[3008]	917	NH 119 272	AF16	500	11	25
AF20		MMMMM	[21] 1.33m NNW of AF16							
[91]	Beinn Fhionnlaidh			3294	[1004]	1.33 NbyW of AF16	127	215	8	
[97]	Beinn Fhionnlaidh			[3297]	1005	NH 115 282	128	205	11	25
AF21		TTTTT; N	[21] .5m ENE of AF16 [G] Renamed 1981.							
[91]	Creag na h-Eige★			3753	[1144]	.5m NNE of AF16		40	8	
[97]	Stob a' Choire Dhomhain			[3763]	1147	NH 131 264	AF16	36	11	25
AF22		TTTTT								
[91]	Sron Garbh#			3500c	[1067]	1.25m E of AF16		118	8	
[97]	Sron Garbh			[3711]	1131	NH 145 263	AF16	40	11	25
AF23		TTTTT								
[91]	An Leth-Chreag★			3443 (3250)	[1049]	.67m WSW of AF25		137	8	
[97]	An Leth-chreag			[3448]	1051	NH 153 269	AF25	124	11	25
AF24		TTTTT; H	[21] .33m W of AF25							
[91]	Tom a' Choinich Beag#			3450a (3250)	[1052]	A small top W of AF25		132	8	
[81]	Tom a' Choinich Beag			[3376]	1029	NH 157 273	AF25	168	11	25
[97]	Tom a' Choinich Beag			[3386]	1032	NH 157 273	AF25	158	11	25
Notes: [91] Dr Heddle's measurement										
AF25		MMMMM								
[91]	Tom a' Choinich			3646	[1111]	2.75m ENE of AF16	40	63	8	
[97]	Tom a' Choinich			[3648]	1112	NH 164 273	41	58	11	25
AF26		TTTTT; N	[G] Renamed 1921.							
[91]	Top N. of Allt Toll Easa			3149 (3000)	[960]	1.13m WSW of AF27		347	8	
[97]	Toll Creagach, West Top			[3120]	951	NH 177 275	AF27	369	11	25
AF27		MMMMM								
[91]	Tuill Creagach			3452	[1052]	1.5m S of L. Mullardoch	75	131	8	
[97]	Toll Creagach			[3458]	1054	NH 194 282	77	120	11	25
AF28		xTxxx	[G] Introduced 1921. Deleted 1974.							
[21]	Sgurr nan Ceathreamhnan, E. Top			3150a (3000)	[960]	.67m ESE of AF03	AF03	353	8	72
AF29		xTTxT	[G] Introduced 1921. Deleted 1981. Restored 1997!							
[21]	Stob Coire Dhomhnuill			3725 (3500)	[1135]	.88m E of AF16	AF15	46	8	72
[74]	Stob Coire Dhomhnuill			3725 (3650c)	[1135]	NH 139 262	AF15	44	8	26
[97]	Stob Coire Dhomhnuill			[3730]	1137	NH 138 262	AF16	38	11	25
AF30		xxMMM	[74] The Munro moves to a new top, 1m N of AF09; see Endnotes. [81] Typo: Easting 091 should be 081. [G]							
	Probably known since 1891, but wrongly located; see AF09. Renamed 1981.									
[74]	Creag a' Choire Aird, South Top			3210a (3150c)	[978]	NH 082 258	167	304	8	26
[97]	Mullach na Dheiragain			[3222]	982	NH 080 259	167	269	11	25/33

No. Yr.	Code Name	Status	Remarks Feet	Metres	Location	Of Mtn.	Top	Sect.	Map
AF31 [97]	xxxxT Stuc Fraoch Choire		[G] Introduced 1997. [3012]	918	NH 052 253	AF03	493	11	25/33
AF32 [97]	xxxxT Stob Coire na Cloiche		[G] Introduced 1997. [3002]	915	NH 075 227	AF03	509	11	25/33
NM01 [91] [21] [97]	MTTTT Creag Dhubh Creag Dubh Creag Dubh		[G] Demoted 1921. 3102 3102 [3100]	[946] [946]	2.5m N of L. Mullardoch 1.25m ENE of NM01 NH 199 350	213 NM02 NM02	390 405 386	9 9 12	82 25
NM02 [91] [97]	MMMMM Carn nan Gobhar★ Carn nan Gobhar		[21] 2.25m N of L. Mullardoch 3251 (3250) [3255]	[991] 992	1.25m WSW of NM01 NH 181 343	152 152	253 245	9 12	25
NM03 [91] [97]	MMMMM Sgurr na Lapaich Sgurr na Lapaich		[21] 2.75m N of L. Mullardoch 3773 [3773]	[1150] 1150	2.5m N of L. Mullardoch NH 160 351	22 24	34 34	9 12	25
NM04 [91] [74]	TTTxx Rudha na Spreidha★ Rudha na Spreidhe		[G] Demoted 1981. 3250c 3400c	[991] 1057	.25m NbyE of NM03 NH 163 356	NM03	268 134	9 9	27
NM05 [91] [97]	TTTTT Sgurr na Clachan Geala★ Sgurr nan Clachan Geala		[21] .63m SbyE of NM03 3250c [3592]	[991] 1095	.5m S of NM03 NH 161 342	NM03	265 79	9 12	25
	Notes: [91] According to Mr Colin Phillip, this top must be fully 3500ft.								
NM06 [91] [74]	TTTxx Creag a' Chaoruinn★ Creag a' Chaoruinn		[G] Demoted 1981. 3000c 3050c	[914] 972	1m SSE of NM03 NH 168 338	NM03	523 333	9 9	27
NM07 [91] [74]	TTTxx Braigh a' Choire Bhig Braigh a' Choire Bhig		[21] 1.13m SbyW of NM03 [G] Demoted 1921. 3303 3317	[1007] 1013	1.5m S of NM03 NH 158 337	NM03	206 211	9 9	27
NM08 [91] [97]	MMMMM An Riabhachan An Riabhachan		[74] This Munro has wandered to and fro [G] Called 'N.E. Top' in 1921/74. See Endnotes. 3696 [3704]	[1127] 1129	Btw. L. Lungard & L. Monar NH 133 344	29 29	49 43	9 12	25
	Notes: [21] [Hill-shaded 1-in. shows actual top to be .5m ENE of this top, on county boundary]								
NM09 [91] [97]	TTTTT An Riabhachan, W. Top An Riabhachan, West Top		[21] 1.5m WSW of NM08 [74] Typo: Top No. 166 should be 167. 3406 [3412]	[1038] 1040	1m WSW of NM08 NH 117 337	NM08	158 147	9 12	25
	Notes: [91] The 3526 pt. on the 1-in. is incorrect. The correct height for this point given on the 6-in. is 3559. It is, however, only a portion of the ridge of the main E summit, the real W top being .33m WbyN from this point, and 3406ft.								
NM10 [91] [97]	MMMMM An Socach★ An Socach		3503 (3250) [3507]	[1068] 1069	1m WSW of NM09 NH 100 332	68 67	113 104	9 12	25
NM11 [81]	xxxTx An Riabhachan, N.E. Top		[G] Introduced 1981. Deleted 1997. See Endnotes. [3665]	1117c	NH 139 348	NM08	57	12	25
NM12 [81] [97]	xxxTT An Riabhachan, S.W. Top An Riabhachan, S.W. Top		[G] Introduced 1981. [3563] [3563]	1086 1086	NH 123 338 NH 123 336	NM08 NM08	91 86	12 12	25 25
SF01 [91] [97]	MMMMM; N Sgurr Ruadh Sgurr na Ruaidhe		[21] 2.5m NNW of L. Beannacharan [G] Renamed 1921. 3254 [3258]	[992] 993	2.5m NNW of L. Bunnacharan NH 288 426	151 151	251 243	9 12	25
SF02 [91] [97]	MMMMM Carn nan Gobhar★ Carn nan Gobhar		3242 (3000) [3255]	[988] 992	1m ENE of SF03 NH 273 439	154 153	273 246	9 12	25
SF03 [91] [97]	MMMMM Sgurr a' Choir Ghlais Sgurr a' Choire Ghlais		[21] 3m NWbyN of L. a' Mhuilidh 3554 [3553]	[1083] 1083	3m NNW of L. a' Mhuillidh, S'farrar NH 259 430	57 60	94 91	9 12	25
SF04 [91] [97]	TTTTT Creag Ghorm a' Bhealaich★ Creag Ghorm a' Bhealaich		[21] .63m ESE of SF05 3378 (3250) [3379]	[1030] 1030	1m WNW of SF03 NH 244 435	SF05	170 159	9 12	25
SF05 [91] [97]	MMMMM Sgurr Fhuar-thuill Sgurr Fhuar-thuill		3439 [3442]	[1048] 1049	1.5m WNW of SF03 NH 235 437	81 82	141 130	9 12	25
SF06 [91] [97]	TTTTT Sgurr na Festig★ Sgurr na Fearstaig		3326 [3330]	[1014] 1015	.5m W of SF05 NH 228 437	SF05	195 185	9 12	25

No. Yr.	Code Name	Status	Remarks Feet	Metres	Location	Of Mtn.	Top	Sect.	Map
EA01		MTTMM	[G] Demoted 1921 (lower than EA02). Reinstated 1981 (higher than EA02)!						
[91]	Maoile Lunndaidh		3294	[1004]	3m N of L. Monar	126	214	9	
[21]	Maoile Lunndaidh		3294	[1004]	.5m NE of EA02	EA02	229	9	82
[74]	Maoile Lunndaidh		3294	1007	NH 135 458	EA02	226	9	26
[81]	Maoile Lunndaidh		[3304]	1007	NH 135 458	122	205	12	25
[97]	Maoile Lunndaidh		[3304]	1007	NH 135 458	125	201	12	25
EA02		TMMxx	[74] Typo: Northing 353 should be 453. [G] Promoted 1921. Deleted 1981. See EA01.						
[91]	Creag Toll a' Choin*		3295 (3250)	[1004]	Shoulder .5m SW of EA01		213	9	
[21]	Creag Toll a' Choin		3295 (3250)	[1004]	2.75m N of L. Monar	123	228	9	82
[74]	Creag Toll a' Choin		3250c	1006	NH 131 453	121	229	9	26
EA03		TTTTT	[21] .5m WbyN of EA02						
[91]	Carn nam Fiaclan		3253 (3250)	[992]	.75m WbyS of EA01		252	9	
[97]	Carn nam Fiaclan		[3268]	996	NH 123 454	EA01	234	12	25
EA04		MTTTT	[G] Demoted 1921.						
[91]	Bidean an Eoin Deirg		3430	[1045]	2.5m NW of Head of L. Monar	84	145	9	
[21]	Bidean an Eoin Deirg		3430	[1045]	1m EbyS of EA05	EA05	154	9	82
[97]	Bidean an Eoin Deirg		[3432]	1046	NH 103 443	EA05	136	12	25
EA05		MMMMM; N	[21] 3.25m NW of Head of L. Monar [G] Renamed 1921.						
[91]	Sgurr a' Chaoruinn		3452	[1052]	1m W of EA04	74	130	9	
[97]	Sgurr a' Chaorachain		[3455]	1053	NH 087 447	78	122	12	25
EA06		MMMMM							
[91]	Sgurr Choinnich		3260	[994]	.75m W of EA05	146	245	9	
[97]	Sgurr Choinnich		[3278]	999	NH 076 446	139	224	12	25
EA07		MMMMM	[21] 4.75m [W] of Head of L. Monar						
[91]	Bidein a' Choire Sheasgaich		3102 (3000)	[946]	4.5m W of Head of L. Monar	214	391	9	
[97]	Bidein a' Choire Sheasgaich		[3100]	945	NH 049 412	224	384	12	25
EA08		MMMMM							
[91]	Lurg Mhor		3234	[986]	3.5m W of Head of L. Monar	159	281	9	
[97]	Lurg Mhor		[3235]	986	NH 065 404	163	261	12	25
EA09		TTTTT	[21] .5m EbyN of EA08						
[91]	Meall Mor		3190 (3000)	[972]	.33m EbyN of EA08		317	9	
[97]	Meall Mor		[3195]	974	NH 072 405	EA08	299	12	25
Notes: [21] The name on both maps is about 1m E. of the top									
EA10		MMMMM; L							
[91]	Moruisg		3033	[924]	2.5m E of Glencarron Station	258	468	9	
[74]	Moruisg		3026	922	NH 103 503	260	498	9	26
[97]	Moruisg		[3045]	928	NH 101 499	255	446	12	25
Notes: [91] 3026 on 1-inch map									
EA11		xxxMM	[G] Introduced 1981.						
[81]	Sgurr nan Ceannaichean		[3002]	915	NH 087 480	275	515	12	25
[97]	Sgurr nan Ceannaichean		[3002]	915	NH 087 480	284	508	12	25
WA01		MMMMM; N	[G] Renamed 1921.						
[91]	Meall a' Chinn Deirg		3060	[933]	5m N of Head of L. Carron	236	432	10	
[97]	Maol Chean-dearg		[3061]	933	NG 924 499	247	429	13	25
WA02		MMMMM							
[91]	Sgurr Ruàdh		3141	[957]	3m NW of Achnashellach Station	194	357	10	
[97]	Sgorr Ruadh		[3156]	962	NG 959 505	195	330	13	25
WA03		MMMMM							
[91]	Beinn Liath Mhor		3034	[925]	1m NbyE of WA02	257	467	10	
[97]	Beinn Liath Mhor		[3038]	926	NG 964 519	258	453	13	25
TO01		TTTTM; N	[91] ind. 'Beinn Alligin' [G] Renamed 1921. Promoted 1997.						
[91]	Spidean Coir' an Laoigh#		3021	[921]	.75m SSW of TO02		479	10	
[81]	Tom na Gruagaich		[3025]	922	NG 859 601	TO02	484	13	19
[97]	Tom na Gruagaich		[3025]	922	NG 859 601	268	470	13	19/24
TO02		MMMMM	[91] ind. 'Beinn Alligin'						
[91]	Sgurr Mor#		3232	[985]	4m NW of Torridon	160	282	10	
[97]	Sgurr Mhor		[3235]	986	NG 865 613	162	260	13	19/24
Notes: [91] Sgurr Mor is the local name. On the 6-inch map this top is called Sgorr Tuaigh									
TO03		TTTTT	[91] ind. 'Liathach' [21] 1m WbyS of TO06 [G] Promoted 1981.						
[91]	Mullach an Rathain		3358	[1024]	1.25m NE of Torridon		182	10	
[74]	Mullach an Rathain		3358	1023	NG 911 576	TO06	195	10	26
[81]	Mullach an Rathain		[3356]	1023	NG 912 577	105	175	13	25
[97]	Mullach an Rathain		[3356]	1023	NG 912 577	108	172	13	25

No. Yr.	Code Name	Status	Remarks Feet	Metres	Location	Of Mtn.	Top	Sect.	Map
TO04		TTTTT; N	[91] ind. 'Liathach' [G] Renamed 'Northern Pinnacles' 1981.						
[91]	Meall Dearg#		3150a (2750)	[960]	.25m NNE of TO03		344	10	
[97]	Meall Dearg (Northern Pinnacles)		[3133]	955	NG 913 579	TO03	355	13	25

Notes: [91] Measured by Mr Norman Collie

TO05		TTTTT; NL	[91] ind. 'Liathach' [21] .5m E of TO03 [G] Renamed 1921. Debatably allocated to TO03 in 1981/97. Location						
			wanders about.						
[91]	Spideanan nam Fasarinen#		3050a (2750)	[930]	.75m E of TO03		444	10	
[74]	Am Fasarinen		2850c	927	NG 920 576	TO06	478	10	26
[81]	Am Fasarinen		[3041]	927	NG 924 575	TO03	465	13	25
[97]	Am Fasarinen		[3041]	927	NG 923 574	TO03	447	13	25

Notes: [91] Measured by Mr Norman Collie

TO06		MMMMM	[91] ind. 'Liathach' [21] 2.25m ENE of Torridon						
[91]	Spidean a' Choire Leith		3456	[1053]	2m ENE of TO03	73	129	10	
[97]	Spidean a' Choire Leith		[3461]	1055	NG 929 579	75	118	13	25

TO07		TTTTT; NL	[91] ind. 'Liathach' [21] .33m ENE of TO06 [74] GR slightly east of top? [81] Error: Top wrongly allocated to						
			TO03 [G] Renamed 1981.						
[91]	Bidean Toll a' Mhuic#		3200a (2750)	[975]	.33m EbyN of TO06		307	10	
[74]	Bidein Toll a' Mhuic		3200a (2850c)	[975]	NG 936 582	TO06	319	10	26
[97]	Stob a' Coire Liath Mhor		[3225]	983	NG 932 581	TO06	267	13	25

Notes: [91] Measured by Mr Norman Collie

TO08		TTxxT; H	[91] ind. 'Liathach' [G] Deleted 1974. Restored 1997.						
[91]	Stuc a' Choire Dhuibh Bhig★		3000a (2750)	[914]	1m EbyN of TO06		514	10	
[21]	Stuc a' Choire Dhuibh Bhig		3050a (2750)	[930]	.63m EbyN of TO06	TO06	470	10	82
[97]	Stuc a' Choire Dhuibh Bhig		[3002]	915	NG 942 582	TO06	510	13	25

Notes: [91] Measured by Mr Hinxman, who made it well over 3000ft.

TO09		TTTTT	[91] ind. 'Beinn Eighe Range'						
[91]	Sail Mhor		3217	[981]	West end of Beinn Eighe		291	10	
[97]	Sail Mhor		[3215]	980	NG 938 605	TO12	277	13	25

TO10		MMMMM	[91] ind. 'Beinn Eighe Range'						
[91]	Ruadh-stac-Mhor		3309	[1009]	NW Spur of Beinn Eighe	120	202	10	
[97]	Ruadh-stac Mor		[3314]	1010	NG 951 611	120	193	13	25

TO11		TTTTT; HL	[91] ind. 'Beinn Eighe Range' [21] .63m S of TO10 [G] Located too far E. and too low until 1981?						
[91]	Coinneach Mhor★		3130 (3000)	[954]	.75m S of TO10		369	10	
[74]	A' Choinneach Mhor		3130 (3000c)	[954]	NG 950 601	TO10	395	10	26
[97]	Coinneach Mhor		[3202]	976	NG 944 600	TO12	288	13	25

Notes: [91] The top lies W from this pt. & is somewhat higher [21] The name on the 6-inch is .75m SE of the 3130 pt.

TO12		TTTTM; H	[91] ind. 'Beinn Eighe Range' [21] .63m WSW of TO13 [G] Promoted 1997.						
[91]	Spidean Coire nan Clach#		3220a (3000)	[981]	.5m WSW of TO13		287	10	
[81]	Spidean Coire nan Clach		[3189]	972	NG 965 597	TO10	314	13	25
[97]	Spidean Coire nan Clach		[3258]	993	NG 966 597	150	242	13	25

Notes: [91] Dr Heddle & Mr Colin Phillip's measurements. This peak is certainly higher than Sgurr Ban & Sgurr an Fhir Duibhe

TO13		TTTTT	[91] ind. 'Beinn Eighe Range'						
[91]	Sgurr Ban		3188	[972]	3.5m SW of Head of L. Maree		321	10	
[97]	Sgurr Ban		[3182]	970	NG 974 600	TO12	307	13	25

TO14		TTTTT	[91] ind. 'Beinn Eighe Range'						
[91]	Sgurr an Fhir Duibhe#		3160 (3000)	[963]	.5m E of TO13		339	10	
[97]	Sgurr nan Fhir Duibh		[3159]	963	NG 981 600	TO12	325	13	25

TO15		TTTxx	[91] ind. 'Beinn Eighe Range' [21] .88m NE of TO13 [G] Deleted 1981.						
[91]	Creag Dubh★		3000c	[914]	1m NE of TO13		524	10	
[74]	Creag Dubh		3050a (3000c)	[930]	NG 986 607	TO10	469	10	26

LF01		MMxMx	[G] Deleted 1974. Reinstated 1981. Deleted 1997 again! See Endnotes.						
[91]	Slioch		3260a (3250)	[994]	1.5m N of L. Maree	147	247	11	
[81]	Slioch, Trig Point		[3215]	980	NH 005 688	169	285	14	19

Notes: [91] Both on the 6 & 1-inch maps the only height given for Slioch is 3217ft. On the 1-inch, however, about 200yds. ESE of this point, on which is the cairn, is a small 3250 cont.. Captain Kirkwood R.E. gave the height as 3260ft.

LF02		TTTTT							
[91]	Sgurr an Tuill Bhain (Slioch)		3058	[932]	.75m E of LF01		436	11	
[97]	Sgurr an Tuill Bhain		[3064]	934	NH 018 688	LF09	425	14	19

LF03		MMMMM; H							
[91]	A' Mhaighdean		3100a (2750)	[945]	3.5m N of LF01	218	400	11	
[21]	A' Mhaighdean		3060a (2750)	[933]	3.75m N of LF01	237	451	11	92
[74]	A' Mhaighdean		3173 (2850c)	[967]	NH 008 751	181	341	11	19/20
[81]	A' Mhaighdean		[3150]	960c	NH 007 748	190	342	14	19
[97]	A' Mhaighdean		[3173]	967	NH 007 749	187	313	14	19

Notes: [91] Only a 2750 cont. is given for this mountain. Dr Heddle & Mr Colin Phillip have both, however, made the height over 3100, which is probably nearly correct

No. Yr.	Code Name	Status	Remarks Feet	Metres	Location	Of Mtn.	Top	Sect.	Map
LF04		MMMMM							
[91]	Mullach Coire Mhic Fhearchair		3320a (3250)	[1012]	4m NE of LF01	116	197	11	
[97]	Mullach Coire Mhic Fhearchair		[3340]	1018	NH 052 735	115	181	14	19

Notes: [91] Mr Colin Phillip's measurement. Dr Heddle made it some 30ft. less

LF05		MMMMM; H	[21] .75m N of LF04						
[91]	Sgurr Ban		3194	[974]	1m N of LF04	177	312	11	
[74]	Sgurr Ban		3244 (3194)	[989]	NH 055 744	151	277	11	19/20
[97]	Sgurr Ban		[3245]	989	NH 055 745	157	254	14	19

Notes: [21] [The actual top on the hill-shaded 1-inch map is .2m S of the 3194 pt. and about 3250ft.]

LF06		xxMMM	[G] Introduced 1974. 'Discovered' by J. Gall Inglis in 1929!						
[74]	Beinn Tarsuinn		3070 (2850c)	[936]	NH 039 727	234	444	11	19/20
[97]	Beinn Tarsuinn		[3074]	937	NH 039 728	238	415	14	19

LF07		xxMMM; L	[G] Introduced 1974. Apparent movement of summit is due to very poor early surveys.						
[74]	Ruadh Stac Mor		3014 (2850c)	[919]	NH 021 758	271	519	11	19/20
[97]	Ruadh Stac Mor		[3012]	918	NH 018 756	276	489	14	19

LF08		xxMMM	[G] Introduced 1974.						
[74]	Beinn a' Chlaidheimph		3000c (2800c)	[914]	NH 061 776	279	541	11	19/20
[97]	Beinn a' Chlaidheimh		[3005]	916	NH 061 775	280	501	14	19

| LF09 | | xxMTM | [74] GR is N. Top, discounted in earlier editions. [G] Introduced 1974. Demoted 1981. Reinstated 1997! See | | | | | | |

Endnotes.

[74]	Slioch, North Top		3216 (3217)	[980]	NH 005 691	165	301	11	19/20
[81]	Slioch, North Top		[3215]	980	NH 004 691	LF01	287	14	19
[97]	Slioch, North Top		[3218]	981	NH 004 690	170	273	14	19

LF10		xxxTT	[G] Introduced 1981.						
[81]	Mullach C. Mhic Fhearchair, E. Top		[3218]	981	NH 056 734	LF04	283	14	19
[97]	Mullach C. Mhic Fhearchair, E. Top		[3218]	981	NH 056 734	LF04	272	14	19

LF11		xxxTT	[G] Introduced 1981.						
[81]	Sgurr Dubh		[3012]	918	NH 061 729	LF04	501	14	19
[97]	Sgurr Dubh		[3012]	918	NH 061 729	LF04	491	14	19

TE01		MMMMM	[91] ind. 'An Teallach Range' [21] 2.75m SSW of Dundonell Inn						
[91]	An Teallach, Bidein a' Ghlais Thuill		3483	[1062]	2.5m SSW of Dundonell Inn	71	123	11	
[97]	Bidein a' Ghlas Thuill		[3484]	1062	NH 068 843	72	112	14	19

TE02		TTTTT	[91] ind. 'An Teallach Range'						
[91]	Glas Mheall Mor		3176 (3000)	[968]	.75m NE of TE01		328	11	
[97]	Glas Mheall Mor		[3212]	979	NH 076 853	TE01	280	14	19

TE03		TTTMM	[91] ind. 'An Teallach Range' [21] .5m SWbyW of TE01 [G] Promoted 1981.						
[91]	Sgurr Fiona		3474	[1059]	.5m SW of TE01		126	11	
[74]	Sgurr Fiona		3473 (3474)	[1059]	NH 064 836	TE01	133	11	19/20
[81]	Sgurr Fiona		[3474]	1059	NH 064 837	70	119	14	19
[97]	Sgurr Fiona		[3478]	1060	NH 064 837	73	115	14	19

TE04		TTTTT	[91] ind. 'An Teallach Range'						
[91]	Sgurr Creag an Eich★		3350a (3250)	[1021]	.5m W of TE03		185	11	
[97]	Sgurr Creag an Eich		[3337]	1017	NH 055 838	TE03	183	14	19

Notes: [91] Dr Heddle's measurement

TE05		TTTTT; H	[91] ind. 'An Teallach Range'						
[91]	Lord Berkeley's Seat#		3300a (3250)	[1006]	200yds. S of TE03		208	11	
[21]	Lord Berkeley's Seat#		3380a (3250)	[1030]	200yds. S of TE03	TE01	179	11	92
[74]	Lord Berkeley's Seat		3436 (3250c)	[1047]	NH 065 834	TE01	153	11	19/20
[81]	Lord Berkeley's Seat		[3435]	1047c	NH 064 834	TE03	136	14	19
[97]	Lord Berkeley's Seat		[3379]	1030c	NH 064 835	TE03	160	14	19

Notes: [91] Mr Colin Phillip's estimate

TE06		TTTTT; H	[91] ind. 'An Teallach Range'						
[91]	Corrag Bhuidhe★		3360a (3250)	[1024]	.25m S of TE03		181	11	
[74]	Corrag Bhuidhe		3400 (3250c)	[1036]	NH 065 833	TE01	175	11	19/20
[81]	Corrag Bhuidhe		[3346]	1020c	NH 065 833	TE03	179	14	19
[97]	Corrag Bhuidhe		[3435]	1047	NH 064 834	TE03	132	14	19

Notes: [91] Dr Heddle's measurement

TE07		TTTTT; NH	[91] ind. 'An Teallach Range' [21] .5m SSE of TE06 [G] Renamed 1921.						
[91]	Top above Cadha Gobhlach★		3040a (3000)	[927]	.5m SSE of TE03		456	11	
[74]	Stob Cadha Gobhlach		3145 (3150c)	[959]	NH 068 826	TE01	368	11	19/20
[81]	Stob Cadha Gobhlach		[3117]	950c	NH 068 825	TE03	381	14	19
[97]	Stob Cadha Gobhlach		[3150]	960	NH 068 825	TE03	337	14	19

Notes: [91] This point is at the NW end of the ridge, of which Sail Liath is at the SE end. The latter is slightly below 3000ft. Dr Heddle's measurement

No. Yr.	Code Name	Status	Remarks Feet	Metres	Location	Of Mtn.	Top	Sect.	Map
TE08		TTTTT; H	[91] ind. 'An Teallach Range'						
[91]	Glas Mheall Liath★		3080a (3000)	[939]	.5m EbyS of TE01		418	11	
[74]	Glas Mheall Liath		3156 (3150c)	[962]	NH 078 841	TE01	357	11	19/20
[81]	Glas Mheall Liath		[3117]	950c	NH 077 841	TE01	380	14	19
[97]	Glas Mheall Liath		[3150]	960	NH 077 840	TE01	335	14	19
Notes: [91] Dr Heddle's measurement									
TE09		xTTTx	[G] Introduced 1921. Deleted 1997.						
[21]	Corrag Bhuidhe Buttress#		3050a (3000)	[930]	.33m SSE of TE06	TE01	465	11	92
[81]	Corrag Bhuidhe Buttress		[3074]	937c	NH 066 831	TE03	424	14	19
TE10		xTTTT	[G] Introduced 1921.						
[21]	Sail Liath		3100a (3000)	[945]	SE end of An Teallach Range	TE01	412	11	92
[97]	Sail Liath		[3130]	954	NH 071 824	TE03	360	14	19
FA01		MMMMM	[91] ind. 'Fannich District' [21] 3m NWbyN of W end of L. Fannich						
[91]	A' Chailleach		3276	[999]	3m NW of head of L. Fannich	136	228	11	
[97]	A' Chailleach		[3271]	997	NH 136 714	144	232	14	19
FA02		MMMMM	[91] ind. 'Fannich District' [21] 1.33m E of FA01						
[91]	Sgurr Breac		3240a (3000)	[988]	1.5m E of FA01	155	276	11	
[97]	Sgurr Breac		[3278]	999	NH 158 711	138	223	14	20
Notes: [91] Mr Colin Phillip's aneroid measurement									
FA03		MMMMM	[91] ind. 'Fannich District' [21] 3.75m SbyW of Braemore Lodge						
[91]	Meall a' Chrasgaidh		3062	[933]	4m S of Braemore Lodge	235	431	11	
[97]	Meall a' Chrasgaidh		[3064]	934	NH 184 733	243	424	14	20
FA04		TTTTT	[91] ind. 'Fannich District' [21] .67m NW of FA07						
[91]	Carn na Criche		3148 (3000)	[960]	.75m ESE of FA03		350	11	
[97]	Carn na Criche		[3153]	961	NH 196 725	FA07	331	14	20
FA05		MMMMM	[91] ind. 'Fannich District'						
[91]	Sgurr nan Clach Geala		3581 (3500)	[1092]	2.75m NNE of head of L. Fannich	52	88	11	
[97]	Sgurr nan Clach Geala		[3586]	1093	NH 184 715	53	81	14	20
FA06		MMMMM	[91] ind. 'Fannich District'						
[91]	Sgurr nan Each★		3026 (3000)	[922]	1m S of FA05	261	476	11	
[97]	Sgurr nan Each		[3028]	923	NH 184 697	267	469	14	20
FA07		MMMMM	[91] ind. 'Fannich District' [21] 3.75m NNW of Fannich Lodge						
[91]	Sgurr Mor		3637	[1109]	3.5m NbyW of Fannich Lodge	42	67	11	
[97]	Sgurr Mor		[3642]	1110	NH 203 718	43	61	14	20
FA08		MMMMM	[91] ind. 'Fannich District'						
[91]	Beinn Liath Mhor Fannaich		3000c	[914]	1m ENE of FA07	281	525	11	
[97]	Beinn Liath Mhor Fannaich		[3130]	954	NH 219 724	209	358	14	20
Notes: [91] Probably about 3200ft.									
FA09		TTTTT; H	[91] ind. 'Fannich District'						
[91]	Meall nam Peithirean★		3000c	[914]	.75 SbyE of FA07		536	11	
[21]	Meall nam Peithirean★		3130a (3000)	[954]	.75 SSE of FA07	FA07	378	11	92
[74]	Meall nam Peithirean		3196 (3100c)	[974]	NH 205 709	FA07	320	11	20
[97]	Meall nam Peithirean		[3195]	974	NH 207 708	FA07	300	14	20
FA10		MMMMM; NH	[91] ind. 'Fannich District' [G] Renamed 1921.						
[91]	Meallan Rairigidh		3109	[948]	2.25m N of Fannich Lodge	209	383	11	
[74]	Meall Gorm, N.W. Top		3174 (3109)	[967]	NH 222 696	180	340	11	20
[97]	Meall Gorm		[3113]	949	NH 221 696	215	370	14	20
FA11		TTTTT	[91] ind. 'Fannich District'						
[91]	Meall Gorm★		3000c	[914]	.67m ESE of FA10		526	11	
[97]	Meall Gorm, S.E. Top		[3025]	922	NH 232 692	FA10	472	14	20
FA12		MMMMM	[91] ind. 'Fannich District' [21] 2m NE of Fannich Lodge						
[91]	An Coileachan		3015	[919]	2m NbyE of Fannich Lodge	268	489	11	
[97]	An Coileachan		[3028]	923	NH 241 680	266	465	14	20
FA13		MMMMM							
[91]	Fionn Bheinn		3060	[933]	2.25m NNW of Achnasheen Station	237	433	11	
[97]	Fionn Bheinn		[3061]	933	NH 147 621	246	428	14	20
FA14		xxxTT	[G] Introduced 1981.						
[81]	Toman Coinich		[3074]	937c	NH 148 714	FA01	425	14	19
[97]	Toman Coinich		[3068]	935	NH 148 713	FA01	422	14	20
WY01		TTTTT	[91] ind. 'Ben Wyvis Range' [21] 1.33m SWbyS of WY03						
[91]	An Cabar		3106	[947]	1.33m SSW of WY03		386	12	
[97]	An Cabar		[3104]	946	NH 450 665	WY03	379	15	20
WY02		Txxxx	[91] ind. 'Ben Wyvis Range' [G] Deleted 1921.						
[91]	An Socach		3295	[1004]	.5m E of WY03		212	12	

No. Yr.	Code Name	Status	Remarks / Feet	Metres	Location	Of Mtn.	Top	Sect.	Map
WY03		MMMMM	[91] ind. 'Ben Wyvis Range'						
[91]	Ben Wyvis, Glas Leathad Mor		3429	[1045]	6.5m NbyW of Strathpeffer	86	149	12	
[97]	Glas Leathad Mor		[3432]	1046	NH 463 683	85	135	15	20
WY04		TTTTT	[91] ind. 'Ben Wyvis Range'						
[91]	Tom a' Choinnich★		3134	[955]	1m N of WY03		366	12	
[97]	Tom a' Choinnich		[3127]	953	NH 463 700	WY03	366	15	20
WY05		TTxxx	[91] ind. 'Ben Wyvis Range' [G] Deleted 1974.						
[91]	Glas Leathad Beag★		3000c	[914]	1.75m NE of WY03		527	12	
[21]	Glas Leathad Beag★, W. Top		3027a (3000)	[923]	2m NE of WY03	WY03	502	12	93
WY06		TTTTT; N	[91] ind. 'Ben Wyvis Range' [G] Renamed 'Glas Leathad Beag, Centre Top' 1921.						
[91]	Top of Coire Lochain★		3000c	[914]	2.33m NE of WY03		528	12	
[97]	Glas Leathad Beag		[3045]	928	NH 492 706	WY03	442	15	20
Notes: [21] Almost a separate mountain									
WY07		TTTxx; N	[91] ind. 'Ben Wyvis Range' [21] 2.75m NE of WY03 [G] Renamed 1921. Deleted 1981.						
[91]	Feachdach		3018	[920]	2.67m NE of WY03		485	12	
[74]	Fiaclach		3018 (3018)	[920]	NH 496 711	WY03	516	12	21
Notes: [21] The name on both maps is .63m N. of top									
GU01		MMMMM	[21] Strathvaich, 3m ESE of GU03						
[91]	Am Fraochagach★		3120	[951]	Strathvaich, 3, ESE of GU03	205	378	12	
[97]	Am Faochagach		[3127]	953	NH 303 793	210	361	15	20
GU02		MMMMM							
[91]	Cona' Mheall★		3200a (3000)	[975]	1m EbyN of GU03	172	302	12	
[97]	Cona' Mheall		[3209]	978	NH 274 816	176	283	15	20
Notes: [91] Mr Colin Phillip's estimate; levels taken from Beinn Dearg									
GU03		MMMMM							
[91]	Beinn Dearg		3547	[1081]	5.5m SE of Head of L. Broom	60	99	12	
[97]	Beinn Dearg		[3556]	1084	NH 259 811	57	87	15	20
GU04		MMMMM	[21] .75m N of GU03						
[91]	Meall nan Ceapraichean★		3000c	[914]	1m N of GU03	282	529	12	
[97]	Meall nan Ceapraichean		[3205]	977	NH 257 825	177	286	15	20
GU05		TTTTT; HL	[74] GR is for E. shoulder of ridge.						
[91]	Ceann Garbh, Meall nan Ceapraichean★		3063 (3000)	[934]	.75m NE of GU04		430	12	
[74]	Ceann Garbh		3075c (3050c)	[937]	NH 266 831	GU04	441	12	20
[97]	Ceann Garbh		[3176]	968	NH 259 830	GU04	309	15	20
GU06		MMMMM	[21] 4.75m EbyS of Inverleal						
[91]	Eididh nan Clach Geala		3039	[926]	5m EbyS of Inverleal	251	459	12	
[97]	Eididh nan Clach Geala		[3041]	927	NH 257 842	257	451	15	20
GU07		MMMMM							
[91]	Seana Bhraigh		3041 (3000)	[927]	6m EbyN of Inverleal	248	454	12	
[97]	Seana Bhraigh		[3038]	926	NH 281 878	262	458	15	20
AS01		MMMMM	[21] 4.25m EbyS of Inch na Damph						
[91]	Ben More, Assynt		3273	[998]	4m EbyS of Inch na Damph	139	232	13	
[97]	Ben More Assynt		[3274]	998	NC 318 201	141	227	16	15
AS02		TTTTT; H	[21] .63m SE of AS01						
[91]	Ben More, Assynt, S. Top		3200a (3000)	[975]	4m EbyS of Inch na Damph		304	13	
[97]	Ben More Assynt, South Top		[3150]	960	NC 324 192	AS01	334	16	15
Notes: [91] Dr Heddle's estimate									
AS03		MMMMM							
[91]	Conamheall		3234	[986]	3.5m EbyS of Inch na Damph	158	280	13	
[97]	Conival		[3238]	987	NC 303 199	158	255	16	15
KH01		MMMMM							
[91]	Ben Clibrig		3164	[964]	3.33m SbyE of Altnaharra Inn	188	337	13	
[97]	Ben Klibreck, Meall nan Con		[3156]	962	NC 585 299	194	327	16	16
Notes: [21] On the 6-inch map called 'Meall nan Eoin'; on the 1-inch 'Meall nan Con'									
KH02		MMMMM							
[91]	Ben Hope		3040	[927]	1.5m E of S end of L. Hope	250	457	13	
[97]	Ben Hope		[3041]	927	NC 477 501	256	449	16	9
EC01		TTTTT	[91] ind. 'Ben Avon' [21] 2.25m NEbyE of EC07						
[91]	East Meur Gorm Craig★		3075 (3000)		.5m N of EC02		422	14	
[97]	East Meur Gorm Craig		[3068]	935	NJ 159 042	EC07	420	8	36
EC02		Txxxx	[91] ind. 'Ben Avon' [G] Deleted 1921.						
[91]	Big Brae		3100a (3000)	[945]	1.5m W of L. Builg		396	14	
Notes: [91] Mr Colin Phillip's estimate									

No. Yr.	Code Name	Status	Remarks Feet	Metres	Location	Of Mtn.	Top	Sect.	Map
EC03		TTTTT; L	[91] ind. 'Ben Avon' [21] 1.75m NE of EC07						
[91]	West Meur Gorm Craig★		3354 (3250)	[1022]	.5m W of EC02		183	14	
[74]	West Meur Gorm Craig		3354	1021	NJ 157 036	EC07	199	14	38/41
[97]	West Meur Gorm Craig		[3356]	1023	NJ 153 036	EC07	173	8	36
EC04		TTTxx; N	[91] ind. 'Ben Avon' [21] .88m NbyE of EC07 [G] Renamed 1921. Deleted 1981.						
[91]	Stob Dubh, Bruach an Fhurain★		3533 (3250)	[1077]	1.5m W of EC02		104	14	
[74]	Stob Bac an Fhurain		3533	1076	NJ 137 034	EC07	113	14	38/41
EC05		TTTxx	[91] ind. 'Ben Avon' [21] .75m ENE of EC07 [G] Deleted 1981.						
[91]	Mullach Lochan nan Gabhar		3662 (3500)	[1116]	.75m EbyN of EC07		55	14	
[74]	Mullach Lochan na Gobhar		3662	1105	NJ 143 022	EC07	80	14	38/41
Notes: [91] Located 300yds. SbyE of the point marked 3608 on the 1-in.									
EC06		TTTxx	[91] ind. 'Ben Avon' [21] .88m EbyS of EC07 [G] Deleted 1981.						
[91]	Stuc Gharbh Mhor		3625 (3500)	[1105]	1m E of EC07		73	14	
[74]	Stuc Garbh Mhor		3625	1120	NJ 147 013	EC07	56	14	38/41
Notes: [91] Located on the County March .5m N of the name Stuc Gharbh Mor on the O.S.									
EC07		MMMMM; N	[91] ind. 'Ben Avon' [21] 6.75m NbyW of Braemar [G] Renamed 1921.						
[91]	Ben Avon		3843	[1171]	6.5m NbyW of Braemar	16	27	14	
[97]	Leabaidh an Daimh Bhuidhe		[3842]	1171	NJ 131 018	17	26	8	36
EC08		TTTxx	[91] ind. 'Ben Avon' [G] Deleted 1981.						
[91]	Stob Dubh an Eas Bhig		3250c	[991]	1m S of EC07		261	14	
[74]	Stob Dubh an Eas Bhig		3400c	1063	NJ 133 002	EC07	130	14	38/41
EC09		TTTxx; N	[91] ind. 'Ben Avon' [21] .63m SW of EC07 [G] Renamed 1921. Deleted 1981.						
[91]	Shoulder .5m SW of Ben Avon		3729 (3500)	[1137]	1.5m N of EC10		44	14	
[74]	Ben Avon, S.W. Top		3700c	1135	NJ 125 013	EC07	45	14	38/41
EC10		MTTTT	[G] Demoted 1921.						
[91]	Carn Eas		3556	[1084]	5m NNW of Braemar	56	93	14	
[21]	Carn Eas		3556	[1084]	5.25m NNW of Braemar	EC07	99	14	65
[97]	Carn Eas		[3573]	1089	NO 122 992	EC07	84	8	43/36
EC11		MTTTT	[G] Demoted 1921.						
[91]	Creag an Dala Moire★		3189	[972]	.67m SE of EC10	181	319	14	
[21]	Creag an Dail Mhor★		3189	[972]	.75m SE of EC10	EC07	327	14	65
[97]	Creag an Dail Mhor		[3189]	972	NO 131 982	EC07	304	8	43/36
EC12		TTTTT	[91] ind. 'Beinn a' Bhuird' [21] 1m ENE of EC14						
[91]	Cnap a' Chleirich★		3811 (3750)	[1162]	1m EbyN of EC14		30	14	
[97]	Cnap a' Chleirich		[3852]	1174	NJ 107 010	EC14	25	8	36
EC13		TTTTT	[91] ind. 'Beinn a' Bhuird' [21] 1.88m NE of EC14						
[91]	Stob an t-Sluichd		3621	[1104]	1.75m NE of EC14		74	14	
[97]	Stob an t-Sluichd		[3632]	1107	NJ 112 027	EC14	66	8	36
EC14		MMMMM	[91] ind. 'Beinn a' Bhuird' [21] 6.75m NWbyN of Braemar						
[91]	Beinn a' Bhuird, N. Top		3924	[1196]	6.5m NW of Braemar	11	18	14	
[97]	Beinn a' Bhuird, North Top		[3927]	1197	NJ 092 006	11	15	8	36
EC15		TTxTx	[91] ind. 'Beinn a' Bhuird' [G] This top was the original O.S. spot height of 3860. Deleted 1974. Reinstated 1981!						
[91]	Beinn a' Bhuird, S. Top		3860	[1177]	1.75m S of EC14		24	14	
[21]	Beinn a' Bhuird, South Top		3860	[1177]	1.75m S of EC14	EC14	24	14	65
[81]	Beinn a' Bhuird, South Top		[3862]	1177	NO 090 978	EC14	23	8	36
EC16		xTTxx	[G] Introduced 1921. Demoted 1981.						
[21]	A' Chioch		3500c	[1067]	.5m ENE of EC15	EC14	122	14	65
[74]	A' Chioch		3500c	1050	NO 096 987	EC14	147	14	38/41
EC17 to stay?		xxTxT	[74] Location and new height is .5m NbyE of EC15 [G] Introduced 1974. Deleted 1981. Reinstated 1997! Here						
[74]	Beinn a' Bhuird, South Top		3860	1179	NO 093 986	EC14	25	14	38/41
[97]	Beinn a' Bhuird, South Top		[3868]	1179	NO 093 986	EC14	20	8	43/36
LL01		MMMMM							
[91]	Beinn Breac, East Top		3051	[930]	East Side of Gl. Derry	243	443	14	
[97]	Beinn Bhreac		[3054]	931	NO 058 971	249	431	8	43/36
LL02		TTTTT	[21] .5m WNW of LL01 [74] Height 929 is 927 in Table 2.						
[91]	Beinn Bhreac, West Top		3000c	[914]	.5m W of LL01		530	14	
[97]	Beinn Bhreac, West Top		[3041]	927	NO 052 972	LL01	448	8	43/36
Notes: [21] [Locally called Craig Derry]									
LL03		MMMMM							
[91]	Beinn a' Chaorruinn		3553	[1083]	Btw. Gls. Derry & Avon	58	95	14	
[97]	Beinn a' Chaorainn		[3553]	1083	NJ 045 013	58	88	8	36
LL04		TTTTT	[21] .75m ENE of LL03						
[91]	Beinn a' Chaorruinn Bheag★		3326	[1014]	.75m EbyN of LL03		196	14	
[97]	Beinn a' Chaorainn Bheag		[3337]	1017	NJ 058 017	LL03	182	8	36

No. Yr.	Code Name	Status	Remarks Feet	Metres	Location	Of Mtn.	Top	Sect.	Map
LL05		MMMMM; N	[21] 2.75m NE of MC11 [G] Renamed 1921.						
[91]	Caiplich, Ben Bynac		3574	[1089]	2.5m NE of MC11	53	90	14	
[97]	Bynack More		[3576]	1090	NJ 041 063	54	82	8	36
Notes: [91] The highest point of Ben Bynac. The 3296 point marked on the 1-inch map is merely a shoulder running up to Caiplich									
LL06		MMMTT	[G] Demoted 1981.						
[91]	A' Choinneach		3345 (3250)	[1020]	1m NNE of Foot of L. Avon	108	187	14	
[74]	A' Choinneach		3345	1017	NJ 032 048	112	207	14	38/41
[81]	A' Choinneach		[3337]	1017	NJ 032 048	LL05	186	8	36
[97]	A' Choinneach		[3333]	1016	NJ 032 049	LL05	184	8	36
LL07		MMMMM	[21] .75m SE of L. Avon [G] Called 'N.E. Top' in 1921/74.						
[91]	Beinn Mheadhoin		3883	[1184]	SE of L. Avon	12	19	14	
[97]	Beinn Mheadhoin		[3878]	1182	NJ 024 016	13	18	8	36
LL08		TTTTx; H	[21] .63m SW of LL07 [G] Deleted 1997.						
[91]	Beinn Mheadhoin, S.W. Top		3750	[1143]	.5m SW of LL07		41	14	
[81]	Beinn Mheadhoin, S.W Top		[3816]	1163	NJ 018 011	LL07	29	8	36
LL09		TTTTT; N	[G] Renamed 1921.						
[91]	Top North of Coire Etchachan		3551	[1082]	.75m E of L. Etchachan		97	14	
[97]	Stob Coire Etchachan		[3550]	1082	NJ 024 005	LL07	92	8	36
LL10		TTTTT	[21] .38m SE of L. Etchachan [G] A top of MC04 until 1974; thereafter, a top of LL11.						
[91]	Creagan a' Choire Etchachan★		3500c	[1067]	3500 c. SbyE of L. Etchachan		115	14	
[97]	Creagan a' Choire Etchachan		[3635]	1108	NO 011 996	LL11	64	8	36/43
LL11		MMMMM	[21] 3.25m NNW of Derry Lodge						
[91]	Derry Cairngorm		3788	[1155]	3m NNW of Derry Lodge	20	32	14	
[97]	Derry Cairngorm		[3789]	1155	NO 017 980	20	29	8	36/43
LL12		xTTTT	[G] Introduced 1921.						
[21]	Stacan Dubha★		3330a (3250)	[1015]	.75m W of LL07	LL07	205	14	74
[97]	Stacan Dubha		[3327]	1014	NJ 012 014	LL07	186	8	36
LL13		xTTTT	[G] Introduced 1921.						
[21]	Sgurr an Lochain Uaine★		3220a (3000)	[981]	.63m NEbyN of LL11	LL11	292	14	64
[97]	Sgurr an Lochan Uaine		[3225]	983	NO 025 991	LL11	266	8	36/43
LL14		xTTxx#	[G] Introduced 1921. Deleted 1981.						
[21]	Little Cairngorm#		3450a (3250)	[1052]	.63m SbyE of LL11	LL11	142	14	64
[74]	Little Cairngorm		3350c	1040	NO 020 973	LL11	166	14	38/41
LL15		xxxTT	[G] Introduced 1981.						
[81]	Bynack Beg		[3163]	964	NJ 035 068	LL05	332	8	36
[97]	Bynack Beg		[3182]	970	NJ 035 068	LL05	305	8	36
MC01		MMMMM; H							
[91]	Carn a' Mhaim		3329	[1015]	2.5m S of MC04	115	194	14	
[21]	Carn a' Mhaim		3400a (3329)	[1036]	2.5m SbyW of MC04	91	171	14	64
[97]	Carn a' Mhaim		[3402]	1037	NN 994 951	95	151	8	36/43
Notes: [21] [The actual top is .33m NW of the O.S. cairn]									
MC02		TTTTT; H							
[91]	Sron Riach★ (Ben Macdui)		3534 (3500)	[1077]	1m SE of MC04		103	14	
[21]	Sron Riach★		3534 (3500)	[1077]	1m SE of MC04	MC04	110	14	64
[74]	Sron Riach		3600c	1110	NN 999 978	MC04	73	14	38/41
[81]	Sron Riach		[3642]	1110	NN 999 978	MC04	67	8	36
[97]	Sron Riach		[3642]	1110c	NN 999 977	MC04	62	8	36/43
MC03		TTTxx	[21] .67m ESE of MC04 [G] Deleted 1981.						
[91]	Top of Coire an Sput Dheirg★		4095 (4000)	[1248]	.5m ESE of MC04		7	14	
[74]	Stob Coire Sputan Dearg		4050c	1249	NN 998 985	MC04	8	14	38/41
MC04		MMMMM							
[91]	Ben Macdhui		4296	[1309]	Btw. Gls. Derry & Dee	2	2	14	
[97]	Ben Macdui		[4295]	1309	NN 989 989	2	2	8	36/43
MC05		TTTTx	[21] .38m NNE of MC04 [G] Deleted 1997.						
[91]	Ben Macdhui, N. Top		4244	[1294]	Btw. Gls. Derry & Dee		4	14	
[81]	Ben Macdhui, North Top		[4249]	1295	NN 991 995	MC04	4	8	36
MC06		TTTTT; N	[21] 1.5m NEbyN of MC04 [G] Renamed 1921.						
[91]	Top of Cliffs above L. Avon		3673	[1120]	1.5m NNW of MC04		53	14	
[97]	Carn Etchachan		[3674]	1120	NJ 003 009	MC04	49	8	36
MC07		TTTTT; N	[21] 1.5m SWbyW of MC11 [G] Renamed 1921.						
[91]	Top of Coire an Lochain★		3983 (3750)	[1214]	1.5m SW of MC11		16	14	
[97]	Cairn Lochan		[3986]	1215	NH 985 025	MC11	12	8	36
MC08		TTTxx	[21] 1.13m WSW of MC11 [G] Deleted 1981.						
[91]	Fiacaill Coire an t-Sneachda★		3500c	[1067]	1m WSW of MC11		116	14	
[74]	Fiacaill Coire an t-Sneachda		3500c	1125	NH 988 032	MC11	54	14	38/41

No. Yr.	Code Name	Status	Remarks / Feet	Metres	Location	Of Mtn.	Top	Sect.	Map
MC09		TTTTT; N	[G] Renamed 1921.						
[91]	Top of Coire an t-Sneachda★		3856 (3750)	[1175]	.88m SW of MC11		26	14	
[97]	Stob Coire an t-Sneachda		[3858]	1176	NH 996 029	MC11	23	8	36
MC10		TTTxx	[G] Deleted 1981.						
[91]	Fiacaill a' Choire Chais★		3737 (3500)	[1139]	.33m W of MC11		43	14	
[74]	Fiacaill a' Choire Chais		3700c	1141	NH 999 039	MC11	43	14	38/41
MC11		MMMMM	[21] 1m NW of L. Avon						
[91]	Cairn Gorm		4084	[1245]	NW of L. Avon	6	9	14	
[97]	Cairn Gorm		[4081]	1244	NJ 005 040	6	7	8	36
MC12		TTTTT							
[91]	Cnap Coire na Spreidhe★		3772 (3750)	[1150]	.75m NE of MC11		35	14	
[97]	Cnap Coire na Spreidhe		[3773]	1150	NJ 013 049	MC11	33	8	36
MC13		TTTxx	[G] Deleted 1981.						
[91]	Sron a' Chano		3250c	[991]	1m N of MC12		264	14	
[74]	Sron a' Cha-no		3300c	1028	NJ 016 066	MC11	185	14	38/41
MC14		MTTTT	[G] Demoted 1921.						
[91]	Creag na Leacainn, S. Top		3448	[1051]	2.5m W of MC11	76	134	14	
[21]	Creag an Leth-choin, S. Top		3448	[1051]	2.5m WbyS of MC11	MC11	143	14	74
[97]	Creag an Leth-choin		[3455]	1053	NH 968 033	MC11	121	8	36
MC15		TTTxx	[21] .38m N of MC14 [G] Deleted 1981.						
[91]	Creag na Leacainn, N. Top		3365	[1026]	2.5m W of MC11		177	14	
[74]	Creag an Leth-choin (North Top)		3365	1026	NH 969 039	MC11	191	14	38/41
MC16		xTTxx	[G] Introduced 1921. Deleted 1981.						
[21]	Fiacaill na Leth-choin#		3550a (3500)	[1082]	.67m WNW of MC07	MC11	104	14	74
[74]	Fiacaill na Leth-choin		3500c	1083	NH 975 034	MC11	101	14	38/41
BC01		TTTTT	[21] .88m NEbyE of BC02						
[91]	Sron na Leirg★, Braeriach		3875 (3750)	[1181]	1m NE of BC02		22	14	
[97]	Sron na Lairige		[3884]	1184	NH 964 006	BC02	16	8	36
Notes: [91] 300yds S of point marked 3839 on 1-inch map									
BC02		MMMMM							
[91]	Braeriach		4248	[1295]	2.25m WbyN of MC04	3	3	14	
[97]	Braeriach		[4252]	1296	NN 953 999	3	3	8	36/43
BC03		TTTxx; N	[21] .75m WbyS of Braeriach [G] Renamed 1921. Deleted 1981.						
[91]	Braeriach, Top above C. an Lochan		4036	[1230]	.75m W of Braeriach		11	14	
[74]	Stob Coire nan Lochain		4036	[1230]	NH 940 997	BC02	11	14	37/38
Notes: [91] See Chapter 4.2									
BC04		TTTTT; N	[G] Renamed 1981.						
[91]	Braeriach South Plateau		4149	[1265]	1.5m SW of BC02		6	14	
[97]	Carn na Criche		[4150]	1265	NN 939 982	BC02	5	8	36/43
Notes: [91] See Chapter 4.2									
BC05		MTTTM	[G] Demoted 1981. Reinstated 1997!						
[91]	Sgor an Lochan Uaine★, Cairn Toul		4095a (4000)	[1248]	.5m WbyN of BC06	5	8	14	
[21]	Sgor an Lochan Uaine (The Angel's Pk.)		4095a (4000)	[1248]	.5m NWbyW of BC06	BC06	8	14	64
[81]	Sgor an Lochain Uaine		[4127]	1258	NN 954 976	BC06	7	8	36
[97]	Sgor an Lochain Uaine		[4127]	1258	NN 954 976	5	6	8	36/43
Notes: [91] Mr Hinxman's aneroid measurement									
BC06		MMMMM							
[91]	Cairn Toul		4241	[1293]	West Side of Gl. Dee	4	5	14	
[97]	Cairn Toul		[4236]	1291	NN 963 972	4	4	8	36/43
BC07		TTTTT; N	[G] Renamed 1921.						
[91]	Top of C. an t-Saighdeir★, Cairn Toul		3989 (3750)	[1216]	.5m S of BC06		14	14	
[97]	Stob Coire an t-Saighdeir		[3980]	1213	NN 962 963	BC06	14	8	36/43
BC08		MMMMM	[21] 1.5m SEbyS of BC06						
[91]	The Devil's Point		3303	[1007]	1.5m SE of BC	123	205	14	
[97]	The Devil's Point		[3294]	1004	NN 976 951	130	207	8	36/43
BC09		MMMMM	[21] 3m SbyW of BC06						
[91]	Beinn Bhrotain		3795	[1157]	3m S of BC06	19	31	14	
[97]	Beinn Bhrotain		[3796]	1157	NN 954 922	19	28	8	43
BC10		MMMTT	[G] Demoted 1981.						
[91]	Carn Clioch-mhuillin		3087	[941]	1.33m SE of BC09	223	407	14	
[74]	Carn Cloich-mhuilinn		3087	942	NN 968 907	226	427	14	38/41
[81]	Carn Cloich-mhuilinn		[3091]	942	NN 968 907	BC09	409	8	43
[97]	Carn Cloich-mhuilinn		[3091]	942	NN 968 907	BC09	395	8	43

No. Yr.	Code Name	Status	Remarks	Feet	Metres	Location	Of Mtn.	Top	Sect.	Map
BC11		MMMMM								
[91]	Monadh Mor			3651	[1113]	2.5m SW of BC06	39	62	14	
[97]	Monadh Mor			[3652]	1113	NN 938 942	40	57	8	43
BC12		Txxxx	[G] Deleted 1921.							
[91]	Leachd Riach*			3250 (3250)	[991]	1m WbyS of BC11		269	14	
BC13		TTTTT; N	G] Renamed 1921. Renamed 1981 again. Allocated to BC02 until 1997.							
[91]	Top above Lochan nan Cnapan			3009 (3000)	[917]	1.5m S of Head of L. Eunach		497	14	
[21]	Stob Lochan nan Cnapan			3009 (3000)	[917]	1.75m S of Head of L. Eunach	BC02	526	14	64
[97]	Tom Dubh			[3012]	918	NN 921 952	BC11	494	8	36/43
FE01		TTTxx	[21] 1.38m E of FE02 [G] Deleted 1981.							
[91]	Diollaid Coire Eindart*			3184	[970]	1.25m S of FE02		324	14	
[74]	Diollaid Coire Eindart			3184	974	NN 905 928	FE02	322	14	37
FE02		MMMMM; N	[21] 3.75m SSW of Head of L. Einich [G] Renamed 1921.							
[91]	Meall Tionail			3338	[1017]	3.5m SbyW of Head of L. Eunach	113	192	14	
[97]	Mullach Clach a' Bhlair			[3343]	1019	NN 882 927	114	180	8	35/36/43
FE03		Txxxx	[G] Deleted 1921.							
[91]	Druim nan Bo			3005 (3000)	[916]	.5m SW of FE02		504	14	
FE04		MMMTT; N	[21] 2.5m SW of Head L. Einich [G] Renamed 1921.							
[91]	Meall Dubh-achaidh			3268	[996]	2.5m SW of Head L. Eunach	143	238	14	
[74]	Meall Dubhag			3268	998	NN 881 955	139	254	14	37
[81]	Meall Dubhag			[3274]	998	NN 881 956	FE02	237	8	43
[97]	Meall Dubhag			[3274]	998	NN 880 955	FE06	230	8	35/36/43
FE05		MMMTT	[21] 1.25m WSW of Head of L. Einich [G] Demoted 1981.							
[91]	Carn Ban			3443	[1049]	1.5m WSW of Head of L. Eunach	78	136	14	
[74]	Carn Ban Mor			3443	1052	NN 893 972	77	143	14	37
[81]	Carn Ban Mor			[3451]	1052	NN 893 972	FE02	129	8	43
[97]	Carn Ban Mor			[3451]	1052	NN 893 971	FE06	123	8	35/36/43
FE06		MMMMM; N	[21] West Side of L. Einich [G] Renamed 1921.							
[91]	Sgoran Dubh, South			3658	[1115]	West Side of L. Eunach	37	59	14	
[97]	Sgor Gaoith			[3668]	1118	NN 902 989	36	52	8	36/43
	Notes: [91] Locally known as Sgoran Dubh Bheag									
FE07		TTTTT	[21] .88m N from FE06							
[91]	Sgoran Dubh, North			3635	[1108]	.75m from FE06		70	14	
[97]	Sgoran Dubh Mor			[3645]	1111	NH 905 002	FE06	59	8	36
	Notes: [91] Locally known as Sgoran Dubh Mhor									
FE08		TTTTT	[21] .75m WbyS of FE07							
[91]	Meall Buidhc#			3185 (3000)	[971]	1m WbyN of FE07		323	14	
[97]	Meall Buidhe			[3202]	976	NH 891 001	FE06	289	8	35/36
FE09		MMMTT	[21] 1.5m WNW of FE07 [G] Demoted 1981.							
[91]	Geal Charn			3019 (3000)	[920]	2.5m WNW of FE07	264	483	14	
[74]	Geal Charn			3019	920	NH 884 014	266	512	14	37
[81]	Geal Charn			[3018]	920	NH 884 014	FE06	490	8	36
[97]	Geal Charn			[3018]	920	NH 884 014	FE06	481	8	35/36
ED01		MMMMM	[21] 1.25m E of L. Cuaich							
[91]	Meall na Cuaich*			3120 (3000)	[951]	5m NE of Dalwhinnie Hotel	206	380	15	
[97]	Meall Chuaich			[3120]	951	NN 716 878	214	368	5	42
	Notes: [91] Located .5m E of point marked Stac Meall na Cuaich on the 1-in.									
ED02		MMMMM	[21] 2.75m ESE of Dalwhinnie Hotel							
[91]	Carn na Caim			3087	[941]	2.75m SE of Dalwhinnie Hotel	224	408	15	
[97]	Carn na Caim			[3087]	941	NN 677 821	232	400	5	42
ED03		MTTxx	[G] Demoted 1921. Deleted 1981.							
[91]	Meall a' Chaoruinn			3004	[916]	1.5m E of Drumochter Pass	279	509	15	
[21]	Meall a' Chaoruinn			3004	[916]	2.75m N of Dalnaspidal Station	ED04	538	15	64
[74]	Meall a' Chaoruinn			3004	[916]	NN 646 777	ED04	536	15	37
	Notes: [91] Called only 'Chaoruinn' on the 1-inch map									
ED04		TMMMM; N	[G] Renamed & Promoted1921.							
[91]	Fuar Bheinn			3064 (3054)	[934]	1m E of ED03		428	15	
[21]	A' Bhuidheanach Bheag			3064	[934]	.88m E of ED03	233	445	15	64
[97]	A' Bhuidheanach Bheag			[3071]	936	NN 660 776	240	418	5	42
	Notes: [91] The point of which the height is given is 1.25m NbyE of the name Fuar Bheinn on the maps. The Perthshire sheet gives 3062, the Inverness-shire sheet gives 3064, while the 1-inch gives 3054									
ED05		MTTTT	[G] Demoted 1921.							
[91]	Glas Meall Mor			3037	[926]	3m NE of Dalnaspidal Station	253	461	15	
[21]	Glas Mheall Mor			3037	[926]	3.25m NE of Dalnaspidal Station	ED04	488	15	64
[97]	Glas Mheall Mor			[3045]	928	NN 680 769	ED04	443	5	42

No. Yr.	Code Name	Status	Remarks	Feet	Metres	Location	Of Mtn.	Top	Sect.	Map
TT01		MMMMM	[21] Btw. Heads of Gls. Feshie & Tarf							
[91]	Carn an Fhidleir			3276	[999]	Head of Gls. Feshie & Tarf	137	229	15	
[97]	Carn an Fhidhleir (Carn Ealar)			[3261]	994	NN 904 842	148	239	6	43
TT02		MMMMM	[21] 1.75m EbyS of TT01							
[91]	An Sgarsoch			3300	[1006]	2m E of TT01	124	207	15	
[97]	An Sgarsoch			[3300]	1006	NN 933 836	126	202	6	43
TT03		TTTxx	[G] Deleted 1981.							
[91]	Druim Sgarsoch★			3128 (3000)	[953]	.75m E of TT02		373	15	
[74]	Druim Sgarsoch			3100c	954	NN 946 835	TT02	394	15	37
TT04		TTTxx	[21] .88m N of TT05 [G] Deleted 1981.							
[91]	Beinn Gharbh			3000c	[914]	.75m N of TT05		531	15	
[74]	Beinn Gharbh			3000c	932	NN 853 791	TT05	458	15	37
TT05		MMMMM	[21] East of Head of Gl. Bruar							
[91]	Beinn Dearg			3304	[1007]	East of Gl. Bruar	122	204	15	
[97]	Beinn Dearg			[3307]	1008	NN 852 777	124	198	6	43
TT06		MMMMM								
[91]	Carn a' Chlamain★			3159 (3000)	[963]	1.5m NW of Forest Lodge	190	342	15	
[97]	Carn a' Chlamain			[3159]	963	NN 915 758	192	321	6	43
TT07		MMMMM	[91] 'Beinn a' Ghlo' app.							
[91]	Carn Liath			3193	[973]	4.75m NW of Blair Atholl	178	313	15	
[97]	Carn Liath			[3199]	975	NN 936 698	181	294	6	43
TT08		MMMMM	[91] 'Beinn a' Ghlo' app. [21] 1.63m WSW of TT10							
[91]	Braigh Coire Chruinn-bhalgain★			3505	[1068]	SW Top of Beinn a' Ghlo	66	111	15	
[97]	Braigh Coire Chruinn-bhalgain			[3510]	1070	NN 945 724	66	103	6	43
TT09		TTTTT	[91] 'Beinn a' Ghlo' app. [21] 1m SWbyW of TT10							
[91]	Airgiod Bheinn★			3250c	[991]	Shoulder, 1m SSW of TT10		262	15	
[97]	Airgiod Bheinn			[3481]	1061	NN 961 720	TT10	114	6	43
TT10		MMMMM	[91] 'Beinn a' Ghlo' app. [21] 8m NE of Blair Atholl							
[91]	Carn nan Gabhar			3671	[1119]	NE Top of Beinn a' Ghlo	33	54	15	
[97]	Carn nan Gabhar			[3678]	1121	NN 971 733	32	47	6	43
TT11		xxxTx	[G] Introduced 1981. Deleted 1997.							
[81]	Carn a' Chlamain, North Top			[3123]	952	NN 914 761	TT06	378	6	43
WC01		MMMMM								
[91]	Carn an Righ			3377	[1029]	1.5m WNW of WC02	101	171	15	
[97]	Carn an Righ			[3376]	1029	NO 028 772	102	162	6	43
WC02		MMMMM	[21] 5.25m NW of Spital of Glenshee							
[91]	Glas Thulachan			3445	[1050]	5m NW of Spital of Glenshee	77	135	15	
[97]	Glas Tulaichean			[3448]	1051	NO 051 760	79	126	6	43
WC03		TTTTT	[21] .88m SbyE of WC04 [81] Typo: Northing 799 should be 779							
[91]	Mam nan Carn★			3224 (3217)	[983]	Btw. WC02 & WC04		285	15	
[97]	Mam nan Carn			[3235]	986	NO 049 779	WC04	262	6	43
Notes: [91] 150yds SSW of the point marked 3217 on the 1-inch is a point on the 6-inch 3224ft.										
WC04		MMMMM	[21] 2m NbyW of WC02							
[91]	Beinn Iutharn Mhor (Ben Uarn Mor)			3424	[1044]	2m N of WC02	88	151	15	
[97]	Beinn Iutharn Mhor			[3428]	1045	NO 045 792	88	139	6	43
WC05		MTTTT	[G] Demoted 1921 (lower than WC06).							
[91]	Carn Bhac			3014	[919]	2.5m N of WC04	269	491	15	
[21]	Carn Bhac, S.W. Top			3014	[919]	.75m WSW of WC06	WC06	520	15	65
[97]	Carn Bhac, S.W. Top			[3018]	920	NO 041 827	WC06	478	6	43
WC06		TMMMM; N	[G] Renamed & Promoted 1921 (higher than WC05)							
[91]	Top of Coire Bhourneasg★			3098	[944]	.75m NE of WC05		402	15	
[21]	Carn Bhac, N.E. Top			3098	[944]	2.5m N of WC04	217	417	15	65
[97]	Carn Bhac			[3104]	946	NO 051 832	221	381	6	43
WC07		MTTTT; H	[G] Demoted 1921.							
[91]	Beinn Iutharn Bheag (Ben Uarn Beg)			3011	[918]	1.25m E of WC04	271	495	15	
[21]	Beinn Iutharn Bheag (Ben Uarn Beag)			3121	[951]	1m EbyS of WC04	WC04	387	15	65
[97]	Beinn Iutharn Bheag			[3127]	953	NO 065 791	WC04	362	6	43
Notes: [21] [170yds. NbyE of the 3096 pt. on the 1-inch map]										
WC08		TTMMM	[G] Promoted 1974.							
[91]	An Socach (West end)			3059	[932]	1.5m ENE of WC07		434	15	
[21]	An Socach (West end)			3059	[932]	1.5m ENE of WC07	WC09	452	15	65
[74]	An Socach, West End			3059	944	NO 079 799	220	420	15	41
[97]	An Socach			[3097]	944	NO 079 799	227	388	6	43

No. Yr.	Code Name	Status	Remarks Feet	Metres	Location	Of Mtn.	Top	Sect.	Map
WC09		MMTTT; N	[G] Demoted 1974. Renamed 1921. Old name restored 1981.						
[91]	An Socach (East end)		3073	[937]	2.5m ENE of WC07	232	424	15	
[21]	Socach Mor, An Socach (East end)		3073	[937]	2.5m ENE of WC07	230	440	15	65
[74]	An Socach, Socach Mor		3073	938	NO 099 806	WC08	438	15	41
[97]	An Socach, East Top		[3077]	938	NO 099 805	WC08	409	6	43

Notes: [91] On the 1-inch, 'An Socach' applies to both tops. On the 6-inch, however, 'An Socach' is only the W top, while the E top is called 'Socach Mor'. The name Socach Mor on the 1-inch is .75m E of the top

No. Yr.	Code Name	Status	Remarks Feet	Metres	Location	Of Mtn.	Top	Sect.	Map
WC10		MTTTT	[G] Demoted 1921.						
[91]	Carn Bhinnein		3006	[916]	2.5m E of WC02	276	502	15	
[21]	Carn Bhinnein		3006	[916]	1m WSW of WC11	WC11	532	15	65
[97]	Carn Bhinnein		[3008]	917	NO 091 762	WC11	497	6	43
WC11		MMMMM	[21] 3.5m EbyN of WC02						
[91]	Carn Geoidhe		3194	[974]	3.5m E of WC02	176	311	15	
[97]	Carn a' Gheoidh		[3199]	975	NO 107 767	180	293	6	43
WC12		TTTxx	[G] Deleted 1981.						
[91]	Carn nan Sac		3000 (2750)	[914]	.75m EbyN of WC11		513	15	
[74]	Carn nan Sac		3000c	920	NO 119 770	WC11	506	15	41
WC13		MMMMM	[21] .5m WbyS from Braemar road summit						
[91]	The Cairnwell		3059	[932]	.5m W from A93 road summit	238	435	15	
[97]	The Cairnwell		[3061]	933	NO 134 772	245	427	6	43
WC14		MMMMM	[97] Error: GR is 091 762 – Carn Bhinnein! Should be 134 792.						
[91]	Carn Aosda		3003	[915]	1m N of WC13	280	510	15	
[97]	Carn Aosda		[3008]	917	NO 134 792	278	496	6	43
WC15		xxxxx	[G] Carn a' Bhutha. 3000c. NO 034 820. A top of WC06. Introduced 1969. Deleted 1974!						
GM01		TTTTT	[21] .88m NWbyN of GM02						
[91]	Meall Odhar		3019	[920]	.75m NW of GM02		484	16	
[97]	Meall Odhar		[3025]	922	NO 156 773	GM02	473	7	43
GM02		MMMMM							
[91]	Glas Maol		3502	[1067]	Head of Glenisla	69	114	16	
[97]	Glas Maol		[3504]	1068	NO 167 765	69	107	7	43
GM03		MMMMM							
[91]	Creag Leacach		3238	[987]	1.5m SSW of GM02	156	277	16	
[97]	Creag Leacach		[3238]	987	NO 154 745	159	256	7	43
GM04		TTTTT							
[91]	Little Glas Maol★		3184 (3000)	[970]	.75m SE of GM02		325	16	
[97]	Little Glas Maol		[3192]	973	NO 175 758	GM02	302	7	43

Notes: [91] A very doubtful top. In the Eastern Grampians it is especially difficult to decide what are to be considered separate mountains, tops, or merely shoulders

No. Yr.	Code Name	Status	Remarks Feet	Metres	Location	Of Mtn.	Top	Sect.	Map
GM05		MMMMM	[21] 2m NEbyN of GM02						
[91]	Cairn na Glasha		3484	[1062]	2m NE of GM02	70	122	16	
[97]	Cairn of Claise		[3491]	1064	NO 185 788	71	111	7	43
GM06		TTTTT	[21] 1m SSW of GM05						
[91]	Druim Mor★		3144 (3000)	[958]	1m SbyW of GM05		354	16	
[97]	Druim Mor		[3153]	961	NO 190 771	GM05	332	7	43

Notes: [91] A very doubtful top. See note to GM04

No. Yr.	Code Name	Status	Remarks Feet	Metres	Location	Of Mtn.	Top	Sect.	Map
GM07		MMMMM	[21] 2.5m SSW of Head of L. Callater						
[91]	Carn an Tuirc		3340	[1018]	2.5m S of L. Callater	112	191	16	
[97]	Carn an Tuirc		[3343]	1019	NO 174 804	113	179	7	43
GM08		xxxTT	[G] Introduced 1981.						
[81]	Creag Leacach, S.W Top		[3094]	943	NO 149 741	GM03	406	7	43
[97]	Creag Leacach, S.W. Top		[3094]	943	NO 149 741	GM03	393	7	43
DO01		MMMMM							
[91]	Tom Buidhe		3140	[957]	Head of Gl. Doll	197	360	16	
[97]	Tom Buidhe		[3140]	957	NO 213 787	204	348	7	44
DO02		MMMMM	[21] .75m NNW of DO01						
[91]	Tolmount		3143	[958]	.75m N of DO01	192	355	16	
[97]	Tolmount		[3143]	958	NO 210 800	202	346	7	44
DO03		TTTTT							
[91]	Crow Craigies★		3014 (3000c)	[919]	.75m E of DO02		490	16	
[97]	Crow Craigies		[3018]	920	NO 221 798	DO02	480	7	44
DO04		TTTTT	[21] 2m ESE of L. Callater						
[91]	Fafernie		3274	[998]	2m ENE of L. Callater	231	16		
[97]	Fafernie		[3281]	1000	NO 215 823	DO06	222	7	44

No. Yr.	Code Name	Status	Remarks	Feet	Metres	Location	Of Mtn.	Top	Sect.	Map
DO05		TTTxx	[21] .5m SWbyS of DO04 [G] Deleted 1981.							
[91]	Creag Leachdach★			3000c	[914]	.75m SW of Fafernie		532	16	
[74]	Creag Leachdach			3150c	960	NO 211 817	DO06	361	16	49

Notes: [91] A very doubtful top. See note to GM04.

DO06		MMMMM	[21] .5m ENE of DO04							
[91]	Cairn Bannoch			3314	[1010]	.5m E of Fafernie	119	200	16	
[97]	Cairn Bannoch			[3320]	1012	NO 222 825	117	188	7	44

DO07		TTTTT	[21] .63m SEbyS of DO06							
[91]	Cairn of Gowal★			3242 (3000)	[988]	.5m SE of DO06		272	16	
[97]	Cairn of Gowal			[3251]	991	NO 226 820	DO06	248	7	44

Notes: [91] A very doubtful top. See note to GM04.

DO08		TTTTT; HL	[21] 1.25m SSE of DO06 [81] Wrong height, GR, etc. Top confused with DO07?							
[91]	Craig of Gowal★			3027 (3000)	[923]	.75m SW of DO10		475	16	
[74]	Craig of Gowal			3000c	927	NO 232 809	DO06	480	16	49
[81]	Craig of Gowal			[3251]	991	NO 226 821	DO06	256	7	44
[97]	Craig of Gowal			[3041]	927	NO 232 809	DO06	450	7	44

DO09		TTTTT; H	[21] .63m NW of DO10							
[91]	Creag-an Dubh-loch★			3100a (3000)	[945]	.75m NW of DO10		398	16	
[97]	Creag an Dubh-loch			[3225]	983	NO 233 822	DO10	265	7	44

Notes: [91] Mr Munro's aneroid measurement

DO10		MMMMM								
[91]	Broad Cairn			3268	[996]	2.5m S of SD08	144	239	16	
[97]	Broad Cairn			[3274]	998	NO 240 815	142	228	7	44

DO11		MMMMM	[21] 5.5m W of Clova							
[91]	Mayar			3043	[928]	5m W of Milton of Clova	246	451	16	
[97]	Mayar			[3045]	928	NO 240 737	253	444	7	44

DO12		MMMMM	[21] 3.5m W of Clova							
[91]	Driesh			3105	[946]	3.5m W of Milton of Clova	212	387	16	
[97]	Driesh			[3107]	947	NO 271 735	219	376	7	44

SD01		MMMMM	[21] 2m E of Foot of L. Callater							
[91]	Carn an t-Sagairt Mor★			3430	[1045]	1.5m E of L. Callater	85	146	16	
[97]	Carn an t-Sagairt Mor			[3435]	1047	NO 208 843	83	131	7	44

Notes: [91] Unnamed on the 1-inch O.S., but on Baddeley's & Bartholomew's maps called Cairn Taggart

SD02		TTTTT	[21] .63m ENE of SD01							
[91]	Carn an t-Sagairt Beag★			3424 (3250)	[1044]	.5m EbyN of SD01		152	16	
[97]	Carn an t-Sagairt Beag			[3425]	1044	NO 216 848	SD03	140	7	44

SD03		MMMMM	[21] 1.38m SWbyW of SD08							
[91]	Carn a' Choire Bhoidheach★			3630a (3500)	[1106]	1.5m SW of SD08	45	71	16	
[97]	Carn a' Choire Bhoidheach			[3642]	1110	NO 226 845	42	60	7	44

Notes: [91] Called Cairn of Corbreach on Baddeley's & Bartholomew's maps. Just N of the Lochnagar track from Braemar is a point 3571 on the 6-inch. The hill rises considerably S of the track; careful aneroid measurements by Mr Munro make it about 3630ft.

SD04		TTTTT; H								
[91]	Creag a' Ghlas-uillt			3450a (3250)	[1052]	1m S of SD08		133	16	
[21]	Creag a' Ghlas-uillt★			3495a (3250)	[1065]	1m SbyW of SD08	SD03	128	16	65
[74]	Creag a' Ghlas-uillt			3500c	1068	NO 242 842	SD03	124	16	41
[97]	Creag a' Ghlas-uillt			[3504]	1068	NO 242 842	SD03	106	7	44

Notes: [91] Mr Munro's measurement

SD05		TTTTT								
[91]	Cuidhe Crom			3552	[1083]	1m ESE of SD08		96	16	
[97]	Cuidhe Crom			[3553]	1083	NO 259 849	SD09	89	7	44

SD06		TTTxT	[21] .5m SE of SD05 [G] Deleted 1981. Restored 1997!							
[91]	Little Pap			3000c	[914]	1m SE of SD05		537	16	
[74]	Little Pap			3050c	956	NO 264 844	SD09	382	16	41/42
[97]	Little Pap			[3136]	956	NO 265 844	SD09	349	7	44

Notes: [91] The name Little Pap on the 1-inch map is about halfway btw. the top & Cuidhe Crom, which is the 3552 top

SD07		TTTTT	[21] 1m ENE of SD08							
[91]	Meikle Pap			3211	[979]	1m EbyN of SD08		295	16	
[97]	Meikle Pap			[3215]	980	NO 259 860	SD09	276	7	44

SD08		TTTTx; N	[21] .33m SSE of SD09 [G] Renamed 1974. Deleted 1997.							
[91]	Lochnagar (Cairn)			3768	[1149]	6m S of Balmoral		37	16	
[81]	Lochnagar, Cac Carn Mor			[3773]	1150	NO 245 857	SD09	37	7	44

SD09		MMMMM	[21] 5.75m S of Balmoral							
[91]	Lochnagar (Cac Carn Beag)			3786	[1154]	.33m N of SD08	21	33	16	
[97]	Lochnagar, Cac Carn Beag			[3789]	1155	NO 243 861	21	30	7	44

No. Yr.	Code Name	Status	Remarks Feet	Metres	Location	Of Mtn.	Top	Sect.	Map
SD10	TTTTT		[21] 1m NbyW of SD08						
[91]	Meall Coire na Saobhaidhe		3191 (3121)	[973]	1m N of SD08		316	16	
[97]	Meall Coire na Saobhaidhe		[3195]	974	NO 242 872	SD09	298	7	44
SD11	MMMMM								
[91]	Mount Keen		3077	[938]	6m SSE of Ballater	230	421	16	
[97]	Mount Keen		[3081]	939	NO 409 869	235	406	7	44
SD12	xTxTT; N		[G] Introduced 1921. Deleted 1974. Renamed & Restored 1981.						
[21]	Stob an Dubh-loch		3470a (3250)	[1058]	1.25m N of Dubh Loch	SD03	135	16	65
[81]	Top of Eagle's Rock		[3448]	1051	NO 237 838	SD03	132	7	44
[97]	Eagle's Rock		[3448]	1051	NO 237 838	SD03	125	7	44
SK01	MMMMM		[21] 5.75m SSE of Sligachan Inn						
[91]	Blath Bheinn (Blaven), N. Top		3042	[927]	5m SSE of Sligachan Inn	247	452	17	
[97]	Bla Bheinn		[3045]	928	NG 529 217	252	441	17	32

Notes: [91] Cuillin names are from Mr Pilkington's new map, & the approximate heights are from careful aneroid measurements by Mr Norman Collie

No. Yr.	Code Name	Status	Remarks Feet	Metres	Location	Of Mtn.	Top	Sect.	Map
SK02	TxxTT		[G] Deleted 1921. Restored 1981.						
[91]	Blath Bheinn (Blaven), S. Top		3031	[924]	5m SSE of Sligachan Inn		471	17	
[81]	Bla Bheinn, S.W Top		[3031]	924	NG 528 215	SK01	476	17	32
[97]	Bla Bheinn, South Top		[3038]	926	NG 528 215	SK01	455	17	32
SK03	MMMMM		[74] Typo: Northing 453 should be 253!						
[91]	Sgurr nan Gillean		3167	[965]	3m SbyW of Sligachan Inn	185	333	17	
[97]	Sgurr nan Gillean		[3163]	964	NG 471 252	191	320	17	32
SK04	TMMMM		[74] Typo: Northing 453 should be 253! [G] Promoted 1921.						
[91]	Bhasteir		3020a	[921]	.33m W of SK03		482	17	
[21]	Am Basteir		3050a	[930]	.5m W of SK03	246	469	17	70
[97]	Am Basteir		[3064]	934	NG 465 253	242	423	17	32

Notes: [91] Located .33m S of point called Sgurr Bhasteir on 1-inch map. See note to SK01 [21] Contours on the 1-inch map cannot be relied on and are therefore omitted here. Also known as Sgurr Dubh a' Bhasteir

No. Yr.	Code Name	Status	Remarks Feet	Metres	Location	Of Mtn.	Top	Sect.	Map
SK05	MMMMM								
[91]	Bruach na Frith		3143	[958]	.67m W of SK03	193	356	17	
[97]	Bruach na Frithe		[3143]	958	NG 461 252	200	342	17	32
SK06	MMMMM; H								
[91]	Sgurr a' Ghreadaidh		3100a	[945]	2m NW of Head of L. Coruisk	217	399	17	
[21]	Sgurr a' Ghreadaidh, North Top		3197	[974]	.33m SSW of SK18	173	314	17	70
[74]	Sgurr a' Ghreadaidh, North Top		3192 (3197)	[973]	NG 445 232	178	329	17	25/33
[81]	Sgurr a' Ghreadaidh		[3192]	973	NG 445 232	181	310	17	32
[97]	Sgurr a' Ghreadaidh		[3189]	972	NG 445 232	185	303	17	32

Notes: [91] See note to SK01

No. Yr.	Code Name	Status	Remarks Feet	Metres	Location	Of Mtn.	Top	Sect.	Map
SK07	MMMMM		[21] 150yds SbyW of SK21 [G] Called 'N. Top' in 1921/74.						
[91]	Sgurr na Banachdich		3167	[965]	Westernmost point on main ridge	186	334	17	
[97]	Sgurr na Banachdich		[3166]	965	NG 440 224	190	319	17	32

Notes: [21] Also spelt 'Banachaig'

No. Yr.	Code Name	Status	Remarks Feet	Metres	Location	Of Mtn.	Top	Sect.	Map
SK08	MTTTx		[G] Demoted 1921 (lower than SK09). Deleted 1997!						
[91]	Sgurr Dearg (Ordnance Point)		3234	[986]	.75m SSE of SK07	157	279	17	
[21]	Sgurr Dearg, Cairn (O.S. Point)		3234	[986]	Close NW of SK08	SK09	282	17	70
[81]	Sgurr Dearg, Cairn		[3209]	978	NG 443 216	SK09	291	17	32
SK09	TMMMM		[G] Promoted 1921 (higher than SK08).						
[91]	Sgurr Dearg ("Inaccessible Peak★")		3250a	[991]	Close SE of SK08		256	17	
[21]	Sgurr Dearg, Inaccessible Pinnacle		3254	[992]	.63m SSE of SK07	148	266	17	70
[97]	Sgurr Dearg, Inaccessible Pinnacle		[3235]	986	NG 444 215	164	263	17	32

Notes: [91] See note to SK01

No. Yr.	Code Name	Status	Remarks Feet	Metres	Location	Of Mtn.	Top	Sect.	Map
SK10	TTTTT; N		[21] 100yds NE of SK11 [G] Renamed 1921.						
[91]	Sgurr Alaisdair★ (N.E. Peak)		3210a	[978]	.5m SE of SK08		297	17	
[97]	Sgurr Thearlaich		[3209]	978	NG 451 208	SK11	285	17	32

Notes: [91] See note to SK01.

No. Yr.	Code Name	Status	Remarks Feet	Metres	Location	Of Mtn.	Top	Sect.	Map
SK11	MMMMM; NH		[G] Renamed 1921. For the height problem, see Chapter 1.5, fn. 3.						
[91]	Sgurr Alaisdair★ (S.W. Peak)		3255a	[992]	Btw. SK10 & SK12	150	250	17	
[21]	Sgurr Alasdair		3309	[1009]	.67m SE of SK08	117	216	17	70
[97]	Sgurr Alasdair		[3255]	992	NG 450 207	154	247	17	32

Notes: [91] See note to SK01

No. Yr.	Code Name	Status	Remarks Feet	Metres	Location	Of Mtn.	Top	Sect.	Map
SK12	TTTTT		[21] 200yds SW of SK11						
[91]	Sgurr Sgumain		3104	[946]	.33m SW of SK10		388	17	
[97]	Sgurr Sgumain		[3107]	947	NG 448 206	SK11	378	17	32

No. Yr.	Code Name	Status	Remarks Feet	Metres	Location	Of Mtn.	Top	Sect.	Map
SK13		TTTTT; N	[21] .25m WbyS of SK14 [G] Renamed 1921.				417	17	
[91]	Sgurr Dubh (W. Peak)		3080a	[939]	1m SW of Head of L. Coruisk				
[97]	Sgurr Dubh an Da Bheinn		[3077]	938	NG 455 204	SK14	412	17	32
Notes: [91] See note to SK01									
SK14		MMMMM; N	[21] .5m EbyS of SK11 [G] Renamed 1921.				382	17	
[91]	Sgurr Dubh (Central Peak)		3110a	[948]	1m SW of Head of L. Coruisk	208			
[97]	Sgurr Dubh Mor		[3097]	944	NG 457 205	228	389	17	32
Notes: [91] See note to SK01									
SK15		MMMMM	[21] .63m SbyE of SK13				464	17	
[91]	Sgurr nan Eag		3036	[925]	1.5m N of Soay Sound	256			
[97]	Sgurr nan Eag		[3031]	924	NG 457 195	265	464	17	32
SK16		xTTTT	[74] Typo: Northing 453 should be 253! [G] Introduced 1921. GRs do not separate it from SK04/SK17				543	17	70
[21]	Bhasteir Tooth#		3000a	[914]	Close W of SK04	SK04			
[97]	Bhasteir Tooth		[3005]	916	NG 464 252	SK04	503	17	32
SK17		xTTTT	[74] Typo: Northing 452 should be 252!				472	17	70
[21]	Sgurr a' Fionn Choire#		3050a	[930]	150yds SW of SK04	SK05			
[97]	Sgurr a' Fionn Choire		[3068]	935	NG 464 252	SK05	421	17	32
SK18		xMMMM	[74] Error: GR 451 238 is NE Peak of Mhadaidh. [G] Introduced 1921.				521	17	70
[21]	Sgurr a' Mhadaidh, S.W. peak		3014	[919]	1.33m SW of SK05	270			
[97]	Sgurr a' Mhadaidh		[3012]	918	NG 446 235	277	490	17	32
Notes: [21] Consists of 4 peaks, 2970, 280, 2910 & 3014. The latter has two tops, about the same height									
SK19		xTTTT	[G] Introduced 1921.				335	17	70
[21]	Sgurr a' Ghreadaidh, South Top		3180a	[969]	.33m SSW of SK18	SK06			
[97]	Sgurr a' Ghreadaidh, South Top		[3182]	970	NG 445 230	SK06	306	17	32
SK20		xTTTT	[G] Introduced 1921.				404	17	70
[21]	Sgurr na Banachdich, Centre Top		3104	[946]	100yds SbyE of SK07	SK07			
[97]	Sgurr na Banachdich, Central Top		[3091]	942	NG 441 223	SK07	397	17	32
SK21		xTTTT	[74] Typo: GR 440 223 should be 441 226. [G] Introduced 1921.				529	17	70
[21]	Sgurr Thormaid★		3007	[917]	.5m SW of SK06	SK07			
[97]	Sgurr Thormaid		[3038]	926	NG 441 226	SK07	459	17	32
SK22		xMMMM	[G] Introduced 1921.				397	17	70
[21]	Sgurr Mhic Coinnich		3107	[947]	.5m SEbyE of SK08	210			
[97]	Sgurr Mhic Choinnich		[3110]	948	NG 450 210	217	373	17	32
SK23		xxxxT	[G] Introduced 1997.				511	17	32
[97]	Knight's Peak		[3000]	914	NG 471 254	SK03			
MU01		MMMMM					331	17	
[91]	Ben More, Isle of Mull		3169	[966]	7m SSW of Salen, Mull	183			
[97]	Ben More, Isle of Mull		[3169]	966	NM 525 330	189	316	17	48

Additional Notes to Table 5.2

Some Errors in the 1891 Table:–

1. Am Bodach (AE04) is marked T411 and Carn Dearg (OT08) is marked T410 (both Tables). AE04 should be T410 and OT08 should be T411.

2. Sgorr Dheirg, Beinn a' Bheithir (AP06) is 3392 in Table 1 and 3362 in Table 2. M106 and T180, are fixed by height 3362, which is the map value.

3. Leachd Riach (BC12) is marked 3250c in Table 2, but plain 3250 in Table 1. The latter marking is correct.

4. Top 1/2 mile west of Saddle is marked 3090c in Table 2 – A typo for 3000c.

5. Sgiath Chuil is not marked 'ap.' in Table 2. It should be.

6. The location of Ciste Dhubh (AF13) is given as '1.5m S of Mam Sodhail'. Presumably this is a typo for '.5m S of ...'

7. Spidean a' Choire Leith (TO06) is located '2m ENE of Mullach an Rathain (TO03)'. Evidently this is a typo for '2m ENE of Torridon'.

8. The Top above Cadha Gobhlach (TE07) is located ' .5m SSE of Sgurr Fiona (TE03)'. Evidently this is a typo for '.5m SSE of Corrag Bhuidhe Buttress (TE06)'.

9. The Mountain Numbers for AF09, AF10 and AF11 are displaced by one line in Table 1. See the Variorum Table entries and Chapter 4.8

Some particularly troublesome mountains:–

1. *Carn Ballach.* The location of this top remains a puzzle. James Gall Inglis firmly put the most north-easterly top of Carn Ballach highest and deleted the S.W. Top, but since 1974 Editors have given Carn Ballach the Grid Reference of this deleted top. Although previous maps were indecisive, providing only a contour for the N.E. top, the 2 cm. map shows a 920m. contour at the S.W. top only, thus making it the higher top. But Gall Inglis' evidence seems clear enough – see *SMCJ* 1939, XXII, 109-116 – and the 4 cm. map shows tiny 920m. contours at both tops. Further investigation is clearly needed.

2. *Creag a' Choire Aird.* This long ramified ridge has caused Table Editors endless trouble, largely on account of very sketchy early survey work. Munro's typo (see 9. above) cannot have helped, and the normally reliable Edred Corner (see *SMCJ* 1916, XIV, 148-152) – although he identified four tops on the ridge – seems to have got heights and distances wrong between Carn na Con Dhu and Mullach Sithidh. Gall Inglis added the following note in the 1933 Tables, 'Creag a' Choire Aird: S. Top (last edn. 'Southern Ridge'); the adverse comment on the inference drawn from the hill-shading should be deleted from the Note, as it does not apply to the new position ".5m. S." of the 3188-foot top. The "1.5m. south" of the last edition seems to have been a clerical error, as H.T.M.'s card index has ".5m. S.", agreeing with John Dow's position, and height of 3215 ft.'

3. *An Riabhachan.* This long ridge has suffered from uncertainties about the location of tops at both ends. A brief period of doubt about whether the most north-easterly top (NM11) might be the true summit led to that top being introduced as a Top in 1981. At the same time the western shoulder of the summit ridge (dismissed in 1891 by Munro) was also introduced (NM12), temporarily providing this simple ridge with 4 Tops!

4. *Slioch.* The summit is unfortunately furnished with two pimply tops with very little between them (LF01 and LF09). This circumstance has led to a pleasant game of ping-pong in the Tables, now resolved in favour of LF09. Occasionally, and absurdly, both tops have been in the Tables at once. See Chapter 6.8 below for Parker's solution of the problem. Similar difficulties afflict Ben Lui, The Saddle, and probably Coinneach Mhor (TO11) and Ceann Garbh (GU05).

Technical Advice to Munroists

6.1 Introduction

THIS SECTION must begin with a disclaimer. It is not intended to be a presentation of up-to-date technical advice. For this the reader should turn to one of the well-known textbooks, such as Eric Langmuir's *Mountaincraft and Leadership*. The purpose of the present section is to set out the techniques used by the pioneers. In selecting material I have emphasised the use of aneroids and other devices to obtain heights, and the particular methods employed to navigate accurately in thick weather.

However, my aim in presenting this material is not solely historical. The history of the Ordnance Survey's attempts to map our mountains accurately shows that there are always errors made and eminences overlooked or misplaced. Although it is not much seen today, I think there is still a place for the amateur surveyor on mountains. After all, current maps give heights which are accurate only to the nearest metre: in other words, they are accurate – always assuming that no observational, instrumental or administrative errors have been made – only to around 5 feet! And of course decisions about Munro status depend on accuracy to a foot: decisions about Corbett status are even more height-critical, since cols must be considered as well as peaks. James Parker's measurements on Slioch (Chapter 6.8) show how useful and decisive amateur surveying can be.

Accurate navigation in thick weather is the key to safe movement on mountains, and there is more to this than knowing how to use a map and compass. Perhaps the essays on navigation by Douglas, Raeburn and Parker may be helpful in suggesting these extra ingredients of sound navigation.

The early writings of the pioneers, notably William Naismith and Harold Raeburn, contained much valuable advice about movement over snow. However, the equipment used – heavy hob-nailed boots and a 5-foot ice-axe of very solid construction – lent itself to particular techniques, especially glissading, which are lethal with modern equipment. On the other hand, the modern crampon makes descent of icy ground a comparatively simple matter. So I have not included any of the period pieces on snow and ice techniques. However, Naismith's well-known Rule, and a modern revision of it by Trevor Ransley, are included.

As light relief, I have framed the section with a hilarious discussion of training and equipment by Joseph Stott and with Geoffrey Dutton's compendium of old-fashioned recommendations for the use of coca leaves as an improvement on glucose tablets, chocolate bars or mint cake! Naturally, on no account should these recommendations be followed, since the use of cocaine is illegal.

6.2 Joseph Stott's 'Practical Hints For Pedestrians'

Robin N. Campbell[1]

Joe Stott, exhausted after carrying his fell-pole up Cruach Ardrain

. . . Stott reserves his most fantastic notions and strongest prejudices for the final chapter of his manuscript. This chapter begins with various admonitions regarding training – the Pedestrian 'must pack inside his skin every ounce of beef and bone and muscle he can accumulate. Therefore let him eat and drink as much as he likes, fish, flesh and fowl, porridge and pudding bread, fruit, beer, wine and spirits . . . When you turn out of bed, never on any account whatever – winter or summer – neglect your bath. Have it quite cold, if you can stand it; if not, as nearly as possible. After your bath, spend not less than a quarter of an hour in your dumb-bell and bar-bell exercise, or Indian clubs if you have them. A most important factor in training of any kind – is a stroll of one or two miles before breakfast. It fill your lungs with pure morning air, it cleanses your brain and your whole body, it gives you a huge appetite for breakfast, and it braces you up for the day's work. If you find walking on an empty stomach disagrees with you, take a wine glass of milk and a biscuit; this will easily keep you going until breakfast. Of course it must depend altogether on your circumstances, as to when you take the rest of your walking exercise. The best plan would be about an hour of walking before lunch and an hour afterwards.

---

[1] *Tir nam Beann: Rambles and Scrambles among the Bens and Glens of Scotland* is a manuscript book written by the SMC's first Editor, Joseph Stott, which gives an entertaining and fascinating account of the mountaineering activities of Stott and his friends in the 1870s and 1880s. This Edinburgh group were known as 'The Tramps' and they contributed about 10 original members to the SMC. The manuscript is now in *NLS Acc. 11538*, item 269. What follows is an extract from my review of Stott's manuscript – 'Stott's Mountaineering Club', *SMCJ* 1974, XXX, 257-263.

Putting it alongside your morning stroll, and any other exercise you may take during the day, it will give you a total of ten or eleven miles. This is quite enough. Walk as much every day of the week, with an occasional long stretch on Saturdays or Sundays, and at the end of a couple of months you should be fit for anything.'

As a result of this regimen, Stott adds, the Pedestrian will have 'a development of muscle as hard and clean-cut as marble.'

Climbing requires practice, too. Even 'the first-rate Roadster' will find 'wind and thigh wanting in him.' If hills and rocks are not readily to hand, then 'a steep stair is a capital substitute. Walk up and down stairs steadily for half an hour with a ten-pound dumbbell in each hand and see how fagged you feel after it.'

Stott now turns to a lengthy treatise on the proper equipment for Pedestrianising, passing through boots to stockings (which must be of thick worsted, 'silk or cotton would be as much out of place on a walk as worsted would be in a Queen's drawing-room') through knickerbockers ('ideal for crawling on your knees') and Norfolk jacket to the vexing question of headgear . .

'I have tried half a dozen different head-gears before deciding on what I always wear now. My first was an elegant affair, made of cambric or linen; light as thistledown, broad in the brim, and set on a wire framework. For the sun it did tolerably well, wind rather badly, but alas! the first drencher of rain caused the crown to collapse and came pouring through, down face and neck, in an abundance that no handkerchief could sop up. Straw hats I have not found much better; polo-caps or glengarries lay you open to headaches and sunstroke; knitted tam o' shanters are hot and uncomfortable. The tweed caps known as deerstalkers, with good flaps or scoops fore and aft, are capital; but better still is a soft hat with a curly brim made of the same tweed as your coat. The brim will turn down, and shoot all rain clear of face and neck onto your shoulders. There should be no thick lining and the hat should be ventilated with four or six airholes. The uses you can put such a headpiece as this to are endless. By day of course it shelters you; by night, if you camp out or are travelling, it serves as a night-cap; you can fill it with water and use it as a washing basin; you can scoop up water with it out of deep wells, if you have no other means of doing so. To my mind a pugaree[2] savours of the Cockney tourist, so do not have one. A large white handkerchief draped over the hat does just as well; and failing the cabbage leaf, a few handfuls of wet herbage thrown loosely into the crown and supplied with cold water now and again, will keep you safe enough. The back of the neck is an even more fatal place in great heat than the head, so do not fail to let the white awning hang well over it.'

The 'Cockney tourist' comes in for abuse in other parts of the manuscript. The Tramps find a bottle secreted in the summit cairn of Carn Liath of Beinn a' Ghlo. It contains a leaflet 'inscribed with various rhapsodies,' among them one to the effect that the depositor had enjoyed 'a bath of ecstasy and prayer.' The Pilot holds forth – 'Confound these hydropathics and the Cockney crew they bring about the country. I suppose a time'll come when we can't go anywhere without meeting a poetry-spouting tourist.' Indeed.

---

[2] 'Pugaree' is an anglicization of Hindi 'pagri' – a turban.

Next comes some valuable advice about care of the feet. After a discussion of various relatively conventional prophylactic measures (meths, alum, etc.) Stott's own method is presented – 'A very good preventative both for footsoreness and blisters, is soaping your stockings. Before putting them on in the morning, take a lump of soap, and, having turned them inside out, rub the whole of the foot over and over till it is quite white and moist. When you put them on, you will find them moist and slimy, but they will keep your feet cool, and prevent chafing. It is useless to soap your *foot,* the soap must be applied to the *stocking.'* A final precaution is to 'change your stocking (at lunch) – the right leg to the left, the left to the right. The six or seven hours of walking you have already done has impressed on your feet the pattern of every stitch in the wool, and the fact of changing puts a stop to this process.' If, however, even this Draconian measure fails then the Pedestrian must 'prick (the blister) and press the water out. Next melt a few drops of tallow into the palm or your hand, and add some drops of whiskey or other spirit. Mix the two into a paste and rub it into the blister as hard as you can.' Stott remarks that this method, obtained from an old Swiss guidebook, has never been known to fail and 'is ever so much better than the old-fashioned and barbarous plan of drawing a worsted thread through the blister and leaving it overnight.'

This obsession with the feet is entirely natural, given the gargantuan expeditions of the Tramps, who thought little of forty miles in a day. Another understandable obsession is with drink: beer is regarded as 'a very bad drink. It heats you, clogs the mouth and makes you perspire profusely.' Milk is held in low esteem, for similar reasons. On the other hand cider and cold tea are highly valued but the former is 'unfortunately, to be had in few places' while the latter 'usually necessitates long waiting'! Whisky is the subject of a lengthy encomium early in the manuscript . .

'Oh! Ho! a fine thing is the good Hieland whiskey. It is the internal and the external medicine of the Pedestrian. It heals blisters and footsoreness, and an application of it to a rheumatic knee-joint is almost sure to do good. Should you feel a trifle 'seedy' in the morning nothing puts you right as a 'nip' will; a 'peg' before a meal puts an edge on your appetite; a drop during a meal enlivens the conversation; and a drop after it acts as a sedative and promotes digestion. When you get thirsty on the road – a thing which will happen often – nothing refreshes you so much as a draught of cold burn water with just a 'soupçon' of the 'craythur' in it, to take the chill off. On a cold, wet day . . a pull at your flask makes you tingle all over with warmth and pleasure; and after climbing a peak or a pass, you would surely never think of leaving the elevation you have won without promoting a similar elevation in your own feelings by means of a dram. Finally, the social tumbler of toddy, over which you fight your battles again in the evening is one of the sweetest memories of the Pedestrian and I defy anyone who has once tasted the potent beverage to refrain from joining the poet in its praise:–

> *Fortune, if thou'llt gie me still*
> *Haill breeks, a scone, and whisky gill,*
> *Tak' a' the rest.'*

The chapter concludes in grand style with a comparison of Pedestrianism with bicycling, to the gross disadvantage of bicycling. There is first a grudging admission – 'the only advantage bicycling possesses is that on good roads it is possible to cover very long distances with comparative ease' – which is then immediately retracted, since 'I say comparative, since nothing that I know of looks more punishing and laborious than seeing a cyclist bent nearly double, painfully propelling his machine up a hill that is easy to anyone else.' Moreover, 'Look at the discomfort of wind, either ahead or across you; the by no means remote chance of something serious going wrong with your machine; the trouble of cleaning it, and stabling it at night.' Now comes the clincher, 'I have not so far touched upon the unhealthy side of this form of exercise; the complaint known as 'bicyclist's back', or the hollow chests, round shoulders, craning necks and knock-knees induced by it. I do not mean to say that amongst the ranks of cyclists there are not to be found many magnificent specimens of manhood and far-famed athletes who are free from the blemishes I have enumerated, but all the same, the class taken as a whole does not shine in noble appearance and 'manly beauty', and as a Pedestrian I have not the slightest wish to be classed with it. I think it is a great pity that so many of our young fellows are constantly to be seen spinning about on bicycles and tricycles – their legs nothing more than a pair of cranks, their arms connecting-rods.' Finally comes a masterstroke, 'Another thing that I look upon as an adverse argument is that many men who were once ardent bicyclists, have now given it up.'

What a strange mixture these Victorian climbers were! Stott's boyish enthusiasm for everything connected with our hills (solemnised annually when the SMC sing the atrocious doggerel of his Song[3]) comes no more clearly from the pages of *Tir nam Beann* than does his precise old-womanish concern with niceties of equipment and technique. What kind of men dance reels in the moonlight in Glenfalloch[4] before retiring to soap their stockings and rub muttonfat and whisky into their blisters?

In *Tir nam Beann*, according to Stott, the first rays of the rising sun simultaneously strike the end of Leith Pier and the top of Buachaille Etive. Clearly, in such a country no Antisyzygies are too Caledonian.

---

[3] See opposite.

[4] In an earlier chapter, Stott describes such a reel outside the Inn at Inverarnan. At the time of writing I had no knowledge of the tradition of male country dancing, maintained by army regiments and disappearing with the end of conscription or possibly as a result of an improvement in public taste! For example, I subsequently learned that in 1950 the all-male membership of the Junior Mountaineering Club of Scotland amused themselves after their Annual Whole-Club Dinner with 'energetic country dancing in the moonlight, the beauty of the background' – this was provided by the slate-heaps of South Ballachulish – 'compensating for the vile lack of polish in the performance and the primitive nature of the music' (*SMCJ* 1950, XXIV, 263). However, it is not long before we discover that these annual proceedings were concluded by 'members retiring to the local dance hall . . where a contingent of the Ladies' Scottish Climbing Club provided very charming and entertaining partners'.

Song of the Scottish Mountaineering Club

Joseph G. Stott
Air– 'The Golden Slippers'*

Oh, the big ice axe, it hangs on the wall,
With the gaiters, and the gloves, and the rope, and all.
But we'll polish off the rust, and we'll knock out all the dust,
     When we go up to the mountains in the snow.
Then our raiment stout shall the cold keep out,
And the good old axe shall again cut tracks,
And the frozen slope shall call for the rope,
     When we go up to the mountains in the snow.
     Chorus

Then our cragsmen bold shall swarm up the shoots,
And shall win their way by unheard-of routes;
While others, never flagging, the tops and peaks are bagging,
     When we go up to the mountains in the snow.
Though the hailstones rattle, like the shot in battle,
And the whirlwind and blizzard freeze the marrow and the gizzard,
Though it thunder and it lighten, still our hearts it cannot frighten,
     When we go up to the mountains in the snow.
     Chorus

For the best of the Club will then be afoot,
From the President down to the last recruit,
And a merry band you'll find us, as we leave the town behind us,
     When we go up to the mountains in the snow.
You may tell Tyndrum that we're going to come,
And at snug Dalmally shall our hillmen rally,
And a lot of other places shall behold our jolly faces,
     When we go up to the mountains in the snow.
     Chorus

Let the Switzer boast of his Alpine host;
But the Scotsman kens of a thousand Bens-
Oh! their names are most supemal, but you'll find 'em in the Journal,
     As compiled by that enthusiast, Munro.
The Salvationist takes his pick from the list,
And the agile Ultramontane finds the exercise he's wantin'–
Each gets climbing that'll please him, as the mood may chance to seize him,
     When we go up to the mountains in the snow.
     Chorus

---

* 'The Golden Slippers' was a music-hall song composed by the negro musician James Bland, and usually known by the first line of its chorus, 'Oh, dem golden slippers!'

Good comrades we, of the SMC,
We're a jolly band of brothers, tho' we're sons of many mothers.
And trouble, strife, and worry – Gad! they quit us in a hurry,
    When we go up to the mountains in the snow.
For our northern land offers sport so grand,
And in every kind of weather do we ply the good shoe-leather;
And from Caithness down to Arran, on the mountains big and barren,
    You can trace our little footprints in the snow.
    Chorus

From the sunrise flush, when the hill-tops blush,
Till the moonbeams quiver on the ice-bound river,
We push attack and foray, over ridge and peak and corric,
    When we go up to the mountains in the snow.
When the long day's done, and the victory's won,
And the genial whisky toddy cheers the spirit, warms the body,
Then the ptarmigan and raven, far aloft above our haven,
    Hear our chorus faintly wafted o'er the snow.
    Chorus

Chorus

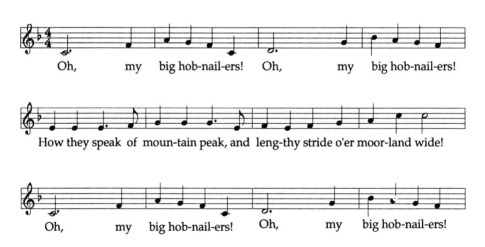

Oh,   my   big hob-nail-ers!   Oh,   my   big hob-nail-ers!

How they speak of moun-tain peak, and leng-thy stride o'er moor-land wide!

Oh,   my   big hob-nail-ers!   Oh,   my   big hob-nail-ers!

Memories raise of   joy-ous days   u - pon the moun-tain - side

6.3 Naismith's Rule

IN *SMCJ* 1892, II, 136 Wm. Naismith described a solo round trip from Crianlarich over Cruach Ardrain, Stobinian and Ben More to Luib, which he carried out on the 2nd of May. He concluded thus: 'Distance 10 miles; total climb, 6,300 feet; time, six and a half hours (including short halts). This tallies exactly with a simple formula, that may be found useful in estimating what time men in fair condition should allow for easy expeditions, namely, an hour for every three miles on the map, with an additional hour for every 2,000 feet of ascent.'[2]

. . . and Naismith Reviewed

Trevor Ransley[1]

NAISMITH'S RULE for estimating the time for a mountain walk has been known, in Scotland at least, for many years and by rough practical verification it has become an accepted and invaluable yardstick. However, when re-reading recently an article in *Les Alpes* for March 1949, I was prompted to question the implications of Naismith's rule in a critical light and to consider the benefits of the method adopted by the Swiss author.

On one aspect of mountain walking, Naismith was completely silent: the time taken for descent. My own practice has varied between ignoring the height difference in the calculation and taking about one-half or two-thirds of the equivalent total time for the ascent. Neither has entirely satisfied me. There is, furthermore, a practical inconsistency in Naismith of the type that can arise from such an empirical simplification. This is that the rise is allowed the same time value whatever the horizontal distance; thus a thousand feet in one mile is given the same time as a thousand feet in four miles. To ignore in effect the gradient seems to me intuitively wrong, for as distance is increased so ultimately the time for a given rise must become of less significance.

Having now criticised a traditional precept, I must be constructive and explain the Swiss method. As with Naismith, it is based on a horizontal walking rate and a vertical climbing rate, but in this case they are not applied separately; instead a resultant is used

---

[1] *SMCJ* 1971, XXIX, 369-372.

[2] It is interesting that Naismith glissaded the north-east slope of Ben More, and possibly was able to use the snow cover to advantage on other descents. Descent of the north-east slope of Ben More in summer conditions is likely to be a much slower process for 'men in fair condition'. So Naismith's Rule may be a rule for fit men, rather than men in fair condition, and this is a supposition confirmed by long and measured experience!

which effectively depends on the gradient. For descent, a different resultant is used, based on the same walking rate but on a vertical descent rate equivalent to double the ascent rate. The mathematics on which the calculations are based are beyond the scope of an article like this and probably outside the interest of most readers of the *Journal,* so that the results are most useful as an easily read chart rather than as a formula. An examination of the chart with this article shows that the objection to Naismith's inconsistency is removed and moreover, not only is provision made for calculating descents, but intuitive results are also

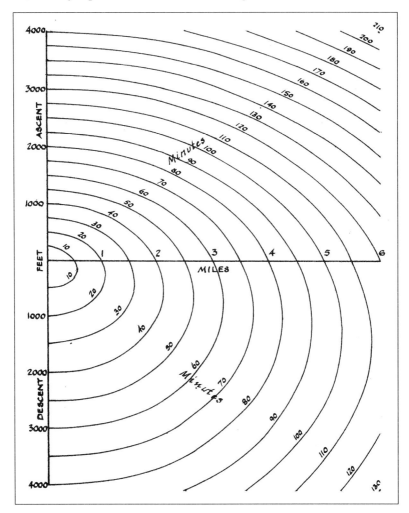

Ransley's Chart to modify Naismith's Rule

catered for. Thus it will be seen that for descents on gentle slopes up to a certain limiting gradient, the time can be less than for a similar horizontal distance alone, and beyond that as the slope steepens so the time begins to increase again.

There are two aspects of specifying a rule for a calculation of this kind: the first is concerned with basic assumptions of the way in which the variables are combined. The second is concerned with the actual constants used and this must now be dealt with. However, I do not intend becoming involved in definitions of average conditions of ground and weather and of what constitutes an average mountaineer; such arguments beset work study in other fields. The Swiss chart is based on 4.5 km/hour for the horizontal rate, 300 m/hour for vertical ascent and 600 m/hour for vertical descent. The English equivalents for these are about 2.8 miles/hour, 1000 and 2000 ft/hour. Since walking in the Alps involves more rugged ground than the average in Scotland, less generous values are appropriate. I have based my version, therefore, on 3 miles/hour, 1500 and 3000 ft/hour. So the walking rate is the same as Naismith but the rate of ascent is markedly and justifiably different. Although Naismith's 2000 ft/hour seems reasonable when included in his particular combination, it is hardly likely that an average person could 'walk' up a near-vertical slope at that speed!

The chart is used in this way: select a point on the horizontal axis equivalent to the measured map distance and select a point on the vertical axis (upper part for ascent, lower part for descent) equivalent to the difference in height of the two points; trace vertically and horizontally to find the point which completes the rectangle on the chart and interpolate by estimation the time from the values shown against the curves which straddle the point. For example, the time for a distance of 4 miles and an ascent of 3500 feet will be about 166 minutes, and for a distance of 2.75 miles and a descent of 1800 feet the time will be about 59 minutes. On a long walk, the total time should be obtained from separate sections of roughly uniform slope. This is not necessary with Naismith, of course.

On one further point Naismith has little to say: the average allowance that should be made for rest, meal stops and minor contingencies. This must be mainly a personal matter, but some average guide is needed and it is perhaps not surprising that work study provides a clue to this recreational but physical activity. Therefore, 25% should be adequate for all normal needs, and all that is necessary to find the total time for an expedition is to calculate the times for the separate sections of ascent and descent from the chart then add 25% to the total. Clearly for practical purposes the final estimate will be rounded up to the nearest hour or half-hour. On this basis the whole walk to Ben Lomond and back from Rowardennan (3.5 miles and 3150 feet) would be allowed five hours.

Most people like to think of themselves as better than average, whether as mortals or mountaineers, but most will also be only too ready to claim on appropriate occasions that conditions of ground or weather are worse than average. Nevertheless, estimates such as those given by Naismith's or this 'Swiss' rule can only be based on average unless we wish to modify them with subjective assessments that seem appropriate from time to time. Since writing the original draft of this article, I have read Eric Langmuir's account of subjective assessments in the excellent *Handbook of Mountain Leadership,* but I am doubtful whether the modifications to Naismith would be easy to use in practice. So we are left with a choice that only experience can help us to make.

6.4 How to Stop a Fall on Hard Snow or Ice

W.W. Naismith[1]

BOOKS and articles on mountaineering rarely give much advice on this subject,[2] and perhaps a few words may not come amiss from an old climber, who in his day has made many experiments on snow, and who will gladly welcome suggestions from younger men.

The authors who deal with the practice of climbing in snow naturally devote themselves chiefly to showing the best ways of *avoiding* slips and falls; but, in spite of all the care climbers may use, mistakes will sometimes happen. It is most important therefore to know exactly what to do if a fall should unfortunately occur; and to practise the thing quietly beforehand, so that it may be remembered in an emergency.

Suppose, then, that an unroped climber, when mounting a slope of hard snow, somehow or other falls out of his steps and finds himself sliding downwards involuntarily on his side, what is he to do?

Two things, in the writer's opinion. *First*, let him instantly turn his face inwards to the slope, and dig his toes into the snow. *Second*, holding the stock of his axe in either hand, let him grasp the axe-head by the blade with his other hand; and then, bringing it low down to the level of his breast-bone, press the pick into the snow – at first gradually, but ultimately with the weight of his body behind it.

The climber will then be practically supported on a tripod, consisting of his axe-head and the toes of his boots, which will plough parallel furrows down the slope, deep or shallow, according to the condition of the surface. As a result, tremendous resistance will be developed, and the slide ought soon to come to a standstill. The ice-axe held in the way described will quickly bring the climber 'right end up', even if he should have slewed round and be sliding down sideways.

In the event of a roped party being upset, and getting adrift on ice or snow, owing to the fall of one of their number, each man must separately do his utmost to stop his own way, and to retard the motion of the others; and the method above described appears to be the best available for all.

Even without an axe, by turning face inwards one has the best chance of arresting a slide downhill on a moderate snow slope. On one occasion the writer remembers proving that on hard-frozen snow set at 32° (measured) it was just possible to stop with the toes alone; but when the angle rose to 35°, the help of the axe was needed.

---

[1] *SMCJ* 1919, XV, 323-324.

[2] Mr George D. Abraham, in *The Complete Mountaineer*, gives on p. 87 a good paragraph about stopping a slip on icy snow; and Mr Gilbert Thomson, in *SMCJ* 1908, X, 23-24, makes some valuable suggestions for braking in sitting glissades. —WWN

6.5 On Route Finding In Mist

W. Douglas.[1]

ONE often hears tales of people being enveloped in mist while among the mountains, and of their being afraid to move until it clears away; also of shepherds and others, well acquainted with their surroundings, going hopelessly astray when suddenly caught in fog. Why is this? The answer is simple – because they have never taught themselves to walk by compass.

The mere possession of a compass will not help one much without the knowledge of how to use it, combined, of course, with his knowing the point of the compass in which his direction lies; this he may get from a map, if he knows where he is, and has the power to read the map aright.

When one sees a gathering storm likely to develop into thick mist, he should at once take a compass bearing of the direction in which his route lies, be it to a hill-top, pass, or inn. If this is got, it simplifies matters greatly, for no consultation of map nor allowance for compass variation is necessary. When once one is in the mist, if the ground is not covered with snow, there will generally be some objects, such as projecting or peculiarly shaped or coloured stones, tufts of grass or heather, visible, according to the density of the mist, within either a radius of a few yards, or of a much greater distance. Lay your course by compass, and try to pick up three objects in line in the direction you want to go. Before you pass the first, pick up another still farther ahead. This is soon done unconsciously, and thus a fairly straight course can be steered with only a glance at the compass every five to fifteen minutes or so.

If the ground be under snow, it increases the difficulties of the situation, for often it is absolutely impossible to distinguish anything ahead. When the mist in the air and the snow on the ground blend in colour, as they often do, then the bewilderment is excessive, and it is often even impossible to see whether the ground ahead is rising or falling, so that one gets many surprises as his foot reaches the ground too soon or too late. Generally, one can tell when he comes to the edge of a precipice, for the different colour of the void space is quite perceptible, and if one is constantly on the *qui vive* there is little danger of his walking over it. When these conditions prevail it is best to rope up, and then the man in the rear becomes the steersman, for the track ahead of him to the man in front gives a fairly good idea of the straightness of the course taken.

When one has had no previous acquaintance with the country that he intends to cross, or with the mountain he wishes to climb, and since his arrival at his base everything has been shrouded in mist so that no clear view of the route has been had, then the art of steering by compass and map can be practised in its entirety.

First, one must know how much to allow for the variation of the compass, which, for our Scottish hills, may be roughly averaged at 18° W. of N. It is well to put a little mark on the compass card at this point (just a shade N. of NNW), and when the needle points to this

---

[1] *SMCJ* 1907, IX, 248-251.

mark, then the card and map are in agreement; if, however, the compass card revolves along with the needle, as many cards do, you will not be able to take advantage of this plan. Next look over the map for distinctive landmarks, such as streams, junction of streams, cols, tops, bridges, and such like things; roughly estimate the time one should take between each, and look out for them when they are due. Tick each off as they appear, and in this way you know exactly where you are and never lose touch of the route. Without taking infinite care, one is certain to go wrong. If all our members were to tell of their experiences in mist, I think few could boast of not being wandered occasionally.

I remember a most laughable incident occurring at our last Ballachulish Meet. A party of half-a-dozen of us, including the President and other old members, of which I was one, attempted to make the round of Beinn a' Bheithir in thick mist. Well, we reached the east top successfully, and also had no difficulty in finding the top of the highest peak. From here we had to round a deep corrie to reach the next top to the east of us. Away we went gaily down the ridge and duly turned at the correct spot, and after going steady for some time, found ourselves at a cairn. It had been snowing all the time and no tracks were visible, but our President was uneasy, and insisted that we were back again at the peak we had left more than an hour before. We scouted the idea, but he soon convinced us that he was right by unearthing the lunch papers we had buried before leaving the top. Moral:– In mist, with a large party, always see that one man is appointed to keep the course, and make him responsible. We did this now, and had not the slightest difficulty in getting to the west top (Sgorr Bhan),[2] and so back to Ballachulish.

Mr Goggs has given us an explanation of his mysterious night's wandering about the head of Glen Lyon,[3] and Mr Corner also has attempted to explain how he found himself at Braemar instead of Glen Shee.[4]

I have often steered a good course in mist, but I well remember the first which gave me the necessary confidence. Many years ago, when at Aviemore, a friend and I started for Ben Macdhui, a mountain then new to both of us. The mist was thick all day, and down almost to Rothiemurchus Forest. We found the group of cairns on the top without much difficulty, and got home again without once missing the slight landmarks we had marked down on the map. We were some eight hours in the mist on that occasion.

Another memorable bit of compass work was done in the company of Mr Naismith. We left Rosthwaite, ascended Grain Gill, found the central gully on Great End, climbed it, crossed Scafell Pike, picked up Mickledore, climbed the North Climb, [Scafell] Pillar and Scafell, descended Deep Gill to Wastdalehead in dense mist the whole day, without either of us having been on these hills before.[5]

---

[2] Since Sgorr Bhan is the *east* top of Beinn a' Bheithir and Sgorr Dhonuill (presumably their first summit) is its *west* top, Douglas and his party certainly deserved to get lost. One must also deplore the leaving of lunch papers in the cairn. This expedition does not show the SMC in a very creditable light.

[3] See Chapter 7.3

[4] See Chapter 7.4

[5] This visit to the Lake District is described by W. Naismith in *SMCJ* 1896, IV, 175.

Since then I have often steered a good course, and I have often been 'wandered' off into some side valley. When this occurred, I have had only myself to blame, for it has been always due to carelessness in reading the map or compass; and that carelessness is often excusable to oneself, for when blizzards are blowing, rain descending, and fingers wet and cold, one is very apt to scamp these operations and trust to the uncertain shifts of the wind for a guide. When once one has lost touch of his landmarks, it is very difficult to pick them up again, and one has then to walk boldly in the faith of the compass, with an uncomfortable feeling all the time that something is wrong somewhere.

The chief point to remember is, to keep in touch with all the outstanding landmarks *en route*, and that is only done by frequently consulting the map, the watch, and the compass. The aneroid is a useful adjunct, but is not absolutely necessary. Tick the points off as they are passed. I remember, in Arran, telling two unbelieving friends of mine, after we had been groping our way in dense mist for a couple of hours, that we were not far off a well with a cairn of stones. When we reached this a few minutes later, they had unbounded confidence in their guide. Don't trust too much to the wind as a guide, for it is apt to change, and don't walk too long without checking the direction with the compass, and timing the distances between points by the watch, and you will not go far wrong.

Bidein a' Ghlas Thuill from the north

6.6 On the Height of Some of the Black Cuchullins in Skye

J. Norman Collie[1]

DURING the last ten years the Cuchullin Hills in Skye, even in spite of the rain and mist of the West Coast of Scotland, have been steadily acquiring a reputation as a district where some of the best rock climbing in the British Isles can be obtained. Descriptions of them have appeared in the Alpine Club Journal, and their attractions have been set forth at length. Still, after all, the district is small, and all the peaks have been ascended; the rugged ridge can be climbed from one end to the other, and the mountaineer will not find much left undone. Although, however, there are no new peaks to conquer, the Ordnance maps still remain; and should anyone seek for information whilst actually on the hills from, let us say the one-inch map (printed May 1885), problems more difficult to solve than the ascents of many of the dark weather-worn pinnacles of rock are often found, and one must certainly possess that faith which is said to be able to remove mountains, before a proper understanding of this map can be obtained which harmonises with the environment.

There are, however, later editions, especially the revised map of six inches to the mile (printed in 1887),which are more correct, yet even in this map we are left in entire ignorance of the heights of most of the hills.[2] Out of the seven highest summits Sgurr Dearg alone has been able to inveigle the surveyor to climb its misty brow; and out of about thirty-three separate peaks amongst the Black Cuchullins, the heights of only eleven have been measured. It was for this reason, therefore, that I began six years ago to try to determine the heights of the various summits omitted by the Ordnance Survey. With the aid of an ordinary aneroid barometer, I soon began to collect some really startling results.

The first was, that all measured heights on the map were quite wrong. This did not much surprise me. But when a few days later I took another series of observations on the same peaks, and found that, after all, the hills on that day were about the same height as when they had been measured years before by the Survey, I was reluctantly forced to conclude that either there had been a fall in the heights of hills, or else my aneroid measurements were untrustworthy. This latter seemed the more probable, for on two

---

[1] *SMCJ* 1893, II, 168-173.

[2] Mr C. Pilkington has produced an excellent map of the Cuchullins, which can be obtained from John Heywood & Co., Deansgate, Manchester. Post free, 6d. —JNC

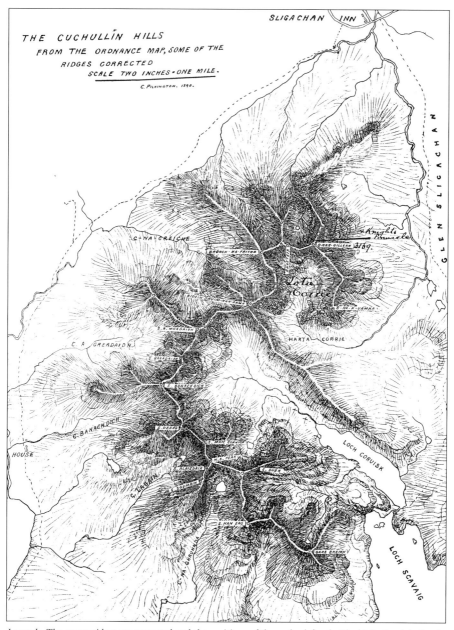

THE CUCHULLIN HILLS
FROM THE ORDNANCE MAP, SOME OF THE
RIDGES CORRECTED
SCALE TWO INCHES = ONE MILE.
C. PILKINGTON. 1890.

Legend: The upper ridges are corrected and the positions of the peaks defined. The highest point of each mountain is at the beginning or end of each name. Bidein-Druim-nan-Ramh has three peaks; the central one is the highest. Mhadaidh has four peaks; the one on the junction of the ridges is the highest. N.E. Peak, Sgurr Alaisdair and Sgurr Sgumain are the three peaks forming the Alaisdair group, and are known collectively as Sgurr Alaisdair. The mountain at the junction of the Sgurr Dubh ridge seems to have no name. The map is rough and incomplete; notes and drawings of corrections will be gladly received by the Scottish Mountaineering Club, or by me. C. Pilkington

separate days, after having carefully set the aneroid before starting in the morning, on my return in the evening the whole of Sligachan Inn was found, according to the aneroid, on one occasion below sea-level, whilst on the next occasion it appeared to be elevated in the air to the dizzy height of over one hundred feet. Obviously there was something wrong; was it the aneroid, or was it something else? I soon came to the conclusion it was something else, for unless the atmospheric pressure remained constant during the whole day, the results I obtained were just what were to be expected — and also the West Coast is exactly the place where the barometer never remains stationary for any lengthy period. Aneroids also, as Mr Whymper has recently shown in a most conclusive manner, at high altitudes rapidly lose on the ordinary mercurial barometer, and that on descending they do not at once return to their normal condition. But as 3,300 feet is the limit of height on the Cuchullin hills which has to be measured, this source of error could not be a very large one. In order therefore to obtain observations which were to be at all reliable, two things were necessary, a steady barometer during the whole time a set of consecutive measurements were being taken, and also a reliable aneroid. I was certain of neither of these two requirements; but by measuring the hills from their tops, and checking the results so obtained by the existing measurements in the Ordnance Survey, a near approximation to the truth could be obtained.

To take an example. I wished to measure the height of the Basteir Tooth at the head of the corrie looking down to Sligachan Inn. Having climbed Sgurr nan Gillean, and setting my barometer at 3,167 feet, the measured height in the Ordnance Survey map, I then climbed along the ridge to the summit of the tooth; the aneroid then marked 3,030 feet. On continuing the climb to the summit of Bruach na Frithe, I found the height of that mountain to be 3,140 feet; and as the Ordnance height is 3,143 feet I concluded that during the couple of hours which I had taken to go from Sgurr nan Gillean to Bruach na Frithe the barometric pressure at sealevel had remained constant; and also, as the greatest ascents or descents were small, both the sources of error, namely a changing atmospheric pressure and a faulty aneroid, were reduced to a minimum, and I therefore took 3,030 feet as the height of the Basteir tooth.

By this method the heights measured on the ridge of the Cuchullin hills, either up or down, rarely exceeded 500 feet; and as the time taken between the measurements was short any rise or fall in atmospheric pressure at sea-level would hardly have time to affect the readings to any great extent, and also any change would be at once noticed by the observed heights not agreeing with those of the Survey. The heights were also checked by means of the clinometer whenever it was possible. By using the clinometer on the summit of the Inaccessible peak, Sgurr Alaisdair appeared to be about twenty feet higher. The observations made with the aneroid corroborated this, for the Inaccessible peak was found to be 3,255 feet, and Sgurr Alaisdair 3,275 feet.

All the heights therefore given in this paper *are calculated from the observed Ordnance heights*, which are taken as being correct to start with, and in no case are they measured by the aneroid from sea-level. They are, in fact, merely a set of differences measured from the top of one peak to the top of the next.

Sgurr nan Gillean	3,167*[3]	Bealach Coire na Banachdich	2,810
Bealach [to Pinnacles]	2,920	Sgurr Dearg	3,234*
1st Pinnacle [=Knight's]	3,000	Inaccessible peak	3,255
2nd Pinnacle [=3rd Pinnacle]	2,920	Bealach	2,690
Basteir Tooth	3,030	Sgurr Mhic Coinnich	3,180
Bealach a' Leitir	2,700	Sgurr Alaisdair, East peak[6]	3,230
Bruach na Frithe	3,143*	Dip between East and West peak	3,050
Bealach at head of Coir' a' Mhadaidh	2,520	Sgurr Alaisdair, West peak	3,275
Pinnacle [An Caisteal?]	2,740	Dip between Sgurr Alaisdair and Sgurr Sgumain	3,050
Lowest point on ridge	2,520		
1st Summit, Bidein Druim nan Ramh	2,820	Sgurr Sgumain	3,104*
Dip between 1st and 2nd Summit	2,730	Bealach between Sgurr Alaisdair and Sgurr Dubh	2,810
2nd Summit, Bidein Druim nan Ramh	2,860		
Dip between 2nd and 3rd Summit	2,750	1st Summit, Sgurr Dubh[7]	3,090
3rd Summit, Bidein Druim nan Ramh	2,810	Dip between 1st and 2nd Summits	2,900
Bealach na Glaic Moire	2,510	2nd Summit, Sgurr Dubh[8]	3,120
1st Summit Sgurr a' Mhadaidh	2,925[4]	Pinnacle (on main ridge)	2,740
2nd Summit Sgurr a' Mhadaidh	2,880	Bealach a' Gharbh Choire	2,620
Dip between 2nd and 3rd Summit	2,820	Sgurr nan Eag	3,020
3rd Summit Sgurr a' Mhadaidh	2,910	Bealach	2,550
4th Summit Sgurr a' Mhadaidh	2,920	Summit on ridge	2,870
Bealach	2,760	Bealach	2,750
An Dorus	2,890	Garsbheinn	2,934*
1st Summit, Sgurr a' Ghreadaidh	3,190	Blath Bheinn	3,042*
2nd Summit, Sgurr a' Ghreadaidh	3,180	Bealach	2,310
Bealach	2,800	Clac Glas	2,590
Pinnacle on ridge[5]	3,040	Bealach	2,080
Bealach	2,920	1st Summit of Sgurr nan Each	2,360
1st Summit of Sgurr na Banachdich	3,167*	2nd Summit of Sgurr nan Each	2,400
Dip between 1st and 2nd Summit	3,020	Bealach	2,090
2nd Summit of Sgurr na Banachdich	3,100	Garbh bheinn	2,649*

[3] Those heights which are marked with an asterisk are the Ordnance Survey heights. —JNC

[4] Notice that no top of Sgurr a' Mhadaidh is measured higher than 3000 feet – it did not appear even as a Top in the 1891 Tables – and that what Collie calls the 1st Summit is reckoned to be the highest. Subsequent members' aneroid heights settled on the values, proceeding westwards, of 2925, 2880, 2910 and 3020 feet (List of Cuillin peaks prepared by W. Douglas, *SMCJ* 1897, IV, 209-213). However, it was not until 1904 that heights were produced by the O.S. – East peak (Collie's 1st Summit) 2970 feet; West peak (Collie's 4th) 3014 feet. —RNC

[5] *i.e.* Sgurr Thormaid. —RNC

[6] *i.e.* Sgurr Thearlaich. —RNC

[7] *i.e.* Sgurr Dubh an Da Bheinn. —RNC

[8] *i.e.* Sgurr Dubh Mor. —RNC

From these measurements it will be seen that Sgurr Alaisdair is the highest hill in the Cuchullins; next comes the Inaccessible peak, the true top of Sgurr Dearg; the third in height is Sgurr a' Ghreadaidh; probably Sgurr Mhic Coinnich is fourth; and Sgurr Banachdich and Sgurr nan Gillean are equal for fifth place. Although I do not claim great accuracy for these measurements, still in the two cases of the comparative heights of Sgurr Alaisdair and the Inaccessible peak, and also of Sgurr Banachdich and Sgurr a' Ghreadaidh, I am sure that the heights are nearly correct, for they were very carefully checked by the clinometer. Perhaps before concluding the note on the Cuchullin hills, it would not be out of place to give a few directions dealing with the best routes to be followed on one or two parts of the ridge, where a great deal of time might be wasted by any one who had not the necessary local knowledge.

Sgurr nan Gillean and the four pinnacles.

One of the most interesting ascents of Sgurr nan Gillean is to climb on to the lowest or fourth pinnacle from the Basteir corrie, and thence over the four pinnacles to the summit. On this route there is a drop, after passing the top of the second highest pinnacle, into a small gully, which faces the first pinnacle (the one next Sgurr nan Gillean). The descent into this gully is on the right hand side at the top looking in the direction of the first pinnacle.

All the gullies leading from Coir' a' Basteir up between these pinnacles can be climbed, with the exception of the one between the second and third pinnacle. The faces of the pinnacles themselves also afford excellent rock climbing.

The Pinnacle Ridge of Sgurr nan Gillean. The highest pinnacle, Knight's Peak, was promoted to a Top in the 1997 revision of the Tables

Basteir Tooth.

In traversing the Basteir Tooth from Sgurr nan Gillean to Bruach na Frithe there is a drop immediately on the west side of the summit; the route continues down on the Lota corrie face till a lower point is reached, where a cairn can be seen on the top of a smooth sloping face of rock, from here descend diagonally across the Lota corrie face (in the direction of Sgurr nan Gillean) till it is possible to climb down on to the loose stones at the bottom of the precipice. This point is from 200 to 300 feet below the top of Bealach a' Leitir.

The ridge from Bruach na Frithe to Sgurr a' Mhadaidh.

In traversing this part of the ridge it is better to go westward, for owing to the lie of the rocks the way is easier to find when going in this direction than when the route is reversed.

The ridge from Sgurr Mhic Coinnich to Sgurr Alaisdair.

Directly beyond the peak of Sgurr Mhic Coinnich on the south side there is a very precipitous drop. This can be turned by descending on the Corrie Labain side just before reaching the summit of Sgurr Mhic Coinnich and then keeping to the left till the bealach is reached.

The ridge between Sgurr Alaisdair and Sgurr Dubh.

If the ridge from the east peak of Sgurr Alaisdair be followed in a southern direction a difficult piece of climbing will be met with, where it is necessary to descend into a narrow cleft in the ridge; this is probably not possible without a rope. After descending into the cleft the opposite perpendicular side has to be climbed, and the hand and foot hold will be found somewhat scanty. It is not necessary, however, to traverse this part of the ridge, for by descending from Sgurr Alaisdair to the dip between it and Sgurr Sgumain, an easier route can be found.

There are several facts which a climber in the Cuchullin hills will find useful to remember. One of the most important is that once on the ridge no water can be obtained, except from rain pools, and there are not many of these to be found.

Another is that very often the descent into the corrie below is by no means so easy as it looks, and it is always best to travel along the ridge till a bealach is reached and then to descend. More than once I have started down from the ridge and found no difficulty for the first 300 or 400 feet, then the angle began to increase in steepness, and finally the face became almost perpendicular from smooth slabs of rock which sloped down at an impossible angle and quite stopped farther progress.

And lastly a rope should always be taken, for although it is not often necessary whilst traversing the ridge, still there are many spots where a dyke has weathered away, or smooth sloping slabs of rock make the use of the rope often, very desirable, and time and security will both be gained.

"WE HAD ALWAYS WANTED TO DO THE DUBHS."
-A. E. Maylard.

I.

Said Maylard to Solly, one day in Glen Brittle,
"All serious climbing, I vote, is a bore;
Just for once I Dubh Bheag you'll agree to do little,
And, as less we can't do, let's go straight to Dubh Mhor."

II.

So now, when they seek but a day's relaxation,
With no thought in the world but of viewing the views,
And regarding the mountains in mute adoration,
They call it not "climbing" but "doing the Dubhs."

These clever verses first appeared on the reverse of the SMC's Annual Dinner Menu, 1st December 1905, and were later published in the Guidebook to Skye (1907, Volume IX, 353), written by Willie Douglas. This excellent guidebook was the basis of the SMC guidebook by E.W. Steeple and G. Barlow, published in 1923, and the verses appeared there too. So far as I know, their last appearance was in W.M. Mackenzie's Climber's Guide to Skye (1958). The excursion to which the verses refer is Ernest Maylard's 'Only a Beautiful Day on the Hills' (SMCJ 1905, VIII, 299). Douglas says the verses were written by 'the Club's poetaster'. This uncommon word is given in Chambers' dictionary as 'a petty poet; a writer of contemptible verses'. Since this is slanderous, and Douglas was a publisher, my suspicion is that Douglas wrote the verses himself!

6.7 Aneroid Barometers

J. Gall Inglis[1]

EVERYONE who carries an aneroid must have noticed how rarely the barometer reading at the top of a mountain corresponds with the Ordnance Survey figures, the discrepancy being frequently 150 feet or more. The whole of this discrepancy, however, may be due not to a faulty instrument, but simply to the temperature conditions under which the reading is taken. Cold air is heavier than warm air, with the result that in summer more than 1,000 feet of air must be traversed vertically to produce the same alteration on the height of the barometer that 1,000 feet does in winter.

Aneroids are graduated in accordance with a table calculated by the late Sir George Airy, which shows the height corresponding to any reading of the barometer in inches, assuming sea-level to be 31 inches, and the mean temperature of the intervening air 50° Fahr. This latter figure represents the average temperature throughout the year, but the heights given in the table are too high in frosty weather and too low in very warm weather by 30 feet per 1,000 feet of rise, or even more.

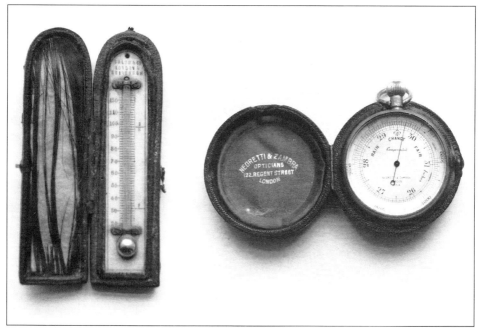

Hugh Munro's Thermometer and Aneroid Barometer

---

[1] *SMCJ* 1907, IX, 243-247. This extraordinary exposition of the difficulties of determining mountain heights using aneroids make the enterprise seem almost impossible. It is worth bearing in mind, however, that most of the heights 'determined' by the pioneers using these methods turned out to be more correct than the mapped heights obtained by triangulation and levelling.

The temperature error, however, which is common to both mercurial and aneroid barometers, may be eliminated as follows, according to Airy's table:–

Add together the temperatures at the upper and lower station. If this sum, in degrees of Fahrenheit, is greater than 100°, *increase* the height by 1/1000 part for every degree of the excess above 100°F.; if the sum is less than 100°, *diminish* the height by 1/1000 part for every degree of the defect from 100°.

For ordinary mountaineering this rule is useless, as simultaneous readings at the foot and at the summit are of course out of the question, but, fortunately, there are means available for obtaining a fairly reliable approximation to them. The Ben Nevis Observatory records show that the difference in temperature between the top of a hill and sea-level is nearly constant, except under abnormal conditions, and that on the average the temperature of the air decreases by about 1°F. for each 275 feet of rise, or 3.6°F. per 1,000 feet. The amount varies slightly according to the season of the year, but the mean variation from the average does not exceed 2°F. on either side, or 12.5 per cent.

	Mean Difference about	Rise per 1° Fall of Temp	Fall in Temp. per 1000ft. Rise
March to May	18°F.	244ft	4.1°F.
June to October	16°	275ft	3.6°
November to February	14°	313ft	3.1°

Knowing, then, that on the top of a mountain, say 3,000 feet high, the temperature will be about 3.6° x 3 = 10.8° lower than at sea-level; to correct for temperature in accordance with Airy's rule, it is only necessary to double the temperature at the time of observation, add 10.8°, and then subtract from 100°, which will give approximately the number of feet to add or deduct per 1,000 feet of rise. Similarly for other heights as in the following table, which gives the winter and spring figures also for the sake of comparison. As the large March-June difference, however, is believed to be due to the cooling effect of the unmelted snowfields, the spring figures should probably be only utilised for the highest mountains, on which the snow lies long, and in considerable quantity.

	Fall in Temperature in °F.		
Rise in Feet	Nov-Feb	Mar-May	Jun-Oct
250	0.75	1.00	1.00
500	1.50	2.00	1.75
1,000	3.00	4.00	3.50
1,500	4.75	6.25	5.50
2,000	6.25	8.25	7.25
2,500	7.75	10.25	9.00
3,000	9.25	12.25	10.75
3,500	11.00	14.50	12.50
4,000	12.50	16.50	14.50
4.407	14.00	18.00	16.00

It is evident from the above table that the higher the altitude of the 'lower station' can be arranged for, the less is the error due to temperature.

The following table, calculated on this basis for a mountain 3,000 feet high, and taking the round number of 10° as the difference in temperature, will give a good idea of the influence of temperature on the readings at different seasons of the year. It will be noticed that in ordinary frosty weather the temperature error for 3,000 feet is about 100 feet, so that in winter climbers nearing the top must expect to have another 100 feet more to climb than the aneroid indicates.

Shade temperature (°F.)
at Time of Observation.

70	Add to aneroid reading 50ft. per 1,000ft. of rise = 150ft.
60	Add to aneroid reading 30ft. per 1,000ft. of rise = 90ft.
50	Add to aneroid reading 10ft. per 1,000ft. of rise = 30ft.
45	Correct
40	Deduct from aneroid reading 10ft. per 1,000ft. of rise = 150ft.
35	Deduct from aneroid reading 20ft. per 1,000ft. of rise = 30ft.
30	Deduct from aneroid reading 30ft. per 1,000ft. of rise = 90ft.
25	Deduct from aneroid reading 40ft. per 1,000ft. of rise = 120ft.
20	Deduct from aneroid reading 50ft. per 1,000ft. of rise = 150ft.

Another source of considerable error is present in those convenient aneroids which have the scale of feet movable with respect to the 'inches' scale. Unfortunately, convenience is obtained at the price of accuracy. The movable scale is graduated in accordance with Airy's table, and when set with '0' at 31 inches will be found to read as follows with respect to the 'inches' scale:–

Sea-level	corresponds to	31.000in. –	Fall for 1000ft. of rise
1000ft.		29.883	1.117in.
2000ft.		28.807	1.076
3000ft.		27.769	1.038
4000ft.		26.769	1.000
5000ft.		25.804	0.965

Readings of 31 inches at sea-level, however, are almost unknown, the average reading being usually reckoned as 29.92 inches. Hence the zero of the shifting scale has to be moved round to 29.92 on the average, or more than an inch, when setting for sea-level, while with a very low barometer it might even be to 29.00. Let us see the result, using the figures in the above table for convenience:–

At sea-level	31.000in.	29.883in.	28.807in.
At 3,000ft. the barometer would stand at	27.769	26.769	25.804
Fall for 3,000ft.	3.231	3.114	3.003

Now as 3,000 feet on the shifting scale is graduated to the equivalent of a fall of 3.231 inches, it is evident that, when the barometer stands below 31 inches, the aneroid must register less than 3,000 feet if the zero of the scale is set accordingly at starting. With the average sea-level reading the aneroid will only register 2,883 feet at 3,000 feet (*i.e.*, 117 feet too low, one tenth of an inch corresponding to about 100 feet), while with a reading of 28.807 at starting it will only register 2,772 feet.

But this is not all. If the dial of an aneroid is examined, it will be noticed that, as a rule, the arc representing 1 inch of mercury gradually decreases in length as the barometer falls, to suit the exigencies of the mechanism. Thus, in addition to the above-mentioned error, there is superadded a second one, due to the large divisions of the scale being shifted round to where there should be shorter divisions.

From the above considerations it will be seen that, where reliable observations of altitudes are desired, the zero from which the barometer is graduated must not be moved. Also, account must be taken of the temperature conditions. It is a curious fact, however, that the 'shifting scale' error compensates the temperature correction fairly well in frosty weather.

In addition to these errors which can be eliminated, there is also another error which cannot be provided against with certainty, being caused by a mechanical defect inherent in the aneroid principle. Every one who has read his aneroid on reaching the top, and then read it again after a few minutes, even, must have remarked that the second reading always gives a height greater than the first. This discrepancy is due to the fact that, as Whymper's observations have proved, aneroid barometers when moved from one level to another always take some time before they adjust themselves permanently to the altered conditions. A special form of aneroid barometer by Watkins, which is 'turned on' every time a reading is taken, claims to have practically obviated this inaccuracy; it is, however, rather bulky for ordinary mountaineering purposes, being about 3 inches in diameter and 2.5 inches thick, though quite light for its size.

This aneroidal error, as it may be termed, is rather important, and very complex, but I may deal with it more fully in another paper in a later number of the *Journal*.

6.8 The Height of Slioch

J.A. Parker[1]

THERE has always been some uncertainty as to whether the correct height of Slioch is 3,217 feet, as given on the 6-inch map, or 3,260 feet approximate, as given in Munro's Tables. With the object of settling the question, if possible, I climbed the hill last Easter and made a careful examination of the summit. My equipment included a $4^{1}/_2$-inch surveyor's aneroid, a 2-inch aneroid, an Abney reflecting level, and a tracing of the 6-inch ordnance map. The aneroids were carefully tested three days later, near Aberdeen, and were found to be working well; the $4^{1}/_2$-inch one being never more than 10 feet out on an ascent and descent of about 500 feet, with intermediate readings on three ordnance bench marks.

Slioch has two tops of almost equal height. The NNW top has a 6-foot cairn which stands almost at the edge of the steep, rocky north-west face of the hill. The second top, which bears about SSE from the other, is a rounded top and has a 3-foot cairn distant about 250 yards from the NNW cairn.

---

[1] *SMCJ* 1935, XX, 401-403. The position of the Munro top of Slioch has of course wandered to and fro between the points investigated by Parker (see Variorum Table).

The 6-inch map shows a cairn, with the level 3216.6 feet, near the edge of the rock-marking indicating the steep NW face of the hill. No other levels are given on the upper part of the hill, the nearest being that of 3058.4 feet on the summit of Sgurr an Tuill Bhain, about 1 mile to the east.

The 1-inch map also shows the cairn and 3,217-foot level at the edge of the NW slope, but, in addition, shows a small circular 3,250-foot contour about 250 yards ESE from the 3,217-foot cairn.

When Munro prepared his Tables in 1891 he adopted the height of '3,260 feet approximate' as being the height of the hill, giving as his reasons the 3,250-foot contour and a note by a Capt. Kirkwood, R.E., in the Visitors' Book at Kinlochewe, stating that the height of the hill was 3,260 feet. That book is not now in the hotel at Kinlochewe and I have therefore not been able to examine the entry.

Slioch from the south side of Loch Maree

Everyone who has climbed the hill must have noticed that the two tops were of almost equal height, but apparently the only entry in the *Journal* is that by Mr Vandeleur (Vol. XVIII, p. 97), stating that to him the two tops "appeared to be much of the same height". In the *Cairngorm Club Journal* for January 1906, Mr E.A. Baker stated that the 3,217-foot point was the "better point for the view", which could hardly have been the case were the other top 43 feet higher.

When I climbed the hill in 1918 I noticed that the two tops were of almost equal height and I therefore assumed that the 3,217-foot cairn must be some way down the steep north-west face, although that was a most unlikely position. My next ascent was in 1933 and I then noticed that from the NNW top I could see the horizon (the West Monar Hills) slightly above the skyline of the SSE top, which proved that the NNW top was the higher.

The doubtful point was, of course, whether or not the NNW top was actually the 3,217-foot point marked on the maps. This was the problem that I set out to solve last Easter.

I climbed the hill via the top of Sgurr an Tuill Bhain and descended by the same route. The aneroids were read in both directions, *i.e.*, from the Sgurr to the NNW top and back again. The 4½-inch aneroid gave differences of level of 150 feet (going up) and 160 feet (coming down), the mean of which added to the height of the Sgurr (3,058 feet) gave the height of the NNW top as being 3,213 feet. The smaller aneroid made it 3,228 feet. These readings proved that the NNW top was actually the 3,217-foot Ordnance Survey point, and this was confirmed by comparing the position of the cairn with the features shown on the 6-inch map.

From the NNW cairn I again saw the distant horizon slightly above the profile of the SSE top (by about 6 feet), and the line of sight through the Abney level passed above the SSE top by about the same amount, my note being 'by about twice the height of the cairn'. The 4½-inch aneroid showed that the SSE top was just a little lower than the NNW one. Looking back from the SSE top the line of sight through the Abney level struck the solid of the NNE top about 9 feet (one and a half times the height of the cairn) below its profile, thus proving that the NNW top was distinctly higher. The 4½-inch aneroid again confirmed, but no horizon observation was possible as the distant hills were clouded over.

My operations from and to the Sgurr occupied almost two hours, during which the barometer was steady. The air temperature would not affect the aneroid readings as the vertical height measured was only 159 feet. The Abney level had been carefully set for the horizontal position on the shore of Loch Maree and was verified after the descent.

The only possible conclusions to be drawn from the above are: that the NNW top is the 3,217-foot ordnance point; that it is the highest summit of Slioch; that the SSE. top is distinctly lower (probably by as much as 5 feet), and that the 3,250-foot contour and 3,260-foot height are not justified by the facts.

In view of the above, I sent a fully detailed report to the Director-General of the Ordnance Survey, and suggested that the 3,250-foot contour should be deleted from future reprints of the 1-inch map. In reply he stated that the whole matter had been investigated and that the contour would be deleted.[2]

---

[2] It may be of interest to the reader to know that the currently accepted heights of the two summit points of Slioch are :- NNW Top 981m (3218ft) and SSE Top 980m (3215ft).

6.9 Aneroids and Munros

J. Rooke Corbett[1]

THE PRACTICE of carrying a pocket aneroid is one to be recommended to all wanderers on the hills. It is a great help in route-finding, and a record of its readings makes an interesting addition to one's diary. When rambling alone I generally keep such a record, partly for future reference, but mainly because, being very careless in compass reading, I often lose my way, and I find it a great help when this has happened to have an exact note of where I was half an hour before, and what the barometer said, whether it overstated or understated the height.

Now for route-finding, when all one wants is to know which is the nearest 250-feet contour line on Bartholomew's map, the pocket aneroid is good enough, but when an attempt is made to determine the exact height of a mountain there are many possible sources of error which may arise. A glance through the footnotes of Munro's tables will show how great differences may arise in the determination of the height of a top by this means.

Let us consider some of these sources of error. First of all, there are those which arise from the carelessness of the observer.

1. It is possible to misread the instrument. The best check on this is to have several observations taken, if possible by different observers or on different instruments.

2. If the instrument has a sliding scale, it is possible to set it incorrectly. A good check on this is to take readings at several points whose heights are already known. It is, however, better not to alter the setting if a discrepancy arises, as part of the discrepancy may be due to some other cause, and any alteration of the setting causes confusion.

3. If the instrument has a sliding scale the scale may slip. This is less likely to happen if the instrument is kept in its case than if it is carried loose in the pocket, but the safe check is to notice the reading at sea-level on the fixed scale and verify this every time a reading is taken.

4. A certain amount of arithmetic is required in deducing the actual height from the aneroid reading whether the scale is fixed or sliding. It is possible to do this arithmetic wrong. If a note is taken of the readings, the crude readings should be recorded so that the arithmetic may be checked afterwards at home.

Then there is another group of errors for which the weather is responsible. The barometer does not really measure altitude. It measures air pressure. It is only when the pressure diminishes uniformly with the altitude that the altitude can be inferred from the barometer readings.

---

[1] *SMCJ* 1932, XIX, 324-332.

J. Rooke Corbett

5. The barometer may rise or fall during the day. This can be checked in the same way as error No. 2. It is also a good practice to return later in the day and take a second reading at the place where the barometer was set. In fact, without this check the readings are almost valueless.

    It is quite unsafe to assume because the weather is fine that the barometer is steady. One of the finest days I had in Scotland last summer was 27th May. I spent two hours on the top of Beinn nan Ramh basking in the sun and enjoying the view of the Kinlochewe Hills, and all the time the barometer was going down at the rate of about 40 feet per hour.

6. The difference in pressure due to a change in altitude varies with the temperature. If the air is cold it will be more dense and the barometer will therefore exaggerate heights. If the air is warm the barometer will understate the height. A table for correcting this is given on p. 107 of the *General Section of the Guide Book* but I do not think much use is made of it in practice. When aneroid readings have been published in the *Journal* this question has generally been ignored.

7. When a wind is blowing there is also the possibility of eddies being formed round a hill, which would give rise to local variations of pressure.

Finally, there are the errors due to the instrument itself.

8. If the barometer has a sliding scale, it will only give correct readings for one barometric height. This is due to the fact that 1,000 feet of air weighs less when the pressure is low than when it is high. If the standard barometric height of the instrument is known, this error may be eliminated by keeping the scale set to that height and using the instrument as a 'fixed scale' barometer.

9. The barometer may be of faulty construction, may be in need of cleaning, or may have suffered from strain or shock. The operative part of an aneroid is a very delicate spring, and if it is taken up the mountains too often a permanent deformation will set in sooner or later. It is, moreover, very sensitive to ill-treatment. The story of the gentleman who accidentally dropped his aneroid on top of Scafell Pike and found, when he picked it up again, that the height of Scafell Pike was 16,000 feet is probably apocryphal, but it points a moral.

    If accurate results are desired, a uniform practice should be adopted when reading the aneroid. The best procedure is to hold it horizontal, tap it gently, and take the reading through a magnifying glass.

Even when cared for like a baby the aneroid is still liable to a serious fault.

10. The aneroid after being taken up a hill does not always reach its final level at once. There is a time lag. The plan usually recommended for dealing with this is to read the aneroid at once on arriving at the point of observation. This works fairly well if one is walking continuously uphill, but in Scotland one usually rises fairly rapidly to about 3,000 or 3,500 feet and then wanders about at approximately the same level. The barometer may give a correct reading when one first arrives at the high level, but will then go on falling and give exaggerated measurements of height.

A good example of this phenomenon is described by J. Gall Inglis on p. 85 of Vol. XIX. of the *Journal*.

I suspect that this last peculiarity of the aneroid may have helped some of the less elevated Munros into the Tables. Take, for example, the case of Meall na Teanga. The height is given in the Tables as 3,050 feet, but the Ordnance Map shows it as between 2,950 and 3,000 feet. I have never been able to make out exactly what happened when the height was fixed at 3,050 feet, but I guess that some one took an aneroid up Meall Coire Lochain, set it on that top at the O.S. height, 2,971 feet, and then went on to Meall na Teanga and registered a further 79 feet of rise, most of which was really time lag. I know that when I was on these tops I took Meall na Teanga first, and my aneroid did not show any change at all in descending to 2,971 feet. Of course in my case the time lag would be acting the other way. I do not doubt that Meall na Teanga is really higher than Meall Coire Lochain. Whether it is really above 3,000 feet is another question. If the estimate of 3,012 feet given in the new Guide Book is correct, the barometer trusted by Sir Hugh Munro must have lost 38 feet and mine must have lost 41 feet.

The procedure recommended as a check on error No. 2 does, in fact, act as a check on most of the above-mentioned errors, and even provides a means of correcting them to some extent.

Let me illustrate this by a few extracts from my notebook. On 20th May 1931 I set out from Kinlochewe, cycled up Gleann na Muice to the fork of the path 2 miles beyond the Heights, ascended Mullach Coire Mhic Fhearchair by the east ridge, traversed over Sgurr Ban on to Beinn a' Chlaidheimh, and returned by Bealach na Croise to my bicycle and to Kinlochewe. The readings were as follows:–

9.09 a.m. –Barometer set at 90 feet at Kinlochewe.

10.14 a.m. –860. Fork of paths.

12.20 p.m. –3,000. Rocky pinnacle $^{11}/_{16}$ of a mile ESE from Mullach Coire Mhic Fhearchair.

12.37 p.m. –2,900. Col.

12.50 p.m. –3,310. Very small cairn on grassy top about $^{3}/_{8}$ of a mile ESE from M.C.M.F.

1 p.m. –3,210. Col.

1.10 p.m. –3,470. Top of M.C.M.F. (O.S. height, 3,326.)

1.35 p.m. –3,475. Same place. This means that the time lag was negligible. I cannot really read this scale to 5 feet.

1.55 p.m. –2,800. Col.

2.10 p.m. –3,410. Top of Sgurr Ban. This was in the 3,200 feet contour ring, 150 yards SW of the cairn.

2.14 p.m. –3,340. Cairn. (O.S. height, 3,194.) There was obviously something wrong here. A drop of 70 feet in 150 yards is a gradient of 1 in 6.5, but the gradient was not more than about 1 in 30. To add to the confusion, the top of Beinn Alligin[2] was visible right over the point where my aneroid said 3,410 feet. I went back to take the reading again, but got –

2.30 p.m. –3,410. That was the tale my aneroid had decided to tell, and it was sticking to it. I gave it up and went on to –

2.55 p.m. –2,160. Col.

3.37 p.m. –3,120. Top of Beinn a' Chlaidheimh.

The top of this mountain is drawn quite wrongly on the new 'Popular' Ordnance Map. The steep slopes, instead of stopping short at 2,800 feet, are continued upwards to a sharp ridge with several tops, of which the two southernmost are the highest.

3.42 p.m. –3,110. Second top with small cairn.

4.32 p.m. –3,120. Back at first top. Again no time lag. One of the worst troubles about this failing of the aneroid is that it is so unreliable. If it always occurred, one would know better what to do about it.

In the interests of science I ought to have returned over Sgurr Ban so as to obtain a further check on the barometer readings without too great an interval of time or height. A real hero would have gone across to Beinn a' Chlaidheimh and back to Sgurr Ban a second time, so as to have a still more perfect check on the doings of the barometer. But I thought the day's journey would be quite long enough without this, and so went by the easiest route to –

8.05 p.m. –970. Fork of paths. (860 at 10.14 a.m.)

8.45 p.m. –200. Kinlochewe.

Now let us see whether we can make any deductions from these figures. The day was fine and the visibility good, but there was a strong and cold east wind. Evidently errors No. 5 and 6 were in operation, probably also No. 7, and perhaps some of the others.

On the way up the aneroid recorded a rise of 3,470 – 90= 3,380 feet, when the actual rise was 3,326 – 90=3,236 feet. If this error was uniformly distributed over the whole ascent, a simple sum in proportion will show that the rocky pinnacle and the grassy top were respectively 450 and 153 feet below 3,326 feet, and their heights would be 2,876 and 3,173 feet.

On the way down, the aneroid recorded a drop of 3,475 – 200=3,275 feet, when the actual drop was 3,236 feet. A similar sum will show that the top of Beinn a' Chlaidheimh is 350 feet below 3,326, and is therefore 2,976 feet.

Or, if we start from the 3,194 point on Sgurr Ban, the barometer showed a drop of 3,140 feet when the actual drop was 3,104 feet. This would make the height of Beinn a' Chlaidheimh 218 feet less than 3,194, or 2,976 feet again.

---

[2] The 1921 height for Sgurr Mor was 3232 ft.

More complicated calculations on the basis that the fall of the barometer was at a uniform rate per hour and that the remaining errors were at a uniform rate per 1,000 feet of height would give results 10 or 20 feet lower.

These figures, of course, cannot be taken as accurate, but they are likely to be nearer to the truth than an uncorrected reading.

In trying to determine the exact height of a mountain from aneroid measurements, we are in the position of a magistrate who has to get at the facts of a case from one or more witnesses of very moderate veracity.

Sometimes there is a considerable degree of unanimity. In the case of Beinn Tarsuinn, for example, my pocket liar and Gall Inglis' coming down from Mullach Coire Mhic Fhearchair and Hirst's coming up from Lochan Fada all agreed at about 3,070 to 3,080 feet, while Parker's made it even higher.

On the other hand, the new Ordnance Map shows the height as between 2,850 and 2,900 feet, the SMC Guide Book gives it as 2,970 feet (on what authority does not appear), and on 16th May 1926 my pocket liar recorded Beinn Tarsuinn as 100 feet lower than A' Mhaighdean.

This brings to notice another point which should not be lost sight of in weighing up the evidence, and this is, that the evidence may not all be before us. When one obtains a reading like that, which does not disagree with the map or the Guide Book, it is, in the journalist's phrase, 'not news'. One does not write to the Journal about it. One is quite likely not to mention it to anybody, and in this particular case I forgot all about it myself, and only discovered it recently on turning up an old notebook.

In the case of Beinn Tarsuinn, however, there is better evidence of height available than any barometer reading, and that is the view to the south-west. If the mountain were no higher than is indicated on the Ordnance Map, this view would be bounded by the ridge of Slioch and Sgurr an Tuill Bhain. If Beinn Tarsuinn were exactly 3,000 feet high, the highest points of Beinn Eighe and Liathach would only just be visible from its summit, showing like small teeth above this ridge. As a matter of fact, a photograph taken from the top of Beinn Tarsuinn shows quite a lot of the ridge of Beinn Eighe.

Of the mountains mentioned by Burn in his notes in Vol. XV. of the *SMC Journal*,[3] the top in the Fannich group between Sgurr Breac and A' Chailleach is certainly over 3,000 feet, though hardly as high as the 3,131 feet given in his note. I had an interesting view of this top last May from Sgurr a' Choire-rainich, near Sgurr a' Mhuilinn. This top appears to be a little higher than Sgurr a' Ghlas Leathad (2,778 feet), but is below 2,800 feet. From it the top in the Fannichs is exactly in line with the highest points of An Teallach, which appear above it as two small teeth, almost too small to be distinguished except with a telescope.

Foinaven deserves further investigation. The cairn does not appear to be quite at the highest point, but when I was up there the weather was too thick for surveying.

---

[3] See Chapter 4.4

Carn Gorm-loch, in Strathvaich Forest, was registered at 2,910 feet by my aneroid, which had been set at 3,120 feet on Am Faochagach, but I think this reading is too low. In 1930 I had a very good view of these two mountains from Seana Bhraigh. Seen from here, they appear as two rounded hummocks standing up in front of the skyline of the Monadh Liath, and a calculation based on their comparative heights above this line made the height of Carn Gorm-loch 2,965 feet.

Among the Cluanie hills my aneroid agreed with Burn's that Faochag was below 3,000 feet, and that Gurr Thionail was 3,065 instead of 2,965 feet. One would, of course, want better evidence than an aneroid reading before saying that the Ordnance Map was wrong.

I should like to support most of Burn's proposals for the amendment of Munro's tables, especially the deletion of Sron a' Chadha and the inclusion of the Little Bynac.

Also, I think an amendment is needed on Beinn Heasgarnich. I traversed this mountain from south to north on 26th April 1930 in search of Stob an Fhir-Bhogha, and kept strictly to the ridge over several hummocks, but in no case did I drop as much as 50 feet until I reached the cairn at 3,530 feet. There is, however, a top farther north, shown on the 'Popular' Ordnance Map, for which my aneroid recorded a rise of 120 feet.

Note.– On 28th May 1931, when on A' Chailleach, I made another attempt to estimate the height of Beinn a' Chlaidheimh, by seeking out the viewpoint on the west side of A' Chailleach from which it was exactly in line with Beinn Dearg Mhor (2,974 feet), so that through a telescope the cairn on Beinn Dearg Mhor looked as though it were on the highest top of Beinn a' Chlaidheimh. I then tried to fix the height of this viewpoint, both by aneroid readings and by another method which may give more reliable results where short distances are concerned. This method is to note with the aid of the horizon (or of a pocket-level) a point or a level with one's eye, and then walk to this point and repeat the operation, counting how many times it has to take place in order to reach the top of the mountain. Then measure the height of your eye above your foot, and a simple multiplication sum will give the height of the summit above your starting-point.

By this method I made the viewpoint 190 feet below A' Chailleach cairn (3,276 feet), and computed the height of Beinn a' Chlaidheimh at 2,997 feet. The aneroid readings made the view-point a little lower.

6.10 Orientation

Harold Raeburn[1]

PERHAPS the most valuable part of mountaineering art is orientation, or pathfinding.

This by no means merely implies the simple and elementary pathfinding involved in finding one's way back by a route followed a few hours before. Though the guide's ability to do [this] used to fill Alpine pioneering amateurs with almost awe-struck admiration, [it] is the veriest ABC of orientation. Far from being an 'instinct' incapable of acquisition by anyone not born an Alpine peasant, this is simply a matter of some little practice in observation, and can readily be learned by anyone of average intelligence who likes to take the trouble.

The simplest and quickest way to learn the elements of the art is, as the guides unconsciously learned it, by walking, not climbing, on hilly ground, and *avoiding* all difficulties.

It is true the expert in orientation is born, not entirely made; that is, no amount of scientific orientation with map, compass, etc, will enable the student of pathfinding to excel the man who has the faculty; be it the sense of space and distance, the 'bump of locality' added to a thorough knowledge of map, compass, and photograph reading. It is also certainly the case, that there are many men, excellent mountaineers in other ways, who always seem to remain in the infants' class in this department.

But if few amateurs can hope to take honours in both natural and scientific orientation, there is all the more reason why they should seek to thoroughly understand the side most guides are deficient in.

There is another form of orientation, in addition to the natural and scientific, much practised in climbing both at home and abroad, but which I consider hardly comes under the definition of mountaineering art. This may be called the artificial or conventional.

---

[1] Harold Raeburn was the greatest climber of the pioneering period in Scotland. This extract from his textbook *Mountaineering Art*, pp. 213-330 (Fisher Unwin, 1920) is included because it offers sound advice, though delivered in the abrupt and forceful manner for which Raeburn was notorious. "Something of Stalin was in his make-up", remarked Lord Mackay in his interesting reminiscences ('Vignettes of Early Climbers', *SMCJ* 1950, XXIV, 169-180). I have applied some editing – in square brackets – to make his peremptory advice a little clearer. —RNC

Conventional Orientation

The most elementary form of this is the finger-post. We must also include here all artificial marks, or indications of routes to be followed, such as scratches on rocks, footsteps in snow, broken bottles, pieces of paper, cairns, and daubs of red paint.

This red-paint guiding device is almost like an eruptive disease in certain parts of the Eastern Alps. Switzerland and France are yet happily largely free from it. It is even carried up actual climbs in some places. I am convinced that these city-cab-horse-blinker methods of orientation are responsible for many accidents, and not a few deaths. Young ignorant fellows follow these marks, thinking that of course everything must be all right. The way or the weather gets too hard for their inexperience; they fall and perish.

This was recognised as a danger so long ago as 1885 – it afterwards greatly increased – by perhaps the most capable and scientific mountaineer of his age (he died aged twenty-four) who ever lived, Dr. Emil Zsigmondy. In his book, *Die Gefahren der Alpen*, he writes: "Auf diese Weise ist der Besuch von diese, schöne Berge fur Leute erleichtert, welche nicht das geringste Stück von Bergkentniss oder Kartenlesen haben, und auch manche Unglücke vorgebeugt."[2]

It has been recommended that, on rock-climbs where difficulty of finding the way back may be feared, cairns should be built and pieces of paper placed at intervals on the way up. In the Eastern Alps packets of papers can even be bought for this purpose

A cairn here and there, at places where it seems probable error might arise, is perhaps useful and legitimate. A climb is not a paper-chase, however, and a leader's eyes would be better employed in observing and noting the terrain than in groping in purblind fashion from cairn to cairn, or from paper to paper.

It is certain that this shoddy method of mountaineering is responsible for the deaths of many young continental climbers.

When a party is reduced to the necessity of following this system, it proves, to my thinking, that they are undertaking a climb for which they are really unfit. It *may* come off all right, but the leader has not sufficient ability, or experience, to justify him in leading the party. A cairned route which they are following may also lead into a *cul de sac* or impossible place where the original climbers had turned back; but there is nothing to indicate this, and the leader of the followers has not enough experience to see this.

The fact is that all these conventional orientation methods, such as I have mentioned, and also meticulous handhold labelling, literary climbing guides, are not mountaineering lore at all. They are merely cribs. Used simply as notes, they are often quite useful. The student who confines himself to the study of cribs, will never make a scholar. The climber who relies upon this form of orientation, will never become a mountaineer.

---

[2] "In this manner is access to these beautiful peaks made easier for people who have not the slightest knowledge of mountain country, or of map-reading, and thus many accidents are produced." —HR

Natural Orientation

Natural orientation is very difficult to explain or teach. If a man has it in him to learn he will pick it up, to some extent, more or less unconsciously.

The faculty should not be described as pathfinding in the sense of being able to follow a known route on a map, or from a description or photograph. Path-making is a better description of it. It means the *knowing* the best way in hill-country where none of these things exist. It also covers every detail of mountain craft on rocks or ice, from the smallest rock-climb to the greatest ice-fall.

In effect it is the faculty of choosing the line of least resistance, the easiest route, even on places sometimes invisible.

On a steep little rock-climb the projected judgment of this may be very short. On a great new peak it may be miles away, but in essence the principle is the same.

This often looks like intuition; but, though there is a certain amount of intuition in knowing how to put together and utilise fragments of knowledge, it is yet really a kind of projected experience, as it were, of similar climbs and conditions, encountered and made, it may be, years ago.

It is thus almost impossible for a young man to be a really good guide, unless he is one of the geniuses for whom ordinary rules are not made.

For those who have not got the faculty, or who, though possessing it in some measure, have not the years of experience, the most reliable methods of orientation are the scientific.

It is always as well to supplement these, when possible, by methods drawn from the practical experience of oneself or of others.

Scientific Orientation

How to read the Map and Compass. – For very accurate bearings the prismatic compass is used. This is a compass to which a prism is attached through which we can readily read off the bearings on the card. In connection with this an instrument called a protractor is used. The handiest form of this is a semicircular plate of celluloid. In the centre of its straight-edge an arrowhead is marked. The curved edge is divided into degrees.

To Find [the] True Bearing from a known point A to a known point B. – Lay the protractor on the map with its longer edge parallel to true north, the inner edge to the left, if B is east of A, right, if west. Place the arrowhead at A. Now read the bearing where the line A B passes the graded edge, and take the figures below 180° if B is east [of A], above 180° if B is west [of A].

To find Magnetic Bearing. – Lay the protractor with the arrowhead at A and its inner edge parallel to magnetic north line. The true bearing is thus 18° [less than the Magnetic bearing].

To find an Unknown Visible Point B on the Map. – Take compass-bearing. Lay the protractor parallel to magnetic north, and with the arrowhead at the spot where the bearing is taken A. The line drawn from A on the correct bearing given by the protractor will pass through B.

To find with the Compass the Time by the Sun.– The sun's true bearing at 6 a.m. is 90°. It moves one degree in four minutes. Suppose the sun's compass bearing is 120°, then the true bearing is 120°-18° = 102°; 90° = 6 a.m. and the excess of 102° over 90° = 12°; 1° = 4 minutes; 12 x 4 = 48. The time is therefore 6.48 a.m.

In most places and countries magnetic north does not coincide with true north. In the foregoing examples I have taken the amount of this variation, as it is called, for the centre of Great Britain in 1920 as 18° west of true north.

In speaking or writing of directions taken, whether in mapped or unmapped districts, it is always better and clearer to give the true directions, and for this purpose we have to know the variations. Tables of this, for most places in the world, are given in the Nautical Almanac. These are revised every few years, as variation is a fluctuating figure.

There are various theories by which variation is attempted to be explained. None are quite satisfactory. The subject is a very intricate one, and cannot be dealt with here.

All maps are published with the true direction, which does not vary. Most good maps have printed on them an engraving of a compass-needle, showing the magnetic variation for the date and locality when and where they were published. The actual variation for subsequent dates can be readily ascertained by means of the Tables of Variation given in the Nautical Almanac.

As an instance of the hopeless confusion into which we should fall if we did not always reckon in true direction away from the locality in which we happened to be, I may take [the case of magnetic variation in] Canada [as an example].

There [in] Halifax [it] is 22° west of true, [in] Vancouver [it] is 25° east of true, a total divergence of 47°.

Orientation in General

Though a prismatic compass is necessary for very accurate bearings, it is often heavy. A good, not too small, compass, with luminous points and floating card, is quite sufficient for ordinary mountaineering: fairly accurate bearings can be taken with this, and of course the prismatic has no advantage over it for steering in mist or darkness.

There has been brought out recently an excellent marching compass, first-rate also for mountaineering, the lid of which forms a circular protractor. It is also provided with luminous points for night work, is legible, and light. It is called the Magnapole.

The compass is one of the most useful tools of the mountaineer and is a very trustworthy guide for *general* direction on the mountains, more especially in mist or darkness. The route indicated by it, the direct route, is rarely the best, or even a possible route. It is essential to work with it in conjunction with the map, or previous knowledge of the district by a member of the party. The element of time, taken from a last definitely located place, must also be taken into consideration, and this made [into]

The Magnapole

a rough dead reckoning, according to the nature of the ground traversed, and its angle. The aneroid is a very great help in orientation under these difficult conditions.

The use of a pedometer has been suggested, but though some hill-walkers seem to have found these of use, I think this can only be the case on very smooth and easy ground.

It is much easier to find the way, apart altogether from climbing difficulties, on Alpine peaks than it is on British hills. An Alpine arête is usually very definite. A glacier, once constituted as such, is as definite as a great river. As in journeying down a river, when we come near rough rapids or falls, we make a portage on the bank, so on the glacier it is usually best to clear off the ice before becoming involved in the *séracs*. We may otherwise, like the first party to descend the Saleinaz Glacier in the Swiss part of the Mont Blanc range, have an exciting time, and spend a cold night out.[3]

Though it is easier to find one's way on Alpine peaks than it is on homeland hills, the consequences of losing it is likely to be more serious on the snows. It is better to learn at home how to find the way.

Water, according to the axiom, always runs downhill. It is therefore, like the compass, an infallible guide to the right direction, supposing we are on a hill, and desire simply to get down. It does not follow, however, that it will always do to closely hug a watercourse. This may drop into a ravine, or plunge over a cataract. Neither of these ways may be convenient. It will, as a rule, be better to keep some distance away from the stream on either hand.

The easiest time and place to lose the way is when leaving a cairn or summit in mist. A very slight divergence here leads to an enormous error in a very short distance.

On arrival at such a point, careful note should be taken of the direction from which the party came, and this should be at once marked by means of an ice-axe, an arrow drawn in the snow, or built with a few stones in the absence of snow.[4]

---

[3] The first descent was made by J.D. Forbes and Auguste Balmat in 1846, by way of the Tour and Trient glaciers and the Fenêtre du Saleinaz. I think, however, it was the second traverse by Alfred Wills' party, recounted in *Peaks, Passes and Glaciers* that Raeburn had in mind. —RNC

[4] Surely a form of 'conventional orientation', which was thoroughly despised earlier! —RNC

The larger the party the easier is the losing of the way. A solitary hill-walker *has* to note everything, and this shortly becomes habitual; he is little likely to go far wrong.

In a large party there are always distractions of various kinds. Unless someone is definitely in charge there are apt to be discussions, perhaps disputes, which consume time, but do not lead to the clearing of either mist or mystification.

One of the most difficult problems in daylight orientation presents itself under the following conditions. These are fairly common on British hills, say the Cairngorms, in March and April. A high plateau, covered with a uniform coating of crusted snow. Mist, and a strong, cold wind, blowing a stream of fine ice-dust across the frozen waste.

The eyes are here at a loss. The angle of ascent or descent can only be judged by the amount of labour necessary to make progress. The sense of isolation is very great, as the visible circle is extremely narrow.

The visible world, being small and restricted, has its visible objects placed, as it were, behind a huge blurred telescope lens. The waving stem of a dead weed is a tree, or a man, a sheep, a woolly mammoth; and a boulder, a beetling cliff.

Constant reference must here be made to the compass, and it is better for both the first and last men to carry and consult one at frequent intervals. It is easier for the last man to detect slight variations from the correct direction, as he has the rest of the party in front of him to check his steering by.

6.11 Steering in Mist by Dead-Reckoning

James A. Parker[1]

IN THE West Highlands the features of the hills are usually so definite that a climber who is steering his way by compass and aneroid through a dense mist for a certain point will easily recognise when he reaches it. It is in fact usually a case of following a compass direction until one runs up against the hill or object that he is steering for. This is the method indicated in Mr Douglas's article[2] with the addition that he recommends that the climber should form an estimate of the time that he should take to reach his goal, and consult his watch as well as his compass and aneroid. The element of time is, however, very uncertain, as in thick weather and in snow the going is very much slower than in good weather. In mist one is also apt to imagine that he has gone much further than is actually the case, and a good instance of this error is mentioned in the Lochnagar expedition referred to below.

In the Cairngorms, where the features of the hills are not nearly so definite as in the West Highlands, I have found the above methods insufficient, and at times have had to resort to steering by dead-reckoning. In other words, before leaving a known point for a

---

[1] *SMCJ* 1916, XIV, 114-117.

[2] See Chapter 6.5

certain goal, I measure the distance to the latter very carefully on the one-inch Ordnance map, note the compass direction, and then actually pace out the distance in the proper direction, the aneroid being, of course, also consulted. The advantages of the method are apparent from the first and second expedition described in the preceding paper.[3] On the first occasion dead-reckoning was not adopted, and after we had left the edge of Corrie Brandy all that we knew was that we had been steering in a certain direction for a known time, but as to how far we had actually gone we were ignorant. And it was only natural, therefore, that after going on for some time, and not encountering any definite object from which we could locate our position, we began to have some doubt as to where we were, and that we therefore did the wisest thing under the circumstances and returned. On the second expedition the weather was quite as bad, but on the outward journey Miller and I knew exactly where we were all the time, and could have pricked off our position on the map at any time. On the return journey dead-reckoning was not used, as we were running towards an easily recognisable object, *viz.*, Glen Darrarie. Steering by dead-reckoning is quite simple in theory, but a few notes on the practical application may be useful.

As the method is, of course, only very approximate, it will usually be sufficient to measure the distance on the map to the nearest eighth of a mile.

When pacing out the distance I count one foot only, and thus reckon fathoms and not yards. Every one hundred fathoms is recorded with the fingers of one hand according to the deaf and dumb alphabet, and a mile[4] can thus be registered without making any notes.

Pacing yards on hilly country is of necessity only very approximate, and large allowances must at times be made, the extent of which can only be estimated for from experience gained in clear weather. Any corrections that are deemed necessary must be made at the time, and are best done by simply omitting to count a step now and again as may be thought necessary.

The mere fact of counting one's steps ensures that the compass will be read at pretty regular intervals, and conduces to accurate steering.

When it is found necessary to verify the direction by consulting the compass, it will be found very convenient to stick the ice axe or stick vertically into the ground to mark the distance paced, go back a few steps, consult the compass, and move sideways until the axe or stick is in the proper direction, and then go ahead again.

It is, of course, advisable to have two compasses with the party, in case one should get out of order, as quite easily happens in very wet weather.[5]

In spite of the very approximate nature of the method, I have found it very successful in the Cairngorms, and always resort to dead-reckoning in bad weather, when careful steering is necessary, and in the absence of definite landmarks.

---

[3] An account of various thwarted expeditions in search of the elusive 'Craig Maskeldie', *SMCJ* 1916, XIV, 108-114.

[4] Presumably nine hundred fathoms!

[5] Or in case the leader should forget which end of his compass is the north-seeking end! See *SMCJ* 1916, XIV, 93 —JAP. [Parker's reference is to a party at a Club Meet at Lochearnhead who managed to come off Ben Vorlich down Glen Artney thinking it was Glen Ample].

The first time that I adopted the method was during a walk from the Cairnwell to Carn Bhinnein in dense mist. Carn a' Gheoidh was found from the Cairnwell by ordinary compass work, but from it dead-reckoning was used for a distance of five furlongs due west, after which a southwest course took us to the peak of Carn Bhinnein.

A long piece of work consisted in walking from the Sneck between Ben Avon and Ben a' Bhuird, to the south summit of the latter hill, *via* Cnap a' Chleirich and the North Top. The weather was of the worst description, *viz*. dense mist, a south-west gale, falling snow, and blind drift! The Cnap, which is a very definite top, was found from the Sneck by ordinary compass work, but beyond it the only definite landmarks were the eastern corries, which were heavily corniced, and which we were most anxious not to see at all, as they were a sort of lee shore. From the Cnap dead-reckoning was adopted for a distance of three miles with a right-angled change of direction left after we had proceeded sufficiently far westwards to ensure that our next tack would clear the edge of the eastern corries. No attempt was made to locate the north summit, as it is simply a theoretical point on a large plain, and to have found it would not have helped us. The weather was very bad, especially on the southern tack, and at one time the leader got forty-five degrees out in a hundred yards stretch. The south summit is marked by a large cairn, and it appeared out of the mist pretty nearly at the distance that we expected.

Another long expedition was from the top of the Stui Buttress to Allt na Guibhsaich, *via* the Ladder path of Lochnagar, in a dense mist which reached down to the 1,500 feet contour. The top of Lochnagar was thickly coated with snow, and the precipice was heavily corniced. In order to find the top of the Ladder we paced out a distance of two miles due east from the top of the Stui Buttress, and then struck north until we came to the edge of the precipice, a short distance to the west of the top of the Ladder. As showing the uncertainty of the 'time estimate', I may mention that after we had been toiling across the seemingly never-ending waste of snow for some time, the second man suddenly said, "Is it not about time that we were going north?", when, as a matter of fact, we had only gone about a third of the two miles, and had we turned north, we would most probably have got into difficulties on the west slopes of the Cac Carn Beag!

Lochnagar

6.12 Drug Addiction in Scottish Mountaineering:
the First Steps of a Descent

Geoffrey J.F. Dutton.[1]

CLIMBERS frequently use stimulants on long or hard routes; the after-effects may be mildly or grossly harmful. Addiction is no subject to be dealt with here. Neither is it new. Whilst preferring, with the old fogeys of 1890-odd in the Club Song, 'The Genial Whisky Toddy,' the Editors feel it is their duty to point out that the more irresponsible younger generation of climber was born very long ago. Here we reprint parts of an account published by Sir Robert Christison, Bart., in *Trans. Roy. Bot. Soc. Edin.* 1876, XII, 478-493, on the effects of cocaine on his climbing performance in Scotland. 'Coke' we now know to be one of the most dangerously addictive of 'hard' drugs; the spectacle of drug-pushing to the young (students at that ...), innocently or no, must engender the gravest concern, must it not? And that dope-peddler Batchelor should be rounded up, if his own excesses have not already brought him to an early grave.

'I was first led to pay attention to the Peruvian custom of chewing cuca by reading, full forty years ago, the 'Travels in Chilé, Peru, and on the River Amazons,' of the German naturalist Pöppig ...

'The conclusion at which he arrived is, that the habit is as seductive and as injurious to health, mind, and morals, as that of tippling in Europe, or opium-eating in the East. He says it is almost confined to natives of the aboriginal red race, has not been adopted by negroes, and is discountenanced among all of European descent; that even those who use it to no great excess must stop their work several tiines a day to chew their quid contemplatively, and are much displeased if disturbed in their placid enjoyment; and that those who have got thus far are apt to become mere slaves to it, surrender every other occupation for it, and, quitting society, pass their time in the wild forests between hunting for their sustenance and lying under a tree chewing their beloved weed, calling up delightful visions and building castles in the air, and so insensible to outward occurrences as to remain thus all night indifferent to cold, torrents of rain and even the howlings of the panther in their neighbourhood. But, in the end, life is cut short about the age of fifty by

---

[1]*SMCJ* 1971 , XXIX, 385-388. Readers will perhaps be familiar with Dr Dutton as the author of the 'Doctor' stories (*The Ridiculous Mountains*, 1984; *Nothing So Simple As Climbing*, 1993; both Diadem Press). He was, however, also Editor of the *SMCJ* from 1960 to 1971.

obstruction, dropsy, or jaundice, or through simple extenuation and exhaustion. When the habit has thus degenerated into a vice, the victim becomes, in the language of the country, a Coquero, and is irreclaimable. If a man of Spanish blood begin to use cuca, he is at once looked on with suspicion; for usually, in the course of time, he abandons himself entirely to it, and becomes an outcast from the society in which he moved ...

'Von Tschudi, indeed, says, that a profligate coquero may be known by his foul breath, stumpy teeth, pale quivering lips, blackcoloured mouth, dim eyes, yellow skin, unsteady gait, and general apathy; but, in his narrative, obviously in part compiled, he does not say he described such a man from actual observation; on the contrary, all three travellers represent in colours more or less strong the great utility of cuca to the Indians in the hard labour they have to undergo.

'Von Tschudi observes that, in his own trials, he found it to be a preventive of that difficulty in breathing which is felt in the rapid ascent of the Andes. He mentions the following instance, which he carefully watched, of the power of the Indians to bear long fatigue without any other sustenance. A miner, sixty-two years old, worked for him at laborious digging five days and nights without food, or more than two hours of sleep nightly, his only support being half an ounce of cuca leaves every three hours. The man then accompanied him on foot during a ride of sixty miles in two days. Nevertheless, von Tschudi was assured by the priest of the district that he had never known the man to be ill ...

'At all events, however, the following experiments .. prove that the leaves may be easily used by most, if not all, persons, so as to produce no unpleasant, unsafe, or even suspicious effects whatsoever.

'My first trials were made in 1870, when I was not aware that any one else in Europe had experimented with it. My specimen was sent to me by a London mercantile gentleman, Mr Batchelor, six years before ...

'Two of my students, out of the habit of material exercise for five months, tired themselves thoroughly with a walk of sixteen miles in the month of April. They returned home at their dinner hour, having taken no food since a nine o'clock breakfast. They were very hungry, but refrained from food, and took each an infusion of two drachms of cuca, made with the addition of five grains carbonate of soda, which was added to imitate the Peruvian method of chewing the leaves along with a very small quantity of lime or plant ashes. I am satisfied, however, that any such addition is superfluous. Presently hunger left them entirely, all sense of fatigue soon vanished, and they proceeded to promenade Princes Street for an hour; which they did with ease and pleasure ...

'I reserved what remained of my good specimen of cuca for further trial during my autumn holidays in the country. On September 15th, while residing at St Fillans on Loch Earn, I ascended Ben Vorlich. The mountain is 3224 feet above the sea, and 2900 above the highway on the lochside. The ascent is for the most part easy, over first a rugged footpath, and then through short heather and short deep grass; but the final dome of 700 feet is very steep, and half of it among blocks and slabs of mica slate, the abode of a few ptarmigan, of which a small covey was sprung in crossing the stony part. On the whole, no Highland mountain of the same height is more easily ascended. The temperature at the side of the lake was 62°; on the summit, 52°. In consequence of misdirection, I had to descend an intervening slope on the way, so that the whole ascent was 3000 feet perpendicular. I took two hours and a half to reach the summit, and was so fatigued near the close that it required considerable determination to persevere during the last 300 feet. I was richly rewarded, however, by an extremely clear atmosphere, and a magnificent mountainous panorama, of which the grandest object was Ben Nevis, forty miles off, shown quite apart from other mountains, and presenting the whole of its great precipice edgeways to the eye. My companions, who, as well as I, were provided with an excellent luncheon, soon disposed of it satisfactorily; but I contented myself with chewing two-thirds of one drachm of cuca leaves. We spent three-quarters of an hour at the top, during which I looked forward to the descent with no little distrust. On rising to commence it, however, although I had not previously experienced any sensible change, I at once felt that all fatigue was gone, and I went down the long descent with an case like that which I used to enjoy in my mountainous rambles in my youth. At the bottom, I was neither weary, not hungry, nor thirsty, and felt as if I could easily walk home four miles; but that was unnecessary. On arriving home at five o'clock, I still felt no fatigue, hunger or thirst. At six, however, I made a very good dinner. During the subsequent evening I was disposed to be busy, and not drowsy; and sound sleep during night left me in the morning refreshed and ready for another day's exercise. I had taken neither food nor drink of any kind after breakfasting at half-past eight in the morning; but I continued to chew my cuca till I had finished the sixty grains when half-way down the mountain.

'Eight days afterwards I repeated the experiment, but used ninety grains of cuca. Being better acquainted with the way, no ground was lost by an intervening descent, so that the perpendicular height to be reached from the highway was 2900 feet. I took two hours and a quarter to ascend, and on reaching the summit was extremely fatigued. The weather had changed, so that the temperature, 51° at the loch-side, was 41° at the top. A moderate breeze consequently caused so much chilliness that my party were glad to redescend in half an hour by which time I had consumed two-thirds of the cuca, taking, as formerly, neither food nor drink. The effects were precisely the same, perhaps even more complete, for I easily made the descent without a halt in an hour and a quarter, covering at least four miles of rugged ground; and I walked homewards two miles of a smooth level road to meet my carriage. I then felt tired, because nearly three hours had elapsed since I consumed the cuca and in that time the Peruvians find it necessary to renew their restorative. But there was no more cuca left, and I was tempted to substitute a draught of excellent porter. I suppose this indulgence led on to the unusual allowance of four glasses of wine during dinner, instead of one or none; and the two errors together, with possibly some discordance between cuca and alcohol, were the probable cause of a restless feverish slumber during the early part of the night; but quiet sleep succeeded, and I awoke quite refreshed and active next morning.

'One of my sons, who accompanied me on both occasions, used cuca the first time, but also took luncheon on the summit. Though not in good condition for such work, he made it out without fatigue; and on the second occasion, when there was no more cuca to give him, he felt decidedly the want of it when he reached the highway at the foot of the mountain.'

CHAPTER 7

Predicaments

7.1 Introduction

SOONER or later, we all come to grief on the mountains. We are caught in a bad storm, we lose the way, we are benighted. More often than not, most fortunately, these incidents do not become accidents, and we can look back on the awful error – whatever it was – with equanimity. In this section these commonplace predicaments are illustrated with stories taken mostly from the pioneering days.

Naismith goes up Ben More Assynt in the dark, completely unequipped for navigation. Indeed, completely unequipped! And suffers the consequences. Munro and Lawson bite off more of the Fannichs than they can chew on a short day and get benighted. Goggs sails into a gross navigational error in Glen Lyon. Corner's compass goes berserk in the Grampians (or perhaps he reads the wrong end!). Goggs, again, encounters unreasonable amounts of rain in Benderloch. Backhouse and Ling wander foolishly about in the Lairig Ghru. A novice blunders about on icy Ben Lui. And absolutely everybody gets whisked about by outrageously boisterous winds!

Next time, it could be you!

7.2 Benighted on Ben More Assynt

W.W. Naismith[1]

THE EDITOR evidently believes that the following narrative of broken mountain-eering laws and the natural consequence thereof, although not edifying, may prove instructive.

Wednesday, 11th July 1900, found me at Oykell Bridge Inn with a fine afternoon at my disposal. Ben More Assynt was only fifteen miles off, two-thirds of which could be cycled. This mountain had been merely a name to me since my school days, and I wanted to make his acquaintance. Unfortunately I had neither map, compass, nor aneroid with me, and only thin boots. To climb an unknown peak in these circumstances was of course madness, and I shall not attempt to palliate the offence.

I left my bicycle with the gamekeeper at Ben More Lodge, on Loch Ailsh, a pretty sheet of water with a wooded island, and started for the hill at 5 p.m. – much too late! The 'packet' of sandwiches given me by the hotel people contained two minute specimens only, and as they were not worth carrying, they were promptly eaten on the way up. The highest

---

[1] *SMCJ* 1900, VI, 82-86.

Gorm Loch Mor

Fionn
Loch Mor

Ben More
Assynt

Conival

Contour interval 250 ft

one mile

River Oykel

Drawn by Adam Kassyk 1997

Benmore Lodge

North

Map to illustrate Naismith's wanderings on Ben More Assynt

point of Sutherlandshire has not, I think, been described in the Journal, and it is probably but seldom climbed from the south. It rises to 3,273 feet, and has several other tops not much lower. Coinnemheall (pron. Connival), 3,234 feet, a mile west-south-west, is separated from Ben More by a dip of about 300 feet.

I followed a track along the left bank of the river Oykell for two miles, then sloped up the hillside, passed a round little loch (Dubh Loch Beag) close on my right, and ascended the grassy southern shoulder of Ben More. The top of that was gained in two hours from the lodge, and another half-hour's hard going along an interesting ridge took me to a knob, which various indications – including the finding of a pocket-comb – pointed to as likely to be the summit. This southern ridge has precipitous sides in several places, and is fairly narrow – somewhat resembling the crest of Aonach Eagach. The rock is 'Old Boy' until within a few yards of the top, when it changes to Cambrian quartzite.

From about six o'clock the weather had shown signs of deterioration. Canisp, Suilven, Cul Mor, Cul Beag, and the Teallachs, which had previously stood out with startling clearness, began to put on their night-caps. A cloud would hide the top of Ben More itself for a few minutes and then disperse, but only to form again. When I reached the first top and looked over, the whole valley to the east was filled with rolling mist, which quickly crept up the slope and enveloped the solitary wayfarer.

Not being certain which was the summit, I proposed to go on over everything as far as Coinnemheall, and descend by its south-east ridge into Glen Oykell, and so home; but this project did not come off. A hundred yards away, and only faintly discernible from the pocket-comb top, was another quartzite summit with a small cairn. From that top, a well-defined ridge – the only one visible – descended until it was lost in the thick fog. Was this the continuation of the main ridge? If so, it ought to run west or south-west at first; and the wind, which had blown steadily all day from the west, ought to be on my 'starboard bow'; and sure enough it was! So, with hardly a passing misgiving, I trotted down the ridge as fast as the rough quartzite permitted, until I had descended probably 1,000 feet.

As the ridge showed no signs of rising to another top, I concluded that the two tops close together must have belonged to Coinnemheall. I therefore quitted the ridge and turned to the left down a scree slope, fully expecting to emerge from the clouds in Glen Oykell. By-and-by the air cleared sufficiently to show me that I was in a strange country! Several lochs with very irregular outlines were not far off, and a herd of deer were grazing in the foreground. The stags were so aghast at seeing a human being come down from the sky, that they apparently forgot to be afraid, and gazed in a sort of spellbound way until I was quite near them. The valley I had dropped into was not that of the Oykell. I must, I thought, have somehow got on the Atlantic side of the watershed, and the precipitous buttress on my left was no doubt the reverse side of Coinnemheall. If so, however, what had become of Suilven and his grotesque neighbours? Even though shrouded in mist, why did I not see their bases?

Oh for a map and compass! Skirting the cliffs on my left, I mounted the ridge beyond, but the buttress had then changed its appearance, and had no resemblance whatever to Coinnemheall. A further considerable descent, followed by a most unwelcome ascent, put me on another ridge, merely to find that the valley on its far side had a stream in it certainly, but it ran the wrong way! Then surely the next ridge was the watershed I was hunting for. No, it wasn't! My preconceived notion that I was on the *west* side of Ben More, and that, by circling round the mountain to my left for a short distance, I was bound to arrive at the watershed at the head of Glen Oykell, was responsible for most of this wild-goose chase.

Once more I decided that a ridge on the horizon *must* be my goal, unless indeed it had evanesced. I even persuaded myself that I recognised the contour of the hills on both sides of the col ahead of me. A tedious up-and-down traverse across two miles of scree and rough ground ended only in another disappointment. I was looking down a new valley, but not the right one.

The night was by this time as dark as a moonless July night ever is. Rain had been falling heavily for some time, and I was wet through, dead beat and painfully hungry. It was already long past the time I had promised to be back at Oykell Bridge Inn, and the prospect of ever getting there appeared remote. Even the whereabouts of Ben More itself was now a matter of uncertainty; and remembering the time I had been trudging since leaving the top, it seemed possible that I had put another hill or two between me and it. It occurred to me that a man might wander for days through a large part of Sutherlandshire without meeting a human habitation, and that I had been told that a 'shower' in those latitudes sometimes lasted for a fortnight. With these dismal reflections I sat down and wound my watch. No sound broke the solemn silence except the distant rush of a burn.

'When things are at the worst they begin to mend.' I had not rested many minutes before I noticed that the fog was 'lifting'. The first thing seen was a corner of the northern sky faintly reddened by the invisible sun, who had then doubtless got as far as Behring Straits on his nightly round. That glimpse gave me the points of the compass approximately. The partial dispersion of the mist also revealed a ghostly apparition which greatly puzzled me. It seemed to be Suilven, but metamorphosed in some extraordinary way. A subsequent examination of the map explained the mystery. I had been looking at a conglomeration of Suilven and Canisp seen in line.

It was at last evident that, whereas I had intended to descend the south side of Ben More, I had actually gone down its north-east side! And a change of the wind, which had chopped round from west to east, if it did not cause the mistake, at least prevented its discovery. As any attempt to continue the circling process round this bulky mountain and its outlying spurs would probably make matters worse, I resolved to attempt, what I ought to have done hours before, namely, to go right over the top of Ben More, and retrace my upward route.

The first difficulty was to find Ben More! After considering the situation I decided to steer if I could south-east, in the hope of knocking up against my friend sooner or later. A mile's walk across comparatively level moorland, with some very boggy bits here and there, brought me to a ridge running in the desired direction, but after a weary grind it ended in an isolated top surmounted by an Ordnance cairn. A slope of terrible quartzite scree went down to a neck between two tarns on the far side, but nothing was at first visible beyond. After a short halt, the shadow of higher ground loomed out of the obscurity.

To descend quartzite scree set at the greatest angle of shaky 'repose', at midnight, in thin boots, and without a stick, is, I contend, an extreme trial of one's equanimity, but 'time saw me through', and a well-marked ridge rose from the dip. At first grass, it soon changed to scree and rock, and became steeper, until it led to the top of something which I felt sure was over 3,000 feet. A ridge running to the left at right angles to that I had come up dipped for a few hundred feet and then rose to a peak whose top was in cloud. The summit I had reached was for the moment clear of fog, but heavy rain made everything hazy. I concluded that it was Coinnemheall, and if so, by holding on south-east into the valley I should find myself at the source of the Oykell.

But there was still a little doubt whether I had actually bagged the highest top of Ben More or not, and after such a long night's work it would never do to leave that question open. So I followed the ridge to the left. It seemed to be absolutely interminable, but, at long and last, at 1.30 a.m., it *did* come to an end between two quartzite tops, which were at once recognised as those I had left exactly six hours before! Hech! Tired but grateful, I allowed myself just five minutes' rest, then scrambled along the southern ridge as fast as the imperfect light allowed. At the rounded shoulder the mist became very thick again, and it looked like going astray once more, but I picked up my bearings before any harm was done.

Four o'clock saw me back at the keeper's cottage. He and his wife, worthy people, insisted in spite of protestations on getting up and preparing breakfast, and never was it more acceptable. Thus fortified, I cycled through a shower-bath to Oykell Bridge, along a road covered with several inches of porridge or some other similar material. When one has once become wet through, and is relieved of the anxiety of trying to keep dry, rain, if it is only heavy enough, becomes almost enjoyable; and so it happened that a bedraggled but tolerably cheery traveller turned up at his inn at 6 a.m., and tumbled in among the blankets, with the reflection that it must not occur again, but that after all he would not have missed the weird experience for a good deal.

7.3 Beinn Dearg and the Fannichs

H.G.S. Lawson[1]

AS that particular portion of Ross-shire in which the Fannich Hills are situated was unfamiliar to me, it was with pleasure that I found myself able to fall in with a proposal of H.T. Munro's that we should take a flying visit to those parts.

Neither of us had much time to spare, but with bicycles it is wonderful how accessible some of the remoter districts really are so long as you are not very particular about damaging your tyres. We accordingly arranged to meet at Aultguish Inn on the morning of 9th March. Munro, who is always good for a little scouting work, decided to take the early train from Edinburgh to Garve on the 8th, and spy out the land, with, as I afterwards discovered, the quiet intention of adding to his already sufficiently weighty bag of peaks. I arrived at Strathpeffer a little after seven the next morning, and started against rather a

---

[1] *SMCJ* 1901, VI, 152-160.

nasty wind, but with the roads much drier than I had ventured to hope. As I have before found that expeditions commencing with the 4 a.m. train for the Highlands are subsequently subjected to modifications, I made inquiries in passing Garve Station, but found that no change had been made in this case. Munro was duly forward with all the impedimenta, the weather looked tolerably decent, and everything seemed well. On reaching the inn I found Munro in the middle of breakfast. The previous afternoon he had gone up Am Fraochagach by a ridge running from near Loch a' Gharbh Raoin, and had found the snow mostly in good condition, requiring a moderate amount of step-cutting high up. Coming down by Strath Vaich, he had had difficulty in crossing a stream in the dark, and had to retrace his steps for a long distance. Eventually he returned to a keeper's house, the occupier of which mounted him on a steed and sent him down the glen in great style. He ultimately arrived at the inn well after midnight. Munro remarked that the outstanding feature of the country was that there were no bridges anywhere, and that where an apology for stepping stones existed, they had evidently been constructed for the use of a SMC ex-President other than himself. I observe the saying at the time, but unfortunately did not pay much attention to it.

The Fannich Hills are grouped pretty much in the shape of a cross, one limb of which runs north-west to south-east, and the other east to west. Sgurr Mor and Carn na Criche being common to both. The south-east to north-west route is well described by Gilbert Thomson[2] in the second volume of the *Journal*, and had been traversed by Munro in 1893. Our original plan had been to go to Beinn Dearg on the day of my arrival, and the following day traverse the Fannichs from east to west, but as the day seemed fine, we altered our plans, and decided to visit the Fannichs first. This turned out to be a most unfortunate decision. As we purposed leaving the road near Loch Droma and descending toward the boathouse at the lower end of Loch a' Bhraoin, bicycles were obviously of little use, and as we were making rather a late start, it was thought best to take a trap which, after depositing us five miles up the road, would drive round to the boathouse and get us back at a reasonable hour. Mr Mackay, our landlord, acted as driver, and at 11.45 we dismounted and started across a very boggy moor for Beinn Liath Mhor Fannaich. The snow, when we reached it, was deep and soft, and continued so till near the summit, which was reached at 2.30. The height of this hill, which is marked only by a contour on the O.S. map, was made to be 3,120 feet. There is a cairn on the top, and another about thirty yards short of the summit. What it is for I know not. We then had a few glissades to the col between this peak and Sgurr Mor. The top of this, on which is a large cairn, was reached at 3.30. Sgurr Mor, 3,637 feet, is the highest of the Fannichs, and seems a very finely shaped hill, but owing to the mist we saw it only in bits. Carn na Criche was reached twenty minutes later (cairn beyond summit), and we were soon trudging up the steep north ridge of Sgurr nan Clach Geala, which is 3,581 feet, and the second highest peak of the range. This was heavily corniced on the east edge. The top was reached by 4.45, but no cairn was visible, though there may possibly have been a small one completely covered by the snow. We hurried down the south ridge in the mist toward Sgurr nan Each, and reached that top (no cairn) at 5.30, and on arriving at the beallach between Sgurr Breac and Sgurr nan Clach Geala at six,

2 *SMCJ* 1893, II, 307-310.

decided we must leave the former peak and A' Chailleach for another occasion. The descent continued over very rough ground down the left side of the burn flowing toward the north. This increased in volume very rapidly, and soon became a powerfully flowing torrent. At that time we didn't expect to have any streams to ford, but intended to keep down the bank till the junction with the outlet from Loch a' Bhraoin, which in its turn we understood would be crossed by a bridge. After a bit we saw a sight which made us consider things, and ultimately demonstrated that it is not only the woman who deliberates that is liable to be lost. On the other side of the stream there appeared what in the fading light seemed to be a first-rate bridle path. Munro, who had descended Meall a' Chrasgaidh (the hill to the right) to the boathouse at the end of Loch a' Bhraoin some eight years previously, was confident that he never had had to ford a torrent like that beside us now. He might possibly have crossed this stream and the outlet from Loch a' Bhraoin by separate bridges, but probably the bridge he had crossed was below the confluence of the streams, and that consequently the sooner we got across this one the better. This we managed with just a little trouble.

The description of the next part of our expedition I approach with some hesitation, and had it not been for the lofty moral example of our ex-Treasurer,[3] who manfully owned up to all his misdemeanours, I admit that an attempt might have been made to conceal certain events which followed. The truth is that two SMC members disgraced themselves by failing to get home on the evening they intended, had to stay the night out, and finally arrived at their destination some twelve or fourteen hours behind time. I shall tell a plain unvarnished tale, but shall extenuate to the extent of pleading that for each of them it was a first offence.

By the time we had got across the stream and were re-shod it was quite dark, and we found that what had appeared to be a path was something quite different. What it was, or what it was for, neither of us ever made out. It seemed to be a narrow artificial and very irregular ridge, and as far as progress was concerned was no better, but soon got worse, than the open moor, with all its soft peat holes and frequent pools of water. We stumbled along this at a snail's pace for an hour or two, wondering when the bridge would appear, and then found our advance barred by a torrent falling down the hillside into the main stream. This tributary formed a series of cascades, and was quite hopeless to cross where we were. The only thing to be done now seemed to be to ascend the bank of stream number two, and see if there were any fordable part. We accordingly climbed up several hundred feet, back to the snow again, but no place where we could get across appeared, nor did there seem to be any prospect of such turning up for a long way. It seemed rather hopeless work following this stream indefinitely, and we thought a look at the map might assist us.

Between us we managed to raise three matches, and before attempting to light the first we carefully arranged the map with a view to having the proper part before us when things became visible. There seemed to be now more wind than I had noticed before, and it was a palpitating moment as the first match was struck. To our joy it stayed in, but to our

---

[3] This is a reference to Willie Naismith, who had just retired as SMC Treasurer. And of course the 'lofty moral example' supplied was his confession of oblivion in Assynt – Chapter 7.2 above.

disgust we found that the map was folded upside down, with a wrong part presented to us. As quickly as possible the map was rearranged, and we found the general district where we were, and then exit first match. Number two seemed always in danger of being blown out; and number three was lighted needlessly soon. For a few precious seconds we drank in as much of the map as we could, and then utter darkness – worse than before.

By this time it was tolerably manifest that unless the moon came out we were landed for the night. For provision for the day we had each taken two sandwiches and a piece of cake, but although extremely hungry, we thought it better to reserve for future use the small quantity of cake that alone remained. No good place could be found to lie down on. The heather and peat hags were as sodden as they could be, and where there was any shelter a snow-drift was sure to be found. All the same, we did lie down for a bit. For the beginning of March, and in the locality we were, the night, though extremely dark, was probably not a cold one, as far as a thermometer reading might indicate. To compensate there were other discomforts. Everything was saturated. Our boots were more or less full of water, frequently there was a drizzling rain, and when it stopped there was sure to be wind, which was worse. We appeared to have seen different things on the map during the half minute or so that it was visible to us, and we endeavoured to reconcile the different impressions that had been made. For the next hour and a half we discussed this in a way that would have done credit to the historical debates that took place during the yachting meet. Afterwards the point as to whether we were as hungry as we had been a couple of hours previously arose, and on this subject it may be mentioned that we agreed that we were not. The reason for this and supplementary questions were next considered for at least an hour, bringing us on to about one o'clock. The coldness of our feet had now become almost unendurable, and as it seemed just a little lighter, we thought that by climbing the hill a little we might find how we really lay by Loch a' Bhraoin. For the best part of an hour we mounted very slowly up the side of the stream, and finally agreed that we saw the loch pointing a good deal higher up the valley than we were. The next question was, where was the bridge? In his former excursion Munro was certain that he came down the shoulder of Meall a' Chrasgaidh almost in a bee-line for the boathouse at the end of the loch; that he had had no difficulty crossing streams, and that he had crossed one bridge, and possibly two. It therefore seemed impossible that the bridge could be lower down the valley; and the only feasible explanations seemed to be that it had been washed away or that we had passed it in the darkness. This was quite possible, as we had failed to see the stream issuing from the loch. By this time the moon, though never appearing, must have risen considerably in the heavens, and things seemed to be distinctly lighter. We then descended to where the streams met, and commenced ascending the main stream, hugging the bank. We felt we were now quite entitled to finish any food we had. This took about a couple of minutes, and at about three o'clock we started up the main stream again looking for the bridge. Often the thought of the whereabouts of our trap and what sort of a time our landlord was having occurred to us. Was he also in the open, or had he a roof over his head? We went very slowly up the rough ground by the side of the stream, and in about half an hour or so passed the junction with the overflow from Loch a' Bhraoin. This, as already mentioned, had not been noticed in the jet darkness as we came down, and the sight of it encouraged us in the hope that we had also failed to notice the bridge. During the next little while several false reports were raised as to the bridge being in sight, but as each of these was found to be groundless, Munro would state that as far as he recollected the bridge was about 300 yards above the particular bend of the stream at which we happened to be. This took place about half-a-dozen times, and by then we were getting much above the direct line between the shoulder of Meall a' Chrasgaidh and where the loch must be. I continued to hope all things regarding this bridge, but began to think that it must be used solely by such people as Mrs Harris, and when we came to a rather sheltered place, suggested a rest, and sat down. Munro went on a bit, I believe did ditto, and eventually returned with no further information regarding the bridge. Obviously we had just to get across without it, and to put in the time till dawn we considered as to whether if admittedly you are as wet as you could be, there was any advantage in stripping when you came to a place where fording was practicable.

Different views were held and acted on when the opportunity ultimately arose, and the matter is still undecided. At six o'clock it was sufficiently light to see what was going on, and ten minutes later we found a place which we thought we could ford. This was managed successfully, and shortly we came in sight of the loch, with a bridge at its outlet. Seven o' clock found us across the bridge, with our driver and a keeper standing at the door of the boathouse. Short explanations followed. The bridge that we had sought so earnestly was a myth, but except in spate the stream, notwithstanding its width, may easily be crossed dryshod. Mr Mackay had fortunately met this keeper on driving up to the boathouse, just as the latter was leaving for some remote cottage. The two of them had sat up in the shanty expecting us every minute. By good luck there happened to be a tin of cocoa and some extraordinary biscuits in the place, and with a good fire they managed to make themselves tolerably comfortable. We gladly joined in a cup of cocoa, and at eight o'clock drove off, rather over twelve hours behind time. The chance of seeing the gorge at Braemore and the Falls of Measach in fine flood was too good to be missed, so when we came to the junction of the Ullapool and Dundonnell roads we dismounted and went through the Braemore grounds. The falls are probably familiar to most SMC members, and have often been described, but I doubt if any have seen them in better form than they were on that Sunday morning. The horse, like ourselves, was feeling somewhat the want of food, and it was nearly noon before Aultguish was reached. On our arrival we were sorry to find that everybody, had stayed up during the night for us, and it was obviously with a feeling of relief that it was seen that everybody was much as usual. By his conduct on the previous night Munro had given away his reputation, and no astonishment was manifested on his account. Glances full of that quality that is said to be cultivated by familiarity were, however, directed at me. The extremely limited amount of Classics I ever knew is now pretty well all forgotten, but one dictum of an ancient sage still stays in my memory. He pronounced that the wisest man was he who thought of wise things and did them, and that the next wisest man was he who said the wise things another did and followed that good example. With fools, however, exactly the contrary holds. The man who did idiotic things solely of his own accord no doubt was a bit of a fool, but he who saw the foolish things one fool did and proceeded to do likewise was a much more hopeless character. The good people of Aultguish showed plainly that they were disciples of that philosopher.

As we had missed the previous day's dinner, that day's breakfast, and it was nearly luncheon time, a compromise was made regarding meals, and shortly a first-rate one, consisting of roast mutton, ham and eggs, and cheese appeared. After that we retired to our rooms, and one at least indulged in rather more than forty winks. We had pretty well spoiled our chances of doing anything that day, but as the afternoon was very fine, we went for a walk along the Garve road and loafed generally.

As we had to catch the evening train at Garve, the next day's programme had to be short, and Beinn Dearg was decided on. We accordingly bicycled as far as the bridge over Abhuinn a' Ghiubhais Li, and then walked up the valley of Allt Mhucarnaich for nearly two hours, crossing the stream just above the junction with a tributary that comes in from the north at about 1,400 feet. From near here we were fortunate enough to see an avalanche on a scale far beyond anything I ever dreamt of occurring in this country. For a width of over a hundred yards the snow suddenly peeled off the face of the shoulder to our left, and came rattling down with a tremendous noise. Munro, who has made such innumerable excursions on the hills during winter, admitted that he had seen nothing like it before, and when afterwards we came to the bed of slip many were the regrets expressed that neither had a camera. The snow was heavy as we ascended farther, but a steady grind took us to the top – large cairn – at about 1.30.

Earlier in this volume Mr A.E. Robertson describes a splendid north face to this mountain.[4] We stayed for more than half an hour on the top, hoping to get a good view of this, but saw it only imperfectly, through a thin shifting mist. There seemed to be something similar at the north-east side, but as one is liable to be greatly deceived regarding the relative size of things in a mist, I shall attempt no description. Two hours after leaving the top brought us to the road again. A mile or two down the condition of the road at last proved too much for us, and Munro had what looked like a nasty spill from his machine, though he professed to be little the worse. The inn was reached at five, and our tour was at an end.

It is always pleasant to have grounds for acknowledging one's indebtedness to one's host, and this sketch would be incomplete without some such recognition. Mine host of Aultguish treated us in every respect very well, and though most irregular hours were kept, seemed to be able to produce excellent repasts at very short notice. He, moreover, plays the game in a sportsmanlike way, for although you engage rooms, occupy them with your baggage, keep the entire establishment up during the night, and then don't turn up till the following noon, no charge for apartments nor attendance appears directly or indirectly in your bill. This point I respectfully commend to the consideration of the ex-Treasurer of the Club should he be contemplating anything further in the nocturnal line. He can start from no better base.

---

[4] 'Ben More Assynt and Beinn Dearg', *SMCJ* 1900, VI, 36-37.

7.4 Stuchd an Lochain and the Upper Part of Glen Lyon

F.S. Goggs[1]

'There they stood, ranged along the hillsides, met
To view the last of me, a living frame
For one more picture! in a sheet of flame
I saw them and I knew them all. And yet
Dauntless the slug-horn to my lips I set,
And blew.' – *Childe Roland to the Dark Tower came.*

A SINGLE word will often set one's thoughts a-roaming, and the occurrence of several black dots against which was printed the word 'Tower' in Bartholomew's Map comprising Glen Lyon, has excited my imagination for several years. First I thought of a Scottish rival to the castellated Rhine, then I imagined I might have discovered the scene of Browning's well-known poem, the last stanza of which is quoted above. The glamour of romance being thus thrown over the upper part of Glen Lyon, I eagerly accepted an invitation from Munro last New Year to accompany him in a third attempt on Stuchd an Lochain. Even apart from the fact that I wished to visit this particular portion of the country, I think every member of the SMC is bound out of gratitude to the compiler of Munro's Tables to assist that enthusiast in what I believe is his intention of beating Robertson's bag of all the three-thousanders by equalling the latter in mountains and surpassing him in tops ascended.

To find the main route or routes to Stuchd an Lochain, I turned to what I hoped were to prove the illuminating pages of the SMC Guide Book. I conned the indices of the Journal, but they were innocent of any such name. I turned up Munro's Tables to make sure the hill was included in the list of the immortals. Yes, there he was right enough, No. 191. I turned afresh to the Guide Book, and diligently traced Stuchd an Lochain's neighbours: all his neighbours were duly scheduled, but not even 'No information' was set against him. He has been absolutely and entirely ignored. I feel I am entitled to ask our Editor for an explanation of this omission. Why this nepotism, this favouritism?[2]   Are not all the 'Munros' entitled by the mere fact of their being ''Munros' to at least a mention in the Guide Book? Of course I am aware that this hill boasts at its foot no Loch Awe Hotel, no Corrie

---

[1] *SMCJ* 1905, VIII, 235-44.

[2] The Editor of the Guide Book frankly admits he was not aware that the claims of this mountain were sufficiently great to entitle it to a place in the Guide Book. He, however, will be pleased to get a condensed report from Mr Goggs which can be printed with other additions at some future time. —WD

Arms or other place of popular resort replete with fireplaces in the bedrooms, hot-water bottles and other luxuries for the aged and infirm; but are our Scottish Bens to be given places of consideration according to the quality of the hotels at their base? Luxury, luxury, luxury, everything is sacrificed nowadays to the goddess Luxury: she conquered the Alps long ago, and now she is devouring the SMC, and the Editor, I regret to think, stands not up against her, but has fallen a victim to her blandishments.

Again, on the ground of antiquity Stuchd an Lochain is entitled to an honoured place. The earliest recorded ascent of Ben Cruachan, which mountain occupies several pages in the Guide Book, took place, according to our esteemed Editor, at the beginning of the last century. I have found the record of an ascent of Stuchd an Lochain in about the year 1590. It reads as follows:–

> 'On the brow of *Stuic-an-lochain* – a huge rock beetling over a deep circular mountain tarn – they encountered a flock of goats. Mad Colin[3] [Colin Campbell of Glenlyon, d. 1596 or 1597] and his man forced them over the precipice. When surveying their work from the top of the cliff, Colin unexpectedly came behind Finlay [his attendant], and ordered him, in a threatening voice, to jump over. He knew it was useless to resist. He said quietly, and as a matter of course: "I will, Glenlyon; but," – looking at a grey stone behind them – "I would just like to say my prayers at yon stone first; it is so like an altar." Colin mused, looked at the stone, and, letting go his hold, bade him go, and be back immediately. Finlay reached the stone, knelt down, muttered whatever came uppermost, and every now and then took a sly look at his master. Colin stood yet on the edge of the cliff, and kept looking on the mangled bodies of the goats. He seemed to become horrified at his own mad work. Finlay lost not his opportunity. He stealthily crept behind his master, grasped him by the shoulders, and shouted, in a thundering voice, "Leap after the goats." The unhappy lunatic supplicated for mercy, in vain. Finlay's grasp was like a vice; and he so held him over the precipice, that if let go he could not recover himself, but inevitably fall over. "Let me go this once," supplicated Colin. "Swear, first, you shall not circumvent me again." "By Mary?" "Nay, by your father's sword." "By my father's sword, I swear." "That will do; now we go home."[4]

Obedient to Munro's fiery cross, the night of 29th December 1904 found our leader, Nelson, and myself eating the crumbs which fell from the table of a Masonic banquet in an adjoining room, into which, the 'tyler' having deserted his post, one of us incautiously wandered. Luckily the intruder was the only Mason in our small party, and so survived to tell the tale.

At 5.30 a.m. next day we were roused. At seven we cautiously felt our way into a two-horse machine, and were soon ploughing through the darkness up Glen Lochay. It had been a wild night of storm and rain, and the west wind was still hurling its misty cloud

---

[3] Mad Colin built the Castle of Meggernie (five miles east of Stuic-an-lochain), probably about 1582. —FSG

[4] From Duncan Campbell (date). *The Lairds of Glenlyon.* pp. 17-18. —FSG

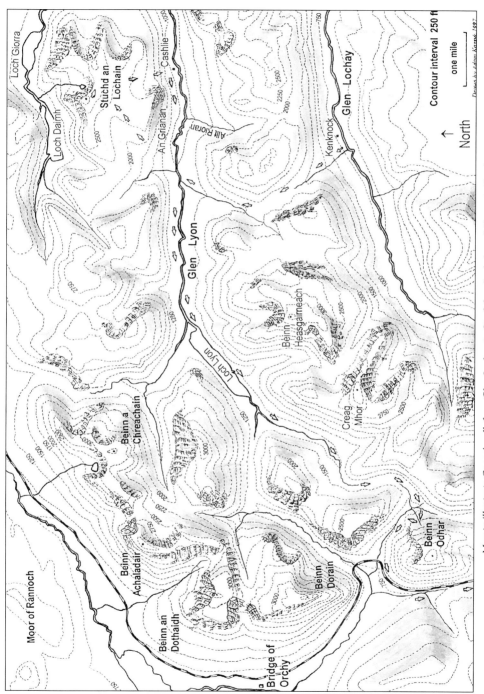

Map to illustrate Goggs' walk from Glen Lochay to Stuchd an Lochain and thence to Tyndrum

battalions down the glen. Ever and anon there was a lull, a few stars peeped out and were reflected in the sullen stream on our left, then with apparently redoubled force came the rainstorm sweeping down the wide glen and completely enveloping it. I did my best to use the driver as a breakwater, but to no purpose, and we huddled together in silence – our close companionship being only broken by the necessity of opening several gates and recovering the driver's cap which blew away. I reconciled myself to a thorough soaking, but determined that come what might, it should not be my fault if Munro did not bag his mountain at this his third attempt.

At eight precisely we reached the farm of Kenknock (745 feet), and leaving the machine to await our return, we struck up Allt Truchill, and soon found an old track[5] which led us well up the east side of the glen. The col marked by a cairn is 1,738 feet, and is half a mile beyond a small lochan which lies some distance below you to the west.

Up to this point the rain had been consistently washing our faces, and we had all I think quietly resigned ourselves to what seemed our inevitable fate. Beyond the col we strained our eyes to get a view of Glen Lyon. We soon made out that there was a glen below us, and a dim wall of mountain with dull silver streaks here and there, proving the existence of burns, loomed up indefinitely on the further side. The path led to a bridge which we crossed, and soon afterwards the track withered away. The circling mists were now distinctly rolling up the hillsides, the rain abated, and hope commenced to rise from her ashes. Soon the river Lyon was clearly seen, one or two farms became visible, and the opposite hills assumed a less vague aspect. On we went with lighter hearts, making for a house we saw marked on the map named Lubreoch, and a ford close to.

There is always a spice of romance and adventure in making an incursion into a little-known Highland glen. The houses named on your map may have been in ruins for the last century, the fords shown thereon may only be passable on one or two occasions in the year; the fact that the map shows no bridge at the point you wish to cross is by no means satisfactory evidence that there is none, or *vice-versa* if a bridge is shown at a particular point, what proof have you that it was not washed away yesterday or ten years ago? We were in a most delightful state of uncertainty this morning as to fords, houses, and bridges. To my mind this uncertainty is one of the chief charms in climbing or walking in the Highlands. Most of us live in towns, and our lives are calculated to the minute. Start for business at such and such a time; keep certain appointments at fixed hours; lunch at a certain place and moment; return home by a stated route at practically a fixed time; dinner at –; bed at –. Hurrah for a day's fling in the Highlands. Unfettered and free, we go where we please. Away with your Guide Book and details of routes: the unknown for me!

To come back to our journey. The day was undoubtedly clearing up rapidly, patches of blue sky appeared, the sun came out, and the hillsides were rain-pearled, sparkling as if with joy. We saw a good broad river below us, and looked up and down for a bridge.

---

[5] This track is marked on the old One-Inch Ordnance Survey Map, but does not appear on the revised One-Inch. It is still fairly well defined, and is certainly worth the trouble of following to any one walking over to Glenlyon from Kenknock. The track starts a quarter of a mile north of Kenknock. Strike the first burn to the west of the farm, and follow it north till it forks: the beginning of the track will be found 100 yards on, inside the fork. – FSG

Not a sign of one! A little further, and we caught sight of a cottage which was evidently that marked Lubreoch on the map. Round another knoll and there was a boat, moored our side of the river, close to the cottage. We luckily found the shepherd at home, but he was none too eager to take us over, as the boat he told us was 'nae ill to coup,' which being translated by Munro for my benefit, I found to mean 'easily upset'. The river, at the ford where the boat was, ran deep and swift, and the navigation of the crossing undoubtedly demanded care. Our ice-axes came in useful as boathooks, and in two journeys the three of us were across.

From the ferry we had the first view of our hill. The sun had drawn up the mists, several waterfalls were racing down in quivering masses of snowy white, and there stood Stuchd an Lochain revealed to our eager eyes, away back over the near hills forming the north side of Glen Lyon, with a light mantle of snow covering his summit. I looked up and down the glen expecting to see picturesque towers on knolls, but none were apparent; and, as Munro anticipated we had enough to do to fill in our day and knew nothing about towers, I reluctantly dismissed them from my mind for the time being.

Along the road east for half a mile, then taking again to the moor, we struck the burn, coming down Allt Camslai, above Pubil Farm, and mounting rapidly, soon reached the open moor, which stretched away to the north-cast, gently sloping right up to the summit of Stuchd an Lochain. The driest route is to keep the ridge to your north, but it matters little, and each choosing our own line, an eagle welcomed us at the summit cairn (3,144 feet) at twelve – four hours after leaving Kenknock.

The view is not extensive, except to the north-west, over the moor of Rannoch, lonely, bleak, and black. The winter so far had been open to an extent rarely known; there was practically no snow up to 2,750 feet, and the country did not present its usual wintry aspect. Nearly 2,000 feet below to the north stands the solitary farmhouse of Lochs, looking like a grey alpine hospice. It is presumably called Lochs from the fact of its being situated between two lochs, Loch Dhamh and Loch Girre, but only the first-named can be seen from an Lochain – a high ridge cuts off any view of Loch Girre. Immediately below (some 750 feet) is Lochan nan Cat; the steep faces round this lochan are broken up, mixed rock and turf. There does not seem to be any regular rock cliff or face.

Munro did not try to dispose of his companions by emulating Mad Colin, and we proceeded east to bag another top. The descent of the first 173 feet is fairly steep, then you rise 34 feet and are over the 3,000 line again (3,005 to be exact), another slight drop below the 3,000 contour, up again, and the cairn at the east end of the summit ridge (3,031 feet) is soon reached, a little more than a mile from the summit itself. Striking due south by the Allt Cashlie, we dropped down on Cashlie Farm (1,000 feet) a little after one, and were hospitably entertained by Mr and Mrs McKerchar[6] inside, whilst certain unscrupulous collies, to make matters even, ransacked my rucksac, which I had incautiously left outside.

---

[6] In 1800 a Macnaughton had Cashlie: his son James took part in Sir Ralph Abercromby's expedition to Egypt, and at the landing of the troops in Aboukir Bay on the 8th March 1801 was the first to reach the shore, after 'a neck-and-neck race between the Highlanders and the 23rd and 40th Regiments.' – from Duncan Campbell (date). *The Book of Garth and Fortingall.* pp. 240-241. – FSG

Wishing to explore upper Glen Lyon, I proposed reaching Loch Awe Hotel, the site of the New Year Meet, by walking to Tyndrum, and taking train thence. As Munro had twice already traversed the glen, it was agreed that I should do the tramp alone, and that he and Nelson should go back to the trap at Kenknock by a nearer way. They crossed the bridge over the Lyon, a quarter of a mile east of Cashlie (this is the last bridge (west) over the Lyon), then west by Dalchiorlich, after passing which farm it is best to keep well up the shoulder of the hill on your left up the trackless Allt Rioran to the well-defined col at its head (1,941 feet). The last 200 feet up and the first 200 feet down the other side are steep, with a number of rocks scattered about. Kenknock is then seen immediately below. My erstwhile companions duly reached their machine in under two hours.

After promising to join them at Tyndrum Station about 7.30, I started west at a good pace, leaving Cashlie 1.40. Every now and then a shower came on, but this only made the glen look finer, the mist magnifying the shoulders of Meall Ghaordie which jutted out like huge cliffs and overlapped each other. The bridge at Invermeran was half broken down, but climbing up the centre buttress and then throwing dignity to the winds, I crawled across the two remaining tree stems, and so reached the further shore. Along the side of Loch Lyon the track dives again and again, and sometimes for a considerable distance, into the loch itself, and the walker is forced to take a track a little higher.

Half a mile past Ardvannoch some malignant sprite lured me to leave the main track and strike off across a bridge over the stream coming down the Abhainn Ghlas, to Tomochoarn. I passed half-a-dozen men here, who stared at me in an interested kind of way, but with true Highland reserve said nothing. It was 3.50 and getting dark, so I hurried on along a rough track which in two and a half miles ended at some sheep-fanks. The glen now became very boggy and very dark, and by coming several croppers I proved both these facts simultaneously. The glens seemed to wind much more than I had anticipated, but being a non-smoker, I could not consult map, compass, or watch.

However, I kept on, and after a time found I had crossed the watershed (1,366 feet). I was then forced up to the left to avoid a gorge of the burn; it was now so dark that to the malignant sprites watching, my motions must have appeared very unsteady, but I drank nothing but burn water, and fed in thought on the plum pudding and jam pieces long since hidden securely by those thieving Cashlie collies. Coming down to the stream again, I tried the other side, but after scrambling up a steep bank and finding no obvious route in the darkness, I re-crossed the stream and stumbled along till a side burn in flood foaming down a deep rocky channel brought me to a full stop. Here, thought I, I must pass the night.

In front of me was a sugar-loaf peak, which I guessed must be Beinn Dorain, and the lights of a train confirmed me in this. The line was evidently not far off; so near and yet so far. I reckoned it must be about 6.30, and now the pride of office came to my rescue. The Librarian of the SMC throwing up the sponge at 6.30 p.m? No! never! I *will* get to the railway line.

The only reasonable course open was to follow the burn up to the sky-line, so putting my not over-willing muscles to work, another 1,000 feet was soon added to the day's play. I then crossed over the prostrate body of my enemy, and was on the open hillside. A light!

Don't be fooled by a will o' the wisp. Again, a light! It does not move. It is far below. It must be a light from a cottage. Feeling my way cautiously with my ice-axe down what seemed a steep stony slope, with here and there a six-foot piece of cliff, I soon crossed the railway metals and found a surfaceman's cottage. It was only 7.30, but all chance of reaching Tyndrum Station in time to join Munro and Nelson was gone. The good lady of the house only spoke Gaelic, but her hospitality was genuine and acceptable. She quickly made some refreshing tea, and after half an hour's rest I followed the metals south for over a mile, then taking to the road I walked into the hall of Tyndrum Hotel at 9 p.m.

Mr Stewart, so well-known as a type of the old-fashioned hotel-keeper, who looks on his guests with personal interest, soon made me comfortable in his private parlour. After making out a telegram to Loch Awe for sending the first thing next morning, I slept the sleep of the just. On consulting the map I found I had in sheer carelessness turned off south half a mile beyond Ardvannoch instead of keeping along the well-defined track due west. I could give half-a-dozen most excellent reasons for making such a mistake, but to tell the whole truth and nothing but the truth, it was a piece of gross and inexcusable carelessness, and when I next do walk abroad at the New Year, I have determined to take a lantern and matches, in addition to brains chastened by experience.

7.5 An Experience of the Hills of Ey

Edred M. Corner[1]

THIS communication is sent to the Journal because the writer had a peculiar experience whilst on the very ordinary round-topped hills of the Forest of Ey. Further, the result of his adventure was that such a day's work was done on the hills as to be possibly worthy of note. The mountains between Glen Shee and Braemar, although a large number exceed 3,000 feet, are of very tame character, and for years have received no mention in the Journal except in Mr H.T. Munro's paper 'A Summer Night on the Glen Shee Hills'.[2] and a section by him in the growing SMC Guide-book. Though these are not hills which offer rock-climbing in any sense, yet they are hills which offer a splendid high-level walk, ever varied in view and interest, a breezy bracing climax and close to a holiday.

After spending a long and rather weary day in a mail cart, which took five hours to get from Blairgowrie to the Spittal, I left the hotel next morning at 7 a.m. The day was dark and lowering, the clouds being about 1,500 feet high; that is to say, only 300 or 400 feet above the Spittal. The wind was cool, strong and gusty, driving banks of dense black cloud up from the south-west. During breakfast a torrential downfall of rain had lasted a quarter of an hour. As it was nearly my last chance of a day on the hills, I decided to set the weather

---

[1] *SMCJ* 1907, IX, 167-174. Dr Corner was an avid topographer, like James Gall Inglis, and contributed 30-odd articles and notes to the *SMCJ*. The 1921 Tables contain many footnotes ascribing heights and observations to Dr Corner. I have been unable to discover any note or reference to his completion of the Munros or Tops, but since he lived until 1951 and was a dedicated bagger, it is almost inconceivable that he did not complete.

[2] *SMCJ* 1898, V, 116-120.

at nought and go forth. The day was very young, 7 a.m., and I hoped, against a steadily falling barometer, that the weather would improve.

Outside the hotel everything was wet and fresh as it only can be in the early morning. Crossing the bridge over the river, I passed through a gate close by the church, and followed the track round the foot of Ben Gulabin, beneath a rocky headland which forms so prominent an object in the view from the hotel. Passing a ruined house, the track took me through some trees to the side of the river. It was here that the particular experience began. The day was cold rather than cool, so that I was intensely surprised to see a flash of lightning. The thunder came crashing, with another torrential shower. I was wet through before 8 a.m. This thunderstorm lasted about three quarters of an hour, after which it brightened a little. The path took me to the Allt Ghlinn Ghailneiche, and over a bridge to its west bank. The rain had stopped, except for showers of a few minutes' duration to prevent me drying.

I followed up the glen until opposite a burn which descended from Carn Geoidh, when I took to the western hillside, and in a few minutes was within the zone of the mist. Passing at least two sets of rocks I arrived at the broad easy ridge of Creag Bhreac, and in due course struck a wire fence which goes more or less north and south over the backbone of Glas Tulachan. Now the wind was from behind, and assisted me, no longer dashing the rain into my face. The fence, acting as a guide, was a great comfort, as it allowed me to go on without constantly consulting map and compass. It was a long and weary trudge of over a mile of slowly rising ridge to the top of Glas Tulachan, the monotony of which was occasionally relieved by glimpses down into its north-east corries. There are two such corries, which, by the fitful glimpses I obtained, might give some sport in winter, but certainly none in summer. Glas Tulachan is 3,445 feet high, and though I have read that it possesses a huge cairn, I only found a small one. In fact, considering that it is the highest hill between Glas Maol, east of the Cairnwell Pass, and Ben a' Ghlo by Blair Atholl, it was a very small cairn.

After passing this I followed the fence for a little distance, and then left it, striking west into Glen Mhor, following the burn which runs north-west from Glas Tulachan. The whole glen seemed a mass of water. Runnels which in the usual course of events could be stepped over easily, and would often be dry, were full and swollen to the size of a decent burn. Frequently they were too wide to jump, and had to be waded. But the additional wet received in this way scarcely made itself felt. Having joined the main burn, Allt a' Gleann Mhor, I seized on the interval between two showers to take an early lunch. It was a hurried meal on account of the quick succession of the showers. All the time I had been in the mist no thunder was heard.

From my luncheon place the col between Carn an Righ and Mam nan Carn was quickly gained. The ascent of Carn an Righ is about 700 to 800 feet from here. It is very easy; grassy at first, becoming stonier as one ascends. The upper part of the hill is made of quartz, hence its fine symmetrical conical shape. The mist was re-entered just above the col. The wind was much stronger and higher on Carn an Righ than on Glas Tulachan. There are two very respectable quartz cairns on the summit of this little-visited hill, 3,377 feet high, but as the wind made it bitterly cold I did not tarry, starting for the saddle again. The height of this

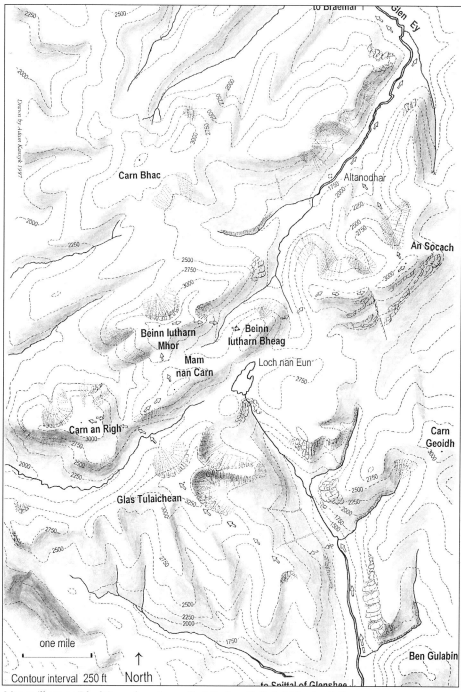

Map to illustrate Edred Corner's route over the hills from Spittal of Glenshee to Braemar

col is about 2,600 feet. It presents no noteworthy features. The ridge of Mam nan Carn rises steeply at first, easing off after about 300 feet, and becoming broad, grassy, and stony in places. About 150 yards south-west of the point marked 3,217 feet, the six-inch Ordnance Survey map gives a point 3,224 feet high. Munro says there is a small cairn on this hill; in the mist I never saw it.

Having passed the summit I steered north-east, and came to the col between Mam nan Carn and Ben Uarn Mor. This is a delightful grassy place with springy turf. The height is about 2,800 feet. A rise of 500 or 600 feet over an easy ground brought me to the large white quartz cairn of Ben Uarn Mor. As I was there ten days after the summer excursion of the Cairngorm Club, I was impressed with the absence of all litter; a fact which shed credit on the members present. By the side of the big cairn I noticed a second and small one, which Mr A.C. Waters told me afterwards was used as the altar upon which the mystic rites of initiation to that Club had been performed. The weather was distinctly drier than it had been, and I had a great discussion with myself as to whether the tops of that out-of-the-way hill Carn Bhac should be visited or not. All was in favour of Carn Bhac when suddenly it began to rain heavily. This decided me, and taking compass bearings, I rapidly descended to the Allt Ben Uarn.

When I was at the fringe of the mist, the first occasion for some time, I noticed the thunder rolling about the hills. The claps at this level were shorter and more frequent than those heard in the morning whilst at a lower level. In a short time I reached the col between Mam nan Carn and Ben Uarn Beg. Its height is about 2,800 feet. An ascent of about 250 feet placed one on the summit of Ben Uarn Beg. It had never ceased to rain since leaving Ben Uarn Mor. The height of Ben Uarn Beg is 3,011 feet, and it has a small cairn on the summit. From this top a bumpy ridge with two tops, 2,845 and 2,742 feet high respectively, leads in a circuitous manner towards An Socach. Instead of attempting the very difficult task of finding my way along this in the mist, I preferred to descend in an east-north-east direction into the corrie between Ben Uarn Beg and An Socach. A steeper pull of some 800 feet landed me on the top of An Socach, 3,059 feet. No cairn was to be seen.

I had scarcely left the mist since leaving Ben Uarn Mor, and it had been raining practically continuously all the time. But now it rained and blew still harder. There was no shelter, and I had to crouch on occasions with my back to the wind behind wholly inefficient stones. It was noticed also that the frequency of electrical discharges from the rocks was much increased. They were very pretty, being chiefly glow discharges which lit up the scene, but were unaccompanied by thunder. When thunder did come it was not the booming sound to which one is accustomed at low levels, but merely a loud and vicious rattle, just like a stonefall on a rocky mountain, such as one hears in Skye or on Ben Nevis.

The surroundings were eerie and unpleasant, such as are apt to get on the nerves of a wet and lonely climber who had been in the mist for some hours. Still I had the summit of An Socach to visit (Socach Mor). It was close and also the last item in the work of a good day. Having been travelling by compass for hours, consulting it every few minutes, I was pretty much at home with the directions and started off for Socach Mor in heavy rain. The ridge between these two tops is nearly level, declining and rising less than 200 feet in a mile. Hurrying along I came at last to the big cairn on Socach Mor, 3,073 feet. It is a stony top, and the electrical glow discharges were very frequent in consequence. The thunder was rattling three or four times a minute, a vicious wind howled through the cairn battering all unsheltered parts with hail. It was a most uninviting state of affairs such as did not tempt me to linger.

Having thus completed my day's work, I consulted my compass to return. But what a surprise! I had been travelling on a ridge running east-north-east with a howling gale behind me coming roughly from the south-south-west. Yet the compass persisted in showing that the north was in the wind's eye. On arriving on the summit I had sat down in the lee of the cairn and should have been facing north ! Had the wind changed, or what had happened? It was bitterly cold and the electrical discharges pretty but very unpleasant, so that, having no inclination to pause and consider, I naturally assumed that the compass knew better, and set off in a direction which appeared to be east-south-east or thereabouts. After descending a few hundred feet I came across water which was running in a south-easterly direction according to the compass, so I followed it, and eventually emerged from the mist and rain close to the main burn of the glen. But I had never been in this glen before. I had meant to be in Glen Baddoch, but this certainly was not Glen Baddoch. The hills were different. It seemed narrower. By-and-by I espied a clump of trees and a house. These were certainly not in Glen Baddoch. Where was I? The compass should help. So it was consulted, and, to my disgust, showed that I was in a glen which ran north-east, not south-east, and certainly was not Glen Baddoch. The map proved it to be Glen Ey and the house to be Alltanodhar Shieling with the clump of trees around it.

Shortly, my position was this. It was six o' clock and I had been travelling with few halts and little food for many hours. I was many miles from the Spittal, with one or two water-sheds in between. Lastly, I was about fourteen or fifteen miles from Braemar, the nearest house of public entertainment. I chose the latter alternative because it was the easiest, there being a road and a track which was mostly downhill. So, having finished my stores of provisions in the lee of the empty shieling, I began the long tramp down Glen Ey. The clump of trees round the house is very thick, making it dark beneath them. The track down the glen was in great part under water, even when it was not diving through the burns. It may be a beautiful glen, but I don't know, as my thoughts were occupied with the problem as to how I, practically a ten-year-old member of the SMC, had come down in the wrong glen. A boyish trick, forsooth, and humiliating in spite of our Librarian's confessions of his lonely wanderings at the head of Glen Lyon.[3]

It was then that the truth dawned on me. The electrical disturbances, whose increase and incessance I had noticed on the Socachs, had turned my compass. It could not have been a magnetic rock, because when I reached running water the compass was as biassed as it had been on the top of Socach Mor. My compass must have been turned, demagnetised, or otherwise affected on the Socach ridge and was deviated for about two hours. This was a curious experience to have on the rounded easy hills of this district.[4]

---

[3] See the preceding Chapter 7.3

[4] James Greig's 'Electrical Disturbances on Beinn a' Ghlo' (*SMCJ* 1907, IX, 290-291), with Corner's article in mind, failed to find any deviation of the compass under similar electrical conditions.

Near the bottom of Glen Ey the keeper met me, I have no doubt on the scent of a trespasser on the last day of July. But his heart was softened when I gave him my news, relating the misfortunes which led to my being in Glen Ey. His news was depressing also–two more miles of glen and five of road to Braemar!

Braemar was reached about 8.30 p.m., but I was still in trouble. I was wringing wet and had no other clothes. This might be considered bad, but worse was to follow. There is one fairy wand in particular which opens the hearts of hotel managers at fashionable places. I lacked that persuader, having left almost all my money at the Spittal. Fortunately, Mr Macdonald of the Fife Arms was the reverse of what might have been expected, for he accepted the word of a wet, dirty, and, I have no doubt, disreputable-looking wanderer. Certainly, Braemar was one of the last places I should have expected to see that night. But I had had an excellent day on the hills, plenty of new experiences, and a kind, genial host and entertainment at my journey's end. Further than this, I met an old friend, and in his company tested the deep truth of the last sentence of Munro's article which I have already referred to. After his day in the Glenshee hills, he dwelt feelingly on post-prandial ease and cigars.[5] There is no doubt that there should be no niggardly finish to a good day.

There was a peculiarity about the thunder which I had not noticed before that day. In the valleys below the mist it possessed all the rolling, booming character with which we are so familiar. In the mist I heard very little of it. This is not surprising, for very few who spend days on mountains can have failed to see a thunderstorm below them and have heard no thunder. But when I was on the tops and still in the clouds, the thunder was again apparent and had changed its character from a long, booming roll to a sharp, short, vicious rattle. This rattle did not seem to accompany the glow discharges, which were more frequent on the sharper and rockier summits, but only the more definite sparkings.

The next day I had to return to the Spittal, and, having found Mr A.C. Waters, SMC, at Braemar, we decided to have a gentle day together. As is well known, near Braemar is the Cairnwell Pass, 2,200 feet high, and traversed by a driving road. That was obviously the key to our 'gentle day', as the road led to the Spittal of Glen Shee. We hired a machine and drove nearly to the top of the pass, from which we ascended a three-thousand footer in half-an-hour without having to hurry! I know of no gentler beginning to a day in Scotland. The name of our hill is Carn Aosda, 3,003 feet high. It is a quartz hill with two cairns. After duly halting, we descended, and, leaving the Cairnwell on the left, passed over Carn nan Sac (3,000 feet) to Carn Geoidh (3,194 feet). It was astonishing how the ground had sucked up the previous day's rain, showing how badly the moisture was needed. Carn Geoidh has two cairns, one being on the south side and not on the summit. A further walk took us to the summit of Carn Bhinnein (3,006 feet), which is, as Munro says, the most shapely top in the district. It is true that it is not separated from Carn Geoidh by dip or distance as are Carn Aosda or The Cairnwell, but in individuality it ranks above them all.

---

[5] After his long night-day on the West Glenshee hills, Munro bicycled for 4 hours from the Spital to his home against wind and over a road 'reduced . . to the consistency of porridge, so that I only reached home at 8 p.m. I have nothing more to add. There are some emotions too sacred to be minutely described in print, such, for instance, as the beatitude induced that evening by a bottle of 'the boy' and a post-prandial cigar.'

It is a rocky knob at the point of intersection of some grassy ridges which enclose grassy corries. The actual summit is composed of quartz, and, contrary to the statement of the Guide Book, has a cairn, and a very respectable cairn too. Here we parted, Waters returning northward to Braemar, I southward to Spittal. Twice on the homeward journey I went to sleep, and twice was awakened by a sharp shower. Such was the last day of a holiday which, no matter how carefully the plans had been made for it, had not followed the course which had been prepared. This has a great and happy result, one can build fresh schemes for the future, and have the additional pleasure of traversing ground which has become familiar from former experiences. It is a very great pleasure to visit neighbourhoods which have been explored before, provided that some time has been allowed to elapse, unless there are special attractions as in Skye. I had not visited this part of the country since 1898. My second visit has made me feel that eight years shall not elapse before I see it again. It is a matter of joy that I have still at least two hills which I wish to climb in this neighbourhood.

The two consecutive days which I had there were a great contrast to each other; one full of storm and mist, the other sunny, particularly on the north side of the range.

7.6 A Fifteen-Hour Walk In Benderloch

F.S. Goggs[1]

TO BE ON THE TRAMP from early morn to dewy eve – to start with lantern, and to arrive at the haven where we would be in company with the evening star, having seen the sun make a complete circuit of the heavens, is an experience which cannot be considered uncommon in the case of those whom the spirit of the mountains calls to Alpine snows ; but in Scotland, to spend fifteen consecutive hours on the hills, though by no means an unprecedented, is yet not a very common proceeding. It might be mentioned as a further fact, which, though by no means unprecedented, is yet not very common, to wit, that during the whole of those fifteen hours it never ceased raining. From the last mentioned fact, any member of the SMC will at once anticipate that the log of the expedition will produce moving incidents of fell and flood.

Most unfortunately, the Club's versatile Honorary Secretary has not yet turned his attention to the science of crystal gazing, and when in December 1911 the Club at its Annual General Meeting decided to hold the Easter Meet at Glencoe, no official warning was given that this might prove to be a difficult matter. As Easter 1912 drew near, however, the railway-men struck, and the service of trains became smaller by degrees and beautifully less, till over many of the branch lines no trains ran. Ballachulish, the most convenient station for Glencoe, is at the end of a branch line, and the problem whether that particular section would be working or not at Easter could only be solved by the famous formula of the Prime Minister, Wait+C. There seemed to be a fair probability that at least one train a

[1] *SMCJ* 1913, XII, 258-266.

day would run from Edinburgh to Oban, so three members of the SMC, having pored over maps for some time, decided to take the train to Taynuilt and from there to trust to Charon and shank's mare.

Rooms were, therefore, engaged at Taynuilt and Clachaig, and the three of us with well-filled rucksacs and the kind of feeling which, I imagine, pervades the minds of those proceeding to the front in some campaign, of absolute uncertainty as to how far you will get and when, if ever, you will arrive at your destination, took our seats in a long and crowded Caledonian train at Edinburgh. At Stirling it was raining heavily, and the downpour accompanied us for the next forty hours. We waited inside and outside every station on the line, and at length reached Taynuilt at midnight – seven and a half hours as against a normal four. Heavy rain and Egyptian darkness did their best to prevent our finding the Temperance Hotel, but the desire for shelter proved strong enough to prevail over all obstacles, and half an hour the wrong side of midnight found us asleep.

At 5.30 we were called, and at 6.40 we started for our distant Mecca – Clachaig. It was still raining, a heavy pall hung over the shores of Loch Etive, and the outlook was as funereal as a wet day anywhere always gives. Bearing in mind the old proverb, 'rain before seven, clear up by eleven,' we hoped for the best. A little before seven, standing on the edge of the rough stone pier jutting out into the loch, one of us yelled for the ferry-boat till his throat was somewhat sore, whilst the two others stayed in the shelter of a small wooden hut, erected for the use of those crossing the loch, which is here only a quarter of a mile wide. Half a dozen quarry-men joined us, and our Charon, ruddy-faced and stoutly built, soon landed us on the further shore. We passed quickly through the quarries with their cranes, their lines of rail, their curious coracle-looking shelters for the men hewing the stones after these have been quarried out of the rock face, etc. We had not come to see these, and were pleased to leave the sights and sounds of strenuous labour behind us and to find a charming track by the loch side, in some places hewn out of the hill, now up, now down, creeping round first one headland, then another; on the one hand – the dim shore across the loch seen through the bare stems and branches, which in two months' time or less would form a leafy screen – on the other, the cliff broken here and there by running streams, and covered with moss and lichen, and ever above the clang of our hobnailers was 'heard the water lapping on the crag.'

One or two solitary cottages were passed, then at Cadderlie the hills retreated and the loch widened – for all that we could see that morning it might have been the boundless ocean. Just after passing Cadderlie we ought to have kept to our right, still hugging the loch side, but a track to our left led us into moss hags and rank ground, and then petered out. However, we struck the track again before crossing Abhainn Dalach by a wire suspension bridge, just beyond which we came across a weary-looking shepherd lolling beside a weary-looking wee haycock. Two or three days later we saw the same shepherd in sunshine, and he seemed to have grown cheerful, but on the day we are speaking of man and nature looked weary and depressed. The shepherd lived a mile and a half away up the glen: we could see his dim habitation in the dreary distance, and we pitied his dismal lot, but looking back now I think it was all a question of weather. We spoke to him, and found he knew of the existence of the hill we were making for, but he had never been up it.

We now left the track and struck north for the Allt Easach, to a point where the burn made a grand display of white horses, flecked with black. Above these falls we continued along the west bank of the stream, mounting very gradually. Beinn Bheag rose on our left and Beinn Mheadhonach on our right: both these low hills had evidently been worn smooth by ice, and although their slopes were overgrown to some extent by moss and turf, quite sufficient black-smoothed rock remained to tell the history of the past. The rock glistened with the water which steadily poured over it: beneath us the saturated turf squelched with a sound as of water-logged boots; out from the watery mist before us came the silver streamlets or foaming cascades, behind us the watery mist was pierced by the same ever-agitated element. Water, water, water, – above, below, all round. The rain was not falling with any special force, there was no particular wind, but the moisture came down – down – down with a kind of silent and resistless persistence, mocking all hope. A pair of herons standing on a sandy spit in the burn resented our intrusion, stretched out their long legs, and flew into the all-devouring mist: some bedraggled sheep moved clumsily away, but most living things thought it was a day on which it was more pleasant to remain indoors than to go out.

As we followed the full burn to its source, it diminished in volume, and at length we saw the side of our hill looming up to the north-west. We then left the burn and struck away up what we found to be a fairly steep slope, with outcrops of rock here and there. Some way up we had some refreshment, but the shelterless wind and rain-swept slopes did not invite a lengthy sojourn. We eventually struck the snow-crusted summit ridge of Sguliaird (or Sgulaird – 6-inch O.S. map) at the foot of the final rise, and soon a big circular cairn loomed through the mist like another distant top (3,059 feet, 1 p.m). The derivation of the name Sguliaird is uncertain, but Mr R. Angus Smith in his book, 'Loch Etive and the Sons of Uisnach,' states that Sgeulee means story-teller (p. 202), so that Sguliaird will mean the story-teller's height.

Our programme for the day was a generous one, and included Beinn Fhionnlaidh and Sgor na h-Ulaidh, and although I expect we all had some secret misgivings as to carrying our task through, no-one hinted retreat. From the summit of Sguliaird the ridge dips north-east to 2,855 feet, then rises to a subsidiary top, 2,963 feet (about one-fifth of a mile from each other), at which point the ridge divides; the main portion goes north at first, then curves to the east to Stob Gaibhre (2,244 feet), whilst a steep rocky spur goes east, the two ridges encircling Coire nan Tulach. Down the spur we went, finding the descent steep and rocky; the rocks were well split up, and afforded us an enjoyable scramble. Taking a compass bearing in the mist, we found we were going too much to the east, and presently a partial clearing showed far below silver streaks running apparently in a wrong direction from our standpoint. We therefore contoured round, struck the main ridge again, and came to a small lochan (2,087 feet), with a hillock (Stob Gaibhre) rising straight up behind. From the hillock we strained our eyes northward, and seeing nothing but veiled and gloomy outlines, the desolation and despair of surrounding nature chilled our hearts, and a proposition to leave the two remaining hills to a brighter day found no opposer.

There could not be much argument about the line of retreat: there was only one – Glen Ure. With the load of two hills off our backs, we trotted gaily down a steep hill-side, avoiding here and there a rocky face, through a small hanging valley, which contained a few stunted trees and was well suited for storing stolen cattle, till we struck a good path not marked on the map. This path leads from Glen Ure farm to the top of the glen, keeping the west bank of the burn all the way, and runs high up the hill side to avoid a deep gorge. Where we struck the path we found ourselves faced by a perpendicular wall of unscalable rock, which formed the east side of the glen; many feet below us was the brawling stream in spate, behind were the steep grassy slopes, down which we had just come, rising to an indefinite height into the mist. The glen was extraordinarily narrow, a deep cut in the hills – a ravine much more nearly expresses its character than the word glen, but the scale of the ravine is large and generous; its sides on a misty day tower to heaven. It is a fitting home for the king of birds who nests here. We none of us remembered a similar glen in Scotland, and were delighted to have come so unexpectedly across such a striking bit of country.

The path led us in some two miles to Glen Ure farm (3.30 p.m.), where a mossy stone bridge, in the middle of a short gorge containing some noble specimens of the fir, spanned the today foaming burn. Under more peaceful weather conditions there are delightfully translucent pools below and above the bridge, and the miniature gorge might well be a haunt of the fairies. The name Glenure takes us back to troublous times, for was it not Colin Campbell of Glenure who was the victim of the Appin tragedy on the 14th May 1752, and for whose murder a Stewart paid the last penalty at the scene of the crime near Ballachulish? If local tradition be correct, Stewart's execution seems to have been as much a murder as that of Campbell, but judicial. Robert Louis Stevenson, in 'Kidnapped', makes the tragedy live before us, and those who prefer cold history unmixed with fiction can find the whole grim story in the series, 'Notable Scottish Trials, Trial of James Stewart (The Appin Murder).'

The farmer at Glenure kindly gave us the use of an out-house, where, protected from the steady downpour, we lit our aluminium cooker, and soon had a luxurious afternoon tea ready. Unpacking, the consumption of many courses, the drinking of much tea, then repacking, took somewhere approaching an hour. We now had a good road under our feet, and after three miles, mostly through wood, found ourselves at Salachail. Here we had a choice of routes – the obvious one by a good track leading to Ballachulish down Gleann an Fhiodh; the other, pathless, but more direct, by Allt Eilidh and the northern part of Allt na Muidhe. Galbraith, with the wisdom of age and experience, plumped for the track; Russell knew that route, and therefore voted for the unknown. I, too, voted for the trackless, so Galbraith gave in to the views of his juniors: whether he will do so again, I am not sure.

After a chat with the keepers at Salachail regarding the route, &c., we took a very rough track from the sheep-fank a quarter of a mile beyond the farm, to the north-east: this led us towards the Allt Eilidh burn, but always kept considerably above it. The water was roaring down a gorge in the glen, and made so much noise that conversation was difficult; in fact, whenever we were near a stream that day, the noise was that of a workshop filled with machinery going at full speed, and the din in our ears persisted even when one had left the burn. Strong wind has the same noisy effect, and I have no doubt both tend to make the climber sleep more soundly when the time comes. We gradually ascended, the burn being always on our right, till we saw a dam, a quarter of a mile long, above us: we then went to cross the stream where it left the reservoir, but one look at the foaming water was sufficient, and we walked back the length of the dam, and skirted the reservoir till we gained the glen beyond it. We were surprised to see this huge loch here, as it was not marked on the map, but under less watery conditions its area is small.

Night was fast coming on, and we stumbled along over rough ground till we struck a narrow track, which led to the col (about 1,050 feet), giving access to Allt na Muidhe. Here the path ceased, and we descended steeply, bearing slightly to the right, till we found ourselves shut in by two streams, the one from the col, the other the stream in Allt na Muidhe. It was imperative that we crossed one burn or the other, and that quickly; but neither looked at all inviting. Glancing up the Allt na Muidhe a black line was seen across the white waters. "A bridge," shouted one of us, and we thought our deliverance was accomplished. On arriving at the 'bridge' we found that we were not yet out of the wood: only one old fir still remained, and that covered with nails, having the business ends uppermost. Whether the worn timber would support 12 stones remained to be seen: an attempt by one of the party to cross it astride, avoiding the nails, revealed a very perplexed mental picture, and as a divided mind never accomplishes anything, neither did he. No one else seemed inclined to experiment on nail points, and as it was getting darker every moment, we ran to look at the other burn, which seemed of the two a trifle smaller.

We were getting desperate now, and as Galbraith was the oldest, we tied a rope round his waist and threw him in. He scrambled out safely on the other side, and we followed in turn. It was now (8.15) quite dark, but we stumbled along the hill side above the roaring torrent of the combined streams, and soon saw on the further bank the light from the keeper's cottage, which rejoices in the name of Gleann-leac-na-muidhe. We then came to the bridge crossing the burn and the road leading to Bridge of Coe. We did not cross this bridge and try to puzzle out the track to Clachaig, because we thought it quite possible that the bridge over the Fionn Ghleann burn might be washed away. As a matter of fact, the bridge is high above the stream, and is not at all likely to be carried away in a spate.

A mile further we arrived at the farm of Achnacon at 8.45, and going in to light our lantern we were told that the rain had been incessant for seventy-two hours, that the river was over its banks, and that it was dangerous to go on. It was arranged at length that the farmer's son and one of his men should accompany us with a swinging lamp. The cavalcade was soon on its way, and we had visible proof that the water was indeed over the roadway. We were piloted over fields, and through hedges, until at length the hard highway at the Bridge of Coe was beneath our feet. We said goodnight to our guides, and at 10.20 we were standing in the porch of Clachaig Inn. We were not wet through, thanks to wettermantels, but we did not despise a change and some warm food.

Three days later a party of five drove from Kingshouse to the school at Lochetivehead in the teeth of a violent storm from the west, and having learned that the bridge over the Kinglass had been washed away two or three years ago, we followed the path on the north bank, which leads through charming birch and mossy woods, under the shadow of the ice-worn slabby face of Beinn Trilleachan. Starting at 10.15 a.m. in a heavy rainstorm of almost tropical violence we thought we were in for a thorough soaking. At mid-day, however, a marvellous change took place, the rain disappeared, the sun came out, and we had some of the most charming rainbow effects any of us had ever seen. The strong wind raised spindrift from the surface of the loch, and the sun shining on the spray made long sections across the loch's surface glisten with all the colours of the rainbow, whilst at the same time broad belts of rainbow hue lit up the mountain sides. We all stood fascinated by the marvellous and charming effect. Was the weather too stormy for the ferry boat at Bonawe to cross? On a favourable answer to this question depended our catching the train at Taynuilt. On reaching the ferry at 3.50 p.m. we found that the boat had only been able to make its first crossing that day an hour previously. The ferry on the other side over the River Awe could not be used that day at all. It was fortunate that we had not come down the south side of the loch, as had we wished to ferry over the River Awe we should have found it impossible. It seems that it is a very rare occurrence indeed for anyone to be prevented from crossing the Bonawe ferry for a whole day – once in several years – but in stormy weather an intending passenger may have to wait an hour or two.

> "This Land of Rainbows, spanning glens whose walls,
> Rock-built, are hung with rainbow-coloured mists,
> Of far-stretched meres, whose salt flood never rests,
> Of tuneful caves and playful waterfalls,
> Of mountains varying momently their crests."
> – Wordsworth. *"Composed in the Glen of Loch Etive."*

7.7 Midnight Wanderings in the Larig

Edward Backhouse.[1]

"YOU CAN'T go wrong in the Larig." So spoke one who ought to know, for every year he treads the familiar way drawn thither alike by the grandeur of the scene and by the warmth of welcome at the further end. But members of the SMC. have no such word as 'cannot' in their vocabulary; and these pages are written to show how two of them accomplished the impossible.

W.N. Ling, T.E. Goodeve, and I left Aviemore for Glen Einich on the Saturday of last Easter, and tramped through wet snow to the lower bothy. We were passed on the way by a large wagonette party, which broke into twos and threes and made, as we did, up the slopes of Braeriach. On the hillside the snow was in good condition, and a strong wind blew cold from the south-east. A thousand feet from the top we walked into cloud and had to search for the summit by means of the compass. The plateau was encrusted with ice, and as we peered along its surface, broken by blocks of stone, the appearance was of a glacier. The compass was still needed to steer us from the top, but soon the clouds showed signs of breaking, and we caught glimpses of the valley. After a while, first one ridge and then another cleared and again was covered. Gradually the open spaces increased. For much of the way a fine cornice hung above the unseen corrie on our left.

---

[1] *SMCJ* 1913, XII, 286-290.

Near the Angel's Peak we met Goggs and Watson walking from Derry to Aviemore. Goodeve joined them, as he had to leave for the south next morning.

Ling and I walked on to Derry Lodge, scarcely needing the other men's tracks to guide us. We left the broad back of the mountain north of the Devil's Peak and hit an easy route to the valley. Before seven, we were enjoying the warm welcome of Mr Fraser and his daughter.

We were greeted next morning by the sight of trees heavily laden with snow, and a thick carpet on the ground, which a persistent fall was deepening every minute. Miss Fraser fervently ejaculated, "I'm glad I'm not a Scottish mountaineer," but it was without the least foreboding that we set out for our walk across the Larig. Our intentions on Macdhui were of course put aside. Up the valley from Derry Lodge we could distinguish the path only by the deeper snow that lay on it; and in the teeth of a violent wind we ploughed our way onwards. To miss the bridge across Luibeg burn caused little delay, but was of ill omen. Over the slopes of Carn a' Mhaim the snow lay less thickly and we made good progress, particularly where we rounded for a short space into the lee of the hill. Here for the first and last time till a roof was above us, we were able to talk without shouting. Once in line with the course of the Dee the wind met us furiously, and we were heartily thankful that the angle of ascent was very gentle. Still the snow fell, sometimes heavily, and then with sparse flakes driven before the wind. Although we could see little but rocks looming from time to time out of the mist, we did not trouble much about the route, as we fondly thought that the course of the stream would guide us. So thinking, we rose gradually at first, and then more steeply, and then so steeply that we resorted to the compass, and found that we were aiming north-west instead of north. Rocks appeared dimly in every direction. We concluded rightly that we must be in a corrie of Braeriach, and turned north-east to contour back again to the main valley.

It is always tiresome to drop when you know that a rise must follow: the annoyance is much more serious when every step is a laborious lift of the foot out of deep snow. So came it that we were impatient of descent and turned too early in a northerly direction. For some time we skirted the hill side without misgiving, rising gradually, as we hoped, in the direction of the pass. But once more we found ourselves encompassed by rocks, and guessed that we were again in a corrie. There are, broadly speaking, two ways out of a corrie; one the streams take, the other is popular with climbers. So as the Larig had proved elusive, we determined to make for the summit plateau of Braeriach, which as everyone knows is a biggish target to hit. We could see snow above us broken here and there by ribs of rock. As we climbed the labour of each step increased, until the heavy man of the party found himself now and again lower at the end of a struggle than when it began. The snow was extremely soft and lay at a high angle on frozen grass, so that the only dependable support was that of the ice axe driven hard into the turf. Progress by the ribs of rock which jutted out from the snow was impossible, as they were covered with ice. Fortunately as we climbed higher the snow improved slightly, and at last appeared the cornice which rimmed the corrie. We went on in hopes of finding a gap, and it was not until we were within some 30 feet of it that we saw that it would be difficult to win through. Straight ahead the cornice was obviously impossible, to the left it was little better; but to the right the curve was broken by a bridge of snow which reached down to the slope below. Ling thought that he might be able to clamber across; but without a rope the bridge could not even be reached with safety, for steep ice slopes were between us and it. So there was nothing for it but to go down once more.

It was 6.30, and all the daylight left us was needed to reach safe ground. And still it snowed. We aimed to the east and went down till the slope rose against us, and then debated whether to turn north towards Aviemore or south to Derry Lodge. We had little idea how far from either we were, and so decided that it was better to take the direction we knew, however sketchily.

The next few hours are best passed over with few words. We found the Dee and followed down, the light fading rapidly. We crossed the stream perhaps five times, sometimes on its frozen surface, more often breaking through to its icy waters. We learnt that it is easier in the dark to step into a stream than to find the way out. A strong wind at our backs chilled us; the snow froze in lumps of ice to our clothes ; we had eaten nothing for many hours, and we trudged on through the deep snow, vainly searching for a glimpse of the bothy in the hope of a little shelter in which to put on sweaters and eat a few mouthfuls. At last we gave it up, and crouching behind a boulder our numbed hands groped clumsily in rucksacks for cakes and dates. Ling's sweater, caught by a blast of wind, was seen no more, and altogether we felt that fate was dealing hardly with us.

But from this point things went better. The snow stopped falling for the first time since we set out twelve hours earlier, the moon had risen, and before long we could discern a black form to our right front, which we took for the Devil's Peak. Soon we could make out the line of the Dee and the low pass which leads to Derry.

We steered a good course round the hillside, and after much weary trudging, the woods of the valley showed as dark patches on the white landscape. Rarely can those woods have neared so slowly; but at last the first trees were reached, the bridge was crossed, and the long stretch to Derry was traversed. Soon after 12.30 we were knocking at the door of the Lodge. Of the hospitality shown us it is impossible to speak too gratefully. A fire was soon burning in the kitchen, and another in the parlour. The first served to thaw and then to dry our clothes; while at the other we sat arrayed in our host's check suits, which adorned impartially my long shanks and Ling's elegant ankles. We drank tea and ate biscuits, consoled by Mr Fraser's sympathy and his daughter's richly deserved chaff. Then to bed, while the Fraser family stayed up till morning (so we afterwards discovered) drying our clothes.

No one who had the good fortune to be in the neighbourhood of Aviemore will soon forget Easter Monday of 1913. We spent it in a successful attempt to cross the Larig, albeit a matter of ten hours was needed to accomplish it. It was a delightful, though at times toilsome, walk. The clouds cast moving shadows on the snowy mountains; at the head of the great corries of Braeriach the cornice curved and hung.

As we sat in the sun by the side of our familiar acquaintance the Dee, we traced our wanderings in the snowstorm of the previous day and drew the obvious morals, which for members of the S.M.C. need not here be repeated. Our initial mistake had been in following up the stream which issues from Garbh Choire instead of the one which falls from the pass. When we first turned back we were high up the slopes of the corrie, and had we gone on could have easily gained the summit of Braeriach and thence probably Glen Einich. Instead we descended and contoured into Coire Brochain. The basin of the corrie was sufficiently flat to mislead us into thinking that we were again on our proper route and that north was our right course; whereas it took us up one side of the corrie and ended in our undoing.

The snow was hard beyond the Pools of Dee, and it was not until we crossed the pass that the way became laborious. But when the sky is clear, it matters little that at every step one is sinking to the knee. After a while the snow grew thinner and through Rothiemurchus Forest it disappeared.

At sunset the glow on the eastern hills was worthy of the Alps. As we strode along the last stretch of road the light was fading, and thrushes sang in the spruce trees their vesper song. In the space of a very few hours we had passed from the depth of winter to the fullness of spring.

7.8 A Far Cry to Lochow

J.F.A. Burt[1]

I FELL in with Murray Lawson at Kingshouse in the summer of 1924, and he invited me, after some days' climbing together, to the 1925 New Year Meet at Lochawe. I felt the need of arriving at my first meet as fit as possible, so planned an approach that involved several days on the hills. Though I had scrambled about the Arran hills since boyhood, my mainland climbing was confined to the previous eight months. I had made no more than three snow ascents, but these were under excellent guidance.

Starting from Aberfeldy, I walked to Fortingal and a memorable dinner. Next day I traversed Carn Mairg, met a car at Bridge of Balgie and finished at Killin. A heavy snowfall now imposed a virtual off-day, but the next again was fine and I entrained for Crianlarich, from which I climbed Stob Garbh and Cruach Ardrain. The snow was pretty deep on the lee-sides, and much marked with tracks of mountain hares (of which, by the way, we had chased hundreds, and killed three, on the road from Bridge of Balgie), ptarmigan and a fox. As I topped one of the hummocks on the summit ridge of Stob Garbh I surprised the last in the next hollow – the only live fox I have ever seen in Scotland.

I plowtered up the short steep snowy slope from the east col to the Cruach Ardrain cairn and struck – or rather, was struck by – a south-west blizzard. I was spun round by the wind and lashed by stinging hail. Completely *désorienté,* I had a hard fight to force myself, in accordance with reason and the compass, to resist an instinctive feeling that the way to Crianlarich lay along the ridge which, in reality, leads to Ben Tulaichean.

---

[1] *SMCJ* 1953, XXV, 120-123.

Happily I funked glissading down the Y-gully and set off for the western ridge. But the vicious wind and hail daunted me. I have always had a horror of the seemingly personal malignity of very high winds, and instead of continuing over the nose of the Grey Height, I made my way down from the west col to the shelter of the glen. Here I floundered about in the failing light among boulders, snow-drifts and the horrors of snow-masked peat hags. But I got down in time for a bath before dinner and the deep healing slumber I always associate with Crianlarich.

I caught the morning train to Tyndrum and embarked on the final stage of my little Odyssey – the traverse of Beinn Laoigh and Beinn a' Chleibh. The path by the side of Coninish Water was easy and pleasant, and all went well until, abreast of the farm, I broke a hookside of my spectacles while cleaning them. After that my memories, though vivid, are naturally a trifle blurred.

Beinn Laoigh, the high point of Burt's long walk from Aberfeldy to Lochawe to join the 1925 SMC New Year Meet

I climbed up, happily enough, to the lip of the great North Corrie. There, frankly, as holding my glasses to my eyes I viewed the onward way, my heart quailed. The snow in the corrie was obviously much deeper than the worst I had experienced the day before. As a matter of fact I learned later that two much more experienced climbers had reached the corrie and, without hesitation, turned back. In my inexperience the idea never occurred to me.

On I went, floundering in soft snow that was frequently up to my waist and once up to my neck. It was not pleasant, but I accepted it as being all in the day's work. But when I found myself, breathless and snow-plastered, at the foot of the Fox's Rake, I felt I must modify my plan. My snow-swim had taken it out of me: the thought of resuming it in the lower pitches of the Rake was unbearable; and for the first time in my life on the hills I felt I had not the necessary reserves of strength. So I turned to the ill-defined buttress on my left. I clawed my way up 1,000 feet of broken rock and snow-covered turf. After the corrie, the going, though none too easy, seemed heavenly. About two o'clock I climbed on to the summit ridge, a few feet from the cairn.

The same screaming south-wester which I had met on Cruach Ardrain greeted me once more, but mercifully, there was this time no hail. I crouched in such shelter as the cairn afforded and ate some sandwiches and crystallised fruit. Then I set off for Beinn a' Chleibh.

That was a nightmare passage. The southern face of Lui was covered with a thin sheet of *verglas,* out of which stuck pebbles and outcrops of rock. These saved me from cutting steps or I should have been benighted. Slithering from jut to jut, I forced my way to the col against the raving wind.

I had some shelter as I plugged up the 400 feet to the next summit, but there the wind met me with redoubled fury, and again my heart failed me. I had only to force my way down over the nose to McLaren's farm, and a plain road to Dalmally awaited me. But I could not face again that demon wind, and sought instead a sheltered gully on the unprospected north face of Beinn a' Chleibh.

I ought to have been killed several times over. In the failing light I glissaded downwards until some sixth sense persuaded me that all was not well. I dug in my heels, produced my glasses, held them to my eyes and perceived that I was on the verge of a 20-foot drop on to what – I could not see in the gloom. I contoured to another gully and repeated the process – including the sixth sense and the 20-foot drop.

As the last gleam of daylight died I scrambled up the railway embankment and sat down by the permanent way. I ate my remaining provisions (I remember the exquisite flavour of some candied apricots) and took stock of my position. Between me and the main road raced a torrent, swollen by the snows: if there was a bridge it was now too dark to find it on the map. I had not thought of this in my panic-stricken flight from the summit. Ahead of me lay about five miles of sleepers to Dalmally.

I have always loathed sleepers. Too near for one to stride from one to the next, too far apart to be taken two at a time, they impose on the walker a frustrated mincing motion most trying to the muscles of the leg. But the path beside the permanent way has snares in the shape of signal wires and was not to be thought of in the dark. So, from sleeper to sleeper I plodded wearily through what seemed eternity. Once I had to step aside, when the west-bound train came along. I gazed up enviously at the figures in the warm, well-lighted carriages, borne in ease and comfort over my *via dolorosa.*

I came ashore at Dalmally Station. Only two miles and a half of sleepers stood between me and Lochawe, but once more I could not take it. I went to the general store and inquired after a car to take me the five miles by road. Someone went off to start it up, and I sat down in the genial light and warmth of the shop, dripping on the floor as the frozen snow melted out of my clothes. The villagers came in to do their New Year's Eve shopping. At last a perspiring man came to say that they couldn't get a sign of life from the car engine, "but there iss the delivery van, of course . ."

"Man dear," said I (we had an Irish housemaid then), "I would gladly go in a hearse!"

So when Murray Lawson came to the porch to see who the latest arrival was, there was I, clambering stiffly out of a grocer's yellow van. He did not so much as raise an eyebrow, but I had a subtle feeling that he did not think it was quite the proper way for a guest to arrive at a Meet.

Nor was it. The whole expedition had been a thoroughly base-over-apex performance. And the moral of that – as the Duchess (no, the other one, in 'Alice') would say – must be that there is a Providence which looks after fools and drunkards; for besides acting like a fool I was at that time climbing-drunk.

> *'How bad and mad and sad it was!*
> *But then, how it was sweet!'*

7.9 The Breath of the Gods

Compiled by W.D. Brooker[1]

THERE are windier places than the Scottish Highlands. In Adelie Land in the Antarctic the average wind speed throughout the year is said to be 60 mph! However our mountain playground is the scene of much boisterous behaviour by Mother Nature. Here are a few examples.

Getting the Wind Up

P.W. Gribbon

THERE is nothing exceptional in a high wind on a hill. It's a common experience to be buffeted and dumped, to go crab-crawling and to lie prostrate.

We sat in the hut. The great outdoors was having a prolonged period of unpleasantness. We were indolent and lethargic and even spiritually debilitated. We had no thoughts of routes. Every hour the chopper man forayed outside to check the lines anchoring the machine on its snow pad, but no one with any sense moved on to the mountain. It needed a diet of high moral fibre to counteract the tedium of our continual hut lurking. Let's go for a wee walk.

We were wafted up Allt a' Mhuilinn with the north-west wind at our tails and we were whisked up the Coire Leis slopes to the long arête leading to the summit of Carn Mor Dearg. There the force of the wind was spinning into a vast eddy and curling back on the southern flank of the arête, and sometimes there was some shelter in the lee. We trod carefully, tripodal with axes, ready to run and crouch and scamper erratically onwards. The arête had hidden quiet corners in a dip in the snow or the back of a rock. It wasn't an escapade beyond the pale of reason. We knew that the arête led to the open broad and gentle slope rising to the summit. Ay, there was the rub.

---

[1] *SMCJ* 1985, XXXIII, 167-174.

When we forsook the shelter of the last rocks, we walked blithely with our eyes open on to an expansive and innocuous sweep of mountain. We were on to a frozen wave of bleakly polished ice, colourless, lifeless, windswept. Only a brisk stamp uphill with our crampons biting the surface, we thought. With a sideways cant, we were compensating the vectors of the wind . Nonetheless we had a problem: how to get up the slope. Leaning and moving, we were going sideways across the icy slope on an unwanted traverse line that took us away from the direct line of the crest. The only answer was to stop and lock, going nowhere.

We were wedded to the slope, hanging on picks fractionally inched into ice, teetering alarmingly on crampon tips. What next? Nothing. Cling on and wait. In front was the obvious slope leading up the crest. A few yards to go, it was so near and yet so far. Behind, under my heels not seen but felt with some disquiet, was the long snow slope that arched and steepened towards the gullies that were furrowed between sharp spines of stones. A few feet to safety, a thousand feet to oblivion. Whose was the choice?

The wind had blown for hours, it was an unrelentingly cruel wind, shifting infinitesimally and offering only a fractional respite in mere morsels of a knot. We would have to snatch the right moment to move. We waited, counting the ice grains a few eyelashes away in incessant sound, the lash of whips, cracklets and spicules. No need to communicate, the plan was known by instinct. We clung and hunched into our innermost cores, womb-hidden and nurturing under tight control our microcosm of instant vital being. We waited perhaps for ten minutes, it could have been longer. Time passed without meaning. Wait, hang on, survive . . . then a break . . Go!

We were flung up on the wings of the wind. Up and over the crest, the sound tearing over the horizon, and we went down, ever downwards, running free and wild, until with a sudden timidity we turned about to face the slope and to start kicking cautiously into the unknown corrie. Drained of adrenalin, we stopped to consider our position.

The upper slopes of the Aonachs merged into the mist. We would have to contour home on a long low level circuit around the flanks of Carn Mor Dearg. We weren't going to complain. There was a time to hold our peace, with thanks.

An Ignominious Retreat

D.G. Pyper

ON January 4th, 1983 I was nearing the end of my Munro tally and on the way back to Aberdeen from Kinlochewe it seemed a good idea to deal with the recently promoted Sgurr nan Ceannaichean near Achnasheen, having already done its near neighbour Moruisg. The weather was quite good, grey and dull with high cloud, but without even the faintest breeze. In fact, the stillness was oppressive.

I leave the road thinking that it should not take long to rattle up and down this upstart. I'll probably be in the pub before afternoon closing. After about an hour I am about 200 feet below the summit plateau. That's good, a wee breeze from the southeast to get rid of the sweat. Another 100 ft and it is no longer so good. My anorak goes on. Where the hell did that wind come from?

I'm on the snow that drapes down from the plateau and it is frozen hard so the axe is needed. This wind seems to be growing stronger by the minute. It's a struggle removing my pack to get the axe without losing my footing. Axe gripped firm, off I go. Just another few feet and I'll be able to toddle along to the summit. But drawing level with the plateau I am hit by a blast of air that throws me back down about 6 ft. Leaning further forward with expectancy and axe at the ready, I try again. I reach my former high point and meet the same unrelenting blast. It becomes a hands-and-knees affair, hauling across the horizontal snow. I hope nobody is watching these ridiculous antics. I begin to realise how serious the situation has become when my body lifts off the snow and my only remaining contact with the mountain is the pick of the axe. I decide the game is up and its time to get to hell out of here, but the problem is to pull the pick out of the hard snow when the rest of me is airborne. The choice is to hang on until the body parts company with the axe at the arm sockets or to extract the pick and be blown away. The decision is taken for me when the axe comes out and I find myself in a sprawling heap 30 ft down the slope. My interest in this summit has dissipated and I waste no time in retreating to the car and the security of the pub.

Even hardened locals who had seen it all were crowding for a space at the window to view the storm and this seemed to alleviate the self reproach I felt at having just failed on a wee Munro. Reflecting over my pint I realised that the only thing that went according to plan was catching the pub before closing time.

An Unexpected Blow: High winds in the Monadh Liath

David J. Broadhead

1984 came roaring in with high winds and deep snow. Having narrowly escaped the clutches of the Highland weather after Hogmanay, it was with some trepidation that Anne Macintyre and I drove North again on the evening of Friday 20th January. Relieved to find the A9 black all the way to Newtonmore, we joined Dave Morris, looking forward to a weekend of cross-country skiing. With such an abundance of snow we were spoilt for choice of possible tours. The weather forecast had sounded optimistic so it seemed an ideal opportunity to satisfy an old ambition. Skiing almost from Dave's front door we planned to cross the Monadh Liath, spend the night out in a bothy then follow the Findhorn down to Tomatin.

Saturday dawned fine and although the morning radio forecast promised a strong southerly wind later in the day, we continued with our plan, confident that with the wind behind us we would make rapid progress. Roger O' Donovan had been in the Findhorn only a week or so previously, so we telephoned him about suitable bothies just before leaving. Speaking from Glenmore Lodge he warned us of a poor weather forecast, with conditions already very severe on Cairngorm. Unperturbed, we stepped out into the sunshine and skied up Glen Banchor and around into Glen Balloch.

The morning passed quickly as we slowly climbed to the bealach between Carn Ban and Carn Balloch, slightly lower than 900 metres. As we entered the mist we were aware of the wind at our back picking up a little, but since it was pushing us in the right direction we were more concerned with staying close together in the poor visibility. On the broad bealach the deep snow had been blown clear and we were laboriously picking our way between iced rocks when suddenly the wind seemed to take us completely by surprise.

The three of us were literally swept off our feet. Like skittles, we were bowled over almost simultaneously. Looking around, I saw the others in the same undignified sprawl as myself. After a couple of unsuccessful attempts to stand up again, with a heavy sack on my back, skis on my feet and a long stick in each hand frightened to let go of anything which might blow away, I felt ridiculously immobilised. Still wearing his skis, Dave crawled across and we considered our situation, shouting in each other's ear. It was tempting to struggle on, lured by the lee side of the hill and shelter in the glen below, despite the perils of skiing down unfamiliar ground in a near white-out, driven uncontrollably by the wind, the possibility of missing the bothy in the dark and a long hard day tomorrow.

Sensible judgment prevailed when Anne joined the discussion, indicating that one of her ski sticks had been snatched out of her hand, leaving us with no alternative but retreat into the teeth of the a gale. In our present position skis were more of a hindrance than a help, so Dave suggested fastening all three pairs to one rucksack, out of harm's way. Still lying flat on the ground I strapped the sack plus skis to my back then with the help of the others fought my way up onto my feet. Clinging to each other we struggled into the gale, a bizarre pantomime performance, Dave's powerful six-foot-plus pulling and Anne pushing while I staggered between them, battling with the wind for control of the ungainly load on my back. Fighting for every step, we slowly made our way off the bealach and down. Less exposed, the edge wore off the gale as we lost height and waded through deeper and deeper drifts of snow until we were glad to be able to put our skis back on our feet.

With every step forward the prospect of a night out (or worse) receded and as the adrenalin wore off we became more aware of the physical discomfort of skiing straight into the blizzard. Two of us without goggles or an adequate face mask had a particularly unpleasant time with crusts of ice building up over faces and eyes.

My cheeks were chapped for a few weeks after. However, by the time darkness overtook us we were in the shelter of Creag Dubh and almost home. When the Cairngorm Chairlift anemometer recorded 161 m.p.h[2] just after 8 p.m. we were sitting in front of a roaring fire, a happy outcome to our little epic. It was not until next morning, listening to the radio, that we gradually learned of the seriousness of the blizzard which had trapped thousands of people all over the Highlands. We were particularly saddened but not surprised when we heard of the five people out on the hills who had not been so fortunate.[3]

---

[2] See J.S. Barton, 'Wind and Weather on Cairngorm Summit', *SMCJ* 1984, XXXIII, 52-56. This is an account of the operation of the Cairngorm weather station maintained by Heriot-Watt University's Department of Physics. Barton gives a further reference, useful to connoisseurs of atrocious weather, – P.D. Baird's 'Weather and Snow on Beinn Macdhui', *CCJ* 1957, XVII, 147-149. Other interesting aspects of our mountain climate, including the likelihood of the return of glaciers, are reviewed in Gordon Manley's 'Scotland's Semi-permanent Snows', *SMCJ* 1972, XXX, 4-15.

[3] All five died in the northern Cairngorms, three descending from Coire an Lochain, two above Coire an t-Sneachda.

Incident in Arran

W.D. Brooker

IN 1949 the spacious days of amateurism were still with us and at Easter I had organised a week's climbing in Arran free of charge by arranging for myself and a school friend to act as mountaineering instructors on an Army Cadet Force course. From the unaccustomed luxury of our officers' (temporary) quarters at Lochranza we had taken a group on to Caisteal Abhail. The wind had been building up to a gale as we crossed Ceum na Caillich and the full blast struck while we were on top, making us cower among the summit blocks. Dashing across an exposed space to secure a small cadet who appeared to be in imminent danger of belng blown away I was myself knocked over by a gust and when I grabbed hold of a rock as an anchor my whole body fluttered for a few moments like a pennant streaming in the wind

It was both bizarre and disconcerting.

The other oddity on that occasion was the loss of our rope (well, His Majesty's rope, really). This was a military item, khaki in colour and made of a glossy manila fibre. It was what was known in those days as 'full-weight' and of fairly massive dimensions. This rope was still brand new and had not been softened by use, so it formed a rigid circular coil rather like a motor-car tyre. Another gust picked this up and sent it bowling and bouncing down the mountainside with great speed. Aberdonian instincts prompted immediate pursuit but thoughts about the comparative intensities of military enquiries into the loss of army cadets and of ropes intervened and we attended to our human responsibilities and never saw the rope again. It didn't really matter since we had our own 'half-weight' nylon for the actual climbing. Or perhaps it did, because one of those cadets is now a minister in Mrs Thatcher's government! If only ...

A Windy New Year

R.N. Rutherfurd[4] was at the 1921-22 New Year Meet in Arran. It was his first SMC Meet and was attended by illustrious members such as W.N. Ling, W. Inglis Clark, J.S.M. Jack, E. C. Thomson and J .H. Bell. His diary has this brief entry for January 1st: "Bus to Corrie, up Glen Sannox with MacLean, Scott and Thomson. Blown flat on Suidhe Fhearghas. Crossed Saddle into Glen Rosa. Rained all the time!"

He further writes:– "I haven't read my 'Climbing Log' for many years but what memories it brings back! What memories of these men once famous in mountaineering! I was there on the invitation of J. H. Bell (not J. H. B. Bell[5]) who had climbed with my uncle, R. G. Napier. I remember conversations with Ling and Inglis Clark in the evening. The latter told me about his first ascent of a mountain, I've forgotten the name, in New Hampshire and how a shepherd and his wife gave him shelter that night. Jack came from

---

[4] Rutherfurd was one of the founding members of the JMCS.

[5] These Bells are frequently confused. The first Bell (John Hart) was born in 1870 and was one of the early members of the SMC. The second Bell (James Horst Brunnerman) was born some 40 years later. Both men were strong climbers and pioneered new routes.

Paisley, and was very good to me. As for the incident on Suidhe Fhearghas I can well remember how all four of us were fighting our way, using our axes, against a tremendous wind. Suddenly I found myself flat on the ground. I rolled over but could not see any other member of the party. Like me they had all been blown flat. The wind eased slightly and when I sat up I caught sight of the others beginning to move. No one was hurt but we were lucky not to have been at the summit of the mountain.

PERHAPS the wind experience to cap them all is described by W. Inglis Clark in a note about that same New Year Meet.[6] It is reproduced here in full.

Wind Phenomenon on Goatfell – At the recent New Year's Meet, at Brodick, a succession of hurricanes rendered mountaineering difficult. Among other excursions was one to the summit of Goatfell, when a series of wind vortices swept down the slopes, tossing members here and there. Owing to the slight sprinkling of snow, the passage of these cyclones was made visible, each circle of wind raising a margin of snow like a wall some feet in height. But the most interesting thing was that each large circle, revolving, say, at 40 miles per hour, had on its margin five vortices ... where the velocity seemed more like 100 miles per hour, and at each of these a pyramid of snow was raised to a height of perhaps 30 feet. The whole circle with its satellites had a rapid movement down the mountain face. To those who were able to look, the sight was an awe-inspiring one. Some of the members were in advance of the writer and, as the circle bore down on them, one could see them brace themselves to resist it; but if by chance they encountered a secondary vortex, resistance was in vain, and they were tossed about with resistless force. No doubt these wind movements accompany every violent storm, but in this case the whirlwinds were rendered plainly visible owing to the snow. The writer could easily recognize the part of a circle in which he chanced to be, but when in the secondary vortex, he was thrown certainly more than 20 feet in a fraction of a second.

[6] *SMCJ* 1923, XVI, 266

Theme and Variations

Give me my scallop shell of quiet: let me go
Over the benty ground and high over the fells,
And further to the west, among the granite wells,
To hear the very streams of Iorsa where they flow:

Or over to Kintyre and Knapdale, and to know
The burning heather again, and all the former spells,
The golden plover's tune, and what the curlew tells;
And, rounding ancient hills, the white bird of the snow.

A highway and a way, they are not hard to win;
The fond wayfaring man, he shall not err therein;
They take you through the woods, above the fallow lea:

For past the red bracken, you find a rocky stair,
And so come out at last on the world open there,
Ridges white to the north, and islands in the sea.

W.P. Ker

CHAPTER 8

The Modern Munroist

8.1 Introduction

UNTIL the 1950s, the traverse of the Munros was a leisurely affair, occupying several years and even taking up the whole active life of a climber in some cases. However, the seeds of rapid completion were already sown by Robertson in the 1890s, who fairly galloped through the West Highlands in separate summer campaigns. However, it was perhaps P.L.J. Heron, operating from the handy base of Fort William, who initiated the common modern practice of bolting down the Munros in a few feverish years – *Munrosis brevis*, as Bill Brooker[1] characterizes this form of the 'disease' in his amusing article reproduced below as Chapter 8.6, and certainly it was Hamish Brown who initiated the practice of multiple completion or *Polymunrosis*. Perhaps the acme of this endeavour was Mark Elsegood's running traverse in 1988.[2] Since the coming together of fell-runners and the Munros, short completions have become shorter and more numerous. This whole aspect of Munro-bagging has been largely ignored here, for reasons given in my Preface, and the interested reader is referred to Andrew Dempster's book[3] for more detail. I have instead devoted the pages of this section to the Ordinary Munroist, who is only ordinarily fit and who has to make do with day trips or weekends with only the occasional week-long expedition. Sandy Cousins (Chapter 8.2), Iain Robertson (Chapter 8.4) and Ivan Waller (Chapter 8.5) all fall into that category, but as their contributions show, they all have interesting tales to tell.

Rapidity and frequency of completion are only two of many changes in Munroing that we have seen in the years since 1950. A casual scrutiny of the list of completers (endpapers) shows that the Munro curve is better than exponential and now soars towards an unimaginable nemesis in which everyone in the world will have completed the Munros by the year 2050! So what was once the pastime of a few despised eccentrics has become a healthy recreation for Everyman (and, of course, Everywoman). However, it should not, I think, be taken too seriously, even though it should equally on no account be scoffed at! So I have included two contributions (besides the Brooker pathology already described) which take a light-hearted approach: Jim Donaldson's attempt to find the mythical Ben Feskineth (Chapter 8.3) and my own ludicrous posthumous completion on behalf of the man who started it all, Hugh Munro.

---

[1] Brooker, following the lead of his predecessor Iain Smart, adopts a sardonic approach to the classification of forms of Munro-bagging which some may perhaps find mildly offensive. However, Brooker also established the 'post' of Keeper of the List as a well-oiled bureaucracy, retaining and responding to all correspondence and perfecting an efficient system of numbering and registration: he has been 'the Bagger's Accomplice' to a degree that former Keepers, beginning with Eric Maxwell, did not quite achieve.

[2] See *SMCJ* 1989, XXXIV, 228-232.

[3] *The Munro Phenomenon*. Mainstream Publishing Co. 1995.

8.2 Hillwalking from Cape Wrath to Glasgow

A.G. Cousins[1]

Sandy Cousins on the summit of Mullach Fraoch-choire

IF YOU LIKE reading accounts of climbers moving slowing up a vertical wall on minute rugosities, swinging over the void on *etriers* secured by thumbnail pitons or traversing unbroken ice walls on daggers and front points, turn to another article – this will bore you. This is no account of a route which was interesting until it leaned back to the vertical and became straightforward. But if you like to wander over the hills and corries of our beautiful country then fill your pipe, pour yourself a glass of malt and come with me on a traverse of Scotland.

For some time I have wanted to spend a holiday climbing and staying in bothies and I decided to combine this into a long trip across Scotland. I suggested the idea to two or three friends, but there was little enthusiasm, so I resolved to go on my own. In the middle of winter I started to plan the trip. I enjoyed the planning and some points may be of interest. For many evenings our front room floor was carpeted by O.S. maps as I chose the summits, ridges, glens and corries of my route. I had to expect bad weather, so to ease the navigation I marked my intended route on the maps, marking changes of direction with the bearing and distance to the next turning point. In this way I hoped to be able to maintain the route 'blind'. Alternative routes on lower ground were noted in case the high tops became too unpleasant.

---

[1] *SMCJ* 1972, XXX, 37-47.

I wrote to various people on my route asking if some simple shelter was available, if they would keep a box of provisions I would send in advance, and if due to estate work or game there was any area on their ground I should avoid. All were most helpful offering some shelter and many offered to provide provisions if I advised my requirements in advance. I hope such hospitality will never be abused. Seventeen supply boxes were sent to various keepers, hotels, houses, and huts *en route*. My route included some spots where there was no bothy or shelter and I intended to bivouac in an emergency polythene bag or whatever shelter I could make if required. However, just before I started Vango provided a nylon Force Ten featherweight (5 lbs.) tent which proved excellent. This gave me freedom to have comfortable secure nights out wherever I wanted. The tent could be satisfactorily set up with only four pegs in a few moments. I even practised setting it up from a sitting position in case I should seriously injure my leg and require shelter. The Super Ariel sac (27 ozs.) with its inflatable tube pad provided by Brown Best gave a comfortable carry with about 30 lbs. load. Hamish MacInnes kindly agreed to be my emergency contact and my wife had a schedule of about six dates when she could expect a telephoned progress report from me. If my call was a day overdue she would advise Hamish who had a copy of my route. From the date and place of my last call he could estimate where I might be. If he heard nothing the next day he could assume something was wrong and set up some search. In this way according to my schedule the longest I could expect to wait if I became immobilised was about six days!

Palatable food is essential if such a trip is to be enjoyed. I selected my provisions from a list of what I liked, modified to tinned and packet varieties, since the food would be packed about two months before use. For simplicity I made up a week's menu and repeated it four times in my food boxes. Although I was never hungry, I lost a stone during the journey. Practically all the food was bought in one visit to a supermarket, and the bill was about five feet long! There would be boxes at most of my night stops, and these boxes would contain my dinner, breakfast for the next morning, and some lunch to carry. I had always one day's emergency food and with the spacing of the food boxes I only had to carry two days' food a couple of times. In some boxes, I had clothes, paraffin, maps, film, batteries, etc. I could leave unwanted items in some boxes and these were posted home by my hosts. Thus the weight carried was minimised. Yes, I did cut short my toothbrush![2]

I arrived at the gear I was to carry by eliminating from a list of desirable items until I had a much smaller list of necessary items. Weight reduction was achieved by discarding containers and using polythene bags, making canvas slippers as an evening change, using a Hely Hansen Polar jacket ($1^1/_2$ lbs.) instead of a heavy woollen pullover, a nylon Ariel sac, home made nylon climbing jacket, and the Vango Tent. The Hely Hansen Polar (brushed nylon) socks were most comfortable and they have now done about 600 miles without any

---

[2] The passion for weight-reduction is strong in the marathon bagger. However, perhaps this was carried to the most extreme lengths by the Alpine climbers Philip Hope and William Kirkpatrick, whose advice can still be studied with profit (see W.T. Kirkpatrick, *Alpine Days and Nights*, Allen & Unwin, 1932). For example, Kirkpatrick provided himself with aluminium collar studs! So far as toothbrushes are concerned, Raeburn's advice (in his *Mountaineering Art*, Unwin, 1920, p. 45) comes to mind, 'Toilet articles are not wanted in a Hut: the less washing at high elevations the better.'

sign of wear. I used Fisher mountain boots which I found very comfortable. One sees very few wearing the kilt these days, but I find it very good for hillwalking. It is much more comfortable than breeches for wet summer weather, and is cooler in hot weather. Even though I had snow and gales I only used my over-trousers twice on the trip. My cromach was no ornament: it served as a bog-tester, fishing rod, spare tent pole, camera tripod, support for crossing rivers, and as a crutch if required. The only preparation I felt I needed was to get used to carrying about 30 lbs., so for about three weeks I walked to my office about three miles each way carrying a load, and I had pleasant, though tiring walks across the Stockiemuir, out to Loch Lomond and across the Campsies at the weekends. About three weeks before I was due to start all my food had been sent off, all arrangements were completed, and I could relax and contemplate the exciting prospect ahead. Just about this time, through a neighbour in the BBC, a couple of chaps came along to film me walking to work – all rather comic, I thought.

On the first of June I arrived with a co-driver by car at Durness in glorious hot sunshine. I had stashed my first food box in the heather where I would cross the main road in a couple of days' time. We were ferried across the Kyle of Durness, then joined the tourist minibus for the run out to the lighthouse. Much of the area is used as a bombing and shelling range, and I heard that a hurried phone call had recently saved the bar being blown off the Keodale Hotel when someone got his bearings wrong! At the Cape Wrath light I was given a warm send off by the Keeper and his wife and set off homeward across the short dry grass of the undulating coast. I was on my first mile when stepping into a hole I almost twisted my ankle. It was a warning to keep alert all day, every day. I had been warned that some character inhabiting one of the bothies was rather undesirable, so I crossed the moor with dirk and cromach at the ready! Topping a rise I had my first view of the beautiful mile of sand at Sandwood Bay. Oyster-catchers greeted me as I crossed the wide beach, which was empty though criss-crossed by footprints. The track from Sandwood took me to the road where my 'chauffeur' met me, and we camped at Oldshore Beg.

We had breakfast in the sunshine early next morning, then he left for Glasgow by car and I set off on foot. This was a day of hot sunshine and the views from the twisting road by Kinlochbervie were a delight. Sitting in a hay-field I shared my mid-morning snack with a tramp and learned something about life on the road, while a corncrake's grating cry rose in the shimmering heat. By lunchtime I reached the Durness Road, and a kestrel flew suddenly from its concealed nest just a foot or so from my foodbox as I retrieved it from the heather. I lunched with some peat cutters then crossed the rising moor towards Foinaven. By late afternoon I was in a corrie below the hill where I intended to bivouac. I felt fit so I carried on up the steep dry mossy grass in warm sunshine and arrived at the top at about 5 p.m. to be greeted by gentlemen from the Yorkshire Ramblers who were just completing the ridge. I camped beside the summit of Ganu Mor and made a most comfortable bed of dry moss. The evening was calm with a slow temperature inversion gradually drawing low mist across the moor below as the lights began to twinkle in the villages along the coast, and on ships in the Minch. With my dinner over it was a delight to sit with glass in hand and watch my cigar smoke drifting slowly from the tent door. Just before turning in I had a walk round the summit, and felt quite excited looking south over the mass of peaks dimly lit by the afterglow of sunset, at the prospect of the great journey ahead, yet relaxed in the knowledge that all my planning was done, and my supplies were in position.

I woke early when the brilliant sun topped the cairn above me and shone hot in the open tent door. Banks of white cloud floated in low over the coast and evaporated over the land below me. By 9 a.m. I was packed and on my way along the ridge to Foinaven. I had a cool drink of Cremola Foam made from snow and continued along the ridge and down to Bealach Loch an Easain Uaine for a lunch stop as twelve fine stags in velvet ambled past me quite unaware of my presence. *En route* throughout the trip I left wax-chalk messages such as 'Sandy 1200 3.6.71' at cairns, bothies, etc., so that if anything went wrong they could help anyone following my route. At Lone Bothy I picked up the food box left for me by the keeper at Loch Stack. I visited the Yorkshire Ramblers, who entertained me to afternoon tea at their camp. This was in true safari style – mess tent, tables, chairs and an ample wine cellar-they do not believe in roughing it in hotels like the SMC! That evening I phoned the BBC's *Today in Scotland* who were going to do progress reports. As they were not ready to record and I could not arrange to phone at specific times, let alone specific days, I decided to scrap the idea. After a pleasant evening with the keeper I returned to my tent and slept very comfortably on a fine bed of rushes.

A cool east wind, which was to continue for a couple of weeks, gave ideal hill-walking conditions next day. I crossed to Kylestrome on an old pony track with the ruins of the old pony shelter at the top of the pass. I noticed 'Beware of the Bull' notices on the track (surely a right of way), which seemed contrary to the Countryside Act. Kylestrome must be among the most picturesque ferry crossings in Scotland, and as usual the seals were bobbing around in the tidal swirls. A tourist took my sack up to the top of the road so I enjoyed an unloaded stroll up to Loch na Gainmhich then I took to the path up towards the high lochan under Glas Bheinn. The path, a good one, goes over a pass to the top of the Glencoul waterfall, the highest in Britain, and well worth a visit. There is also an easy walk to the waterfall along the steep shore of the loch. An eagle passed low above me on the way and plovers with their beautiful plaintive alarm cry kept flying ahead of me, unfortunately warning deer of my coming, as shown by the continual scatter away ahead of me. With my tent at the edge of the lochan, I was able to sit in my sleeping bag and try a few casts as wisps of mist drifted into the corrie. My rod was made by screwing a couple of rings into my cromach, and fixing my reel to the handle. I enjoy camping in these isolated corners, and the wee tent gave a feeling of comfort and security should the weather change as it was really watertight. My pocket radio was good company and reception was usually very good on the high ground.

Thick mist surrounded me next morning and my set line bore no trout, though I've had good fish from the lochan before. This was a grey day on the grey quartzite tope of Glas Bheinn, Ben Uidhe, Conival and Ben More Assynt. I was taking Dextrosol a couple of times a day and, though it was difficult to assess the effect, I felt I was going well. I stopped for lunch making a little boulder howff and entertained myself singing – hoping there was no-one around in the mist. I considered going along Breabag, but the glen below me was too tempting and soon I was down in sunshine again washing my underwear in a burn and enjoying a smoke on the long trudge to Benmore Lodge. There the keeper put me up in the bothy and I dined well from my food box. That evening in the keeper's house with its fine old hunting engravings we sat cracking about game and salmon until about midnight. His friendly deerhound could stand easily resting its paws over my shoulder.

The walk from the lodge to Coire-mor bothy was on road and track all day. A tourist took my sack along to Oykell Bridge, where I collected my food box and enjoyed a delicious lunch in the hotel. I found I had a yen for fresh meat and vegetables. For a while I walked with an elderly shepherd moving his lambs and ewes away from the road. I met the keeper and he took my sack up to Corriemulzie so I enjoyed the long walk up the glen without a load. From the lodge I followed the track to the bothy under Seana Braigh. This is a grand bothy in a fine situation. After such a good lunch I had little appetite for dinner. I was tired after some 20 miles of road-bashing, but enjoyed the evening sitting at the door of the bothy sipping Drambuie, listening to an opera and watching deer playing like children in the shallow lochan in front of me. My pipe smoke drifted out on the calm air, and waiting for me across the loch towered the sharp peak of Creag an Duine, as I turned in on a warm straw bed.

I was away by 8.30 in the morning. It was calm and grey and I climbed slowly and steadily to the narrow ridge leading to the Seana Braigh plateau. Having my route and bearings previously marked on my maps was useful as I was in mist until midday. I came on some ptarmigan chicks near the summit and the hen flapped around trying to distract me as I photographed the chicks at my feet. By lunchtime the sky cleared and I lunched on the big open flat before Eididh nan Clach Geala in bright sunshine. The high ground around me was ringed with deer watching me like Red Indians in a Western. At the summit I found the boulder howff I had made three years ago. I crossed Meall nan Ceapraichean and rather wearily climbed across snow patches to Beinn Dearg, then started the long descent and good path to Loch Droma *via* Lorguill. This had been a fine day's hill-walking with a great feeling of being alone in a huge group of mountains and high plateau with sunlit peaks all around as far as one could see. I was however looking forward to my friend Bill Donaldson's arrival. I had just finished an enjoyable dinner when he arrived and camped beside me.

The second week began with the welcome sound of sizzling bacon for breakfast and – luxury – fresh bread! We climbed in cold mist and sleet showers to Meall a' Crasgaigh, Am Biachdaich, Sgurr nan Clach Geala and on to Sgurr nan Each – what beautiful names – as the weather cleared to sunshine. I had planned to go down to Nest bothy, but Bill, a Munro-bagger, lured me eastward along the Fannichs with promises of steak his wife had for us at camp at Fannich dam. We crossed Sgurr nan Clach Geala again, Carn na Criche, Sgurr Mor, Beinn Liath Mhor Fannaich, Creachan Rairigidh, Meall Gorm and An Coileachan. There were several stone howffs along the tops. We could see across Scotland from the Beauly Firth on one side to Loch Torridon on the other. This was one of the big days of the journey involving 19 miles, 6400 feet of ascent and 10 summits.

Next morning we drove back west to Achnasheen so that I could rejoin my route and Bill vanished into the wilds of the Loch Carron hills. I climbed Fionn Bheinn in sunshine and snow showers, an easy ascent made interesting by the antics of ptarmigan distracting me from their chicks, and the views of the Fisherfield hills. As often happened on the journey familiar hills reminded me of climbs I had enjoyed and friends I had been with there. Back on my route again I passed Loch Gowan and crossed the pass on a good path to Scardroy. This is a lovely spot. Rugged hillsides plunge down to the wooded loch and the bright green fields beside the river are dotted with a few tidy houses. The friendly atmosphere was confirmed when the keeper put me in his bothy complete with kitchen, hot bath and room with fire. My dinner (all from my box) that night was typical: chicken soup, beef stew, potatoes, carrots, peas, rice and fruit, Drambuie, cigar, tea and lemonade. Breakfast next day was fruit juice, cereal, kipper fillets, oatcakes, etc., and lunch as usual was shortbread, biscuits, tea, jam and sweets.

From Scardroy I went up Coire Mhoraigein and on to Sgurr Coire nan Eun and An Sidhean. The tops were misty and I found that with my radio on in my pocket the volume altered as I altered course, thus I navigated for about a mile on a steady course which landed me right at a col I wanted. I went down the Allt na Chois to Loch Morar, and along the path to the Lodge where Bill joined me in the evening. The keeper gave us the use of an excellent bothy with stove, cooker, and beds.

Our round of the Strathfarrar hills, Beinn na Muice, Carn an Daimh Bhain, Sgurr na Muice, Sgurr na Fearstaig, Sgurr Fhuar-thuill, Creag Ghorm a' Bhealaich, Sgurr a' Choire Ghlais, Carn nan Gobhar, Sgurr na Ruaidhe, and Garbh-Charn, was done in a mist driven by a strong northerly wind with occasional blasts of sleet, a wild day indeed. I found polythene bags made good gloves. We were both weary as we trudged back along the road to the bothy and I found my boot was holed at the toe.

The low cloud continued next day when we crossed the dam, waded the Uisge Misgeach and climbed Carn nan Gobhar, Sgurr na Lapaich with its interesting rock ridge to the summit, and the An Riabhachan tops, flanked by slopes of deep old snow. From Coire Mhaim we went down to Socach bothy (private and locked) where the landowner had delivered my food box. This bothy, the Seldom Inn, was most comfortable.

The anticyclone had steadied up again next day and we set off in shirt sleeves along to the west end of Loch Mullardoch, where we separated, Bill going to Sgurr nan Ceathreamhnan and I to Mam Sodhail via Beinn Fhionnlaidh. It seemed a long hot grind and then as I topped the ridge to Carn Eige the cloud came in and I had cold sleet showers and dark mist again. I was not usually conscious of my load on the hills but often felt it at the end of the day especially if I had to finish along a road. I had map and compass work all afternoon as the ridge twisted round deep corries and passed looming shapes on the ridges. 'This', I found myself thinking, 'is what hillwalking is all about'. One has to be confident to navigate and to read the ground. I crossed Ciste Dubh, Carn Coulavie and emerged from the mist at Bealach Coire Ghaidheil, where I waited for Bill. He arrived and we found we had passed within a few feet of each other minutes earlier in the mist. We spent the night in the deserted Alltbeithe hostel. By mistake my map for the next days' route was in my box awaiting me at Cluanie Inn, so I made a rough sketch from a map in the hostel.

A sprinkling of new snow on the summits glittered in the early sun next morning as Bill left for Mam Sodhail and home, and I headed south over Mullach Fraoch-Choire with its interesting wee pinnacle ridge and A' Chralaig, reaching Bealach Coir-a-Chait for a lunch stop. On route I had a glimpse of Ben Nevis four days' journey away. It was like seeing an old friend and I felt quite pleased that I was going well. All I had to do was relax mentally, keep going steadily and enjoy this beautiful hill-walking. I was averaging about 14 miles and 3500 feet per day. The hills were very dry and I had to seek about for tea-water for lunch. From Sgurr nan Conbhairean I skirted the north corrie to another top. I had intended to stop the night down in Prince Charlie's cave, and could see the boulders of the howff a long way below me, but I decided to head for Cluanie as it was still early in the day. A golden eagle drifted along the edge of the ridge beside me for a few yards with its beady eye looking at me from under its wing. I went down the Allt Coire Lair to the road, trudged wearily along to the Inn, and camped. I dined (poorly) in the Inn and the staff kindly gave me luxuries like milk, eggs, bacon and bread – very tasty! Two weeks and two hundred miles lay behind me.

Ascot Day was one of mixed showers and sunshine on the south Cluanie hills. I went up Druim Shionnach along the ridge to Creag a' Mhaim then back along to Aonach air Chrith and Maol Chinn Dearg, all interesting narrow ridge walking, then steeply down to camp in Glen Loyne at a ruined bothy. I found that one boot was deteriorating a bit and did some sewing repairs as best I could, but began to wonder if this could be the end of the trip. With rain squalls lashing the tent I felt depressed. However, I was dry and snug, and things which seem problems at night are often minimal next morning so I pushed despair aside, lit a fresh cigar, sipped more Drambuie and settled in my bag.

Up into the mist again in the morning I walked rather carefully, avoiding straining my boot, and from the Bealach I followed the ridge to Gleouraich then back over the Bealach to Spidean Mialach as the weather cleared to sunshine by the time I reached the Quoich dam. It was a joy to walk down beautiful Glen Garry in warm sunshine with the birds singing and the dark cattle flicking their tails in birch tree shades. At Greenfield, south of Loch Garry, the farmer insisted I avoid the midges, though I had felt none on the trip, by giving me a room in his house. I attacked my boots with glue and nails and soon they were as good as new again. We talked late, and here as throughout the trip I found the folk I met most interesting and hospitable.

Fedden, the ruined house, was my lunch stop next day. I surprised some young ducks into their first splashing attempts at flight along a burn, and photographed a dappled new born red deer calf, crouching in the heather as the hind barked nervously from a distance up the hillside. On the way to Cam Bealach I came on a small adder and I was surprised at the needless cold shiver I felt. I climbed Sron a' Choire Ghairbh in cold sunshine and crossed to Meall nan Teanga. This top seemed a kind of milestone and I sat down for a time looking around. Northward I looked back over the glens, lochs, peaks and ridges forming the distant horizon and realised I had crossed that seemingly enormous distance. I thought of John Hinde's R.A.F. party who had done a similar journey in 1968, of Hugh Munro's love of hills, of past members of the SMC who had explored these hills, and I felt in a small way part of that great company. To the east and west lay country I did not know well, Knoydart and the Grey Corries of Lochaber. The southward view was dominated by the great dark hump of Ben Nevis streaked white, high over the glittering waters of Loch Linnhe, and islands that seemed to float in shimmering sunlight. I was leaving the new country and crossing into familiar country. Even though I had been climbing around the country for some twenty years, over sixty of the tops I had just been on were new to me. Lord, what a beautiful country! The noises of civilisation floated up from the Great Glen as I crossed to Meall Coire Lochain, Meall Odhar and trotted down to Ruigh-na-Beinne into the forest and down to Mile Dorcha. I kept my mind off my seemingly heavy load and tired legs until I flopped down in my tent at Gairlochy. On the way I saw a wren and earlier I had seen an eagle – our smallest and largest birds in the same day. Some tourists invited me into their caravan for supper and a cheery evening. The midges were fierce.

Before breakfast I telephoned a report to *Today in Scotland* and was amused to listen to it later during breakfast in the early sunshine. Walking along the canal to Inverlochy I thought how useful the SMC canoeists might have been. I had a desire for some fresh meat so I had a good steak lunch in the café at the Distillery then went up the familiar path to the CIC Hut. The hut is much improved due to the efforts of the Custodian and his work squads. There I met the first people I had seen on the hill (excluding Bill Donaldson), since Ceann Garbh sixteen days earlier. The longest I had gone without seeing anyone even in the distance, was about 30 hours.

In the small hours I woke with toothache. I had had some twinges since Scardroy but this was different. I telephoned the police and was told to report there and a dentist would be 'standing by'. A quick breakfast and I was in Fort William in a couple of hours. There was no record of my call at the police station, but I was directed to a dentist. Other pale-faced casuals arrived as I waited my turn. A man from Mallaig awaited a verdict on his last few choppers. 'Next please', and the pain vanished as I found it was my turn.

'Are you the fellow on the long walk?'

My ready story was cut short by 'Open wide'. Tap, tap. 'Oops! There it is!' Zip, zip, the bits fly and the hole is sealed. I was just entering Glen Nevis again when a car passed and with a happy wave the man from Mallaig with toothless smile roared past. Early in the afternoon I was back at the hut, and I climbed the *Arête* and soon reached the summit of Ben Nevis. I could just see my last top Ben Lomond and almost felt regret that the end was in sight. I dropped quickly down to the car park at the head of Glen Nevis and noticed there that the chaffinches hopping about kept the humans in mobile cages! The path through the gorge had been thoughtfully repaired and improved so that it still looked 'natural'. Steall Hut was a welcome sight. I was a day ahead of schedule and unfortunately missed some Lochaber JMCS friends who came up next evening to meet me.

Steall Hut to Lagangarbh Hut was a walk I had not done before and I recommend it for its variety of ridges, wild scenery and good walking tracks. The morning was wet as I made my way up through a jungle of dripping birches onto the misty slopes of Sgurr a' Mhaim, along the narrow south ridge with the impressive though easy gap and on to Am Bodach, where the weather improved and the sun came out. The Loch Leven hills looked wonderfully rough and the sea lochs were like water-filled trenches. I followed the ridge past An Garbhanach and on to the double top of Na Gruagaichean. Because I still had to go a long way I was reluctant to go out to Binnein Mor so I headed down to Kinlochleven, where I had a good high tea before following the water pipes and the Devil's Staircase to reach Glencoe in the lovely soft evening light. There was a halo round the sun foretelling wild weather to come in a few hours. As I cleared the last rise the Buachaille rose

Sandy Cousins strides out over the Highland hills

majestically before me with Lagangarbh nestling below. I remembered my first visit to the hut on a snowy February day years ago when I was a new boy, all eyes and ears to catch the pearls of wisdom and technique from the old hands. I may be a bit sentimental but I think the SMC is more than a Club, it's a living tradition. The Hut was empty of people but full of memories as I turned in.

It was raining heavily from low cloud scudding in from the west next morning, when I crossed the Coupal just above the waterfall and went up Sron na Creise. On the ridge the cold front weather really hit me with a full gale so that I could hardly move and squalls of hail and rain came across like wire. I wandered a bit and, being sure that the top of Clach Leathad lay in one direction, I had to force myself to trust my compass which told me it was in another direction. The compass, as usual, was right. For the second time on the trip I had put my day's map in the box ahead of me, but I had again made a sketch map and had been over this ground a few times before. On the Bealach before Stob Gabhar I was briefly below the mist so I stopped to fill up with some chocolate and Dextrosol to heat me up, and wrung out my socks. The roar of the wind on the ridge was awe-inspiring and I had to keep just the right distance from the edge to seek the slightly calmer area one gets due to the uplift of the wind. At the summit I could just get shelter enough to eat more. As the rain had forced through my clothes I was a bit chilled, so I set off down the familiar fence posts and soon emerged below the mist. The forecast had been for clearing skies in the late afternoon. I sat down for a rest just below the mist and quite suddenly the rain stopped, the cloud shredded and the warm sun shone from huge patches of blue. It was 4 p.m. How's that for timing? I took off my wet clothes and hung them around me to dry off as I walked to Bridge of Orchy. Looking back at the sunlit hills there was no hint of the wild conditions I had just come through. The proprietor at Bridge of Orchy added fresh food to my food box, and I dried off my gear as I slept in Glencoe Ski Club Lodge.

After wading across the Orchy I strolled down sunny Glen Orchy and across Am Mam to the Dalmally road where I collected my box at a house, lunched and set off up Ben Laoigh. New tree-planting may soon affect access to the west side. At over 3000 feet on the south ridge I found a trickle of water and a flat site for my tent. During dinner I watched a lovely sunset over Cruachan as the evening shadows crept across the Arrochar hills.

The burbling of sheep in thick mist around me woke me at about 6 a.m. and I visited the summit a few feet above me. Early mist cleared as I crossed Ben Oss and Ben Dubhchraig on my way to Glen Falloch. On the road some tourists leapt out to take my photograph and one was nearly run over in the process! From Ben Glass farm I headed through the tangled woods on the east side of the loch to Ardleish, where I dined from my box. A short way down the loch I climbed over the Maol an Fhithich ridge with unfamiliar views of the loch and the Arrochar hills, and went down the rough Garrison Glen to Inversnaid as I listened on my radio to Bill Sproul and party telling of their trip to the Hindu Kush. As usual the midges at Inversnaid were vicious.

Real Loch Lomond weather (low mist and drizzle) greeted me in the morning and I was soon soaked on my way through the dripping woods to Rowchoish. I hope this side of Loch Lomond is left unspoilt for those who enjoy rough walking away from the rumble and peeps of the traffic on the west side. Climbing through the wood I emerged on the high moor below Ben Lomond and watched a troop of some forty wild goats with kids. One sees so much more wild life when one is quiet and alone on the hills. At 4.30 I arrived at the familiar triangulation pillar at the summit and camped in mist and strong wind in a calm spot where the uprising wind lifts over the summit. After dinner, feeling a little disappointed that expected friends had not turned up, I listened to a concert from Glasgow then slept soundly.

The walk to Drymen and to Glasgow is marred by the danger from traffic. Even where corners are being realigned there is no footpath. In Drymen I stayed with a friend. The last day's walking was one of enjoyable reflection. The view back northward to the hills, the cry of the curlew on the Stockiemuir Road, the scent of bog myrtle, these reminded me of the sights and sounds of the trip. The crisp early morning light with mist drifting in the corries, sunlit ridge-walking, wild days scrambling past dark shapes in the mist, the soft colours of the highland evenings in the hills – I can close my eyes and see them all.

Approaching Bearsden I had a panoramic view of Glasgow. I was home.

8.3 Ben Feskineth – a Lost Munro?

James C. Donaldson[1]

IT WAS IMPOSSIBLE to give details of Ben Feskineth in the 1981 edition of The Tables as the information available was very sketchy. The position of this mountain is still not clear, but as rumours of its existence may be circulating it has been decided to make public such facts as are known.

During the summer of 1980 the writer came across a copy of a *Guidebook to Scotland* published by Adam & Charles Black. This was the 19th edition published in 1872. It contained a page which named the principal peaks of Scotland and, as good Edinburgh men, Messrs. Black had seen fit to include Arthur's Seat in the list, albeit the lowest eminence of all. But, somewhat higher up the list, appeared the entry – Ben Feskineth, Perthshire, 3530 feet and immediately there was the electrifying thought that there might yet be another Munro discovered neither by Munro nor the Ordnance Survey and that not even Colin Philip nor Hamish Brown had come across it during their perambulations of Scotland. Investigation became of the utmost importance.

The book in the writer's hands had belonged to a Mr George Burnet who, it was easily ascertained, died shortly after 1900 at not a great age.   His copy was the special 'Pedestrian's Edition' and there is a note in it by the publishers that a 'few copies have been printed on thin paper for the use of pedestrians.' From this it seemed reasonable to assume that he was an active mountaineer and as such might well have been an early member of the SMC. A thorough search of the journals right up to 1900 followed but there was no record of Burnet as a member. However, at the Dalmally Meet of 1894 a guest of the name of Burnett (two Ts – but the journal Editor has never been immune from error – no initials given) attended, apparently as the guest of either Tough or Brown, being out on the hills with one or both of these celebrated climbers on each day of the Meet. He never figures again in the pages of the *Journal*.

But, like the dog that failed to bark,[2] the significant feature of this Meet may be that Munro himself was not present. Surely, if he had been there Burnet would have mentioned this mountain that was listed in his book but not in Munro's Tables, in which case the mystery might have been solved there and then.

There followed some months of inaction broken only by a moment's excitement when a climber was encountered who claimed to have actually climbed Ben Feskineth. But the euphoria quickly subsided when it was established that he really meant Ben Heasgarnich. Now, the heights of the two peaks are the same and it did seem possible that confusion might have risen in Black's mind but, as a visit to the National Library Map Room quickly showed, this was not the case. Along with their guidebooks the Blacks had commissioned Mr John G.

---

[1] *SMCJ* 1981, XXXII, 131-133. Donaldson's tenure as Master of the Tables – like that of the contemporary Keepers of the List, Iain Smart & Bill Brooker – was tempered by a measure of wit and gentle deprecation of Munroing, which is well exemplified by this whimsical piece.

[2] An allusion to Arthur Conan Doyle's Sherlock Holmes story *Silver Blaze*.

Bartholomew to produce a set of maps of Scotland with a scale of 4 miles to the inch. They are beautifully drawn maps and that of Perthshire, while it shows a croft called Feskinninch at the foot of Loch Lyon, clearly names Benheasgarnich (*sic*) in its proper place. There is no Feskineth, while the O.S. map for the same period has a different name for the croft.

The next step was to find out what help the National Library itself could give. Two editions of the book were made available for inspection, one being the same edition as had already been seen, the other the 15th edition published in 1861. This earlier edition also mentioned Feskineth but gave its height as only 3521 feet, which was at least evidence that by 1872 recognition that some mountains were capable of changing their height[3] was already established. In neither edition does Ben Heasgarnich appear in the list of principal peaks. In both editions the editors invited corrections, but while in 1861 they offered to send a free copy to anyone returning a guidebook annotated with corrections they did not do so in 1872. One assumes that the offer was withdrawn having been found to be too expensive. But it is reasonable to suggest that someone must have pointed out that they had the height of Feskineth wrong in 1861. Otherwise it would not have been changed. But if the height was corrected why not the name if that was wrong? The index to the guide is no help: although comprehensive it includes neither Feskineth nor Heasgarnich.

The likely explanation of the mystery may well be that Feskineth is really Heasgarnich but as the possibility of another Munro is involved a decision one way or another cannot be lightly made.

Another explanation that has been put forward relates to the astonishing rate of growth of the mountain already referred to – nine feet in only eleven years. Perhaps, like a mushroom, its rapid burgeoning was followed by a brief maturity and equally rapid collapse. Who knows, perhaps only The Doctor[4] can provide a satisfactory solution to the problem? If he could be persuaded to lead a team of investigators suitably qualified for so important a matter, readers might expect a report in a subsequent *Journal*.

To finish on a lighter note, Black's Guide provides much practical information within its pages. Of particular interest to climbers are the prices charged for coffee and whisky: sixpence for a cup of the former and threepence for a glass of the latter, in 1861. But by 1872, while the cost of coffee was unchanged, the price of whisky had doubled! –'O MIHI PRAETERITOS REFERAT SI JUPITER ANNOS.'

---

[3] See *SMCJ* 1977, XXXI, 191 for discussion. – JCD

[4] The intellectual anti-hero of Geoff Dutton's stories. See Chapter 6.12, footnote 1.

8.4 From Sea to Shining Sea!

Iain A. Robertson[1]

THE IDEA that had gestated in my mind was of a high-level walk across Scotland, from the easternmost extremity to the westernmost extremity. This general proposition allows for considerable variation in the route that might be chosen, and in my case it was purely idiosyncratic involving those hills and passes for which I had a personal preference. It was certainly not the most direct route, nor that incorporating most Munros, nor any other specific criteria. The scope for singularity in such enterprises is great and forms one of the attractions, both in planning and execution. The starting and finishing points were, however, immutable – the lighthouses of Buchan Ness and Ardnamurchan. I had originally expected to do the trip solo, but John Rogers volunteered to accompany me, which, as well as providing welcome companionship, probably stiffened the resolve to see the project accomplished. Although travelling together, we were each self-sufficient in terms of food, tent and other equipment. Members of our respective families had agreed to bring supplies of food and clean clothes to convenient points where our route crossed arterial roads, and so we did not have to carry more than five day's food at any one time. That we did the trip in 1983 during what the newspapers subsequently described as 'the warmest July for 300 years,' was entirely fortuitous.

The first of the chosen hills was Bennachie; and I had decided that the most interesting way of getting to it from Buchan Ness would be to follow the coast south to the estuary of the Ythan, and from there strike inland. Thus the first two days involved no high-level walking at all, though they were not without interest. On the day that we set out there was a haar, and we were pursued down the coast by the boom of the Buchan Ness foghorn. The haar rendered the Bullers of Buchan invisible, but if anything, enhanced the Gothic atmosphere surrounding Slains Castle. The sun was dispersing the fog by the time that we reached the Sands of Forvie nature reserve so that we had some opportunity to view the wildlife . It is an area of dunes and tussocks, not unattractive, and quite different from anywhere else we passed through during the trip. The second day was entirely on metalled roads; from Newburgh to Chapel of Garioch, and the sun beat down mercilessly all the day. In the late morning, Pitmedden House provided garden seats and orange squash – I have a vague recollection of flowers in a formal garden as well. Back on the road, the book that I was reading was in danger of turning to pulp as drops of perspiration rained down on it.

---

[1] *SMCJ* 1985, XXXIII, 140-147.

At mid-afternoon the 'Oldmeldrum Arms' emerged from the haze; we approached it with the single-mindedness of desert travellers approaching an oasis, not even a plaque to the memory of a native of Oldmeldrum, described thereon as 'the father of tropical medicine,' could detain us. The barman stood at the door watching our approach with passive gaze.

"Are you open?" we croaked. "Naw, we're closed," he said. Then, perhaps sensing our desperation; "Oh, but I'll gie ye a drink though."

We ordered four pints straight off. Inquiries at Chapel of Garioch resulted in the offer of a campsite in the grounds of Pittodrie House, "just vacated by the Rhynie girl guides." During that evening there was satisfaction in gazing at the distinctive outline of the Mither Tap of Bennachie rising beyond the trees that verged on our campsite, for the Lowlands of Buchan were now behind us and the start of the high-level walk proper was at hand.

The next morning the weather was a repetition of that of the previous day – hot and hazy. Although not the highest top of Bennachie, the Mither Tap is the dominant one, and as we approached it over heathery slopes, the bulk of the great tor and the surrounding fortifications became more impressive. Though lacking the altitude to be in one of the canons of 'the collectable mountains,' yet it was quite worthy of being the first hill of the trip. After a pause on the summit during which we could distinguish little about us through the haze, we continued our traverse of Bennachie by the less frequented Oxen Craig and Watch Craig, and then descended for another road section from Keig to Montgarrie. Of the two, Keig was the more interesting as it had (a) a licensed grocer, and (b) topless sunbathers. Beyond Montgarrie are the Correen Hills, of which Lord Arthur's Cairn is the highest. The whole area has a network of farm roads and other tracks, and at about 1100 feet, just beyond the last farm, we set up camp for the night. That evening the weather had turned thundery, and there was much rumbling among the hills further to the west, but we escaped with a shower of rain that lasted a mere half hour – the only rain we had until the trip was completed. The rain cleared the atmosphere, and the rest of the night was calm and still with only the faintest murmurs of civilisation drifting up from the Howe of Alford below. The only other sounds audible were the calls of curlews, peewits and oyster-catchers.

The next morning we followed a track the mile or so that led to the top – where there is indeed a large cairn – then across further moorland through an enormous colony of gulls and so down to the village of Lumsden. The Ladder Hills beyond Lumsden do not feature prominently in Scottish mountaineering literature; this is not surprising as their charm probably lies more in the glens that give access to them than in the hills themselves. However, for our purposes they provided the highest level route to the main Cairngorms lying west beyond the Lecht. Forming as they do the watershed between those rivers such as the Deveron which flows north into the Moray Firth, and the Don which flows east into the North Sea, the Ladder Hills provide in clear weather pleasant views over the 'whisky glens' and beyond to distract one from the rather tiresome going, consisting largely of deep heather interspersed with deeper peat hags. As we were not blessed with clear weather, I will comment no further apart from observing that for country so apparently devoted to the shooting of grouse, there were remarkably few to be seen. The gulls we saw in the colony on Lord Arthur's Cairn must have outnumbered the grouse we saw on both the Correen and Ladder Hills by several thousand to one.

The Lecht and Cock Bridge were reached on the afternoon of the fifth day, and a telephone call that evening ensured that food and clean clothing were delivered to us on the following day. By the time that this was accomplished it was mid-afternoon, and so we confined ourselves to walking the seven miles or so over into Glen Avon where we camped on the bank of the river beneath the northern corries of Ben Avon. As the guidebook notes, the northern face of the mountain is the finest.

The next morning we selected the ridge that forms the east side of the corrie containing Lochan nan Gabhar – one of the green coloured lochans characteristics of the Cairngorms – for our ascent to the plateau. This ridge proved a good viewpoint from which to see the adjacent corries, and it had a discontinuous spine of granite outcrops which one could wander over or around according to one's whim. The day was both cooler and clearer and from the plateau we could look back over the country that we had traversed as far as the Buck above Lumsden, as well as viewing the hills to the south from Lochnagar to Beinn a' Ghlo. The descent to the Sneck showed the extent of the snow remaining in the corries of Beinn a' Bhuird; then, as we walked west over Beinn a' Bhuird and the Moine Bhealaidh, we had before us the panorama of the main Cairngorm plateau, stretching from Derry Cairngorm to Bynack More. As the fitful sun of the morning had given way to an afternoon of continuous sun, we opted to camp that evening by Loch Etchachan, the highest campsite of the trip. It was also one of the stillest nights, the wind dropping almost entirely, but the morning dawned with most of the tops shrouded in mist. This put paid to a tentative plan to diverge from the planned route to take in the four 'four-thousanders,' and so from the top of Ben Macdui we dropped down into the Lairig Ghru by the spur that is marked by a cairn in memory of the crew of an Anson aircraft that crashed there in August 1942. A steepish descent over boulders concentrates the mind when one is carrying a large pack, the normal adjustments to balance are just not enough, as we both discovered. The re-ascent up on to Cairn Toul and into the mist again was also something of a grind, albeit for different reasons. The requirement for keeping to high-level meant that we next had to head toward Gaick, and so our route off Cairn Toul was down by Loch nan Stuirteag – gulls audible but not visible – over Monadh Mor and down to the Feshie/Geldie watershed where we set up camp.

After the grandeur of the main Cairngorms, the hills of Gaick seemed somewhat pedestrian. However, on the next day the weather was a quite remarkable combination of sunshine and clear atmosphere. Specifically, my route for that day was: An Sgarsoch, Carn Ealar, Beinn Bhreac and Leathad an Taobhainn, which meant I was virtually skirting that upper section of the Feshie where it flows easterly, then north-easterly, before turning back upon itself to flow eventually into the Spey. As I tramped my way over an unending succession of peat hags, I was rewarded with a constant backdrop of the Cairngorms, while to the south the Perthshire hills could be seen to their termination above Rannoch Moor, with Ben Cruachan distinct beyond the Moor. Further round, the Ben Alder group, Creag Meagaidh and the Monadhliaths completed the horizon. Also, in almost continuous succession herds of red deer came into view, paused, and then trotted off. The last part of the day, after crossing the line of the Minigaig near its highest point, involved a descent to Gaick Lodge by the glen of the Allt Gharbh Ghaig, a spectacular gorge with a stalkers' track gouged out of its wall. John had been off on his own that day doing some of the Atholl hills farther to the south, and when we met up in the evening he claimed to have been talking with a female ghillie in a bikini. As well as being a contradiction in terms, I felt that this may have been a riposte to my topless sunbathers at Keig whom John had failed to spot, being too deeply engrossed in his book. Sometime during this, the ninth day of the trip, we passed the half-way point in our journey.

The next day was a short one, ten miles or so to Dalwhinnie for food and clean clothes. Gaick Lodge by Loch an t-Seilich is hemmed in by slopes which rise with uniform steepness to the surrounding plateau. Our route followed one of the many stalkers' tracks that radiate from the lodge. We zig-zagged interminably upward until at last we reached the high ground where we crossed over a hump graced with the name A' Mhairconnaich, and so down to the aqueduct from Loch Cuaich that led us gently to Dalwhinnie. As at Cock Bridge, we dined that evening at a hotel.

Eating during the trip consisted of four or five days of dehydrated foods prepared individually in camp, interspersed with some excellent meals enjoyed at hotels adjacent to the replenishing points. We did not, however, stay in any of the hotels, sleeping in the tents every night until the trip was completed.

A late morning start from Dalwhinnie allowed another shortish day. The requirement of keeping to high-level took us along the ridge of the Fara which provides a delightfully airy walk down the west side of Loch Ericht. The weather, although not sunny, was quite clear and we had the opportunity to inspect our route for the following day beyond Loch Pattack, as well as looking down the length of Loch Ericht. It was on the Fara that we met two Austrian youths, one wearing green wellies, making their way across country from Kinlochleven to Dalwhinnie. We later discovered that they had been nonplussed to find no resident warden or food for sale at the Culra Bothy. That evening we camped beside the path to the Bealach Dubh, just beneath the Lancet Edge, which, though not the termination of the ridge that lies to the north of the Bealach Dubh, is its most interesting means of access. That evening we met a geologist, camping nearby, who was engaged in preparing a geological map of the area. He told us a tale about a helicopter that had been engaged by the Ordnance Survey to lift a load of sand and cement to the top of Ben Alder. On the appointed day, however, the helicopter had gone adrift in the mist and the load had been deposited on a sub-top of Ben Alder at some distance from the actual top. Could it be that the pilot did not have an accurate map?

The next morning the tops disappeared into the cloud, so that the Lancet Edge, Geal Charn, Aonach Beag and Beinn Eibhinn were a navigational exercise – more successful than that of the Ordnance Survey helicopter. After descending to the Uisge Labhair, we re-ascended on the south side to take in Sgor Gaibhre and Carn Dearg to the south-east of Loch Ossian. By the afternoon the cloud had lifted from these tops and we had limited views to Rannoch, though the higher hills remained shrouded. We then descended to Loch Ossian near the youth hostel, walking on from there to erect the tents on 'the Road to the Isles' just beyond Corrour Station. That evening, as a purely extra-curricular activity, we climbed Leum Uilleim which rises from the moors south-west of Corrour Station.

The next two days, which were to see us to Fort William, provided quite outstanding weather conditions. On both the sun shone from an almost cloudless sky, and the visibility was such that the view was bounded only by the ultimate horizon. To have such weather conditions on what were probably the most scenically spectacular sections of the trip was indeed fortunate . To start with there was the walk to the foot of the Grey Corries. The descent from Corrour Station to Lochtreighead presents varied and unfamiliar views of the Mamores, Ben Nevis and the Aonachs. From Creaguaineach Lodge, the start to the Lairig Leacach is unusual in that, for the first half mile or so, it is confined within a rocky gully, almost a dry gorge. Thereafter, the glen opens out and the path proceeds by the Allt na Lairige, which has many fine pools and waterfalls. A strong urge to stop for a swim was kept in check by the incessant attention of clegs which infested the glen.

The Grey Corries brought a difference of opinion within the party. John went for Stob Ban as the Munro outlier, while I preferred the true eastern termination of the ridge at Stob Coire na Ceannain. This latter is a narrow ridge enclosing a south-east-facing corrie and it makes a pleasant ascent. The party united again on Stob Choire Claurigh and the rest of the day was taken up with the magnificent traverse of the Grey Corries. The ridge itself is set off on either side by fine corries and subsidiary ridges, but on this particular day it seemed as if the better part of all Scotland's mountains were on view. From the perfect detail of the Mamores across Glen Nevis to the far hump of Ben Wyvis; from Wester Ross to Perthshire, an army of hills was ranged for our inspection, upstanding and outstanding – a memorable sight. The late afternoon found us at the col that separates the Grey Corries from the Aonachs, and here we set up camp. That night there was an almost-full moon which hung over the Mamores, illuminating them splendidly and throwing shadows across the face of the Aonach Beag immediately above our tents.

The next morning our approach to Aonach Beag was dictated by the necessity to avoid the snow patches that still filled some of the deeper gullies. But once on the southern shoulder of the mountain we tramped up the rim of the eastern corrie, surely as wild and remote a fastness as any in the Highlands. The particularly bald and mossy summit brought the full extent of Ben Nevis into view, dominating the landscape both by its bulk and its grandeur. A quick detour to Aonach Mor (this was one of the few occasions when we were able to dump the sacks), and then a descent on steep grass to the foot of the east ridge of Carn Mor Dearg, where fortunately we came upon a spring. The day was almost without wind, and on the successive re-ascents I confess that the heat was really getting to me despite my Downs-type sunhat (a knotted handkerchief). On the Carn Mor Dearg Arête we met a garrulous gentleman from Worcestershire who enthused that, "all this was much superior to the Malverns". When I at last hauled my sack on to the summit of Ben Nevis, I found it quite thronged. The world and his wife and bairns disported themselves in the scantiest of summer clothing, consuming gallons of fizzy drinks, and generally congratulating themselves on having reached Britain's highest summit – which they were well entitled to do, considering the heat and the condition of some of the upper stages of the tourist track. That evening we booked into the Glen Nevis campsite and enjoyed our first shower for fourteen days, Fort William being reached on the fourteenth day of the trip.

The high-level rule should have led to a crossing of the Corran Ferry, or a hike over the moors to the north of Loch Eil. But I had hills that I particularly wanted to climb on the west side of Loch Shiel, which precluded the former, and I could see little merit in the latter; and so the next day, after further supplies had been delivered, we took the road to Glenfinnan. No more need be written of this walk, save that we only reached the end of Loch Eil that day, and did the further five miles to Glenfinnan as a preliminary to the next day. This marked another parting of the ways as John planned a more extensive traverse than I, and I also wished to fulfil a long-held ambition to visit Glen Aladale.

The day was sunless, though by no means cold, when I reached Glenfinnan. The route on to Beinn Odhar Mhor and Beinn Odhar Bheag beyond it is less than obvious, involving 'down' as well as 'up'; however, they are both hills of character and they command good views over and beyond Loch Shiel. The prospect to the west that day was obscured by cloud. The next hill, Beinn Mhic Cedidh has had fame thrust upon it by its recent elevation to Corbett status. The cairn is as yet minute, but it will no doubt grow with the visits of the faithful. My two-Corbett stint for the day completed, I descended over grassy slopes into Glen Aladale where I pitched my tent by the burn some two miles up from Loch Shiel. The glen is a quiet place, difficult of access except by boat down the loch, and given over to forestry, though not all the ground is planted. It appeared very little visited as the path was quite overgrown when I walked down in the evening to Glenaladale House which stands deserted. The glen has the genuine feeling of remoteness, and I was glad to have passed that way.

The next day was the last among the hills. I climbed over the Bealach of Coire Mhoir and down Glen Glutanen to the Bealach na Lice, and from there down Glen Moidart to Assary where I met up again with John. The glens Glutanen and Moidart are really one glen, but they are constricted at the Bealach na Lice by a narrow gorge which, like a wasp-waist, divides the whole into two parts. In upper Glen Moidart there are the extensive ruins of the old settlement of Ulgary. Although upper Glen Moidart is mountain country, the scenery becomes more lush as one descends to sea level, and the lower portion of the glen is dense with rhododendrons. There followed a road section to Acharacle where we left the main road which continues along the south side of Ardnamurchan peninsula, to follow the track along the north coast. That evening we reached Gortanfern on the track to Ockle; part of this track is being improved to 'forestry road' standard. Gortanfern was the most midge-infested campsite of the entire trip, which ensured a quick getaway the following morning.

Ardnamurchan, despite considerable encroachment by the tourist industry, retains much character, and this is probably best seen along the less-frequented north coast. The last section of the track before Ockle is like a transplanted stalkers' track winding among the low hills. After Ockle one is in almost continuous sight of the sea, but the weather that day was again dull and hazy, and the furthest we could see was the outline of the island of Muck to the north. That part of the route from Swordle through Kilmory to Faskadale, where there is a fishing station, is metalled road. Beyond Faskadale there is a marked path across what was, during a previous geological age, the roots of a volcano, which explains the many outcrops of gabbro in the area. From Glendrian we took the path to Altnaha, and from there positively the last ascent of the trip over the Bealach Ruadh – all of 400 feet high – to Achnasaich and the final two miles of road to the Ardnamurchan lighthouse. The very minute that we reached the lighthouse it started to rain. Thus ended our trans-Scotland walk.

Any feelings of achievement were perhaps slightly diminished by the knowledge that we still had a further six miles to walk back to Kilchoan. But there was certainly a feeling of satisfaction: we both grin broadly from the photograph that we had taken standing in the rain in front of the lighthouse, and I even managed to persuade John that we should take bed and breakfast that evening. Then there was the bottle of wine that we had with our dinner at the Kilchoan Hotel, so we must have been feeling good. I do not seek to proselytize, but there is much to be said for being free to take off to the hills and keep on going without the necessity of returning to a car, hut, camp or whatever. It is a different facet of the mountain experience, and it allows even the most familiar hills to assume a fresh role as links in an extended chain of mountain episodes.

The statistics of the trip in round figures are: 250 miles, 42,000 feet of climbing and eighteen days from lighthouse to lighthouse.

8.5 That Elusive Final Munro

Ivan Waller[1]

'Existing Munroists who are fit and well will be expected to do the new Munros and Tops as soon as possible, as the accomplishment of this objective presents no insuperable task'

Munro's Tables, 1981

EVER SINCE 1925 when I was $18^{1}/_{2}$ years old and first climbed Schiehallion, I have enjoyed walking and climbing in the Highlands and Islands of Scotland, but I was 62 before my wife gave me my first copy of Munro's Tables and I studied the mysteries of this book for the first time. I found that I had about 40 of these 3000 foot mountains to my credit plus a similar number of tops, the satellites surrounding these heavenly bodies, which altogether added up to 543 summits, though lately reduced to 517.

Ten years later we were on Broad Cairn together above Loch Muick when I realised that I was exactly half way, and round the bend so to speak without a moment to lose. This was odd because up till then it had never occurred to me that I would ever be able to do them all, but two years later on 8 June 1980 I traversed Lurg Mhor in thick mist and arrived on Bidein a'Choire Sheasgaich to become No. 207 in the list of Munroists and to earn a fizzy celebration which my wife had waiting for me in the van down in Attadale.

Little did I suspect the machinations which Munrosis had in store for me. I remained in fact very pleased with myself until one day watching the Lake District Mountain Trial, I met Neil Mather and Stan Bradshaw who were running in this 17 mile fell race, and they

---

[1] *SMCJ* 1985, XXXIII, 175-177.

told me that they also had completed that summer but they of course had done the Tops as well, so off I had to go again, a poor pedestrian with 58 to climb. It was during the following year 1981 that the second edition of the Metric Tables was published and the newly introduced twin summit of Ben Lui became my final Munro Top. The weather was perfect, it was the day after the Royal Wedding which I had watched on the television in Tyndrum and my celebrations amply covered both events.

Did I say final? Yes, but I soon found that another Top had crept unannounced into the tables, Carn na Con Dhu, 3 km out along the north-cast ridge from Sgurr nan Ceathreamhnan towards Loch Mullardoch. I rode up on my scooter, set up base camp near the Cluanie Inn, walked in to Alltbeithe Youth Hostel in Glen Affric, made an early start on Sunday morning when there was no deer stalking, to climb my latest final on 13 September 1981 and was rewarded on my return to Alltbeithe by the vision of the Warden's girl friend sun bathing in the nude.

A year went by during which I climbed two fine Welsh 3000-ers which I had missed out, Elidir Fawr in the Glyders and Yr Elen in the Carnedds. In the autumn I joined one of Hamish Brown's very good parties to do the Irish Munroes (note the 'e' as in the Irish whiskey). After Lugnaquilla and Galtymore for starters and two superb courses on Macgillycuddy's Reeks I celebrated my final summit for the Grand Slam on Brandon Mountain together with Matthew Moulton, another ³/4 century old completer and the others on 11 October 1982.

There followed a year of resting on my laurels and doing a few nostalgic Lake District rock climbs, but the lull was soon broken by my discovery of a Top I had missed, which had sprouted from 911 to 916 metres, Creag na Caillich at the Killin end of the Tarmachan Ridge. Furthermore, a brand new Munro, Beinn Teallach north of Tulloch Station, had been promoted from Corbett status. Ever on the trail I did these two finals in May this year 1984 using the West Highland Line and the Killin Post Bus, youth hostels and a night on the waiting room floor at Tulloch. Soon after this I went with my wife to Glen Shee and did yet two more final Munros, which I had had on my conscience for several years, ever since Jim Donaldson had told me that although I had stood many times on the summits of the Cairnwell and Carn Aosda on skis, they did not count because I had used the ski-lifts! Two hours sufficed to make an honest old man of myself, only to learn that Sgurr a' Choire Bheithe, a remote Corbett in the Rough Bounds of Knoydart had started to rear its head to Munro status, and there it waits.

In the meanwhile by way of an insurance against more new Munros and Tops appearing I am doing the ' Metros,' the name I have given to the Scottish summits between 900 and 914.4 metres. The word refers to metrication and has nothing to do with the motor car or the Paris underground railway. One of the additions to my original list of the Metros has the apt but ominous name of Finalty Hill!

8.6 Rampant Munrosis: the Scottish Disease

W.D. Brooker[1]

IT IS JUST over a hundred years since the 'Tables giving all the Scottish Mountains exceeding 3,000 feet in Height, by Hugh T. Munro,' appeared in the *Journal* of September, 1891. This was rightly regarded as an important event and the culmination of a considerable and dedicated effort. At the outset, Munro himself 'had little idea of the enormous amount of labour and research which it would entail – a labour which, even if it bad not been altogether abandoned, would have been vastly increased but for the invaluable assistance given by Colin Philip ...' Even Stott, who like his editorial successors was not easily impressed, declared that it 'had occupied over three hundred hours during some five months ... it forms a contribution ... whose value it would be difficult to exaggerate. There is little doubt that the lists will receive the study they deserve at the hands of all who are interested in the mountains of Scotland.'

Prophetic words! And yet few would have imagined, not even the Compiler himself, that the Centenary of his work would be celebrated by a feature article in *The Times* (Colour Magazine, 30 March, 1991), that the word 'Munro' was to enter the English language *(The Oxford Guide to English Usage,* p. 25), and that the name of Hugh Munro would become more widely known than that of any other of the founders of the Club. Munro readily admitted that the work to which he gave such commitment was incomplete. Many of the original heights given were approximate and based on aneroid readings. In 1913 he was revising the Tables and wrote 'the issue of the third edition of the revised 1-inch Ordnance Survey Map has thrown considerable extra light on the subject, and also involved a large amount of extra work; for not only has every name and height to be checked on the 1-inch, but the 1-inch and 6-inch have again to be compared to see if they agree ..' etc., etc. He ended with a list of 76 tops whose precise heights remained uncertain and sought confirmation of his own readings from aneroid-bearing Members of the Club.

This will be a familiar scene to successive Masters of the Tables who have had to wrestle with the results of orogenetic frenzies by the Ordnance Survey. Even today, a hundred years on, doubts can arise. The latest 1: 10,000 map shows Ganu Mor on Foinaven at 914 metres. This is rounded to the nearest metre and according to the O.S. the true height lies between 913.8 and 915.2 (2998 and 3002.6ft), and raises the interesting question as to

---

[1] *SMCJ* 1991, XXXIV, 598-603.

whether this, and not Ben Hope, is the most northerly Munro. Not that it really matters, since Foinaven is a superb mountain and should be climbed anyway. If it is elevated, we should not be too surprised since (1) J. Rooke Corbett pointed out in 1932 that the cairn did not appear to be on the highest point and suggested it deserved further investigation, while in 1920[2] (2) A R G Burn had mentioned that on Heddle's *Geological Map of Sutherland* (1881) it was marked as 3013 and that Munro himself bad been told by a local source that it was over 3000 feet.[3] A pity he omitted it from the Tables, but perhaps his aneroid was not at its best when he was there!

It was the pioneer Complete Munroist, A.E. Robertson, who seems to have been the first to use the term 'Munros' (within inverted commas), for the mountains which reached 3000 feet in height. This usage seems to have continued until 1929 when J.H.B. Bell dispensed with the inverted commas in two footnotes he added to an article about his local Lomond Hills. These notes are worth quoting here as they scurrilously caricature the two main styles of activity in the mountains. The distinction was more imagined than real of course, but it may have been more applicable in the days before Munrosis developed as an endemic disease among Scottish hillgoers. 'A salvationist, to the ultramontane,[4] is a somewhat low-grade person, hardly a climber, who endeavours, by the easiest way, to reach the summit of any sort of Scottish hill which exceeds 3000 feet in height above sea level. Such a hill is called a Munro ..', and, 'The ultramontane is, in the Lomond sense, a crazy and irresponsible person who climbs any nearly vertical face of rotten rock and vegetation by the most difficult way. He seldom visits the summit of a hill, and he is forbidden by his creed to remove any loose rocks or vegetation, which must be allowed to remain, in order to lure to destruction a future aspirant to ultramontane glory.'

What Bell did not fully appreciate was that the oft-derided peak-bagging activities of many salvationists and even some dedicated ultramontanes were symptoms of a new ailment which was to affect large numbers of Scottish hillgoers in the years ahead – Munrosis, the Scottish Disease. It is a weakness of the currently available means of detection that Munrosis is only identified with any certainty when the disease has run its course and the sufferer becomes a mere statistic. Even so, the rate of spread is impressive. Over fifty years were to pass before the first ten cases were recorded and it took another thirty years for them to reach 100. A glance at the accompanying graph will show that since then the rate of growth has been exponential or even explosive, with the disease having run its course in almost 850 recorded cases in the hundred years since Munro first published his work. Additionally, cases which come to light long after they are concluded suggest there must be an unknown number of undetected and hence unrecorded instances in which the condition has taken effect. It should be remembered that these figures apply to cases which are complete and there must be very many sufferers who are abroad in the Scottish hills today but who will not appear in the statistics until later.

---

[2] See Chapter 6.9

[3] See Chapter 4.4

[4] The terms Salvationist and Ultramontane are due to the Loretto headmaster Hely H. Almond. They are discussed above in Chapter 1.7

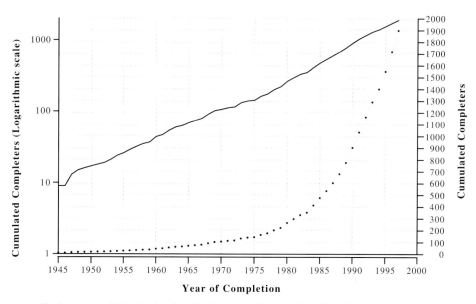

The lower curve (right-hand scale) plots the accumulated number of completers by year of completion from 1945 to 1997. The upper curve (left-hand scale) plots the same data on a logarithmic scale. Since this is a straight line, it confirms the exponential growth of completers in recent years.

The true nature of the affliction was probably not fully appreciated until the 1980's. *The Scotsman* carried a brief report by Peter McCue on 'Chronic Munrosis – a severe form of obsessional neurosis peculiar to Scotland.' The October 1984 edition of *Scottish Medicine* published a much fuller description entitled 'The Scottish Disease' by Dr Iain B. McIntosh, a Stirling G.P. This paper revealed such understanding of the condition that it seemed likely the writer must himself be afflicted, as can be seen from these extracts:-

'Unique to Scotland, this is a highly contagious affliction which affects teenagers and the not so young of both sexes. Predominant in the male, it takes an acute or chronic course and in the obsessed can threaten life and limb. An acute episode can progress to ultimate recovery in months but in its chronic state it can last a lifetime, with latent intermissions and relapses resulting in fitful bursts of over-activity and mad, compulsive behaviour . . .

'Those affected are disabled by an obsession which can interfere with social life, destroy a marriage and severely strain a marital relationship . . . Social effects are minimised when husband and wife suffer together and support clubs have flourished in recent years . . .

'Medical services have been expanded to meet the needs of this group and volunteers provide emergency care for those who suffer from exposure, hypothermia and trauma in pursuit of their obsession . . . Many of the young feed their obsession, submit themselves to intense exposure and overactivity for a year or two and win free of the condition.

'For a few the cycle restarts to further blight their lives, although paradoxically, with passing years, overweight and smoking lead to a compulsion-free existence as breathlessness and fatigue prevent overexposure to this bizarre activity. With advanced years this strange state burns itself out, allowing the very elderly to escape from its malign influence.'

Over the last twenty years, Dr Iain Smart of the University of Dundee, in association with the writer, has carried out studies which have considerably advanced our understanding of Munrosis and successfully identified a number of variants. Some of these findings are summarised as follows:–

Incubation. The period taken by this preliminary phase varies greatly from individual to individual. There appears to be some correlation between its length and the time taken for the condition to run through its cycle. Many long term sufferers have experienced lengthy incubation, sometimes visiting a mountain for the climbing it affords and not even going to the nearby summit after the climb. At this stage such persons may totally ignore even easily accessible Munros if they lack climbing interest. Then discerning companions may notice signs of aberrant behaviour – a tendency to extend and distort a day on the hill beyond its natural length in order to take in an additional top – the possession of a map (often surreptitiously) on which some summits have been underlined in red. These are indications that incubation is over and the disease has developed, even if not fully admitted by the sufferer. It should be said here that nowadays, like bastardy, Munrosis has a much readier and more open acceptance than in the past when in many quarters it carried a social stigma. Today it may even be flaunted!

As was mentioned earlier, if incubation is brief or entirely absent there is often an intense period of overactivity in which the disease may burn itself out in a few years or even in months. However it may well recur and if so, it is likely to do so again and again until age or infirmity put an end to the obsession. Recurrence may take the form of extending the compulsion to include the adjacent summits known as Tops or even those mountains Furth of Scotland which exceed 3000 feet. Some will win free at this point, sated with what is called 'A Grand Slam', but there are others who have been known to suffer transference to the Corbetts, which were not part of the original Tables.

Munrosis vulgaris, sometimes called *M. inadvertens* – the most common form in which the condition only takes full hold when the victim, having enjoyed normal mountain activity for years, suddenly discovers (or has it pointed out by a misguided person) that only 50, or 100, or whatever, Munros remain to be done and the full tally might as well be completed.

Secondary Munrosis is the increasingly common situation in which an already Complete Munroist finds that a second cycle gets underway through the well-intentioned, but probably ill-advised, practice of accompanying a spouse or other close associate experiencing the first cycle of the disease. Such involvement is liable to lead to –

Polymunrosis – where the condition recurs in cycles. The best known of a growing number of documented cases of *Polymunrosis* is that of (62) Hamish M Brown who, having breathed a sigh of relief in 1965, has found himself on a treadmill which has rotated seven times (so far). A further complication endured by Brown is that on at least two of these circuits he has been pursued by dogs which have succeeded in stowing away in his rucksack at critical places such as the Inaccessible Pinnacle of Sgurr Dearg.

That a shared burden is more easily borne appears to be confirmed by the fact that about 30 cases of *M. matrimonialis* have been recorded. Here completion occurs simultaneously by husband and wife, often hand in hand. *M. familiaris* is rarer, but instances of entire families succumbing certainly occur. At least three have been recorded, one of which included the most extreme case of *M. juvenilia* on record, that of (493) David Kale who had gone through the complete course of a bout of Munrosis by the age of 13 years and 10 months.

At the other end of the spectrum are examples of *M. venerabilis* such as (207) Ivan Waller who was 73 and had taken 55 years to resolve his condition. A similar case was that of (646) Iain Ogilvie who having spent no less than 66 years in thrall must surely represent the extreme case of *M. longus.* Younger sufferers not infrequently experience very intense but mercifully short episodes. Notable cases of *M. brevis* were (607) Mark Elsegood and (777) Hugh Symonds, at 66 and 67 days respectively. (383) Martin Moran at 83 days is in the same category but since these were entirely in winter the designation of *M. hibernalis* is also appropriate.

Whether persons with a solitary tendency have a liability to Munrosis or whether the condition itself encourages those afflicted to seek isolation (for obvious reasons) is not resolved, but a significant proportion of Munro activity is carried out alone and a few cases of complete *M. soloensis* have been recorded. Another rare variant which may well have gone some way to make the condition easier to bear is *M. claravistitis,* the experience of a clear view from every summit.

The ingenuity of Man is well known and the motive for alleviating the burden of Munrosis powerful; thus a few like (237) Haswell Oldham have found their personal solution in the pursuit of *M. elegans* – the ascent of every Munro by an obvious sporting route, Lochnagar by *Eagle Ridge*, Beinn a' Bhuird by *Mitre Ridge,* Nevis by *Tower Ridge* and so on. Unfortunately some Munros lack such sporting features and on them ingenuity may be tested. Oldham ascended Mount Keen on ski with the aid of a parachute!

A variant which has not yet been recorded but which would appear to suit the needs of some in that it represents the ultimate in secrecy, solitude and anonymity would be *M. nocturnalis.* Other variants which would successfully disguise Munrosis and perhaps dilute its effect, although they would certainly extend its duration, are *M. vovoensis* – never ascending more than one Munro on any one day and *M. totoyoyoensis* – similar, but with a return to sea level between each Munro. Refinements in the ways in which a sufferer might respond to the obsession and thus obtain diversionary relief are *M. incrementalis* – starting with Beinn Teallach and concluding with Ben Nevis, or the reverse – *M. decrementalis.* More complicatedmight be *M. alphabeticus,* and so on.

However the variant that commands itself to my own ambition would be *M. terminalis* – dilution of the effects by spreading the activity over the entire lifetime so that the final heart attack or whatever it is to be takes place on the way down from the last summit. Mind you, it would require meticulous planning, but what a way to go!

8.7 A Posthumous Completion

Robin N. Campbell[1]

AS NOTED in my recent article about Munro,[2] Sir Hugh died with three Tops to go; Carn an Fhidhleir (Feshie), Carn Cloich-mhuilinn and the Inaccessible Pinnacle, the first two Tops being Munros in the 1891 list. When carrying out the research for this article I formed the opinion that something should be done about this regrettable state of affairs. Lighthearted and tasteless discussions with friends explored the possibilities and eventually arrived at the goal of constructing an effigy of Munro and transporting the object to the three missing Tops. I believe it was my friend Paul Brian who made this ingenious proposal, but he may well wish to deny this now.

In 1991 I found myself in the position of having to address the great gathering of Munro-baggers on November 23rd[3] with little to say, so I resolved to set the effigy project in motion. It was late October before I managed to acquire a kilt (Hunting Fraser) and Glengarry bonnet at affordable (Oxfam) prices. The Munro tartan is a red and yellow abomination which would put the most somnolent deer to startled flight. I cannot imagine that Sir Hugh would have worn it on the hill; surely he would have preferred the douce and furtive hues of the Hunting Fraser. Once these essential items had been obtained, construction of the effigy could proceed with some confidence that it would be completed. However, I took the precaution of paying a visit to the grave at Lindertis – to seek permission, as it were. No ominous event occurred, so I thought it safe to proceed.

I fashioned a mask for the head, using gauze strips loaded with plaster over a clay mould of Sir Hugh's face, and painted it with tempera-based colours. Latex hands were found in a joke shop: rival manufacturers of these curious products obligingly offered different hands. Ears were fashioned from Fimo clay. Limbs and head were made from stuffed tubular bandages, fixed to a trunk of supernumerary pillows and reinforced with coathanger wire. A visit to the barber provided hair for wig and whiskers, and amusement for the staff. The effigy, when finally assembled in early November, weighed 30 lbs., stood about 5ft. tall and had cost about £100. If I say so myself, it bore a tolerable resemblance to Munro and was sufficiently life-like – or death-like – to frighten visitors to my house severely. It was too bulky to fit in a rucksack but, protected by plastic bags and folded in Z, it could be strapped to a packframe. We were ready.

On Sunday 10th November, we left Forest Lodge in Glen Tilt, accompanied by my colleague Dr Helen Ross, in darkness and steady rain, at 7.30 a.m. The approach to Carn an Fhidhleir involves climbing over a shoulder of Carn a' Chlamain to the Tarf Bothy, which we reached around 10 a.m. The weather meantime worsened considerably, the rain turning

---

[1] *SMCJ* 1992, XXXV, 121-122.

[2] See Chapter 1.7

[3] This well-attended and popular event took the form of a dinner in the Roxburghe Hotel, Edinburgh. It was organized by Bill Brooker, the Keeper of the List, with the purpose of celebrating the Centenary of the Tables, and all recorded extant Completers were invited. It is likely that a similar event will be organized to celebrate the Centenary of Robertson's Round in 2001. On this future occasion the Roxburghe Hotel will hardly suffice: perhaps the multitude might just squeeze into Murrayfield or Hampden Park!

Munro ready for Carn an Fhidhleir

to sleet and a lively westerly beginning to blow. Dr Ross gave it up about a mile beyond the bothy and Munro and I proceeded alone. On the final ascent to the summit the winds were so strong that at times, furnished as I was with a kind of sail, I dared not move for fear of being whisked away. Much snow had fallen and this became a whirling mass of icy spindrift in the fiercest gusts. We reached the cairn about 1 p.m. Since there was plainly to be no photo-opportunity, Sir Hugh declined to leave his cocoon, and so we immediately began to descend in the teeth of the gale. When we reached the Allt a' Chaoruinn the winds eased and it began to snow heavily. I have a decrepit left knee which acts up worse than usual in heavy winds and it was now providing me with a good deal of discomfort. We collected Dr Ross at the Bothy and left for the final leg around 3.30. Our progress was slow and painful, so much so that we were engulfed by darkness at the top of the pass. By the time we reached the edge of Glen Tilt our torches were more or less done for: the descent path could not be found and we slid down to the Tilt, for the most part on our backs. Parts of poor Munro extruded through the plastic bags in protest. As I limped towards Forest Lodge, I fancied I heard him murmur "Even worse than 1908", recalling his previous attempt to climb this troublesome mountain, which had foundered in thick darkness and torrential rain.

Munro exhausted after his ascent of Carn Cloich-mhuilinn

Although I had originally planned posthumous ascents of all three Tops, this unexpected onset of winter ruled out the Inaccessible Pinnacle, so we had to be content with an ascent of Carn Cloich-mhuilinn on the following Sunday. This was uneventful and, although the mountain was snow-bound and conditions at the cairn were far from ideal, Munro dismounted and I was able to take a number of photographs. Due to an oversight, we were obliged to celebrate his posthumous completion of the Munros with coffee. I remarked that since his earliest recorded Munro had been Ben Lawers in 1879, his completion time of 112 years would take some beating. Since he was now qualified to attend his own Dinner I smuggled him into the Roxburghe Hotel on the following Saturday. He occupied a table on his own and remained modestly shrouded by a dustcloth until I exposed him to the assembled baggers at the conclusion of my speech. Despite the atrocious bad taste of this outlandish stunt, it received a generous reception from the gathering. It was perhaps fortunate that no member of the Munro family had attended ...

Sir Hugh remains intact and patiently awaits his visit to the Inaccessible Pinnacle, to be celebrated in early June, this time with champagne. In the meantime I have not neglected his spiritual welfare: I offer him readings from the early Journals, usually taken from his own work, and an occasional verse of the Club Song. I trust that members will realise that although this posthumous completion served less worthy purposes at the Roxburghe Hotel, my motive in bringing it about has been to delight the Shade of Munro and to honour his memory.

Later ...[4]

Sir Hugh Munro, in the form of a full-sized effigy, completed his round of the Tops on Wednesday 10th July 1992 with an ascent of the Inaccessible Pinnacle of Sgurr Dearg. An attempt had been made on Tuesday 9th, in the company of Robin Campbell, Derek Pyper and Helen Ross, but unexpected bad weather sent the party back to the Hut. Wednesday offered better conditions and in the early afternoon Campbell, Munro and Ross set off for the summit. A passing climber, Mr James Kenyon of Accrington, was roped in for the final attack. Campbell, Kenyon and Munro ascended the Pinnacle by its East Ridge, while Ross remained below in order to take photographs. After descending, the party enjoyed a bottle of champagne before returning to Glen Brittle. Sir Hugh's traverse of the 538 Tops of his 1891 Tables was begun in May 1879 with an ascent of Ben Lawers. At the time of his death in 1919, 535 Tops had been visited. Carn an Fhidleir (Feshie) and Carn Cloich-mhuilinn were ascended last year, leaving only the Inaccessible Pinnacle to be accounted for. His round has therefore occupied a period of 113 years and must be considered as a strong candidate for the Slowest Completion of the Tops.

Munro about to set out for the Inaccessible Pinnacle with his guide and porter, Robin Campbell

[4] *SMCJ* 1993, XXXV, 304.

Index of Past and Present Munros and Tops

This is an index of substantial references to every Munro and Top. Hill-names followed by an asterisk are those in current use. Hill-names are followed by the unique codes used in the Variorum Table. Boldface entries are Variorum Table locations. Normal brackets enclose optional elements; square brackets enclose alternatives; curly brackets enclose sub-section names.

A' Bhuidheanach LA16   160, **181**
A' Bhuidheanach Bheag* ED04   83, **197**
A' Chailleach {Fannich}* FA01   60, **192**, 237
A' Chailleach {Monadhliath}* ML08   64, **182**
A' Chioch {Cairngorms} EC16   **194**
A' Chioch {Cluanie}* ES05   **185**
A' Choinneach Mhor TO11   101, **190**
A' Choinneach {Cairngorms}* LL06   55, 100, **195**
A' Chralaig* ES04   **185**, 294
A' Ghlas-Bheinn* AT01   60, **186**
A' Gruagach MA04   **177**
A' Gruagach, N.W. Top MA05   **177**
A' Mhaighdean* LF03   59, 89, 102, **190**
A' Mharchonaich* WD03   58, **180**
Airgiod Bheinn* TT09   **198**
Am Basteir* SK04   143, **201**
Am Bathaich(e) QO01   93, 103, 105, 107, 116, 148,
  153, **184**
Am Binnein BQ11   **171**
Am Bodach {Glencoe}* AE04   **176**, 202
Am Bodach {Mamores}* MA11   55, **177**, 296
Am F(r)aochagach* GU01   63, 101, **193**, 254
Am Fasarinen* TO05   **190**
An Cabar* WY01   **192**
An Caisteal* BQ02   64, **170**
An Cearcallach* LA06   **181**
An Coileachan* FA12   60, 109, 110, **192**, 292
An Garbhanach* MA09   56, 93, 148, 165, **177**, 296
An Gearanach* MA08   11, 56, 121, 166, **177**
An Leth-chreag* AF23   **187**
An Riabhachan (N.E. Top)* NM08 57, 160, **188**, 203,
  294
An Riabhachan, N.E. Top NM11   57, **188**, 203
An Riabhachan, S.W. Top* NM12   **188**, 203
An Riabhachan, W. Top* NM09   **188**, 203
An Sgarsoch* TT02   38, 62, 103, **198**, 303
An Sgor(r)* LY08   **171**
An Socach (W. End) {Cairnwell}* WC08 62, **198**, 268
An Socach {Affric}* AF10   63, 121, **186**, 203
An Socach {Mullardoch}* NM10   63, **188**
An Socach {Wyvis} WY02   109, **192**
An Socach, E. Top/End {Cairnwell}* WC09 138, **199**
An Stuc* LT03   53, 105, 141, **172**
An Tudair* AF14   102, **187**
Aonach air Chrith* SS03   58, **184**, 295
Aonach Beag {Ericht}* EL04   52, 93, 120, 142, 148,
  150, **179**, 304

Aonach Beag {Nevis}* NE08   53, **178**, 305
Aonach Eagach BL05   **175**
Aonach Meadhoin* NS07   58, 103, 120, **185**
Aonach Mor* NE07   58, **178**, 305
Beinn a' Bhuird, N. Top* EC14   61, **194**, 245, 303
Beinn a' Bhuird, S. Top* EC15   **194**, 245
Beinn a' C(h)lachair* EL09   52, 103, 161, **180**
Beinn a' Chaor[a/ru]inn Bheag* LL04   104, **194**
Beinn a' Chaor[a/ru]inn {Derry}* LL03   62, **194**
Beinn a' Chaor[a/u]inn (Centre Top)* LA02 52, 108,
  109, 168, **181**
Beinn a' Chaor[a/u]inn, N. Top* LA03   52, **181**
Beinn a' Chaor[a/u]inn, S. Top* LA01   52, **180**
Beinn a' Chlaidheim(p)h* LF08   116, 161, 166, **191**,
  234-5, 237
Beinn a' Chleibh* LU01   51, 113, **170**, 281
Beinn a' Chochuill* CR08   66, **174**
Beinn a' Chomhainn SE03   **171**
Beinn a' Chreachain* OR06   **173**
Beinn a' Chroin (E. Top)* BQ04   64, **170**
Beinn a' Chroin, W. Top* BQ03   **170**
Beinn a' Chuirn* OR08   64, 108, **174**
Beinn Achaladair (N. Top)* OR04   **173**
Beinn Achaladair, S. Top* OR03   **173**
Beinn Achallader, N. Top OR04   57, **173**
Beinn Achallader, S. Top OR03   **173**
Beinn an Dothaidh* OR02   53, **173**
Beinn an Lochain AR05   66, 166, **170**
Beinn B(h)uidhe* AR08   66, **170**
Beinn Bheoil* EL15   55, **180**
Beinn Bhreac (E. Top)* LL01   62, 138, **194**
Beinn Bhreac, W. Top* LL02   109, **194**
Beinn Bhrotain* BC09   61, 84, 161, **196**
Beinn Chabhair* BQ01   55, **170**
Beinn Chaluim (N. Top) MF06   58, **173**
Beinn Chaluim, S. Top MF07   **173**
Beinn Cheathaich* MF09   **173**
Beinn Creachan OR06   55, **173**
Beinn Dearg {Atholl}* TT05   57, **198**
Beinn Dearg {Guisachan}* GU03   63, **193**, 293
Beinn Dheiceach MF09   66, 109, **173**
Beinn Doireann OR01   **173**
Beinn Dorain* OR01   53, **173**
Beinn Dubh Chraige LU04   **170**
Beinn Dubhchraig* LU04   64, **170**, 298
Beinn Eibhinn* EL03   52, 150, **179**, 304
Beinn Eunaich* CR09   11, 66, **174**

Beinn Fhada (Centre Top)* CO12   **176**
Beinn Fhada (N.E. Top)* CO07   **176**
Beinn Fhada {Kintail}* AT03   161, **186**
Beinn Fhionnlaidh {Affric}* AF20 63, 109, 110, **187,**
    294
Beinn Fhionnlaidh {Appin}* AP03   63, 88, **176**
Beinn Gharbh TT04   **198**
B(h)einn Ghlas* LT06   53, 108, **172**
Beinn Heasgarnich* MF03   55, **173,** 300
Beinn Ime* AR03   66, **170**
Beinn Iutharn Bheag* WC07   54, 99, 105, 108, 110,
    141, **198,** 268
Beinn Iutharn Mhor* WC04   54, 99, **198,** 268
Beinn Laoigh LU02   **170,** 298
Beinn Liath Mhor Fannaich* FA08 60, 101, 138, **192,**
    254, 292
Beinn Liath Mhor* WA03   59, 113, **189**
Beinn Mhanach* OR09   64, **174**
Beinn Mheadhoin (N.E. Top)* LL07   62, 86, **195**
Beinn Mheadhoin, S.W. Top LL08   109, **195**
Beinn na Lap* OT07   12, 63, **179**
Beinn na Socaich* GC04   109, **178**
Beinn nan Aighe(n)an* ET01   64, **174**
Beinn nan Eachan* LT12   105, **172**
Beinn nan Eachan, E. Top LT13   **172**
Beinn nan Eachan, W. Top LT12   **172**
Beinn Narnain* AR02   55, **170**
Beinn Oss* LU03   **170,** 298
Beinn Sgritheall* SG01   **183**
Beinn Sgritheall, N.W. Top* SG02   **183**
Beinn Sgulaird* AP04   56, **176,** 273
Beinn Tarsuinn* LF06   105, 148, 160, 165-6, **191,** 236
Beinn Teallach* LA18   **182,** 308
Beinn Tulachan BQ05   **170**
Beinn Tulaichean* BQ05   64, 113, **170**
Beinn Udlamain* WD02   58, **180**
Ben Alder* EL13   52, **180**
Ben Attow AT03   56, **186**
Ben Avon EC07   61, **194,** 303
Ben Avon, S.W. Top EC09   **194**
Ben Bynac LL05   **195**
Ben Challum (N. Top)* MF06   **173**
Ben Challum, S. Top* MF07   **173**
Ben Chonzie* SE03   66, **171**
Ben Clibrig KH01   62, **193**
Ben Cruachan* CR02   49, 51, **174**
Ben Hope* KH02   62, 89, **193**
Ben Klibreck KH01   **193**
Ben Lawers* LT05   53, **172,** 316
Ben Lomond* AR01   55, **170,** 298
Ben Lui* LU02   51, 53, 168, **170,** 203, 280-1, 308
Ben Lui, N.W. Top LU05   **170,** 203, 308
Ben Macdhui (Main Top)* MC04   24, 51, 55, 62, **195,**
    303
Ben Macdhui, N. Top MC05   **195**

Ben More (Isle of Mull)* MU01   63, 88, **202**
Ben More Assynt* AS01   62, **193,** 249-53, 292
Ben More Assynt, S. Top* AS02   **193**
Ben More* BQ10   51, **171**
Ben Nevis* NE01   48, 49, 53, 58, **177,** 296, 305
Ben Oss LU03   64, **170**
Ben Sgriol SG01   20, 56, 59, 88, **183**
Ben Sgriol, N.W. Top SG02   20, **183**
Ben Starav* ET03   64, **174**
Ben Starav, S.E. Top ET09   **174**
Ben Uarn Beag WC07   **198**
Ben Uarn Mor WC04   **198**
Ben Vane* AR04   66, **170**
Ben Vannoch OR09   **174**
Ben Vorlich (S. Top)* AR06   55, **170**
Ben Vorlich {Loch Earn}* SE01   51, **171,** 247-8
Ben Vorlich, N. Top* AR07   **170**
Ben-y-Hone SE03   **171**
Bhasteir SK04   **201**
Bhasteir Tooth* SK16   60, 104n, 105, 148, **202,** 220-1,
    223
Bidean a' Glas Thuill TE01   **191**
Bidean an Eoin De[i/a]rg* EA04   57, 99, 105, 108,
    148, **189**
Bidean nam Bian* CO09   50, **176**
Bidein a' Choire Sheasgaich* EA07   25, 57, **189,** 307
Bidein a' Ghlais Thuill* TE01   63, **191**
Bide[a/i]n Toll a' Mhuic TO07   102, **190**
Big Brae EC02   61, 109, 110, **193**
Binnein Beag* MA07   63, **177**
Binnein Mor* MA06   53, **177**
Binnein Mor, S. Top* MA03   **176**
Bla(th) Bheinn (N. Top)* SK01   **201,** 221
Bla(th) Bheinn, S. (W.) Top* SK02   109, **201**
Blaven SK01   60, **201**
Braeriach South Plateau BC04   99, 115-6, 121, **196**
Braeriach* BC02   22, 50, 51, 55, **196**
Braigh a' Choire Bhig NM07   109, **188**
Braigh Coire Chruinn-bhalgain* TT08   57, **198**
Broad Cairn* DO10   66, 142, 148, **200**
Bruach na Frith(e)* SK05   60, **201,** 220-1
Buidh' Aonach LA16   **181**
Bynack Beg* LL15   100, 104, 161, **195,** 237
Bynack More* LL05   55, **195**
Ca(i)rn Etchachan* MC06   86, **195**
Caiplich LL05   100, **195**
Cairn Bannoch* DO06   55, 66, **200**
Cairn Gorm* MC11   24, 51, 55, **196**
Cairn Lochan* MC07   115-6, 141-2, 148-50, **195**
Cairn na Glasha GM05   55, **199**
Cairn of Claise* GM05   **199**
Cairn of Corbreach SD03   55, **200**
Cairn of Gowal* DO07   98, **200**
Cairn Taggart SD01   55, **200**

Cairn Toul* BC06   22, 51, 55, **196**, 303
Caiste[a/i]l* GC06   **178**
Carn a' Bhutha WC15   161, 165, **199**
Carn a' Chlamain* TT06   57, **198**
Carn a' Chlamain, N. Top TT11   **198**
Carn a' Choire Bhoidheach* SD03   **200**
Carn a' Gheoidh* WC11   **199**, 245
Carn a' Mhaim* MC01   62, 86, **195**
Carn an Fhid(h)leir* TT01 36, 37, 62, **198**, 303, 314-5
Carn an Righ* WC01   55, **198**, 266
Carn an t-Sagairt Beag* SD02   **200**
Carn an t-Sagairt Mor* SD01   **200**
Carn an Tuirc* GM07   55. 142, **199**
Carn Aosda* WC14   66, **199**, 270
Carn Ballach (N.E. Top)* ML07 64, 99, 168, **182**, 203,
    285
Carn Ballach, S.W. Top ML06   99, 109, **182**, 203
Carn Ban (Mor)* FE05   64, 98, 116, 148, **197**
Carn Ban* ML03   93, 107, 113, 114, 116, **182**, 285
Carn Beag Dearg NE04   109, **178**
Carn Bhac (N.E. Top)* WC06   62, 103, 119, **198**
Carn Bhac (S.W. Top)* WC05   161, **198**
Carn Bhinnein* WC10   66, 99, 105, 108, **199**, 245, 270
Carn Clioch-mhuillin BC10   **196**
Carn Cloich-mhuillinn* BC10   15, 34, 61, 116, 166,
    196, 316
Carn Dearg (N.W. Top)* ML04   64, **182**
Carn Dearg (N.W. Top)* NE03   160, **177**
Carn Dearg (S.W. Top)* NE02   **177**
Carn Dearg Meadhonach* NE05   109, **178**
Carn Dearg {Ericht}* EL08   55, **180**
Carn Dearg {Ossian}* OT08   12, 64, **179**, 202, 304
Carn Dearg, S.E. Top* ML05   **182**
Carn Ealar TT01   **198**
Carn Eas* EC10   61, 105, 108, 148, **194**
Carn Eig(h)e* AF16   57, **187**, 294
Carn Eite AF16   **187**
Carn Fuaralach NS08   58, 120, **185**
Carn Geoidhe WC11   66, 99, **199**, 270
Carn Ghluasaid* ES13 58, 113, 116, 142-3, 148, 153,
    186
Carn Gorm* LY09   53, **171**
Carn Liath {Atholl}* TT07   57, **198**, 206
Carn Liath {N. Laggan}* LA15   **181**
Carn Mairg {Lyon}* LY04   53, **171**
Carn Mairg {Monadhliath} ML03   64, 99, **182**
Carn Mor Dearg* NE06   53, **178**, 282-3
Carn na Caim* ED02   9, 64, 83, **197**
Carn na Coire Mheadhoin* ES06   **185**
Carn na Con Dhu* AF09   141, **186**, 203, 308
Carn na Criche {Cairngorms}* BC04   141, 148-9, **196**
Carn na Criche {Fannich}* FA04   **192**, 254, 292
Carn nam Fiaclan* EA03   57, **189**
Carn nan Gabhar {Atholl}* TT10   57, **198**
Carn nan Gobhar {Mullardoch}* NM02   63, **188**, 294

Carn nan Gobhar {S'Farrar}* SF02   57, **188**
Carn nan Sac WC12   **199**, 270
Carn Sgulain* ML09   64, 109, **182**
Ceann Garbh* GU05   101-2, 119, 160, **193**, 203
Ceum na h-Aon Choise AT02   103, **186**
Chno Dearg* OT05   **179**
Ciste D(h)ubh {Affric} AF13   **187**, 203, 294
Ciste Dhubh {Cluanie}* NS09   58, **185**
Clach Leathad* BL07   64, **175**, 297
Clachlet BL07   **175**
Cnap a' Chleirich* EC12   **194**, 245
Cnap Coire na Spreidhe* MC12   **196**
Cnoc Dearg OT05   63, **179**
Coinneach Mhor* TO11   60, 141, 148, **190**, 203
Coire Odhar ES03   **185**
Cona' Mheall {Guisachan}* GU02   63, 160, **193**
Cona(-)mheall {Assynt} AS03   **193**, 249-53
Conival(l) {Assynt}* AS03   62, 138, **193**, 292
Corrag Bhuidhe Buttress TE09   63, **192**, 203
Corrag Bhuidhe* TE06   **191**
Crags above Coire Ard Dhoire LA09   **181**
Crags above Glac Bhan OT04   **179**
Craig Coire na Fiar Bhealaich* QO05   **184**
Craig of Gowal* DO08   **200**
Cralic ES04   56, **185**
Creag a' Bhragit BQ13   109, **171**
Creag a' Chaoruinn {Affric} AF11 63, 102, 121, **187**,
    203
Creag a' Chaoruinn {Mullardoch} NM06   109, **188**
Creag a' Chaor[a/u]inn {Cluanie}* ES12   **186**
Creag a' Choir' Aird (N. Top) AF07 89, 168, **186**, 203
Creag a' Choir' Aird, E. Top AF08   109, **186**, 203
Creag a' Choir' Aird, Southern Ridge AF09   47, **186**,
    203
Creag a' Choire Aird, S. Top AF09   160, **186**
Creag a' Ghlas-uillt* SD04   98, 104, **200**
Creag a' Mhaim* SS01   58, 142, **184**, 295
Creag an Dail Mhor* EC11   61, 108, **194**
Creag an Dala Moire EC11   121, **194**
Creag an Fhithich* LT04   **172**
Creag an Leth-choin (S. Top)* MC14   105, 108, **196**
Creag an Leth-choin, N. Top MC15   **196**
Creag an Lochan LA11   119, **181**
Creag Coire nan Each* AF11   **187**
Creag D(h)ubh {Mullardoch}* NM01   63, 105, 108,
    141, **188**
Creag Dubh {Torridon} TO15   105, 148, **190**
Creag Ghorm a' Bhealaich* SF04   **188**
Creag Leacach* GM03   55, 109, 142, **199**
Creag Leacach, S.W. Top* GM08   **199**
Creag Leachdach DO05   98, 103, **200**
Creag Meag(h)aidh* LA04   52, 103, **181**
Creag Meaghaidh, E. Top LA05   109, **181**
Creag Mhor {Lochay}* MF04   55, **173**
Creag Mhor {Lyon} LY02   53, 161, **171**

Creag Mhor {N. Laggan} LA08   109, **181**
Creag na Caillich* LT14   **172**, 308
Creag na h-Eige AF21   **187**
Creag na Leacainn, N. Top MC15   **196**
Creag na Leacainn, S. Top MC14   51, **196**
Creag nan Clachan Geala AF05   **186**
Creag nan Damh* SS07   58, **184**
Creag Peathraich EL10   64, **180**
Creag Pitridh* EL10   93, 142, 148, **180**
Creag Toll a' Choin EA02   119, **189**
Creagan a' Choire Etchachan* LL10   86, 150, **195**
Creag[-/]an Dubh-loch* DO09   150, **200**
Creise* BL10   **175**
Crom Leathad LA12   119, 121, **181**
Crow Craigies* DO03   150, **199**
Cruach Ardrain (S.W. Top)* BQ07   58, 64, **170**, 279
Cruach Ardran, N.E. Top BQ06   109, **170**
Cuidhe Crom* SD05   **200**
Derry Cairngorm* LL11   62, **195**
Diollaid a' Chairn* EL07   150, **180**
Diollaid Coire Eindart FE01   98, **197**
Driesh* DO12   66, **200**
Drochaid an Tuill Easaich* ES11   **186**
Drochaid G(h)las* CR04   100, **174**
Dru(i)m S(h)ionnach* SS02   58, **184**, 295
Druim Mor* GM06   98, 103, **199**
Druim nan Bo FE03   84, 98, 109, **197**
Druim Sgarsoch TT03   161, **198**
Druim Shionnach, W. Top* SS08   **184**
Eagle's Rock* SD12   **201**
East Meur Gorm Craig* EC01   **193**
Eididh nan Clach Geala* GU06   63, **193**, 293
F(r)aochag SA07   103, **184**, 237
Fafernie* DO04   55, **199**
Feachdach WY07   121, **193**
Fiac(h)lach WY07   **193**
Fiacaill a' Choire Chais MC10   109, **196**
Fiacaill Coire an t-Sneachda MC08   30, **195**
Fiacaill na Leth-choin MC16   **196**
Fionn Bheinn* FA13   59, **192**, 292
Fuar Bheinn ED04   119, **197**
Gairich* DK06   **183**
Gaor Bheinn (N. Top) FI01   **182**
Gaor Bheinn, S. Top FI02   **182**
Garbh Chioch Bheag* DK03   **183**
Garbh Chioch M(h)or* DK02   105, 138, 166, **182**
Garbh Mheall LY12   55, **172**
Garbh Mheall, S.E. Top LY13   **172**
Garbh-leac ES04   **185**
Geal Charn (Drumochter)* WD04   64, **180**
Geal Charn {Feshie} FE09   64, 98, 108, 116, **197**
Geal Charn {Monadhliath}* ML01   64, 103, 138, **182**
Geal Charn {S. Laggan}* EL11   **180**
Geal-Charn {Ericht}* EL05   52, 98, 120, 150, **180**, 304

Glas Bheinn Mhor* ET05   64, **174**
Glas Leathad Beag (Centre Top)* WY06   100, 105, 116, **193**
Glas Leathad Beag (W. Top) WY05   141, 150, **193**
Glas Leathad Beag, E. Top WY07   **193**
Glas Leathad Mor* WY03   160, **193**
Glas M(h)eall Mor* ED05   64, 83, 108, 116, 148, **197**
Glas Maol* GM02   55, 103, **199**
Glas Mheall Liath* TE08   **192**
Glas Mheall M(h)or* TE02   105, 121, 148, **191**
Glas Thulachan WC02   55, **198**, 266
Glas Tulaichean* WC02   **198**
Gleoura(i)ch* QO04   58, **184**, 295
Gleoura(i)ch, E. Top QO05   **184**
Gulvain (N. Top)* FI01   63, **182**
Gulvain, S. Top* FI02   **182**
Knight's Peak* SK23   **202**, 221-2
Ladhar Bheinn* KN03   59, 89, **183**
Leabaidh an Daimh Bhuidhe* EC07   **194**
Leachd Riach BC12   108, 109, **197**, 202
Little Cairngorm LL14   85, **195**
Little Glas Maol* GM04   85n, 98, **199**
Little Pap* SD06   **200**
Lochnagar (Cac Carn Beag)* SD09   55, 62, 104, **200**, 245
Lochnagar, Cac Carn Mor SD08   **200**
Lochnagar, Cairn SD08   **200**
Lord Berkeley's Seat* TE05   **191**
Luinne Bheinn* KN02   59, **183**
Luinne Bheinn, E. Top* KN06   **183**
Lurcher's Crag MC14   **196**
Lurg Mhor* EA08   25, 57, **189**, 307
Mam Coire Easain BL08   108, **175**
Mam nan Carn* WC03   99, **198**, 268
Mam Sodhail* AF15   19, 93, 148, **187**, 294
Mam Soul AF15   57, 63, **187**
Maoile Lunndai(c/d)h* EA01   57, 119, 168, **189**
Maol Chean-dearg* WA01   60, **189**
Maol Ch[i/ea]nn-dearg* SS04   58, 160, **184**
Marcaonach WD03   **180**
Mayar* DO11   66, **200**
Meall a' Bharr* LY05   **171**
Meall a' Bhuiridh* BL09   64, **175**
Meall a' Chaoruinn ED03   64, 83, 108, 119, **197**
Meall a' Chinn Deirg WA01   **189**
Meall a' Choire Leith* LT09   53, **172**
Meall a' Chrasgaidh* FA03   60, **192**, 292
Meall a' Churain* MF11   66, **173**
Meall an Fhuarain Mhoir* AT02   **186**
Meall an t-Snaim* LA14   **181**
Meall an/na Teanga* WL02   103, 108, 160, **182**, 234, 295
Meall Buidhe {Feshie}* FE08   98, **197**
Meall Buidhe {Knoydart}* KN01   59, 89, **183**
Meall Buidhe {Lyon}* LY12   **172**

Meall Buidhe {Orchy}* OR05   **173**
Meall Buidhe, S.E Top* KN05   **183**
Meall Buidhe, S.E. Top LY13   **172**
Meall Chuaich* ED01   12, **197**
Meall Chuirn MF11   119, **173**
Meall Coire Choille-rais* LA07   **181**
Meall Coire Coille na Froise LA07   **181**
Meall Coire na Saobhaidhe* SD10   **201**
Meall Corranaich* LT08   53, **172**
Meall Cruidh* ET02   **174**
Meall Cuanail* CR03   51, **174**
Meall Dearg {Glencoe}* AE03   66, **176**
Meall Dearg {Torridon}* TO04   105, 148, **190**
Meall Dubh-achaidh FE04   64, 98, **197**
Meall Dubhag* FE04   113, 116, **197**
Meall G(h)las Choire* EL02   **179**
Meall Garbh {Lawers}* LT02   53, **172**
Meall Garbh {Lyon}* LY07   53, 161, **171**
Meall Garbh {Tarmachan}* LT11   **172**
Meall Garbh {Treig}* OT06   **179**
Meall Ghaordie* MF01   53, **173**
Meall Glas* MF08   119, **173**
Meall Gorm (N.W. Top)* FA10   109, **192**, 292
Meall Gorm, S.E. Top* FA11   **192**
Meall Greigh* LT01   **172**
Meall Gruaidh LT01   50, 66, **172**
Meall Liath* LY03   **171**
Meall Luaidhe LY06   **171**
Meall Mor* EA09   25, 57, **189**
Meall na Cuaich ED01   55, 83, **197**
Meall na Dige* BQ14   113, **171**
Meall nam Peithirean* FA09   **192**
Meall nan Aighean* LY02   **171**
Meall nan Ceapraichean* GU04   63, 101, 102, 119,
    160, **193**, 293
Meall nan Con* KH01   **193**
Meall nan Eun* ET07   64, **174**
Meall nan Tarmachan* LT10   **172**
Meall nan Tarmachan, S.E. Top* LT15   **172**
Meall Odhar* GM01   85, **199**
Meall Tionail FE02   64, 98, **197**
Meallan Rairigidh FA10   60, **192**, 292
Meikle Pap* SD07   **200**
Monadh Mor* BC11   62, 161, **197**, 303
Moruisg* EA10   61, **189**
Mount Keen* SD11   9, 66, **201**
Mullach an Rathain* TO03   105, 107, 113, 116, 121,
    148, 166, **189**, 203
Mullach C. Mhic Fhearchair* LF04   59, 89, **191**, 234,
    236
Mullach C. Mhic Fhearchair, E. Top* LF10   101, 161,
    191, 234
Mullach Cadha Rainich* AF17   102, **187**
Mullach Clach a' Bhlair* FE02   **197**
Mullach Coire an Iubhair EL11   52, **180**

Mullach Coire nan Nead* EL01   **179**
Mullach Fraoch-choire (Centre Top)* ES01   **185**, 294
Mullach Fraoch-choire, N.E. Top ES02   **185**
Mullach Fraoch-choire, S. Top ES03   **185**
Mullach Lochan na(n) G[a/o]bhar EC05   **194**
Mullach na Dheiragain* AF30   **187**
Mullach na(n) Coirean (N.W. Top)* MA16   56, **177**
Mullach na(n) Coirean, S.E. Top* MA15   **177**
Mullach Sithidh* AF07   **186**, 203
Na Gruagaichean* MA04   108, 110, 122, 142, **177**, 296
Na Gruagaichean, N.W. Top* MA05   **177**, 296
Northern Pinnacles TO04   **190**
Puist Coire Ardair* LA09   **181**
Ridge S. of Creag a' Choir' Aird AF09   121-2, **186**,
    203
Ruadh Stac Mor {Letterewe}* LF07   116, 138, 161,
    166, **191**
Ruadh-stac-Mhor {Torridon}* TO10   60, **190**
Rudha na Spreidh[a/e] NM04   109, **188**
Sail Chaorainn* ES08   142, 148, **185**
Sail Chaoruinn ES09   103, **185**
Sail Liath* TE10   105, **192**
Sail Mhor* TO09   102, 105, 113, 116, 121, 141, **190**
Saileag* NS05   58, 142, **185**
Saoiter Mor AF14   63, **187**
Schi[c/e]hallion LY01   50, **171**
Scour Gairoch DK06   63, **183**
Scour Ouran NS01   56, **184**
Seana B(h)raigh* GU07   63, **193**, 293
Sgairneach M(h)or* WD01   64, 160, **180**
Sgiath Chuil* MF10   119, **173**, 202
Sgor a' Bhuic NE13   **178**
Sgor a' Choinnich Beag GC01   **178**
Sgor a' Choinnich Mor GC02   56, **178**
Sgor a' Mhaim MA13   55, **177**
Sgor an Lochan Uaine* BC05   15, 22, 51, 84, 105, 108,
    121, 141, 166, 168, **196**
Sgor Choileam FI03   56, **182**
Sgor Choinnich* OT10   12, 64, 108, 121, 141, 148, **179**
Sgor Gaibhre* OT09   12, 64, **179**, 304
Sgor Gaoith* FE06   98, **197**
Sgor Iutharn(a)* EL06   98, **180**, 304
Sgor na Ciche DK01   56, **182**
Sgor na h-Eilde MA01   **176**
Sgor na h-Eilde Beag MA02   **176**
Sgor na h-Ulaidh* AP02   63, 88, **176**
Sgor nan Coireachan {Dessary}* DK04   63, **183**
Sgor nan Coireachan {Finnan}* FI04   63, **182**
Sgor(r) an Iubhair* MA12   55, 138, 142-3, 149, 168,
    177
Sgor(r) nam Fiannaidh* AE01   64, **176**
Sgoran Dubh Mor* FE07   22, 51, 98, **197**
Sgoran Dubh North FE07   **197**
Sgoran Dubh South FE06   98, **197**
Sgorr Bhan* AP07   **176**, 216

Sgorr Dhearg* AP06   53, **176**, 202, 216
Sgorr Dhonuill* AP05   53, **176**, 216
Sgorr Ruadh* WA02   59, **189**
Sgurr (n)an Fhir Duibhe* TO14   **190**
Sgurr a' Mhoraire Beag QO03   **184**
Sgurr a' Bhealaich Dheirg* NS06   58, **185**
Sgurr a' Bhuic* NE13   **178**
Sgurr a' Chaorachain* EA05   **189**
Sgurr a' Chaoruinn EA05   57, 99, **189**
Sgurr a' Choir Ghlais* SF03   57, **188**
Sgurr a' Dubh Doire* AT04   103, **186**
Sgurr a' Fionn Choire* SK17   **202**
Sgurr a' Ghreadaidh (N. Top)* SK06   61, **201**, 221-2
Sgurr a' Ghreadaidh, S. Top* SK19   **202**, 221
Sgurr a' Mhadaidh (S.W. peak)* SK18 61, 104n, 165, **202**, 221
Sgurr a' Mhaim* MA13   **177**, 296
Sgurr a' Mhaoraich Beag* QO03   **184**
Sgurr a' Mhaoraich* QO02   **184**
Sgurr a' Mhoraire QO02   59, 103, **184**
Sgurr Ala(i)sdair (S.W. Peak)* SK11 26, 61, 67, **201**, 220-2
Sgurr Alaisdair, N.E. Peak SK10   **201**, 221
Sgurr an Doire Leathain* SS05   58, **184**
Sgurr an Fhuarail* NS08   **185**
Sgurr an Lochain Uaine* LL13   86, **195**
Sgurr an Lochain* SS06   58, 142-3, **184**
Sgurr an Tuill Bhain* LF02   **190**, 229-30
Sgurr Ban {Letterewe}* LF05   59, 89, **191**, 234-5
Sgurr Ban {Torridon}* TO13   59, **190**
Sgurr Breac* FA02   60, **192**
Sgurr Choinnich Beag* GC01   **178**
Sgurr Choinnich Mor* GC02   **178**
Sgurr Choinnich* EA06   57, **189**
Sgurr Creag an Eich* TE04   **191**
Sgurr Dearg (Cairn) SK08   35, 61, 168, **201**, 221
Sgurr Dearg (Ordnance Point) SK08   119, **201**
Sgurr Dearg, Inaccessible Pinnacle* SK09   15, 34-6, 38, 93, 118-20, **201**, 220-2, 312, 317
Sgurr Dubh a' Bhasteir SK04   **201**
Sgurr Dubh Mor SK14   26, 61, 67, **202**, 221
Sgurr Dubh an Da Bheinn SK13   26, 61, **202**, 221
Sgurr Dubh {Letterewe}* LF11   **191**
Sgurr Dubh, Centre Peak* SK14   **202**
Sgurr Dubh, W. Peak* SK13   **202**
Sgurr Eilde Beag* MA02   **176**
Sgurr Eilde Mor* MA01   63, **176**
Sgurr Fhuar-thuill* SF05   63, **188**
Sgurr Fhuaran* NS01   19, **184**
Sgurr Fiona* TE03   63, 105, 166, **191**, 203
Sgurr Leac nan Each* SA01   **183**
Sgurr M(h)or* TO02   **189**
Sgurr Mhic C(h)oinnich* SK22 61n, 104n, 143, **202**, 221-3
Sgurr Mor {Dessary}* DK05   63, **183**

Sgurr Mor {Fannich}* FA07   60, **192**, 254, 292
Sgurr na Banachaig SK07   **201**
Sgurr na Banachdich (N. Top)* SK07   61, **201**, 221-2
Sgurr na Banachdich, Centre Top* SK20   **202**, 221
Sgurr na Carnach* NS02   19, 56, 105, 141, **184**
Sgurr na Ciche* DK01   **182**
Sgurr na Ciste Duibhe* NS03   56, **185**
Sgurr na Creige {N. of Saddle} SA06   153, **183**
Sgurr na Creige {W. of Saddle} SA02   **183**
Sgurr na Fearstaig* SF06   **188**
Sgurr na Festig SF06   **188**
Sgurr na Forcan* SA05   **183**
Sgurr na Lapaich {Affric}* AF18   19, 63, 105, 108, 110, 115-6, 141-2, **187**
Sgurr na Lapaich {Mullardoch]* NM03   57, **188**, 294
Sgurr na Ruaidhe* SF01   **188**
Sgurr na Sgine* SA08   59, **184**
Sgurr na Sgine, N.W Top* SA11   **184**
Sgurr na(n) Clachan Geala* NM05   **188**
Sgurr nan Ceannaichean* EA11   **189**, 283-4
Sgurr nan Ceathramhan {Cluanie} ES01   56, **185**
Sgurr nan Ceathramhan, N.E. Top ES02   **185**
Sgurr nan Ceathreamhan (E. Top)* AF03   58, 89, **186**
Sgurr nan Ceathramhan, Centre Top AF03   **186**
Sgurr nan Ceathramhan, E. Top AF28   **187**
Sgurr nan Ceathramhan. W. Top* AF04   **186**
Sgurr nan Clach Geala* FA05   60, **192**, 254, 292
Sgurr nan Conbhairean* ES10   58, **185**, 295
Sgurr nan Each* FA06   60, **192**, 254, 292
Sgurr nan Eag* SK15   27, 61, **202**, 221
Sgurr nan Forcan SA09   **184**
Sgurr nan Gillean* SK03   60, **201**, 220-2
Sgurr nan Saighead* NS10   141, **185**
Sgurr nan Spainteach* NS04   **185**
Sgurr Ruadh {Achnashellach} WA02   **189**
Sgurr Ruadh {S'Farrar} SF01   57, **188**
Sgurr S[g/q]umain* SK12   26, 61, **201**, 221
Sgurr Thearlaich* SK10   26, 61n, **201**
Sgurr Thormaid* SK21   **202**, 221
Sgurr Thuilm* FI03   **182**
Shoulder .5m SW of Ben Avon EC09   **194**
Slioch (Trig Point) LF01   59, 168, **190**, 203, 228-30
Slioch, N. Top* LF09   **191**, 203, 228-30
Snechdach Slinnean ML02   99, **182**
Socach Mor WC09   **199**, 268
Spidean a' C(h)oire Leith* TO06   **190**, 203
Spidean Coir' an Laoigh TO01   **189**
Spidean Coire nan Clach* TO12   2, 60, 102, 105, 113, 116, 141-2, **190**
Spidean Dhomhnuill Bhric* SA02   **183**
Spidean Mialach* QO06   58, **184**, 295
Spideanan nam Fasarinen TO05   101, **190**
Sron a' Cha(-)no MC13   103, 108, **196**, 237
Sron a' Choire Ghairbh* WL01   63, **182**, 295

Sron a' Choire* LA10	103, **181**
Sron a' Ghaothair LA10	109, **181**
Sron a' Ghearrain* BL02	**175**
Sron an Isean* CR07	95, **174**
Sron Chon a' Choirein LY10	**172**, 263
Sron Chona Choirein* LY10	172
Sron Coire a' Chriochairein* LA13	**181**
Sron Coire na h-Iolaire* EL14	55, **180**
Sron dha-Murchdi LT07	109, **172**
Sron Garbh Choire {N. Laggan} LA13	**181**
Sron Garbh {Affric}* AF22	**187**
Sron Garbh {S. Laggan} EL12	**180**
Sron na Lairig(e)* BC01	**196**
Sron na Leirg BC01	**196**
Sron nan Giubhas BL04	**175**
Sron Riach* MC02	31, 86, **195**
Stacan Dubha* LL12	86, **195**
Stob a' Bruaich Leith* BL01	**175**
Stob a' Choire Dhomhain* AF21	**187**
Stob a' Choire Leith* GC08	**178**
Stob a' Choire Mhail MA17	**177**
Stob a' Choire Mheadhoin* OT02	**179**
Stob a' Choire Mheadhonaiche OT02	58, 121, **179**
Stob a' Choire Odhair* BL06	64, **175**
Stob a' Choire Odhair* KN04	59, **183**
Stob a' Coire Liath Mhor* TO07	**190**
Stob a' Ghlais Choire* BL11	108, **175**
Stob an Cul Choire* NE09	109, **178**
Stob an Dubh-loch SD12	**201**
Stob an Duine Ruaidh* ET08	**174**
Stob an Fhir-Bhogha MF02	160, **173**, 237
Stob an Fhuarain* AP01	**176**
Stob an t-Sluichd* EC13	164, **194**
Stob Bac an Fhurain EC04	109, **194**
Stob Ban {Grey Corries}* GC12	63, **179**, 305
Stob Ban {Mamores}* MA14	56, **177**
Stob Binnein* BQ11	**171**
Stob Cadha Gobhlach* TE07	**191**
Stob Choire a' Mhail* MA17	**177**
Stob Choire an Easain Mhoir OT01	58, **179**
Stob Choire Claurigh (S. Top)* GC09	56, 95, 120, **179**, 305
Stob Choire Claurigh, N. Top GC13	**179**
Stob Coir' an Albannaich* ET06	64, **174**
Stob Coire (an) Easain* GC03	95, 120, **178**
Stob Coire (na) Gaibhre* GC11	**179**
Stob Coire a' Chairn* MA10	56, 93, 121, 148, **177**
Stob Coire Altruim* CO03	99, **175**
Stob Coire an Fhir Dhuibh NE10	160, **178**
Stob Coire an Laoigh* GC05	56, 120, **178**
Stob Coire an Lochain {Cairngorms} BC03	**196**
Stob Coire an Lochain {Dochart}* BQ12	**171**
Stob Coire an t-Saighdeir* BC07	84, **196**
Stob Coire an t-Sneachda* MC09	**196**
Stob Coire Bhealaich* NE12	**178**
Stob Coire Cath na S(g)ine* GC07	**178**
Stob Coire Coulavie AF12	**187**, 294
Stob Coire D(h)u(i)bh* LA17	**181**
Stob Coire Dheirg* ET04	**174**
Stob Coire Domhnuill* AF29	**187**
Stob Coire Easain* OT01	**179**
Stob Coire Etchachan* LL09	**195**
Stob Coire Leith* AE02	**176**
Stob Coire Lochain* AF19	**187**
Stob Coire na Ceannain* GC10	56, **179**, 305
Stob Coire na Cloiche* AF32	**188**
Stob Coire na Cralaig* ES03	150, **185**
Stob Coire nam Beith* CO10	**176**
Stob Coire nan Ceann GC10	**179**
Stob Coire nan Dearcag AF06	**186**
Stob Coire nan Lochan* CO11	105, 148, **176**
Stob Coire Raineach* CO06	99, 105, 107, 116, 141, **175**
Stob Coire Sgreamhach* CO08	105, 141, **176**
Stob Coire Sgrenach CO08	**176**
Stob Coire Sgriodain (N. Top)* OT03	63, **179**
Stob Coire Sgriodain, S. Top* OT04	**179**
Stob Coire Sputan Dearg MC03	**195**
Stob Dearg {Buachaille}* CO01	**175**
Stob Dearg {Cruachan}* CR01	**174**
Stob Diamh* CR05	95, 100, 108-9, 111, **174**
Stob Dubh an Eas Bhig EC08	**194**
Stob Dubh* CO05	99, **175**
Stob Dubh, Bruach an Fhurain EC04	**194**
Stob Garbh {Crianlarich}* BQ09	**171**, 279
Stob Garbh {Cruachan}* CR06	51, **174**
Stob Ghabhar* BL03	53, **175**, 297
Stob Gharbh Mhor EC06	**194**
Stob Glas Choire BL11	**175**
Stob Lochan nan Cnapan BC13	**197**
Stob na Broige* CO04	99, 105, 108, 116, 141, **175**
Stob na Doire* CO02	99, 105, 116, 141, **175**
Stob nan Clach* MF05	**173**
Stob Poite Coire Ardair (W. Top)* LA11	**181**
Stob Poite Coire Ardair, E. Top LA12	**181**
Stobinian BQ11	10, 51, **171**
Stuc a' Choire Dhuibh Bhig* TO08	102, **190**
Stuc a' Chroin* SE02	51, **171**
Stuc B(h)eag AF01	**186**
Stuc Bheag* AF02	**186**
Stuc Fraoch Choire* AF31	**188**
Stuc G(h)arbh Mhor EC06	**194**
Stuc Mor AF02	105, **186**
Stuc Mor* AF01	148, **186**
Stuchd an Lochain* LY11	53, **172**, 259-63
Taynuilt Peak CR01	**174**
The Angel's Peak BC05	15, 15n, **196**
The Cairnwell* WC13	66, **199**, 245, 270

The Devil's Point* BC08 15n, 21, 51, 62, 83n, 84, 142, **196**

The Saddle* SA04 56, **183,** 203

The Saddle, E. Top SA09 **184**

The Saddle, Trig Point SA10 **184**

The Saddle, W.Top SA03 **183**

Tigh Mor (na Seilge) (N.N.E. Top)* ES07 58, 103, **185**

Tigh Mor (na Seilge), Centre Top ES06 **185**

Tigh Mor (na Seilge), S.S.W. Top ES08 116, **185**

Toll Creagach* AF27 **187**

Toll Creagach, W. Top* AF26 **187**

Tolmount* DO02 54, 66, 142, **199**

Tom a' Choinich Beag* AF24 160, **187**

Tom a' Choinich* AF25 57, **187**

Tom a' Choinnich* WY04 **193**

Tom Buidhe* DO01 66, **199**

Tom Dubh* BC13 **197**

Tom na Gruagaich* TO01 105, 113, 141, 148, **189**

Tom na Sroine* NE11 **178**

Toman Coinich* FA14 60n, 101, 150, 161, **192,** 236

Top above C. an Lochan BC03 99, **196**

Top above Cadha Gobhlach TE07 **191,** 203

Top above Lochan nan Cnapan BC13 99, 103, **197**

Top btw. Cruach Ardran & Stob Garbh BQ08 109, **171**

Top btw. Mam C. Easain & Stob Glas Ch. BL10 **175**

Top btw. Mam Sodhail & Sg. na Lapaich AF17 **187**

Top half mile N. of Saddle SA06 **183,** 202

Top N. of Allt Toll Easa AF26 **187**

Top N. of Coire Etchachan LL09 **195**

Top of An Cul Choire NE09 **178**

Top of C. an t-Saighdeir BC07 **196**

Top of Cliffs above L. Avon MC06 **195**

Top of Coire a' Chaoruin LA14 **181**

Top of Coire an Lochain MC07 **195**

Top of Coire an Sput Dheirg MC03 31, 86, **195**

Top of Coire an t-Sneachda MC09 **196**

Top of Coire Bhealaich NE12 **178**

Top of Coire Bhourneasg WC06 119, **198**

Top of Coire Coulavie AF12 102, **187**

Top of Coire Dearg MA15 **177**

Top of Coire Dubh {N. Laggan} LA17 **181**

Top of Coire Dubh {Orchy} OR07 108, 109, **174**

Top of Coire Lochain {Affric} AF19 **187**

Top of Coire Lochain {Wyvis} WY06 102, **193**

Top of Coire nan Dearcag AF06 **186**

Top of Coire nan Laogh MA03 **176**

Top of Eagle's Rock SD12 **201**

Tuill Creagach AF27 63, **187**

Tuill Creagach, W. Top AF26 **187**

Uinneag a' Ghlas[-/]Choire EL02 **179**

West Meur Gorm Craig* EC03 **194**

General Index

This index consists mostly of names of people and of hills not included in the previous index. No attempt has been made to index references to Munro or Robertson, and topics are only very selectively indexed. Footnote references are marked by a small 'n'.

A' Chioch, Mull 88

Abraham, George D. 214n

Airy, Sir George 225-7

Aitken, Robert 32n

Alexander, Henry 15n

Allan, Elizabeth 79

Almond, Hely H. 32

Andrewhinney Hill 128

Arran Hills, The 286-7

Arran Murder, The 49

Baddeley's Guide 162

Baines, Jack 133, 153

Baird, Mr. of Knoydart 17

Baird, P.D. 285n

Baker, E.A. 229

Barlow, Guy 26n, 245

Barrow, Walter 13

Bartholomew, John 300

Barton, J.S. 285n

Battenberg, Prince Henry of 30

Bearhop, Derek A. 122, 123n, 166

Beinn a' Bhuiridh 53

Beinn Alligin 63

Beinn Bhreac (Feshie) 303

Beinn Dearg Mhor 237

Beinn Mhic Cedidh 306

Beinn na h-Eaglaise 127

Beinn Odhars, The 306

Bell Craig 144

Bell, James H.B. 36n, 46, 49, 79, 93, 286n, 310

Bell, John H. 286

Ben Alder Lodge (McCook) 52, 55, 64

Ben Wyvis 36, 50

Bennachie 302

Bicycling, Evils of 208

Bidein Druim nan Ramh 221

Birkscairn Hill 144

Bishop of St Andrews 40

Black Tongue, The	64, 66
Black's Guide	162, 299-300
Black, Dr. John S.	49, 55
Black, Hugh	55
Bland, James	209n
Bonsall, Prof. Frank F.	33, 117, 121, 126, 137, 147
Bradshaw, Stan	307
Brian, Paul	314
Bridge, George	130-1, 133-4
Broadhead, David J.	284-5
Brooker, Wm. D.	282, 286, 288n, 314n
Brown, H.M.	145, 156, 166, 288, 299, 308, 312
Bullough, Sir George	10n
Burn, Ronald G.	32, 34, 36, 38, 60n, 79-82, 90, 160-1, 236, 310
Butterfield, Irving	133, 153
Buxton, Chris	133, 153
C.I.C. Hut	71ff, 296
Cairngorms, Character of	30
Campbell, Colin of Glen Lyon	260
Campbell, Colin of Glenure	274
Campbell, Duncan	260
Campbell, Robin N.	126, 150, 153
Carn Gorm Loch, Strathvaich	101, 161, 237
Carr, Herbert R.C.	129, 133
Cassie, Mr. of Hopeman	49
Christison, Sir Robert	246ff
Clach Glas	60, 221
Clark, Mrs. W. Inglis	60, 61
Clark, R.W.	153
Clark, W. Inglis	16n, 60-1, 73-4, 77-8, 286-7
Clements, E.D.	133-4
Clothing, Ideal	206
Coats, Wilf L.	161
Cobbler, The	55
Colley, Sir George	13, 42, 43
Collie, J. Norman	26, 118
Copland, Alexander	15n
Corbett, J. Rooke	60n, 80, 90, 127, 133, 160-1, 310
Corner, Edred	84, 160-1, 203, 216, 265n
Corrieyairack Hill	132
Craigellachie, Aviemore	21
Creag an Duine, Seana Braigh	161
Crockett, S.R.	55
Cuillin Ridge, Structure of	28
Dawson, Alan	132, 133
Dempster, Andrew	153, 288
Derry Lodge (Frasers)	20, 24, 29-30, 277-8
Dewey, Michael	132, 133-4
Dillon, Paddy	132-3, 153
Docharty, Wm. McK.	130, 133
Donald, Percy	111-2, 128, 133
Donaldson, James C.	32n, 34, 165-6, 299n
Donaldson, Wm	293
Douglas, Wm.	33, 34n, 38n, 39, 50, 53, 101, 221, 243, 245
Dow, John	80, 147, 160-1, 203
Doyle, A.C.	299n
Drumleys House	13, 39
Drummond, James	55
Drummond, Peter	46
Dutton, Prof. Geoff J.F.	32n, 300n
Elsegood, Mark	288, 313
Elton, Robert R.	73
Emslie, W.T.	129, 133
English Hills, The	144-6
Fara, The	304
Fasnakyle House	18
Feet, Care of	207
Fielding, Gen. W.	42
Foinaven	101, 161, 236, 291-2, 310
Forbes, Prof. J.D.	242
Fraser, Alexander	39
Garbh Bheinn, Blaven	221
Garden, Wm.	31, 38, 80
Garsbheinn, Skye	28, 221
Geddes, Jack	50
Glen Aladale	306
Glen Clova	15
Glen Isla	16
Glenquoich Lodge	18
Glomach, Falls of	19
Glover, George T.	16
Goggs, Frank S.	216
Goodeve, T.E.	276
Graham, Fiona	131-2, 133
Grant of Rothiemurchus	21
Grant, Ewen	50
Gribbon, Phil W.	282-3
Grieg, James	269
Grieve, Tom	71n
Griffin, A.H.	153
Guisachan House	18n
Hall, Herbert	163
Hall, Robert	163-4
Harker, Dr. Alfred	28, 61
Harvey, Rev. James	57
Herman Law	128, 144
Heron, P.L.J.	288
Hewitts 132	
Hillshaw Head	144
Hinde, John	295

Hirst, J. 161, 236
Hodge, E.W. 129, 133, 153
Hope, Philip 290n
Howie, W. Lamond 55, 58
Inglis, H., *Contour Road Book* 62n
Inglis, James G. 100n, 126, 160-1, 165, 203, 234, 236
Inglis, Robin G. 33, 114n, 126
Irish Hills, The 88, 144-5
J.M.C.S., Customs of 208
Jack, J.S.M. 286
Johnson's Maps 162
Kale, David 313
Kenyon, James 317
King, W. Wickham 29
Kinloch House, Rum 10n
Kirkpatrick, Wm. 290n
Kirkwood, Capt. 229
Kirriemuir Observer 40n
L.S.C.C. 208
Ladder Hills, The 302
Lairig Ghru (Learg Grumach) 21, 276-9
Langmuir, Eric 204, 213
Lawson, Murray 279
Leathad an Taobhainn 303
Leum Uilleim 304
Lewis, Gwyn 133, 153
Liathach 63
Lindertis House 14, 16, 38, 40, 314
Ling, Wm. N. 34, 117-8, 276, 286
Lister, George A. 129, 133
Loch Etchachan 24
Lodge, Prof. R. 13n
Lowther Hill 144
Lynam, Joss 134
MacInnes, Hamish 290
Mackay, A.M. (Lord) 238
Mackenzie, R.J. 32n
MacLaren, Maud 58
MacRobert, Harry 36, 72
Magnetic Variation 215, 241
Manley, Gordon 285n
Marilyns 132
Marsh, Terry 131, 133
Mather, Neil 307
Matheson, Wm. 115
Maxwell, D.C. 129, 133, 145
Maxwell, Eric 288n
Maylard, A. Ernest 55, 245
McConnochie, Alex.I. 20
McCue, Peter 311
McIntosh, Dr Iain B. 311

McIntyre, Anne 284-5
McKenzie, John 26, 29
Meall Coire Lochain (Lochy) 234
Meall Gorm, Strathvaich 101, 161
Methuen, Jack 58
Middle Hill 144
Mitchell, Ian 46
Moncrieff, Alex. 56, 58, 66
Moran, Martin 313
Morris, Dave 284-5
Moss, E. 129, 133
Motoring, early 12, 13
Moulton, Matthew 308
Mowbray, Norman 73
Mt. Brandon 308
Mulholland, H. 133, 153
Munro, Miss A.K. 42
Munro, Selina (Byrne) 44
Munro, Sir Campbell 44
Munro, Sir Hugh T. —
    Card Index of Tops 36, 100, 107-9, 165
    Copy of the Tables 36, 86, 101, 165
    Death in Tarascon 39, 45
    Grave 15, 39, 314
    Military Career 44, 45
    Opinions about Landowning 38n
    Political Activity 44
    Rheumatism 34
    Writings 4, 6, 8
Munro, Sir Thomas 44
Munro, Sir Torquil 13, 14, 39
Naismith, Wm. W. 39, 55, 72, 211-3, 216, 255
Napier, Graham 72, 286
National Library of Scotland 1n, 163, 300
Nuttall, John & Anne 133, 153
O'Donovan, Roger 284
Ogilvie, Iain 313
Oldham, Haswell 313
Ordnance Survey 2, 118, 120, 122, 142, 150, 161, 204, 218-21, 230, 309
Parker, James A. 55, 56, 60, 61, 78, 80, 90, 133, 153, 160-1, 203-4, 236
Parry, Charles W. 91
Peacock, A.W. 100
Peyton, Mr. of Broughty Ferry 49
Philip, Rev. J.A. 40
Phillip, Colin B. 25, 26, 32, 33, 42, 118, 161, 299, 309
Pilkington's Map of Skye 119-20, 218
Pitkin, James (Aneroids) 50
Pöppig, Dr 246
Prothero, the Misses 26
Purchase, David 114n

Pyatt, E.C.   153
Pyper, Derek G.   283-4, 317
Raeburn, Harold   29, 51n, 290n
Ramsay, George G.   42, 52, 53
Ramsden, Sir John   52
Reid, George R.S.   51, 57, 58, 59
Reid, Walter   16n
Rennie, J.   13, 55
Robertson, Kate (McFarlan) 53, 55, 56, 60, 63, 64, 66
Robertson, Rev. A.E. —
       Applies to join SMC   53
       Brief Record   35, 48, 49, 63n, 64n
       Cycle Tour 1898   58-60
       Cycle Tour 1899   62-64
       Defects of his Round   36, 46, 47
       Memorial Bridge   77
       Notebooks   35, 46, 49, 51n, 53n, 63n
       Photography   46, 77
       Struck by Lightning   48
Rogers, John   301
Ross, Helen E.   314-5, 317
Ross, John M.   32n
Rothiemurchus Forest   24
Rum, Isle of   10-11
Rutherfurd, R.N.   286
Salvationist & Ultramontane   32, 310n
Scottish Mountaineering Trust   2n, 122
Sellar, R.T.   89
Semaphore on Sgoran Dubh   22, 98
Separation, Concept of   111-4, 121, 125
Sgor na h-Aide   56
Sgurr a' Choire-rainich (Conon)   236
Sgurr a' Ghlas Leathad   236
Sgurr nan Each, Blaven   221
Sgurr Thionail, Quoich   103, 161, 237
Shiel Dod   144
Simpson, F.H.F.   129, 133
Skiary Inn   17, 59
Smart, Iain   288n, 312
SMC Meet in Skye, 1923   79
SMC Minute-books   39
SMC Yacht Meet of 1897   13
Smith, J. Parker   18n
Smith, R. Angus   273
Smith, Robin C.   155
Smith, W.P. Haskett   153
Smythe, Frank   78
Sow of Athole   58
Speirs, Wm. B.   73
Steeple, E.W.   245
Stob Law   144

Stott, Joseph G.   32, 42, 52, 69n, 205n, 208n, 309
Strathcona, Lord   66
Strathfarrar Hills, The   294
Streaps   11
Swatte Fell   144
Symonds, Hugh   313
Talla Cleuch Head   144
Tarascon, Provence   39, 45
Tarfessock   144
Tarmachans, The   53
Taylor, Alex.   55
Thomson, Edward C.   36, 80, 160-1, 286
Thomson, Gilbert   214n, 254
Tod, Harry   53
Tough, Wm.   53
Training, Ideal   205-6
Tramps, The   32, 205n
Trowgrain Middle   128
Tschudi, Von   247
Twain, Mark   32
Tweedmouth, Lord   18
Vandeleur, C.R.P.   229
Variorum Table   170-202
Variorum Table Key   168-9
Variorum Table Notes   202-3
Variorum Table Sections   167
Veitch, Prof. John   39
Wainwright, A.   133, 153
Wall, Claude W.   129, 132-3
Waller, Ivan   91
Walsh, A. St. G.   133, 153
Warburton, Peter   162
Waters, A.C.   268, 270
Watkins' Aneroid   228
Watson, Adam   15n
Weir, Tom   32n
Welsh Hills, The   144-5, 147, 308
Wettermantels   51n
Whisky, Uses of   207
Whymper, Edward   220, 228
Whyte, Dr.   49, 50, 55
Wills, Alfred   242
Wilson, Gordon   89
Wilson, John D.B.   49
Winans, W.L.   18n, 57
Wright, D.S. Blythe   156
Wright, Nick   153
Yeaman, E.J.   131, 133
Young, James R.   100, 108
Zipf's Law   156
Zsigmondy, Dr. E.   239

J.S. Huddart Mark Sinclair Elsa Yates
Robert W. Yates Pat Eady Ken Parnham
David Rhodes Geoffrey D. Carter
Irene Cook Ken G. Telfer Mark Wrightam
Gibson McGeachie Lynne McGeachie
George D. Ferguson Adrienne Simcock
Peter Simcock Jamie F. Stone
Patricia A. Horner Douglas Marr
Anthony J. Sanford
Linda M. Moxey-Sanford Derek Blackburn
Jack Escritt John Nelson Ann Landers
Pedro Landers Robin W. Dempsey
Christopher M. Huntley Martin J.B. Lowe
Richard P. Wood Mike Futty
Alun Gwyn Thomas Elizabeth M. Thomas
Ian R. Mitchell Eric Drew
Derek R. Snowdon Alan Chow
Cameron McNeish William F. Buchanan
Marian P. Elmes John Neave John Baxter
Peter Lockett Michael Gairey
Colin A. Simpson Gordon Keir
Irene I. Clark J. Alan Fyfe Peter Newley
Heather King Dorothy Spencer
Graham J. Gainey James G. Benson
Peter Collin Bob Sharp Peter N. Jones
John Whyte Thomson Tony Heath
John Starbuck Anne R. Robson
Andy Harrison Iain Smith
David N. Gothard Robert B. Gunn
Joyce C. Stephens Neil Heaton
George Herraghty Dave Foy Mike Dixon
Stephen Dunn Ron A. Henderson
Bob Connell Howard A. Sowerby
Thomas Cull Ian Cumming J.R. Anderson
Andy Sargeant Derek Finlay Jack Harrison
Robert Alexander H.H. Mills
William Redford James Entwistle
Alan R. Munro Alan D. Armstrong
Brian J. MacDonald Ian Dargie
John A. Stark John Pownall
William Watson Alan M. Henry
Brian Gardiner R. Keith Bootle
Patrick M. Leahy Stuart F. Ingham
Stuart Irvine Donald C. McCallum
Lindsay D. Munro Roderick C. Munro
R. Bramley Derrick Harman
Charlie Ramsay Tom M. Millar
Allan Bantick Nigel Orr Cedric Y. Harben
David Lowther Mary McIlroy
Anthony Wragg W.D. Borthwick
Janet Hartley Roger Hill-Cottingham
Matthew Glover A.G. Brooks
Gordon Berry R. Martin Adams

1992

A.G.F. Aitken Clifford Simpson
James I.R. Tees Jane Wainwright
Haydn Thomas W. Alan Fortune
Martin Douglas Kydd Peter Douglas Buck
William Platts Gordon Taylor
Barbara Redford Andrew Naylor
James G. Halkett Iain A. MacLeod
Eric Ivison Fred Goodyear Paul M. Child
Mick Biggin Elda Morrison
Alexander J. Sim Iain K. Mitchell
James Gordon Dave Park Rod Harrison
Mark Douglas Peter Bailey Steve Fallon
David Todd G. Watters John C.B. Kelly
Richard Gatehouse Frank A. Mellor
Jennifer Mellor David C. Seivewright
David Hoyle Smith Roger Coates
Simon Bolam William A. McKenzie
Alexander R.B. Taylor Bill Faimaner
Susan M. Miller John B. Jones John Nuttal
Veronica Gray John Peel Frank Malloy
John B. Mitchell Alistair J. Montgomery
Dave Dawson Hedly Horsler
Valerie Horsler Ian B. Pyper
M.J. Poznanski Sandy Wood A.W. Ridler
David Murray Patricia J. Brodie
Patrick J. Temporal Jeffrey C. Stone

Jim Wright John B. McKeown
James W. Marshall Meryl Marshall
C.D. Evans James Anthony Fenner
Tim Pickles James Dignall Penny Barron
Christina B. Morton John C. Chappell
Alan Fielding Terry Barclay
Calum N. White Brendan J. Hamill
Margaret Barnett Christopher Barclay
Christopher J. Angwin Nancy Thomson
Christopher Bantoft David I. Harris
Richard Wiles Mark Rigby Peter Reynolds
Duncan Hunter Pamela L. Clark
Margaret Hall George S. Deas
Graham Benny Christopher G. Butcher
Brian Ewing Denis A. Oidgeon
Colin H. McNab Raymond Shaw
Nettie Geddes Jim Cunningham
Margaret Riley Ronald H. MacGregor
Andy Murphy W.H. Smith Callum Sword
Marjorie Langmuir Geraldine Newlyn
John Hendry Margaret Hendry
Herbert S. Clarke Marion K.W. Clarke
Betty Hamer John Hamer Wattie Ramage
Allan Kernohan James C. Ashby
Ian Dickson Terence M. O'Brien
Gordon McI. Bruce Norman F. Hazelton
Rory Gibson Andrew Johnston
Stephen Crabbe Andy Whitehead
Gilmour Strang Levan Bryn
Winifred Graham Iain B. McIntosh
Aida Sutton Alan Sutton Paul Krebs
K. Higgins Graham Daniels Alan D. Grant

1993

Stephen P. Evans Christopher Dyos
W.H. Jones G. Dobrzynski
Robert Robertson Colin Wilson
David Thatcher David I. Nixon
David Waterson R.M. Kerry Alan Keegan
Mike J. Westmorland Rita Norrie
John T. MacLeod David Douglas
C. Knowles Margaret Russell Peter Collins
Eric Cook Sandra Stead Mike Heckford
Brian D. Panton Charles M. Mackay
Iona Bowden Roy Bowden
Garth B. Fenton Elaine S. Fenton
Harry Kirkwood Jeanette Barr
Bernhard Lapp Ian Collie W.R. Shipway
Peter Drummond Peter McPhail
Christine E. Tulloch David I. Hill
Dave Peck Theodore Cadoux
Chris J. Upson Mike Fry John B. Matthews
John Johnson Peter Lincoln Bill J. Bowers
Karin Froebel J.S. Burrows Donald Rich
David Slater David Unsworth Linda Aitken
William Aitken Mary Hepburn
Alan H. Holmes George W. Morl
John Martin Roy D. Williamson
Margaret L. Brooker David Baker
Kenneth Brown Jean M. Gayton
Robert J. Tait Carole Baillie
Michael Baillie David Jaap
William Sinclair Carl Morris
Jack Berryman Charlie Sutherland
David Haworth Dorothy Wilson
Maurice E. Twentyman Ian Donnelly
Joyce Cosby Brian Cosby Valerie Moffat
Andrew Moffat John F. Wilson Chris Lee
Iain S. MacDuffie Jeff J. Burgum
W.P. Maxwell Martin C. Powell
Heather Ogorman John Holder Iain King
James A.D. Convery Arthur W. Ager
Dave Stanford Robert L. Plumb
Heather Coakes R.J. Anderson
Roger C. Henshaw Michael Atkins
John G. Carrie James L.W. Baxter
Richard T. Griffiths Duncan Foster
Norman Carrington Janey Brogan
David Brogan S.G. Singleton Morag Wylie
Gordon Hopper Innes Sutherland
Frank Martin Christine M. May

Timothy J. May Una S. Woods Keith Yates
David A. Cryle Michael Hanlin Ian Gray
Brian Cowie L. Hunter Tom W. Boyd
Michael J. Donaldson Dorothy McLean
Joan Wilson Dave Kennedy Brian Welsh
G. Fraser Ritchie Alan Findlay
John M. Barrett Allan P. Lees
Andrew Balsillie N. Kenworthy
Martin J. Darling Iain Roberts
David D. Taylor Bill Robertson
Irving Notman Dave Marshall William
G.J. Joss

1994

Tony M. Deall Bill R. Johncocks
Peter Swindells David Smith
Nigel P. Morters Adrian M. Lodge
Carol Lodge Lorraine Nicholson
Harry Blenkinsop John D. Taylor
Kevin Borman David Williams
Robert J. Shapperd David Fisher
Steve Simpson Anne Lochead Keith Work
Julian P. Ridal Alistair Maitland
J. Sebastian Grose William Beattie
Alex D. Grant David W. Duncan
Graham T. Illing Michael McLaggan
W. Harvey Condliffe Keith Moody
Roberta Taylor Charles M. Taylor
Eiona Conacher John G. Aird
Barbara V. Watson Celia Goodman
Audrey M. Litterick Charles Leggat
Fiona Wallace Terry A. Fuller
Michael J. Smyth Neil S. Dunford
J.H. Calvert N.S. Hunnisett Leigh Sayers
Catherine S. Gray Robert P. Gray
Robert W. Gray Ian Forder Ken A. Butcher
Frankie S. Cumming Ian McVittie
Charles G. Elliott Ben S. Cooper
Ian J. Brownell Raymond Hay
Gillian M. Green John E. Green
John Mackay Fraser MacGillivray
Kenneth W.C. Stewart Alex K. Kirk
J.P. Fish F. David Smith G.W. Hollins
Christine C. Macleod Rhoda McKinnon
David Bonham Irene Crawshaw
Grahame Crawshaw Pat Craven
Brian Norman Gerry Callaghan
George Middleton Alistair Patten
Carol Harper Keith Harper
Margaret Beattie Carole Strang
Martin Horn Murray Smith Carole George
Iain McManus Iain A.B. Wallace
Ken Naismith Lyn S. Wilson
Jeremiah J. Scott Graham Wanless
Clare Parnell Simon Halliwell
A. Julian Spencer W. Lofthouse
M. Lofthouse J. Weir Brown Stephen Sharp
Richard Burt John D. Shiel John M. Griffin
Ruth Hannah C.P. Herdman
Moira Broadhead A.Stuart Duncan
John G. Proud Allan J. Gordon
Ian H. Anderson John King
John B. Boyling Stephen Hartley
James Martin A.H. Blandy
Richard R. Cooper Geoff Scott
W. Michael Gollan Colin D. Grant
Thomas G.F. Rankin

1995

Chris Andrews Lorna McLaren
George Galloway Hugh Insley
Ron Fosberry George C. Gilchrist
A.L. McLaren Gordon Birnie
Douglas R. MacLeod George Page
Ron Johnson Kate Potter Alan Bellis
Graham W. Beckett Patrick J. P. Nelson
Charles D. M. Black Jacqueline Cummings
Barry M. Rose J. B. Murphy
David M. Mollison Derek R. L. Borthwick
Bill Patullo Peter Goodwin
Dominic Goodwin Anne Hill Martin E. Hill
Gillian M. Shirreffs Richard C. Shirreffs